D0499938

JANE AUSTEN'S NAMES

Jane Austen's
* Names *

Riddles, Persons, Places

MARGARET DOODY

The University of Chicago Press   Chicago and London

MARGARET DOODY is the John and Barbara Glynn Family
Professor of Literature at the University of Notre Dame.

The University of Chicago Press, Chicago 60637
The University of Chicago Press, Ltd., London
© 2015 by The University of Chicago
All rights reserved. Published 2015.
Printed in the United States of America

24 23 22 21 20 19 18 17 16 15   1 2 3 4 5

ISBN-13: 978-0-226-15783-2 (cloth)
ISBN-13: 978-0-226-19602-2 (e-book)
DOI: 10.7208/chicago/9780226196022.001.0001

The University of Chicago Press gratefully acknowledges
the generous support of the Institute for Scholarship in the
Liberal Arts, College of Arts and Letters, University of
Notre Dame, toward the publication of this book.

Library of Congress Cataloging-in-Publication Data
Doody, Margaret Anne, author.
Jane Austen's names : riddles, persons, places / Margaret Doody.
      pages ; cm
Includes bibliographical references and index.
ISBN 978-0-226-15783-2 (cloth : alk. paper) —
ISBN 978-0-226-19602-2 (e-book) 1. Austen, Jane,
1775–1817—Language. 2. Names in literature. 3. Names, Personal,
in literature. 4. Names, Geographical, in literature. I. Title.
PR4038.L33D66 2015
823'.7—dc23
2014026046

CONTENTS

FIGURES

ACKNOWLEDGMENTS

Many friends contributed to this project. I am grateful to fellow scholars, especially Julia Douthwaite, Laura Haigwood, Jocelyn Harris, Jayne Lewis, Robert Mack, Roger Moore, Peter Sabor, and Douglas Murray for cheering the work on generally and for supplying information on particulars. Doug Murray's unpublished essay on Box Hill has been extremely useful, as has Roger Moore's consideration of General Tilney's abbey. Roger Short supplied an unusual reference. Janine Barchas most kindly sent me copies of her articles prefiguring her important *Matters of Fact.* I am particularly grateful to Deidre Lynch and Claudia Johnson who read the manuscript in earlier stages and made helpful suggestions. Gratitude goes to Claudia for remarkable insights over the years, and for continuing discussions and engagement with Austen's life and works.

Debts extend over time and space. I am grateful to David and Marilyn Butler for friendship over decades, with fond recollections of the house in Woodstock Road, and conversations with Marilyn on Edgeworth, Burney, and Austen. Jane Hurst of the Curtis Museum in Alton, Hampshire, most generously supplied her detailed knowledge of Alton and of the Austens' life in the Chawton region, making the past present. The late Henry Rice, descendant of Edward Austen, and his wife Anne have supplied me with deep and wide-ranging knowledge of Austen's family and their connections and environment. I am grateful to Sandy Lerner and to all at the Chawton Library for its resources and for the excellent conference in July 2013. My thanks to staff at the British Library, the Bodleian Library, the Ashmolean Museum, and the National Portrait Gallery, London. Thanks are also due to Sara Weber of Special Collections at the Hesburgh Libraries, University of Notre Dame.

Emphatically grateful expressions are owed to Kurt Milberger, efficient assistant extraordinary, who patiently acquainted himself with the entire manuscript in various phases and brought new zeal to the hunt for the artworks.

This is my opportunity to say "thank you" to Alan Thomas, editorial director at the University of Chicago Press, for believing in the book. I am also grateful to Randolph Petilos for patient work with the manuscript and for answering numerous inquiries.

All who teach will know how sincerely I mean it when I offer heartfelt thanks to my students in the class "Jane Austen and Her World." Their eyes bring fresh enlightenment, and their new insights persuade me that Austen is inexhaustible.

A NOTE ON TEXTS

All references to Austen's works (unless otherwise indicated) are to the Cambridge edition of *The Works of Jane Austen* (Janet Todd, general editor): *Juvenilia,* ed. Peter Sabor, 2006; *Northanger Abbey,* ed. Barbara M. Benedict and Deirdre le Faye, 2006; *Sense and Sensibility,* ed. Edward Copeland, 2006; *Pride and Prejudice,* ed. Pat Rogers, 2006; *Mansfield Park,* ed. John Wiltshire, 2005; *Emma,* ed. Richard Cronin and Dorothy McMillan, 2005; *Persuasion,* ed. Janet Todd and Antje Blank, 2006; *Later Manuscripts,* ed. Janet Todd and Linda Bree, 2008. Citations of major novels refer to volume number (in roman numerals) and chapter number (in arabic numerals). Quotations from *The Watsons* and *Sanditon* are drawn from transcripts in the *Later Manuscripts* volume. Conventional abbreviations for all titles of more than one word are employed: for example, *S&S.*

The following works will be cited by short titles followed by volume and page references without endnotes:

Johnson, *Dictionary:* Samuel Johnson, *A Dictionary of the English Language; In which the words are deduced from their Original, and Illustrated in the different Significations by Examples from the best Writers.* 2nd ed. 2 vols. London: W. Strahan, for J. and P. Knapton, T. and T. Longman, et al., 1755.

Shakespeare Plays: Samuel Johnson, ed., *The Plays of William Shakespeare . . . to which are added Notes by Sam. Johnson.* 8 vols. London: J. & R. Tonson et al., 1765.

Mills: A. D. Mills, *A Dictionary of British Place Names.* Oxford: Oxford University Press, 2003.

ODNB: Oxford Dictionary of National Biography. Oxford: Oxford University Press, 2004. www. oxford.com.

Reaney & Wilson: P. H. Reaney, revised with additions by R. M. Wilson, *A Dictionary of English Surnames.* Oxford: Oxford University Press, 2005.

References to the following works will be cited in endnotes by short form of title, with volume and page numbers:

Camden-Gibson, *Britannia: Britannia; or, A Chorographical Description of Great Britain and Ireland. Together with the Adjacent Islands.* Written in Latin by William Camden . . . and Translated into English, with Additions and Improvements, Revised, Digested and Published with large ADDITIONS by Edmund Gibson, D.D. 3rd ed. 2 vols. London: R. Ware, J. and P. Knapton et al., 1753.

Camden-Gough, *Britannia: Britannia; or, A Chorographical Description of the Flourishing Kingdoms of ENGLAND, SCOTLAND, and IRELAND and the Islands Adjacent; From the Earliest Antiquity.* By William Camden. Translated and Enlarged . . . By Richard Gough, F.A. & R.SS. Illustrated with Maps, and other Copper-Plates. 3 vols. London: T Payne and Son; G. G. J. and J. Robinson, 1789.

Family Record: William Austen Leigh and Richard Arthur Austen-Leigh, *Jane Austen: Her Life and Letters; A Family Record.* 2nd ed. New York: Russell & Russell, 1965. First published 1913.

JAAFR: Deirdre Le Faye, *Jane Austen: A Family Record.* 2nd ed. Cambridge: Cambridge University Press, 2004. (Not to be confused with the 1913 *Family Record.*)

PART I

England

Chapter 1

Words, Names,
Persons, and Places

Fiction, Names, and Riddles

"The name of Newton-Priors is really invaluable!—I never met with anything superior to it.—It is delightful.—One could live upon the name of Newton-Priors for a twelvemonth" (30 November 1814; *Letters*, 284).

So Jane Austen wrote in the autumn of 1814 to her niece Anna (daughter of Jane's brother James). Before her wedding to Benjamin Lefroy three weeks earlier Anna had been writing a novel; now Jane Austen encourages her niece, even after marriage, to continue. Anna's aunt has read a new chunk of manuscript. As a mark of Anna's promise she singles out her invention of a name. "Newton Priors" strikes Jane Austen as a particularly happy name for an imaginary place.

Presumably Austen appreciates Anna's wit in playing with the real place name "Newton Abbot(s)," combining the common "Newton" (i.e., "new" + *tun,* settlement or town) with the ecclesiastical, medieval, and important "Priors." A "Prior" is a cut below an "Abbot." Perhaps Anna Austen's characters have been living on the site of a priory but behaving in a manner not consonant with the priory's origins. Austen is always interested in cultural layers of the past and especially in ecclesiastical foundations. Her own novels display an acute attention to the shimmer of historical significance within names. Austen achieves meaning that goes down deep into layers of English history and relationship to the land.

Would Austen be bothered with such details? An artist cannot do anything slovenly. Jo Modert's groundbreaking essay "Chronology within the Novels" made us aware of the kind of care that Austen could put into apparently casual details.[1] Building on work by R. W. Chapman, Mary Lascelles, and Vladimir Nabokov, Modert taught us to appreciate Austen's subtle evocation of human time, the "hidden calendar game for the reader" in *Emma*. Jane's pianoforte arrives on Saint Valentine's Day; Frank almost confesses the true state of affairs to Emma on Shrove Tuesday (22 February), a proper time for confessions. The Box Hill expedition takes place on Midsummer Day (New Style). Midsummer madness briefly reigns. Mr. Knightley proposes to Emma on Old Midsummer Day.

Names of places and persons in Austen's novels are chosen with equal care. The name of an estate or a village is never insignificant. First names and surnames always matter. The question of naming brings out a poetic complexity in Austen—as well as different kinds of comedy. Jane Austen's family was highly conscious of names. There is evidently a family joke regarding the first name "Richard," as we see early in Austen's extant letters: "Mr. Richard Harvey's match is put off, till he has got a Better Christian name, of which he has great Hopes" (16 September 1796; *Letters*, 10). The joke is echoed in the third sentence of *Northanger Abbey* ("Her father was . . . a very respectable man, though his name was Richard"). Why is "Richard" so funny? The merriment evoked goes beyond an association of the name with Shakespeare's King Richard III or with Sir Richard Crofts, villain of Charlotte Smith's *Emmeline: The Orphan of the Castle* (1788), one of the young Jane's favorite novels. Current American slang would make "Dick" a word obscenely signifying hypermasculinity, but the evidence of slang dictionaries of Austen's day indicates that "Dick" is associated with effeminacy, male weakness, or failure—or with being a poor substitute for something else: "That happened in the reign of Queen Dick, i.e. never; said of any absurd old story. I am as queer as Dick's hatband; that is, out of spirits, or don't know what ails me."[2] Another dictionary adds that "Dickey" is "A sham shirt," also "An ass. Roll your dickey: drive your ass. Also a seat for servants to sit behind a carriage."[3] "Roll your dickey" seems to be getting close to the contemporary American meaning, but with an additional suggestion of imbecility or incapacity. In *Pride and Prejudice* the port-drinking attorney Mr. Philips is about to fire his servant—another unlucky "Richard" (*P&P*, I, ch. 14). Austen seems unable to contemplate the name "Richard" without associations of bumbling or failure, deficiency in masculinity—all emerging in the harsh reflections on poor Dick Musgrove in *Persuasion*. But "Dick" is funny even when submerged in another form; "Miss Dickins," that "excellent Governess" of the young Lady Williams (a "Kitty"), eloped with the butler ("Jack and Alice," *Juvenilia*, 18).

Names encountered in daily life provided amusement. The death of a farmer "Clarinbold" or "Claringbo[u]ld" stimulated Jane to a comic flight:

> Everything quite in Stile, not to mention Mr. Claringbould's funeral which we saw go by on Sunday. I beleive [*sic*] I told you in a former Letter that Edward had some idea of taking the name of Claringbould; but that scheme is over, tho' it would be a very eligible as well as a very pleasant plan, would any one advance him Money enough to begin on. (15–16 September 1796; *Letters,* 9)

A name like other property is really not needed anymore by someone whose funeral has gone by. The departed farmer's surname might now be taken by somebody else as a commodity—if the purchaser could afford it. The joke about Edward becoming "Claringbould" has a slight edge. Austen has noted that her brother Edward is fond of gaining lands, and this brother is indeed going to change his surname. Adopted and made the heir of the Knight family early in life, Edward eventually left off being an "Austen" and became a "Knight."

Names might seem as unalterable and fated as a birthplace, cementing a lasting identity. Women's surnames are alterable, changing upon marriage, but a man's surname stands for his permanent identity and inheritance. That supposition is not always borne out by facts. The eighteenth century went in for dramatic changes of name. Power of will overrides the "natural" or "given." Voltaire, for one, invented his own name, as did the Italian poet Metastasio. The Czarina we know as "Catherine the Great" (1729–96) began as Prussian Sophie-Friederike Auguste. A number of men around Jane Austen altered their names. The father of the Harris Bigg-Wither who was to propose to Jane Austen (with a one-day success) had been, wonderfully, "Lovelace Bigg." On receipt of an inheritance, Lovelace Bigg changed his surname to Bigg-Wither, although only his male heirs used the double-barreled form. James Leigh, Jane's mother's brother, had changed his name to "Leigh-Perrot" in order to inherit the property of his great-uncle Thomas Perrot at Northleigh in Oxfordshire. If Great-Uncle Thomas imagined he was preserving his familial property as well as his family name, he would have been grievously disappointed. James Leigh-Perrot tore down the inherited house at Northleigh, selling the land to the Duke of Marlborough. Uncle James, with the proceeds of his inheritance, acquired property in a more prosperous area between Maidenhead and Reading.[4] There he built a fine new house, calling the place "Scarlets."

Throughout these decisive changes to his property and location, he remained "Mr. James Leigh-Perrot," solemnly honoring as heir the legacy of the surname although—against the true intention of the bequest—Thomas had cashed in the inherited estate and shaken off the ancestral region.

Surnames announce a place in the power structure; they represent tribal membership, property, activity, location, and continuance. According to Christian tradition, in Heaven (or presumably Hell) we shall wear only our first names; just like a title ("Mr.," "Duke," "Dr."), a surname is a social tag of which we shall have no need once we take leave of society. Yet "owners" of names, fancying them as a kind of property, are reluctant to let their existence and strength fade from the world. They may attempt to fasten their names to survivors, often with mixed results. Both the fixedness and the mutability of personal names stimulated Jane Austen's curiosity and comic sense. Surnames are such awkward describers. Are they nouns—objects in themselves? Or perhaps they are but transient adjectives that can be sold as goods in Vanity Fair. The most notable case of name change within Jane Austen's novels is the case of the half-orphan Francis Churchill Weston, transmogrified into Francis ("Frank") Churchill, when after his mother's death the infant is taken in by a maternal uncle and his wife. "Churchill," once given as a middle name in compliment to the maternal surname, later becomes Frank's surname as well. Status and financial expectations depend on those whose name he carries about with him, not on his flourishing biological father. In the same novel, Harriet Smith bears what is obviously a made-up surname to conceal her illegitimacy; the very anonymity of that surname draws attention to it as artifact and mask.

Jane Austen consistently responds to the sound and meaning of names, even those encountered by chance in newspapers. In April 1805 she expresses comic dismay on reading in the papers of a marriage "of the Rev. Edward Bather, Rector of some place in Shropshire, to a Miss Emma Halifax—a Wretch!—he does not deserve an Emma Halifax's maid Betty" (21–23 April 1805; *Letters*, 104–5). The clergyman with the absurd surname (reminiscent of someone in a bathing machine) has comically offended against taste in uniting himself with a woman of such an elegant and novel-worthy a name as "Emma Halifax"—a woman with the first name that Austen had given her new heroine, Emma Watson, combined with an aristocratic surname (employed in *Catharine*). The novelist in mock distress contemplates an elegant "Emma Halifax" doomed to become "Emma Bather"; a low-class "Betty Bather" would have been more appropriate.

Jane Austen's sensitivity to names is closely related to her penchant for riddles and wordplay. She feels the attraction of puns. Lord Chesterfield preferred to believe that such forms of "false wit" (along with old sayings and proverbs) had happily disappeared: "The reign of King Charles II. (meritorious in no other respect) banished false taste out of England, and proscribed Puns, Quibbles, Acrostics, &c."[5] During the eighteenth century it had become officially established among the educated and well-bred that puns are grossly old-fashioned and "low." They are, however, a favorite English form of wit; Shakespeare is full of them. In *Northanger Abbey,* we are told that the heroine's parents "seldom aimed at wit of any kind; her father, at the utmost, being contented with a pun, and her mother with a proverb" (*NA,* I, ch. 9). Reverend Mr. Morland appears unaware that proverbs and puns have been banished since the reign of Charles II. Actually, eighteenth-century literature is very hospitable to wordplay. A favorite device in poetry and prose is "periphrasis," a talking around a noun (concrete or abstract) without employing the normal word. (A famous example is "While *China*'s earth receives the smoking Tyde" in Pope's *The Rape of the Lock.*[6]) Such roundabout description offers new angles of vision within a sort of riddle. Riddles combine immediate mental activity with philosophic perception that *any* words are odd. The strangeness of the notion that words can stand in for things, or reality, exercised John Locke and others. A riddle makes us look afresh at the strangeness, the arbitrary weirdness, of language. We shall not understand Austen if we do not love riddles.

In Jane Austen's lifetime there was a decided taste for works of riddles and "charades." Every reader of *Emma* remembers Harriet's manuscript "riddle book." Such collections are no new thing. In *The Merry Wives of Windsor,* young Slender asks Simple, "You have not the book of riddles about you, have you?" to which Simple replies, "Book of riddles! why, did you not lend it to *Alice Shortcake* upon *Allhallowmas* last, a fortnight afore *Michaelmas?*" (*Merry Wives,* act 1, sc. 2; *Shakespeare Plays,* 2:459). Master Slender apparently hopes for aid from his "book of riddles" to support him in courtship. So too Mr. Elton in his (hopeless) courtship of Emma has apparently eked out his slender wits in consulting one of many published books of enigmas. Both the riddle of "Woeman" recollected by Mr. Woodhouse (but already collected by Harriet) and the gallant riddle attributed to the Reverend Mr. Elton in the ninth chapter of *Emma* appear in at least one of the published "riddle books." Mr. Elton's elaborate charade on "Courtship" is not his invention— nor Austen's. It can be found in the second volume of *A New Collection of Enigmas, Charades, Transpositions, &c.* (1791). This set of verses is treated *as if* Mr. Elton were the ingenious original author—but that is Austen's joke. the smiling Mr. Elton simply plagiarized his text, adding a couple of pointed lines of compliment (aimed at Emma, but misread as directed to Harriet).

A number of printed collections like the one Mr. Elton got hold of (perhaps already possessed) appear throughout the eighteenth century. As in Slender's case (and Mr. Elton's) such riddle collections are advertised as aids to courtship. They have titles like *Delights for Young Men and Maids: Containing Near an Hundred Riddles with Pictures, and a Key to Each;* this seems to have been reprinted at regular intervals between circa 1725 and circa 1755. Riddles evidently suggest sex—and/or marriage—disjunction, conjunction, the bringing of unlikely elements together. We find *Women's Wit; or, A New and Elegant Amusement for the Fair Sex* (offering "*Puzzling Enigmas, Rebusses & Riddles*") published "By a Lady" (ca. 1780).[7]

Like Harriet Smith—or Miss Nash of Mrs. Goddard's school—the Austen family compiled a manuscript collection of riddles, eventually published in 1895, as *Charades &c. Written a Hundred years ago By Jane Austen and Her Family.* This collection is innocuous enough but does testify to the family fondness for puns. One of the three riddles ascribed to Jane Austen, however, has a darker tone than one might expect:

> When my first is a task to a young girl of spirit,
> And my second confines her to finish the piece,
> How hard is her fate! but how great is her merit,
> If by taking my whole she effects her release!

The answer to Riddle No. XVIII is "HEMLOCK."[8] Certainly this excessive revolt against sewing may record hyperbolically the author's occasional genuine revulsion at the constant feminine task. Austen hyperbolically urges a classical suicidal escape from the imposed dullness of female life, equating a reluctant young seamstress with Socrates.

We do not truly know Jane Austen if we do not recognize that she is very fond of puns and plays on words. "Of *Rears* and *Vices,* I saw enough. Now, do not be suspecting me of a pun, I entreat," cries Mary

Crawford—her disclaimer ensuring that we shall all indeed think of an obscene pun related to homosexuality in the Navy (*MP,* I, ch. 6). This is denied by some; John Wiltshire's annotation asserts Jane's innocence. But the young author of the "History of England" shows that she already knew about homosexuality:

> His majesty [King James I] was of that amiable disposition which inclines to Freindship [*sic*], and in such points was possessed of keener penetration in Discovering Merit than many other people. I once heard an excellent Sharade on a Carpet, of which the subject I am now on reminds me . . .
> Sharade
> My first is what my second was to King James the 1st, and you tread on my whole. ("History of England," *Juvenilia,* 187)

Austen knows that Robert Carr was the king's "pet"—and what the term means ("keener penetration"). Miss Fanny Carr (a doubly suspicious name) in *The Watsons* is the best friend of Miss Osborne. Tom Musgrove, airing his French, calls her "a most interesting little creature. You can imagine nothing more *naive* or *piquante*" (*Later Manuscripts,* 323). This description serves rather to confirm than deny a sexual connection between Miss Osborne ("not critically handsome") and Fanny Carr, so often referred to together.

Mary Crawford may be officially rebuked by the outcome of *Mansfield Park.* Yet—disturbingly—Mary shares Jane Austen's own kind of wit. In her more risqué vein Jane writes to Cassandra in 1808: "I must notice a wedding in the Salisbury paper, which has amused me very much, Dr Phillot to Lady Frances St Lawrence. *She* wanted to have a husband I suppose, once in her life, and *he* a Lady Frances" (24–25 October 1808; *Letters,* 151). Jane Austen's joke lies in combining the sound value of the sound of the groom's name as "Fill-it" with the "dirty" connotation of "Lady Fanny." In contemporary British slang, "Fan" and "Fanny" both refer to the female genitals—as we see in Fielding's *Shamela,* in which Shamela's prostitute mother resides at "the Fan & Pepper Box."[9] This slang meaning is reflected in the name of the heroine of John Cleland's *Memoirs of a Lady of Pleasure,* better known as *Fanny Hill.* But every female, good or bad, possesses a "Lady Fanny" ("Lady Frances"). Austen's joke here raises a question as to why she names her apparently most modest heroine "Fanny."

Nobody is likely to be more conscious of the poetry of names than a novelist trying to shape characters. It is vital to the success of a story to find the right, the significant, name for a character (who is, at bottom, all signifier). Some novelists are more successful at name invention than others. Henry James's characters are easy to remember by their names, and Trollope at his best can be superb—by which I mean "Archdeacon Grantly" and "Glencora Palliser," not the "Sir Omicron Pie" sort of caper. The task becomes the more challenging if the writer cannot choose the pointedly generic, calling a schoolmaster "Thwackum," or allegorical, as in "Allworthy." Austen is not as fond of open allegory as Fielding or Richardson and offers us less of overt Eden. To be sure, Uncle "Gardiner" in *Pride and Prejudice* takes us gently back to Adam, and in *Emma* even the most delicate of beautiful maidens (to whom the author has given her own first name) retains Eve's taste for the apple— if only baked apples. Jane Austen, while producing multiple meanings, avoids *obtrusive* allegory—but not all allegory.

Persons and Places

The design of the present work is to concentrate on the meaning of names occurring within the separate major novels, taken in order. (*Northanger Abbey* is made to stand for the first of Austen's mature novels.) Comments on the intermediate works *Catharine, Lady Susan,* and *The Watsons* are interspersed with discussions of the major novels, and their titles given in italics to distinguish these novelistic works, even if unfinished, from short pieces. The personal names of characters— including allusions and implications both historical and literary—are treated first. The discussion of place names, real and imaginary, follows. We look first at who the characters are (according to their names) and then at where they come from and where they find themselves.

We don't see Jane Austen in the creative kitchen. But we do get some little glimpses of her ideas about naming characters when she converses by letter with nieces who are trying to write fiction. The experienced novelist enjoys Anna Austen's introduction of a striking comic surname, even though Anna's husband Ben does not care for it: "We have no great right to wonder at his not valueing [*sic*] the name of Progillian. *That* is a source of delight which he hardly ever can be quite competent to" (28 September 1814; *Letters,* 277). Writing to her much younger niece Caroline about the story that Caroline sent her, Austen says she approves of Caroline's authorial treatment of the heroine Olivia, "but the good for nothing Father, who was the real author of all her Faults & Sufferings, should not escape unpunished.—I hope *he* hung himself, or took the sur-name of *Bone* or underwent some direful penance or other.—" (6 December 1814; *Letters,* 288).

Austen's names for characters and their acquaintances not only form part of the connective tissue of her narrative but are also expressions of her poetic power. She appreciates the weight of history borne by names. For we are not original in our names; they come from somewhere else. And that "somewhere else" is a hinterland of tribes and histories, political arrangements, loyalties and battlefields. Surnames are not only remnants but conductors of history, exhibiting Anglo-Saxon origin, or Norman—or perhaps Danish or Celtic. Ethnicity and political division are caught in names. First names, too, have reference to saints and monarchs, heroes and eras. Names refer us to violence, to wear and tear and conflict. The past recurs in the present. Like it or not, we bump into it.

Jane Austen has also paid maximum attention to her choice and description of places. Heroines belong to or come from a particular place that defines them. Yet they hardly ever stay put. Austen's heroines—and some of her leading men, too—are caught in a state of displacement. Darcy, with all of Pemberley behind him, is out of place when we first meet him. Austen's most interesting characters ("good" and "bad") are in motion. We take our "being" with us from one place to another, and "being" has to adjust. The cultural forces that shape an English person include not only the social and financial status of the birth family, but also the place of birth—of which the most important single unit in England is the county. Austen carefully tells us (with the one exception of Lady Susan) what county each of her heroines was born in. There are important differences between Wiltshire, native county of Catherine Morland, and Hertfordshire, home of Elizabeth Bennet. Colonel Brandon is from Dorset—very different from Mr. Darcy's Derbyshire. In her choice of real places as settings, and in her invention of imaginary towns and estates, Jane Austen is acutely aware of whether a place name is Saxon, Danish, or Norman French. Personal names become place names and vice versa; a name can be a kind of place. Mr. Bingley's surname, for instance, name of a Yorkshire town, is of mixed Danish and Saxon origin, harking back to the Danish invasions and settlements of the eighth to the eleventh century. Charles Bingley and his sisters are "of a respectable family in the north of England," and their fortune is "acquired by trade" (*P&P,* I, ch. 4). That the Bingleys' ultimate "north" is Yorkshire is substantiated by the fact that the seaside resort the Bingleys go to is Scarborough (*P&P*, III, ch. 12). Beneath their aspirations, their pretensions to London polish and southern gentility, this family retains attachment to its ancestral region.

We don't usually think of Austen as concerned with what we call "ethnicity"—not, at least, until she is about to produce her first black character in *Sanditon*. The Enlightenment had inherited from antiquity forms of what might be called "disdainful ethnography." Foreigners and their behavior can be dealt with as amusingly grotesque—especially if they are dark or of mixed race. Such an ethnography is hinted at in a discussion of foreign dancing engaged in by William Price and Sir Thomas with his knowledge of "the balls of Antigua" (*MP*, II, ch. 7). (See below, ch. 11.) These male travelers' recollections, expurgated for female consumption, would offer, like accounts of other travelers, vignettes of dances (picturesque, absurd, slightly distasteful) in Sicily, the Iberian Peninsula, and the West Indies.

Racial thinking at home in England extends beyond attitudes to black Africans to deprecation of Celtic characteristics. Henry Crawford, as Mr. Rushworth points out, is short (nowhere near six feet). He is initially considered "black and plain"—not because of his skin color but because his hair and eyebrows are black and his eyes dark (*MP*, I, ch. 5). He looks like one of the dark Celts, and his small, wiry, and dark-haired sister likewise; Mary is a complement and no threat to the tall blonde Bertram girls. Austen occasionally refers to skin color. Of Emma Watson, "well made & plump," we are told, "Her skin was very brown, but clear, smooth and glowing" (*Watsons, Later Manuscripts*, 293). Elizabeth Bennet, according to Miss Bingley, in her summer travels "is grown so brown and coarse!" (*P&P*, III, ch. 3). Such descriptions touch upon the issue of race. Elizabeth is not a blonde like her mother and elder sister; she has "dark eyes" as Darcy notes, and her figure is "light and pleasing" (I, ch. 6)—more like Mary Crawford than female Gardiners or Bertrams. Does Austen have some slight preference for the dark people, whose skin browns in the sun? If Mr. Rushworth and Maria Bertram are Saxon standard-bearers, they do not come off very well in morals and intellect.

Austen is consistently sensitive to ethnic differences within the British Isles. Who descends from Normans?—or Danes? Who is Scots or Welsh? Lady Catherine De Bourgh's married surname is that of one of William the Conqueror's trusted aides who immediately took over one of the most important coastal fortifications. Lady Catherine, by birth a Norman Fitzwilliam, is still manning the defenses against vulgar Saxons. In contrast, Celtic backgrounds are more than hinted at in names like Wynne, Price, Campbell, Griffiths, Hamilton.

History, uncomfortable history, is everywhere in the Austen novels. In *Emma,* an accumulation of Saxon references is interrupted by a recollection of violent Tudor politics. We cannot elude history. Each of us carries it with us—in our first name, last name, birthplace. Austen's central characters seem to have a fair amount of freedom. Yet they are imprisoned by genealogy, dwelling place, customs. They make mistakes, bumping into their own presuppositions and conventions, often without noticing such collisions. Biases and assumptions abound. Not only Elizabeth Bennett possesses "prejudice." Austen takes exploration of this condition to an unusual depth, without offering simple moral solutions as if all we are faced with were merely a "problem." In the poetics of her novels she scores the background and the influences with complex counterpointing of reference. Historical events and historical personages repeatedly intrude—including Queen Elizabeth, a bone of contention from *Catharine* onward. When Mrs. Percival wishes "to see the Manners of the People in Queen Elizabeth's reign, restor'd again," her niece protests. "I hope you do not mean . . . to restore Queen Elizabeth herself . . . for if she were to come again. . . . She might do as much Mischeif [*sic*] and last as long as she did before" (*Catharine, Juvenilia,* 251). Personages domineering and scandalous—too irritating to be merely allegorical—lurch into the worlds of their successors. Even the most minor character carries old history in the inevitable label—first name + surname. Austen also puts a lot of thought into references to offstage persons mentioned by characters proper. Such supernumerary personages do not truly dwell within the story, but are contributors to it. The halo of references to persons outside the immediate story (which I have termed "the penumbra") grows more complex and more effective in the later novels. Within the names of onstage contemporary characters old conflicts are revived; religious and political allegiances freshly reanimated. Old scandals are resurrected with the use of names like "Palmer," "Weston," "Dashwood."

Janine Barchas in *Matters of Fact in Jane Austen* (2012) has done a magnificent job of tracing the contemporary presence in Austen's England of important families bearing the surnames given to some of the novelist's most important characters. Barchas is most interested in the currency and immediacy of such reference. I am more interested in Austen's figurative use of language (including names), as well as in the long reach of Jane Austen's historical memory and her creative play with history. References target old enmities and regional tensions. Her play with British memory extends back to the coming of the Saxons, the conflicts with Danes. She turns repeatedly to particular "trouble spots" of history: the Conquest of 1066; the reign of Henry VIII and the Dissolution of the Monasteries; the reign of Elizabeth; and the late Restoration, particularly the time of Monmouth and James II. We find consistent recognition of civil wars, including the Wars of the Roses as well as the great Civil War of the 1640s. Painful events, civil wars, dissensions, successes, and failures leave their mark and are recognizable in surnames—and in place names.

Jane Austen possesses a strong sense of place. Various commentators including Deirdre Le Faye and Maggie Lane have noted her acute comprehension of the social geography of London and of Bath. But she is most at home in the countryside and the network of small towns. Austen uses the names of real places to great effect, creating concealed harmonies or interesting dissonances between place name and person. In *Persuasion,* for instance, the casual reference to "Taunton" as the market town and legal center can stir memories of the Bloody Assizes, particularly in conjunction with the constant reference to "Wentworth," the name of Charles I's supporter Lord Strafford, condemned to death by Parliament. The beheading of Strafford is intricately related to the attempted rebellion led by Charles II's illegitimate son the Duke of Monmouth and the subsequent Bloody Assizes at Taunton and elsewhere. No set or string of events is ever entirely over. Austen's England is a place of strains and tension, of disharmonies potentially revived or momentarily perhaps foregone. In her imaginary place names Jane Austen's poetic invention is at its happiest; her linguistic understanding gets full admission to the historical games she is playing. "Mansfield Park" is a name that greatly repays unpacking, but so too is "Combe Magna," or "Highbury"—or "Pemberley."

The employment of so many significant names from mixed eras emphasizes the central importance of anachronism. This may seem a strange thing to allege of an author who is as scrupulous as to details of time, place, and distance. In 1816 Austen writes a somewhat apologetic "Advertisement" to the novel that she thinks she is going to publish soon, fretting over the fact that this work was written some years before:

> This little work was finished in the year 1803 . . . some observation is necessary upon those parts of the work which thirteen years have made comparatively obsolete. The public are entreated to bear in

mind that thirteen years have passed since it was finished, many
more since it was begun, and that during that period, places, manners, books, and opinions have undergone considerable changes.
("Advertisement," *Northanger Abbey*)

The author is acutely aware of complex change between 1803 and 1816.
Austen's scrupulous sensitivity to the contemporary is an aspect of her
deep allegiance to history and respect for changes in places, manners,
fashions, books, and opinions. But her respect for the impact and complexity of historical life urges her toward a subtle probing of conflicts
and oppositions, unsettled and sliding layers of difference. Austen mis-
chievously if often quietly brings to the feast apples (not baked) of discord. One of her prime techniques is to throw carefully into her mix references to different periods and occasions of open and painful conflict.
These can make their subtle but prickly appearance simultaneously: the
long discord between Norman and Saxon; the Dissolution; the Civil
War, coloring the Cavalier gentlemen's hatred and distrust of the Puritans and all mere traders—all of which are summoned into *Pride and
Prejudice,* for example. Because we bear names and live on sites of this
earth that have been settled and fought over, we are living in a world
dense with anachronism. Influences emanating from different moments
of time strike simultaneously upon us during our own moment in the
sun. Past lives matter to us—are in some sense already *in* us. Anachronism is the deep truth about history. The only way in which we can write
history is to be more or less unconsciously anachronistic. Miss Tilney
tastefully approves of the contemporary historians who write fine modern speeches for persons we might not really like to hear from—like
Caractacus (*NA,* I, ch. 14).[10] Eleanor doesn't realize that her taste—
like that of her approved historians—is colored by prejudices. Historians enchant readers into unconscious excursions into anachronism.
The publications of history writers constitute only a tiny—even largely
unimportant—portion of what we feel and obscurely know as history
in the life into which we get plunged at the time we are born and named.

Anachronism is inevitable—it is entailed upon living within the
product (material and immaterial) of multiple times. What is General
Tilney's "Northanger Abbey" but an anachronism several times over?
Austen is very good on private memory and its interpretation and *mis*-
interpretation of the immediate past that we call "the present," as well
as of the longer past. Although "Eight years and a half is a period!"
as Wentworth says (*Persuasion,* II, ch. 10), eight years may seem noth-

ing to the emotional consciousness. But the past of long-gone history keeps poking through too. The past shapes and colors the present. Lady Catherine De Bourgh cannot get out of her Norman-ness or her Kentish assumptions of superiority.

D. W. Harding claims Austen divides personages into characters and caricatures.[11] Harding elaborates on E. M. Forster's distinction (in *Aspects of the Novel*) between "flat" and "round" characters; Forster stresses the difference between those personages with serious interior lives and those whose actions and reactions are not only exaggerated but unvarying. Harding admits that there are moments when a "caricature" develops more human propensities. Actually, it is hard truly to exaggerate or caricature. There is no action or speech so outrageously foolish or absurd—invented by any comic or satiric dramatist, poet, novelist, or standup comic whatsoever—that it has not been equaled and surpassed in what we term "real life." What Austen captures is really the way that we, dear readers, think of ourselves. Each of us imagines Self as three-dimensional, serious, and possessing potential for change. We feel entitled to look upon Others (outside our immediate circle and affectionate concern) as predictable, unvarying—in Forster's term, "flat." Austen altered narrative when, as John Mullan succinctly puts it, she "introduced free indirect style to English fiction, filtering her plots through the consciousness of her characters."[12] In reading, we are always in or near to a characteristic consciousness, but that consciousness makes itself known as "real" by being partly wrong—even deluded. If we got out of that center, the "flat" character, if freshly taken on as eyes to see through, would become "round" and an Elizabeth Bennet or Mr. Darcy would become "flat"—as indeed Darcy is "flat" to Mrs. Bennet. And Mr. Bennet is "flat" to Charles Bingley—we find out near the very end that Bingley always considered Mr. Bennet "eccentric" (*P&P,* III, ch. 13). A number of Austen's characters, as Mullan notes, do not even speak—Captain Benwick is a prime example.[13] Yet we are persuaded of their reality, their consciousness being eked out by that of highly verbal observers.

The mirthfulness of her "caricature" is an aspect of Austen's mercy—the sense that we are all not above limitation. The Lockean consciousness is an ironic assemblage of blunders, and being conscious is full of pitfalls. Elinor Dashwood draws an ardently unreasonable picture of the moral virtue of the timid and dishonest Edward Ferrars. But we get so caught up in Marianne's more blatant error that we don't see Elinor's, because we are persuaded that *she* is a character fully "round," with a developed consciousness—so we are more likely to believe her. Austen's brilliant use of *style indirect libre,* one of her greatest contributions to the Novel, induces the all-too-human reader to participate in human falsehood, prejudice, and error—to know mortal fallibility from within. "We are conscious of many frailties," Jane Austen says in her written prayers; "Be thou merciful, Oh Heavenly Father! to Creatures so formed & situated" (*Later Manuscripts,* 574). The further the device moves us (comically) to humility, the more we take in of how Austen's characters are "formed & situated" in tribe, time, and place. *Style indirect libre* can leave us claustrophobic, imprisoned in one mind. Contact with the natural world, if never unmediated, yet comes as refreshment to the reader as well as to the character. Austen allows us little breaks, moments to enjoy what is "not-mind" like baked apples, weather, a hedgerow.

Austen is fully aware that human beings are produced—by culture and circumstances not designed by them—before arriving (if they ever do) at judgments and choices. In *Mansfield Park* she examines ruthlessly the circumstances of personality production, exhibiting constraints and pressures inflicting permanent damage. No one in the novel is left off the hook. Austen is truly a moralist, and asks for accountability. But accountability must allow some mercy, as we are inevitably conditioned by so much, including the acts and words of generations passed away before we came to be. The ingenious tangle of national histories represented in her fiction through the medium of names speaks of the problematic nature of being in time and in history. Even a consciousness is not a freehold possession.

Austen's poetics is a poetics of anachronism, of multiplicity. Persons reflect places, and places reflect times and individuals. Times collide with each other, one event or concept seeps into others, adding color and flavoring like wine in water. Austen's fiction is at one level—and this is in itself a great achievement—a perfect mastery of all the techniques of "realism." But in her earliest surviving works the teenage Austen gave naturalism and realism—and all formulas of rhetoric—good kicks in the backside. She engages a new kind of surreal comedy. It is foolish to believe that she was committed heart and soul to "realism"—which is merely another set of games with words. Her mature fiction (retooled to fit the tastes of circulating libraries) works so well—and never loses its capacity to startle and surprise—because of its odd density and because its assumed stabilities are counteracted by mercurial instability. Her apprehension of her England resembles Freud's strange suggestive picture (presented early in *Civilization and Its Discontents* and then hastily withdrawn) of a Rome with all its different eras and constructions simultaneously visible. Names in any one novel reflect different phases of "England" converging. Austen refuses to accept history as one-way linear development. She is not writing historical novels, like her mother's cousin Cassandra Cooke, author of *Battleridge* (1799)—though a published work by a novelist in the family may have been an encouragement. Austen is a historian of her immediate present, as many now realize—but she is more than that. Without having to use "Gothic" trappings, she has fully comprehended the tumult of the Gothic, its exploration of the pain of the past and the confusions of different times pressing against each other. Within Austen's acutely observed present, there are the other times, interbraided in twining motion like streams of water down a cascade. We sense an unsubdued flux of old pains and human seasons. Austen seeks to capture the truly absurd simultaneity, the perfectly real anachronism of culture and of individual being. In her resonant references we do not have to choose between one historical allusion and another, or between literary or historical allusion, or between metaphor, wordplay, description, and recall. Austen's poetics is complex, multiplex under its simplicity, evocative rather than (as it pretends) totally naturalistic. In an "Emma Woodhouse" of "*Hart*-field" we find reference to Emma Hart (Lady Hamilton) and to Queen Emma, to the rich family of Watson-Woodhouse and to a woodshed, to perfection and ego, to queenship and hardship. Puns, playfulness, history, comedy and tragedy, historical realities of grandeur and loss—these all at work at once. They are not driving us toward a simple one-to-one equivalence but toward a poetic rather than prosaic encounter with the complex contradictory texture of life.

Austen's poetics is more than the laughter of the foam upon the waves of time. The persons she imagines always have a place upon the earth—the literal earth. She begins *Catharine,* her earliest surviving serious attempt at full-length fiction, with a handmade bower of greenery. "Kitty" and the Wynne sisters have created their "fine shady Bower" of fertile Devonshire's green life, a tribute to affection, female sexuality, and the natural world (*Juvenilia,* 242). Of all these things Catharine's aunt harbors great suspicion. For Mrs. Percival (first of Austen's great hypochondriacs) feminine sexuality is to be repressed. The outdoor world is likewise dirty, inimical, a threat to health. Austen's heroines like touching the earth, being on it and of it. *The Watsons* begins with splashing through the mud, which also soils Elizabeth Bennet's skirts. We have not recognized Austen if we do not see and feel her deep affinity with the land itself, with the physical earth that we depend on so much and over which we make so many foolish claims. We carry about a deep deposit of our mundane earthiness. Personal names and place names bend back toward the land and our humble relations with it. *Hurst*—or *ley* or *haigh* or *shaw*—may meet us in the language of names, incorporating old languages, earlier generations' contact with the real earth. Austen distrusts the "picturesque," the "sublime"—and even the "beautiful"—as if the very categories are somewhat dishonest. Certainly she holds no brief for the "pretty." In her fictions we are never away from mud and earth and air and season and changing light and rain and the generosity of the earth that we love to translate and spiritualize into self-pleasing aesthetics (sometimes very stupidly) and upon which we deeply rely every day for sustenance and life itself. Place names become personal names, and personal names can be attached to places. They belong to that fragile and deep poetic of the human to which Jane Austen responds. The spot of earth does not need us. Jane Austen knows this very well—though she also knows we like to behave as if it did. Earth does not name us nor desire our names. We need it.

Chapter 2

Names as History

INVASION, MIGRATION, WAR, AND CONFLICT

Jane Austen is very conscious of English history, its strata of significance, its detritus—and both its comedy and its pain. On Saturday 26 November 1791 she completed her "History of England." The author who wrote this satire at age sixteen, a constant reader of history books, shrewdly observes historians' pride and prejudice. She is sharply aware of past divisions and discords and the traces they leave. Whether the advent of the Normans was a great civilizing event or represented loss of freedom was freshly debated in Austen's time, under the pressure of the war against Revolutionary and then Napoleonic France. Ann Radcliffe in a travel book of the mid-1790s could assume that England should be proud of having a language still essentially Germanic, resisting takeover by Latinate French. Commenting on the ease with which one can read a sentence in German, Radcliffe remarks,

> So permanent has been the influence of our language which the Saxons acquired by their establishment of more than five centuries amongst us; exiling the antient British tongue to the mountains of Scotland and Wales; and afterwards . . . resisting the persecution of the Normans; rather improving than yielding under their endeavours to extirpate it.[1]

Radcliffe's linguistic comments reflect a version of the "Norman yoke" theory. The English had sturdily *resisted*. Not having a French-derived name could be a source of patriotic pride. The author (whose married surname is Anglo-Saxon "red cliff") seems happy enough regarding the Saxon conquest of "the antient British tongue." Linguistic takeover is "persecution," a threat to meaning. Something of this point of view—

or John Bull prejudice—can be felt in Mr. Knightley's critique of Frank Churchill: "No, Emma, your amiable young man can be amiable only in French, not in English. He may be very 'aimable,' have very good manners, and be very agreeable; but he can have no English delicacy towards the feelings of other people" (*Emma*, I, ch. 18). George Knightley makes this decided critique before he has even met Frank.

The invocation of history has emotional value. In asking the reader to take on the English history known to Austen and her English contemporaries, I am using their vocabulary, with full use of capital letters marking the significance and importance of persons (Prime Minister, Lord Chief Justice) and events (Black Death, Bloody Assizes, Black Act). Not "the conquest" but the Conquest, not a "civil war" but *the* Civil War. There is a frisson of memory and anxiety attached to such phrases, which should not be comfortably homogenized and modernized out of recognition. History summons fear, excitement, sorrow. Major conflicts leave permanent scars. History's rise into narrative consciousness is accompanied by rising tensions. Names carry with them records of population movements and the wounding effects of historical events. In eighteenth-century England there was rising interest in the Anglo-Saxon background, an interest partly defensive and certainly increasing as the French threat became more real. Information was lavishly offered to the reading public so that the meaning and origins of old personal and place names could be readily understood. The reader of Edmund Gibson's and then of Gough's editions of Camden's *Britannia,* for example, can find out that "BERT is the same with our *bright;* in the latin [*sic*] *illustris* and *clarus.*" "EAD in the compound . . . denotes *happiness,* or *blessedness.* Thus *Eadward* is a happy preserver." "MUND. is peace: from whence our Lawyers call a breach of the peace, *Mundbrech.* So, *Eadmund,* is happy peace."[2]

The strongest punctuation marks in English history are invasions and civil wars. The earliest inhabitants of the islands (according to the history known in Austen's time) were of the tribal groups collectively called "Celts" like their relatives in Brittany. From these Celts we get the terms "Britons" and "Britain" (Latin *Britannia*). The first major invasion tracked in written history was the incursion of the Romans in 55/54 BC under Julius Caesar. Serious attempts were made to attach Britain under the Emperor Claudius in 43 AD. Efforts to subdue Caledonia (Scotland) never succeeded. Britons fought back, most notably the heroic if unsuccessful revolt led by Queen Boadicea, head of the

Iceni tribe, in 61–63 AD. At the death of Septimius Severus in 211 AD expansionist plans ceased. Eventually a Rome pressed by barbarian invasions at home took back its troops.

The Romans, who valued the British Isles chiefly as a fortifiable redoubt protecting territory in Gaul, left roads and settled encampments. The names of some cities bear the Roman suffix *-caster* or *-ceaster* meaning fortified camp—hence "Doncaster," "Chester." The cathedral city of Winchester where Jane Austen died was once a Roman fortified town, though its name also refers to pre-Celtic *Venta*—a name figuring in Jane Austen's last literary work, her deathbed verses on Winchester and Saint Swithin.

Fresh invasions came from northern Europe, incursion of Frisians and Jutes (from Jutland). The largest groups of newcomers were the Saxons and the Angles; according to Bede, emigrating Angles emptied their region of Germany. These Germanic tribes came intending to settle. The Saxon influx, widespread and continuous, permanently changed the face of the country, its culture and its language. The Britons were largely driven to marginal regions (Wales, Cornwall, Scotland). In the twentieth century these areas became called the "Celtic fringe," although, as Linda Colley points out in *Britons* (1992), this term is too simple; other peoples exist in these margins, while the Welsh and Scots did not "see themselves as fellow Celts."[3] This mysterious margin of otherness explains why, even after her shaky conversion through Henry's rebuke, Catherine Morland cannot quite believe that the temperate human nature of the practical "midland counties of England" extends throughout the island: "Catherine dared not doubt beyond her own country, and even of that, if hard pressed, would have yielded the northern and western extremities" (*NA*, II, ch. 10). Celtic British names tended to fade from a landscape increasingly English in possession. Settlements and landmarks were given Saxon names; the dominant tongue becomes "Anglo-Saxon," the new English.

The Saxons divided into little kingdoms or territories ruled by what we should call "warlords." A Renaissance term for the political arrangement of the period from circa 500 to 850 AD is the "Heptarchy" or "seven kingdoms." The regional differences of these small states leave their traces. Egbert of Wessex (ca. 769–839 AD), who united Kent, Surrey, Sussex, and Wessex, was called "Wide Ruler," the first declared ruler of a greater whole. Life was severely disrupted by prolonged and energetic attempts by the Danes to invade and colonize. Their warriors came by sea; these are the "Vikings," fighting "Spear Danes," celebrated and described in *Beowulf.* Indeed, that Anglo-Saxon poem, sometimes described as "the first English epic," is in subject matter entirely Scandinavian. The Danes came as settlers, not mere pirates. By 870 AD the Danes dominated; of the seven Saxon kingdoms only Wessex was free. Alfred the Great, son of the king of Wessex and eventually king of the West Saxons, fought a determined war, driving the Danes back. In 886 he retook London, the capital henceforward. King Alfred the Great is customarily acclaimed (if a trifle sentimentally and without perfect accuracy) as the first unifying ruler of the English.

Throughout, the work of colonizing continued: the labor of clearing the forest, creating areas fit for tillage and livestock, and making Saxon (or Danish) settlements. Settlement was largely the operation of the common people. New "pioneer" inhabitants set to work, systematically hewing down the forests and establishing small fortified farms or clusters of dwellings amid modest fields of cleared arable land. This tremendous effort is strongly similar to the efforts made in North America by English migrants from the seventeenth through the nineteenth centuries. By the eleventh century the Saxon settled land was in a flourishing state, with life-sustaining agriculture, fine pasturelands, and wildlife supporting good hunting. Well-watered, fertile, cultivated, and settled, this land was likely to be coveted by neighbors.

The Normans—originally "Norsemen" (Scandinavians, Vikings)—had taken a portion of western France close to England ("Normandy"). By the eleventh century they were French speaking, with French customs. They noted the attractions of the green nearby island, so similar to Normandy. The English fighting force was overtasked in combating the Danes. In January 1066 Harold Godwinson (son of a Saxon father and a Danish mother) was king, but his succession was challenged by his own brother Tostig and by Harold Hardrada of Norway. Hardrada and Tostig won a battle near York, but a few days later were surprised and defeated by King Harold and his army. Harold had managed—amazingly—to march his army from London to Yorkshire in four days. But immediately after the battle the army had to hurry southward, more than two hundred and forty miles, to meet the challenge of the Norman invasion led by William of Normandy. King Harold's men, weakened and fatigued, met the invading army on the south coast. The English failed to repel the invader. On 14 October 1066, Harold, King of England, was killed in the combat. The Battle of Hastings was a total victory for the Normans—the only English defeat on English home territory.

In Austen's day this invasion story was more than mere schoolroom reading. There was a most realistic fear that Napoleon could succeed as William of Normandy had done, crossing the English Channel with a sufficient number of ships to carry armies and taking possession of the coast. Naval captains and army officer as well as historians thought hard about the Battle of Hastings and the effectiveness of William's purpose-built invasion flotilla of seven hundred ships. Napoleon was preparing a similar invasion fleet.

The Norman Conquest is the most important single *event* in English history. The coming of the Angles and Saxons had extended over centuries. The action of one October day was final and defining. The immigration of the Angles and Saxons had made the country "England"; the coming of the Normans changed what "England" was to mean. Normans took over and administered the conquered country. The new King William demanded that a record be made of all lands and who held them (primarily for tax purposes). This record came to be known as the "Domesday Boke" (Doomsday Book). Completed with amazing efficiency by 1086, the Doomsday Book is an invaluable source of information as to the names and ethnicities of landholders as well as recording cultivation, settlements, and productivity.

The Normans not only took note of the settlements—they changed the landscape. In their ardent desire for deer-hunting grounds—for the *chase*—the Normans enclosed a great deal of woodland, sending settlers and villagers packing. For centuries to come, hunting on horseback is the mark of the aristocracy. The Normans and their descendants hunted the wild deer so vigorously that eventually there were no more deer in the south. The wildwood also receded under pressure of agriculture and growing population. There had been other changes. Astonishingly, in 1066 there were no rabbits in England. The Normans imported rabbits. This new species belonged to the rich Norman landowners; rabbits' warrens, or burrows, were watched over by "warreners." (Hence come new surnames: "Warren," "Warrender"). The poor were forbidden to kill and eat not only deer but also rabbits, despite damage to their gardens and crops.

The stories of Robin Hood in the free greenwood express resentful resistance to the Norman authority over food and land. The "forest laws" against "poaching" and related "crimes" were a constant source of bitter discontent. Working-class men were likely to defy the landowners' claim to absolute possession of all that hopped or ran or swam or flew and to become "poachers." Unlicensed persons taking game to which their position gave them no recognized right were treated as thieves, subject to severe punishment. (For a poor man to kill a deer merited death.) The advance of settlements diminished the noble deer chase, save in Scotland. Foxhunting was the substitute.[4] But struggles regarding field, forest, and stream continued. New specific laws, such as the "Black Act" of 1723, aroused great hostility.[5] The engrossing of rights to all game among the ruling classes was one of the outstanding—and enduring—instances of the "Norman yoke."

With the Doomsday Book the use of surnames became regularized in England. Throughout the world, one single name per person has been customary. Identification by surname arises first among the noble and the landed. Surnames are also convenient for governments concerned with taxation. The power of "lords" (or warlords) rested on bloodlines and complex genealogies which long made surnames essential. Common people, with less use for an official last name, were often defined by occupation: "Carpenter," "Wright," "Fletcher" (maker of arrows). (This tendency never quite dies out; the electrician in my village in Canada was popularly called "Johnny Kilowatt.") A poor man might be defined as the son of a man identified by a first name: "Robin's-son." A person could also be defined by location: "John who lives by the brook," "Martin from the grove." Men might also be called by the name of the town or region whence they—or their forebears—came: "Lincoln," "Cornwall." Locative descriptions crystallize into surnames.

William did not relinquish his claim to the west of France, and this dual territory provided a cause for war and an excuse for invasions of France by the English for centuries. (The claim of the English king to rule France was maintained until 1688.) Relations between England and France have had a peculiar kind of intimacy mixed with constant hostility as the two nations competed for territory and colonies, influence and trade. British historians and philosophers of the eighteenth century often presented the Norman Conquest as advantageous, linking England with the Continent and European civilization. Opposition to this optimistic history proposed that England had suffered under "the Norman yoke" and that Anglo-Saxon laws and customs had been more inclined to favor justice, equality, and the rights of the common people. Among historians opposing Norman rule is David Hume, whose work Austen knew. (Jane Austen's uncle James Leigh-Perrot gave her a copy of Hume's *History*.) Hume takes the view that Norman invasion introduced dominance by a proud aristocracy and monarchy, as well as too much power given to the Church—all depriving the English of their lib-

1. W. Bromley, *Battle of Hastings* (1804). Engraving after a painting by Philip James de Loutherbourg. Photograph: © Trustees of the British Museum.

erties. Hume disapprovingly remarks that the loss in October 1066 and subsequent submission arose from temporary weakness in the English:

> But tho' the loss . . . was considerable, it might easily have been repaired by a great nation. . . . The people had in a great measure lost all national pride and spirit, by their recent and long subjection to the Danes; and as Canute had . . . much abated the rigors of conquest . . . they regarded with the less terror the ignominy of a foreign yoke.[6]

The Battle of Hastings loomed large in the English imagination at the turn into the nineteenth century. *This* time they were determined to resist the French yoke. In 1804 the great theatrical scene-maker Philip de Loutherbourg drew a historical picture for a patriotic new series and new edition of Hume's *History*. That picture, the frontispiece, is *The Battle of Hastings* (fig. 1).[7]

After 1066, language and customs changed. All important political or legal discourse was conducted in Norman French. The aristocracy became almost entirely Norman, although there was intermarriage. The names of titles vary from the antique "Duke" or Anglo-Saxon "Earl" to specifically French versions of a name of rank, such as "Viscount." We can notice in Austen's novels a clear (if sometimes unobtrusive) line separating Norman names from names of common English (Anglo-Saxon) origin. Locative names ("Hill"), filial names ("Jenkinson"), and work names ("Chapman") indicate the commonest Englishness. (All of the above appear as servants' names.) References to places include various terms for settlement or village such as *-wick* (a settlement on the site of a *vicus,* or Romano-Briton settlement) or a Danish *-by*.

The Conquest was followed by a sequence of civil or internecine conflicts, tribal wars, and struggles for power. Some aristocrats held large territories, very like the old kingdoms, and commanded fighting men. European nobles all have their roots in "warlords" who could control regions and command armed men.[8] The true power of medieval lords was unignorable. Hence the thirteenth-century invention of Parliament placed the House of Lords above the House of Commons. Parliament represents a great advance; the nobles should come and talk with each other and argue things out instead of resorting first to the sword. Creating a centralized government under one king took a long while. Inevitably, the monarchy was weak and the nobles strong.

The Wars of the Roses in the fifteenth century center upon the struggle for dominance between two strong dynasties, each with an attractive emblem—and control of very large regions: Lancashire (Red Rose) and Yorkshire (White Rose). The progress of events was dramatized by William Shakespeare in plays that offer a vivid—if not strictly accurate—account of events and personalities. Shakespeare shows us conflict brought on by the weak King Richard II, soon overthrown by the aggressive Lancastrian Bolingbroke who becomes King Henry IV. After a brilliant (but ultimately meaningless) retaking of some of France under the dashing Henry V, England succumbed to divisions; the weakness of the pious Lancastrian King Henry VI led to defeat by the determination of the York dynasts.

The Yorkists, proud of success, put their own man on the throne, King Edward IV. He died, leaving two young sons under the care of their uncle, the Duke of Gloucester, as Protector. Richard of Gloucester took the throne for himself; his enemies claimed he had murdered the little princes in the Tower. This last Yorkist king, Richard III, was defeated at the Battle of Bosworth Field in 1485 by a new force, Henry Tudor. Technically, Lancaster won the Wars of the Roses, and the Red Rose was supreme, but Henry Tudor founded a new dynasty, shoring up his connection with the Yorkist cause through marriage.

Shakespeare's "History Plays" offer us a factually elastic, action-driven but complex version of the Wars of the Roses, with a built-in Tudor bias. Shakespeare's dramatic story constitutes the version of that civil war most familiar to readers of Austen's time, although they could rely for "real solemn history" on David Hume and Oliver Goldsmith, whose texts were standard in the schoolroom. Jane Austen was familiar with such histories, as well as with Shakespeare's plays, when she inscribed in *Volume the Second* her satiric work "The History of England from the reign of Henry the 4th to the death of Charles the 1st." As Devoney Looser says, "Her *History* deconstructs historical material and then reconstructs it in a fictional mold, claiming with tongue in cheek that truth 'is very excusable in an Historian.' Austen's truths . . . are present-day truths. Her history is self-conscious about contemporary use and apprehensions of the past."[9] Austen is always conscious of appropriation of the past. She sees through self-interested defenses of material appropriations. Historians offer current alibis to the powerful. Under the title of her "History" she adds, "By a partial, prejudiced and ignorant Historian" (176). In this playful work with a serious point, the "Historian" is openly coat-trailing, defending the Stuart cause throughout and taking the "wrong" side in the Wars of the Roses. Under "Henry the 6th" she writes,

> I cannot say much for this Monarch's Sense—Nor would I if I could, for he was a Lancastrian. I suppose you know all about the Wars between him and the Duke of York who was of the right side; if you do not, you had better read some other History, for I shall not be very diffuse in this, meaning by it only to vent my Spleen *against,* and shew my Hatred *to* all those people whose parties or principles do not suit with mine, and not to give information. ("The History of England," *Juvenilia,* 178)

She roots for the underdog, including Richard III. (How pleased and amused she would be at the recent discovery of Richard's skeleton beneath a car park—and his sudden surge in popularity.) A developed satirist, Jane Austen is already aware that written histories are political stories, myths fostered by the winners and uttered for the benefit of the historian's contemporaries. All historians reflect "prejudices." The past cannot come to us uncolored by old or new preferred beliefs and allegiances. Austen's own "prejudiced and ignorant Historian" goes against the stream in preferring the *losing* side in all major struggles. She is attracted to protests and resistances.

The Tudor King Henry VII did not assume kingship without protest. Perkin Warbeck (1474–99), claiming to be the younger of the two Princes in the Tower, made an attempt to take the crown. Warbeck was cordially entertained by the house of Burgundy and welcomed in Scotland; support for this new "Edward V" in Cornwall and the southwest aroused the new Tudor government to action. The new claimant was welcomed in Taunton in Dorset—an area strongly associated with rebellion and refusal to knuckle under to authority. Such West Country rebellions are customarily unsuccessful. Warbeck's forces were defeated; he was captured and made to confess himself a Flemish impostor. Doubts in his favor, however, survived. Mary Shelley was to write a novel, *The Fortunes of Perkin Warbeck* (1830). Jane Austen supports Warbeck, and the other "pretender" Lambert Simnel, in a sexual extravaganza that dissolves heterosexual marital and familial dynastic claims: "For if Perkin Warbeck was really the Duke of York, why might not Lambert Simnel be the Widow of Richard" ("History," *Juvenilia,* 179).

Dynastic claims did not cease, even after the squashing of Warbeck and Simnel. Alternative claims arose, like that made by Lady Jane Grey after the death of the Catholic Mary I. The Tudors had forcefully unified England (and were trying to pull in Scotland) but were faced from the outset with fresh ideological splits. Before the Tudor era, some forms of Protestantism were already on the march, and there was considerable discontent with Rome. Henry VIII did not invent English Protestantism, but he took the Reformation movement in particular directions. Having been *Defensor Fidei,* Defender of the Faith, in his youth, Henry VIII withdrew his allegiance to the papacy over the issue of annulment of his marriage to Katherine of Aragon (often termed "a divorce"). Henry's marriage to Anne Boleyn, a dynastic matter, could have been countenanced, but the embattled Pope Clement VII was unwilling to conciliate the King of England at the price of alienating Katherine's nephew, the powerful Emperor Charles V.

The Tudor period, not least the reign of Henry VIII, fascinates, with its extravagance, its jousts and witty poetic courtiers, its court of discarded queens and multiple beheadings. Austen shares this fascination in her "History of England." She defends "Anna Bullen":

> This amiable Woman was entirely innocent of the Crimes with which she was accused, of which her Beauty, her Elegance, and her Sprightliness were sufficient proofs, not to mention her solemn protestations of Innocence, the weakness of the Charges against her, and the King's Character. (*Juvenilia*, 181)

The treasonable "Crimes" of which Anne Boleyn was accused were (as Austen knew) adultery with four men of the court and incest with her brother. (Both Hume and Goldsmith—like Austen—deny any basis for the charges.) Anne's long "letter to the King . . . dated on the 6th of May" (181) to which Austen refers is reprinted in a numerous standard histories. Not only was Anne beheaded in 1536, but her brother and all the accused men were likewise executed.

King Henry's boldest move—guided by Thomas Cromwell—was the seizure of Church lands in the Dissolution of the Monasteries, beginning in 1536 when the smaller foundations were dissolved. These Church lands—to which the Crown had *no* legal right—were forcibly taken and privatized; Henry VIII used the treasures and rich demesnes to obtain much-needed funds or to reward certain followers. Protest and backlash ensued. In the northeast, particularly in Lincolnshire and Yorkshire, there was an effort to defend the Church and keep the monasteries, popular with the people as they provided social services and education, as well as some assurance of food and protection in difficult times. This protest movement was called "The Pilgrimage of Grace." It briefly rose to armed rebellion, taking some territory including the port city of Hull. Henry VIII ruthlessly put down the Pilgrimage of Grace, executing the ringleaders in 1537.

In Austen's mature fiction we shall keep bumping into characters from Henry VIII's time, and issues unresolved. Questions regarding the seizure of church lands were current in Austen's era. The issue was contemporary, not archaic. In France, the "Jacobins," revolutionaries who had seized the controls from the moderate constitutionalists, demanded the subjugation of the Catholic Church to the French state and the dissolution of all monasteries and convents. (Arguments pro and con are succinctly presented in letter 8 of Charlotte Smith's pro-Revolution novel *Desmond,* 1792).[10] The new government seized Church property. Monks and nuns were thrown into the roads, penniless and homeless, to survive as best they could. Some of the multitude of priests ejected for not conforming to new rules and oaths made their way to England. Among those who spoke up in their favor was the novelist Frances Burney, now Madame D'Arblay, wife of an émigré. Burney's pamphlet *Brief Reflections Relative to the Emigrant French Clergy* (1793) both promoted charitable support of these exiles and pointed out the illegality of the arbitrary measures taken against them. It was embarrassing for English conservatives to contemplate such predatory attacks upon property and usurpations of Catholic Church lands by an arbitrary revolutionary government that the English upper classes hated—for there was an uncomfortably clear parallel to what had happened in England in the sixteenth century. Consideration prompted renewed complaint regarding the sixteenth-century depredation, which had deprived the English people of lands that ought to have been used for the public good. Jane Austen seems always to have been antipathetic to the Dissolution and what it meant. Her "prejudiced Historian" in 1791 makes a mock defense of Henry VIII:

> The Crimes and Cruelties of this Prince, were too numerous to be mentioned, (as this history I trust has fully shewn;) and nothing can be said in his vindication, but that his abolishing Religious Houses and leaving them to the ruinous depredations of time has been of infinite use to the landscape of England in general, which probably was a principal motive for his doing it, since otherwise why should a Man who was of no Religion himself be at so much trouble to abolish one which had for Ages been established in the Kingdom. ("History," *Juvenilia,* 181)

This ironic comment seems a direct riposte to William Gilpin, the travel writer. Austen (like some of her characters, such as Henry Tilney) knew his picturesque *Observations* very well. "At a very early age she was enamoured of Gilpin on the Picturesque," says her brother Henry in 1817, without taking note of her critiques of Gilpin ("Biographical Notice," in *Memoir,* 140–41). William Gilpin, as can be seen in his *Observations Relative Chiefly to Picturesque Beauty* (1786), is always happy when contemplating the ruins of abbeys and their "picturesque" properties. To Gilpin, contemplating the ruins of abbeys is a delightfully English visual treat:

> To these natural features, which are, in a great degree peculiar to the landscape of England, we may lastly add another, of the artificial kind—the ruins of abbeys; which, being naturalized to the soil, might indeed, without much impropriety, be classed among it's [*sic*] natural beauties.[11]

Austen's remark that Henry VIII "was of infinite use to the landscape of England" by ruining the abbeys is a satiric reflection—not a distortion—of Gilpin's complacent view.

William Gilpin occasionally registers an uneasy consciousness of the original function of these charming remnants, but almost always hastens to encourage his English and Anglican readers into full enjoyment of the ruins *as* ruins. The charities of such places only encouraged laziness. So he indicates looking at Tintern Abbey, where there are beggars: "As if a place once devoted to indolence, could never again become the seat of industry."[12]

Catholicism encourages beggary. Abbeys are homes of indolence. These are Whig axioms. In 1798 Gilpin returns to the issue in discussing the ruins of Glastonbury Abbey. Gilpin initially appears to be unusually fair to Glastonbury Abbey's function:

> Above four hundred children were not only educated in it, but entirely maintained. Strangers from all parts of Europe were liberally received. . . . While the poor from every side of the country waited the ringing of the alms-bell; when they flocked . . . to the gate of the monastery, where they received, every morning, a plentiful provision for themselves and their families; all this appears great and noble.
>
> On the other hand, when we consider five hundred persons, bred up in indolence and lost to the commonwealth; when we consider that these houses were the great nurseries of superstition, bigotry and ignorance; the stews of sloth, stupidity, and perhaps intemperance; when we consider, that the education received in them had not the least tincture of useful learning, good manners or true religion, but tended rather to vilify and disgrace the human mind; when we consider that the pilgrims and strangers who resorted thither, were

idle vagabonds . . . and when we consider, lastly, that indiscriminate alms-giving is not real charity, but an avocation from labour and industry . . . filling the mind with abject notions, we are led to acquiesce in the fate of these great foundations, and view their ruins, not only with a picturesque eye, but with moral and religious satisfaction.[13]

Monasteries, in short, must have been bad because they were Catholic, and anything Catholics do is an affront to Protestant ethics and industry. Gilpin makes no attempt to allow for different historical circumstances—for instance, the value in the Middle Ages of teaching local boys Latin and thus giving them access to the learning of the Western world or the importance of monastic labor in breaking new land and introducing better land management without immediate increase in the population. In reality, monks over the centuries had not been "lost to the commonwealth," but their contribution must be erased. As for *giving* something to somebody, patently that is always wrong—according to Whig economics, soon to be powerfully backed by Malthus. The only purpose a great work of architecture and human endeavor such as Glastonbury Abbey can serve is in the picturesque loveliness of its ruins.

In her novels, Austen implicitly combats Gilpin's biases. Two novels have at their center privatized abbeys, and there are other references to lost religious sites. Jane Austen distrusts the cult of the picturesque, suspecting it under its softness as a sharp mode of justifying destruction in the past (and hence in the present). The picturesque, mediating hedonistically between the beautiful and the sublime, offers consolation for the ruination of time and a soothing antidote to *others'* pain and travail. Austen's suspicion of the "Gothic" and the picturesque more generally seems to arise from a sense that a fondness for ruins masks not only a fondness for destruction, but also a political argument. Picturesque ideology might have been created to justify anti-Catholicism and disdain for common needy folk. Austen will not allow the connection to escape her. No wonder that Henry and Elinor Tilney, innocent beneficiaries of the partial destruction and wholesale theft of Northanger Abbey, register approval alike of Whig historians and of Gilpin's picturesque theories.

Chapter 3

Civil War, Ruins, and the Conscience of the Rich

Shakespeare's last "history play" is *Henry VIII,* which links the Tudor victory of Henry VII to Henry VIII's early reign and cautiously exhibits the religious split of the mid-sixteenth century. This is the play that Henry Crawford was reading aloud at Mansfield Park—and did not finish. However cautious Shakespeare needs to be, the story delineated in *Henry VIII* is anxious and sad. The most sympathetic and moving role is that of Katherine of Aragon, victim of Henry's decision to divorce. The play is best known for the speeches of Cardinal Wolsey, a superb example of rise and fall on Fortune's wheel. Austen comically recalls Shakespeare's Wolsey in that light in "Love and Freindship [*sic*]": "What an ample subject for reflection on the uncertain Enjoyments of this World, would not that Phaeton and the Life of Cardinal Wolsey afford a thinking Mind!" (*Juvenilia,* 129).

Austen repeatedly returns to the world of the Tudors. In her first (uncompleted) serious courtship novel, *Catharine* ("Kitty, or the Bower"), the aunt's name "Percival" (changed from lowly "Peterson") is chivalrously medieval or Arthurian. "Percival," a Norman name, and in Arthurian lore a synonym for purity, is in marked contrast to "Dudley," a name associated with male sexuality and sexual trespass. Robert Dudley, Earl of Leicester, was notoriously a favorite and supposed lover of Queen Elizabeth. Mr. Dudley, the clergyman in *Catharine,* is true to his ancestry: "The younger son of a very noble Family . . . more famed for their Pride than their opulence, tenacious of his dignity . . . forever quarrelling" (*Juvenilia,* 245). This neighbor gives a party, inviting Catharine's aunt, a hyperchaste admirer of Queen Elizabeth, in comic parallel to the elaborate festivities at Kenilworth put on for "the Virgin Queen" by Robert Dudley. Jane Austen's collateral ancestor Alice Leigh had married Robert Dudley, the son of that Earl of Leicester.

That Robert Dudley soon deserted Alice, whisking off with his mistress Elizabeth disguised as his page.[1]

Mrs. Percival's relatives, the careless, rich, and successful Stanley family, are presumably descendants of the celebrated Stanley who led the charge of the English against the Scots at the Battle of Flodden and later married the widowed mother of the man who was to become the first Tudor king, Henry VII. That Stanley, originally Yorkist, treacherously fought Richard III at Bosworth—and placed the crown on his stepson Henry's head. The successfully treacherous Stanleys in *Catharine* are in thematic opposition to the unsuccessful Wynne family. Austen's contemporary Wynnes were Stuart loyalists. In her "History of England" Austen lauds the sixteenth-century Duke of Norfolk for remaining loyal to Mary Queen of Scots; the Howards also remained faithful to Catholicism through the centuries of disabilities. "Howard," family name of the Dukes of Norfolk, is England's most ancient aristocratic surname. Austen gives it only to Mr. Howard the clergyman, undoubtedly the designed future husband of Emma Watson.

Conflict between Catholic and Protestant in England became more insistent as the sixteenth century proceeded, although much of the new nation state's attention was turned outward. In Elizabeth's reign England began to explore, claim, and colonize lands in North America and the Caribbean. Spain's effort to invade England with the great Armada of 1588 was beaten off. Protestants became split among themselves. To some extent, Lutherans and the newer Calvinists influenced each other, though greatly at odds in important respects. The Anglican compromise suited many but not all. Catholics mourned their banished international sacramental Church, while dogmatic Puritans were anxious to get rid of bishops and of all Anglican sacramental elements that seemed too much like Catholicism. Fission into smaller and contesting groups of "Dissenters" would become a feature of the late sixteenth and seventeenth centuries, with a multiplication of sects and creeds. Yet, after the threat of Spain had passed, England on the whole enjoyed economic prosperity; well-off inhabitants of country towns created public structures such as Corn Exchanges, almshouses, and schools and rebuilt and enlarged private houses.

The British—and their American progeny—have a fatal attraction to civil war. Dissonances played out primarily as religious difference, but a struggle of some sort was on the cards. Once the power of the great nobles had been beaten back, kingly power and the new mercantilist class, formerly aiding each other, were likely to come into conflict.

Tensions culminated in the great Civil War of the 1640s. The Wars of the Roses had been dynastic and regional. The English Civil War was a truly *political* conflict in the modern sense, with warring ideologies and "culture wars," although regional concerns were not absent. In the 1630s Charles I endeavored to undertake an unpopular war to bring the Scots to heel over the Anglican religious settlement. Lowland Protestant Scotland stoutly resisted. (Highlanders tended to remain Catholic.) Scots aristocrats and commoners signed the "Covenant"—a Covenant with God resisting the Prayer Book and standing true to Calvinist faith. Endeavoring to impose uniformity, Charles I engaged in an unpopular war with Scotland. His English antagonists knew he could be beaten when Charles had to recall Parliament to ask for funds.

The English Revolution of the 1640s marks the division between Royalists or "Cavaliers" favoring the monarch and, on the whole, the Anglican Church as established (or even Roman Catholicism) and the Puritans, or "Roundheads," favoring some kind of theistic Protestant republic (supported by Calvinist Presbyterians and Independents). Parliament became more Puritan just as the country had outgrown the medieval financial arrangements for servicing the state. The growing nation-state was too big for its old cradle. Any ruler was going to be strapped for cash, and Parliament held the purse strings. Charles I had tried to find new ways of raising revenue and doing without Parliament. (Curiously, Oliver Cromwell, dictator during the 1650s, was to face exactly the same fiscal problems and to pursue similar methods, including dismissing Parliament.)

King and Parliament (now knowing its own power) fell out to the point of armed conflict. Royalist forces, though much better versed in warfare, did not win sufficiently decisively in the Battle of Edgehill (23 October 1642). Parliamentary forces gained time in which to learn the arts of warfare and regroup. Oliver Cromwell designed his "New Model Army," an efficient fighting force commanded by General Thomas Fairfax. This army eventually won decisively at the Battle of Naseby (14 June 1645). Parliamentary forces were eventually successful in capturing the king, after a second round of Civil War in which the Scots took the Stuart side. In a highly unconstitutional court of picked members of Parliament (from which all elected MPs who might vote in King Charles's favor had been excluded) "the man Charles Stuart" was declared guilty of high crimes and sentenced to death.[2] King Charles I was executed on 30 January 1649—a date commemorated by the Anglican Church as a day of fasting and penitence after the Restoration for over a century. The English Civil War—the most important event in England after the Norman Conquest—affects all subsequent political developments. It is the mother—or grandmother—of the American Revolution in the following century.

Printed books were not the only sources for direct information regarding Civil War as objective reality. The Civil War left physical traces—as in the old Church of Saint Lawrence at Alton, where Jane's brother Frank's infant son was baptized in 1809. In December 1643, the King's forces at royalist Alton under Ludovic Lindsay, sixteenth Earl of Crawford, were surprised by Parliamentary forces under General Waller. Crawford escaped with most of his army to Winchester, leaving Colonel Richard Boles with a hopeless task as the Battle of Alton raged on 13 December. Some thousand Royalist soldiers were captured; Waller's troops drove the defenders back to the churchyard. Surviving Royalists made for the church and fortified it as well as they could, but after prolonged resistance the parliamentary forces broke in and killed all within; Colonel Boles was cut down on the steps of the pulpit. The church floor ran with blood.[3] You can still see—as Austen could still see—bullet holes and other damage from the battle.

The Commonwealth government was severely Puritan. The Puritans closed the theaters, destroying buildings like Shakespeare's indoor theater at Blackfriars. Swearing was legally punishable, as was going for a walk or playing the lute on Sunday or celebrating Christmas. Government devolved into the personal rule of the Lord Protector, Oliver Cromwell. In the 1650s for the first and only time England was ruled by a dictator. Cromwell was at first almost entirely engaged in wiping out the opposition, defeating the young Charles II at the Battle of Worcester 1650, after invading and most dreadfully pacifying Ireland. He defended as "a righteous judgment of God on those barbarous wretches" the massacre committed in September 1649 at Drogheda, where men, women, and children were slaughtered. The hatred of Cromwell in Ireland has never died.

Oliver's son was unwilling to take on the job after the Protector's death; his generals squabbled among themselves. The Restoration of 1660 brought back the monarchy in the person of King Charles II, son of Charles I, whom Royalists considered a murder victim and religious martyr. Royalist sympathies can be indicated in use of the names "Charles," "Charlotte," or "Caroline," as is clear in a favorite novel of Jane Austen, Samuel Richardson's *Sir Charles Grandison* (1753–54). Such names are still meaningful in Austen's world. Charles Bingley and his sister Caroline hint at an assumed Tory royalism on the part of the Yorkshire father keen on rising into the elite through wealth acquired in trade.

The Civil War was not finished in 1660. Charles II's reign was a very bumpy ride, characterized by efforts of Puritans and republicans within and outside of Parliament to unseat King Charles. At the same time, the nation had to raise revenue for a navy to fight off the rising power of Holland and to face the ambitions of France in the New World as well as the Old. Charles II's marriage to the Portuguese Catherine of Braganza brought no heir, but a wonderful dowry—Bombay, soon the headquarters of Britain's design upon the wealth of India. Charles II was justifiably suspected of being too well connected with France and French interests. (He got funds from Louis XIV in the secret Treaty of Dover.) At one point it was claimed that the Catholics in England, the "Papists," had a secret but wide-ranging plot to assassinate members of the government and take over the country. Reference to the alleged "Popish Plot" provided fuel for anti-Catholic propaganda for decades. Charles's party could claim victimization through the "Rye House Plot," a Protestant conspiracy to assassinate Charles II and the Duke of York on return from Newmarket races in the spring of 1683. (The plot failed because the royals came home early, owing to a fire at Newmarket.) Important persons were allegedly implicated, including republican leaders of the "country" party, William Lord Russell and Algernon Sidney. Both were executed and became martyr-heroes of the Whig cause.

The deep divisions of the Civil War led to the differentiation of two political parties, "Whig" and "Tory." These are not official political parties in our modern sense—our idea of the political party grew out of them. They are not "constitutional" in origin; rather, they are a new formation for which official structure had eventually to make room. Both terms are insults. "Whig" is short for "Whiggamore," meaning a Scottish cattle-robber; a "Tory" is an Irish thief or bandit. Whigs are thus identified as ultra-Calvinist criminals, and Tories as Catholic predators. Each is identified with a disdained Celtic group originating in a fringe area. The nineteenth century saw efforts to clean up the names of established political parties, as "Liberal" or "Conservative"—but the eighteenth-century parties truly are "Whigs" and "Tories."

Internal political divisions morphed fairly rapidly into a two-party system, which seems to suit the agonistic nature of the English-speaking world. Eighteenth-century "Tories" are traditionally associated with the Anglican establishment and with landowners, while "Whigs" generally incline to Protestantism and attract members of trading and commercial classes (although there were also great Whig landowners and aristocrats and some Tory businessmen). Landed property was subject to taxation, while the profits from trade and financial dealings were not taxed. Whigs were likely to be enthusiastic supporters of expensive wars that enlarged trade routes and sustained colonies, but Tory landowners would have to pay for wars enriching untaxed traders in the City of London.

When Charles II died in 1685, his openly Roman Catholic brother James succeeded, despite strenuous objections. His was the last Catholic regime in England, making significant the statement of Mrs. Rushworth in *Mansfield Park* that the chapel at Sotherton was "fitted up as you see it, in James the Second's time" (*MP*, I, ch. 9). Were the Rushworths once practicing Catholics, who briefly came into the open— but who have forgotten or suppressed the inconvenient memory? If so, their loyalty is not *worth* a *rush*. James's first marriage (to Anne Hyde, an English commoner) had issue in only two female children: Mary and Anne. His second marriage to the Italian princess Mary of Modena had issue in a son; his opponents spread the rumor that the baby was not his nor the queen's, but was smuggled to the bedroom in a warming pan. Antipathy to James precipitated the insurrection of James Scott, Duke of Monmouth, illegitimate son of Charles II—and an Anglican Protestant. The Duke of Monmouth, aided and abetted by Anthony Ashley Cooper, Lord Shaftesbury, made his first attempt while Charles II was still alive, during the Exclusion Crisis, an attempt to change the constitution and exclude the Catholic Duke of York (later James II) from the succession.[4]

The second attempt of James Scott, Duke of Monmouth, to gain the crown came after the death of his father. Monmouth proposed religious toleration for Catholics and for various Protestant sects. In summer of 1685 Monmouth came with a modest force from Europe, landing at Lyme Regis. He tried to move toward Bristol, narrowly bypassing Bath. He went through a form of coronation at Chard in Somerset (a few miles from Crewkerne) and was received as King of England at Taunton, in the area that had supported Perkin Warbeck. Driven back from Bristol, he retraced his steps, taking refuge near Bridgewater. The young duke and his small force were defeated on the pleasant green and level fields of Weston Zoyland, at the Battle of Sedgemoor, 6 July 1685. Monmouth was captured, quickly tried, and beheaded.

Monmouth knew the risk he took. But his local followers, many of

them poor working people, were cruelly punished. Trials conducted by
five judges led by Lord Chief Justice Jeffreys (who mocked his victims)
were held in August and September 1685 in Winchester, Salisbury,
Dawlish, Taunton, and Wells. A couple of women were sentenced to be
burned for treason; many rebels were hanged and or transported. These
Bloody Assizes were never forgotten. The cruel aftermath of the Monmouth rebellion, as well as James's zealous attempts to bring England to
rapid acceptance of Catholicism, ignited a strong reaction. Protestant
leaders led by Henry Sidney formally called on the assistance of James's
son-in-law, William of Orange, husband of James II's daughter Mary
and Protestant ruler of Holland. William invaded in 1688, landing on
15 November at Torbay in Devon. He marched on London, gathering
military support. Some of James's generals defected to the Protestant
side—not least in importance, John Churchill. James II yielded, fleeing
from London on 18 December 1688, to take refuge in France. His departure simplified matters for William of Orange, whom many thought
a Dutch usurper. William became England's monarch (in theory, joint
ruler with his wife Mary). This coup of 1688 (often invoked during the
run-up to the American Revolution) was described by Whig patriots as
the "Glorious Revolution." This nearly bloodless "Revolution" resulted
in a new disposition of power, and a new understanding of the constitution of England. After this point, no Catholic could be heir to the
throne or wed with a member of the royal family.

Perpetual disabilities were put upon Catholics. They already were denied the vote. Until 1829, no Roman Catholic could vote in England.
Catholics regularly paid double taxation and were not allowed to live
within five miles of Parliament. (Hence Alexander Pope inhabited a
villa at Twickenham, instead of residing in London.) Absolute distrust of Catholics was widespread among Protestants and republicans.
One of the claims to be registered by American colonists against King
George III is that the king has been too kind to French settlers in Que-
bec, allowing them to remain and govern themselves, practicing their
own religion.

The world into which Austen was born was a long-term result of the
settlement of 1688–89. Anxiety about future rebellion led to the Act of
Union of 1707, uniting England and Scotland as one kingdom. Some
Scottish laws and customs were permitted to remain, including the old
marriage laws, even after English law had radically altered under Lord
Hardwicke's Marriage Act in the 1750s. In Scotland (as formerly in England), a couple had only to get up before witnesses and declare them-

selves married to *be* married. Couples not permitted to marry under the new English law (designed to protect the dowries of girls of good family) could speed to Scotland. Once married in Scotland they were married in Britain. Hence arises the popularity of a Scottish border village, Gretna Green, to which Lydia's friends hope she has eloped to marry Wickham.

Union did not prevent further civil war. The Stuart heir, the "Old Pretender," attempted to gain the crown after the death of Anne in 1715. There was a more ambitious effort in 1745, with the attempted invasion of "Bonnie Prince Charlie," inadequately backed by France. Briefly successful, Bonnie Prince Charlie won over Scotland and brought his troops into England as far as Derbyshire. But the anticipated uprising in his favor among English "Jacobites" did not occur. Hard pressed, his army turned back to Scotland; in the Battle of Culloden his followers were mowed down by the English army commanded by George II's son, the Duke of Cumberland ("Butcher Cumberland"). Fields and cottages were burned or otherwise destroyed, and many of this desolate population emigrated to North America. Samuel Johnson critically notes the desolating effect in his account of his journey to the Highlands.

Bonnie Prince Charlie himself was saved, largely owing to the enterprise of a twenty-four-year-old woman with access to a boat. In June 1746, two months after disastrous Culloden, Flora MacDonald took the disguised prince away in a rowboat; she and her rowers got him to safety in the Isle of Skye. Flora, imprisoned briefly in the Tower of London, was freed in 1747. She became famous, a Scots heroine legendary in her lifetime. Her portrait was painted (fig. 2). Dr. Johnson, who met her on the Isle of Skye, speaks of her in the highest terms: "Flora Macdonald . . . a name that will be mentioned in history, and if courage and fidelity be virtues, mentioned with honour." Johnson adds a personal impression to dispel the image of a virago: "She is a woman of middle stature, soft features, gentle manners and elegant presence."[5]

There were new attempt to reincorporate Scotland imaginatively, through pleasing representations of wild landscape and heroic people. There was even a vogue for Scottish songs and fashions—although the true clan tartan was outlawed. (Linda Colley in *Britons* has described the process of integration of the Scots into the imperial project.) Edinburgh, "the Athens of the North," produced major philosophers including David Hume and Adam Smith. King George III was criticized for favoring the Scots too much—he put his own tutor Lord Bute into the position of Prime Minister.

2. Allan Ramsay, *Flora Macdonald* (eighteenth century). Photograph: © Ashmolean Museum, University of Oxford.

The young Austen mocks the vogue for things Scottish in the 1780s in "Love and Freindship" and "Lesley Castle." Matilda and Margaret Lesley dwell in "an old and Mouldering Castle,"

> which is situated two miles from Perth on a bold projecting Rock, and commands an extensive veiw [*sic*] of the Town and its delightful Environs. But tho' retired from almost all the World (for we visit no one but the M'Leods, The M'Kenzies, the M'Phersons, the M'Cartneys, the M'donalds, The M'Kinnons, the M'lellans, the M'kays,

the Macbeths and the Macduffs) we are neither dull nor unhappy."
(*Juvenilia,* 144)

The catalog of Scots names piles up in overt barbaric absurdity, culmi-
nating in characters from Shakespeare's *Macbeth.* The new Lady Lesley,
a southern urban gold digger, despises the northern castle, its inhabitants and culture.

> These girls have no Music, but Scotch Airs, no Drawings but Scotch
> Mountains, and no Books but Scotch Poems—And I hate every-
> thing Scotch. (*Juvenilia,* 159)

"Catholic Emancipation" (allowing Irish Catholics with property the vote) began to be raised; an attempt in 1780 to change anti-
Catholic law had ignited the Gordon Riots. In 1800 a new Union of
Ireland with England and Scotland resulted theoretically in one nation:
"the United Kingdom of Great Britain and Ireland." This moment of
change in 1800 is marked in *Emma,* when Henrietta Bates catches herself referring to Ireland as a separate *kingdom*—and then recollects the
new Union. The tempting half-promise of Catholic emancipation in
Ireland was not fulfilled. Only Anglicans could be MPs in the new Irish
Parliament. Maria Edgeworth is the most popular of politically minded
writers in favor of developing a progressive Ireland under the guidance
of "the Irish Ascendancy," the Protestant landowning class of which
she—or, more exactly, her father—was a member. Protestant English
speakers would run a new nation, educating the young; native Irish
Catholics could be retrained. Only in *Castle Rackrent* (1800), written
without the influence of Richard Edgeworth, does Maria set forth a
more disconcerting vision of the reality. Differing greatly from Edgeworth (whose work she admired), Austen offers no social-political pro-
grams. She is certainly awake to ethnicity; names and references in her
fiction exhibit sharp understanding of where the Scots and Irish stood
in ruling English eyes.

Around the time she wrote her "History of England" Jane Austen
wrote comments in the margins of her (actually her brother James's)
copy of Oliver Goldsmith's *History of England.* Her notes (now accessible in the Cambridge *Juvenilia,* thanks to Peter Sabor) give us some
insight into her historical and political positions. In these marginalia,
Jane Austen overtly challenges the Whig view of history and espouses
the causes of Catholics, Mary Queen of Scots, and Charles I—and also

of Monmouth, James II, Queen Anne, and all Stuarts. Here she applauds Lucius Cary, Lord Falkland (the Cavalier hero), as "a great & noble Man" (*Juvenilia,* 320). Under the description of Oliver Cromwell as "son of a private gentleman of Huntingdon," who "inherited a very small paternal fortune," she writes, "And that was more than he deserved" (321). Cromwell's assault on Drogheda and the massacre elicits the exclamation "Detestable Monster!" (323). Goldsmith reports a speech by one of the Protestant lords at the time of the "Popish Plot" in favor of getting rid of all Catholics altogether: "I would not . . . have so much as a popish man or a popish woman to remain here . . . not so much as a popish cat to mew or pur [*sic*] about our king." Austen underlined this speech, writing sarcastically, "Elegant creature what charming eloquence" (328). She annotates the portrait of James II, "Poor Man!" (329).

After the description of the horribly botched beheading of Monmouth, Goldsmith condescendingly describes his character; Austen adds, "Sweet Man!" (329). When Goldsmith points out that James II never refuted the warming-pan rumor, Austen adds indignantly, "It would have been beneath him to refute such nonsense" (332). William of Orange is described by her as "A Villain." A reference to a leading supporter of William, "Henry Sidney, brother to Algernon, and uncle to the earl of Sunderland," elicits her terse comment on the Whig Sidneys: "Bad Breed" (332). We should remember Austen's dislike of the Sidneys and what they stand for when we consider the role to be played by Sidney Parker in *Sanditon.*

Goldsmith's summation of the Stuart dynasty (which ended with the death of Queen Anne) is totally negative: "A family, who less than men themselves, seemed to expect from their followers more than manhood in their defence; a family that never rewarded their friends, and never avenged them of their enemies." Austen writes a counterdescription: "A Family, who were always illused, Betrayed or Neglected Whose Virtues are seldom allowed while their Errors are never forgotten." Goldsmith deals with the Old Pretender as "a poor leader" and the Jacobite cause as one that "all the sensible part of the kingdom had forsaken." Austen annotates: "Sensible! Oh! Dr. Goldsmith thou art as partial an Historian as myself!" (337). Austen is deeply aware that "Historians" are "partial, prejudiced and ignorant." What schoolchildren are induced to accept as objective "truth" is an upbeat story of England, a story of Whig progress, laced with condescending remarks upon the alternatives.

Austen presents herself in these remarks on history as a historical contrarian. Her views *may* reflect those of her family, but we cannot be altogether sure. To be a landowning Tory is to be wrapped in certain traditional views, but there is also a tradition of Tory self-awareness. Fielding is more Tory than Whig, but no reader of *Tom Jones* (set during the attempt of Bonnie Prince Charlie in 1745–46) can miss the comedy of Squire Western's clichéd Stuart Toryism. Austen, however, goes in an unorthodox direction in her reiterated support of English Roman Catholics and of Catholicism. This is rather an embarrassment in Austen studies. Those who see the author's religion as of any importance have tended to follow members of her family in stressing an unobtrusive quiet Anglicanism. Like her brother Henry, who insists in the last sentence of his "Biographical Notice" that "her opinions accorded strictly with those of our Established Church" (*Memoir,* 141), they wish see Jane as the respectably pious daughter of a good clergyman. Readers uncomfortable with religion would prefer Austen as a potential secularist, which her portraits of clergymen might substantiate. Austen's resemblances to Wollstonecraft (a rationalist Deist) are occasionally striking. Both believe women are—or can be—"rational creatures." (See Claudia Johnson in *Women, Politics and the Novel.*)[6] Yet I cannot detach the Jane Austen I know from her defenses of Catholicism. There are no indications that she engaged in Catholic practices like praying for the dead, as Frances Burney did. But Frances Burney's grandmother was a Catholic, and Burney married a French Roman Catholic. Austen had no such contacts or influences within her own circle—as far as we can see.

Jane Austen's imaginative straying from the confines of Anglicanism seems both emotional and theoretical. Emotionally, she may have wished for some more ritual, more room for greater emotional response. (In this period English women of the upper classes were not to attend funerals, presumably lest they should "make a scene" by weeping.) Intellectually, Austen's stated (and implicit) sympathy for Catholicism poses an ironic challenge. She unmasks the English gentry's claims to tradition and conservatism. How can you be truly "conservative" if you endeavor to erase and deny such a big piece of the past? On what "right" do you rest your own claims? What is "tradition" worth when you have changed everything to suit yourselves? And then—why did you make so many ruins and call it progress? Pretensions to tradition and conservation of values mask an ugly but coherent acquisitiveness, a destructive greed. Jane Austen ultimately does not believe in the claims of her own "little platoon." Their claims are based on finesse and chicane. Artificial elegancies hide the brutality of power.

Within her novels there are numerous historical whispers of England's unhappy religious conflicts. Austen would appear to agree with Samuel Johnson's view as recorded by Hester Thrale: "Severity towards the poor was, in Dr Johnson's opinion (as is visible in his 'Life of Addison' particularly), an undoubted constant attendant or consequence upon Whiggism."[7] The big takeover of monastic lands can be taken as an expression of nascent Whiggism attended with "severity towards the poor." Austen had an ear to hear William Gilpin's cheerful ability to bear injustices done to others without repining.

Even Oliver Goldsmith, an Irishman making himself an acceptable historian for ruling-class English youth, cannot quite support everything Protestant and commercial. At the advent of George I "the Whigs governed the senate and the court; whom they would, they oppressed; bound the lower orders of people with severe laws, and kept them at a distance by vile distinctions, and then taught them to call this— Liberty." Here Austen agrees, writing in the margin, "Yes, This is always the Liberty of Whigs & Republicans" (*Juvenilia,* 338). Goldsmith cannot avoid noticing the widespread corruption and fraud of the South Sea Bubble debacle in the 1720s: "A spirit of avarice and rapacity had infected every rank of life about this time." Goldsmith follows this account by an unhappy story of a poor couple who killed their child and then hanged themselves. Austen writes in the margin, "How much are the Poor to be pitied, & the Rich to be blamed!" (344). Her nephew James Edward Austen-Leigh, coming upon this comment, disagrees: "Both should be forgiven far from deserving to be blamed" (344). But Austen meant that "the Rich" *should* be blamed.

Austen lived most of her life in a world at war, from the outbreak of the American Revolution in her first year of life to the victory over Napoleon two years before her death. The dangers and constraints imposed by war were visible, including repercussions at home in austerities and discontent—even hunger in rural England. Current conditions are analyzed in Frederick Morton Eden's three-volume sociological treatise, *The State of the Poor; or, The History of the Labouring Classes in England* (1797). Eden notes the rise in the Poor's Rate (local taxation) in relation to a decline in employment owing largely to the war. He hoped people could be persuaded to give. "The sordid, perhaps, may be rendered more dull in the times of distress, but the liberal and humane will never weigh their charities to the mere observance of the law."[8] Matters got worse in the new century. On 1 July 1809 (the year and season the Austen women moved into Chawton Cottage), there was a meeting at the Swan Inn in Alton of local landowners including Jane's brother "Edward Austen Esq." Each subscribing one guinea, they formed the "Alton Association for Preventing Robberies, Theft and Misdemeanors, Protection of Persons and Property, and Prosecuting Offenders." Their (awkwardly named) Association promised rewards for information regarding various felonies, including "Stealing Pigs, Poultry, or Fish, or any sort of Fruit from any enclosed Ground." They resemble Mr. Woodhouse, so alarmed at a theft of turkeys. The Alton Association planned its defense of "Hop-Poles . . . Rails, Posts . . . Tools of any Sort . . . Hay, Straw, or Corn" and threatened those guilty of stealing "Turnips, Carrots, Potatoes . . . from any Field." They are determined to procure sufficient information to prosecute offenders "for every Felonious Act."[9]

Austen does not create poor or working-class characters, but she takes notice of the background of work and want, and frequently scrutinizes the capacity of the rich to keep good things to themselves—and to waste them. The Bertram children amuse themselves in "wasting gold paper" while their elders waste gold (*MP*, I, ch. 2). All of her novels deal with "the conscience of the Rich"—to borrow C. P. Snow's title. Her writings show how little conscience "the Rich" have. Lady Denham praises herself for giving her deceased husband's heir "his Gold Watch" even though "it was not in the Will. He only told me, & that but once, that he shd. wish his Nephew to have his Watch." Lady Denham certainly weighs her charities according to the law and is "mean," as Charlotte inwardly exclaims: "Thus it is when Rich People are Sordid" (*Sanditon*, ch. 7, *Later Manuscripts*, 479).

Jane loved her family. Her own welfare was bound up with theirs. But one can see from time to time in her letters a certain moral embarrassment or cool understated criticism regarding the family pursuit of riches—as in the little joke about brother Edward's taking the name "Claringbould" to get more land. In a letter from Godmersham in 1808 Jane Austen builds on a joke that she and Cassandra might be able to fall in with Elizabeth's "very sweet scheme of our accompanying Edward [their nephew] into Kent next Christmas" if they only had the money: "A Legacy might make it very feasible;—a Legacy is our sovereign good" (26 June 1808; *Letters*, 133). Part of the joke is that wealthy Edward's wife Elizabeth (née Brydges) sketches the "sweet scheme" without any suggestion of helping to pay for it. Beyond that, there is a more uneasy jest. Jane Austen understands and sympathizes with—is necessarily even party to—the family's anxious hopes that uncle James Leigh-Perrot (or somebody) is going to leave James (or some member of her family) a valuable legacy. Yet the more critical part of Jane Austen, the part that stuck close to the novelist (if necessarily held in abeyance much of the time in daily life), recognizes with amusement and recoil that this desire is morally and spiritually mistaken. "A Legacy" ought not to be any Christian's "sovereign good." Hoping for good from somebody's death may be natural, but not virtuous. Austen knows from within how the conscience can harden in relation to money. The "Rich" *do* deserve to be blamed. They have large resources of complacency and teach themselves how to suppress sympathy and conscience. We watch John Dashwood perfecting himself in this disgraceful moral art under the tutelage of his wife, the forceful Fanny.

In Austen's eyes, Whig ideology puts private property ahead of duty or community. Those enriched persuade themselves of their entitlement to prosperity. Austen's Church of England itself is complicit in a system of profit and property exchange. The novelist occasionally gives startlingly naked glimpses of the English Church at work. John Dashwood is astonished to hear that Colonel Brandon has parted with the vacant living of Delaford, offering it to Edward Ferrars. It perplexes John that the landowner has not tried to make anything by the advowson:

> "For the next presentation to a living of that value—supposing the late incumbent to have been old and sickly, and likely to vacate it soon—he might have got I dare say—fourteen hundred pounds. And how came he not to have settled that matter before this person's death? . . . I wonder he should be so improvident in a point of such common, such natural, concern!" (*S&S*, III, ch. 5)

Austen undoubtedly knows that there is a traditional word for trade in church property and offices: "simony"—forbidden by canon law. But this sin of blasphemous greed, this misuse of Church and of religion, is taken for granted, "common" and "natural" in Austen's world, just as John finds it "common" and "natural" to calculate other people's life expectancy in terms of money. Those who would call themselves "Tories" and think themselves "conservative" turn sacred things to private commercial advantage. (Even Brandon uses the living to soothe his own feelings rather than considering parishioners.) Perhaps Catholicism meant for Austen an older version of a community, of property used in common and food raised as on monastic lands for common good. Austen constantly shows us what property is and what it means. Particularly sensitive to the relation between land and food production, Austen constantly indicts those who set the land aside for ornament and boastful show.

PART II

Names

Chapter 4

Naming People

FIRST NAMES, NICKNAMES, TITLES, AND RANK

First Names: Statements of Value

"What's in a name?" Juliet Capulet asserts that a name, a mere verbal label, is unimportant. The opposite theory is espoused by Sterne's Walter Shandy, who believes "that there was a strange kind of magick bias, which good or bad names . . . irresistibly impress'd upon our characters and conduct." Many men, Walter believes, "might have done exceeding well . . . had not their characters and spirits been totally depress'd and NICODEMUS'D into nothing."[1] Alastair Fowler reminds us that this issue was raised in Plato's *Cratylus,* where Cratylus who believes names signify real qualities in the person argues with Hermogenes who thinks them artificial.[2] When he changed the name of shy young Tyrtamos, illegitimate son of a dry cleaner, to Theophrastus ("divine speaker"), Aristotle seems to have believed in the psychological value of names to their wearer.

Walter Shandy's opinion is the view of all novelists in making up names for characters—they must be significant. In what we call "real life" a label affixed by parents—a "given name"—is not supposed an essence. Yet it can be experienced as an archetype of the self. Names depend upon religion, ethnicity, region of origin, and lineage; they relate also to political orientation and fashion. At different times, groups have moved toward the now standard Western custom of two names. In England until the late twentieth century the common term for a "first name" was "Christian name," assuming that every individual was a Christian from his or her christening (though not all Protestants practice infant baptism). Within the Catholic (and Anglican) tradition a child should be named after a saint. Governments have often backed up acceptable names or ruled on the unacceptable.[3] English Jews were expected to employ the Standard English spelling and pronunciation of recognizable Old Testament names.

Middle names, now common, were largely reserved for aristocracy and royalty. Jane Austen's siblings Henry, Cassandra, and Francis all were given middle names, while the other children were not. Cassandra's middle name was Elizabeth—which may explain jokes against Queen Elizabeth in Austen's early fiction and the bossiness of her characters named "Elizabeth"—most of them eldest sisters.

The Conquest had rapidly altered English first names:

> The Norman-French names given by apparently English people to their children were generally the names most commonly used by the Normans . . . : Geoffrey, Gilbert, Henry, Robert, Peter, John etc. and the women's names Agnes, Alice and Maud. (Reaney & Wilson, xxi)

By Austen's time a few of these old standard names had been dropped. Anglo-Saxon kingly names like "Edward" and "Edmund" had remained in continuous use, but many Anglo-Saxon names seemed rough and strange. "Matilda" ("honourable lady of the maids")[4] introduced by Normans, perhaps seemed Germanic—and besides, Queen Matilda was associated with a civil war; her name survived better in the common "Tilly" (Reaney & Wilson, 303). Austen in early works uses "Matilda," which also appears in the spoof Gothic tale spun by Henry Tilney. The names of Plantagenet, Tudor, and Stuart kings remained permanently acceptable, and so did their Eleanors and Margarets, but some noble ladies' names, like "Adela," "Edith," or "Philippa," drop out by the eighteenth century. Biblical names were acceptable over centuries; glossaries of the meanings of Hebrew names often accompanied a Bible.

The rise of Puritanism in England marks a change in naming. Terms for moral and spiritual qualities, like "Patience" or "Salvation," were attached to humans. That strong observer William Camden notes the trend, in evidence before 1605, registering displeasure at such "singular and precise conceit."[5] The custom becomes more aggressive during the Civil War period. Names of minor Old Testament characters (e.g., "Jedediah") were called into use, and Catholic saints' names discarded. In reaction, Anglicans of the eighteenth century strenuously avoid any Puritan tinge. They *never* employ "Mercy," "Faith," or "Prudence." Formerly acceptable Old Testament names became frowned on. When her niece Anna names a character "Rachel," Austen disapproves: "The name of Rachael [*sic*] is as much as I can bear" (9–18 September 1814; *Letters,* 276). Perhaps Austen felt extra dislike because her own great-aunt Rachel Lord had forbidden the marriage of her daughter Elizabeth to a mere Lieutenant Wentworth. The couple married secretly in 1720; when Wentworth came back from Continental wars as a lieutenant-general, Rachel eventually gave in.[6] It is not hard to imagine that this family history is a background to *Persuasion*.

Jane Austen's own grandmother was a "Rebecca," her godfather was a "Samuel," yet these names in her fiction register as "low." "Rebecca," possessed of a "forbidding Squint" and "greazy tresses," tries to remedy her deficiencies with "Patches, Powder, Pomatum, and Paint" ("Frederic and Elfrida," *Juvenilia*, 6). Later, "Rebecca" is the name of Mrs. Price's Portsmouth slavey. Staunch Dissenters sustained Bible names, as in "Josiah" Wedgwood. In Goldsmith's *The Vicar of Wakefield* (1766), Parson Primrose has named his son "Moses"—but that shows what an old-fashioned provincial innocent this Anglican parson is. At the turn into the eighteenth century, we easily find names like "Jonathan" (as in Swift) and "Samuel" (as in Richardson and Johnson), but they begin to dry up. Smollett's Scottish parents named him "Tobias," pleasantly memorable in an era in which male novelists and poets (like the rest of the governing class) seem to be turning into Henrys (Fielding, Brooke) or Williams (Beckford, Godwin, Blake, Cowper, Wordsworth).

We might suspect anti-Semitic prejudice in the recoil from Old Testament names, but the same phenomenon can be observed in relation to the New Testament. Matthew Prior the poet was already out of the swim at his birth in 1664, the child of a Nonconformist artisan in Dorset. Matthew, Mark, Luke—the Evangelists—where are they in the Augustan age? Waiting for the nineteenth century. "Stephen," name of the first Christian martyr and of an English king—popular among Elizabethans—goes totally out of use. Austen uses it once, for a servant in Bath. "Christopher," once good enough for a family like the Hattons, is not in vogue after the time of Christopher Wren. In "Sir William Mountague" Austen rightly gives the name "Sir Christopher Mountague" to an ancestor several generations back. In *Mansfield Park*, "Christopher Jackson" is the estate carpenter (*MP*, I, ch. 13). Old "religious" names descended to the working class. Some names in good repute like "Thomas" or "James" had perhaps ceased to be regarded as "religious," despite New Testament antecedents. One of the greatest Christian saints, Paul, does not seem to have men named after him in England at any period before the nineteenth century. Probably "Paul" seemed too Continental, too Catholic, like "Peter"—also largely absent among the Anglican well-bred.[7] ("Lord Peter Wimsey" could be invented only in the twentieth century.)

Religion and ethnicity created barriers—or tests. "Kenneth" was the name of ancient Scottish kings, but nobody south of the Highlands would name a child "Kenneth"—or "Keith" or "Donald," surnames of Scots clans or families.[8] "Kevin" is altogether Irish. "David"—name of a stellar king in the Bible—as the name of Welsh kings becomes considered a quintessentially Welsh name.[9] A non-Welsh "David" is likely to come from Scotland, like David Hume, or from the provinces, like David Garrick. An aristocratic "Lord David Cecil" would be practically inconceivable.

The name pool evaporated as a number of traditional names became objectionable for various reasons, while innovations were looked on askance. A first name like "Bridget" gives away a person's Irish Catholic background, marking her as "low." Hence the comic incongruity of a "Lady Bridget Dashwood" in "A Collection of Letters" (*Juvenilia*, 194). The joke is employed by Mary Crawford in the chapel at Sotherton, when she imagines "the former belles of the house of Rushworth. . . . The young Mrs. Eleanors and the Mrs. Bridgets—starched up into seeming piety" (*MP*, I, ch. 9).[10] Mary thinks back to a time long ago when such names could be worn by women in the upper ranks—and she may have picked up on the chapel's hidden Catholic past.

Medieval names like "Hugh" or "Alice," going strong in the Renaissance, disappear from polite society. We come upon "Alicia"—Lady Susan's confidante is "Alicia Johnson," and Elizabeth Elliot and Lady Russell know a "Lady Alicia." An archaic name may sometimes be excused as a burden of fine lineage. In "Jack and Alice" in *Volume the First*, the titular heroine Alice Johnson and her brother have names both vulgar and antiquated, unsuited to the drawing room or polite fiction. Jack Johnson, his repetitive name varied only by a grossly plebeian nickname, makes no figure at all. Alice, with her flushed face and tendency to "drink a little too much," elicits one of Austen's best comic sentences: "She has many rare and charming qualities, but Sobriety is not one of them" ("Jack and Alice," *Juvenilia*, 26).

"Susan" goes downhill; it is the name of Charles Adams's cook. In Scotland, "Susannah" remained acceptable. (Susannah Burney, sister of the novelist, was Scottish on her father's side.) Austen constantly treats "Susan" as low. "Lady Susan," like "Lady Bridget," is a kind of oxymoron. We know that in 1803 Austen submitted a novel with the title "Susan" to a publisher. This unpublished manuscript, which the author endeavored to reclaim in 1809, is generally thought to be an early version of *Northanger Abbey*. If so, it seems likely that the heroine Susan as originally planned was more of a simpleton and country bumpkin than Catherine Morland is.

A traditional source of renewal of the national name pool has been royal marriage. "Philip" was imported when Philip II of Spain married Mary Tudor. The names of Charles I's queen, Henrietta Maria ("Henriette Marie"), appealed to some loyalists and to those of Catholic inclinations; these names hovered between the exotic and the familiar. The Duke of Monmouth's mistress was Lady Henrietta Wentworth. "Henrietta" was probably made more acceptable by Charlotte Lennox's novel *Henrietta* (1758; reissued 1787, 1789, 1798). "Maria" retained a slight foreign flavor. It hints at Catholic leanings, as in the case of the (officially Anglican) novelist Regina Maria Roche. The association of "Maria" with dangerous Catholicism was repeatedly signaled by contemporary political figures, not only Queen Maria Theresa of Austria, but also Clementina Maria Walkinshaw and Maria Fitzherbert, mistress—or wife—of the Prince Regent.

One of the few sources of new names in England in the mid-eighteenth century was the Hanoverian dynasty. Their European Germanic names could still seem very foreign. "George," however, was a good choice, the name of England's patron saint. George II married Caroline of Anspach, a fairly popular queen and regent who ensured the currency of the name "Caroline"—a form of "Charles" carrying (in England) Stuart associations. George II's children by Caroline were Frederick, Anne, Amelia, Caroline, William, Mary, and Louisa. These names already had currency or rapidly gained it. "Amelia" (adopted by Fielding for a heroine) becomes acceptable, and "Louisa" becomes naturalized.

George III played up his name, which at its Greek root (*ge-ourgos*) means "farmer" or "worker of land."[11] "Georgic" describes a form of poetry describing agriculture, husbandry, or viticulture. Taking marked interest in agricultural improvements, the King George III represented himself as "Farmer George." This persona is represented in favorable propaganda, as in the print showing King George rewarding an industrious hay maker (fig. 3). The persona is also satirized in Gillray's caricatures of "Farmer George and His Wife." King George III and Queen Charlotte strove to be exemplary. Their marriage embodied marital happiness—no royal mistresses! Their fifteen children (born between 1762 and 1783) have the following names: George, Frederick, William, Charlotte, Edward, Augusta Sophia, Elizabeth, Ernest Augustus, Augustus, Adolphus, Mary, Sophia, Octavius, Alfred, Amelia. The first five

ECONOMIC CHANGES   231

" FARMER GEORGE ": THE KING REWARDING AN INDUSTRIOUS
HAYMAKER NEAR WEYMOUTH.

3. Anon., "George III Rewards a Haymaker near Weymouth" (1807). Photograph: © The British Library Board.

names on this list are traditionally English, as are the Tudor stalwarts "Elizabeth" and "Mary." Queen Charlotte herself had ensured the continuing strength of "Charlotte"; its appeal increased when it was given to the Prince of Wales's daughter and heir, Princess Charlotte (b. 1796).

"Augusta" and "Sophia" had already gained new currency from the Hanoverians. Fielding's *Tom Jones* with its spirited, dark-haired heroine Sophia ("Sophy") had for decades helped to naturalize the romantic (and theological) "Sophia" ("Wisdom"). Camden objected heatedly to this name, believing that Holy Wisdom is an attribute of Christ alone and that its use is blasphemous.[12] Admiral Croft finds the names "Henrietta" and "Louisa" unusual and hard to recall—presumably they still seem to him foreign or newfangled—but his wife's name "Sophia" (or "Sophy") seems to him completely normal, utterly English. Not all

Hanoverian names rose into English common use. Nobody at the time seems to have recognized the importance of being Ernest. "Adolphus" has never appealed. Surprisingly, King Alfred the Great attracted few eighteenth-century supporters in the name game.

The extravagant brood produced by George III and Queen Charlotte may be mocked in Austen's "Edgar and Emma" in *Volume the First,* where we are presented with the inordinately numerous family of Mr. and Mrs. Willmot [*sic*]: "Their family being too large to accompany them in every visit, they took nine with them alternately." As well as five unnamed daughters, they produce from their traveling coach Robert, Richard, Ralph, and Rodolphus. Hoping to see their eldest son, Emma enquires after the rest of the family, and Mrs. Willmot kindly replies in detail:

> "Amy is with my sister Clayton. Sam at Eton. David with his Uncle John. Jem and Will at Winchester. Kitty at Queens Square. Ned with his Grandmother. Hetty and Patty in a convent at Brussells [*sic*]. Edgar at College, Peter at Nurse, and all the rest (except the nine here) at home." (*Juvenilia*, 36)

The heroine, in despair at not seeing her adored Edgar, gives way to grief and "retiring to her own room, continued in tears the remainder of her Life." The comedy consists partly in Emma's being able to distinguish or care about one individual in such a crowd. An undifferentiating but demanding philoprogenitiveness floods the world with Willmots. Their offspring are named—promiscuously and unfashionably—according to various principles, with tendencies both strongly Protestant and strongly Catholic. Among the parental principles is a taste for alliteration. Willful Willmots override fashions in employing old and "low" nicknames like "Sam," "Jem," and "Patty," along with the completely unfashionable "David" mixed in with Old English "Edgar" and pretentious Germanic Continental imports like "Rodolphus."

Poetic and Novelistic Names

Not only kings but writers change the namescape. Macpherson, author of poems allegedly by the Celtic bard "Ossian," seems to have invented the female name "Malvina," but employs genuine ancient Celtic heroic names, including "Oscar."[13] Names from romances appear in the sixteenth century, including "Guy," "Roland," "Bevis," and "Tristram" and

"Lancelot," which Camden considers too fantastical. He heartily disapproves of pagan names like "Cassandra" and "Diana."[14] Novelists are
both inventors and promoters of names. Samuel Richardson derives
his "Pamela" from Sir Philip Sidney's classically based invented name
for his heroine in *Arcadia*. All "real-life" Pamelas are ultimately descendants of Richardson's and thus of Sidney's Pamela. Richardson's invention "Clarissa" is a Latin superlative of *clara* (brilliant, shining)—and
there is a Saint Clara. Novelistic names eventually become bestowed
on real babies. (In 1810 a pair of my own collateral ancestors named
a child "Clarissa.") All Clarissas, living and fictional, are named after
Richardson's heroine—including Clara (originally "Clarissa") Barton,
Virginia Woolf's Clarissa Dalloway, and probably the Clarice who opposes Hannibal Lector. Fiction writers import names from classical,
religious, or literary tradition. Rousseau's novel *Julie ou la Nouvelle
Héloïse* (1761) and Henry Mackenzie's epistolary *Julia de Roubigné*
(1777) gave cachet both to "Louisa" (variant of Heloisa) and to the classical "Julia." ("Louise," however, was not yet English.) Julia Melville in
Sheridan's *The Rivals* is rational and kind. Julia, younger of two sisters in
Radcliffe's *Sicilian Romance,* possesses some of the qualities of a Marianne Dashwood. ("Julius," unlike its female counterpart, never "took.")
"Charlotte" was popular before there was a Queen Charlotte, largely
because of Richardson's vivacious and witty Charlotte Grandison.
Frances Burney uses a Catholic saint's name for the heroine of *Cecilia*
(1782); in *Camilla* (1796) she deploys classical (even Virgilian) names
for the heroine and her sisters Eugenia and Lavinia. But a real Eugenia
Wynne met Admiral Nelson, and Austen knew a real "Camilla" with
the contrasting last name of "Wallop"—the less-than-lovely surname
of the earls of Portsmouth. Extraordinary names like "Ethelinde" are
designed by novelists partly to avoid the charge of holding a particular
real person up to scrutiny.

Good upper-class parents ought not to give their child an uncouth or
elaborate name; Maggie Lane has commented that Austen uses "latinate" names like "Maria" and "Isabella" only for "pretentious or shallow
young women."[15] Yet among Austen's connections were people with
fancy Latin- or Greek-based names. Her father's sisters were "Philadelphia" and "Leonora." One of Jane Austen's best friends had a Greek-
derived first name: "Alethea Bigg." Jane Austen never gives any character
in her mature fiction as improbable a name as her family's "Cassandra,"
though she adopts it as a tribute in "The beautifull [*sic*] Cassandra."
"Cassandra," as Camden reveals, means "inflaming men with love."[16]

The name of the unhappy Trojan princess, doomed to prophesy the truth but never to be believed, was given to female Leighs not in classical reminiscence but as proud reminder of the connection to that Duke of Chandos who had married Cassandra Willoughby.

In her earliest surviving works Jane Austen conducts vigorous experiments with names, savoring their various implications. "Frederic and Elfrida," the first story in *Volume the First,* unites the first name of Smith's hero Frederic Delamere with the name of a Saxon queen. Characters include the sisters Rebecca and Jezalinda Fitzroy. "Jezalinda" is pure invention, in affectionate mockery of Mrs. Smith's "Ethelinde" combined with "Jessica" and "Jezebel" (*Juvenilia,* 6; see Peter Sabor's note, 376). The surname "Fitzroy" is high if naughty Norman, meaning "illegitimate son of the King"—the name of the Duchess of Cleveland's son by Charles II. In "Love and Freindship" Laura bears the name of Petrarch's beloved. This heroine (or antiheroine) becomes attached (if not exactly legally married) to Edward Lindsay. As Lindsay is the surname of Ludovic Lindsay, the commander who left Alton in the lurch, Laura conceals that surname "under that of Talbot." John Talbot, Earl of Shrewsbury, loyal Lancastrian and "Terror of the French," figures strongly in Shakespeare's *I Henry VI.* Laura conceals her husband's Scots name and identity under the cloak of English patriotism and heroism. Edward's sister has the medieval name "Philippa," while Laura's friend "Isobel" has a modern daughter "Marianne." "Edgar and Emma" offers two Dark Age or early medieval Saxon names, one of which will be used later. "Lesley Castle" contrasts the food-obsessed cook Charlotte Lutterell with her sentimental sister Eloisa. Eloisa's alliterative fiancé Henry Hervey dies shortly before the wedding, leaving Eloisa prostrate and Charlotte anxiously forcing everyone to devour the store of prepared eatables. "Eloisa" is a reference to the heroine of Rousseau's *La Nouvelle Héloïse,* while "Charlotte" points to the domestic and practical heroine of Goethe's *The Sorrows of Young Werther* (1774), first seen cutting slices of bread.

English people in this period—of any class—do not name their children after minerals or precious stones, or flowers, fruit, or plants. Nobody is going to be Precious Jade or Peach Blossom—or any European equivalent. No Ruby or Violet will be found, no Pearl or Jasmine. Even our recent taste for such names has its limits; there are people named "Jonquil" and "Pansy" (for I have encountered them), but one does not meet persons named "Convolvulus," "Calceolaria," or "Artichoke." In Austen's period we shall find nobody named "Rose" or "Lily" or "Marigold." "Rosamond" might seem like an exception, but it is not, for "Rosa Mundi" is one of the epithets for the Blessed Virgin Mary and thus acceptable as a saint's name, though it signals Catholicism. (Edgeworth presumably named her Protestant child heroine "Rosamond" in order to appeal to Irish Catholic readers.)

A successful romance novel, *The Flame and the Flower* by Kathleen E. Woodiwiss (1972), set supposedly in England in 1799, has a heroine named "Heather Simmons"—which is delightfully ridiculous! No woman of *any* class would be so called in 1799. The hero's name is only a fraction more likely: "Captain Brandon Birmingham." In the 1790s "Birmingham" would signify low-class industry, Dissenters, and vulgarians. A male child *might,* however, be christened "Brandon," owing to the peculiar English Protestant custom of using surnames as first names in allusion to a family line. Camden remarks on this new practice: "In late years Surnames have been given for Christian names among us, and no where else in Christendome." Surprisingly, the Catholic-leaning historian favors this innovation: "It seemeth to proceed from hearty good will and affection of the Godfathers . . . or from a desire to . . . propagate their own names."[17] Commonly the mother's maiden surname is thus propagated in a male. Surnames were first employed as "Christian names" to prevent loss of connection with the mother's old and aristocratic family.

Eventually, surnames of English noble families, Norman and Saxon terms like "Neville," "Howard," and "Stanley," became generally available first names. "Shirley," a surname, made the second switch from being an all-boy first name to all-girl under the indomitable force of Shirley Temple. (Celtic surnames like "Meredith" and "Kelly" have recently become first names for girls.) Heroes' surnames—Clive, Nelson, Lincoln—provide new mines of first names. In her mature fiction Austen generally avoids giving a character a surname as a first name—though there are two interesting exceptions.

Nicknames

Nicknames express the affections, but are also conventions subject to fashion. The day after Jane's birth her father wrote to his sister, "We have now another girl, a present plaything for her sister Cassy, and a future companion. She is to be Jenny, and seems to me as if she would be as like Henry as Cassy is to Neddy."[18] George Austen's happy employment of nicknames reflects an old-fashioned taste. (He was not as well born as his wife.) We may doubt that the Knights who adopted Edward called the heir anything as undignified as "Neddy." Among polite people, nicknames came to seem "low"—at best, to be kept strictly within the family. That "Jenny" was used within the family is testified by its presence on the handle of young Jane's parasol in the "Rice Portrait" (fig. 4). Probably the green parasol was a gift of her father who still saw in Jane his little girl, his "Jenny," and not the nubile young lady she was becoming. When the Austen sisters are grown, they address each other in personal letters by full first name. Austen early recognized that old nicknames like "Jenny," "Kitty," and "Peggy" were out of keeping with pretensions to caste. Charlotte in "Lesley Castle" is characteristically insensitive in addressing her old friend Margaret Lesley as "Peggy" (*Juvenilia*, 145). That Lady Williams was once "Kitty" is comic ("Jack and Alice," *Juvenilia*, 18). In revising her story of "the Bower" Austen changed her heroine's name from "Kitty" to "Catharine."

An acquaintance or friend should be referred to formally, not even by first name—nor by last name alone, save by those entitled to use surname address. Male upper servants (butler, valet) were addressed by last names only. Among elite males, surname address and reference is standard. Mr. Bingley refers to and addresses his friend as "Darcy." Mrs. Elton breaks gender (and class) bounds when referring to Mr. Knightley as "Knightley" and also affronts class proprieties when referring to Miss Fairfax as "Jane"—evidence that she sees Miss Fairfax as of a lower class than herself. Emma speaks of Harriet Smith to Mr. Elton as "Miss Smith" and not as "Harriet." She addresses Harriet by her first name, however, while Harriet addresses "Miss Woodhouse," not "Emma."[19] To use first names is to take a liberty; Mary Crawford calls Miss Price "Fanny," but, as Maggie Lane remarks, Fanny stoutly holds out against calling her "Mary."[20]

When Elizabeth Bennet is visiting Netherfield, Mr. Bingley's sisters should refer to her as "Miss Elizabeth Bennet" (as Bingley does), but they sneeringly begin to call her "Miss Eliza Bennet" to her face and "Eliza Bennet" behind her back (*P&P*, I, ch. 8). This nicknaming (picked up from Sir William Lucas) is intentionally demeaning.[21] At home the second Miss Bennet is "Lizzy"; she is "Eliza" to Sir William Lucas and to her close friend Charlotte (who also uses "Lizzy"). Affectionate usage, reserved for the few, should not become public. In Austen's later novels, nicknames are not customarily employed for adults. There are three outstanding exceptions: the male "Tom" and "Frank" and the female "Fanny." "Tom" is natural when the son has

4. Ozias Humphry, *Jane Austen* (ca. 1789) ("Rice Portrait"). Photograph courtesy of Anne Winston Rice.

the first name of the father. Frank Churchill's use of "Frank" is natural as the son of a "Francis," but continued use after father and son have separated reflects the bearer's projection of boyish charm. "Frank" permits a continuous pun regarding a plotter who is anything but "frank." Fanny Price is a special case. The name "Fanny" Dashwood may reflect her mother's lack of gentility. Nancy Steele vulgarly uses her nickname ("Nancy" for "Anne") in public. That Nancy has an equally mannerless friend named "Martha Sharpe" (a New Testament first name already demoted) clarifies her lower-middle-class milieu. Nicknames descended to—and were associated with—servants. In *Emma,* "Patty" is the name of the Bateses' only servant. "Patty" will become a nickname for "Patricia" (not in use in the eighteenth century), but in Austen's time "Patty" (like "Matty") is a nickname for "Martha."

Names for pets are, like nicknames, terms of affection, but animal names, and even animals, are extremely rare in Austen's works. The Watsons' horse who wisely proposes to stop at the milliners is unnamed. Animals turn up at odd moments. Osborne Castle contains, according to young Charles Blake, "a monstrous curious stuff'd Fox there, & a Badger—any body would think they were alive" (*The Watsons, Later Manuscripts,* 304). This description comically indicts the Osbornes: "Anyone would think they were alive"—but they aren't, not quite. Osborne Castle's people, like its dead trophies, are "stuff'd." Lord Osborne may share some qualities of the (now moribund) fox and badger (slyness and shyness). Only two characters, male and in the same novel, have names for animals. The mare that Willoughby tries to give Marianne is "Queen Mab," referring to a fantasy world elaborated by Mercutio in *Romeo and Juliet*—a reminder that love is dreamy and magical, rarely realistic. Sir John Middleton, irked that his generous gesture was followed by Willoughby's injury to Marianne, exclaims, "It was only the last time they met that he had offered him one of Folly's puppies and this was the end of it!" (*S&S,* II, ch. 10). John Willoughby did not need the gift—he himself is one of the puppies of Folly. The mare Edmund gets for Fanny's use is utilitarian, unnamed. Lady Bertram, with all the ingenuity of which she may be supposed capable, calls her pug dog "Pug." Despite momentary play with puppies in *Northanger Abbey,* Austen—unlike Burney—does not recognize animals as important affectional objects. She seems determined to keep her young women away from pussycats and birds. Intimacy should be kept to human relations. Intimate terms, however, should be private, secured from the coarseness of the world.

Chapter 5

Titles, Status, and Surnames

AUSTEN'S GREAT SURNAME MATRIX

Titles: Rank and Class

We are accustomed to dealing with issues of "class." But "class" covers attributes like education or purchasing power, things that can be achieved (at least theoretically) by ability and effort. "Rank" is more like having blue eyes—not an achievement, just a fact. Class and rank differ, as Tom Keymer explains:

> Where "class" would be measured in terms of . . . productivity and income . . . "rank" placed primary emphasis on lineage, implying that social status was more or less inalienably conferred by birth and descent.[1]

Lady Catherine De Bourgh, daughter of an earl, upholds her own order, not herself individually, when she "likes to have the distinction of rank preserved" (*P&P*, II, ch. 6). (But she also admits—or her guileless toady admits for her—that externals like dress *do* matter to upkeep of rank.) Elizabeth prefers class, inwardly judging that Lady Catherine is not noted "for extraordinary talents or miraculous virtue"; therefore "the mere stateliness of money and rank, she thought she could witness without trepidation" (*P&P*, II, ch. 6).

The desire to believe in an ordained series of grades in society, constant and inalienable, beyond the transitory measure of money, did not readily die out—despite disconcerting flexibility in practice. Titles have constantly been bestowed on British "commoners" for diverse reasons, military performance and/or political loyalty chief among them. Medieval knighthood was supposed to be won through prowess in battle, but a knighthood became a convenient gift for other services; hence the term "carpet knight" for one knighted in the palace and not on the field of battle. Sir William Lucas, a local businessman, became mayor of Meryton and was given a knighthood just for making a speech, an address to the King George III—expressing loyalty to a monarch perhaps not actually present. Sir William's knighthood would have been a political move, to reward middle-class supporters of King George III. If it were given just after the first crisis over the king's illness, then it would indeed be very recent indeed (1789–90). Knighthoods were cheap and did not clutter up the landscape by passing to descendants.

The title of baronet is inherited, but baronets are not peers and have never sat in the House of Lords. James I, in want of cash, forced all men in receipt of a certain income to buy a baronetcy; from this point the title became devalued. Old families, like the husband of Richardson's Pamela, disdain a mere "novel Honour"; Mr. B. complains that the title of "Baronet" follows "Knight" into devaluation, "hastening apace into like Disrepute."[2] Keymer points out that Debrett's new *Baronetage of England* (1808) was needed because "233 new baronetcies had been created between 1760 and 1800."[3] Hence Sir Walter Elliot's contempt for "the almost endless creations of the last century" (*Persuasion*, I, ch. 1). The king was in theory supreme arbiter of promotion in rank, but the dominant party in Parliament could have a very large say. George III not only chose Pitt the Younger as Prime Minister, but also created new peers to give Pitt more supporters in the House of Lords.

Titles or honorifics in use among the aristocracy are a bugbear to Americans and to many modern British readers—save those who actually mix with the titled. The complex code allowed one to see where on the rungs of the golden ladder a person might be placed. The wife of a duke is a duchess—for example, "the Duchess of York." The eldest son of a duke has a courtesy title of his own (one of his father's less important titles)—for example, the Duke of Omnium's son is "Lord Silverbridge." The second (or later) son of a duke is "Lord" + first name + last name ("Lord Peter Wimsey"), and his wife is Lady + husband's first name ("Lady Peter"). The wife of a viscount is addressed as "Lady" but may be referred to in third person as "Viscountess." The daughter of a duke, earl, or marquis is "Lady"+ first name + last name; she retains that title in marriage to an untitled person. Keymer cites the odd instance of "a member of the Watson-Wentworth dynasty, whose father was a marquis" who "took on the oddly conflicted name of Lady Henrietta Alicia Sturgeon on marrying her footman in 1764."[4] The honorific "Lady" is used of a baronet's wife or knight's wife, but only with her husband's surname, not with her first name ("Sir William Lucas and Lady Lucas"; "Sir Thomas Bertram and Lady Bertram"). Introduced to a "Lady Russell" or a "Lady Middleton" we know her husband is—or was—only a knight or baronet. Mr. Collins's patroness Lady Catherine married a baronet, but we know she is of higher rank by birth—for if she were merely a baronet's wife she would be only "Lady De Bourgh." Sons and daughters of a baronet (e.g., Anne Elliot) don't rate a title. "Honourable" is a title for the son or daughter of a baron (see Jessica Mitford's *Hons and Rebels*). The appellation is rarely used, save on very formal occasions; John Yates (the foolish young man who marries Julia Bertram) is referred to as "Mr. Yates" rather than as "the Honourable Mr. Yates." Visiting cards are formal, retaining all the elements of a title; hence, to someone like Sir Walter Elliot, they are valuable for showing off: "They had the cards of Dowager Viscountess Dalrymple, and the Hon. Miss Carteret, to be arranged wherever they might be most visible" (*Persuasion*, II, ch. 4).

Below the titled honors are other subtle signs of gradation, sometimes the mere production of self-regarding fantasy. We see this most clearly in *Emma,* with a central character who pretends that her own or her family's position is a matter of unalterable superiority, true rank, and not a product of economic power in a changing society. Jane Austen constantly represents the conflict—and the fluctuation— between "rank" and "class." The conservative ideal did not match the contemporary flow of social change—if it ever had done so. Sir William Lucas, in trade, is made a knight for commercial and political reasons. Mr. Darcy has no title, though we can work out that he is the grandson of an earl. Mr. Knightley has no title, and one cannot imagine that he should care about one. Knights and baronets are fairly common characters in Jane Austen's novels, but we rarely meet genuine aristocrats— at the rank of baron or above. Keymer points out that Lord Osborne is the man of highest rank in Austen's oeuvre. The few true aristocrats that Austen introduces to us are disagreeable (Lady Catherine), warped (Lord Osborne), or vapid (the Dowager Viscountess Dalrymple). Belief in rank as a value in itself is rendered despicable in the character of Sir Walter Elliot, who dislikes merit and clings to his inalienable birthright. He will truckle to titled ladies for the inane pleasure of being reputed to be related to (and keeping company with) persons of rank—an unwittingly humble sign that he sincerely believes in rank as pure value.

Among titles we should include the important "Mr." and "Mrs."— short for "Master" and "Mistress." A male of the laboring class without any property and thus not a master of anything was *not* "Mr."—nor was his wife "Mrs.," however truly married. "Miss," also short for "Mistress," is respectful, a term supposedly reserved for the daughter of a master of property. In Richardson's *Pamela* the heroine's parents are referred to as "Gaffer and Goody Andrews," semi-affectionate patronizing terms for persons with nothing. Worthy village women of some little standing but no significant property could be called "Dame." Describing her Christmas charities to the poor Austen mentions gifts of stockings "to Mary Hutchins, Dame Kew, Mary Steevens & Dame Staples" (24–26 December 1798; *Letters,* 31).[5] Young women of no background are referred to merely by their first or last names or both: "Jane Eyre." Skilled female servants are referred to by their surnames (as if male), like Lady Bertram's maid Chapman. Unskilled and lowly maids carry only a first name (or nickname). On the other hand, a single woman who owned property or was in charge of—"mistress" of—valuable property and had command over others, was a "Mistress" or "Mrs." (like "Mrs. Hughes" and "Mrs. Patmore," housekeeper and cook in Downton Abbey). In *Catharine* the heroine's aunt "Mrs. Percival" is a maiden lady, yet she owns real property, and thus is "Mrs."

These terms are respect forms. Men may sometimes address women by their first names, while women seldom address or refer to men of their own age and class by anything other than "Mr. + surname." Courtship and marriage do not confer equality of usage. Mr. Knightley calls Emma "Emma," while she may speak truly when she says, "I will promise to call you once by your Christian name"—once *only,* at the marriage ceremony. It stills seems too "low" for her to call her husband by his Christian name. Emma's youthful experiment in calling him "George" was evidently a trying out of a fraternal relationship (*Emma,* III, ch. 17). Mrs. Elton is "low," trying to deformalize propriety by referring to "Mr. E." In speech to third parties, the proper title of friend, lover, or spouse should be preserved. As Horatio Nelson lay dying below decks in the *Victory* he is recorded as saying, "I am a dead man, Hardy. . . . Pray let my dear Lady Hamilton have my hair."[6] He addresses his friend by surname, but refers to his mistress correctly and formally in bequeathing a lock of hair. When your remaining life is measurable in minutes, would it not be more natural to say, "Give Emma my hair"? It would seem so to us, but probably not to Nelson—or Hardy.

Surnames: Public Selves, Statements of Context

According to Christian orthodoxy, a surname is not related to one's truest identity. In heaven, so the theory goes, we shall have neither title nor surname. Nobody shall be "Lord this" or "Lady that"—neither will anyone be "Mrs." or "Colonel," "Dr." or "Professor." The surname likewise is essentially not real, therefore not used in baptism—however hard for human pride to swallow. Americans may still wish their baby christened "John Warden Bryson III"—although the numbering of a son by generation is a form of title and like the surname should not accompany one to Paradise or even to the font. Yet surnames, which bestow tribal, regional, and familial identity, often seem more important than the first name.

Surnames are our inescapable public selves, indicating lineage and origins. In her "Collection of Letters" in *Volume the Second* Austen creates the enigmatic Miss Jane (née Annesley). Miss Jane's father's name is associated with dispute and questions of identity. The case of "the Annesley Claimant" focused public attention for years on the possibility that a true heir had been spirited away by a false claimant to his name and estate. A man claiming to have been kidnapped turned up to claim name and fortune. Smollett in *Peregrine Pickle* (1751) drew upon this story from "real life."[7] "Miss Jane" tells her confidante that she secretly married Captain Dashwood, by whom she bore two children. Dashwood was killed in the war and the children died. Seeing no reason to insist on the vanished marriage, and because she could never hear "the name of Dashwood . . . without emotion," Miss Jane gave up on a married name or any surname, either her father's or her husband's: "I dropt all thoughts of either, and have made it a point of bearing only my Christian one since my Father's death" (*Juvenilia*, 196). Both surnames are highly problematic. "Annesley" indicates an uncertain claim to identity (later it will be the surname of Georgiana Darcy's middle-aged companion). "The name of Dashwood" was so strongly associated with carousal, seduction and rape, atheism, and disturbance that a number of people might not hear it "without emotion." (Austen will use that name again). The central joke in this story, however, lies in the mysterious Jane's contrarian assumption that she *can* do without a surname if she pleases—as if it were merely a matter of personal choice, like using a nickname. Miss Jane defies the tradition that moves a woman from father's to husband's name. She belongs to no male, to no lineage or place. This "Miss Jane" seems an avatar of Jane Austen, claiming an impossible freedom, an unknowable identity.

First names may become place names, place names become surnames, and surnames become first names. Surnames in effect "place" you. As verbal terms they most commonly stem from indications of location, occupation, or affiliation. Names of common occupations like "Wright" and "Smith" crowd the annals of the poor. Terms indicating locations (a field, a hill, and a grove) supply the foundational common English surnames. This is clear in the fictional name "John o' Nokes," or "John-a-Nokes" ("John who lives by a group of oaks") long used in out-lining law cases:

> John-a-Nokes and Tom-a-Stiles: two honest peaceable gentlemen, repeatedly set together by the ears by lawyers . . . having for several years past been supplanted by two other honest peaceable gentle-men, namely, John Doe and Richard Roe.[8]

"John-a-Nokes" and "Tom-a-Stiles" became figures of speech partly be-cause they represent an archetypal pattern. Many surnames originally bore direct reference to a natural feature or landmark. The name even-tually became portable and abstract. Descendents of an earlier settled "Nokes" family move far from the original stand of oaks but keep the label generations after the namesake trees have disappeared. English sur-names (like those in other languages) often suggest a strong earthy asso-ciation, relationship to a particular spot on the earth, now forgotten, ab-stracted into a linguistic sign. Anglo-Saxon terms for natural things, or the work of man with nature, endure at the heart of numerous English surnames. On her mother's side Jane Austen could claim relation to the aristocracy, yet the name "Leigh" is simply a strong old name, referring only to the basic unit of settlement: *ley,* a clearing in the woods. Jane's own surname (like that of all named "Austin," however spelled) ulti-mately derives from "Augustine," first missionary to the Anglo-Saxons, buried in Canterbury (*Cantwaraburg,* "Stronghold of the people of Kent," Mills). Augustine is rapidly anglicized to "Austin" as in "Austin Priors." "Austin"/"Austen" is a regional name taken by Kentish folk who worked in or around Canterbury Cathedral, the church of "St. Austin," or worked for the monastic order, the "Austin friars."

A poor man might be defined through simple filiation, as the son of a man referred to by his first name: "Robin's-son," "Jenkins's-son." "John-son" is simply "John's son." This Scandinavian formula was standard among Danish settlers. Despite devotion to Samuel Richardson and Samuel Johnson, Austen finds such *-son* names dull and saves them for unimportant persons. ("Mr. Robinson" is the Musgroves' apothecary.) Characters with speaking parts usually have more interesting names. The name of the region, town, or county from which settlers came offers other locative descriptions that crystallize into surnames. In Austen's novels, locative names ("Hill"), filial names ("Jenkinson"), and work names ("Wright") indicate the commonest Englishness. (The three just cited pertain to servants.)

English people could usually tell at once whether a surname was English, Norman-English, Scottish, Welsh, or native Irish. Many English tended to think of the Scots and the Irish—along with the Welsh—as rude and uncivilized. Scottish or Irish Protestant aristocracy was inferior to "real" English aristocracy. Immigrants to England often changed their names, getting rid of a "Mac" or "O." Frances Burney's father, Charles Burney the musicologist, dropped the "Mac" from "Macburney." In Austen's novels a clear (if sometimes unobtrusive) line separates Norman names from names of common English (Anglo-Saxon) origin. A Norman name is likely to indicate influence, power, inherited status, or high rank. *Pride and Prejudice* plays most fully with indications of Norman descent and aristocratic assurance—all caught in the comic figure of Lady Catherine De Bourgh. But characters with Norman surnames are not always easily laughed off, and some disagreeable people in Austen's novel have names of Anglo-Saxon derivation.

The surnames of Austen's characters are often deft references to historical struggles past and present. In *Mansfield Park* young William Price—with his Welsh surname—has endured, and will endure, strenuous physical effort and real danger in defending the nation (and its colonies) against the French in the Napoleonic naval battles. The English have struggled against the Welsh and still keep them under, but they are lucky to have a Price to fight for them. Past historical conflicts like the Norman Conquest, the Wars of the Roses in the fifteenth century, the English Civil War in the mid-seventeenth century, and the "Glorious Revolution" of 1688–89—all leave their mark. Austen deploys historical names like "Fairfax," "Churchill," and "Russell" with subtlety and effect. Samuel Richardson was the first English novelist to incorporate into his narrative figurative and realistic historical names with complex poetic signification. In *Clarissa* he uses Harlowe (otherwise "Harlow") as his heroine's surname, a pun on "harlot" and "Harlowe." The name of the town in Essex ("Harlow") is, however, a realistic locative. That Clarissa's first stop after leaving home is Saint Alban's in Hertfordshire suggests that her family's house is in Essex on the borders of Hertfordshire and that the name of her rising and self-important family came from a town not far from where they live now. Richardson also deliberately uses names of historical import, like "Lovelace," "Byron," and "Grandison," names of extant families with particular Civil War histories.[9] Charles Grandison (a kind of virtuous counterpart to Bonnie Prince Charlie) gets into an honorable entanglement with a Continental Catholic girl named "Clementina," a parallel and contrast to Bonnie Prince Charlie's entanglement with his Scottish (and Catholic) mistress Clementina Walkinshaw.

Austen saw what Richardson was up to and learned how to use and refine his play with names. Other authors had already taken note. Frances Sheridan's heroine in *The Memoirs of Miss Sidney Bidulph* (1761) offers an unusual instance of a heroic male surname used as a female's first name. The heroine's name honors Algernon Sidney, a kind of Whig patron saint, executed under Charles II for a part in the Rye House Plot. In *Emmeline,* Charlotte Smith has her heroine turn from the emotional Frederic Delamere to the rational, stable, and kind hero Godolphin, who bears a name of political importance in the Age of Anne. Sidney Godolphin, originally a moderate Stuart supporter, became associated with the Whigs and John Churchill, Duke of Marlborough. As Lord High Treasurer, he stabilized finances and forwarded the Act of Union with Scotland. Jane West makes a similar move in *A Gossip's Story* (1796) when the reliable suitor with the politically resonant surname "Pelham" is refused by the overromantic and wrongheaded Marianne Dudley (another historical surname, from the Elizabethan era, Dudley had already been used by Austen in *Catharine*).

The young Jane Austen combats the Whiggish compromise indicated by Emmeline's choice. Jane sets no store by any "Godolphin." Contrariwise, playing her role as reader with vigor, she insists on taking Frederic Delamere as the undeniable romantic hero, an ardent and idealistic lover unjustly treated: "Elizabeth the torment of Essex may be compared to the Emmeline of Delamere" ("History of England," *Volume the Second, Juvenilia,* 186). Austen enjoys conflating the historical and the fictional. Annotating Goldsmith's *History,* where he writes "Lord Delamere took arms in Cheshire," she comments, "I should have expected *Delamere* to have done so, for it was an action unsuited to *Godolphin*" (*Juvenilia,* 334).

Austen's Great Surname Matrix

Austen's choice of historically current names constantly circles about one particular nexus, which might be termed "the Fitzwilliam-Wentworth complex." R. W. Chapman drew attention to the connection of the D'Arcy family with the Fitzwilliams, and in 1953 Donald Greene succinctly explained and elaborated upon such connections in his important essay "Jane Austen and the Peerage":

> Robert D'Arcy, fourth and last Earl of Holdernesse (1718–1778) and William Fitzwilliam, fourth Earl Fitzwilliam (1748–1833) were both great men in Whig political circles. . . . In 1782 (when Jane Austen was seven) the Marquessate of Rockingham became extinct, on the sudden death of Charles Watson Wentworth, of Wentworth Wood-house in Yorkshire, Marquess of Rockingham, Prime Minister of Great Britain. . . . The Wentworth and Woodhouse families were united in the thirteenth century, when one Robert Wentworth married a great heiress, Emma Wodehous [*sic*]. The senior line of the Wentworth Woodhouse family achieved a baronetcy under James I. A sister of the first baronet married the heir of the D'Arcys, and the eldest son of the first baronet was the great Thomas Wentworth, Earl of Strafford, Charles I's ill-fated minister. Strafford's only son left no issue, and his estate descended to the children of his sister Anne Wentworth, who had married Lord Rockingham, head of the Watson family. It was a later Anne Wentworth who, in 1744, married the third Earl Fitzwilliam; and on the death of her brother the Prime Minister . . . the fortunes of the Watsons, Wentworths, and Wood-houses all devolved on the Fitzwilliams.[10]

Greene also draws attention to the fact that Austen knew many persons of the aristocracy and was "distantly related to the magnificent Fitzwilliams and Cavendish's themselves."[11] The Duke of Chandos had married as his second duchess Cassandra, who was "sister of Thomas Willoughby, Lord Middleton." "Middleton" and "Willoughby" are certainly names familiar to readers of *Sense and Sensibility*. Greene's summary contains the maiden name of one heroine (Emma Woodhouse) and the married name of another (Anne Wentworth).

Jane Austen's imagination played upon grand names, grand estates, and great expectations. The young Jane made free with the printed "Form of an Entry for Marriage" and filled in the blanks (reproduced in

Juvenilia). First, she invents a bridegroom grandly named "Henry Frederick Howard Fitzwilliam of London"; on her second try, the groom is "Arthur William Mortimer of Liverpool" who is to marry "Jane Austen of Steventon." Elizabeth Jenkins, who discovered this document, points out that we here see in a line not only first names given to Austen's characters—save for "Mortimer"—but also surnames that appear in Austen's fiction: "Howard" (Rev. Mr. Howard will surely win Emma Watson) and "Fitzwilliam" (the name of Darcy's maternal line, supplying his first name).[12] But the third choice is dramatically different: "This Marriage was solemnized between us Jack Smith & Jane Smith late Austen"—and "Jack Smith" and "Jane Smith" are the only witnesses listed to their own wedding. From the highest end of the social and financial scale Jane plunges to the very lowest—rejecting momentarily the grand identities in a fantasy of lower-class alliance.[13]

Austen's ambitious and playful use of aristocratic surnames is adumbrated in the early story "Sir William Mountague." The absurdly faithless hero is introduced in a lengthy sentence on his lineage:

> Sir William Mountague was the son of Sir Henry Mountague, who was the son of Sir John Mountague, a descendant of Sir Christopher Mountague, who was the nephew of Sir Edward Mountague, whose ancestor was Sir James Mountague, a near relation of Sir Robert Mountague, who inherited the Title and Estate from Sir Frederic Mountague. (*Volume the First, Juvenilia,* 47)

The solemn list mocks the books of peerages and baronetage, the illogic of the boring genealogical transmission through the sacred patrilineal line by right of primogeniture. The objective list also shows some hitches in this masculine line: Sir Christopher is only a *nephew* of the man from whom he inherits, and Sir Edward himself inherited from an undefined "near relation" of a former inheritor (leaving open a possibility of illegitimate succession). The achievement of being a son endows Sir William at age seventeen with "a handsome fortune, an ancient House and a Park well stocked with Deer" (47). (Deer serve as a remaining sign of Norman privilege.)

"Sir William Mountague" refers us to a real family, the Montagus (variously spelled). The Norman name, derived from the original seat at Montaigu-Les-Bois, means "pointed mount (hill)." The original Montagu family, first granted English lands in Wiltshire by King William, achieved more spectacular properties later, most notably the magnificent manor of Beaulieu ("beautiful place") in Hampshire. Beaulieu (now a showplace) was created out of the monastery of Beaulieu Abbey, purchased in 1538 by Thomas Wriothesley, first Earl of Southampton. It came to the hands of the Montagues when Ralph Montagu, third Baron Montagu, married Elizabeth Wriothesley, daughter of the Earl of Southampton. A descendant, Ralph Montague (1638–1709), made a duke under Queen Anne, was considered by Swift "as arrant a knave as any in his time." (He may be the model for Lovelace's uncle Lord M. in *Clarissa*.) Expert in gallantry and dalliance, Ralph may also furnish a model for Austen's philandering character. Another inspiration for Austen—as well as a source of the particular spelling—is probably Amelia Opie's first novel, *The Dangers of Coquetry* (1790), published when Opie was only eighteen. Opie's "Edward Mountague," though virtuous, is torn between two women.

Amelia Opie set out to expose the dangers posed by both a female and a male coquet. Austen's little antihero Sir William Mountague is a male coquet par excellence. The names of the ladies with whom he is involved are those of prominent aristocratic or gentry families. Their names are titles in themselves. Sir William outdoes Mr. Watt in "Three Sisters" (or Frederick Wentworth among the budding Musgroves) in an inability to distinguish between good-looking sisters or female relations. He is at first equally attracted by each of the three Clifton sisters. The real Cliftons, descended from one of King William's knights, fought for the Royalists in the Civil War and were heavily fined by Cromwell. Jane's contemporary Sir Arthur Clifton (b. 1780) became an army officer who was to fight at the Battle of Waterloo.

Sir William Mountague would do well to marry a Clifton, but his aspiring mind urges him to look higher. He next falls in love with "a young Widow of Quality," Lady Percival. "Percival" (or "Perceval") is Norman French, with strong associations with a hero of the Grail cycle. The British Percival family included Irish peers, earls of Egmont. Spencer Perceval, seventh son of the second earl, was a rising politician at the time Austen wrote the story. He became Prime Minister and is the only person in that office to have been assassinated (in 1812). Jane Austen certainly could not have known of the more exciting aspects of Spencer Perceval's career when she wrote this story, or *Catharine* in which she will use the name again.[14] Here, Lady Percival is only the widow of a Percival; we find out a bit later she is really a "Wentworth" by birth.

The Percivals would be an important connection—and the Wentworths even more so. But Sir William the butterfly leaves Lady Percival and falls in love with "Miss Arundel." The Arundel (or Arundell) family of Cornwall, Norman in origin, was ancient. Sir John Arundell fought for Henry VI at the Battle of Tewkesbury (1471), and Arundells were staunch royalists in the Civil War. The direct line died out in 1701, the estates going to an *heiress;* recollection of this fact might make a "Miss Arundel" seem especially desirable. But Miss Arundel "preferred a Mr. Stanhope":

> Sir William shot Mr. Stanhope; the lady had then no reason to refuse him; she accepted him and they were to be married on the 27th of October. But on the 25th Sir William received a visit from Emma Stanhope the sister of the unfortunate Victim of his rage. She begged some recompense, some atonement for the cruel Murder of her Brother. Sir William bade her name her price. She fixed on 14s. Sir William offered her himself and Fortune. They went to London the next day and were there privately married. (48)

"Stanhope" is the surname of the Earl of Chesterfield, Philip Dormer Stanhope, author of published letters addressed to his illegitimate son on manners and morals. Dr. Johnson memorably said that these *Letters* "teach the morals of a whore, and the manners of a dancing master."[15] Austen appears to agree, valuing the life of a male Stanhope at fourteen shillings. Emma Stanhope, of this louche family, provides a surprising bride for fickle Sir William.

If Sir William is still seventeen, his marriage to Emma Stanhope—like many marriages in Austen's early comic works—would not be legal. Marriage in any case does not prevent Sir William from wandering:

> Chancing one day to see a charming young Woman entering a Chariot in Brook Street, he became again most violently in love. On enquiring the name of this fair Unknown, he found that she was the Sister of his old friend Lady Percival, at which he was much, rejoiced, as he hoped to have by his acquaintance with her Ladyship, free access to Miss Wentworth. (48–49)

Faithless Sir William works his way through serious of flirtations among the aristocracy. Hesitating among the Clifton girls he soon flies higher. He marries into the Stanhopes, while soon hoping to enjoy an adulterous fling with a Wentworth lady, to whose sister he has earlier been attracted. Traditionally, male straying from a marriage to have an affair did not count—legally or socially—as "adultery." Sir William's marriage—if it is one—would not be ended by any illicit arrangement with an unmarried female of any rank.

The Wentworths were the wealthiest and most important of all the families Mountague encountered. Some of the estates of doomed Lord Strafford descended to the Watson family. Thomas Watson Wentworth—who had added the "Wentworth"—became first Marquess of Rockingham. His son and heir, Thomas Watson, begot the Marquess of Rockingham who became Prime Minister. A Wentworth had married into a local Woodhouse family in the fourteenth century; the Woodhouse lands went to the Watsons when the second Earl of Strafford died without an heir.

In the prosperity of the eighteenth century, the house on the estate of Wentworth-Woodhouse in south Yorkshire was gigantically rebuilt. The excessively rich Watson Wentworths felt superior to the descendants of the unhappy beheaded loyalist; these "real" Wentworths had inherited the title of Lord Raby, but not the estate. The secondary branch of that family—really the neglected primary branch—built "Wentworth Castle" in joking retaliation, a pseudo-medieval contrast to the great Augustan mansion.[16] So, the question regarding any Wentworth is, "does he or she belong to the rich side of the family—or just the poor side?" Sir William was foolish to stray among Stanhopes, if he might have rich pickings marrying among Watson Wentworths. But if the Wentworth young lady is only of the poorer (if more noble) branch, she would do for mere dalliance.

This use of "Wentworth" in *Volume the First* indicates that Austen is early attracted to the ironic use of aristocratic surnames. Already we can see her beginning to turn to the Great Name Matrix. She makes free with the blue bloods and makes fun of them—and of readers who pursue stories of high life. Throughout her career, Austen finds her strongest surnames—in particular for central male characters—within the complex that Greene adumbrated and that Janine Barchas has further illuminated in *Matters of Fact*. Barchas points to the exploits and scandals of these powerful families and the interconnectedness of their names both within English life and within "Jane Austen's Fictive Network": "Austen's fascination with the Wentworths, first noted by Donald

Greene, grows increasingly overt from text to text, linking Darcys and Woodhouses to Watsons and Vernons to Bertrams and Wentworths."[17]

The central name is *Wentworth*. This is the center from which other names radiate in what I have termed the Great Name Matrix. This name, however, like the solution to a riddle, is concealed until very late. "Wentworth" is used directly at last, as the hero's surname, in Austen's last completed novel, *Persuasion*. (In *Sanditon* Austen is moving away from the Great Name Matrix, choosing a different social milieu.) Sir Walter dismisses Frederick's brother (and thus Frederick and Mrs. Croft too): "Mr. Wentworth was nobody . . . nothing to do with the Stafford family" (*Persuasion*, I, ch. 3). These Wentworths are invisible to Sir Walter as relations of Lord Strafford, probably because they do not belong to the *rich* Watson Wentworths. Austen leaves us to guess that they probably belong to the purer if poorer line.

Thomas Wentworth, Earl of Strafford, is the object of Austen's admiration (fig. 5). Her regard seems to be based not his Stuart loyalty alone but on his self-sacrifice. Confronted by a hostile Parliament determined to sentence him to death (even after the trial failed to find guilt), Thomas Wentworth told King Charles I not to try to save his own life at the expense of the king's life and the security of the kingdom. Wentworth passed the ultimate test, putting the welfare of somebody else and some greater good ahead of his own, at the cost of life itself. He is thus the eternal opposite of flaunting show-off landowners, self-interested privatizers, and money-centered successes. "Wentworth" represents a moral value that ultimately does not rest on the well-being of the self. Captain Frederick Wentworth (who, like Thomas Wentworth, Lord Strafford, has sufficient egotism and pigheadedness) risked his own life for England, while a Sir Walter Elliot would never risk a hair for the greater good.

All of the lush Wentworth-Woodhouse estate was to be gathered together and inherited by the earls Fitzwilliam, through Rockingham. If "Wentworth" is a name signifying royalist devotion, the name "Fitzwilliam" reeks of successful Whiggery and Gargantuan wealth. When the young fourth Earl Fitzwilliam took his seat in the Lords as a dependable liberal Whig, his uncle, Charles Watson-Wentworth, second Marquess of Rockingham, was Prime Minister. On his coming of age, Fitzwilliam's estates provided a handsome income of £6,900 per annum. When Rockingham died childless in July 1782 William Fitzwilliam be-

5. Anthony van Dyck, *Thomas Wentworth, First Earl of Strafford* (ca. 1633). Photograph: © National Portrait Gallery, London.

came in a moment the richest man in England. This highly newsworthy young Fitzwilliam's accession to a wealth almost beyond the dreams of avarice—though nothing is—led the young Jane Austen at Steventon to imagine for herself a bridegroom of this wealth-encrusted name. (Fitzwilliam had actually married Lady Charlotte Ponsonby in 1770.)

In Parliament, Fitzwilliam was looked on as the leader of his party. He fell out with Burke, supporting Pitt's suspension of Habeas Corpus in 1794. Pitt made him Lord Lieutenant of Ireland. In Ireland, Fitzwilliam advocated Catholic Emancipation, antagonizing John Beresford, leader of the Ascendancy. Recalled, Fitzwilliam protested against mistreatment and Beresford accused him of libel. The two men prepared for a duel in June 1795, but a magistrate put an end to their proceedings. The Whig coalition formed after Pitt's death fell into disagreement, especially on the ending of the slave trade, which Fitzwilliam opposed. In 1811 it was bruited that the Prince of Wales as Regent would ensure that Fitzwilliam became Prime Minister. He never got there. Before Jane Austen's death Fitzwilliam's role had dwindled. Later, Lord Holland praised him in temperate terms: "With little talent and less acquirements, he was, throughout his life, one of the most considerable men in the country."[18]

This most famous Fitzwilliam of Austen's day is an unavoidable exemplar of the Whig party rejoicing in inordinate riches and power. The example inspires the comic set of Fitzwilliams in *Pride and Prejudice*. These include not only Lady Catherine (née Fitzwilliam) and Colonel Fitzwilliam (looking for a rich wife) but also Fitzwilliam Darcy, accustomed to wealth and privilege and unused to making himself agreeable. The Darcy name also connects through the matrix to the Wentworth-Woodhouse connection. The chief significance of the surname, however, lies elsewhere. "Darcy" cuts against the proud Whiggish arrogance of the Fitzwilliams. Thomas Lord Darcy was beheaded in 1537 for his part in the rising against King Henry VIII called "The Pilgrimage of Grace." Henry was determined to put down with a strong hand what really began as a protest movement and then developed into open revolt against the Dissolution of the Monasteries. The Duke of Norfolk (a Howard) and a Fitzwilliam were among Darcy's chief opponents. Defeated, Thomas Darcy was not taken north to be executed but was beheaded on Tower Hill, as an example to anyone else who might think of protesting against Henry's (or Thomas Cromwell's) designs.

One of Thomas Darcy's female grandchildren married Henry Babington, and a son of this marriage, Anthony Babington, became a page to Mary Queen of Scots and was executed in 1586 for the "Babington plot." The Darcys are thus associated with the cause of Austen's beloved Mary Queen of Scots, as well as with a doomed defense of the threatened monasteries.

Thomas Darcy's support of the people of Lincolnshire and Yorkshire against the command of Henry VIII cost him his life. The martyred Thomas Darcy's great-grandson married Margaret of Wentworth-Woodhouse; their estate descended to the first Earl of Holdernesse, ancestor of the Earl of Holdernesse of Jane Austen's own time.

Fitzwilliam Darcy and Frederick Wentworth offer fascinating examples of Austen's play with English surnames at once contemporary and historical. "Fitzwilliam Darcy" is the major case of Austen's use of a surname as a first name. The usage indicts a certain pompous pride in adhesion to a maternal surname signifying immense wealth and power. Frederick Wentworth, his first name taken from the young Austen's favorite fictional hero (the emotional and impulsive Delamere), is the only Austen hero worthy to bear that surname. Looking at Austen's two most sexually attractive heroes, we see that each has a spiritual dimension; each bears the surname of a man who gave his life for something he held more important than himself. Darcy's surname redeems the crass acquisitiveness and self-satisfaction found in his unchristian "Christian name." Part of the comedy lies in the fact that "Fitz-William" is a sign of illegitimacy; *fitz-* (*fils-*, son) is the prefix used to describe a Norman aristocrat's son born out of wedlock. Some surnames originally conveyed a lot of information. A "Fitzwilliam" might rejoice to think he was the son of William the Conqueror himself. But whoever the first Fitzwilliam was, he was a bastard.

Chapter 6

Personal Names
(First and Surnames)
in the "Steventon" Novels

Personal Names in *Northanger Abbey*

SURNAMES IN *NORTHANGER ABBEY*

The heroine's surname is based on a common formation; there is a real "Morland" far north of Catherine's Wiltshire. Anglo-Saxon *mor* means marshy ground, or moor. "Morland," "land in a marsh," would once have described the quality of the land a family occupied. The surname belongs to a well-known painter, George Morland (1763–1804), who depicted rural scenes, including workers and their animals—a connection made by Janine Barchas.[1] Catherine's surname, however, seems to function chiefly like a strong pun; her family needs "more land." Catherine's father occupies a rectory or parsonage; he can farm the glebe land that goes with it, but only as occupant for life. Neither does General Tilney's second son, also a clergyman, own any land, even though he slightly improves some of the land belonging to his parsonage—not to himself— at Woodston.

Catherine's genuine—and permanent—landless state makes more ironic the misidentification of her as a great heiress, appointed to inherit the properties of Mr. and Mrs. Allen who kindly take her to Bath. The estate of Ralph Allen of Prior Park, as Janine Barchas points out, had been in transition when Austen was first writing the novel. Wealthy Ralph Allen's Prior Park would have been juicy pickings; John Thorpe in his drive passes that unignorable estate. Thorpe wills himself into believing Catherine rich, desiring to confuse "old Allen," (temporary) guardian of Catherine, with the Prior Park Allens of great fortune.[2]

Mr. and Mrs. Allen of Fullerton are only quietly well-to-do. Mrs. Allen can afford fine clothes, but Mr. Allen mildly objects to his horses going to Salisbury for shopping. Were this childless couple to leave Catherine their property (which never crossed their minds), they could not supply grandeur. Limited in education and social talents, the

Allens are a trifle uncouth. Camden, quoting Scaliger, says that "Alan" is "thought to signify an hound."[3] The name "Allen" or "Alan" refers to a barbarian horde ("Alans" or "Aluns"), which, like the Goths, ravaged central Europe in the Dark Ages. Pope refers to them in his mock-epic *The Dunciad;* Dullness is "Great nurse of Goths, of Aluns, and of Huns!"[4] Austen introduces "Huns" with "Hunsford" in *Pride and Prejudice.* In *Northanger Abbey* the heroine is traveling with some well-intentioned barbarians. Mr. Allen does not think of accompanying his womenfolk to the Upper Assembly Rooms and seeing to introductions before escaping to his card game. Miss Tilney is properly chaperoned by Mrs. Hughes, of the Welsh name, a former schoolfellow of Eleanor's mother.

Mrs. Allen has no notion of how to be a chaperone, but chats about her own clothing and its price. Henry laughs when Catherine says that at home the only thing she had to entertain her was to go and call on Mrs. Allen—"What a picture of intellectual poverty!" (*NA,* I, ch. 10). (The intellectual wealth of his Life with Father is not much better.) Henry unkindly finds relief from the imbecility of the childless matron's remarks by mimicking her to her face without her catching on.

The Master of Ceremonies links Catherine with Henry Tilney. But Mrs. Allen makes a connection for Catherine in introducing Isabella and John Thorpe, children of Mrs. Allen's old schoolfellow. "Thorp(e)," an Anglo-Saxon term showing Scandinavian influence, refers to a hamlet or village. This commonplace term serves as suffix to many place names. Mrs. Allen's other friends have equally unprepossessing names. Neither the Skinners nor the Parrys are in Bath this year. "Parry" (or "Perry") is Norman-French for a pear tree, *poirier.* "Perry," a rural alcoholic drink, is to pears what cider is to apples. (Mr. Perry of *Emma* is but a rural apothecary.) "Skinner" is an occupational name; the labor of taking skins off dead horses, cows, and mules was inevitably disgusting if necessary. Dr. Skinner, the Allens' neighbor, came to Bath for the gout. He is presumably a Doctor of Divinity; Fullerton can hardly support two clergymen, so we may assume Dr. Skinner is retired. Thorpe, Parry, and Skinner make a comic low-caste combination reflecting upon Mrs. Allen.

Morlands and Thorpes have humbly locative surnames—dwellers in marshy land or in a village. They belong to places; they are not owners. The Tilneys enter at another level; their name is about possessing. The name derives from an Old English place name, "Till-ney," which means "Tilla's isle." There are several places named Tilney/Tylney, notably in the eastern county of Norfolk; former generations of our Tilney family may have moved east-west instead of north-south. Tudor Tilneys were important. Edmund Tilney (1535–1610) was son of Philip Tilney, usher of the Privy Council. Edmund's grandfather, Sir Philip Tilney, was attached to Thomas Howard, second Duke of Norfolk, who married Tilney's cousin and later his sister. These marriages "allied the Tilneys to virtually every important family in the country" (*ODNB*). Through rich marriages Edmund acquired lands in Middlesex and Surrey. A successful courtier in turbulent times, Edmund Tilney became Master of the Revels and in effect licenser of plays. Such association with the theater offers another and comic connection between "Tilneys and trapdoors" (*NA*, I, ch. 11).

In the eighteenth century, one Richard Child took the name of Tylney; he had married Dorothy Glynne, daughter of John Glynne and Dorothy (née Tylney)—a rare example of a surname descending from a female. Richard was created first Earl Tylney in 1731. Austen may have transposed the comic name "Richard" from the genuine Richard Child to Catherine Morland's father. Antiquated "Dorothy" features as the servant in Henry's mock-Gothic tale. Later, Earl Tilney, born a Long, added the surname of Tilney when he became Earl Tilney. In 1805 Catherine Tilney-Long at age fifteen became enormously wealthy when her younger brother died in 1805. Barchas suggests that Austen in revising the manuscript of *Susan* (already finished and sold in 1803) made her heroine a "Catherine" in honor of the teenaged heiress Catherine Tilney-Long.[5]

In contrast to Edmund and such successful land-acquiring Tilneys, Charles Tilney, son of Edmund's cousin, participated in the plot to free Mary Queen of Scots known as the Babington Conspiracy of 1586. As we have seen, Anthony Babington, leader of the ill-thought-out plot (which entailed killing Queen Elizabeth), was a great-grandson of Thomas Lord Darcy of the Pilgrimage of Grace. Loyalty to Mary of Scots would have appealed to Austen. This episode—not dealt with by Barchas—suggests that while there is one branch of Tilneys (or Tylneys) who are power seeking, land hungry, and self-aggrandizing, there is another branch that is loyal and not averse to risk and self-sacrifice. It is easy to see where General Tilney belongs—whereas in the end Henry opts for some risk.

General Tilney married a "Miss Drummond" with a hefty dowry. Janine Barchas points out that this is ill sorted.[6] Drummonds were staunch Jacobites, starting with James Drummond the fourth earl. If

Miss Drummond were a secret Catholic or Catholic sympathizer, she could not have been altogether happy in living in a confiscated and secularized monastery, rendered subordinate to the dictatorial general's stern self-indulgence. As a Scot she is also an alien, commanded to assimilate herself to a triumphant English conqueror who took her twenty thousand pound dowry to wife.

General Tilney is at first uncritically admired as "tall, and handsome, and Henry's father" (*NA*, II, ch. 1). In appearance and domination he resembles Henry VIII who took the abbeys. Though he cannot say "off with her head!" he dismisses Catherine in summary judgment. General Tilney laments missing the two distinguished friends who failed to keep him company in Bath; the Marquis of Longtown and Mr. Courtney. "Mr. Courtney" may be connected to Edward Courtenay, first Earl of Devon (1526–56), a descendant of Edward IV, who became involved in various plots (involving assassinations) to put Elizabeth on the throne. This friend, probably a congenial Tudor supporter of aristocratic descent, would not, one imagines, have sympathized with the ardent feminist heroine of Mary Hays's daring *Memoirs of Emma Courtney* (1796).

Northanger Abbey, once "a richly endowed convent," had "fallen into the hands of an ancestor of the Tilneys on its dissolution" (II, ch. 2). General Tilney, then, descends from a successful courtier of Henry VIII, present at the original land grab. Tilneys ingest everything. General Tilney is obsessed with himself and his sacred mealtimes. We can savor the comedy in the sentence, "The dining-parlour was a noble room" (II, ch. 6). Feeding *oneself* is not "noble"—not in the moral sense, though perhaps elites do eat everything up. General Tilney's estate seems devoted to working for his table. He boasts to Catherine of the trouble his gardens and hothouses give him: "The utmost care could not always secure the most valuable fruits. The pinery had yielded only one hundred in the last year" (*NA*, II, ch. 7). Pineapples, a signal of great wealth, first signaled ownership of West Indian plantations—a luxury food par excellence. Growing pineapples in English hothouses could consume a fortune in fuel required to keep a "pinery" warm. General Tilney displays the comically negative qualities of a nouveau riche like Mary Robinson's Sir Edward Clarendon in *Angelina* (1796). Clarendon, who bought his title and assumed a saliently Tory name, has purchased an abbey that he insists on showing off to Lord Acreland, to whom he designs to marry his daughter. At Clarendon Abbey Acreland complains of "the stupid vulgarity of my wealthy host" as he is "dragged, scorching in the sun, to view the Gloucestershire hills from the farthest end of the park." (The imaginary Clarendon Abbey may not be too far from imaginary Northanger in Gloucestershire.) Greedy Clarendon also forces Acreland to eat and drink too much:

> "You see, my Lord, we know how to live,'" said Sir Edward this morning, while cutting a pine apple at breakfast; "don't imagine that all good things are confined to the tables of the nobility: I assure your Lordship, that my pinery is one of the first in the kingdom, let the other be where it will; to be sure it has cost me a world of money—but no matter for that; life is not life, my Lord, without good eating."[7]

Robinson's character exemplifies Tory conventions regarding vulgarity. With his newly minted name, his purchased abbey, and his "pinery," this boaster is of the mercantile class. Austen's greedy and vulgar owner of an abbey, however, is a genuine Tory—no interloper but an *inheritor*. Yet his remarks strongly resemble those of the freshly minted abbey owner—save that General Tilney knows enough to add the untruthful disclaimer: "Though careless enough in most matters of eating, he loved good fruit—or if he did not, his friends and children did" (*NA*, II, ch. 7). General Tilney shows off like any vulgar merchant. General Tilney's name puns on the word "till," but there is no real tillage of the land in order to feed the population visible on the Northanger estate. Everything seems designed to go into the general's giant kitchens and down his capacious gullet, as if he were a modern Cyclops.

FIRST NAMES IN *NORTHANGER ABBEY*

Acquisitive General Tilney's first name is presumably the Hanoverian "Frederick"; his eldest son would be named after him. Camden comments that "Frederic" (along with "Frery" and "Fery," its short forms) "hath been now a long time a Christian name in the ancient family of Tilney, and lucky to their house, as they report."[8] General Tilney seems a bit wary of his elder son. He is not trying to find a spouse for him. No doubt Frederick is sulkily aware of what is expected, and wishes to sow his wild oats first. The father comes down heaviest on his only daughter Eleanor, preventing her marriage, while he seems anxious to settle the more malleable and less important younger son.

Henry Tilney has the Christian name of a line of English kings, the name of Austen's favorite older brother, the mercurial and witty Henry.

The name "Henry" recurs in Austen's mature works; the other "Henry" who aspires after an Austen heroine is the witty and deceptive—if charming—Henry Crawford. There are similarities between these Henrys. Both sometimes use their wit for mockery of women. Henry Tilney, a man of peace, not of war, has allied himself with his sister against the masculine and military leading team of his household. To a lesser extent Henry Crawford does this too, keeping his bond with his sister while maintaining his relation to Admiral Crawford. Henry Tilney's position imposes a certain unwilling submissiveness. Tethered to a living in his father's gift and on his estate, he must endure the paternal beck and call. Henry has some incentive to marry early; a family of his own at Woodston will provide good reason for not spending time in his father's house.

Henry Crawford is restless, impatient, dissatisfied with things as they are and with himself. Henry Tilney is likewise unsatisfied. His response to unpleasant constraint is sarcasm. He cracks his wit on others—he plays off Mrs. Allen to her face, as even Catherine notices. Henry's parodic response arises from a genuine aversion to cliché—and after meeting his father, we can understand, for General Tilney's conversation is all heavy cliché. Henry Tilney's playfulness and irritation are qualities shared with Shakespeare's Prince Hal—kept in check by the fact that this young man is *not* the heir. If Austen is critical of the kind of takeover Northanger Abbey represents, then General Tilney is an usurper (like Henry IV), and his younger son, like Hal, participates in a suppressed guilty awareness of usurpation. Yet Henry Tilney as a clergyman endeavors—to a very limited extent—to carry on the original work of the abbey.

Captain Frederick Tilney has all the sense of entitlement that being an heir can give him. The most noteworthy member of the English royal family to carry this name in the eighteenth century was "poor Fred," Prince of Wales, heir to George I, who died prematurely. "Poor Fred" and his father became decidedly at odds, a pattern repeated by successive Hanoverians, including George III and his eldest son. Slightly more docile than a typical Prince of Wales, Frederick Tilney does all he can to evade his father. "Frederick" will be the name of Austen's true war hero of *Persuasion*—a man who also has a rebellious streak and a strong sense of his own worth. The name is given to the first "hero" in Austen's stories, the self-regarding Frederic of "Frederic and Elfrida." Captain Tilney shares the name of Austen's favorite fictional hero, Charlotte Smith's Frederic Delamere, but has little of Frederic Delamere save his impatience. Frederick Tilney is evidently expert at rapid seduction, as impatient as his father to get at dinner. Annoyed by Catherine's presence when he is trying to speak with Isabella, he is openly rude (*NA,* II, ch. 3). Like his father, he performs by cliché. Throughout his life, Henry will need to please—or at least not offend—this selfish elder brother. Henry's choice of Catherine as a bride is probably his one piece of effective self-assertion in a lifetime.

Catherine Morland's first name (the author's second choice) is the name of a saint (Saint Catherine of Alexandria, patron saint of maids and virgins). In eliminating "Susan" in rewriting Austen may have borrowed the heroine's name from her old unfinished story. The name signifies purity, though Austen here does not emphasize that by the spelling "Cath*a*rine" used in the early unfinished novel. Miss Morland is comically unsullied by impurity, pretensions, or deceit. "Open, candid, artless . . . knowing no disguise"—so Henry Tilney defines her, ironically pretending to be speaking of Isabella (II, ch. 10). Catherine's brother James, more naive than his sister, is taken in for a longer period by the Thorpes. Austen has given the heroine's endearingly foolish brother, an Oxford student who will be a clergyman, the name of her own eldest brother—James Austen, former Oxford student and also a clergyman in the making. Perhaps Jane wishes to cut her officious eldest brother down to size; she never gives his name to a strong or clever character. The father of Catherine and James, the Rev. Mr. Morland, is "a very respectable man, though his name was Richard" (I, ch. 1). This first name, always amusing to Austen, is associated with lack of intellect. A "Richard" is not well suited to rule. His unfortunate nickname would be "Dick."

Eleanor Tilney's dignified name is realistically appropriate to her rank. In *Ethelinde* Eleanor is the first name of the horsy gentlewoman Miss Newenden. It is the name of a powerful and effective queen, Eleanor of Aquitaine, wife of Henry II, who managed things for him in his absence. But Eleanor Tilney is never allowed to manage things. Essentially the same name is given to the most developed and morally authoritative female character in *Sense and Sensibility.* Elinor Dashwood, another half-orphan, may have her flaws and serious misfortunes, but she is not required—as Eleanor Tilney is—to yield to daily oppression. A kind of upper servant to her father, Eleanor must point out to Catherine how little power she actually has; presumably the general's wife had nearly as little. Eleanor most misses departed Mrs. Tilney.

John Thorpe's short and common first name, in use in all classes, cannot tell us much, but his manners quickly inform us that he is under-bred and crudely pretentious. Isabella Thorpe's showy given name, pre-sumably her mother's choice, is the name of a Spanish, not English, queen. On the fictional level her name is peculiarly appropriate for an advocate of Gothic novels. "Isabella" is the name of the heroine (or one of the heroines) of Walpole's *The Castle of Otranto* (1764), the first Gothic novel. The alternative heroine of *Otranto* is Matilda, unfortu-nate daughter of cruel Manfred (a position a bit too like Eleanor's). That name turns up in Henry's parodic story as author of "the memoirs of the wretched Matilda" (II, ch. 5).

Maggie Lane says that names like "Isabella" are suspect. Yet, Emma's elder sister—placid and maternal—is an "Isabella." Mr. Woodhouse, however, says that Emma's sister was nearly christened "Catherine" (*Emma,* I, ch. 9). Perhaps Austen substituted "Isabella" for Emma's sis-ter because "Susan" had just been changed to "Catherine Morland." John Thorpe fully abets the family project of finding a husband for Isa-bella and pushing on to a match. In order to further Isabella's courtship of James Morland, John reluctantly takes his younger sister Maria driv-ing with him. (The outing successfully results in an engagement.) But John would not drive his sister Anne, according to Isabella, "because she had such thick ancles" (*NA,* I, ch. 15). In this early work Austen al-ready shows us an "Anne" who is left behind and denigrated. Anne finds solace with friends: "Catherine was. . . . glad that Anne should have the friendship of an Emily and a Sophia to console her" (*NA,* I, ch. 14). These two names are in vogue. The inadequate introduction of these girls by their first names alone (instead of as "Miss Sophia Somebody," etc.) adds to our impression that Anne Thorpe is young and unformed.

The author makes some use of the penumbra, absent acquaintances, while sharply limiting the number of persons that the heroine encoun-ters in Bath. Isabella strives for gentility when she refers formally to her friend "Miss Andrews" of Putney, "One of the sweetest creatures in the world" (I, ch. 6). Unlike Pamela *Andrews,* the Putney friend seems dull, if lowborn. Miss Andrews is "amazingly insipid," despite one violently colorful appearance in "puce-coloured sarsenet" (I, ch. 6; ch. 15). "Miss Andrews" is largely a fictional character, a foil of Isabella's invention. Isabella also mentions a "Captain Hunt," one of her admirers "at our as-semblies last winter." If Hunt is fortune hunting—possibly like Captain Hunter in *The Watsons*—he could not take much interest in Isabella. Such banal names give us an impression (substantiated by "Putney"—see discussion in chapter 10) that the Thorpes' social circle is middle class—or lower middle class—and undistinguished. John's friend "Sam Fletcher" has a doubly plebeian name—a low nickname plus an occupational surname. A "Fletcher" is a "maker of arrows" (from Old French *fleshier*). The arrows fit in well with Thorpe-ish reference to *hunting*, which John claims ardently to pursue. The old Normans pursued deer through the greenwood, firing at them with bow and arrow. But Isabella is really the member of the family on the hunt.

The narrative has a high proportion of references to games and sports, starting with Catherine's "cricket, base ball, riding on horseback, and running about the country" (I, ch. 1). During this period there was new patriotic interest in traditional English games. Catherine's pastimes may establish her as a true undiluted *Anglo-Saxon* woman. Flirting, dancing, courtship, seduction, and fortune hunting are more dangerous courtly games. Game playing is involved not only in the hazards of courtship but in the world's most serious entertainment. That grand entertainment is the pursuit and acquisition of possessions—to which we are led by the "pool of commerce" during the evening "spent together at Thorpe's" (I, ch. 11). The most amusing caper of this high-ranking if lethal game is the assumption of the right to transform a well-endowed convent by force into a personal mansion, while maintaining as a core principle the unquestionable absolute right to property.

Names in *Sense and Sensibility*

SURNAMES IN *SENSE AND SENSIBILITY*

The novel's most striking—even astonishing—surname is "Dashwood." The name is old, a mixture of Norman French and Anglo-Saxon: "de Dashwood." (Dashwoods existed in Norfolk prior to the Norman Conquest.) In *Sense and Sensibility,* on a poetic level (important even amid the historical references), the name indicates "dashed from the wood," like the fallen leaves that Marianne loves. Throughout the novel, things fall or are dashed away.

"Dashwood," however, is most immediately remarkable because of its strong associations with a scandalous personage, a connection explored by Janine Barchas in chapter 5 of *Matters of Fact.* The most famous person to bear that surname in Austen's era was Sir Francis Dashwood, fifth Baron Le Despencer (1708–81). Francis was a politician—a not too successful Chancellor of the Exchequer (1762–63) and Postmaster General (1765–84). His real achievement, however, was founding what was popularly called "the Hell-Fire Club." This loose group met for several years in the ruins of Medmenham Abbey, remodeled by Francis Dashwood to suit carousals. The scene of orgiastic operations then moved to his own home at West Wycombe Park. One notable achievement in landscape gardening at Wycombe was creating through the lawns, bushes, and founts of his gardens an anatomically complete representation of the female form, apparent to a viewer placed at the right vantage point. Hogarth depicted Dashwood in monkish robes, blasphemously contemplating the image of a naked female.

The Austens and the wicked Francis Dashwood were connected. Francis's father's daughter Rachel would marry Sir Robert Austen of Bexley in Kent. Robert Austen preceded Francis Dashwood as MP for New Romney; Sir Francis's successor in that office in 1761 was none other than Thomas Knight of Godmersham, who adopted Jane Austen's brother Edward. Barchas does not explore this connection, but Thomas Knight was well acquainted with Sir Francis and could probably have told his own stories about him. Francis Dashwood's third wife was Mary King, and the next heir took the name of Dashwood-King. Sir John Dashwood (1765–1849), the fourth baronet, married a Mary Anne Brodhead from whom he became estranged. Sir John attempted to sell everything in order to spite her—an event that Janine Barchas connects with Fanny Dashwood's desire to dispute her mother-in-law's right to china and household furnishings. Dashwoods supplied much public gossip, but nothing exceeded in flamboyance the rich and deviant Francis. Janine Barchas suggests that "in her choice of the name *Dashwood*, Austen seems to court an audience for her first published novel by appealing to contemporary sensationalism."[9]

Austen, however, had already used the name in the story of the mysterious "Miss Jane" in "A Collection of Letters" (1792). Miss Jane, daughter of the "the late Admiral Annesley" consented to a secret marriage with Captain Henry Dashwood, killed in America. Her children by that marriage died, and Miss Jane determined to remain "Miss Jane," without the trouble of a surname. "I could not prevail upon myself to take the name of Dashwood (a name which after my Henry's death I could never hear without emotion)" (*Juvenilia*, 195–96). In that early story the name "Dashwood" is associated with secret sex and with disappearance—the vanishing of love. In the first chapter of *Sense and Sensibility* we are given the situation of a Mrs. Dashwood, who accepts the surname of another "Henry Dashwood." He too vanishes in death.

Her entirely legitimate marriage is reduced by her stepson and his wife to insignificance. Mrs. John Dashwood even denies the union, to the extent of denying that her husband's half-sisters are any true relation at all.

The name "Dashwood" thrust into prominence at the outset of a novel should offer a certain spicy resonance, expectations of sexual secrets. Ironically the sins of *these* Dashwoods are not sensational, the Dashwood family of Sussex having lived in "so respectable a manner" (*S&S*, I, ch. 1). John Dashwood and his mean-minded Fanny are not at all given to scarlet misdeeds. They are guilty of the commonplace sins: greed, avarice, and coldheartedness. Their coldheartedness, though not the self-centeredness of the seducer—that will be supplied by Willoughby—is in its way a perversion. The couple blasphemes continuously against moral and religious laws. They will do what they want with "their own" estate, assuming absolute license to possess and dismissing loyalty, stewardship, filial piety, or promise-keeping. Austen's worst sinners all break promises, like Isabella who "promises faithfully" what she does not deliver. No promise breaker in Austen's works is worse than John Dashwood, breaking a promise made to his dying father. But such a sin is not material for social opprobrium or delightful scandal.

The Dashwood sisters are, however, treading nearer the edge of scandal than they quite know. Fanny regards any hint of Edward's interest in Elinor (or hers in him) as an outrageous trespass. Elinor is cast as the dangerous seductress. Elinor's seduction and disgrace would please her sister-in-law, but Elinor's marriage to Edward would be a social catastrophe. Elinor is too realistic—and too self-disparaging—to attempt to "entrap" Edward, although she falls in love with him before she believes that he cares for her: "I am by no means assured of his regard for me," she admits to Marianne (*S&S*, I, ch. 4). Elinor is a dangerous romantic who has already overstepped a boundary. Throughout, Elinor's unrealistic adulation of Edward's intelligence and morality demonstrates a clouded judgment. Readers are effectively seduced into ignoring this fact by the pull of Marianne's more overt sexuality and romantic wishes.

Marianne is in great danger of succumbing to sexual overtures; her unsupervised journey to Allenham with Willoughby offers sufficient room for unkind gossip to consider her already fallen (like the first and second Elizas). Within the novel we hear of no slurs on her reputation—although these would have been realistic. Marianne's sexual and emotional enthusiasm makes her open as a target for any man remotely like one of the "monks" of Medmenham and High Wycombe. A "Dashwood" is notoriously the seducer, not the seduced. But both Dashwood girls are in emotional and sexual danger.

Sir John Middleton suggests an old-fashioned, countrified middle way between greed and generosity. His Saxon name means a *tun* (settlement) between other landmarks. The name "Middleton" (freshly celebrated since 2011 when a "commoner" became the wife of Prince William) has aristocratic connections; the Cassandra Willoughby who married the Duke of Chandos was "sister to Thomas Willoughby, Lord Middleton," as Donald Greene pointed out. Jane Austen was connected (through the Leighs) to the *Willoughby* family who owned *Middleton* Hall. Yet she makes Sir John Middleton in his rural Devonshire a mere country squire, content to be so. This Middleton family is of a very middling nature, both in manners and style of living, although there is no real middle ground between Lady Middleton's cold formality and Sir John's old-fashioned genial hospitality. Lady Middleton is formal because she fears being vulgar, aware of her mother's unacceptable City manners—or lack of them. Ironically, the frankness and spontaneity of Sir John and Mrs. Jennings (old-fashioned rural Tory and City Whig) make them better company for each other. They have not yielded to falsehood. Elinor's continuing problem is that she must check spontaneity, guarding conduct and words, and operating with a degree of falsehood that Marianne theoretically bars.

Mrs. Jennings's surname refers us to a historical personage not exactly bad and not exactly good. Sarah "Jenyns" or "Jennings" (1660–1744) became the wife of John Churchill and then Duchess of Marlborough (fig. 6). She is one of the most powerful women in English history. General John Churchill went back on his oath to King James II, changing sides to support the invasion of Mary and William. The family fortunes of the Churchill family were built on that timely act of successful treachery, in which John Churchill's handsome and intelligent wife Sarah was an active assistant. A strong-minded woman, Sarah became a great friend of Princess Anne (later queen). Sarah could be good-humored and a lively conversationalist. But the two ladies fell out, as Sarah in her chosen role as "Mrs. Freeman" spoke her mind to the Queen Anne too frankly. Sarah's temper was unreliable; she fell out with her own daughters and seems to have quarreled with the queen merely about a right of way through the park. This female Jennings was a politician who worked tirelessly for the Whig cause—and that of the

6. Godfrey Kneller, *Sarah Churchill (née Jenyns* [Jennings]*), Duchess of Marlborough* (ca. 1700). Photograph: © National Portrait Gallery, London.

Churchills. From a relatively modest position this commoner developed into one of the most loved, admired, and feared of women.

Sarah was a target of satire, not least in Tory Delarivier Manley's popular satiric novel *The New Atalantis* (1709), a roman à clef pillorying many glamorous courtiers. Among these is the redoubtably beautiful Barbara Villiers, Duchess of Cleveland, former mistress of Charles II.[10] In *The New Atalantis* both John Churchill and his wife come off as treacherous schemers and—like most of the inhabitants of "Atalantis"—given to illicit sex. It is suggested in the novel that John

Churchill got his start up the ladder by sleeping with Barbara Villiers, then still the royal mistress. (See the champagne scene early in *The New Atalantis*.)

Jane Austen makes Mrs. Jennings a vulgarian who comes from the merchant classes of the City of London. (Such a person would be almost inevitably a Whig.) Mrs. Jennings has successfully proceeded on an upward trajectory. Shrewdly, she sent her daughters to fashionable schools where they could learn the gentry's manners and accomplishments and thus change classes. She married both daughters off and up—to country gentlemen. This *bourgeoise* mother (a grandmother several times over) is a nosy, noisy, and dominant matriarch. Yet, unlike her namesake, she is not given to fits of ill temper, but exhibits generous good nature. Austen's first impulse seems to have been to make Mrs. Jennings almost a caricature of gossipy vulgarity, but as the novel progresses the author, like Elinor, seems to have felt the attractions of this strong and practical female personality.

Even cheerful Mrs. Jennings has experienced grief. Her widowhood gives her a share in the novel's themes of loss. One of the numerous signs that her manners are not those of a gentlewoman is her relating to Elinor all the details regarding the last illness and death of her husband. Both Austen and Elinor appear to find this a rude mark of her low class (just as they do Mrs. Jennings's open reference to her daughter's pregnancy). Yet, in expressing her feelings about her husband and airing her memories, Mrs. Jennings shows an unabashed if lower-class respect for bodily travails and for emotional experience—a respect lacking in other central characters. Here as in *The New Atalantis* we find a drinking scene involving an all-female party, but it is sympathetic and gracefully comic: Mrs. Jennings offers to Marianne a remedy that pleased her husband, "the finest old Constantia wine"; the much-tried Elinor drinks it (*S&S*, II, ch. 8). Mrs. Jennings's fearless acceptance of bodily facts and her experience in nursing later make her a powerful resource; she is a staunch friend to the Dashwood girls during Marianne's disappointment and illness.

How suitable that the name of Mrs. Jennings's good wine should be "Constantia"! Mrs. Jennings exhibits the virtue of *constancy*—a virtue in remarkably short supply in the world of *Sense and Sensibility*. Constancy is not a modern virtue. It is more the style to discard persons of little use to personal advancement. Mr. Palmer, for example, when in town "was careful to avoid the appearance of any attention to his mother-in-law, and therefore never came near her" (*S&S*, II, ch. 5). The sympathetic central characters all experience loss and are disparaged or discarded by somebody. There is an autumnal tone to the novel, especially at its opening. Marianne regrets the leaves that will change color and fall without her being at Norland to see. She imagines that while she changes place the trees are eternally in place. Marianne does not realize that the John Dashwood will not only ignore arboreal beauty but also cut down trees for fun and profit. Her woods themselves will eventually be dashed away. Many things pass away in the course of the novel, things that will not return, like the girls' father or Willoughby's love—or his former image.

Willoughby's name fits in with the "wood" or "tree" theme. This Norman Norse name (*Wilgebi*) came into England with the Norman Conquest, when Sir William de Willoughby was given a land grant. The name means "a settlement in a place of willows." This aristocratic Norman name, as we have seen, plays its part in Jane Austen's mother's family, most notably in the Cassandra Willoughby who married the Duke of Chandos.[11] The surname "Willoughby" also exhibits a remarkable novelistic history. It is the surname of Sir Clement Willoughby, the bantering rake in Frances Burney's *Evelina,* who pursues the heroine not as a wife but as a mistress. A more emotive and lovable Willoughby is the hero of Charlotte Smith's *Celestina* (1791). George Willoughby suffers from his father's determination that he must marry a wealthy woman to save his estate. The young man is attracted to Celestina, the lovely orphan girl whom his mother has taken from a convent in France. The couple decide to brave poverty and marry—but on the eve of their wedding Willoughby is told (by interested parties) that he and Celestina are brother and sister. Shocked, Willoughby departs, leaving his beloved uninformed. In Smith's novels a heroine is often traduced by lying deceivers, so it is understandable that Marianne clings to the hope that others are "leagued together to ruin me in his opinion" (*S&S,* II, ch. 7). Both Marianne Dashwood *and* the naive contemporary reader, therefore, have literary and emotional grounds to hope that our John Willoughby might yet be faithful, that there may be a complex explanation for disappearance and unkindness. Celestina (like Smith's reader) comes to believe that Willoughby is planning to marry the rich Miss Fitz-Hayman to save his estate, as indeed he half-heartedly designs. An awkward and intense encounter at a party surely informs a critical scene in Austen's novel.[12]

In an early story Austen experimented with a faithless "Willoughby"; "Edward Willoughby" is the absconding lover lamented by Sophia, who has often been rejected before: "I am not conscious of being more sincerely attached to Willoughby than I was to Neville, Fitzowen, or either of the Crawfords" ("A Collection of Letters," *Juvenilia*, 194). Repetition makes Sophia's fate less pitiable. Burney and Smith both exploit the labile nature indicated by the name, the tendency to bend like the willow to circumstances. The name implies a yielding quality traditionally expected of the female. In the old Anglican marriage service of Elizabethan usage the wife was to swear to be "buxom" in bed and at board—"buxom" meant possessing the yielding qualities of a tree in the wind. (Comically, the word later attaches to secondary female characteristics.) If a man bows like the willow tree, you cannot lean upon him. Some willows weep, and all bow. Willow is also an emblem of forsaken love. Traditionally, forsaken lovers were to wear the willow. (See Desdemona's "Willow Song" in Shakespeare's *Othello*.)

If "Willoughby" has a plangent elegiac tone, signifying aristocracy, weakness, and lost love, the name "Ferrars" is as shocking as "Dashwood." This name of humble origin, based on *fer* (iron), refers to the work of a "farrier," a man who makes iron horseshoes. The *iron* element in Mrs. *Fer*rars is discernible. Little does she know that she can be worsted by *Steele*—a tempered, more enduring, and flexible form of iron. Although the surname derives from a common and low form of work, it went upward. "Ferrars" was the family name of the Earl of Derby. It also became the name of a title. Barchas associates the Ferrers/Ferrars family with Catholicism,[13] but that is not the dominant association in *Sense and Sensibility*. The famous—or infamous—bearer of the title in the eighteenth century was Laurence Shirley, fourth Earl Ferrers (1720–60). (The third Earl Ferrers had been "confined as a lunatic": *ODNB*.) Laurence Shirley shot and killed his steward, probably because the steward was going to testify for Laurence's wife in a case of marital separation. Laurence Shirley had imprisoned his spouse in his house in Leicestershire. (Imprisoned wives seem common enough to justify Catherine Morland.) The aristocratic murderer pleaded insanity but was sentenced to death. Earl Ferrers/Ferrars, wearing his wedding suit, was hanged at Tyburn on 5 May 1760. His execution allowed Britons to boast that all Englishmen were equal before the law.

To this list of scandalous names—including the title of the hanged earl—we should add the name of "Mr. Palmer," husband of Lady Middleton's sister. The word "palmer" means "bearer of palm branches" and refers to one who has been on a pilgrimage, especially to the Holy Land. The historical associations, however, are not at all pious. Mr. Palmer may be supposed descended from an issue of Barbara (née Villiers), or "Barbara Palmer," wife of the complaisant cuckold Roger Palmer during her sexual connection with Charles II. "Roger Palmer" is a highly comical name. The first name has a commonly known "dirty" slang sense, "Roger" being an active verb and also a noun. (The obscene meaning, if often ignored, is presented in the pirates' "Jolly Roger.") Barbara Villiers, a devout royalist, became a Roman Catholic. Her son by Charles was given the surname "Fitzroy" and some rights of his own (fig. 7). It is entertaining to see the success of one of her (presumably Tory) male descendants. Mr. Palmer, an MP, has married (for money) the daughter of a Cit (Mr. Jennings, the merchant) with strong Whig associations such as Charlotte Palmer's maiden name "Jennings" implies.

"Brandon" is both Norman ("de Brandune") and English; Anglo-Saxon "Brandon" can mean a "hill where broom grows." The Scandinavian *brand* could refer to a "firebrand" or "sword." The name "Brandon" thus carries within it a suggestion of violence and fire—as in Richardson's troublemaking "Parson Brand" in *Clarissa* (whom Lovelace calls a "fire brand"). Jocelyn Harris points out that the surname of Richardson's "Mr. B." is implicitly identifiable as "Brandon" in the 1801 edition of *Pamela* in which B.'s residence is "Brandon Hall."[14]

"Brandon" might be taken as another scandalous historical name; Patrick Parrinder connects it with the surname of Charles I's executioner.[15] A more likely historical source is Charles Brandon, first Duke of Suffolk, brother-in-law to Henry VIII.[16] Brandon married his fourteen-year-old ward Katherine Willoughby, an heiress whom he had originally designed as a match for his son and heir. (Katherine presumably had no say in the matter.) Similarly Colonel Brandon's brother took in marriage his father's unfortunate ward, the first Eliza. In both cases a duty of guardianship was grievously abused. At his death, however, Charles Brandon was praised by Henry VIII, who claimed that "his brother-in-law had not made any attempt to injure an adversary, and had never whispered a word to the disadvantage of any one."[17] Our Colonel Brandon, if not as unrealistically inoffensive as the eulogized figure, is certainly unwilling to give offense.

From the Ferrars family's point of view, Brandon is a troublemaker, a firebrand. Under the influence of Elinor, he offers Edward an occupation and a means of livelihood. Yet branded, marked by his past, he seems eternally fated to be almost passive. Young Brandon in the end bowed to his father's will and acquiesced in the financially motivated marital rape of Eliza by his elder brother. He gives up and goes away.

7. Peter Lely, *Barbara Palmer (née Villiers), Duchess of Cleveland with her son, Charles Fitzroy, as Madonna and Child* (ca. 1664). Photograph: © National Portrait Gallery, London.

He carries a sword but is not dangerous. True, he fights a duel with Willoughby, but it is inconsequential.

In *Sense and Sensibility* Austen experiments with the introduction of an ambitious penumbra with multiple associations and gradations of class and activity. Unimportant personages referred to but not appearing as characters supply depth to the class relationships and history. "Old Gibson," a farmer, used to occupy East Kingham Farm, which John Dashwood purchases. The name means "son of Gilbert"; probably a Norman family owned that farm or rented it from the king, long ago. "Lady Courtland," friend of Robert Ferrars, presumably courts those who possess land. The "Careys" with their West Country Norman name live in the Barton neighborhood. "Mrs. Carey" is the caretaker of the heroine as a child in *Emmeline;* the handy Carey family takes *care* of Margaret when Mrs. Dashwood dashes to the endangered Marianne. We also hear of a nearby family named "Whitaker," a suitable West Country landowner's name deriving from "wheat-acre" or "wheat field." Robert Ferrars has a friend named "Elliott" who lives near Dartford (in Kent) and owns an immense "cottage" in which he and Mrs. Elliott (with the judicious advice of Robert) give a party and a dance for eighteen couples. It would be nice to suppose that this fashionable Elliott— who must be as silly as Robert—is related to the proud family of *Persuasion.*

Mrs. Ferrars endeavors to promote a union between her shy son Edward and "the Hon. Miss Morton, only daughter of the late Lord Morton, with thirty thousand pounds" (*S&S*, II, ch. 11). Miss Morton is one of the shadowy gray characters who crowd the margins of this story, interfering with other lives without even appearing. The name "Morton" derives from an ordinary locative, meaning "settlement on a moor or on marshy ground" (Mills). This name has a tang of death about it (*mors, mortis*). Miss Morton is a desirable match now that her father is "the late," leaving her a clear share of his property. The dead lord offers another instance of bereavement, and Miss Morton balefully stands for the mortality of Elinor's own erotic hopes. We have actually *no* assurance that Miss Morton falls in with the scheme of Mrs. Ferrars, who seems to imagine that her giving Edward a thousand a year would provide sufficient financial inducement. Is her son's union with the daughter of Lord Morton just a pipe dream of the unsociable and stingy widow?

Mrs. Jennings introduces an aura of the bourgeoisie. Her friends are City people, not landowners, but "in trade." She pauses in Kensington Gardens to speak to a "Mrs. Clark," whose low name is derived from the occupation of writing and copying. The "Parrys" and "Sandersons" are City friends whom she invites to dinner. "Parry" (also featured in *Northanger Abbey*) is a drink of pear juice. Sanderson, "son of Sander" (or Alexander), is northern and Nordic. Mrs. Jennings's friend "Mrs. Taylor" passes on gossip about Miss Grey's engagement. Her married surname is derived from the craft of a maker of clothes—a low name. (This occupational surname will be used for a character favorably seen in *Emma*.)

Anne Steele's unguarded public remarks on acquaintances give away her original place in life. Unlike her aspiring younger sister, she fails to bother to pretend. In search of potential "beaux" she does not rule out office clerks "provided they dress smart and behave civil." She cites "Mr. Rose at Exeter, a prodigious smart young man, quite a beau, clerk to Mr. Simpson, you know" (*S&S,* I, ch. 21). "Rose" (also "Royce"), an English name of Norman origin, is sometimes a Jewish surname, making it "low" according to English prejudice. Simpson, "son of Sim or Simon," is a Devonshire name (Reaney & Wilson). Anne has gossiping friends in London, Miss Godby and Miss Sparks, who don't believe any man in Edward's position would "give up a woman like Miss Morton, with thirty thousand pounds" (*S&S,* III. ch. 2). "Godby," old Scandinavian ("farm of a man called Gauti": Mills), derives from a place name in Leicestershire. "Sparks" is Old Norse *spraec,* lively, sprightly. (Mrs. Austen refers to "my own Sprack wit.")[18] "Godby and Sparks" sounds like a comedy team. These persons are obviously "low," like all the Steele connections.

Anne Steele likes to be teased about Dr. Davies, a Doctor of Divinity, of (probably) Welsh origins. Other Celtic names include the two apothecaries; talented men from the "Celtic fringe" succeed in this lower branch of the medical profession. Mr. Donavan, who attends Charlotte Palmer's baby and the hysterical Fanny Dashwood, has an entirely Irish name. (Non-Norman Irish names are rare in the Austen novels). Harris, the apothecary who attends Marianne, has a name indicating Scottish origins. After their ejection from Fanny Dashwood's house, the Steele sisters stay with friends, the Richardsons. Jocelyn Harris thinks the surname a hidden tribute, to Samuel Richardson.[19] The great novelist would scarcely be flattered by association with the Steeles' acquaintances.

The Steeles' most interesting connection is their uncle, Edward's tutor "Mr. Pratt." His name suggests to us the part of the anatomy that figures in a "pratfall." In Austen's time it is differently comic—Old English *praett* means "a trick," or (adjectivally) "cunning" or "astute." The comic surname will serve for one of Wickham's coterie in the militia. Yet, there *is* a very famous Pratt of an old Devonshire family, Charles Pratt (1714–94) (fig. 8). As Attorney General, Pratt led for the prosecution in the trial of Lawrence Shirley, Earl Ferrers, for murder in April 1760. This successful prosecution assisted Pratt's rise; eventually he became Lord Chancellor. Pratt was made Baron, then Earl, Camden (1786). Charles Pratt consistently favored freedom, arguing against imprisoning radical Jack Wilkes and sympathizing with American colonists. He took a strong line against general search and seizure. We owe it to Pratt that "an Englishman's home is his castle"—a phrase coined by a journalist in honor of Pratt's decision in 1763 (*ODNB*). A Pratt might well be a person tough to tangle with—somebody on the side of the underdog. Other Pratts must have been left in Devon. Should we not consider Lucy partly Pratt? We see in what a lawyerly fashion she cites evidence for her cause, laying her proofs before the astonished Elinor. In a case of Pratt *v.* Ferrars we know who *must* win—though Mrs. Ferrars won't be hanged.

Sense and Sensibility mocks while it investigates the pretensions of class and blood. There is plenty of low life, not only in the penumbra but at the very center. The names in this novel play with the concepts of "low" and "high." Beneath the surface of the story—as beneath the appearances characters keep up—old scandals bubble. Scandal incites curiosity—that great engine of novel reading. Within the novel we follow Mrs. Jennings's lead and more successfully ferret out the two seduced girls hidden within Colonel Brandon's story. The ineluctable archetypal plot is repetitive. Men take what they want—birds, animals, lands, money, and women. Willoughby did not seduce Marianne, but it is, frankly, hard to doubt that he could have succeeded had he harbored such designs as she later fears he did (*S&S*, II, ch. 10). Marianne's connection to Sir John Middleton probably saves her from being taken by Willoughby as an amorous partner. She is not a "Nobody" as Evelina appeared to Sir Clement Willoughby. The discerning John Willoughby helps himself to young Eliza Williams, seeing she has no status or family.

  Sense and Sensibility uniquely employs personages who do not appear directly in speaking roles and yet are powerful drivers of the plot. Four such noncharacters function *like* characters. All are female: Eliza

8. Francesco Bartolozzi, *Charles Pratt, First Earl Camden* (1795). Mezzotint engraving after a portrait by Thomas Gainsborough (ca. 1772). Photograph: © National Portrait Gallery, London.

the elder; her daughter Eliza Williams; Mrs. Smith of Allenham; and Miss Grey. Eliza the First is the driver of the entire plot insofar as it concerns Marianne. Colonel Brandon's one true love, Eliza was abused by her guardian and forced to marry his elder son. Eloping from the imposed husband, disgraced, and then abandoned, she became a prostitute. Her illegitimate daughter is given the surname "Williams"— Welsh and lower class. This second Eliza, a mere girl, visits Bath with a school friend and is picked up and seduced by Willoughby, who leaves her moneyless and pregnant. By the time we understand this affair we will already have seen Willoughby leaving Marianne abruptly, without explanation. This break, so vivid to us, evidently is Willoughby's standard modus operandi. Presumably he had not recognized the schoolgirl Eliza's connections to a gentleman's family. Substitution and displacement are constantly at work. The two Elizas are scapegoats for male sexual and financial sin. Colonel Brandon is still in love with his first love, who has two duplicates: her distressed daughter and Marianne. Willoughby attracts both. Substitution and displacement also work in Elinor's story. Edward would like to replace Lucy with Elinor, but cannot, until Lucy, constant in desiring Mrs. Ferrars's heir, replaces Edward with Robert.

Mrs. Smith, with the commonplace last name, is the owner of an estate that Willoughby expects to inherit. He takes Marianne to *Allen*ham—"home of barbarians"—and teaches her how to be greedy for someone else's house. At this juncture Marianne unpleasantly begins to resemble Fanny Dashwood. Mrs. Smith, revolted by news of Willoughby's seduction of Eliza Williams, threatens to disinherit him if he does not marry the girl. She cuts off immediate financial supplies. In this tale of steel and iron (Steele and *Fer*) a mere "Mrs. Smith" becomes the "Smith" who forges fate. Willoughby rushes to London and throws himself into marriage with Miss Grey to pay his debts and insure his future.

The woman Willoughby eventually marries has a surname repeating that of the jeweler who owns the real shop, Gray's in Sackville Street (*S&S*, II, ch. 11). That the Sophia Grey possessing fifty thousand pounds of dowry—the young woman who so ruthlessly marries Willoughby—had an aunt called "Biddy Henshawe" suffices to inform us that Willoughby's fiancée is not of a gentle family (II, ch. 8). "Biddy," old-fashioned nickname for "Bridget," is hopelessly lower class; "Biddy Tipkin" is a young woman of the City with dreams of refinement in

Richard Steele's comedy *The Tender Husband* (1705). "Henshawe" sounds as if it referred to a "shaw" or wooded place populated by hens. Miss Grey's guardians are named "Ellison" ("Son of Ellis" or "Elias"), a Scandinavian formation of a name probably northern. Mrs. Ellison's chat in a stationer's shop in Pall Mall is overheard; her unguarded discussion of private affairs in public indicates imperfect gentility. Miss Grey has recently risen from the ranks of tradesmen.

Whether Miss Grey derives her fortune from the sale of jewelry or from a goldsmith artisan in something like Gray's shop (another metallic reference), she purchases Willoughby's family jewels with her gold—her dowry of fifty thousand pounds (II, ch. 8). Miss Grey is gray and shadowy to us. We see her in the background at the fatal party; she dictates the letter that the willowy Willoughby sends. She does not speak in our hearing, but she puts an end to Willoughby as a single man.

The Steele sisters have a type of surname most unusual in Austen. "Steele" was made famous by Sir Richard Steele, author of the *Tatler* essays and of dramas like *The Conscious Lovers*. Lucy Steele is both a tattler and a conscious lover—and a manipulative one. Lucidly and ruthlessly Lucy edges Elinor out of the competition for Edward, confronting her with the evidence that it is Lucy's own hair (not, as Elinor dreamed, her own) that Edward sports in his ring. Lucy, hard as steel, recalls Pope's *The Rape of the Lock:* "What wonder then, fair Nymph, Thy Hairs should feel / The conqu'ring force of unresisted Steel?"[20] Lucy *Steele,* strong and resilient, is a "conquering force"—a match for any *Ferrars,* worker in iron. The Steele sisters are the only characters in major Austen works named after an inorganic substance. Other names refer to places, plants, other humans, or human activities. But the Steeles—or at least Lucy—can be inhumane and dauntless.

The novel plays with cutting implements. Edward, explaining Lucy's marriage to the women of Barton Cottage, absently "took up a pair of scissors . . . spoiling both them and their sheath by cutting the latter to pieces" (III, ch. 12). Willoughby cut off a lock of Marianne's hair. Colonel Brandon wears and wields a sword—the major steel weapon. But Lucy truly knows how to play with edged tools. Elinor gets only what Lucy does not want. Lucy, taking everything she wants from the Ferrars family, is indeed the force of unresisted Steele.

In all its comedy the novel is darkly shadowed and plays perversely with perverse things. It is hard to find the good where even the good are deluded. The story is haunted by theft and violence of the past. The well-meaning are beneficiaries of past sins. Brandon in his profession has supported the British depredations in India, the offense at the core of the trial of the Austens' friend Warren Hastings. He benefits from what his ruthless father and brother have taken, including what they in effect stole from the father's ward. Colonel Brandon is undoubtedly a gentleman—the only one in the story. But he defends nobody, stands up for nothing. A subordinate agent of exploitation (at home as in India), Brandon leads a life shadowed by the past, escaping into memories. He loves Marianne because she reminds him of someone else.

FIRST NAMES IN *SENSE AND SENSIBILITY*

Edward Ferrars bears the Saxon name (*Ead-ward* = "riches" + "guardian") a pre-Conquest royal name, the name of Edward the Confessor (ca. 1002–66), and most recently of Edward VI, defender of Protestantism who died young. It is an ironic Christian name for shy Mr. Ferrars, who has no riches to guard. Robert Ferrars's French-derived Norman first name (the name of a French king) contrasts with the decided Saxon Englishness of "Edward." In *Ethelinde,* the silly Clarinthia Ludford says that her brother's name Robert is too common nowadays and she is changing it to "Rupert"—and the family goes along with her.

Three important male characters are named "John." The name of Christ's favorite disciple (author of the fourth Gospel) was the name of a bad pope and of England's "Bad King John," forced to sign Magna Carta. "John" is more common than aristocratic—see John Thorpe. In *Sense and Sensibility* "John" appears with ingeniously varied colorations: Christian name of John Dashwood, the girls' mean half brother; of Sir John Middleton, the generous country squire; and of the charming and deceptive Willoughby. The surname "Jennings," commonplace if old, is derived from the *ingas* or followers of a John/Jan. "John" appears a blank, on which its possessor can write what he pleases. Every "John" in Austen's fiction has a core of inconsiderate self-centeredness. This may manifest itself in diverse ways, including Sir John Middleton's rage for making people participate in social gatherings and John Knightley's impolite aversion to them

Female characters' first names in this novel are more strikingly varied. Sophia Grey's first name in the Christian tradition means "Holy Wisdom"—but her wisdom is unholy. A perversion of the Sophia Western who rewards Tom Jones, Miss Grey purchases her late chance of a respectable marriage to a handsome man. Lady Middleton is a "Mary"—a favorite name of Austen's for cold, selfish, and irritating females. This elder daughter's correct coldness puts her in parodic parallel to Eleanor, reserved elder daughter of Mrs. Dashwood. Mrs. Jennings's other daughter, Charlotte Palmer, is conventionally named after George III's queen. Like other Charlottes in Austen's oeuvre—including Charlotte Haywood in *Sanditon*—she is practical, steadily if irritatingly cheerful, and unintellectual. Charlotte Palmer (née Jennings) approaches a comic version of *Werther*'s Charlotte, like the madly practical cook Charlotte Luttrell in "Lesley Castle." Lady Middleton's younger sister, Mrs. Palmer is Marianne's counterpart and parodic opposite. Rather than indulging melancholy, she greets blights and stolen hens with an empty laugh (III, ch. 6). It is assumed by Elinor—and by most readers—that grumpy Mr. Palmer blundered in marrying this inanely cheerful woman. But he probably got what he wanted—someone who will put up with his regular spurts of ill nature.

It was pointed out long ago that "Nancy" and "Lucy" reflect the names of Harriet Byron's cousins and best friends, the Selby sisters in *Sir Charles Grandison*.[21] Anne Steele's nickname "Nancy" (once acceptable for Richardson's Anna Howe and Anne Selby) is now old-fashioned. Vulgar Anne Steele has something in common with Anne Thorpe and even Anne Elliot. Annes are pushed around by siblings, regarded as useless to familial ambitions. "Lucy" was rendered cutely common as the name of "Lucy Lockit," the jailer's daughter in Gay's *The Beggar's Opera* (1728). Austen already associated "Lucy" with provincial life and with lower middle-class status. In "Jack and Alice," Lucy declares, "I am a native of North Wales and my Father is one of the most capital Taylors in it" ("Jack and Alice," ch. 5, *Juvenilia,* 22). This Christian name is a tribute to Saint Lucy (Santa Lucia); it means "light" or "illuminator." Saint Lucy's Day, the year's shortest day and longest night, is honored by the lighting of candles. Saint Lucia as a light-bringer is an ironic patron for the younger Steele sister. Lucy is a Lucia *a non lucendo*—far from shedding light, she sheds darkness.

Elinor, like Henry Tilney's sister, bears the name of an English queen consort (differently spelled). Like Eleanor Tilney she is left with an important if thankless position in the family, filling in for a departed parent. Margaret Dashwood, chatty and curious, is the most attractive of Austen's Margarets, who have in common a certain degree of pushiness and self-interest though they lack power and even competence. Austen inserts this third sister in *Sense and Sensibility* to break the spell of the dominant binary.

A key term in the novel, rather than merely an individual name, is "Marianne." It is already Austen's custom in naming characters to set up patterns of binaries: northern versus southern, for example, or Anglo-Saxon versus Norman. In *Sense and Sensibility* she introduces a gallery of characters with questionable credentials and many lines of opposition: Tory and Whig, gentle and middle class. But she raises the conflict to another level in putting the French Revolution at the center of this novel's name game. "Marianne" is a realistic name; one of Austen's connections was a "Marianne." The compound combines two regnant English queens. But in this period it is unignorably revolutionary. Austen joking claimed to her niece Anna, "I think I *can* be stout against any thing written by Mrs. West" (28 September 1814; *Letters,* 277–78). But it is hard to doubt that she read *A Gossip's Story* (1796) as soon as it appeared; West's novel (an influence also detectable in *Emma*) is in the immediate background of *Sense and Sensibility.* The two novels have major motifs in common: the retirement to a dull plain place of impoverished parent and daughter; the rejection of a man who has seduced and abandoned a hapless girl; a young lady with too much sensibility and desire for romance; a sour mother-in-law who (like Mrs. Ferrars) regards herself as superior to the woman attached to her son.

In Jane West's novel, Mr. Dudley, father of the two heroines Louisa and Marianne, runs into financial difficulties. Louisa, at her father's desire, endeavors to reconcile herself to accepting the addresses of Sir William Milton, who could supply a respectable establishment. Father and daughter, however, are repelled on discovering that Sir William has seduced and abandoned a poor girl and her offspring. Louisa, after telling Sir William "I cannot reconcile my heart to a husband deficient in moral principle,"[22] is much happier to accept a simple life in a cottage with her father: "I always had a turn for oeconomy and management; am quite a cottager in my heart, I assure you." Her father warns her, "A cottage life . . . is not so pleasant in reality as in theory."[23] Indeed it is not. Louisa, for all her moral fiber, finds it hard at times to adjust, but presses bravely on. Marianne, well-meaning but not given to self-denial, has meanwhile turned down the plain and virtuous Mr. Pelham. She finds a rich and handsome husband, but her new relatives' belief that she is an intruder from a lower class injures her feelings, and her own sensibility poisons her happiness. In West's novel (as in Austen's) the "Marianne" figure is not condemned nor rejected, even though she is imperfect.

Austen borrows many elements of the contrasting sisters' experience, including loss of money and status, masculine callousness, and removal into a cramped unbeautiful residence. But Austen recomplicates the sites of virtue. Jane West more clearly espouses the self-controlled sister. A libertarian search for perfect happiness will foster conflict and self-indulgence. In making her second heroine "Marianne," West intentionally challenges revolutionary values, though the character remains sympathetic.[24] Austen, like West, both criticizes such new values as independence, honesty, spontaneity, and admits their attraction.

"Marianne," a common name in Provence, had become the name for the new French Republic, the home of liberty. In 1792 a Provencal poet composed in Occitan a song, "La Guérison de Marianne"— "The Curing of Marianne." The song, translated into Parisian French and sung to a well-known tune, "Two Little Savoyards," describes the illness of the girl:

> *Marianne, trop attaquéee d'une grosse maladie,*
> *Etait toujours malheureuse et mourant de misère.*

"Marianne, attacked by a great malady, was always unhappy and dying of her misery."

Various remedies fail to help: "The remedies of Louis are not good; nobody ever gets cured by those. But an ounce of Equality and two drachms of Liberty have freed her lungs."[25] "Marianne" as idea and image became an emblem of the new French state of Equality and Liberty. The young woman with the red Phrygian cap was to replace the image of Saint Mary with an attractive youthful embodiment of a new spirit. Association of "Marianne" with new revolutionary ideals explains the name of both West's and Austen's second sister. In *Sense and Sensibility,* spoiled little Annamaria, Lady Middleton's little daughter, bears the same name reversed. Jane Austen may have known some version of the song "The Curing of Marianne," or "Marianne's Recovery"— which might almost serve as a subtitle of her novel. Lucy is an opposite of Marianne, claiming neither revolutionary nor conservative enlightenment. Lucy's new lights are only the old base values of self-interest.

"Marianne" contains the Catholic "Maria," linking this Dashwood sister to the unfortunate Maria Stuart. Her counterparts—and rivals—

are named Eliza (Elizabeth). These rivals are victims. Yet the victims are winners too, and Marianne, if a survivor, is not exactly the victor. Eliza the First has already won the competition for the heart of Colonel Brandon; Eliza the Second received the sexual attentions of Willoughby. Each Eliza is thus a dominant "Elizabeth" in disguise. The fate of Marianne is controlled by her rival queens, ill fated and headstrong—a new twist on the relation of Queen Elizabeth and Mary Queen of Scots. Marianne, in both her loves (Willoughby and then Brandon), comes second to a dominant Eliza. Elinor also comes second in Edward's halting love career.

A whirlwind of sinful names hurtles about us in the novel: Ferrars, Dashwood, Marianne. (The presence of "Pratt" underlines the significance of Ferrars/Ferrers.) Even Mrs. Jennings has a dubious if magnificent historical counterpart in Mrs. Churchill (née Jennings). Mrs. Jennings's son-in-law Mr. Palmer basks in the status bestowed by a glamorous prostituted ancestress. Seduction, treachery, betrayal, murder, cruelty, crime, and (rarely) punishment—all are found here. Sensibility runs riot in history and in current affairs. Great energies—financial and sexual—can spin out of control.

The conflicts set up in the novel are never brought into true balance. "Sense" means giving up and settling in Dorset. Marianne gives way to her family. Ang Lee's film romanticizes Marianne's wedding, but Marianne is an object of exchange, a means of settling a debt. She is pushed by her family to repay Colonel Brandon: "They each felt his sorrows, and their own obligations, and Marianne, by *general consent*, was to be the *reward* of all" (III, ch. 14; italics added).

Elinor gets the man she humbly craved, a wobbly "Ead-*ward*" who cannot guard anything but will need her guardianship. Edward always wanted a young woman who can replace his mother by telling him what to do. His new job in an exceedingly small rural parish will, happily, demand no more social performance than he is up to. The bashful man is again hidden away—as in Plymouth. Lacking any sense of calling, Edward Ferrars when we last see him seems more concerned with his cows than his parishioners. But perhaps people *should* come second to cows, in a story in which almost everyone of importance (including Mrs. Dashwood) is doomed to come second—never first.

The two Elizas have power only to haunt. This whole story is not told in the Gothic manner, but it is a tale of hidden crimes and the haunting of the present by the past. Sophia Grey is a gray phantom—but powerful. So is the unseen Mrs. Smith. Persons unimportant to readers (and to major characters) cut into important lives. Disappointment and scandalous possibility menace potential growth. John Dashwood callously dwells on Marianne's loss of looks. "At her time of life, any thing of an illness destroys the bloom for ever! Hers has been a very short one" (II, ch. 11). The woods decay and fall. Everything loses its first careless bloom. We have to make do with what comes after, as the leaves become dashed from the wood.

Names in *Pride and Prejudice*

SURNAMES IN *PRIDE AND PREJUDICE*

Fitzwilliam Darcy doesn't quite have a *Christian* name. That it is a surname is emphasized in the advent of "Colonel Fitzwilliam." At the heart of *Pride and Prejudice* there is aggressiveness, and that aggressiveness centers on "Fitzwilliam." As noted earlier, the Fitzwilliams were the richest family in England. The name speaks of Norman dominance and conquest. No Austen character other than Darcy has such a double dose of Norman in their name. The "Fitz" connotes original bastardy— "Fitz-William" hinting at an original begetting by the Conqueror himself. "Bennet" is also a Norman name, if not at once recognizable as such. Introduced by the Normans, it is a French version of Benedict/ *benedictus,* "blessed." The English pronounced the name of Saint Benedict ("Benoit" in Chaucerian French) as "Bennet." We can also hear a kind of pun, on *bien né* or well born. At the time the novel was written, however, "Mrs. Bennet" would sound like "Mrs. Bennett," the clever author (Agnes Maria Bennett) of lowly origins and improper life whose books and opinions sold well. Elizabeth Bennet is generated by fiction writing. Elizabeth's claim to be Darcy's equal is just, at least insofar as the Norman origin of surnames is concerned. "Fitzwilliam," however, is strongly secular, while Elizabeth's surname carries religious meaning. There was a church of Saint Bennet in Gracechurch Street, in the City of London. Burned down in the Great Fire of London (1666), it was rebuilt; Protestantism did not interfere with the name. The Bennets, messy and faulty as they are, are truly "blessed."

Lady Catherine De Bourgh, Elizabeth Bennet's chief antagonist, was "Lady Catherine Fitzwilliam" before her marriage to Sir Lewis De Burgh or de Bourgh (variously spelled by Austen). Sir Lewis's first name indicates an admiration of French absolute monarchs. "Burgh" is rooted in English/Germanic *burh,* or "burg," that is, fortification. The first De Burgh—or de Burg—was a companion of the Conqueror to whom William gave the responsibility of guarding Dover castle and hence of keeping Dover: "Hubert de Burg [*sic*] was appointed constable of this castle."[26] So, the founder of the De Bourgh family was a conquering ruler in Kent. There are other big De B(o)urghs of note, including the Hubert de Burgh, sheriff and later Earl of Kent, who remained faithful to King John and then Henry III. Hubert lived largely, at one point facing penalties for having greedily helped himself to treasure and revenues.[27] Successful invaders and conquerors, De Bourghs hold the fort, looking down on those whom they control. Lady Catherine, aggressively Norman, sits within her fortress of Rosings.

The Bingleys' surname, contrasting with all these Normans, comes from the Danelaw, combining Old English and Norse. *Bing* + *ley* means "clearing made by 'Bing.'" The Old Norse root word "bing" means horse. "Bing" might refer to someone living beside or working in a horse stall—Old Norse *bingr*. An Early Modern "Bingley" is likely a descendant from a native of Bingley in West Yorkshire, cited in Gough's Camden in 1789 as a busy town with canals and locks.[28] Our Bingleys originally came from Yorkshire. They followed the path of migration from a northern county toward south and center, like others including the higher-placed Elliots of Kellynch.

"Charles Bingley," however, is not a name new to fiction; it belongs to a secondary male character in Regina Maria Roche's *The Children of the Abbey* (1796). The heroine, attending a ball where she evokes admiration, attracts the envy of the mean Lady Euphrasia Sutherland.

> "Can it be possible," said Lady Euphrasia, replying to a young and elegant officer who stood by her, in a tone of affectation, and with an impertinent sneer, "that you think her handsome?"—"Handsome!" exclaimed he with warmth, "I think her bewitchingly irresistible."

We then find out the elegant officer's name: "Sir Charles Bingley, who was Colonel of a regiment quartered in an adjacent town."[29] Roche's story combines some of the ingredients of *Pride and Prejudice:* sneering female rivals and would-be superiors, a scene at a ball, and a charming young officer who combines the roles of Austen's Charles Bingley, Colonel Forster—and George Wickham as he *should* be.

The elder of Bingley's sisters has married a southern English gentleman named "Hurst" (common Anglo-Saxon for a "wood" or "thicket"). If named for a feature of landscape, Mr. Hurst has no apparent landed property. Rather than a man on his way up, like Charles Bingley, Hurst looks suspiciously like someone on his way down. Card games seem an important source of income; evidently Darcy at Netherfield tells his host at one point that there is too much card playing. Among the likely problems looming before Charles Bingley and Fitzwilliam Darcy after marriage are not only the irritations of dealing with Wickham and Lydia, but also, most probably, the oncoming financial crash of the Hursts.

Mr. Collins's name is ordinary, if slightly comic. Derived from "Col" (old nickname for "Nicholas"), "Colin" is diminutive; "Collins" originally meant "son of little Colin." The author of the first *Baronetage* (1720) was a Collins. Another Collins was one of England's most articulate atheists of the eighteenth century; Anthony Collins (d. 1729) published *A Discourse upon Freethinking* and other controversial writings, evoking the ire of Jonathan Swift. It may have amused Austen to give the name of this most notorious freethinker to her starched, ignorant, and sycophantic clergyman.

The surname of Sir William Lucas, the naive new-made knight, is not without some distinction. In antiquity it indicates someone from Lucania, hence the Late Greek name "Luke" (*Loukos*), name of the author of one of the gospels. The Lucas family had Royalist associations in the Civil War; the poet Katherine Philips (1632–64) gave one of her best friends and poetic addressees the name "Lucasia."[30] Perhaps Katherine Philips's achievement as a poet softens the "low" surname Austen uses for Mrs. Bennet's vulgar sister and her nonentity of a husband, Mr. Philips the attorney. "Philips" derives from the Greek name "Philip" ("lover of horses"). This first name, although apostolic, had become disused; Welsh associations register "Philips" as a "low" surname.

"Wickham" is not foreign and definitely not Norman. It comes from Old English *wick* (from Latin *vicus*, Romano-British settlement) + *ham* (habitation or home). This doubly locational term is the name of a town in Buckinghamshire. "Wickham" was already the name of a fictional rake—or his fictional name, the pseudonym adopted by the villain-hero of Mary Robinson's *A Natural Daughter* (1799). The gossiping Sir Lionel Beacon describes his friend:

> "An amazing good fellow, but astonishingly run out."
> "By gaming?" said Mr. Morley.
> "By all sorts of sport. A capital dasher. Has debauched more wives and daughters than any man of his age in the three kingdoms."

"And what is he doing in Derbyshire?" said Mr. Morley.

"That is more than I know. . . ." replied Sir Lionel. "Some snug intrigue. . . . An amazing fine fellow, only five and twenty, and astonishingly knowing." . . . .

"And how does he call himself?" said Mr. Morley.

"His real name is lord Francis Sherville. . . . His travelling title is
Mr. Wickham," added the baronet.[31]

Robinson's fake Mr. Wickham with Derbyshire connections is heart-
less, deceitful—and mobile. In Robinson's novel, however, Sherville's
discovery of his illegitimate baby daughter has a softening influence
upon him—as we doubt it would have done in the case of George Wickham.

George Wickham is not quite playing at being Wickham, for he cannot doff his "travelling title." He has no title, family, or lands to fall
back on. A name meaning "place-place" seems comical for such a root-
less man. In a novel greatly concerned both with stability of place and
with the crossing of boundaries, Wickham is a no-place. His surname,
however, is sturdily Anglo-Saxon, and his first name suits patriotic persons, stable and stationary. Yet George Wickham is a force of instability,
though his charms take in two of the most rational characters, Mr. Bennet and Mrs. Gardiner. To complicate matters further, within this
novel mobility is one of the cardinal virtues. Wickham, free-floating
and predatory, seems the antithesis of Elizabeth Bennet, even if she is
briefly sexually attracted to him. But Elizabeth too is mobile, and she
does need a stranger.

Wickham comes surrounded with giddy male companions, attractions in themselves, like the king's posse in *Love's Labours Lost*. His best
friend is Denny—surname from the French Christian name "Denis"
(patron saint of France). "Chamberlayne" whose surname suggests bed-
rooms and undressing, plays at cross-dressing. A woman named "Pen
Harrington," another immodest Penelope in Austen's gallery, is present
when Chamberlayne dresses as a lady. Wickham's environment shim-
mers with gender play, an impression of fluid attachments. Wickham is
nominally under Colonel "Forster"—a form of "Forrester" and a good
name for one who comes from afar, from the wilds (cf. Italian *fores-
tiero*). There are subtle hints that Forster early attracts the eye of Lydia,
but the colonel soon marries. His young wife Harriet becomes Lydia's
best friend; the name of the thoughtful Harriet Byron in *Sir Charles
Grandison* seems unmerited. In Brighton, Harriet Forster may have en-

couraged Lydia in the liaison with Wickham in order to deflect Lydia's attention from her spouse.

Other characters playing an offstage role have significant names. Mrs. Younge, untrustworthy governess of Georgiana Darcy, proved susceptible to Wickham's charm and bribes; she colluded with him in his planned elopement with the heiress. Later the keeper of a boarding house in London, she is traced by Darcy, who rightly suspects that Wickham will again turn to her for help. In championing youthful sexuality without regard to consequences the woman is a bawd but also eternally "young." Youthfulness is her primary value.

Mrs. Reynolds, the housekeeper at Pemberley who exhibits the Darcy portraits, bears (as many have noticed) the surname of England's most celebrated portrait painter, Sir Joshua Reynolds, former President of the Royal Society. "Reynolds" is a fairly "high" name, Norman with roots in Old German and Old Norse, and related to "Reginald." Other characters in a service role include Mrs. Jenkinson, Anne De Bourgh's companion/attendant. Her Scandinavian name structure indicates common origins. Edward Gardiner's man of business or solicitor is called simply "Haggerston," a harsh Anglo-Saxon surname based on *hagger* ("hacker," "cutter") (III, ch. 7, ch. 8). A *haggers-tun* is a woodcutters' settlement. This Haggerston can hack his way through the dense thickets of Wickham's debts.

Lady Catherine indulges in the unmannerly habit of referring to persons not known to her companions, including "the Miss Webbs," "Lady Metcalfe," and "Miss Pope." "Webb" has been previously used in "Evelyn"; the all-too-benevolent Webbs give all they have to Mr. Gower—including their daughter. Lady Catherine's exemplary Miss Webbs *all* play the piano—unlike the Bennet girls—although "their father has not so good an income as yours." Lady Metcalfe ("meat-calf") has expressed profuse gratitude at Lady Catherine's having found her a governess in a Miss Pope, reportedly exclaiming "you have given me a treasure" (II, ch. 6). Miss Pope's name might indicate piety, authority, or expertise in English poetry. Meeting a Calf who met a Pope as a Treasure provides a poetic undertone of the ridiculous. Lady Catherine resembles Mrs. Elton in dragging unknown names into the conversation, as well as in insistent matching of employers with governesses. Her patter makes her more comical and less formidable.

Mr. Jones, apothecary of Meryton, prescribed draughts for Jane when she was ill. His "shop-boy" spreads the news that "the Miss Bennets" have left Netherfield (I, ch. 15). A Welsh form of "John," Jones is an archetypically "low" name. The inclusion of a "Jones" offers the reader a light hint to look to Fielding's novel for Wickham's effective presentation of himself to Elizabeth. (It is not only in *Northanger Abbey* that we find a female Quixote deluded by her reading.) George Wickham's artful story, a fresh adaptation of *Tom Jones,* makes Darcy's father into a Mr. Allworthy, Wickham into kind impetuous Tom, and Mr. Darcy into an evil Blifil.

Between flirting with Elizabeth and running off with Lydia, Wickham flirts with a Miss King. A "nasty little freckled thing" as Lydia complains (II, ch. 16), Mary King, present from the first assembly (where she dances with Charles Bingley), is not on our radar until Wickham turns from Elizabeth to her. Mary King's inheritance of ten thousand pounds makes her briefly interesting to Wickham. "Mary King" was the name of one of the wives of the sinister Francis Dashwood. Presumably Miss King has a narrow escape from Meryton's handsome Bluebeard who wants only her little fortune. Miss King is sent off to live with an uncle in commercial Liverpool—a banishment from the edge of fashion into outer darkness. Another stupid and willful "Mary," Miss King is no princess, but (if against her own will) she succeeds in avoiding Wickham's trap.

Elizabeth Bennet, like the roaming Wickham, needs to move in order to find what she wants. In changing places she unconsciously pursues a mate who is named after a place (like Bingley and Wickham). "Darcy," a Norman name ("D'Arcy"), is derived from the French place name "Arcy"; "Darcy" entered England with one of William the Conqueror's knights. The Irish branch of the Darcy family in Galway and Ulster is deep-rooted. There are genuine historical connections between Darcys and De Bourghs. John Darcy, made chief justice in Ireland, married Joan de Bourgh, daughter of the Earl of Ulster. When William de Bourgh was murdered, John Darcy endeavored as "*justiciar*" to pursue his murderers; later that same year he led Irish forces against William Wallace (*ODNB*). In Austen's era "Darcy" was the surname of the family of the Earl of Holdernesse. Austen may have been thinking of the Darcys while writing *The Watsons,* in which the most aristocratic (and most awkward) character is Lord Osborne. The blue-blooded notable of that surname in Austen's era was Francis Osborne, eventually fifth Duke of Leeds (1751–99). While Marquess of Carmarthen, Osborne married Lady Amelia D'Arcy. But in 1778 his marchioness ran away with Captain Jack Byron (father—by another union—of the

poet). Lord Osborne's self-indulgent awkwardness and voyeurism in relation to Emma Watson augur an unsatisfactory marriage partner—just
as Amelia D'Arcy discovered. Perhaps Austen would not care for anyone who wronged a D'Arcy.

The surname occurs in other fiction. In Susannah Minifie's *Barford
Abbey* (1768) the object of the heroine's interest, shy "Lord Darcey," has
just come of age; his guardian Sir James has dinned into him "that he
must marry *prudently;* which is, that he must never marry without an
immense fortune."[32] In Charlotte Smith's one-volume novel entitled
simply *D'Arcy* (1793), the titular "hero" is a heroine—D'Arcy Beau-
foy is a girl! Her name signifies "Darcy Beautiful-faith." Fitzwilliam
Darcy's faith may be beautiful, but we cannot at first see through the
Fitzwilliam arrogance to his goodness. The other side of Darcy is the
spiritual aspirant, the self-sacrificing Lord Darcy.

FIRST NAMES IN *PRIDE AND PREJUDICE*

Edward Gardiner lives up to his name: he is a true *Ead-ward*—guardian
of riches. He spends his own money and time to protect the Bennet
family, valuing his kin as his treasure. Edward Gardiner is a strong contrast to the weak, vacillating and untruthful Edward Ferrars.

Mr. Bingley's parents have mimicked staunch royalists in giving
their children the names "Charles" and "Caroline" (like the Grandison siblings). This may have been intended to make their family seem
old and conservative. Sir William Lucas with the Whiggish first name
has named his daughter "Charlotte," presumably after Queen Charlotte. His second daughter is "Maria," perhaps a reaching after upper-
class Stuart elegance. Loyal even before knighthood was bestowed upon
him, Sir William is trying to become a good Tory. Charlotte Lucas is
certainly as practical as any Charlotte of them all. She lets nothing go
to waste and efficiently consumes leftovers, including putting a friend's
leftover suitor to use as a husband.

George Wickham has a strong first name, the name of the patron saint
of England, recurrent name of Hanoverian monarchs—and the name of
Austen's own father. It will be the first name of Mr. Knightley. "George"
suits landowners and land workers. The value of such earthy occupation
is reflected in the surname of Mrs. Bennet's brother (also Mrs. Bennet's
maiden surname). They are Gardiners—"gardeners," people close to the
earth and sustenance. City merchant Edward Gardiner yet sustains the
primal values, true to Adamic roots. Wickham targets as marital pros-

pects only those females who bring ready money—not lands. Wickham forsakes—perhaps abhors—that primal georgic work. His father, the elder Mr. Darcy's steward, participated in it, rather as Jane's great-uncle Francis served the Duke of Dorset and others as steward and agent.

Darcy's father named his daughter "Georgiana." This female version of "George" arose in the Hanoverian era. The most famous "Georgiana" was Georgiana Cavendish (née Spencer, 1757–1806).[33] Married off to the Duke of Devonshire on her seventeenth birthday, Georgiana recorded her first discomforts in her marriage and in London society in her novel *The Sylph* (1779). The Duchess of Devonshire, as famous for beauty and charm as her collateral descendant Princess Diana, was a fashion leader and a celebrity. The Devonshire marriage, however, was most unhappy, and her attempt at escape did not work. Georgiana's image, widely circulated in paintings, prints, and caricatures, inspired lesser folk to choose the new name. Within *Pride and Prejudice,* the name invokes the beautiful duchess, suggesting charm and a dangerous tendency to sexual adventure.

The background presence of Georgiana Cavendish contributes to the novel's exploration of female sexuality. In one of the novel's most amazing statements Mr. Bennet earnestly offers Elizabeth a warning of future perils if she married a man she could not love or respect: "Your lively talents would place you in the greatest danger. . . . You could scarcely escape discredit and misery" (III, ch. 17). He is warning his own favorite daughter that in a bad marriage Elizabeth could be tempted to adultery—as Jane Austen knew from the case of Elizabeth, Countess Craven. Mr. Bennet shows an unexpected sympathy for the power of the female sex drive. Such sympathy is entirely lacking in Sir Thomas Bertram—who totally misreads his daughter Maria. Not surprisingly, a teenaged "Georgiana" could be tempted into an elopement by a charmer like Wickham. Georgiana Darcy is not (like the duchess) brutally thwarted by an abusive husband but saved by the kind concern of a brother. Still, the misadventure has not helped her lack of self-confidence.

The names of the first four Bennet girls are traditional names of saints and of English queens, two regnant. Jane Bennet has the name of a queen, the humble and self-sacrificing Jane Seymour. She was presumably named after her mother, Mrs. Bennet, also good-looking in youth—and neither humble nor self-sacrificing. Mary Bennet's first name, that of the greatest Christian female saint, is almost always attached by Austen to negative characters—from the silly greedy Mary who will marry Mr. Watt in "Three Sisters" to the self-pitying Mary Musgrove of *Persuasion*. But if Mary Bennet was named after her mother's sister-in-law, then Mrs. Gardiner is a rare excellent "Mary." "Kitty" is another "Catherine," weak and recessive where Lady Catherine, like Catherine the Great, is overbearing. But Lady Catherine is more ineffectual than she realizes. Most "Catherines" in Austen's oeuvre are somewhat clueless. Lady Catherine's daughter Anne, named after her aunt (Darcy's mother), bears the name of England's last powerful queen regnant. Anne De Bourgh, however, is shy, weak, and in bad health—probably doomed to die young.[34] Again we see an "Anne" pushed around by her family and to some extent ignored.

"Lydia" is a different sort of name. Lydia is a region in Asia Minor, known for making purple dye. Names of their native regions were often given to slaves; the "Lydia" in the New Testament may be a freedwoman. Anything "Lydian" is exotic and highly colored, associated with luxury and hedonism. Lydian music connotes erotic pleasure, as in Dryden's *Alexander's Feast:* "Softly sweet, in *Lydian* Measures, / Soon He sooth'd his Soul to Pleasures."[35] In Richard Brinsley Sheridan's *The Rivals* (1775), a play performed by the Austens at Steventon in 1784, the novel-reading "Lydia Languish" desires to be loved for herself. She wishes to throw away her fortune and elope romantically with a handsome young man—unbeknownst to her, the very man her guardian has picked out for her to marry. Captain Absolute will certainly not risk Lydia's fortune (the main but not sole reason why he is attracted to her); elopement plans are a charade on his part. Lydia Languish will never ride in a fast carriage behind galloping horses speeding to Gretna Green. Neither will Lydia Bennet. Lydia Bennet thinks she is loved for herself and engages in an "elopement" that brings sex and no marriage—social disgrace—until she is "rescued" by being legally tied to her cad.

Darcy's first name reeks of wealth pride, greed, and illegitimacy—not blessedness. It is not properly a Christian name, *not* a name invoking divine grace. Mr. Darcy may be hampered in the spiritual race by such a worldly name. It differs from the humbler ordinary "William" of Mr. Collins and Sir William Lucas. The proposals of a "William" and of a "Fitzwilliam" are both rejected by Elizabeth—at first. After all, Mr. Collins is not wrong in suspecting that an elegant female may be persuaded to accept on the second try.

Elizabeth Bennet's first name is a "Christian name," but it also suggests pride and haughtiness—if also wit and intelligence. She is a contrast to the two Elizas of *Sense and Sensibility,* although these possess the sexual energy that Mr. Bennet saw in his daughter. "Elizabeth" is the name of a biblical saint (Saint Mary's cousin, mother of John the Baptist) and of England's most powerful queen. Important Elizabeths in Austen's fiction vary—including the good-natured vulgar Elizabeth Watson, the cold Elizabeth Elliot and the frightening Mrs. Norris. Yet these are all eldest daughters, and they are all domineering. Except for the deceased Lady Elliot, Austen's Elizabeths—including Fanny Price's youngest sister, irritating Betsey—share an assertive quality, entirely discernible in Elizabeth Bennet. Perhaps Elizabeth Bennet is more engaging and less overbearing than the more off-putting of Austen's Elizabeths because she is in the humbler position of second daughter, not the eldest. That is, Elizabeth Bennet is in the position of Jane Austen, not of Cassandra Elizabeth Austen. Although in her "History of England" and in *Catharine* Austen protested herself an admirer of Mary Queen of Scots and an opponent of Elizabeth, she gave her most loved character the name of England's strong, victorious, and witty queen.

In revenge for the cheated and shadowy Elizas of *Sense and Sensibility,* Elizabeth Bennet is life and power. She wins what she wants and needs. In this novel Austen shows that important mistakes can be rectified. We can learn as we go. Strong people develop. *Pride and Prejudice* is the Enlightenment novel par excellence, advocating freedom and progressive alteration. The very word "prejudice" is an Enlightenment word—and once you recognize an attitude as a prejudice you are already changing. In *Emmeline* Charlotte Smith allowed her heroine to change her mind, to switch from one man to another—a daring move that Austen repeats. Surprisingly, Austen here pursues her themes without protracted or insistent use of *style indirect libre* (or "free indirect style") already beginning to appear as a feature in *Sense and Sensibility.* There are subtle touches of it, but the author refrains from extensive use. *Style indirect* quietly emphasizes character's delusions; Elizabeth is not exhibited as inwardly contaminated by her delusions regarding Wickham. This novel works largely on objective narration and dialogue. Characters look *outside* themselves.

That does not mean that even the best are good at handling the external world. *Pride and Prejudice* presents a multitude of socially inept persons. Obvious cases are Mrs. Bennet, Mary Bennet, and Mr. Collins, but the list takes in almost everyone, including Darcy the stiff and Elizabeth—sometimes aggressive and vulgar. Most characters go awkwardly through social meetings, drawing at hazard on whatever resources they can command at the moment. Mary Waldron convincingly argues that Mr. Collins has studied Lord Chesterfield on "the art of compliment."[36] Lady Catherine does not realize she needs social training, but Elizabeth's remarks comparing manners to piano playing suggest kindly that we all need intelligence and practice (II, ch. 8). Mr. Darcy fears "strangers"—but strangers are our salvation.

Social meetings, awkward and artificial, occasions for boorish errors, are also the bases of enlightenment. The novel exhibits in the names of its characters—Norman, Saxon, and Danish, low and high—the English variety of origins, classes, and attitudes, parties in historical conflicts and regional differences. All of these need to be shaken up together and put in a civil condition. Learning to compromise with and respond to each other is a vital unfinished process. This novel's enduring appeal lies in the support that its "love story" offers to our Enlightenment hope that personal or conventional estrangements and inherited aversions can be overcome. We can create a new culture, however far from perfection we are on any given day.

Mr. Darcy's behavior at the Meryton Assembly is rather like that of the "bear" (*ours*) on which the French place name "Arcy" is supposedly based. His name almost sounds and looks like "dark" (some suppose the name to be based on Erse terms for "dark," *O Dorchaidhe*). A dark and glamorous bear wanders into a ballroom and the expectations of sexual courtship as if he had wandered into a riddle. The not-quite-a-Beast bear does *not* dance with the not-quite-a-Beauty. Their successive encounters with each other are something like a blundering dance. Every savage *can't* dance—it takes time.

Darcy's baser side, his bearishness, supported by pride and shyness, is accompanied by his high side. In trying to explain himself and his defects to Elizabeth, he blames his parents a little, saying they "allowed, encouraged, almost taught me to be selfish and overbearing... to think meanly of all the rest of the world" (III, ch. 16). Yet, as he has just stressed the goodness of his father ("all that was benevolent and amiable"), we can deduce that the haughty and overbearing attitudes were transmitted by the Fitzwilliam parent, his mother, Lady Catherine's sister. Fitzwilliam Darcy's true spiritual nature is hidden within his surname, the name of a Tudor hero beheaded for a leading role in the Pilgrimage of Grace. Mr. Darcy's best ancestor is not the land-guzzling Conqueror from whom he (illegitimately) descended, but the man who would lay down his life for what he believed a cause of grace. Darcy is on a Pilgrimage of Grace, though he does not know it. He is reconciled with those officially "below" him in *Grace*church Street (the street where the church of Saint Bennet [Saint Benedictus, Saint *Blessed*] is still to be found). The dwellers in Gracechurch Street reflect the first paradise—and Adam and Eve's first occupation—in the name "Gardiner." And Darcy joins himself to the impudent, witty, somewhat vulgar blessed one, who is also a queen: Elizabeth Bennet.

All novelists, even those who resist, play to some extent with allegory—or perhaps allegory plays with them. This outline of *Pride and Prejudice* in terms of Grace and Pilgrimage and Blessedness is not meant to be taken even as seriously as the comic allegory in *Tom Jones,* with its Allworthy and Paradise Hall. But Austen's playful meaning is entwined about the characters. There are many small jokes and verbal games along the way in this "light and bright and sparkling" novel. The best joke within a character's name is a very light touch of riddle indeed. A Mr. *Morris* is the original owner of the Netherfield estate, which he rents to Charles Bingley, thus setting off the entire celebratory and playful "Morris Dance" of the story.

Chapter 7

Personal Names in the "Chawton" Novels

Names in *Mansfield Park*

THE PENUMBRA OF *MANSFIELD PARK*

This novel presents us with varying locations and with a number of characters who travel within England and globally. Central characters have a variety of acquaintance. Austen builds up the sense of a larger Britain—and British Empire—through unprecedented use of persons who do not appear directly but create the impression of a wider world. Sir Thomas Bertram, however, appears exceptionally friendless. Despite a career as an MP, landed gentleman, and plantation owner, he prefers isolation. Eventually the author has to scare up "an old and most particular friend," a Mr. Harding sufficiently "hard" to perform his task of conveying bad news about Maria in a series of (paraphrased) letters (III, ch. 16). Edmund (unlike his elder brother) also lacks friends but acquires one (with sisters) with whom he can stay during preparation for ordination. This "Mr. Owen" is referred to only by his surname, antique and Welsh (like "Price"). The sole reference to a working person on Mansfield lands comes from Edmund: "Which way did you turn after passing Sewell's farm?" he asks Henry. "Sewell" from *Saeweald* ("sea-power"), a common Saxon name, suggests "sow well"—a name for a good farmer. While the young gentlemen are hunting and shooting, the real farming work is done.

Tom Bertram, unlike his father, seeks multiple friends. His acquaintance constitutes a penumbra on its own, admitting into the narrative a shower of comic down-market names: "Maddox" (from "Magog," "fortunate," Welsh and low); "Holford" ("ford in a hollow," place in Somerset); "Anderson" (Norse, not genteel); "Sneyd" (from Old English *snidan*, "to cut," suited to a tailor or cutter). Tom prefers friends beneath his social level. The comical fuss of Andersons and Sneyds about being "out" or "not out" shows how families rising from the middle middle class affect this distinction as a badge of social position.

Portsmouth introduces a varied penumbra of persons surrounding the Price family—predictably low. Mr. Price, ignoring Fanny at her first arrival, greets William with information:

> "I have been to Turner's about your mess. . . . Captain Walsh thinks you will certainly have a cruize to the westward. . . . But old Scholey was saying just now, that he thought you would be sent first to the Texel." (*MP*, III, ch. 7)

Turner was a genuine naval supplier of Portsmouth. "Walsh," based on Anglo-Saxon *waelisc* ("foreigner"), originally referred to the dark-haired Celts, especially of Wales. "Scholey," originally signifying a dweller on low-lying ground, has northern associations like the place name "Scholes" (from Old Norse *skali*). "Old Scholey" may be another retired Marine. William Price frets that Lucy Gregory of Portsmouth won't pay attention to him before he is promoted. "Gregory" (medieval surname of Greek origin) is found in northern England and Scotland.

Northern and Scottish names dominate the Price connection. "Campbell" is the surname of the young surgeon on board the *Thrush*. "Mrs. Admiral Maxwell," according to Mrs. Price, was Mary Price's godmother, who gave the little girl the present of the silver knife. Mrs. Maxwell's name thus vulgarly rendered demonstrates how highly this lower-middle-class neighborhood values the professional title as status. Government-bestowed titles, military or civilian ("General," "Sheriff"), do not carry over to the wife; Admiral Croft's wife is, correctly, "Mrs. Croft." "Maxwell," from Saxon "Macca's *wella*" ("Maccus's pool") is the name of "a salmon pool on the Tweed" (Reaney & Wilson). Admiral Maxwell is a Scotsman who has made good in the Navy. Austen seems aware of the advantages England gained from the Act of Union. Smollett's Lismahago in *Humphry Clinker* (1771) points this out: "They [the English] got an accession of above million of useful subjects, constituting a never-failing nursery of seamen, soldiers, labourers, and mechanics, a most valuable acquisition to a trading country, exposed to foreign wars, and obliged to maintain a number of settlements in all the four quarters of the globe."[1]

Away from Portsmouth, aristocratic names enter the penumbra. The Honorable John Yates has visited the home of the Ravenshaw family. "Ravenshaw" sounds comically Gothic. A "Ravens-shaw" would be "a wood full of ravens"—a dark place inhabited by birds of prey. Lord

Ravenshaw, patron of family theatricals, had at least the good taste to cancel the performance when the dowager died, a decent observance of which Yates complains (I, ch. 13).

Mrs. Rushworth (Maria) visits a couple named "Aylmer," who have a holiday home in Twickenham (III, ch. 14). "Aylmer" is Old English ("son of Elmer"). The most distinguished "Aylmer" was Matthew Aylmer who served in the Royal Navy early in the eighteenth century. Admiral Aylmer became a Vice Admiral, eventually Rear Admiral, of the whole English fleet and was made Baron Aylmer. Admiral Crawford's acquaintance could well extend to the families of eminent naval men. "Of *Rears,* and *Vices,* I saw enough," as Mary notoriously remarks (I, ch. 6). Maria's Aylmers could be imagined as descendants of Admiral Aylmer. We can assume that some of this Twickenham family knew Admiral Crawford, who once, as Mary relates, took "a cottage at Twickenham for us all to spend our summers in" (I, ch. 6). Almost certainly Maria Rushworth has been introduced to these convenient Aylmers through Henry Crawford, who saw they could assist him in his clandestine affair. (Presumably the Aylmers had assisted Admiral Crawford in his illicit loves. Was that why he moved temporarily to Twickenham?)

Mary Crawford alludes to her friend Lady Lascelles, who two years previously owned or rented "one of the best houses in Wimpole Street," the house to be occupied during "the Season" by the new-married Rushworths (III, ch. 9). The real Anne Lascelles was the wife of Edward Lascelles (a Norman surname from the French place name *Lacelle*). Edward was made a Baron in 1796, so Anne became "Lady Lascelles." She was never Lady Anne Lascelles, dying in 1805, before her husband was made first Earl of Harewood. The Lascelleses' family fortunes had notoriously been built on the Barbados slave trade under Edward's uncle, ruthless Henry Lascelles of Yorkshire, whose life is described with elegant detestation by Adam Nicolson in *The Gentry*.[2] The family business center was in Mincing Lane in the City, but Henry Lascelles bought a house in Richmond, that suburb of costly villas. There wealthy Henry cut his throat on 6 October 1753. Henry Lascelles's vault in Northallerton church was opened in February of 1814 (the year of *Mansfield Park*'s publication), reviving public memories of his "unprincipled" dealings, including contribution to the South Sea Bubble fiasco.[3] Naming "Lady Lascelles" not only helps to date the time frame of the novel, it also reinforces the theme of slavery—associated with wealth and self-destruction.

MAJOR SURNAMES IN *MANSFIELD PARK*

Sir Thomas Bertram is the master of Mansfield. Most characters are connected to him either directly or through his wife. "Bertram" is ultimately of Germanic origin: *berht hraben* = "bright raven" (a bird of the god Odin). "Bert" functions in Anglo-Saxon names (noted by Camden), but "Bertram" is not Anglo-Saxon but Germanic Norman. That surname became a first name before William left Normandy; Camden notes the barony of the Verdon family, "the first of whom, Bertram de Verdon, came over to England with the Normans."[4] A Bertram's property is registered in the Doomsday Book. Eventually the family had a crest with the motto "J'avance." Austen's Bertrams, tall and blonde, seem more Germanic than French.

Sir Thomas marries Maria, most beautiful of the three Ward sisters. "Ward" (Old English *weard*) can mean a guard—or a person or thing guarded. A legal ward is a person under the governance of another, as an orphan not yet twenty-one can be "a ward of the court." Fanny on coming to Mansfield is her uncle's ward (without formal documentation). The Ward sisters, apparently parentless, must be wards of their uncle "the lawyer." Maria's having attracted Sir Thomas Bertram is greeted with near incredulity at "the greatness of the match" (*MP*, I, ch. 1). Reading the opening paragraph of the novel carefully, we can see that Maria was passive in this "match." Perhaps younger than Marianne Dashwood when she became "the reward" of Brandon's sorrows, Maria as a submissive *ward* was urged, even pushed, by her uncle into becoming "Lady Bertram." Thus, that "it is every young woman's duty to accept such a very unexceptionable offer" is understandably "the only rule of conduct, the only piece of advice" she can pass on to Fanny (III, ch. 2). Sir Thomas's lecture to Fanny when she tries to refuse Crawford sufficiently informs us what pressures were put upon her less resistant aunt (III, ch. 1). Maria Ward will not run the risk of being termed "willful and perverse" or meet the fierce rebuke "you think only of yourself" (III, ch. 1). "Ward" is "*Ead*-ward" with the treasure cut out. The noun "wards" also means bolts and locks such as vex Maria Bertram facing the locked iron gate at Sotherton. A "warder" watches over someone locked up. The Ward sisters are under surveillance, under guard, locked in. The second Maria, more rebellious than her mother, urgently desires to get away from fences and iron gates, locks and bars.

"Bertram," old and aristocratic, is a literary name. "Bertram" is the first name of Shakespeare's most ungracious hero—or antihero. In *All's*

Well That Ends Well, Bertram figures in a story of attraction and repulsion, adoption and rejection, across class boundaries. Helena, orphaned daughter of a physician, has been taken in and brought up by the Count and Countess of Roussillon. Helena shrinks from calling the gentle countess "mother"—she does not wish the countess's son Bertram to be her brother. Knowing her love is hopeless, she pines for the young man whom she sees every day:

> My imagination
> Carries no favour in it, but Bertram's.
> I am undone; there is no living, none,
> If Bertram be away, it were all one,
> That I should love a bright particular star,
> And think to wed it, he is so above me.
> (*All's Well,* act 1, sc. 1; *Shakespeare Plays,* 3:93)

The countess realizes Helena must be in love with someone: "this thorn / Doth to the rose of youth rightly belong." "Young Bertram," far from reciprocating Helena's concealed passion, disdains the girl as a low dependent: "She had her breeding at my father's charge" (act 2, sc. 3). Helena, heir to her father's prescriptions and remedies, takes matters into her own hands, goes to Paris and offers to cure the sick King of France. As her reward for success, Helena requires Bertram for her husband. Bertram obeys the royal command but angrily leaves his nominal wife directly after the marriage ceremony, turning eventually to another woman. Only plot mechanics and the ruthlessness of Helena's passion reunite the persistent, painfully constant woman and her pouting adolescent spouse.

Fanny Price, who is all reaction and rarely takes initiative, would never dream of actively seeking to get the man she wants. Yet Helena's initial secret torment is very like the condition into which Fanny falls. Fanny is further handicapped by not being able fully to admit to herself what her feeling actually is. Guilt—at an almost incestuous illicit desire—intervenes. The audience or reader of Shakespeare's *All's Well* is likely to feel that Helena has married beneath her, that Bertram, surly and petulant, is too immature and selfish to be worth so much effort. Bertram, whose father died when he was young, dislikes the maternal trammels and hates the quasi-paternal power of the king. He grumbles against wardship in the first scene: "I must attend his majesty's command to which I am now *in ward,* ever more in subjection" (act 1, sc. 1; *Shakespeare Plays,* 3:92; italics added).

Mansfield Park is not a repetition of *All's Well,* but the play is a lively background to the novel. Fanny, once the target of her uncle's "medicinal project," is recalled as healer to a family smitten by illness, guilt, and sorrow. She gains a place as a feminine quasi-physician achieving importance from the needs to which she can minister, the pains that she can remedy—and at last gains the Bertram whom she desires. Images of stars and roses found in Shakespeare's play appear in the novel. A young girl is enslaved in a hot rose garden where elder women command that the roses of youth be plucked and dried. Fanny and Edmund associate in stargazing. Fanny's desire to go on the lawn and search for stars with Edmund is a mode of loving her "bright particular star." But Fanny is not permitted even go out to the night lawn by herself. Austen's novel traces in most of its characters that feeling of being "in ward." We find out what it means to be under guardianship, "ever more in subjection."

Sir Thomas Bertram is averse to obligations save those he creates or administers. He apparently shook off his wife's connections in Huntingdon, save for Maria's two sisters. Sir Thomas also appears—strangely—to have no relatives of his own aside from his offspring. The captive and largely isolated Lady Bertram becomes trained by her marriage into almost total passivity. Hoisted up to a position and style to which she was not accustomed, the subjugated Maria (née Ward) has made no rash moves, depending on quiet observation and her husband's instruction. She could not possibly participate in educating her daughters, because she doesn't know what they should know. By the time we meet her, Lady Bertram has spent the greater part of her lifetime in schooling herself out of spontaneity or opinions; she borrows any acceptable clichés she finds floating about her.

Mrs. Norris, eldest of the three sisters, wants to lead but is a social dependent. A clergyman was found who is willing to marry her, patently for the reward of the living of Mansfield. "Norris" might derive from the French for "north" or *nourrice* ("nurse"); Mrs. Norris, harsh as the north, is most un-nurturing. "Norris" is the surname of John Norris, cruel proslavery delegate portrayed by Thomas Clarkson, leading writer for the abolition.[5] Moira Ferguson sees Mrs. Norris as Sir Thomas's overseer, Fanny Price substituting for the slave.[6] Elizabeth Ward's husband, an Anglican clergyman, has the surname of that other John Norris, the mystic John Norris of Bemerton (1657–1712). This John Norris upheld a

Platonist view of the nature of the soul and cosmos; spiritual love is one of his great subjects.[7] Austen might be amused at the contrast between this idealistic English divine and the time-serving Reverend Mr. Norris (surely his first name must have been "John"?) with his unspiritual and unloving wife.

The third and youngest Ward sister, Frances, disregards golden opportunities arising from the Bertram connection. "Miss Frances married, in the common phrase, to disoblige her family" (*MP,* I, ch. 1). This reflects Sir Thomas Bertram's view—he is the "family" whom she really "disobliged." Probably the Mr. Price who courted Frances Ward was culturally and economically not really "beneath" the life to which Frances was accustomed. She moved a long way from her sisters, to the south coast and the bustling aggressive port of Portsmouth. Her overburdened untidy life with many children was probably not a surprise, although her husband's disability and drinking made him a poorer provider than anticipated. She has to cave eventually and ask for help. But Frances Price (née Ward) at least is free of having to act in a constant charade.

On marrying Mr. Price (presumably a "William") Frances Ward assumed an ungentle surname. "Price" is a name of Welsh origin, originally "ap-Rhys," "son of Reese." The Welsh were disdained by the English as natural inferiors, so a Welsh name was inevitably "low." There is a pun in the use of this surname, for this family pays the real *price* for the luxury of Mansfield Park. Members of Fanny Price's family know the price of an empire. They belong to the category of British folk that most fully pays the cost in supplying labor and cannon fodder. Their sailors and marines fight the French and maintain colonies like Antigua.

"Crawford," like "Price," is a name from the "Celtic fringe." This is a Scottish name, either from Gaelic *cru* (bloody) + "ford" or Old English *craw* ("crow") + "ford." The "crow" would fit in well with the "raven" of the Bertrams. (Ravens and crows were long associated with battlefields, for these birds feast on the dead.) The comic "Lord Ravenshaw" fits in well with the ravens and crows of Bertrams and Crawfords. Carrion birds abound.

The real Crawford family seems to originate in Lanarkshire in Scotland. The 1789 *Britannia* discusses their residence under "Lothian."[8] A George Crawford (spelled also as "Crawfurd") had published *A Genealogical History of the Royal and Illustrious Family of the Stewarts* in 1710 and compiled and published *The Peerage of Scotland* in 1716. A Crawford, it seems, might well be a Stuart enthusiast and supporter of Scots aristocracy. Any resident of the Alton-Chawton area, however, would most vividly recall the Battle of Alton and the royalist commander, Ludovic Lindsay, sixteenth Earl of Crawford. From the Alton point of view the Earl of Crawford left the loyalist town and his army in the lurch and treacherously skedaddled to Winchester, leaving the remnant of his men—and the locals—to be destroyed by Waller's forces.

Is a "Crawford" loyal and noble—or treacherous? Henry Crawford, the hidden Scot, is, like the Ward sisters of Huntingdonshire, a kind of displaced person trying to fit in. The novel explores the vulnerability of that condition of displacement—the condition of the Ward sisters; of Fanny, William, and Susan Price—and of the Crawfords also. Austen's novel suggests that this condition may be more likely to foster hesitation than strength, rendering obstacles harder to overcome. Only for William is this untrue, but even he needs patronage to gain promotion. Henry's situation is externally fortunate. His Scots uncle Admiral Crawford has risen to some position and a degree of wealth. Henry owns an estate in Norfolk—not a county that Austen quite trusts; Mrs. Ferrars owns an estate there that she would give to Edward if he married to please her. *How* Henry came by the Norfolk estate is not clear. His position requires persistent self-fashioning as an English gentleman. One of the means he uses is the declaration of loyalty to Shakespeare; Shakespeare, he says, is "part of an *Englishman's* constitution" (III, ch. 3; italics added). Henry's situation fosters uncertain loyalties, uncertainties even in impersonation of Englishness.

If Henry Crawford the English gentleman is a "hidden Scot," he is hidden in plain sight. That he is a "Celt" in origin emerges clearly in his looks. First adjudged by the Bertram girls as "absolutely plain, black and plain" (*MP*, I, ch. 5), Crawford is disparaged by Rushworth: "Nobody could call such an under-sized man handsome. . . . I should not wonder if he was not more than five foot eight" (I, ch. 10). Black-haired and dark-eyed Henry lacks the height and blond coloration of English upper-class males. Henry does not look Anglo. His sister finds favor with the Bertram sisters precisely because Mary, short, dark and vivacious, does not vie with their Germanic good looks: "Had she been tall, full formed, and fair, it might have been more of a trial" (I, ch. 5). Fanny—or Austen—may suspect that Henry Crawford's impersonation of an English gentleman is inauthentic. Do some traits of his persona result from the acting required of the successful immigrant?

Mary Crawford displays a supposedly Celtic talent: she plays the harp and plays it well. It is no wonder that Edmund falls for this seduction, a relief from his Puritan household. Harp playing aligns Mary with contemporary literary heroines, especially those who represent the Celtic nations of Britain—as, arguably, Mary herself does. The first of these in importance is Glorvina, heroine of Sydney Owenson's *The Wild Irish Girl* (1806), which Austen had read (17–18 January 1809; *Letters,* 166). Important novels published in 1814, the same year as *Mansfield Park,* present impressive and important Celtic harp players: in Scott's *Waverley,* the Scots aristocrat Flora MacIvor; in Burney's *The Wanderer,* the beautiful homeless Juliet, a French-educated gentlewoman who is half Welsh.

Late in Austen's novel, the Scottish associations of Henry and Mary Crawford are stressed through the uncompromisingly Scottish names of Mary's friends. A formerly close friend is "Janet Fraser," whose step-daughter Margaret is vainly interested in Henry as a marital prospect. (Another hapless if pushy Margaret.) "Fraser" is the name of a clan from East Lothian, along the river Tweed. Janet's maiden name was "Ross," a Scottish surname derived from a place, "ross" being a Celtic word for "hill spur . . . heathy upland" (Mills, 395). Janet's sister Flora Ross became "Lady Stornaway" on her marriage. "Stornaway" (Old Norse *stjor-navagr* or "steering bay") is—and was—the chief town and administrative center of the Outer Hebrides, as far away from the cultural center as one can get and still claim to be in Britain. We associate Mary with distant "Stornaway" shortly before the author will expel her from the novel. Stornaway represents the outer fringe indeed.[9]

In this novel some of the male and almost all the major female characters are foreign to their position and are continuously required to adjust to a more or less alien culture. The Scottish references circling about Mary Crawford serve quietly but effectively to make her a stranger. Orphaned, she has had to live in London with her uncle Admiral Crawford and her ill-used aunt, because there was nowhere else to go. The offensive womanizing uncle is the true blood relation. Admiral Crawford, like Colonel Campbell in *Emma,* benefited from the British government's willingness to employ and promote talented Scots in the armed services. Like Fanny, Mary is a foster child, taken in—and into wardship—by prosperous relatives. Although Mary's brother has an English estate, her uncle Admiral Crawford and probably her beloved aunt must be Scottish immigrants, either directly or by immediate descent. No wonder Mary's social and affectional associations remain Scots-oriented. Her most dependable relative is her half-sister on her mother's side.

Mrs. Grant, although not a Crawford, may be presumed to be a Scot also, and to have married a clergyman of Scottish descent. "Grant" is a simple name with a number of possible derivations; one meaning is "crooked," as in a bend in a river.[10] But by far the largest number of "Grants" are Scots, members of Clan Grant. Their name may mean "dark, swarthy," or it may be derived from French *grand,* meaning "important" or "senior." But Austen has her own pun on the name; Dr. Grant is *granted* so much for doing so little. Mary's observations of him as a selfish bon vivant and a poor husband are undeniably true, like so much else of what she says. Mary is a truth teller, which elicits censure; others hush or disregard her.

Prices, Crawfords, and Grants are incomers, nomadic migrants or descendants of recent migrants from the Celtic fringe. That fact might suffice to render them heroic or deeply suspect. In this novel, the characters best rooted in English soil and least nomadic are not favorably presented. The most rooted person is Mr. Rushworth, descended from generations of owners of the extensive lands of Sotherton. Yet his name comically indicates the shallowness of a reed in a marsh. That name is also strikingly Puritan. John Rushworth of Acklington Park, Northumberland, was clerk to the House of Commons; in 1642 he recorded Charles I's invasive attempt to arrest five members of Parliament. During the Civil War, John Rushworth acted as secretary for General Fairfax, carrying messages from Parliament to the front; he was known for diligence and speed "although once hoodwinked by a royalist messenger carrying the Great Seal" (*ODNB*). John Rushworth later wrote document-based histories, including the most complete description of the trial of Thomas Wentworth, in his *Tryal of Thomas Earl of Strafford.* There was, however, an earlier Catholic William Rushworth, a secret Catholic missionary, whose arguments for Catholicism were answered by leading Anglican divines (*ODNB*). What side are the Rushworths on? What is the true history of Sotherton Park? Did it pass during the Restoration from a Puritan family to one secretly Roman Catholic? Maria's Mr. Rushworth is a *James*—a Royalist name. Yet in Austen's flicker of comic historical reference he resembles the Puritan messenger *rush*ing about importantly: Julia saw him "posting away as if upon life and death, and could but just spare time to tell us his errand" (*MP,* I, ch. 10). Dislikable Mr. Rushworth resembles—perhaps descends from—that officious Puritan enemy of the martyred Wentworth.

The Rushworths of Sotherton, whatever they once were, have sunk into comfortable inanity. At the turn into the nineteenth century they cannot uphold *any* demanding tradition or cause—royalist or Parliamentarian, Catholic or Puritan. Since Mr. Rushworth is of "the same interest" (I, ch. 4) as Sir Thomas, we may deduce that Rushworths are Whigs, but that is all. Rushworth's ultra-English entertainments entail extinction of animal life and talking about it. Maria is "*doomed* to the repeated details of his day's sport" (I, ch. 12; italics added).[11]

The Honourable Mr. Yates, who introduces acting and *Lover's Vows* to Mansfield and runs off with Julia, is another young man of perfectly English fatuity. Younger son of a baron, irresponsible Yates scampers about on visits. His surname (an Old English word meaning "gates") refers primarily to a gatekeeper. Unlike gate-preserving Rushworth, Yates is less a gate*keeper* than (as we would say) a gate*crasher*. Tom asks him to be "our manager" of their theater company, recalling Mary Ann Yates (1728–87), the actress who (with Frances Brooke) was once joint manager of the King's Theatre (*ODNB*). Yates later refers to Tom as "Mr. Manager," aware that Tom has taken the position for himself. (I, ch. 13, ch. 14.)

Servants at Mansfield Park have modest surnames: Jackson, Ellis, Lee, and Chapman. "Ellis" is Norman "Elias." "Chapman" indicates somebody who sells or barters; it has the same root (*ceapan*) as "Cheapside." The governess, honored as "*Miss* Lee," has a common surname derived from *ley*, essentially the same as the "aristocratic" name of the Leighs. (Did the author imagine herself as a Miss Leigh, parked forever upstairs in a schoolroom with spoiled children—the fate menacing Jane Fairfax?) Lee is often a gypsy name; Miss Lee bows out quietly and pursues her nomadic lonely way.

Wilcox the rheumatic coachman drove the Mansfield party to Sotherton in the depths of winter. His medieval English surname comes from nicknames for "William." "Wilcox" can lend itself to sexual puns (as it does in Forster's *Howards End*). A suitor ought to be making all the effort that Wilcox makes—his cock should be willing. But the supposedly male "sex drive" is largely absent; there is no sign of it in lackadaisical Mr. Rushworth. It was Mrs. Norris who eagerly insisted on the drive over ten miles of bad road. As Mrs. Norris boasts to Sir Thomas, *she* got that coach to move "in the middle of winter and the roads almost impassable" (II, ch. 20). Although Fanny is the heroine of the novel, Mrs. Norris functions as the novel's Driver. Mrs. Norris drives the whole plot. She causes things to happen in the first place.

The most impressive name for a servant is "Baddeley." The Bertrams' butler is the only servant with a small speaking role and even at one moment an amused point of view (III, ch. 1, end). The name means owner of a "bad *ley*"—poor land. Yet that name suggests pretensions to gentility. A William de Baddeley lived in Essex in the thirteenth century; the family has a coat of arms and a crest. Baddeley the butler may be of as good blood as Tom Bertram—or better. In casting *Lovers' Vows* Tom is most willing to undertake the role of Butler—suggesting that he and his butler might be interchangeable. And there is a little pun in the name—for almost everybody here is behaving "badly."

FIRST NAMES IN *MANSFIELD PARK*

The Crawfords and Their Associates

The negative aura of "Mary" in Jane Austen's works cannot be missed. Mary Crawford is the heroine's opposite and antagonist. Yet Mary is defensible and infinitely more complex than previous female antagonists to the heroine: Isabella Thorpe, Lucy Steele, Caroline Bingley. Lucy, strongest of these, is malevolent but easy to read. During the Bath interlude Austen wrote *Lady Susan,* an exercise or "riff" borne out of Mme De Staël's controversial and successful epistolary novel *Delphine* (1802; translated into English 1803).[12] Austen later recommends De Staël's second novel *Corinne* (1807) (28 December 1808; *Letters,* 160–61).[13] De Staël's Delphine d'Albémar, a young widow, is exploited by the attractive—but cynical and self-interested—Sophie de Vernon. Delphine finds Mme de Vernon "the wittiest, most charming, most enlightened person I can imagine,"[14] while scheming Mme de Vernon writes witty letters to others disparaging Delphine and her naïveté. Sophie de Vernon maneuvers her friend into sharing Delphine's own inheritance. Pretending to assist the courtship of Delphine by Léonce, Mme De Vernon deliberately steals Delphine's lover for her own daughter.

Ungrateful while appearing affectionate, Sophie de Vernon is beguiling even to the reader. This representation of attractive doubleness seems to have challenged Austen to present her own complex character to which she gives the same surname: Vernon. De Staël's antiheroine eventually explains. When fatally ill, Sophie de Vernon confesses her deceitfulness to her friend, offering some justification. Finding her youthful thoughts and feelings were of no interest to others, "I shut everything I felt inside, and thus early acquired the art of dissimulation." Married off at her guardian's direction and against her desire she "felt hatred for a

society that did not come to my defense."[15] Sophie, seeing her powerless-
ness, decided that all was fair in a battle she fought alone. Delphine's affection returns for "that fascinating and guilty woman."[16] Austen wants
to present her own attractive siren, duplicitous yet truthful, without
staging a justification—or killing her off. But the strength, energy, and
intelligence of Lady Susan cannot be discounted. Creating a Lady Susan
enabled Austen later to come up with someone as complex as Mary
Crawford, a counterweight heroine rather than comic female villain.

Mary is a sojourner in an alien culture searching for the truth in a land
of cover-up. Many readers—like other characters within the novel—
have been overeager to identify Mary as a dashing representative of the
evils of London, an enchantress of the Town. She may be wealthy and
dashing, but her clan "home" is Scotland and her major connections
are Scots. Perhaps it is a tinge of Scottish bluntness or some effect of
Scottish philosophy that induces Mary openly to notice uncomfortable
points about human arrangements and behavior. Interlocutors shut her
down when she gets too close to the truth—especially truth about the
position of women and the miseries of marriage. She lets on that she
notices the selfish greed of her brother-in-law and its effects on her sister. She suffered especially from having to observe for years the effects
of her uncle's constant and confident infidelity upon the health and
spirits of his wife. Openly acknowledging that she notices—and is offended and hurt by—such things is, as Edmund says, "very indecorous"
(I, ch. 7). Mary is at fault for *not* acting, not representing naive placid
cheerfulness—such as is caricatured in hapless Lady Bertram.

Mary refers to friends with Scottish or northern first names, like
"Janet," the generally preferred version of "Jane" in Scotland—and in
parts of the north of England. (Compare "Janetta" Macdonald in "Love
and Freindship.") No Home Counties girl would use it.[17] Another
friend is "Flora Ross"—a Jacobite name. Flora Ross must be one of the
many girls of Stuart-supporting Scots families named after Flora Macdonald, rescuer of Bonnie Prince Charlie. Walter Scott named his Flora
MacIvor in *Waverley* in honor of that actual heroine. "Flora" ought to
have positive associations for Austen, a Stuart sympathizer

Henry Crawford has the first name of Jane Austen's most amusing
brother, whose flirtation with Eliza de Feuillide during family theatricals the young Jane had occasion to notice. Henry read the novel.
"Henry is going on with Mansfield Park; he admires H. Crawford—I
mean properly—as a clever, pleasant Man" (2–3 March 1814; *Letters*,
256). Austen seems amused at her brother's inability to see his reflec-

tion. "I once saw Henry the 8th acted—Or I have heard of it from some body who did," Crawford claims uncertainly (*MP,* III, ch. 3). But he *has* seen Henry VIII "acted"—impersonated by Sir Thomas, Tom, and himself. (There are touches of Henry VIII in fat, short-tempered Dr. Grant, as well.) Crawford, who reads aloud from Shakespeare's *Henry VIII,* displays some traits of that king: charm (in youth), bossiness, egotism, carelessness of others, and relations with a number of women. In the play, King Henry casts off the virtuous Queen Katherine, moving to marriage with Anne Boleyn; Wolsey, the intriguer, builds up great power and is thrown down. The destruction of the Old Religion is represented in Shakespeare's *Henry VIII* by Katherine, the most sympathetic and dramatically powerful of the characters with the possible exception of Wolsey (and both fall). This play covers the time in which the abbeys were lost. Shakespeare's somber drama exhibits a violent and unstable world. Further destruction is waiting in the wings, despite the forecast of the happiness of Queen Elizabeth's reign—and Mr. Crawford left before the group reached the ending.

Prices

The most important Price to us is Fanny—whom we know by no other name. We mentally refer to her as "Fanny"–though we don't think of Elizabeth Bennet as "Lizzie." (The nickname, natural to a child, is used among Fanny's two families.) But no one employs a more dignified first name; the Crawfords, who didn't know her as a child, use "Fanny" among themselves. Her diminutive is strangely highly sexed, yet childish. We tend to consider Fanny Price as a child or childlike—perhaps she never fully grows up in our eyes or the eyes of others.

The Price family with its numerous children offers a wide range of first names, if not as extensive as the range of Willmots. John Price is an invisible brother, presumably the one who is "clerk in a public office in London." There is a "Richard" (another hapless "Dick"), presumably the "midshipman on board an Indiaman" (*MP,* III, ch. 7). Sam, the eldest brother still at home by the time of Fanny's visit, has the old-fashioned biblical name and low nickname, like Sam Watson, apprentice surgeon. The only other Old Testament name in *Mansfield Park* is "Rebecca," the name of Jane Austen's grandmother—here the name of the Prices' overworked and much-scolded servant girl, probably a child herself.

Susan, fourteen when we meet her, is the next girl after Fanny. Next in the line of boys is little Tom. A baby when Fanny left home, he, like his rich cousin the heir, was named after Sir Thomas, who became this baby's godfather after the thaw set in. (This pregnancy is referred to in Mrs. Price's letter to Mrs. Norris in the first chapter.) Little Fanny loved Tom, but naturally he does not recollect her. Charles has arrived since Fanny's departure; he is eight years old when Fanny first meets him in Portsmouth. The youngest child is Betsey, "about five," a spoiled little girl, the only female child to whom Mrs. Price is disposed to be indulgent. One child is missing: "Another sister, a very pretty little girl, whom she had left there not much younger when she went into Northamptonshire, who had died a few years afterwards. . . . Fanny . . . had preferred her to Susan; and when the news of her death had at last reached Mansfield, had for a short time been quite afflicted" (*MP,* III, ch. 7). Betsey "brought the image of little Mary back again." But Betsey is a disappointment, spoiled, overassertive, and sulky. Little Elizabeth, christened after unpleasant Aunt Norris, nicknamed Betsey, possesses that dominant streak we see in all of Austen's "Elizabeths."

Betsey never met Fanny before, never knew lost Mary, and has no concept of love's connection with grief. Departed sister "Mary" seems a late invention of Austen, conjured up when the author must attend to emotional relations within the Price family. Hidden little Mary casts another light on Miss Crawford as Fanny sees her. Fanny can virtuously resist allowing that alien "Mary" to become a sister. The place of a *sister* Mary is already taken. Sister Marys are amiable nowhere else in Austen. Mary Bennet and Mary Musgrove are characterized by negative and unhelpful responses to the problems of existence. A decided departure, Mary Price is the most amiable of sister Marys—perhaps because she is so totally dead. Or perhaps just because she is authorially summoned to shove out the Mary whom Fanny perfectly repudiates. Yet dead little Mary is associated with her one hurtful memento—a knife, signifying severance, pain, and discord. (Proverbially, a knife should not be given as a gift, as it cuts friendship.)

Susan's love for lost Mary, visible in the undignified squabble over the silver knife, attracts Fanny's attention. Susan, or Susannah, name of a beautiful woman in a book of the Apocrypha, carries associations of physical stature, sexuality, and energy—associations deliberately played with in *Lady Susan,* in tension with the "low" social status of this Christian name. In Austen's works, the name "Susan" always entails an emphasis on physicality—visible even in Susan Fitzgerald of "Lesley Castle" and differently in the initial descriptions of Catherine Morland, a quondam "Susan." Susan Price, shrewd and robust, possesses energy along with a sense of order rare in the Price household. Susan is free of Fanny's shyness and weakness. William recollects early liveliness in Fanny: "We used to jump about together many a time did not us? When the hand-organ was in the street?" (II, ch. 7). His innocent recollection introduces the streetiness and contaminating commonness that the Bertrams originally feared. Readers, like the Bertrams, readily assume that the original move to Mansfield was good for Fanny's health—but was it? Might Fanny have been stronger—more like Susan—if she had stayed where she was?

> Looking forward to her visit to Portsmouth, Fanny is delighted:
> The remembrance of all her earliest *pleasures,* and of what she had *suffered* in being torn from them, came over her with renewed strength, and it seemed as if to be at home again would *heal every pain* that had since grown out of the separation (III, ch. 6; italics added)

Once she allows herself to think of it, she remembers Portsmouth as full of pleasure. *Suffering* was caused by transplantation; Mansfield has brought about unhealed *pain.* Sadly, the doubly displaced Fanny cannot fit back into Portsmouth. Susan, who never left home, took on the role of elder sister that Fanny unwillingly abandoned. Not given to reading, Susan prefers activity. (She has that in common with other Austen "Susans," from *Lady Susan* to *Sanditon.*) In a manner impossible to Fanny, Susan transplanted takes on the Bertram household.

> Her more fearless disposition and happier nerves made everything easy to her there.—With quickness in understanding the tempers of those she had to deal with, and no natural timidity to restrain any consequent wishes, she was soon . . . useful to all; and after Fanny's removal, succeeded so naturally in her influence . . . as gradually to become, perhaps, the most beloved of the two. (*MP,* III, ch. 17)

There is something unnerving as well as admirable in Susan's easy conquest of Mansfield Park. Aunt Norris was not altogether mistaken in her jealous fear of the Prices as encroachers. Susan replaces in Lady Bertram's lax life not only dutiful Fanny but also Mrs. Norris. She supplies what Elizabeth Norris had and Fanny Price never could offer—dynamism and drive.

"Fanny" Price is singular in many respects among Austen's heroines.

From the outset she is denied her full first name. She is always referred to by her cute and sexually suggestive nickname, connecting her with the primary female body part and with childishness. Fanny and the elder Frances Price are at odds. In judging her mother "a dawdle, a slattern" (III, ch. 8), Fanny seems unreasonably critical. The girl has no experience of bringing up some nine or ten children in a small house with a low income and insufficient help. Fanny herself is often inefficient or ineffectual, even though she possesses some "spirit of . . . independence, and nonsense" of which Mrs. Norris complains (III, ch. 1).

Fanny tends to freeze in *inward* resistance. Her bolder mother initially expressed outward resistance, turning her back on the Bertrams. The likeness between mother and daughter is underlined by the shared name. Yet they will never truly recognize their likeness. Frances the First (Fanny Ward) resisted pressure, going her own way. She is better equipped to ride through the roughness of life than her eldest daughter. Frances the First has given birth to and bred a fine group of young people for England. Fanny's elder brother William Price is the only admirable specimen of manhood to be met with in the whole of the novel. Courageous, practical, lively, affectionate, and strong, he has the virtues that nobody else can combine. His kingly name indicates that he is conqueror—an empire builder, a coming leader of men.

Bertrams

Sir Thomas Bertram bears a "Christian name" associated with a skeptical disciple, the Doubting Thomas of the New Testament. "Thomas" is associated with noncompliant saints and clerics: Saint Thomas à Becket, Sir Thomas More. Both came to sticky ends. Sir Thomas's first name (not a kingly one) is perhaps not perfectly matched with his aggressive surname.

Each parent has the first child of the same sex as namesake, expected to reduplicate the parent. Thomas the heir's nickname distinguishes him from his father—and Tom wants to be matey, disliking pomposity and distance. Sir Thomas, by contrast, has absolutely no concept of equality. He values inequality. Maria Bertram and her mother both have the popular variant of "Mary" (pronounced in the English manner). The name of Wollstonecraft's daring and ill-used heroine in *The Wrongs of Woman* is also first name of a novelist esteemed by Austen.

But "Maria" is ambiguous. It is hard not to believe that a primary influence upon Austen in choosing this name for her transgressive young female character (and thus for Lady Bertram) was the notorious Maria Fitzherbert, secret "wife" of the Prince of Wales. Maria (née Smythe) (1756–1832), was related to the Earl of Sefton. Born (like Austen) in Hampshire, she was a Roman Catholic. The death of her second husband Thomas Fitzherbert in 1781 left her with a little house in Mayfair and a handsome income of £2,500 per annum. In 1784 she met George, Prince of Wales. "Prinny" was then young and charming, not the fat fellow he became later. Richard Cosway's portrait of him in this period captures a sexually ambiguous glamour, an appeal enhanced by contemporary fashion (fig. 9). Maria became his mistress; George then wished to marry her. In Maria's house in Park Street on 15 December 1785 (a day before Jane Austen's tenth birthday) the two went through the marriage ceremony conducted by an Anglican chaplain in Holy Orders. But the marriage was illegitimate, banned according to constitutional riders issuing from the "Glorious Revolution." A member of the royal family had to receive permission from the reigning monarch to marry. No member of the royal family could be permitted to wed a Roman Catholic. Maria Fitzherbert was impossible—King George III and Parliament made that clear. Pope Pius VII, however, recognized the marriage, increasing English antipathy. "A wife and no wife," Maria inspired caricatures.

Weakened by debts—to be paid if he married according to legislators' wishes—the Prince of Wales consented to marry Caroline of Brunswick in 1795. When they actually met on their wedding day George was repelled, becoming very drunk. According to report, the couple had intercourse only three times. Caroline gave birth to the legitimate heir, Princess Charlotte, in 1796. (Princess Charlotte was to die in 1817, not long after Austen's death.) Thereafter, the royal "couple" lived apart. The Prince of Wales and his supporters wanted to obtain grounds for divorce. In 1806 the "Delicate Investigation" of Caroline by four commissioners and Spencer Perceval, conducted in hopes of evidence of Caroline's adultery, fueled the anger of liberals and radicals. When the queen wrote to her husband an open letter stating her grievances, Jane Austen was sympathetic: "Poor Woman, I shall support her as long as I can, because she *is* a Woman,& because I hate her Husband" (16 February 1813; *Letters,* 208). The notorious "trial" of Queen Caroline in 1820 was mounted in hopes that her husband, now a King George lacking an heir, could remarry. Caroline died not long after being barred from the prince's coronation in the summer of 1821.

Roger Sales in *Jane Austen and Representations of Regency England*

9. Richard Cosway, *King George IV* (1780–82). Photograph: © National Portrait Gallery, London.

(1994) sees Austen's third published novel as a "condition of England" novel, reflecting the era's instability. Tom Bertram is a careless Regent who abrogates his responsibility; Maria, venal in marrying solely for money, is sexually reckless, attaching herself to Crawford when there is no chance of his marrying her.[18] Sales's account introduces relevant material but seems too fixed in judgmental certainty. The novel itself allows us to see the characters from more than one aspect. Many En-

glish people considered Maria Fitzherbert a true wife and wronged
woman. Others saw a wicked seductress. Several novelists used "Maria"
as the name for a wife who leaves her husband—Wollstonecraft sympathetically, Jane West less sympathetically.

The age was an age of breakages and fresh starts—an age of divorces.
Austen in "Lesley Castle" had gaily imagined a new design whereby
the family broken by the adultery of "the Worthless Louisa" refashions
itself. By dint of becoming Roman Catholic in Italy each member of the
unhappy pair can choose a new partner and "are at present very good
Freinds [*sic*]" (*Juvenilia,* 143; 175). The first wife of the Earl of Morley,
impatient with his infidelity, had eloped with Sir Arthur Paget, whom
she married as soon as her divorce was final (shortly before the birth of
her child by Sir Arthur). In 1808 Lord Paget had left his wife to elope
with Lady Charlotte Wellesley, a married woman, marrying her after
her divorce—and his own. "What can be expected from a Paget, born
& brought up in the centre of conjugal Infidelity & Divorces? . . . I ab-
hor all the race of Pagets," Jane wrote in 1817, impatient at the news that
the eldest daughter of Lord Paget was engaged to the heir of the Duke
of Richmond (13 March 1817; *Letters,* 333). But she admired the new
Countess of Morley, and the Austens had been on friendly terms with
the Cravens until Lady Craven eloped with a lover and still kept up
with her daughters. Given the new acceptability of divorce in high life,
it is little wonder that Mary Crawford thinks that Maria, after being
divorced by Rushworth, should marry Henry: "And, when once married, and properly supported by her own family . . . she may recover her
footing in society to a certain degree" (*MP,* III, ch. 16). This plan cannot
work, as Henry refuses to marry Maria.

Continuing problems regarding the royal princes ensured that Maria
Fitzherbert was not forgotten, even if by the Regency that relationship
had officially ended. The scandal of "Maria," the royal mistress/wife, emphasized the name's Catholic and Continental associations. Maria Fitzherbert also posed questions as to what constitutes "marriage." Queen
Caroline was to say bitterly that she committed adultery but once—
in lying with the husband of Maria Fitzherbert. Perhaps the Prince
of Wales *really* was married to Maria Fitzherbert, and all the rest was
sham. This is a story in which everybody is pitiable and everybody be-
haves improperly—and everybody is unhappy. In that respect the royal
scandal truly resembles *Mansfield Park.*

If the novel's "Maria," the elder Bertram daughter, introduces into
Austen's novel the problems of female sexuality (as society saw it), that

theme is reinforced by the name of her sister Julia. Julia Bertram may have been in part inspired by the teenaged Julia Judith Twisleton, with whom the Stoneleigh heir James Henry Leigh fell in love; they abruptly married in 1786. Julia's brother Thomas, still a schoolboy, eloped to Gretna Green with a girl with whom he had acted in a play—rather like Yates. Mary-Cassandra, Julia's sister, committed adultery with much publicity; Jane Austen (with "a very good eye at an Adultress") correctly identifies her at a ball in Bath.[19] "Julia" was a Roman first name applicable to females born of the Julian clan. Emperor Augustus's daughter Julia, beautiful but reputedly wayward, seems to have erred sexually somehow. The poet Ovid was thought to be privy to her bad behavior (if only by knowing about it), an offense punished by permanent exile. Augustus cast off his daughter Julia, exiling her to an island where the emperor ordered her to be slowly starved to death. The banishment of the historical princess is reflected in the sentence passed upon Maria Rushworth (née Bertram), exiled from home by paternal decree and kept on short allowance. The Bertram girls in childhood boast of their historical knowledge, including "the Roman emperors as low as Severus; besides a great deal of the Heathen Mythology" (*MP*, I, ch. 2). The Bertram sisters may recite the names of Roman emperors but pick up no useful warnings from imperial lives.

The central "Christian name" among the Bertrams is "Edmund." In its Anglo-Saxon staunchness it is a total contrast to Continental "Maria" or Roman "Julia." Attention is deliberately drawn to it by Mary Crawford's dislike of the "the sound of Mr. *Edmund* Bertram," which is "so younger-brother-like," and by Fanny's indignant rhapsody:

> "To me, the sound of *Mr.* Bertram is so cold and nothing-meaning—so entirely without warmth or character!—It just stands for a gentleman, and that's all. But there is nobleness in the name of Edmund. It is a name of heroism and renown—of kings, princes, and knights; and seems to breathe the spirit of chivalry and warm affections." (II, ch. 4)

Mary thinks of the inferior status implied by inserting a given name between title and surname, whereas Fanny dwells on the aura of the first name. In this speech she can employ that cherished first name—though she never uses it in direct address, for she calls Edmund "cousin" while he calls her "Fanny."[20]

"Edmund," despite the "nobleness" felt by Fanny, is an ambiguous name. If we look into Shakespeare we can find that "Edmund" and "Bertram" are both rather bad fellows, though in different ways. To put these two names together constitutes a comical catachresis. In Shakespeare's *King Lear* the good (elder) son and heir of the Duke of Gloucester is named Edgar, and the bad (younger) son is the bastard Edmund. Edmund Bertram is a younger son, but legitimate, and good where his brother is "bad." The name is, as Fanny insists, kingly. The most common explication of the Anglo-Saxon name "Edmund" is that it means "wealthy protector," although Edmund Gibson said it meant "happy peace." "Edmund" became a popular name in England on account of King Edmund of East Anglia, martyr and saint. In 903 he was buried at the Benedictine abbey of Beodericsworth, a royal town in Suffolk, which became known as Bury Saint Edmund's. A magnet for pilgrims, the abbey became rich and powerful until laid waste by the Dissolution.[21] Edmund is certainly the name of a true Saxon king. But this king came to grief.

According to the most popular version of his story, King Edmund, tortured by Danes, refused to renounce his religion. He was then condemned and executed by being shot full of arrows. This story of "the martyrdom of King Edmund" is told in Gibson's Camden:

> For there, this most Christian King, because he would not renounce Christ, was by the most inhuman Danes (to use the words of Abbo) *bound to a tree, and had his body all over mangled with arrows. And they, to increase the pain and torture, did, with showers of arrows, make wound upon wound, till the darts gave place to one another.* And as a middle-aged [i.e., medieval] poet has sung of him:
>
> *Iam loca vulneribus desunt; nec dum furiosis*
> *Tela, sed hyberna grandine pluma volant.*
> New wounds, repeated left no room for new,
> Yet impious foes still more relentless grew,
> And still like winter-hail their pointed arrows flew.[22]

The story of the killing of Edmund is told in Joseph Strutt's "Supplement" to *Antiquities, Manners, Customs, &C. of the English,* with an illustration, *Condemnation and Execution of Edmund* (fig. 10). In this depiction, we see in the top strip the English king being condemned by the Danish leader. In the second strip, Edmund is tied to a tree with three archers shooting at him.

10. Joseph Strutt, *Condemnation and Execution of Edmund* (1792). Plate 2 from *Supplement to The Regal and Ecclesiastical Antiquities, Manners . . . &c. of the English.* Photograph: © The British Library Board.

Metaphorically, this is what happens to Edmund Bertram. Whenever he stands up for something, he gets shot at. When he stands up for family prayers, he is criticized and changes no practices—least of all those in his parental home. Camden's editor Bishop *Edmund* Gibson (1669–1748) in 1705 published *Family-Devotion; or, An Exhortation to Morning and Evening Prayer in Families,* a tract "reprinted well into the nineteenth century" (*ODNB*). Edmund Gibson argues much as Edmund Bertram does at Sotherton:

> For if Men think not of these Things at the most seasonable Times . . . it is not likely that they will fall into such Thoughts in the *midst* of their Business or Pleasures. It is to be fear'd, that there are too many Persons and Families, who are sunk into this unthinking State."[23]

Unlike Edmund the bishop, Edmund Bertram is not applauded. His little attempts to change his sisters' behavior or to get the play project cancelled all attract hostility and come to nothing. Edmund is the butt of jokes and sneers. Sir Thomas Bertram finds it convenient to allocate to Edmund the impossible task of monitoring the family's behavior without delegating to him any authority whatsoever. He is supposed to rule without power. A trifle scared of Tom, whom he cannot quite manage, Sir Thomas doesn't want to put paternal authority totally to the test. (It helps if we imagine Tom as looking something like Cosway's insolent Prince of Wales.) Sir Thomas trusts Edmund—and disparages him. Edmund is comfortably at hand to blame when things go wrong. "Sir Thomas's look implied 'On your judgment, Edmund, I depended; what have you been about?'" (*MP,* II, ch. 1). Edmund is a Regent without any writ, a ruler with no scepter. Responsibility without power is no Regency at all.

Tom occasionally jabs Edmund with reminders that Mansfield Park will belong to him. *He* is true Regent: "Manage your own concerns, Edmund, and I'll take care of the rest of the family" (I, ch. 13). Unlike constant King Edmund, the younger Mr. Bertram, target of unreasonable demands, is not quite able to martyr himself. He always gives way, even participating in *Lovers' Vows.* He betrays Fanny's cause, joining his father in pressing her to marry Henry Crawford. Alternating between delicate indecisions and a tendency to cave in, Edmund the bullied is never happy with a moral position. He just gets shot at again. Unable to repel the slings and arrows of outrageous fortune, he is easily depressed—and expects to be discouraged.

The combination of "Edmund" with "Bertram" is negative. "Edmund" is a hapless kingly saint (though in *King Lear* his name belongs to an ill-fated thorough bastard). "Bertram" is Shakespeare's sulky ill-judging boy. Both are shot at. Helena in *All's Well* regrets that she has unintentionally driven Bertram into danger:

> and is it I
> That drive thee from the sportive court, where thou
> Wast shot at with fair eyes, to be the mark
> Of smoky muskets? O you leaden messengers,
> That ride upon the violent speed of fire,
> Fly with false aim . . .
> . . . do not touch my lord:
> Whoever shoots at him, I set him there.
> (*All's Well That Ends Well,* act 3, sc. 4; *Shakespeare Plays,* 3:341)

The king, speaking his exasperation with Bertram, imagines shooting the lad: "Tho' my revenges were high bent upon him, / And watch'd the time to shoot" (act 5, sc. 3; 3:341). Helena's incompetent adolescent Bertram and the passive martyr Edmund, pierced with a hail of arrows—both are marks to be shot at.

Henry Crawford wanted to make "a small hole in Fanny Price's heart" (*MP,* II, ch. 6). The cruel metaphor conveys the result of shooting with a bullet rather than an arrow. Henry seems an invulnerable shooter, not the prey. But his sister sees Henry as a target: "And then, Fanny, the glory of fixing one *who has been shot at* by so many" (III, ch. 5; italics added). In a story where there is little happiness to be found, Henry both evokes and assails the happiness of others—but he too is shot at, most disastrously by Maria. (He does procure happiness for William Price, who can now be literally shot at with more distinction.)

As in Shakespeare's *All's Well,* at the end of this story leading characters are tamed. At the end of *Mansfield Park,* characters do (however reluctantly) what others would have them do—or disappear. Saved from disappearing into the grave, Tom knuckles under. Edmund settles for submission and makes no further heady excursions into exogamy. Having thrown one daughter away, Sir Thomas, like an unrepentant King Lear, finds a superior substitute. Sir Thomas forgets his early warnings against endogamy and the unsuitability of "cousins in love, &c." (I, ch. 1). "Fanny was indeed the daughter that he wanted" (III, ch. 17). She was not the wife or lover that *Edmund* wanted. Emotional dependency and sexual attraction are different things. Jealousy is always the test of love in Austen. Edmund was never jealous of Henry Crawford but promoted an engagement between Henry and Fanny.

Edmund not sexually attracted by Fanny? Never mind. Fanny was attracted to him, as Helena to Bertram. Yet if it is not right for a woman to marry without love, a man also should be free *not* to marry where he does not love. Like a good boy, however, Edmund gives his father the daughter he wants. Shakespeare's title *All's Well* is ironic, and Austen's ending is troubling. We are assured in the very last sentence that Fanny *will* be happy in the parsonage—still within the domain and control of Sir Thomas Bertram. Formerly Fanny has never been able to approach the parsonage "but with some painful sensation of restraint or alarm" (III, ch. 17) Have "restraint" and "alarm" really passed from her life—or Edmund's? The pair sink back into safe wardship. "I was in safe hands"—in Edmund's chilling phrase (I, ch. 11). Is all well—or are things too true to be good?

Names in *Emma*

PENUMBRA IN *EMMA*

Surrey and Its Past

In *Mansfield Park* names proliferate, fitting the centrifugal movement of the characters. This is a novel of Empire, even while the center attempts to remain fixed. In *Emma,* Jane Austen locates the action in one very English place (Highbury) but deploys a number of names of various origins, indicating different regions, activities, and social levels. Local names in *Emma* are current and credible in relation to class and place.[24] Austen keeps true to the geography and history of Surrey. The background of old Highbury and of Emma's area of Surrey is reflected in typical names of the region. Temporal change is consistently registered in the mobility of Highbury's inhabitants—or visitors—on their way up or down the social scale. Yet the community is bound together by little rituals and observances. The time scheme of the novel emphasizes the liturgical year and the rural calendar, as if Time (properly observed) can bind people together.

"Lower" denizens of Highbury blend in complicated ways with the "higher." Mr. Knightley works closely with William Larkins, his agent or steward. The suffix "kin" means "small" or "little"; the root *Lar* is nickname for "Lawrence"—"little Larry." A "lark," morning songbird of rural fields, is also slang for a festivity or jest. William Larkins adds to festivity by carrying the apples to the Bates household. One of the few visible working-class males, he is a connector. "Farmer Mitchell" (surname derived from "Michael") supplied an umbrella to Mr. Weston (it rains a lot in Highbury), enabling initiation of courtship. That Mr. Weston refers to him as "Farmer Mitchell" not "Mr. Mitchell" allots him the "yeoman" status into which Emma wants to push Robert Martin.

Harriet Smith refers to people connected with her school, including Miss Nash (head teacher) and Miss Prince. Miss Nash has a collection of three hundred riddles. She admires Mr. Elton and also his yellow curtains. Her name may be suggested by Beau Nash, for Miss Nash is the school's *arbiter elegantarium,* the setter of style and judge of taste, even if her origins are humble. Her sister married a linen draper. Miss Prince is the inferior teacher, second to Miss Nash. Neither of these is entertained at Hartfield.[25] Harriet also refers to "the two Abbots," schoolfellows at Mrs. Goddard's. This would be a local name, reminding us that Donwell Abbey once had an abbot whose servants might be surnamed "Abbot." This surname is highly appropriate to the county of Surrey; George Abbot (1562–1633), born in Guildford, became Archbishop of Canterbury. Miss Bickerton, another "parlour-boarder" at Miss Goddard's, panics at the gypsies and runs away leaving Harriet to shift for herself. "Bickering" is quarreling, and a Bicker-*ton* suggests a querulous settlement. But the place name "Bickerton," pleasantly georgic, refers to "farmstead of the bee keepers" (Mills).

Henrietta Bates, a prolific source of names, increases our sense of the dimensions of Highbury. Most names mentioned by Miss Bates reflect Surrey (county of her birth, if not of her parents) and its past. She roots the story in a region with an active population. "John Saunders," probably a local blacksmith, is the man to whom she would have taken her mother's spectacles to be mended. There is a "Sanders Place" in Surrey, its owner claiming descent from a pre-Conquest owner, Watkin de Sanderstead. Such touches prove how alert Austen is to the local culture of the region she portrays.

"Wallis" is the surname of the local baker; "Wallis" (Norman French *waleis,* "foreigner") was used from the Middle Ages for a Welsh or Cornish person. The Bates family lacks cooking facilities, so their apples are baked in the Wallis oven. While some say that Mrs. Wallis "can be uncivil and give a very rude answer," Miss Bates asserts, "They are very civil and obliging to us, the Wallises, always" (II, ch. 9). People working in hot kitchens are often portrayed as irritable, but Miss Bates needs to keep on the good side of Mrs. Wallis.

At the ball at the Crown, Miss Bates is in her element—she knows *everybody*. From her confusing delighted monologue (III, ch. 2) emanate multiple names reflecting the locality. The Otway family is greeted by Miss Bates; the name can indicate somebody coming from an "Otterway." The dramatist Thomas Otway wrote two of the best-known English tragedies, *The Orphan* (1680) and *Venice Preserv'd* (1682). In including an "Otway," Austen plays with the tragic potential of a story like that of Highbury's Orphan Jane. The "Dr. Hughes" turning up at the Crown with a son (an ever-comic "Richard") must be a Doctor of Divinity; were there another medical practitioner in Highbury we should have heard of him. "Hughes" originated in Carmarthenshire in south Wales and to the English ear remains a Welsh name. Mrs. Stokes is the active landlady of the Crown Inn. "Stokes" is a sturdy common surname, deriving from the Old English word for tree stump (*stocc* or "stock"). On the outskirts of Cobham, a Surrey town close to fictional Highbury, lies the village of Stoke d'Abernon. A Mrs. Gilbert attends the ball at the Crown, but "does not mean to dance," probably because she is past thirty. The name "Gilbert" means "bright pledge" or "hostage," in reference to the Germanic custom of sending a child to be adopted into the home of a potential enemy. (It would have made a suitable name for Frank.) "Gilbert" fits the locality. "FitzGilbert" was the name of the Norman family who first took over the village of Stoke d'Abernon. Mrs. Gilbert's husband is probably descended from some inferior branch of the FitzGilberts.

In another connection, Miss Bates mentions "old John Abdy" and his son the hostler. Employed by the Crown Inn, young John takes care of both riding horses and the draught horses. Although he has a good job, he is unable to take care of his elderly bedridden father without some parish assistance. Aged, rheumatic, and bedridden, John Abdy was parish clerk when Miss Bates's father was clergyman. (Such a "clerk" was expected to read psalms and lead the responses.) The old man was literate, but his circumstances are poor. "Abdy" means "one employed at an abbey" (Rainey and Wilson)—a name well suited to the area of Donwell from its pre-Dissolution days. Miss Bates's knowledge of the parish exhibits a much wider and more sympathetic view of Highbury than Emma's. Was Henrietta Bates a kind of unofficial curate to her father? She ought now to be numbered among the working women, for she is keeping up with the parish while looking after her invalid and decaying mother in their cramped apartments—no light task. Mr. Elton has the sense to listen to her advice.

Penumbra of the External World: Associates and Personal Circles

Jane Austen's delineation of Highbury makes extensive use of persons the reader only hears of, creating a variegated halo of Surrey associations and a more complex picture of Highbury. Austen also gives to visitors or new residents coming into Highbury their own individual halo of new associations. *Emma* is extremely resourceful in producing faraway persons who do not appear directly or dramatically. Different groups revolve around secondary or tertiary characters. The associations of names familiar to them and nobody else creates and substantiates the personalities of these characters, as well as establishing the constant existence of a world beyond Highbury's borders.

Jane Fairfax's Friends. Jane's status in the novel means that absent persons important in her life take on more weight than such shadowy persons usually do. "Campbell," name of a surgeon on William's ship referred to in *Mansfield Park,* turns up again in *Emma.* Still mute, this "Campbell," has moved upward in rank and narrative importance. Generous Colonel Campbell and his wife took in the orphaned Jane Fairfax to be cared for and educated with their own daughter. "Campbell" is the name of a major Scottish clan, whose traditional head is the Duke of Argyll. The Campbells fought against the English at the Battle of Flodden (1513); they were defenders of Mary Queen of Scots and of the Old Pretender.[26] Later generations of Campbells made their peace with the government and played their part as empire builders. Scots, mere apothecaries in Austen's early fiction, become noticeably evident in her later fiction as able members of the armed services, like Crawford in the Royal Navy. Yet Colonel Campbell (and his no doubt Scottish wife) might be looked down upon by English officers and civilians.

Jane's friend Miss Campbell does not marry an English gentleman but an Irishman, Mr. Dixon, who is "not strictly speaking, handsome" but "far from it—certainly plain" (II, ch. 3). The Scots name "Dixon" ("son of Dick") was carried to Northern Ireland by Scottish settlers in Ulster; Elizabethan policy furthered the suppression of the natives by encouraging Protestant settlers. Oliver Cromwell ruthlessly put down the native Catholics, and William of Orange followed suit; subjugation of the native Irish supposedly ensured the permanence of Protestant settlements and the power of English landowners—the "Ascendancy." Mr. Dixon with an estate in Northern Ireland must be by descent a Protestant and by attachment an "Orangeman."

Austen's running joke against the name "Richard" or "Dick" works against Mr. Dixon. He who is so "plain" might be part Celt—like "black and plain" Henry Crawford. Dixon may also be relatively poor. Miss Campbell (neither beautiful nor highly talented) takes him on faith; they met at a resort. An Irish gentleman might seem more obtainable than an English one. The Campbells, much better off than the Bates family, are limited by what we would term their ethnic identity.

Such problems are brought openly into the conversation when Emma asks Mr. Knightley "about your friend Mr. Graham's intending to have a bailiff from Scotland. . . . But will it answer? Will not the old prejudice be too strong?" (I, ch. 12). "Graham" is a Scottish name—appearing in "Love and Freindship," where the heroines "rescue" Janetta from her affianced Graham (*Juvenilia,* 122). "Graham" resonates. James Graham, Marquis of Montrose, is a Scots and Stuart hero. An aristocratic Covenanter who fought for Charles I and then for Charles II, Montrose was captured and executed with cruel spite. Johnson in his *Journey to the Western Islands of Scotland* admires "the great Montrose"—but the English don't usually think of romantically loyal heroes when thinking of Scots. The "old prejudice" might even hamper Jane Fairfax, protégée of Campbells, in pursuit of employment in teaching. In Richardson's continuation of *Pamela,* Mr. B. considers employing a Scots tutor for his son. But "this person" must have had "the native Roughness of his climate filed off and polished by Travel and Conversation" and "should, by all means, have conquer'd his native Brogue."[27]

Mrs. Elton's Circle. A cloud of names is introduced by the former Miss Hawkins. It is a rule in etiquette not to talk to your present company about persons they cannot know. Fortunately for us, Mrs. Elton—like Lady Catherine De Bourgh—repeatedly breaks this rule. She creates an extravaganza of names, not rooted in Highbury and its corner of Surrey but floating about in comic fireworks. One of her friends has the last name "Jeffreys" (from *Galfridus*); its strongest association is with the notorious Judge Jeffreys of the Bloody Assizes. Other female friends of Augusta Hawkins include "the two Milmans," both of whom gave up music after marriage. "Milman" is low, meaning "worker at a mill." One of the Milman sisters is "now Mrs. Bird"—ironic, as she stopped emitting any music after she caught a husband. Yet another Milman sister is now "Mrs. James Cooper." "James" is the name of Austen's elder brother, and Cooper is the surname of some of her cousins. There are aristocratic Coopers—the first Earl of Shaftesbury chief among them. But Austen is quite ruthless in her commandeering of names. A "cooper" puts the hoops on barrels and tightens them so they are sound and don't leak. The name refers to common labor on a basic product.

Mrs. Elton's friend Mrs. Jeffreys is "Clara Partridge, that was" (II, ch. 14). This surname reminds us of Fielding's Partridge in *Tom Jones,* Tom's putative father and sidekick. Partridge, a semiliterate schoolteacher, is a gossip and devout coward—a partridge is a timorous game bird. How can one have a famous (*clara*) partridge? Here is another bird to go with "Miss *Hawk*ins" and Mrs. *Bird.* One of the best names of Mrs. Elton's gallimaufry is "A cousin of Mr. Suckling, Mrs. Bragge" who "moves in the first circle" (II, ch. 17). *Bragge* ("active," "lively") comes from the Norse *braggi,* a hero. The concept readily transfers to someone who only *thinks* he is heroic: "to brag" is to boast (usually foolishly) of oneself. The popular card game "Brag," an ancestor of poker, is the subject of a verse by Austen: "Alas! poor Brag, thou boastful Game!—What now avails thine empty name?" (*Later Manuscripts,* 249). Mrs. Elton might herself be termed "Mrs. Brag."

Mrs. Elton is most insistent that Jane Fairfax should take a post as governess with "Mrs. Smallridge." The surname is locative; Small-ridge near Axminster is defined by the "small ridge" in the area. At Mrs. Smallridge's home Jane would have the advantage of dwelling only four miles from Mrs. Elton's alliterative sister Selina Suckling at Maple Grove. The "small" in this potential employer's name indicates her small importance, while the "ridge" indicates that she is prickly or difficult. Mrs. Smallridge's four children will undoubtedly be spoiled brats.[28]

The most oft-repeated name of all Mrs. Elton's horde is that of her brother-in-law—"Suckling." This name was an Old English word for a baby, one still sucking at the breast—the Old English suffix *ling* is diminutive. The Cavalier poet Sir John Suckling (1609–42) was still known and quoted. (His family name came from an ancestor who held land by socage and was a "socling.") The real poet's father actually made a second marriage to a Jane Hawkins (*ODNB*). So there is a genuine association of these two names. Austen is making comic fun, indicating the newness of Mrs. Elton's brother-in-law's family—little shoots that come out of nowhere. Any claim on their part to gentility is in its earliest infancy.

The funniest name of all Mrs. Elton's numerous acquaintances, however, is "dirty": "People of the name of Tupman" who "came from Birmingham" (II, ch. 18). A "tupman" keeps "tups"—rams—whose greatest use is servicing ewes to produce more sheep. (The same word is the
root of the surname "Tupper.") "Tup" and "tupping" were current—
the sense that of a well-known four-letter verb beginning with "f" and
the participle/gerund that goes with it. Iago taunts Brabantio about his
daughter's consorting with Othello: "Ev'n now, ev'n very now, an old
black ram / Is tupping your white ewe" (*Othello,* act 1, sc. 2; *Shakespeare
Plays,* 8:324). Dickens picks up the name "Tupman" for comic use in
The Pickwick Papers.

CENTRAL SURNAMES IN *EMMA*

Going Up and Going Down

"Woodhouse" is an Anglo-Saxon locative meaning "house in (or by)
a wood." A De la Woodhouse was given land after the Conquest. The
family name, as Janine Barchas demonstrates, connects with the Wentworths.[29] Emma in reaction to Mr. Elton's proposal defensively muses
on her superiority of rank: "He must know that the Woodhouses had
been settled for several generations at Hartfield, the younger branch
of a very ancient family—and that the Eltons were nobody" (I, ch. 16).
Mr. Elton may *not* know all of this. We cannot be sure how distantly
self-aggrandizing Emma and her father may link to the "very ancient
family" of Wentworth-Woodhouse. In the property and manners of
Emma's father we see no hints of old aristocracy, nor does Mr. Woodhouse mention any relations save his own progeny. Knightleys provide
assistance, status support, and descendants. Mr. Woodhouse's family
may have been "settled in Hartfield" for a while, but not as true landowners. "The landed property of Hartfield was inconsiderable. . . . But
their fortune from other sources was such as to make them scarcely secondary to Donwell Abbey itself" (I, ch. 16).

Emma, who thinks Harriet incurious about her background, is not
too curious or clear about where her own money comes from. "Other
sources"—investments now, perhaps commerce? Given the history
of the Wentworth-Woodhouses, income might well come from coal
mines.[30] (The treatment and condition of miners was little better than
those of slaves.) Emma, "an imaginist," represents her father's power
as she *imagines* it, but Mr. Woodhouse plays little or no part in the

power regimes of Highbury. (For those who do, see "Male Leaders and Suitors," below.) Choosing Harriet Smith as a friend, Emma consciously condescends to descend—a ploy useful to her defensive need for superiority. "Smith," commonest of English laboring names, covers the shame of Harriet's real mother as well as the name of an unknown father. Emma thinks Harriet stupidly placid regarding her unknown identity, but Harriet's favorite reading matter—stories of orphans, half-orphans, women abused or neglected by parents—is an index of her inner concerns. Emma, casting herself as the parish's Great Lady, is playing a role above her station. She is *not* landed gentry. There is no doubt that she marries up. And her money in stocks and shares, perhaps ultimately derived from coal under the ground, will be plowed back into the cornland of Donwell.

As well as invoking the Great Name Matrix, Emma's surname may conceal a pun, in a novel whose "*Emma*grammatology" contains multiple wordplays.[31] Separated into its syllables, a "wood-house" is a homely shed for fuel. That is its meaning in the first volume of *Clarissa,* in which a "Woodhouse" (always capitalized) is the site in which secret messages are deposited—a go-between. Lovelace "behind a stack of wood" surprises Clarissa "returning from the Woodhouse."[32] Frank uses Miss Woodhouse as an unconscious go-between, a cover or false address for contact with a secret love. One of the older meanings of "wood" (*wode*) is "mad." Is the Woodhouse home a "wood-house"—a "mad-house"? Not only her father but Emma can obsess as well as fantasize.

Austen builds up a Highbury full of personalities, activities, and the acquisition of objects—a piano, a dining table, possibly a carriage. The histories of inhabitants vary. Some persons are recent comers to the "populous village, almost amounting to a town"; others arrive within the course of the year (*Emma,* I, ch. 1). Mrs. Bates, elderly widow of the late vicar, seems at first glance a fixture at Highbury, where she and her middle-aged daughter are living in semigenteel poverty. They have no relatives aside from an orphan niece. Evidently the vicar was a stranger to the village. The Bates family were always newcomers. Without kin, save for Jane who "had yet her bread to earn" (II, ch. 2), the lonely female family has descended, depending upon neighbors for social standing and even supplementary economic support. "Bates," first recorded in the thirteenth century, is derived from the Hebrew first name "Bartholomew" (ironically "rich in land"). This respectable but not high name could be derived from an occupation, a "batter" or "beater" of metals. In this all-female Bates family sexual partners are dead or absent—so it is a surprise when one member of the family attracts a lively male.

Miss Bates's clergyman father has recently been replaced by the young Reverend Philip Elton. His surname might have been suggested by the name of the teenage orphan Clara Elton, heroine of Agnes Maria Bennet's *Juvenile Indiscretions* (1786) whom we see first at a school, like Harriet Smith. The name "Elton" could mean a beautiful or noble town (*Aethel* + *tun/ton*). More probably, it means "eel-*tun*," a settlement rich in eels, like "Elton" in Huntingdonshire. Eely Mr. Elton is on the lookout for a wife who can bestow social and financial advantage. Impossible that Emma would marry someone from "Eel-town"!

"The charming Augusta Hawkins" arrives in midnovel; a woman from the Bristol area searched successfully for a husband in Bath. Her attraction lies largely in her "possession of an independent fortune, of so many thousands as would always be called ten" (II, ch. 4). "Hawkins" derives from Anglo-Saxon *hafoc,* or hawk, relating to the elite practice of hunting with a hawk or falcon. This lady is "a little hawk," or more correctly the descendant of someone who looked after a hawker's little bird. Miss Hawkins descends like a hawk upon her prey, an eel from Eel-town only too anxious to be caught.

Mr. Weston has been steadily moving up, a rise facilitated by freedom from rearing his son. The Coles are another family moving up. The name "Cole" means "dark" or "swarthy," also "coal" (cf. German *Kohl*). The family, with more gentility than one might expect, acquired a crest in the reign of Henry IV. The most famous "Cole," however, is "Old King Cole" in the rhyme or song:

Old King Cole was a merry old soul,
And a merry old soul was he;
He called for his pipe, and he called for his bowl,
And he called for his fiddlers three.

This suits the Cole family of Highbury, jolly folk, given to entertaining.

The Cox or Coxe family (name spelled both ways in the text), local representatives of the legal profession, are present at gatherings but don't have speaking parts. "Coxe" is most probably derived from the Old English and modern British English word for what the delicate Americans call "rooster." It might, however, be simply locative (from "haycock") for somebody living by a hay field. Slightly pejorative, the name indicates a person "cocky" and vulgar. In 1800 Austen comments on meeting again "two Miss Coxes": "I traced in one the remains of the vulgar, broad featured girl who danced at Enham eight years ago." (20–21 November 1800; *Letters,* 61). Emma inwardly describes William Coxe as a "*pert* young lawyer" (I, ch. 16; italics added). The "dirty" meaning is not quite absent. The cocky Coxes are on their way up. Mr. Perry the apothecary is another professional man; his work gives him access to all sorts of households. "Perry" may originally have indicated someone who lived near pear tree(s); the alcoholic drink made of pear juice, agreeably associates the apothecary with healthful pleasure.

Women are active in this narrative, and not just in the upper levels of the novel's society. The novel presents a number of working women. Mrs. Goddard runs her own school. "Goddard," a Germanic name that arrived with the Normans, means "good" plus "hardy." The best-known Goddard is the medieval bishop who founded the hospice for travelers in what became Saint Goddard's Pass. Homely Mrs. Goddard is connected thus with the "Swisserland" of which Frank Churchill dreams (III, ch. 6). Closer to home, "Goddard" is also the name of the sympathetic London apothecary who treats Clarissa in Richardson's novel. Miss (Anne or Anna) Taylor, Emma's governess, is another of Highbury's working women. Attractive and gentle, if not in her first youth, she has a "low" surname deriving from a working occupation. However, it also suggests piety and daily goodness; Jeremy Taylor, seventeenth-century Royalist clergyman, was the author of the still-current devotional classic *Holy Living.* Mr. Weston, who first married up and was looked down on by his wife, looks downward for his second wife. Miss Taylor's refinement and education, however, will be of advantage to their children. Upon her marriage Anna Taylor gains a comfortable house with servants and a carriage. She moves up.

Jane Fairfax and Anna Taylor, governesses future or past, represent the height of professions for working women—not very high. Working women on the lower end of the scale populate the novel. Most servants mentioned are female. Important servants are called by their last name, like "Serle," Mr. Woodhouse's cook, who knows how to boil an egg and make gruel. Norman "Serle"/"Searle," relating to armor, may denote someone who scours armor rather than an armor wearer. Mr. Knightley's housekeeper is "Mrs. Hodges," a pure English surname derived from an old nickname for "Roger." Mrs. Elton's housekeeper "Wright" appears to act not only as housekeeper but also as hairdresser and lady's maid. "Wright" meaning "maker" is also a name element in words like

"Cartwright." Such common surnames are workaday names at the lower level. The Bateses' little slavey "Patty" doesn't rate a surname.

Obliging Mrs. Ford is one of the many active working women encountered in a novel in which women's economic role is a quiet theme. (Her pleasant efficiency suggests that the Ford family is making money and moving up.) Ford's shop is one of the signs of blending and connection. "Ford" refers to a place where a watercourse may be crossed without a bridge. The name is poetically resonant, indicating getting through obstacles, overcoming difficulty. In Ford's shop people meet without the bridges of formality. Center of Highbury, Ford's shop is a place of crossings, where top people meet and mingle "with the second rate and third rate of Highbury" (*Emma,* II, ch. 1). It is in Ford's shop that Harriet remeets the Martins after refusing Mr. Martin. Harriet shops there, and Miss Bates, and so does Frank Churchill, who buys a pair of gloves in order, he declares, to make himself a citizen of Highbury: "It will be taking out my freedom" (II, ch. 6). Frank will allow himself a good deal of freedom before he is done with Highbury.

Emma complacently quotes *A Midsummer Night's Dream* (I, ch. 9); some critics see the novel as thematically related throughout to that play.[33] There is enough "Midsummer madness" certainly in the strawberry party and the Box Hill expedition, on Midsummer Eve and Midsummer Day (New Style). *The Merry Wives of Windsor,* however, also seems a presence here, with its grittier, more prosaic vision of the summer world of folly and courtship. (Windsor is visited by Frank and Mr. Churchill, once free of that un-merry wife Mrs. Churchill.) In Shakespeare's Windsor play we find a "George" (Page) and a secretive "Frank" who is also a "Ford"; jealous of his wife, Frank tries to keep an eye on her, in a plot full of hidden games. Young Frank Ford is a masquerader, playing at being "Mr. Brooke." (Mr. Weston's Frank is a masquerader, his buying gloves is partly a blind, and "Mrs. Ford" makes a good merry wife of Highbury.) When Frank purchases gloves at Ford's shop in order to become "a true citizen of Highbury" (*Emma,* II, ch. 6) is he taking out citizenship in the comic world?

Emma resents the rise from the middle class of those beneath who manifest unpleasant symptoms of budding gentility. Her father does not seem struck by the Coles' inferiority to himself; in general, Mr. Woodhouse does not share Emma's snobbery. "Snobbery" is an inappropriate term. In Austen's day—as in Thackeray's—"snobs" are low persons who intrude on the genteel and attempt to mimic them. "Snob" is *not* commonly used for the truly genteel trying to hold the line. But gentility—as this novel demonstrates—is elastic and relative. Austen actually creates and fully delineates a modern "snob" in Emma Woodhouse. That Emma is not quite alone, however, in her lingering feeling that the Coles are still "low" is reflected in one telling adjective used by Miss Bates, who refers to "the worthy Coles" (III, ch. 2). The spoken qualifier "worthy" indicates that the speaker regards the person spoken of as socially inferior, if meritorious. Nobody speaks of "the worthy Weston"—though Mr. Weston has done almost exactly what Mr. Cole is doing now. He rose through joining his brothers in trade in London, prospering sufficiently in business to buy a small property in Highbury. But Mr. Weston married into the gentry. And he is a native of Highbury.

Orphans and Rival Heroines

Austen populates her tale with numerous orphans or half-orphans: Jane, Emma, Isabella, Frank. There is also the parentless, dispossessed Harriet. Frank lost his mother, as did Jane at age three; Emma and Isabella lost their mother, but not in infancy. Surviving fathers have qualities that make them unsatisfactory as parents. Jane lost both mother and father (and from her mother she has inherited a fatal disease.) To varying degrees, all of these orphans or half-orphans need reassurance. Isabella is happiest, having early found a substitute parent in her husband and in her own parenting. The other orphans are secret, cautious, distrustful, and maneuvering, in very different ways.

Jane Fairfax and Frank Churchill challenge Emma Woodhouse and George Knightley for central roles. They are insider-outsiders—both having lived away from Highbury, though one parent lived or lives there. They bring strangeness, glamour, and interesting names. In Susanna Minifie Gunning's *Anecdotes of the Delborough Family* (1792), a Captain (later Colonel) Fairfax elopes with Lucy Darlington, daughter of a rich banker. After he dies, Lucy loses all their money and then dies also, leaving a son in the military and a daughter. Orphaned "Emely" Fairfax is brought up as a lady and well educated by Sir James Edmonds, an affectionate but elderly benefactor. The backstory of Jane Fairfax may owe something to this earlier "Miss Fairfax." (Gunning's Miss Fairfax has to share the narrative center with her brother and does not have the story to herself—but Jane also never has a story to herself.)

Undoubtedly, Jane Austen exhibits a political consciousness in pairing a Jane *Fairfax* with a Frank *Churchill*. These two characters wear labels of historical-political significance that put them at odds. "Fairfax" is Anglo-Saxon, meaning "fair-haired" (*faeger* + *feax*). It is odd that the young woman bearing this surname should be so noticeably dark-haired. Jane's surname, not very common, is that of Oliver Cromwell's most powerful and efficient general, Thomas, third Lord Fairfax (1612–71). Antipathy seems natural between a Woodhouse, connected to the Stuart-supporting Wentworths, and a Fairfax who assisted the chief regicide.[34] In Gunning's novel the traditional Whig gentry (Fairfax) are warned against allying themselves too closely with the interests and attitudes of the new moneyed class. Jane's father Lieutenant Fairfax heroically died "in action abroad," patriotically fighting the French (II, ch. 2). There is no alliance with the moneyed class, but perhaps Jane can bring one about in connecting with Westons and Churchills.

Characters in *Emma* are engaged in rivalries for the affections and loyalties of other characters—and of the readers. The opposition between Emma and Jane, who (unbeknownst to themselves) are twin rivals for the post of heroine, forms the central axis of the novel.

Austen is playing with a novel mentioned by Harriet—a broad clue persistently misunderstood by readers. Regina Maria Roche's *The Children of the Abbey* pits the heroine Amanda Fitzalan, virtuous and beautiful, though poor, against the objectionable rich young woman, Lady Euphrasia. Austen (who had already drawn on Roche's novel in *Pride and Prejudice*) reworks the situation, and even particular scenes, especially that in which the elegant heroine's playing and singing charms the company and humbles the haughty and more privileged young woman. At a party in Portman Square, Lady Euphrasia and her set plan to embarrass the ignorant Irish girl. Lady Euphrasia's best friend, Miss Malcolm, exclaims, "I have no patience with such creatures forcing themselves into society quite above them."[35] When required to play and sing, Amanda far outdoes Euphrasia: "Her style became so masterly and elegant, as to excite universal admiration, except in the bosoms of those who had hoped to place her in a ludicrous situation." Lady Euphrasia reacts angrily:

> "I declare, I never knew anything so monstrously absurd," exclaimed Lady Euphrasia, "as to let a girl in her situation learn such things, except, indeed, it was to qualify her for a governess or an Opera singer."[36]

Here we have a template for central situation in Austen's *Emma,* even a particular scene: the party at the Coles (*Emma,* II, ch. 8). Elegance is a trump card in both narratives. Emma is not crudely and overtly malicious like Euphrasia—though she *is* malicious. She experiences "mixed feelings," all the more once Frank begins to sing with Jane. A sense of her inferiority to Jane makes Emma all the more likely to yield to the temptation of pseudo-pitying her, as well as sharing unkind gossip—which she herself manufactures. At moments, Emma unconsciously indulges inner gloating over the prospect of Jane's talents descending into the thankless work of a governess. After the Coles' party the naively sycophantic Harriet comfortingly voices the opinions Emma would *like* to be allowed to indulge:

> "Well, I shall always think that you play quite as well as she does. . . . And I hate Italian singing.—there is no understanding a word of it. Besides if she does play so very well, you know, it is no more than she is obliged to do, because she will have to teach." (*Emma,* II, ch. 9)

Austen switches the poles of Roche's narrative; in the new narrative focus, readers' sympathies go to the "the mean girl," while the talented disadvantaged beauty has to fight (often in vain) for an equal place in the narrative.

Male Leaders and Suitors: Knightley, Martin, Churchill, Weston

Emma—probably rightly—counts the Woodhouses among the leading families of Highbury, although feeble Mr. Woodhouse turns to Mr. Knightley for management of his monetary and business affairs. The undeniable leadership and economic power of Highbury reside in Mr. Knightley. If not without limitations, Mr. Knightley is no mere sign of social stability but an active force. Some readers find his name too allegorical, a Spenserian outcropping of conservative chivalry. But it is sufficiently realistic. Mr. Knightley is in a middle state; he has no title with which to decorate his name—a "real" knight would be called "Sir George Knightley." "Martin" is in this text arguably a more interesting name than "Knightley," common as "Martin" appears.

"Martin" originates in Latin *martianus,* a fighter, follower of Mars, god of war. *Martianus* became a Roman proper name. In the fourth century AD a young Hungarian of good birth named Martianus was a mounted Roman warrior. As he was riding through the streets of

Amiens, a shivering beggar asked for his help; Martianus took his sword and cut his own cloak in two, giving half to the beggar. That night, he dreamed a dream in which Christ appeared as the beggar, and told the young man that he had shared his cloak with the Savior and yet was not baptized. Martianus not only underwent baptism, he also became such a convinced Christian that he gave up war and tried to work for peace. When his commanding officer rebuked him for cowardice in not going into battle, the young man offered to strip himself naked of clothes as well as weapons and so to face the opposing army. Saint Martin is— oddly—the patron saint of soldiers. But he ought to be the patron of all who struggle for peace.

Saint Martin became a popular object of devotion, particularly at Tours. His saint's day, Martinmas, or the Feast of Saint Martin, is 11 November (Armistice Day). Many churches and towns took on the name. (I was born in Saint Martins-by-the Sea, New Brunswick.) Saint Martin's popularity did not diminish after the Reformation; Saint Martin-in-the-Fields was rebuilt after the Fire of London, retaining its name and importance, if not the fields.[37] Saint Martin's image, variously and widely reproduced, is that of a knight riding upon a horse, taking out his sword to slash his cloak in half. It is an upper-class icon—a man of the knightly class, on a beautiful prancing steed. Sharing his coat with the beggar, half and half, may seem ungenerous—why not magnani- mously give the whole? On the other hand, the division is a statement of *equality*. It expresses *sharing* rather than condescending *donation*. Saint Martin, we are told, was laughed at for "the figure he made" in his half- cloak but did not care. Martin is an egalitarian saint; in the army "he contented himself with one servant and him he treated as if he were his equal."[38] Martin was clear thinking: "Though a stranger to secu- lar learning, he was in his discourses clear, methodical . . . and power- fully eloquent." His friend Sulpicius adds that he "never heard any man speak with so much good sense."[39] Compare Mr. Knightley on Robert Martin: "He always speaks to the purpose; open, straight forward, and very well judging" (*Emma*, I, ch. 8).

Saint Martin represents a manliness that is not belligerent and not afraid to give. All of this could easily be known to Jane Austen—from, for instance, the Rev. Alban Butler's multivolume *Lives of the Primitive Fathers, Martyrs and Other Principal Saints* (quoted above). Informa- tion about saint's days appeared in almanacs or diaries, like one for 1789 in which Saint Martin comes just ahead of Saint Swithin—subject of Jane Austen's last composition. We may take it that Robert Martin's first proposal to Harriet is made at Martinmas. Though he is rejected, his power ultimately prevails.

The yeoman status of Mr. Martin, so unpleasing to *Emma*, is expressed in his "ordinary" surname. But Martin, the unmounted knight who never does a mean or ungenerous thing, is a counterpart of "Mr. Knightley." Robert Martin is the second "knight" in Highbury—and in Austen's novel. In the spiritual order the two men balance each other and are not, as Emma thinks, at different ends of a vertical scale. *Mansfield Park* almost piercingly illustrates the struggles and pain required to sustain inequality. In that novel most characters accept or actively pursue inequality, damaging others—and themselves. In *Emma* efforts to venerate or impose inequality will generally be thwarted.

"Churchill" is a most eminent if irritating name, its power bursting into the center of the novel. The name "Churchill" began as a locative, referring to a person who lives "by the church on the hill." "Churchill" became the name of an exceedingly famous family—of dubious glory in the eyes of Stuart supporters. Austen used the name before; in *Lady Susan* the Vernons' estate in Sussex is "Churchill," which may make the Vernons somewhat suspect. Jane Fairfax's surname on its brighter side reflects a Puritan love of truth as well as courage—and constancy. Courage and constancy do not apply to Frank Churchill. As we have seen, John Churchill switched sides during the invasion of the Prince of Orange, breaking his oath. Treachery gained him honor and rewards from the new King William III. John Churchill later successfully led the British forces against the armies of Louis XIV on the Continent. Churchill was made Duke of Marlborough by Queen Anne; Blenheim Palace (named for his victory at Blenheim in 1704) was supposedly a gift from a grateful nation.

John Churchill—devious, inconstant, and self-interested—had dash and flair. He knew how to seize a chance. That surname hints at ruthlessness, dishonesty—and a happy outcome, through calculation and luck. A Churchill betrayed a Stuart king; to that extent the name can pair well with that of a Stuart-killing Fairfax. Frank's adoptive surname (his mother's)—already his middle name also—bodes continuous success. The irritable and imperious Mrs. Churchill, his aunt, in her controlling qualities (at least as these are seen by the Westons) somewhat resembles the formidable Sarah Churchill (née Jennings).

Frank Churchill, however, is at birth a *Weston*. He and his father presumably have the same name: Francis Weston. The Weston pair, father and son, however disarming, introduce in their very names elements of sexuality, gamesmanship, gallantry, and danger. "Weston," indicating a westerly village or incomer from the west, is "the name of an old Surrey family" as Fiona Stafford points out.[40] But the name "Francis Weston" directly connects with one of the most colorful and bloody episodes of the reign of Henry VIII—that period to which Austen perpetually returns. Sir Francis Weston was an attractive young courtier, companion of Henry VIII, good at games and sports. The Tudor writer George Cavendish, defensive biographer of Wolsey, disapprovingly refers to Francis Weston as one "that wantonly lyved without feare or dreade . . . following his fantzy and his wanton lust." The poet Thomas Wyatt laments his loss: "Ah! Weston, Weston, that pleasant was and young, / In active things who might with thee compare?"[41] In 1536 when he was only twenty-five, handsome young Francis Weston was one of the men beheaded for alleged adultery with Anne Boleyn (or "Anna Bullen"). Some careless flirtatious words spoken to Henry's Queen were used against him. Francis and others were collateral damage in Henry VIII's effort to get rid of Anne Boleyn and marry Jane Seymour.[42]

Certainly, Miss Taylor's husband has a happier fate. Francis Weston the elder in middle age successfully marries his Anne; he keeps a steady head, despite his good fortune and his love of company and good times. But he is loose-lipped. In *Battleridge,* the historical novel by Jane Austen's mother's cousin, a character of that name has some similar characteristics: "Mr. Weston, in his good-natured manner then retailed the harmless part of the neighbourhood's gossip."[43] Mr. Weston in *Emma* is a persistent gossip; yet, combining innate good nature with the civility inculcated by trade, he usually avoids offense. He is sufficiently a courtier to make elaborate compliments, as he does at Box Hill.

His son, "Frank Churchill Weston Churchill," more strongly resembles the Tudor young gentleman and is the same age. Our Francis Weston too is good at games, plays, and flirtation—sometimes going too far. Frank flirts, offering his "attentions" to Emma, attentions that— so he claims—were returned "with an easy, friendly, good-humoured playfulness" (III, ch. 14). That is probably a good description of the real relation between the Tudor Francis Weston and Anne Boleyn—but "playfulness" did not save them.

"The child of good fortune," as Emma says (III, ch. 14), Francis Churchill Weston Churchill escapes the ill luck that might befall someone so fond of playing on the edge. To borrow Wyatt's phrase, Austen's Frank Churchill is "pleasant and young" and good at "active things" (like riding and dancing). But he is dangerous to himself and others, plunging the woman he loves into misery. At the end, however, he pays for nothing. Like Henry VIII rather than Francis Weston, he gets his Jane. Frank is not Henry VIII; he is not a ruler. By station and temperament he is a mere courtier, however well he thinks of himself, in his jangling fusion of the airy and doomed Francis Weston with the devious successful Churchill.

FIRST NAMES IN *EMMA*

Austen employs "Emma" in early works, as well as for her two Surrey heroines, Emma Watson and Emma Woodhouse. Germanic in origin, "Emma" is a royal name. Though it should lead the list of first names, it will here be discussed last, in order to give it its full due. Names of secondary and minor characters offer some range of choice. Poor Miss Bates's name, "Henrietta," might indicate a faint Catholic (or high Anglican) sympathy—or merely her mother's reading of Charlotte Lennox. We know Miss Bates's name only because her mother calls her "Hetty." Nobody else calls her by her first name. As Maggie Lane points out, once her mother dies she will never hear her first name again.[44] Other first names in *Emma* have been recycled from Austen's earlier works. The outstanding "odd" names are "Philip," "Augusta," and "Selina."

Mr. Elton's "Philip" is unusual; the name of a saint, it was a bit too Greek and foreign for eighteenth-century gentry. "Augusta Hawkins" is an oxymoron, the bird of prey or ugly saleswoman ("hawker") in conflict with a grandiose empress. "Augusta" (feminine form of "Augustus") came in with the Hanoverians. It indicates the Hawkins family's social climbing—we last heard of it in the "Miss Sneyd" encountered by Tom in Ramsgate. This name connects with some contemporary scandal. In 1793 Augustus Frederick, Duke of Sussex, married Lady Augusta Murray, in contravention of the Royal Marriages Act. The marriage was declared void in 1794, but the couple continued to live together until 1801.

The Hawkins parents named their other daughter "Selina." They had not caught on to the fact that upper-class people tended to shun "fancy" or classical names, preferring tried-and-true names of monarchs and saints. Like "Julia" and "Augusta" this is a non-Christian "Christian name." Austen may have recollected Lady Selina Dangle in Susannah Gunning's *Anecdotes of the Delborough Family.* "Selina" had already been used negatively by Mary Robinson in *Angelina;* the villain is the delightfully fashionable and malicious "Lady Selina Wantworth"—a play on the "Wentworth" that so attracted Austen. These novels may also have influenced Frances Burney's choice of the name in *The Wanderer* for Selina Joddrell, the feminist Elinor's foolish younger sister. The Joddrell girls' disagreeable aunt is named Mrs. Maple, perhaps feeding into Austen's name for the Sucklings' "Maple Grove." Selina Suckling (née Hawkins) is supposed to visit Highbury but never appears. Like the moon after which she is named, she is inconstant and sometimes invisible.

A number of names in *Emma* are names of Austen's own family members, comically demoted. "William" has descended since *Mansfield Park,* reserved for "low middle" characters who do not participate directly in the dialogue, like William Larkins or William Cox. "James" is the name of the Woodhouse coachman. "Harry" (a nickname for or version of "Henry") is a footman. "Henry" remained in high estimation, but "Harry," like other nicknames, did not. (In the twenty-first century it has gone up again with Prince Harry.)

The person of lowest estate in *Emma* is the Bateses' servant "Patty." She is probably an orphan charity child, adding to the novel's orphan population. Patty makes apple dumplings as well as cleaning, washing, and fetching fuel and (probably) water. She is furthest from the pileup of monarchical names and pretensions. Mrs. Elton rightly notes that Patty has too much to do to be asked to fetch letters from the post office. It is disconcerting that Jane Fairfax, acutely aware of the menacing slavery of her own position as a governess, is not bothered by the position of her little slavey.

Unusually dispassionate regarding her own name, Austen had already used "Jane" variously—for a sweet Jane Bennet or a vulgar Jane Watson. Jane Fairfax, proud, talented, and beautiful, is reserved; Jane Bennet, who favors candor, also gives too little away. Jane Fairfax, in striking contrast to Emma, is a dark-haired, secretive, and probably consumptive heroine. In creating Lady Susan Vernon in response to de Staël's counter-heroine, Austen raised her powers to the intricacy of Mary Crawford. In *Emma* the character of the counter-heroine is not quite as complex, but the narrative's use of her is very complex indeed. We cannot know Jane Fairfax on first reading. Jane Fairfax is in striking contrast to Emma, "the picture of grown-up health," assured of her place in the sun. Blonde Harriet Smith, cheerful and a little stupid, stands in also as an opposite or complement to both these rival queens. Miss Woodhouse's initial reaction to Harriet seems unconsciously based on Emma's own reading of two novels: *Sir Charles Grandison,* with its blonde orphan heroine Harriet Byron, and *Evelina,* in which the pretty girl, apparently a bastard, is at last acknowledged as the daughter of Sir John Belmont. Emma in her way is a Quixote, like Catherine Morland—or Elizabeth Bennet, upon whom *Tom Jones* has made too deep an impression.

The first name of Mrs. Weston (née Taylor) is the name of a British queen and also of a major saint—Virgin Mary's mother, grandmother of Jesus. Mr. Weston refers to his wife as "Anne," but Miss Taylor's baptismal name may be "Anna," the name given to her baby daughter—the name of one of Jane Austen's favorite nieces. Mrs. Weston conceives and produces a child during the course of the action; the other character to bear a child in the course of an Austen novel is fatuous Charlotte Palmer. "Anna" or "Anne" is a good name for a motherly character, and Miss Taylor was Emma's substitute mother. But Austen's "Annes" are often left behind, overlooked, secondary—even in *Emma,* where Anne Cox's hopes of Robert Martin come to nothing. Austen is about to use "Anne" for her forsaken heroine in *Persuasion.*

Robert Martin dignifies a first name that last served for silly Robert Ferrars. Mr. Knightley's first name is "George," the name of the king, and of Jane Austen's father, and of course of England's patron saint. The character dignifies a name last adorning Wickham—Austen does not reserve it for virtuous characters. But Mr. Knightley is truly what King George III claimed to be, patriotic land worker and husbandman. George Knightley, the true "Farmer George," is unalterable King of Highbury. Mr. Knightley's younger brother, the barrister, is "John"—a name not reserved to high or low; it is also the name of the hostler and his bedridden father. John Knightley is slightly self-regarding and sometimes sharp-tempered. Austen characters named "John" hug their own limitations and do not excel in control of temper or regard for others—see John Thorpe, John Dashwood, and John Willoughby. Sir John Middleton, though likewise tactless, is an exception in good will and a decided contrast to John Knightley in his love of hospitality and social gatherings.

Mr. Weston and his son are both named "Francis"—name of Austen's great-uncle and of a brother. Naturalized in England, Francesco/Francis is the Christian name of a great medieval saint and French kings. Anything but "Frank," the witty young gentleman is neither honest nor open. Was Frank Churchill forced into deceit through his secret engagement? Or did he choose the secret engagement because of its scope for his talent in masquerade, dissimulation and equivocation? Frank probably will never care overmuch for candor, though his last letter belatedly shows how well he can assume it. George Knightley, disliking Frank before he meets him, takes out his incipient jealousy in an anti-Gallican remark—Frank may be "aimable" but not really "amiable" (I, ch. 18). He associates "Francis" with Frenchness. But then, Mr. Knightley does not know he is jealous. Frank arouses jealousy when he flirts—or pretends to flirt—with the Queen of Highbury. He does not pay with his head—he gets away unscathed, successfully using Emma as a cover.

As in all of Austen's novels, but most expansively here in *Emma,* names capture verbal comedy as well as political and social stresses. Their syllables provide puns, charades, and riddles—openly in the novel with Mr. Weston's riddle on Emma's first name, "What two letters of the alphabet . . . express perfection?" (III, ch. 7). The comic battle in the novel is the fight for supremacy among rival would-be monarchs of little Highbury. Emma would be Queen of Highbury, but Jane has a claim, and Augusta Elton has imperial ambitious to reign and go first. Miss Bates supports that claim: "Dear Mrs. Elton, how elegant she looks! . . . Now we all follow in her train. Quite the queen of the evening!" (III, ch. 2). How galling to Emma to hear Augusta Elton proclaimed queen of the ball at the Crown! And what could the venue be named but the *Crown*? Francis (Frank) has the name of a French monarch and a strange position as son and heir, an irresponsible Prince of Wales. Even the rising Mr. Cole has the name of a comic king. Emma—who always wants to be first—wins the position at last, like Queen Alice in *Through the Looking-Glass.* Emma puts an end to the game by marrying King George—Mr. Knightley. Like her predecessor Queen Emma, after marrying one monarch she may give birth to another.

The historical Queen Emma, wife of two Saxon kings (Ethelred II and Canute), and mother of Edward the Confessor, was Norman but acceptably identified as English.[45] Emma remained especially popular in Austen's native Hampshire, especially Winchester where the queen once lived. The historical Queen Emma, handsome, clever, and, rich—*and* well-born—was wife of two kings and mother of another. But she did not have an easy time. At one point she had to flee for her life; to protect her sons she learned to navigate the power politics of Danes and English. Her son Edward the Confessor, jealous of her offspring by Canute, was particularly hard on her. The most colorful of the stories asserts that, not content with stripping her of her possessions, Edward

11. William Blake, *The Ordeal of Queen Emma* (ca. 1790?). Private collection. Author's photograph.

accused his mother of having carried on "a scandalous commerce with Alwin, bishop of Winchester." Tobias Smollett in his *History* includes the traditional tale: "As he [the Norman archbishop] could not prove his allegations by evidence, he insisted upon her proving her innocence by undergoing the fiery ordeal. She accordingly walked, blindfold, over twelve burning plowshares, without being hurt, to the astonishment of. . . . spectators."[46] David Hume stoutly denies this tale: "The invention of monkish historians . . . propagated and believed from the silly wonder of posterity."[47] But this long-cherished story, complete with Saint Swithin intervening on Queen Emma's behalf, retained its appeal. The familiarity of this Ordeal is proved by the picture *The Ordeal of Queen Emma* painted by William Blake (fig. 11). Blake's immediate target is the injustice of kings and religious hierarchies.[48] Emma Woodhouse passes through her own comic and critical Ordeal of Emma while we provide the spectators. And—despite setbacks and comic failures—she succeeds in being Queen Emma of Highbury and the unrivaled heroine of the story.

At the time the novel was written, however, it would be impossible to ignore associations with another leading "Emma," often seen in prints, portraits, and caricatures. The most celebrated "Emma" of the period is the woman born Amy Lyon, daughter of a blacksmith. She acted as a maid to actresses in London, and then became part of a show as "Goddess of Health" in the quack James Graham's "Temple of Health." This enterprise offered sexual rejuvenation; its chief feature was a bed on which the patient(s) could experience electric shocks. After further adventures Amy Lyon became the mistress of the Honorable Charles Greville and at his instigation changed her name to "Emma Hart." Under this new name she became a favorite subject of the artist Romney (fig. 12). Greville eventually needed to break off this affair and marry. He sent his mistress to Naples for a vacation to visit his aging uncle, Sir William Hamilton; on arrival in Italy Emma discovered her long-term relationship had ended.

Sir William Hamilton, a connoisseur, delighted in Emma's beauty and encouraged her in an act she devised herself, part mime, part dance. In Emma's famous "Attitudes," she posed as and interpreted famous women of literature and history, including Medea and Cleopatra. To Greville's chagrin, Sir William Hamilton married Emma in 1791. Horatio Nelson visited Napoli in 1793 and returned after the Battle of the Nile, badly wounded, having lost one arm. Lady Hamilton helped to nurse him back to health, and the hero became Emma's lover (fig. 13). For a time the three lived in London, a ménage à trois. Sir William died in 1803. Lord Nelson was killed at Trafalgar in 1805, believing a grateful nation would look after Emma. Nelson was wrong; Emma died in debt. But her beauty, his heroism, and their love affair had streaked across Britain like a meteor.

A few touches in Austen's novel hint at an affinity between respectable Emma Woodhouse and the notorious and delightful Emma Hamilton. Austen is unlikely to have known of Cornelia Knight's opinion that Emma Hamilton was "a singular mixture of right and wrong," though that would describe her heroine.[49] Austen's Emma does not exactly indulge in literal performance of "Attitudes," although she certainly has a variety of poses and mental postures. As an artist, she makes her surrogate Harriet pose and perform, even if afraid of her "not keeping her attitude and countenance"—an *attitude* in which Harriet undoubtedly has taken instruction from Emma (I, ch. 6). "Hart-field" contains the old surname of Emma Hart. Mrs. Weston says, "There is health not merely in her bloom, but her air, her head, her glance." Emma is "the complete *picture* of grown-up *health*"—like the "Goddess of Health" in James Graham's show (I, ch. 5; italics added). Austen's Emma, if tech-

12. George Romney, *Emma, Lady Hamilton* (1785). Photograph: © National Portrait Gallery, London.

nically "virtuous," is not exactly constant or right thinking: she plays with Harriet as a doll, she unwittingly leads Mr. Elton on, she invents as well as circulates malicious rumors, and she mentally toys with Frank as a suitor. Only when pricked by jealousy does she see that Mr. Knightley is what she wants. Jealousy makes her vulnerable. She sustains self-respect but is saved from being in love with herself. Her beautiful survival shines on others.

Judgment is disarmed by multiplicity, the multifaceted nature of being. But multiplicity needs community in good times and bad. Who

13. William Beechy, *Horatio Nelson* (1800). Photograph: © National Portrait Gallery, London.

could not imagine a communal monument where Emma standing outside Ford's shop watched the children at the baker's window? A First World War monument to the fallen, such as most English towns and villages possess. On it we would read the names of Martin and Knightley and Cole and Ford. Highbury does not dwell in separation, and the whole community survives. Not only Emma but all *Emma*'s characters attract warmth in our sympathy or laughter, in contrast to the cold judgments that close down *Mansfield Park,* where there is no beautiful survival, where exogamy is forbidden, and nothing is shared.

Names in *Persuasion*

In *Persuasion,* Austen finally comes to the heart of her labyrinthine Great Name Matrix and discovers the riddle: the central name from which all others branch is "Wentworth." Austen expands her exploration of ethnicity and dissonances seen in *Mansfield Park* and *Emma.* In a mobile and shifting world, it is increasingly hard to "place" a person. Political identities and ideologies raise conflicts, yet sometimes resolution or compromise may be possible. Ignorance about others and oneself is an obstruction, but we need to take risks. *Persuasion* is a study of love and risk—perhaps partly a response to Sir Walter Scott's criticism in his 1815 review of *Emma* that Austen sacrificed romantic feelings to realism, caring nothing for love.[50] Anne Elliot, "forced into prudence in her youth . . . learned romance as she grew older—the natural sequel of an unnatural beginning" (I, ch. 4). *Persuasion,* like *Emma,* begins as a novel of rural life, but it continues the work of *Mansfield Park* as a study of war and Empire.

SURNAMES IN *PERSUASION*

Elliots and Their Central Associates

The most important surname is "'Wentworth," first encountered as surname of an absent personage of no account.

> "You misled me by the term *gentleman.* I thought you were speaking of some man of property: Mr. Wentworth was nobody, I remember; quite unconnected; nothing to do with the Strafford family. One wonders how the names of many of our nobility become so common." (*Persuasion,* I, ch. 3)

Sir Walter complains that he could not recognize in an allusion to "a gentleman" a mere curate. This Rev. Mr. Wentworth (brother of Frederick) is not truly "a gentleman" but "nobody," owner of no property. Such Wentworths must be riff-raff, no connection of the beheaded earl. It was indeed easy to lose sight of the less showy line of Wentworths in favor of the superopulent Fitzwilliams or the glamorous Watson-Wentworths and Wentworth-Woodhouses mocked by Mary Robinson in her comic invention of the "Wantworth" family. Sir Walter's ability to close his eyes to reality provides a clue that the opposite of what he says is likely to be the case—Frederick and his siblings *are* related to the martyred Strafford. Sir Walter consistently deceives himself regarding the progress of names. Throughout the centuries, service has been rewarded by titles continuously raising "common" names to the elite.

"Wentworth" is an English Anglo-Saxon name, and Austen values it not only for its historical associations but for its punning meaning—Frederic *went,* but he was *worth* something. And Old English *weorth* means "valiant" as well as "worthy." "Elliot" is an ancient name, sometimes connected with the Hebrew for "the Lord on High" or with "Elias" (Hebrew prophet Elijah). Information in Sir Walter's *Baronetage* tells us that members of our imaginary Elliot family acted as sheriff or served as MPs for a borough (a "pocket-borough"?). Raised to the dignity of a baronetcy in the reign of Charles II, an ancestral Elliot was perhaps rewarded for loyalty at the Restoration; there is no indication of military service. How loyal were they? Was one of the three parliaments they sat in the Long Parliament—or Rump Parliament? Sir Walter married Elizabeth Stevenson; the simple Nordic genitive is the kind of surname Austen usually attaches to working-class or bourgeois persons. (A "Mr. Robinson," the Musgroves' apothecary, attends little Charles.) Sir Walter maintains no connection with the Gloucestershire Stevensons. Marriage brought no additional status, though presumably an infusion of much-needed money—as Sir Walter's heir achieved wealth in marrying a butcher's rich granddaughter (II, ch. 9). The deceased wife and mother, meekest of Austen's Elizabeths, is but a short line of type, her appearance and nature in shadow. She lived to regret that "youthful infatuation which made her Lady Elliot" (I, ch. 1).

The *Baronetage* kindly picks up the Elliots in Cheshire (whence the Leighs sprung into history), on their move southward (like the Leighs).[51] Once the Elliots would have lived much further north; Sir Walter's name is Scottish. The most important "Elliots" of Austen's day were Scots, Whig politicians with Scottish titles. Sir Gilbert Elliot (1751–1814) was born in Edinburgh, eldest son of the third baronet and his wife Agnes, a daughter of Hugh Dalrymple who had "Murray-Kynynmund" tacked onto his name. The real Dalrymples were a legal dynasty, a family of lawyers and judges from Berwick on Tweed. "Dalrymple" is a Gaelic locative meaning "a dweller in the territory of the crooked stream." Gilbert Elliot and his brother were sent to Paris with David Hume as their tutor. In 1776 he became a Whig MP and a friend of Edmund Burke. In 1797 he added his mother's multiple surnames to his own, becoming Gilbert Elliot Murray-Kynynmund. That year he was made Baron Minto—as a consolation prize for not being supported in his bid for a seat in Parliament. He was able to insert his feckless brother Hugh into the governorship of the Leeward Islands, ruled from Antigua. Gilbert's chief advisor was his cousin William Elliot (who also craved a seat in the House of Commons). That cousin William Elliot had turned decidedly against reform can be seen in a letter he wrote to Sir Gilbert during the French Revolution:

> Reform, as you observe, implies innovation; and innovation, which is in itself dangerous, cannot fail of leading to destruction when the people are under the dominion or frenzy.[52]

Austen's mature William Elliot shares such views: "his feelings . . . were only too strict to suit the unfeudal tone of the present day" (*Persuasion*, II, ch. 3).

Sir Walter expresses his "feudal" views in adulation of rank and title. In making "Lady Dalrymple" Sir Walter's admired relative, Austen endorses the Scottish origin of her family of Elliots—despite Sir Walter's emphasis on English gentility, purity of name, and heritage. Tweedside lawyers are hardly glamorous. Yet Sir Walter is infatuated with his own relationship to Lady Dalrymple. If the history of the real Elliots is imagined to obtain, starting with the marriage of Gilbert Eliot to Agnes Dalrymple, then the Dowager Lady Dalrymple is Sir Walter's relation only through his maternal line.

Jocelyn Harris first noted the nominal connection with "Mrs. Grace Dalrymple Elliot, a fashionable demi-rep called 'Dally the Tall,' who supplanted Mrs. Robinson in the affections of the Prince of Wales."[53] Janine Barchas has elaborated on the scandals that sprouted after Sir John Eliot married Grace Dalrymple; *Persuasion* may "fold in high-society scandal." There is a hidden joke, a potentially dirty meaning, in wishing to see "Lady Dalrymple."[54] Sir Walter utters the name of his dull relative in reverent adulation, unaware of any comic implications.

The most notable—and *inglorious*—Dalrymple of Jane Austen's day, however, was not the courtesan Grace but General Sir Hew Dalrymple (1750–1830). When Sir Hew took over from Wellesley as commander in the Iberian Peninsula, England had just won a great victory, defeating the French army in Portugal. But in August 1808 General Hew Dalrymple signed an armistice agreement, "the Convention of Cintra," allowing the French soldiers to be evacuated from Portugal—with their loot. The British government was greatly chagrined; there was an official inquiry in November-December of 1808. Hew Dalrymple was contemptuously known as "the Dowager" from that time.[55] *Persuasion* has an inset political joke: "Dowager Viscountess Dalrymple" (*Persuasion,* II 4) might almost be the recently disgraced General Dalrymple in drag—befitting his soubriquet.

The dowager's daughter, the Honorable Miss Carteret, has inherited a name of humble origins, whether French *quartier* or English "carter" (a hauler). George Carteret, one of the eight original proprietors of Carolina, in 1664 received half of New Jersey. In Richardson's *Clarissa,* Lovelace mocks the real monument set up in Westminster Abbey to commemorate a Dame Elizabeth Carteret; "this Dame in effigie" has "one clumsy foot lifted up" so as to "make one imagine, that the Figure . . . was looking up to its Corn-cutter."[56] Sir Walter speaks excitedly of Lady Dalrymple and Miss Carteret as "family connections among the nobility of England and Ireland!" (II, ch. 5). Curiously, he does not mention Scotland. "Noble" persons with Scots or Irish titles are generally considered somewhat inferior to those with purely English titles and lineage. Sir Walter's truckling to these people shows his abject neediness, his sincere adulation of mere title, and his actual distance from the top layer of the highborn in either kingdom.

Sir Walter, unreasonably fastidious, has a large blind spot. His merely Scottish (or Scots-Irish) background strikes him not at all. The *Baronetage* soothes him with the past—but it serves as "consolation" in a distressed hour because it spares him from noting too much of the past. He seems unconscious that title and lands were produced by no acts of military valor. Yet perhaps he does notice, subliminally—he resents fighting men and the honors accorded them. Sir Walter hates some aspects of the aristocratic ideal. In a novel that highlights courage, fortitude, and risk, Sir Walter, a middle-aged failure, is altogether deficient. Wrapped not only in the general falsehood of mere title, but also in his personal cocoon, Sir Walter is not only unwilling but unable to see—let alone admire—*noblesse* of spirit.

In contrast to the sleekly pragmatic and sycophantic Elliots we have a fiery "Russell." Norman "Russell" means "little Red" (as in "red-haired"); "Don Roussel" is a comic term for a fox. This surname has extremely strong Whig connotations. Lord William Russell was among those accused of participating in the Rye House Plot to kill King Charles II; for this he was beheaded in 1683. Russell and Sidney, Whig aristocrats, are republican martyrs and heroes. Russells and Elliots were on opposite sides in the Civil War and during the Restoration. The name "Russell" was highly visible in Austen's youth; the Duke of Bedford (1765–1802) was a Russell. (That duke's younger son, Lord John Russell, was to be author of the Reform Bill of 1832.) If an Elliot and a Russell might be at odds, a Wentworth and a Russell would inevitably come to open hostility. Both sides have literally gone to the block for opposing beliefs. Eventually—so we can hope at the end of *Persuasion*—after Waterloo has been won and the true peace can commence, Lady Russell and Frederick will come to terms with each other.

Lady Russell's name suggests red hair. We also have "sandy-haired" Colonel Wallis, who, despite this defect, is sufficiently good-looking for Sir Walter not to mind walking with him. The name, a variant of "Wallace," refers to various groups of borderland Celts. (In *Emma* the surname served the baker of Highbury and his wife.) Red-haired Colonel Wallis is likely one of the Britons of Strathclyde, a "North Briton." We hear of other Scots in the army and navy. Wentworth might have been asked to take "Lady Mary Grierson" and her brood in his ship. "Grierson" is a version of MacGregor; Lady Mary's husband is apparently a Scottish naval captain. Colonel Wallis, like Colonel Campbell (in *Emma*) and Admiral Maxwell (in *Mansfield Park*), is a Scot making his way upward through wartime service—something Sir Walter does not in this instance seem to resent. (Is Sir Walter subconsciously appeased by the colonel's Scottishness as well as his good looks?) We find another Scot, at a different level. The Elliots' gardener is "Mackenzie," an old Scots name, *Mac + Coinneach* meaning "son of *Coinneach* (comely)" (Reaney & Wilson). (How suitable that even Sir Walter's gardener should be named "son of a handsome man"!) The gardener's combination of Scottish identity and working-class skills seems normative, but in this narrative a number of Scots names turn up among persons in different classes.

Aside from the Wallis couple, Sir Walter does not introduce names of many acquaintances. He recollects "old governor Trent" as a gentleman who once lived in Monkford; Trent (name derived from the river) sounds like a retired colonial governor. Mary mentions a dinner party given by the Pooles. "Poole," another watery name, is Anglo-Saxon, neither rare nor aristocratic. The range of political allegory and aesthetic play within the novel is brought down to earth—literally—with

Mrs. Clay. Mrs. Clay, of the primal Adamic material, is as common as dirt. Her father is Mr. Shepherd, another allegorical name—he guides his ignorant sheep (weak Sir Walter and his daughter) to where he wants them to go. Shepherd is the first driver of the action. He decides that Kellynch will be let and finds the Crofts to rent it. He sends Sir Walter and his eldest daughter to Bath, saving them from themselves by shelving them inexpensively, probably permanently. And he sends Anne bumping into the world where she will find better things than in Kellynch.

Navy People

The names of the navy men and those associated with them offer an interesting and highly varied collection. "Wentworth" ought to be considered chief among the names of naval men, although it is first introduced as the surname of a clergyman, Frederick's brother Edward. Mrs. Croft, Admiral Croft's wife, is Frederick's sister. "Croft" is a common noun, originally indicating a small enclosed field, or a peasant's piece of land, and then the peasant's simple cottage. There were, however, Norman "Crofts"; a "Richard de la Croft" existed in 1230 (Reaney & Wilson). And among the baronets of which Sir Walter might read, Croft of Croft Castle obtained the title in 1671. This long-surviving family died out in the 1790s for want of an heir—which, as Janine Barchas notes, adds an extra significance to the childlessness of the admiral and his wife, "a fact treated unfeelingly . . . as a practical boon."[57] In Admiral Croft Austen redeems the name of the villain of *Emmeline,* Sir Richard Crofts, the mean lawyer of low Scottish origins who persecutes Emmeline at Lord Montreville's bidding. Charlotte Smith uses "Crofts" to indicate someone low in every respect.[58] The word conjures up the most humble kind of dwelling—a "croft" is the very opposite of a Kellynch Hall. The Crofts of *Persuasion* are natural, spontaneous, and unpretentious, in total contrast to the vanity and arrogance of Sir Walter and Elizabeth. Their speech is also colloquial, in contrast to the heavy preworked speech patterns of a Sir Walter.

Sir Walter offers a negative list of naval men as emphatic proof of the offensively low personnel. "A man is in greater danger in the navy of being insulted by the rise of one whose father, his father might have disdained to speak to." The father of Lord St. Ives was "a country curate, without bread to eat." Sir Walter is not put out by the fact that Anglican clergy are ill paid, but offended that "I was to give place to Lord

St. Ives, and a certain Admiral Baldwin." The ugliness of naval life in-
trudes in Admiral Baldwin: "His face the colour of mahogany, rough
and rugged to the last degree, all lines and wrinkles, nine grey hairs of
a side, and nothing but a dab of powder at top." Sir Walter inquires of
Sir Basil Morley, "a friend of mine," who this "old fellow" might be and
is astonished to hear that instead of being, as he estimates, sixty-two,
Admiral Baldwin is only forty. Such degrading sights should be elimi-
nated: "They are not fit to be seen. It is a pity they are not knocked on
the head at once, before they reach Admiral Baldwin's age" (I, ch. 3).

Sir Walter trusts for information to another baronet, whose unusual
first name "Basil" means "king" (in Greek) and whose Anglo-Saxon
surname "Mor-ley" means "clearing near a marsh or moor."[59] "Lord
St. Ives," as new-made baron, takes precedence over the baronets. He
took as title the name of his home town—Saint Ives, Cornwall (on the
"Celtic fringe"). This coastal town, named after a Celtic female saint,
was engaged for centuries in boat building and the export of tin; many
of its inhabitants were seamen. Sunburned Admiral Baldwin's name
predates the Norman Conquest: *bald* + *win* equals "bold" + "protector." "Bald" puns on the advancing *bald*ness of Baldwin's pate. He is the
kind of doughty fighter on whom English safety has always depended.

Sir Walter never considers what evils might ensue if the ruling class
did *not* contribute fighting men. Sir Walter and those like him have
adopted a kind of perverse "feminine" role in which they are protected,
sheltered even from sun and rain, and never expected to fight—bearing
out Mary Wollstonecraft's charge that the very rich, treated like invalids
or women, do not know enough of the world and are therefore unfit for
power.[60] Sir Walter wrongly identifies soft privilege as characteristic of
rulers and, with unconscious male jealousy, verbally caricatures active
Admiral Baldwin.

This novel plays even to a disturbing extent with variation and
changes in gender expectations. Sir Walter in the patriarchal position
acts "feminine," gazing into looking glasses. But the most hardy and
courageous of men are also "feminine," like Captain Harville with his
domestic talents. Conventions of gender differences are questioned in
relation not only to war and love, but also to business, economics, pastimes, and the rubs of daily life. Mrs. Croft, more alert than her husband
in business regarding the rental, corrects her husband's inexperienced
driving by putting her steadying hand on the reins. There is no perfect
"feminine" or "masculine" way of being.

In the second volume, naval persons in Bath are referred to by Admiral Croft with approbation, canceling Sir Walter's diatribe. Croft sees men differently, though he does characterize or "brand" Admiral Brand (Old Norse surname) and his brother as "Shabby fellows!" for stealing men from fellow captains (II, ch. 6). Croft's friend "Captain Brigden" carries the word "brig" (or ship) within his name, though the surname originally means "homestead by a bridge" (Old English *brycg*). Sir Archibald Drew is accompanied by a grandson starting a naval career. "Drew" probably comes from Old French *dru,* "sturdy." "Archibald" comes from Old Germanic via French ("Archambault," "Archbald"); *ercan* + *bald* = "truly bold." This man is *genuinely bold,* strong twice over. This name picks up and reinforces the "bald" Admiral Baldwin. These names contain ancient untitled sterling honor.

Naval characters appear dramatically at the novel's center. Captain James Benwick has a first name belonging to Austen's eldest brother (used most recently for a coachman in *Emma*). "Benwick," Anglo-Saxon *bean-wick,* means "bean place" or perhaps "grassy place." It is the name of a town in Cambridgeshire. "Harville" is a little grander, perhaps. It sounds French, but comes from Old English ("Herd" + *welle*), "place by a well." The Harvilles, poor and struggling, practice the true "old English hospitality" that the Elliots have forgotten (or never known), though the Harvilles are living in "rooms so small as none but those who invite from the heart could think capable of accommodating so many" (I, ch. 11). As in the name "Croft," naval officers' big-heartedness is attached to small accommodation.

Musgroves and Inland Rural Life

Mary Musgrove (née Elliot) feels she has bestowed honor upon mere Musgroves. Jane Austen had once known of a Miss Musgrove (5 September 1796; *Letters,* 8), and one of her own godmothers was Jane Musgrave. The name signifies "mouse-grove," though *mus* might refer to other animals like the weasel (*mustela*) that Charles Musgrove pursues. "Charlton Musgrove" in Somerset reflects the owner of the manor, Richard de Mucegros. That hamlet could have confirmed the choice of a name suitable to Somerset. Austen had already used her godmother's form of that surname in *The Watsons,* in which flirting Tom (originally "Charles") Musgrave is too lightweight to interest Emma Watson, though he attracts her sisters. In *Persuasion* the Musgrove young people have youthful vivacity and charm but seem lacking in intellect, depth, and steadiness. Austen uses "Musgrove" or "Musgrave" for slightly ambiguous rural characters.[61]

The family of Musgroves rose to possession of a motto, "*sans changer*"—"without change." But the Musgroves in *Persuasion* are changing. In touches like the veranda tacked on to the remodeled farmhouse and the girls' harp, we see awkward transition from old rural life. The senior Musgroves, an old-fashioned couple, are relatively uneducated, hospitable, and fond of domestic enjoyments. They possess a certain antique fortitude. They have lost a child to the war; they nearly lose an adult daughter to a serious accident. Unlike Sir Walter, they love their children. Watching that unromantic daily parental love can be hard on Anne, who has not experienced parental love since her mother's death.

The novel reflects and inspires a quiet nervous tension, as various disasters occur to the characters in illness, accident, or enemy action. Mary Favret in *War at a Distance* points out that the alarm and anxiety of a time of war color and infect the novel. Remarking on the recurring image of the fallen human figure in *Persuasion,* Favret suggests that the death of Dick Musgrove (whom Anne mentally rejects so heartily) may have "involved some sort of fall, because falls—to boys and young women—just happen throughout this novel."[62] The Musgroves in their rural peace are affected by the Napoleonic conflict; no inland refuge is unaffected by naval battles. The alarms of war combine with everyday concerns; anxiety seeps through and around time. Anne's fiercely mocking and surprisingly angry rejection of "stupid and unmanageable" Dick Musgrove, Favret argues, is a little more comprehensible if we realize that—according to the novel's time scheme—the lad's death happened not long after Anne had physically recovered from the illness that followed her loss of Wentworth. The intelligence of the boy's death "had worked its way to Uppercross, two years before" the time of the main action (I, ch. 6). So—two years ago Anne had heard of a death that took place at a time when she was just recovering from grief. The death of Dick would have underlined the possibility of Frederick Wentworth's death throughout the past two years. He could be dying on some foreign shore or at sea—could already be dead—even buried at sea. And Anne would not know. Anne doesn't want to hear more of the Musgroves' grief because it jangles her own. Wentworth is now in the same room with her but ignoring her—and already Anne knows he thought her "so altered he would not have known [her] again" (I, ch. 7).

When her lost lover is in close proximity, and Mrs. Musgrove is engaging his attention, Anne loses herself—or consoles herself—in the Kellynch mode. She already resented the unnecessary fuss made over Richard, her judgment blending with Sir Walter's tone to form a brutal narrative: "The Musgroves had had the ill fortune of a very troublesome, hopeless son; and the good fortune to lose him before he reached his twentieth year" (I, ch. 6). This judgment is in tune with her father's style of lethal contempt: "a pity they are not knocked on the head at once." Now, with Mrs. Musgrove separating her from Frederick, who is dutifully enacting sympathy, Anne seeks the relief of perfect contempt by focusing on Mrs. Musgrove's appearance: "He attended to her large fat sighings over the destiny of a son, whom alive nobody had cared for" (I, ch. 8). This is a complex instance of *style indirect libre*. Anne tries to catch herself: "Personal size and mental sorrow have certainly no necessary proportions. A large bulky figure has as good a right to be in deep affliction, as the most graceful set of limbs in the world." But she explodes again into a Kellynch aesthetic of offense: "There are unbecoming conjunctions . . . which taste cannot *tolerate*." Exactly so does Sir Walter judge—and judge of women: "He had counted eighty-seven women go by, one after another, without there being a *tolerable* face among them" (II, ch. 3, italics added).

The mental insulting of Mrs. Musgrove is one of the few moments when we see Anne as her father's daughter—and it is a low moment. Anne has brought something of Kellynch with her to Uppercross. This is a moment of painfully blended anachronism, with a heroine caught in the phase of first love eight years ago *and* in the pain of the present, reflecting her conditioning of painful endurance with her father's voice in her ears. Anne is guiltless of *speaking* her contempt, unlike Emma sharply putting down Miss Bates—but both characters are motivated by angry jealousy that they take out on the least armed female target. Anne relieves herself according to family habit. Her disparagement of stupid "Dick" inwardly crystallizes a permanent anger at the status of Walter's stillborn son, important enough to be mentioned in the *Baronetage,* while she—a living daughter—has been so much neglected.

If we read back from Anne's interior outburst to Sir Walter's disparaging speeches, we may discern that the baronet hides from himself his own rage of disappointment and a kind of postponed mourning. After all, he lost his wife and though he perpetually searches for beautiful women he has not acquired one. Efforts to marry again have apparently been rebuffed for financial reasons. While time drifts on, other men—despite imperfections of which their mirrors should inform them—are gaining honors. All *four* Elliots—Sir Walter, Elizabeth, Mary, and Anne—are responding in different ways to a similar fear of being left out, unwanted, passed over.

In Bath, Anne is most happy to see Mrs. Musgrove again, because Mrs. Musgrove wants to see her. "Mrs. Musgrove's real affection had been won by her [Anne's] usefulness when they were in distress." Anne now participates in the family affection and rejoices in it. "It was heartiness, and warmth, and a sincerity which Anne delighted in the more, from the sad want of such blessings at home" (II, ch. 10). *Now* Anne can express coherently what Musgroves offer that Elliots lack—but she is no longer on the outside looking in.

When he appears at Uppercross, Wentworth is an uncanny creature of resurrection. Being alive is an attribute not to be taken for granted. Frederick talks in a rational joking way about dangerous experiences—including the possibility that the wretched ship of his first command might easily have gone to the bottom. "'I should only have been a gallant Captain Wentworth, in a small paragraph at one corner of the newspapers; and being lost in only a sloop, nobody would have thought about me.' Anne's shudderings were to herself, alone" (I, ch. 8). But her retrospective horror and complex grief blending past and present are interrupted by Mrs. Musgrove's lamentations. Anne cannot always be passively shot at by life; she must fight back. Seeing Wentworth alive does nothing to repair emotional loss, heightened by jealous apprehension of fresh loss (as the Musgrove girls flirt with the new Wentworth and he with them). Anne's responses are colored by recognition of the random possibility of death. Death and loss render her aggressive. Anne, who has partly died but cannot be mourned for, wishes to delete from significance all her rivals—including the dead Musgrove sibling openly mourned for. She does not lose outer self-control. What Anne loses in the early scenes at Uppercross is *perspective*—one of the great themes of this novel.

Charles Hayter: Representation and the Art of Perspective

Mary Musgrove looks down on her husband's cousins the Hayters. Charles Hayter, a clergyman, is heir of Winthrop. The walk to Winthrop is undertaken by Louisa in order to reunite Henrietta with Charles Hayter, leaving Wentworth for herself. "Hayter," probably from *atte heyt,* refers to one living upon or near a hill, though it sounds like the word for "hedge," *haigh*—and an important hedgerow figures in the scene. The most striking fact about Charles Hayter's name, however, is that it is the name of an artist. Charles Hayter (1761–1835) was a well-known painter of miniatures. Janine Barchas observes that the introduction of a "Charles Hayter" stresses the importance of a miniature within the novel, when Captain Harville is commissioned to reset a "small miniature painting" of Benwick.[63]

Charles Hayter was the undoubted expert on the "two inches of Ivory." In 1813 "Mr. Hayter, Portrait Painter (In Miniatures and Crayons)" published *An Introduction to Perspective, Adapted to the Capacities of Youth, In a Series of Pleasing and Familiar Dialogues.* The work on perspective also contains *instructions* on painting miniatures on ivory. In an oft-quoted letter of 1816 Jane Austen wrote to her nephew James Edward comically protesting her innocence of theft in the disappearance of "two Chapters & a Half" of his manuscript:

> What should I do with your strong, manly, spirited Sketches, full of Variety & Glow?—How could I possibly join them to the little bit (two Inches wide) of Ivory on which I work with so fine a Brush, as produces little effect after much labour? (16 December 1816; *Letters,* 323)

This ironic allusion to herself as a mere miniaturist—in a letter written on her own birthday!—should be set beside the commentary of the literal miniaturist, Charles Hayter. He forcefully addresses his reader on the subject:

> There should be but *one* distinction between large and small pictures, namely, "the difference of their size"; to prove which I have only to refer you to Mr. Bone's enamels . . . the small dimensions of a work ought not to lessen its importance, for a good miniature must contain all that a good life-siz'd picture should, except *quantity.*[64]

(*Bone* probably amused Austen.) Here follows detailed advice on ivory and brushes. Hayter also urges his student to work diligently: "Wait patiently and attentively for the completion of your picture, before you indulge your flatterers with the opportunity of praising you. It is an intoxicating tribute, and should be received with great caution."[65] Austen subtly turns the tables on James Edward, offering him the "intoxicating tribute" before his work is finished. It seems likely that she was reading Hayter's little treatise in the year preceding this birthday (her last) when she picks up the issue of the "two Inches of Ivory." She knows that her works are art, possessing all the qualities that could be desired, except mere "*quantity.*" Throughout *Persuasion* she has been deliberately working in a very stripped-down mode.

In his illustrated work Charles Hayter discusses composition related to perspective: the horizon line, the position of the eye. He explains the "*bird's eye* view" or, as young Eliza suggests, "a balloonist's."[66] A drawing or painting, Hayter says, has a kind of fourth wall or window through which the artist views the picture, the "transparent plane." Hayter advises, "in every thing you draw, you are to conceive you are drawing, on a glass or transparent plane, *objects* which are supposed to be on the other side."[67]

Austen herself is an expert in metaphorical perspective and indicates that she knowingly deals with the "transparent plane," with points of view and differing sight lines. She has already excelled in the use of perspectives. In *Persuasion* she draws the different perspectives quickly and clearly into complex relations. Human perspective on life is overtly discussed:

> Anne had not wanted this visit to Uppercross, to learn that a removal from one set of people to another, though at a distance of only three miles, will often include a total change of conversation, opinion and idea. She had never been staying there before, without being struck by it, or without wishing that other Elliots could have her advantage in seeing how unknown, or unconsidered there, were the affairs which at Kellynch-hall were treated as of such general publicity and pervading interest. (I, ch. 6)

Changing moral sight lines may be painful but must happen when vantage points are altered. The wrench is better than deluding oneself in the belief that an individual view is universal, that everyone shares one single perspective. Slippage of perspective is indicated in the introduction of the miniature of Benwick into the narrative, for he "gives himself away" in effigy twice, to a different object and a different vision. The portrait of Benwick remains the same object, while the eyes that will look upon it, bestowing meaning, change altogether. Fanny Harville's viewpoint having vanished, there remains that of Louisa, who has shifted her ground most painfully to let go the vision of Wentworth and accommodate a vision of Benwick.

A number of references to seeing through windows and to lines of sight are found in *Persuasion,* in which *looking* is a master motif.[68] And how do we see? Often through the transparent plane. The plane is not always perfectly transparent, nor the vision entirely clear. On her last evening at Uppercross, Anne looks through the windows of a forsaken and dreary house: "A small thick rain almost blotting out the very few objects ever to be discerned from the windows." Next day in Lady Russell's carriage she can "look an adieu to the cottage" through "the misty glasses" of the coach windows (II, ch. 1). External influences may not impede transparency. Sitting by a window in Molland's, Anne looks out the window at the rainy street and descries "most decidedly and distinctly" Captain Wentworth walking down it. But next day Lady Russell, rather than noticing Wentworth walking down Pultney Street, appears engrossed in looking out for "drawing-room window-curtains"—fabrications that deliberately render a plane not transparent but opaque (II, ch. 7). Mary looks out of the inn window and sees Mr. Elliott and Mrs. Clay, despite Anne's protestations that Mr. Elliot is away (II, ch. 10). In *Persuasion,* what is seen through a window is reality, if limited reality. But the transparent plane cannot alter the perversity of objects on the other side. Questions of vision, perspective, and proportion are raised in the amusing encounter with Admiral Croft looking into a print shop window:

> "But what a thing here is, by way of a boat. Do look at it. Did you ever see the like? What queer fellows your fine painters must be, to think that any body would venture their lives in such a shapeless old cockleshell as that. And yet, here are two gentlemen stuck up in it mightily at their ease, and looking about them at the rocks and mountains, as if they were not to be upset the next moment, which they certainly must be." (II, ch. 6)

We don't know whether the picture is a contemporary work of scenery and sensibility—or even a print of one of Raphael's Hampton Court cartoons, a New Testament theme representing the disciples fishing in a boat.[69] According to Sir Joshua Reynolds, "How much the great style exacts from its professors to conceive and represent their subjects in a poetical manner, not confined to mere matter of fact, may be seen in the Cartoons of Raffaelle."[70] Admiral Croft, looking through his own "transparent plane," is slightly perturbed by loss of "mere matter of fact" and a threat to stability. Croft cannot even look into a print shop without seeing the possibility of accident and overthrow—offered in abundance in this novel in Austen's own picture of life, a story stressing the ever-present possibility of disaster.

The introduction into the novel of a "Charles Hayter" is Austen's secret smile at her own secret understanding of art and perspective. Charles Hayter the character never speaks in the narrative but is known through the various perspectives of others. Nobody possesses the perfect command over space and time that renders one perspective or point of view totally coherent or satisfactory. Anne Elliot herself has fragmented and vertiginous points of view. And time is very odd—in a novel in which the hero's name contains a verb in the past tense. Is anything finished or begun? Is the war actually finished? As Mary Favret says, "Anne's love for Wentworth, in fact, has to break through such false peace and tidy chronology into the stir and roar of a messier, potentially traumatic history."[71] The novel ends with a prospect of unfinished war and unpredictable suffering that yet must be anticipated but cannot be controlled.

Mysterious Mrs. Smith and Verbal Art

Anne's old friend Mrs. Smith, crippled and poor, is a treasury of nominal penumbra. Through her we gain an impression of Bath's variety and perspectives. Her landlady is "Mrs. Speed" (speed can be helpful to an invalid). Nurse Rooke (also called "Mrs. Rooke" as a courtesy title) attends both Mrs. Smith and Colonel Wallis's wife in childbirth and lying-in. Nurse Rooke, who sounds like a large member of the crow family, does not "rook" her patients in fleecing them, but does extract money from them for charitable uses. Useful, efficient, self-reliant, neither idealistic nor romantically attached, this working woman knows her own value. She also comforts patients by telling them the news, putting them back in the social picture. Nurse Rooke picks up information and disperses it from house to house, as crows or rooks pick up shiny objects and place them elsewhere.

Although Mrs. Smith cannot get about, she benefits from news. For Anne the concert was a momentous singular event, but Mrs. Smith knows more about such a regular feature of Bath life. Mrs. Smith presumes the Ibbotsons were there, and "Old Lady Mary Maclean" who

14. Thomas Rowlandson, *The Concert* (1798). From *The Comforts of Bath*. Photograph: Bridgeman Art Library.

"never misses" (II, ch. 9). The Ibbotsons' Norse name suggests northern origin. "Maclean" is yet another Scots name, derived from the Gaelic: "Son of the servant of St. John." Lady Mary Maclean is another respectable wealthy upper-class migrant from the "Celtic fringe." In her widowhood Lady Mary came to Bath in order to save money. "The little Durands were there, I conclude . . . with their mouths open to catch the music; like unfledged sparrows. . . . They never miss a concert." These Durands are probably two aging ladies, whose persistent attendance exhibits their *endurance*. Mrs. Smith's verbal caricature resembles Rowlandson's visual caricature of Bath concerts (fig. 14).

Mrs. Smith herself is apparently of Scottish ancestry. When Anne was sent to boarding school after the death of her mother, "Miss Hamilton, now Mrs. Smith, had shewn her kindness in one of those periods of her life when it had been most valuable" (II, ch. 5). "Hamilton" has been Anglo-Saxon ("settlement on a flat-topped hill"), but since the Middle Ages the name is predominantly Scottish. Medieval Hamiltons intermarried with the Stuarts. The second Earl of Arran, a Hamilton, was Regent of Scotland during Mary Stuart's infancy. He sheltered Mary in 1568 after the queen made her escape from prison in an island on Loch

Leven. The third Marquess of Arran, ardent royalist, was made Duke of Hamilton by Charles I. That first Duke of Hamilton was captured by the "Roundheads" at the Battle of Preston, taken to London, and beheaded. His successor to the dukedom was killed defending Charles II in the Battle of Worcester. The fourth duke of Hamilton supported the Jacobite cause and died in a duel. Hamiltons (not excluding the Sir William who collected volcanoes and married Emma Hart) seem energetic, loyal, and ill-fated.

Mrs. Smith is not above reproach in her plan to put to personal use Mr. Elliot's courtship of her friend. But this former Miss Hamilton, another Scot eking out her resources in Bath, along with Lady Mary Maclean, the Dowager Lady Dalrymple (and the Elliots themselves), is in peculiarly grim circumstances:

> She was a widow and poor. Her husband had been extravagant and at his death, about two years before, had left his affairs dreadfully involved. She had had difficulties of every sort to contend with and in addition to those distresses had been afflicted with a severe rheumatic fever, which, finally settling in her legs, had made her for the present a cripple. (II, ch. 5)

Once she realizes Anne will not marry William Elliot, Mrs. Smith relates his part in her story. Mr. Elliot, her husband's best friend, led him, she claims, into extravagance. Named as executor in Mr. Smith's will, Mr. Elliot refused to act, thus leaving Mrs. Smith without resources, too poor "to purchase the assistance of the law" (II, ch. 9). This account turns Anne altogether against the charms of Mr. Elliot. (Later, her husband will help in straightening out Mrs. Smith's affairs.) The commonness of "Smith," pointed in the case of Harriet Smith, attracts comment within the novel. Sir Walter Elliot loathes the little vulgar name: "A widow Mrs. Smith,—and who was her husband? One of the five thousand Mr. Smiths whose names are to be met with every where" (II, ch. 5). Yet this Mrs. Smith is unique. In financial straits and poor health, she maintains her vivacity and eventually speaks the story of her wrongs.

Charlotte Smith, poet and novelist, had dared to speak of her own wrongs. Through the perverse incompetence of her husband and a legal error of her father-in-law, she lost her fortune and was hard pressed to support her children. Charlotte (née Turner) made a name as a writer. Subscribers to *Elegiac Sonnets* numbered eminent writers, including

Burney and Cowper. Her novels were popular, although her more radical works were less well received in the mid-1790s. The 1797 edition of *Elegiac Sonnets* includes an engraving based on her portrait by Opie (fig. 15). Under the picture is a verse inscription:

> Oh! Time has Changed me since you saw me last,
> And heavy Hours with Time's deforming Hand,
> Have written strange Defeatures in my Face.[72]

"Defeatures" may have influenced Keats's "misfeature" in his 1818 sonnet "The Human Seasons."[73] Charlotte Smith, like Anne Elliot, has undergone change, sorrow as well as time revising her appearance. Charlotte Turner Smith's end was indeed melancholy. A Chancery suit leached away the family money. Increasing illness and sharp poverty hampered her writing. By 1798, as she complains in the preface to *Marchmont,* she did not even have access to books. In pain from gout and arthritis, she praises the kind generosity of her "physician at Bath" for "every skilful exertion which I could not purchase" as he tried to save the life of her dying daughter and to attend herself.[74] Charlotte Smith died in poverty in 1806, some months before the Chancery suit wound to an end.

Like Jocelyn Harris, I certainly believe (and have long taught) that the poems Anne recollects during the autumnal walk to Winthrop come from *Elegiac Sonnets* and that the sufferings of the heroine's fictional friend reflect those of Mrs. Smith the novelist.[75] Harris does not note the fact that both Charlotte Smith and Anne Elliot are written on by the unkind "Time and heavy Hours": "You were so altered he would not have known you again" (*Persuasion,* I, ch. 7). "Oh! Time has changed me since you saw me last," exclaims the poet—aligning herself with the battered sailors and ugly women condemned by Sir Walter. Austen's own opinion of Charlotte Smith's works is higher than modern critics have been willing to understand. Smith's narrative techniques offered valuable models to the young Austen. Smith is a strong predecessor in expressing the unorthodox belief that a woman should not marry without love. In her last completed novel Jane Austen inscribes a sadly playful wish that the author to whom Austen knew she owed a debt, the Mrs. Smith who did indeed go to Bath, could have been cured there, finding friends who would restore her income and welcome her companionship. Sir Walter Elliot has never heard of *that* Mrs. Smith whom Jane Austen loved—the sort of Mrs. Smith who is *not* "to be met with everywhere."

P. Condé sculp.

Oh! Time has Changed me since you saw me last,
And heavy Hours with Time's deforming Hand,
Have written strange Defeatures in my Face.

Published May 15th 1797. by Cadell and Davies Strand.

15. Pierre Condé, *Charlotte Smith (née Turner)* (1797). Engraved from a portrait by John Opie (1792). Photograph: © National Portrait Gallery, London.

FIRST NAMES IN *PERSUASION*

Many of the Christian names in *Persuasion* are Austen standards: an elder sister Elizabeth (as in *The Watsons*); a difficult sister Mary (as in *Pride and Prejudice*); an authoritative cousin William. Mr. William Walter Elliot discards "Walter" but retains the conquering Whiggish "William" without the valor of William Price. The baronet's unusual first name sounds like a family inheritance from Elizabethan times. Sir Walter Raleigh appears in Austen's "History of England" as held in "great veneration" if imperfectly praiseworthy as "an enemy of the noble Essex" (*Juvenilia*, 186). Raleigh risked his life at sea and in battle, fighting against Spain or exploring South America; he was everything actively patriotic that Frederick Wentworth is and our misnamed "Sir Walter" is *not*. Elizabeth Elliot, haughty and vain, has too long been Virgin Queen of Kellynch, a cold maiden "out" for "thirteen revolving frosts." Sir Walter and his daughter are stubborn living anachronisms, stuck in a mock-Elizabethan diorama.

Other names repeat those of earlier novels. There is—or was—a delicate and lovable Fanny (already dead). There is an apparently sober, slightly weak (if poetic) James. Three personages are named "Charles": Charles Musgrove, Tory squire given to field sports; his little son, the Charles who dislocates his collarbone; and cousin Charles Hayter, clergyman heir of Winthrop. The reiterated royalist name seems to allude to a pro-Stuart past, indicating the politics of Musgroves and Hayters.[76] Mrs. Smith's deceased husband was yet another "Charles"— which does seem rather too much of a good thing. The first name of Lady Russell's deceased husband is "Henry." Henrietta Musgrove's first name was last used for Miss Bates. But, as Jocelyn Harris notes, the name of the Duke of Monmouth's mistress, Lady Henrietta Wentworth, is evoked within a text that presents us with a "Henrietta" and several honorable "Wentworths."[77]

Henrietta's sister Louisa has a slightly more modern Continental first name, last used as the first name of Mrs. Hurst (née Bingley). Admiral Croft cannot remember Louisa's first name, which seems to him new-fangled: "I always forget her Christian name. . . . I wish young ladies had not such a number of fine Christian names, I should never be out, if they were all Sophys or something of that sort" (II, ch. 6). "Louisa" is not beyond the Austen pale; Jane's brother Edward's daughter Louisa was born in 1804. "Sophia" meaning "Wisdom" is appropriate for brave and sensible Mrs. Croft. That name, once equally an import, had become familiar. Admiral Croft uses the affectionate English diminutive "Sophy," breaking with traditional etiquette in referring to his wife not only by her first name but even by her nickname. Yet we don't look down on him for this breach. *Persuasion* favors the colloquial and informal—at least when backed by genuine simplicity and affection.

Austen takes care in naming major characters in *Persuasion*, but at the third-tier level when in want of a name she tends to call everybody "Charles" or "Mary." Wentworth was nearly asked to ferry a Lady Mary Grierson with her children. Mrs. Smith's landlady Mrs. Speed appears to be a "Mary," unless that is the name of her maidservant. A Lady Mary Maclean was presumably a member of the concert audience. We don't know Mrs. Smith's own first name. Yet why should that not be "Mary"? In a ballad known as "The Four Marys," "Mary Hamilton" is the apocryphal doomed lady-in-waiting to Mary of Scots, probably conflated with the real Scottish Mary Hamilton, lady-in-waiting to Czarina Catherine, executed in Russia in 1719. Hamiltons' lives are touched with disaster.

A few unusual first names appear. Pagan "Penelope," name of Odysseus's faithful wife, earlier used for Emma Watson's disagreeable and contriving sister, is now the property of the middle-class widow looking for a mate. Penelope Clay cannot afford to be faithful to the memory of her dead husband—nor to Sir Walter. She tires of throwing time and attention away on him and on Elizabeth (perhaps Penelope's true erotic admirer). A "Lady Alicia," blue-blooded model of meanness, happily for Elizabeth set an example by not inviting relatives to dinner (II, ch. 10). Biblical names are for servants. Mary Musgrove's nursery maid is "Jemima" (Hebrew, "dove" or "bright day"), name of Job's eldest daughter born after his ordeal. "Jemima" was the name of niece Anna's first infant. "As I wish very much to see *your* Jemima, I am sure you will like to see *my* Emma," Jane wrote (December 1815–January 1816; *Letters*, 310). Perhaps Austen registers discontent with the biblical attachment of Evangelical Benjamin Lefroy. Literature associates this name with servitude. In Wollstonecraft's *The Wrongs of Women* (1798), Jemima, illegitimate and abused, becomes an attendant at a madhouse. In the cancelled chapter 10 of *Persuasion*'s second volume, a "Stephen" serves the Crofts in Bath. Had Austen forgotten the maiden name of the heroine's mother—"Stevenson"? Or is she underlining its commonness?

Hitherto Austen has used "Anne" for subordinate and inferior characters. Silent Anne De Bourgh and vulgar Nancy Steele are both beginning to wither on the vine—as Anne Elliot feels she is doing. Shyness, weakness, social incapacity, and even aging go with an "Anne." Anne Thorpe (of the thick ankles) doesn't get taken for a drive. Anne Taylor, like Anne Elliot, is no longer in her first youth when she finds her second spring. Anne Elliot bears the name of a major female saint and the last Stuart monarch. But—in marked contrast to Emma—she is a queen ignored. A woman of quiet strength, Anne is often left out, her best qualities mishandled as exploitable resources. A middle child, Anne has been easy to overlook, but not to deceive. Younger Mary was deceived, kept ignorant of William Elliot's failed or nonexistent courtship of Elizabeth and of Anne's broken engagement to Wentworth. Mary's constant fear that she is being kept out of things has some psychological justification.

There was a famous "Ann Elliot," an actress (1743–1769), mistress of the dramatist Arthur Murphy, and later of Frederick, Duke of Cumberland (fig. 16). She is recollected in the *Life of Arthur Murphy* (1811) by Jessé Foot, whose description makes her seem a little like Austen's Emma: "Somewhat above the middle stature . . . her eyes were dark hazle [*sic*] and her hair a beautiful brown." Foot memorably remarks, "Every thing about her was sylphic and enchanting."[78] The enchantment of the short-lived graceful Ann floats over the heroine of *Persuasion,* a woman of "slender form" with "delicate features and mild dark eyes" (*Persuasion,* I, ch. 8; ch. 1). This is not how Anne sees herself, but the actress suggests the "sylphic" young woman Frederick first saw.

The name "Frederick" (attached historically to a real "Ann Elliot") appears in a variant version in a story by twelve-year-old Jane Austen— her first story in *Volume the First.* "Frederic and Elfrida" offers another case of a postponed wedding; Elfrida suffers from too great a delicacy to come to the point. Years fly by. Only when Elfrida sees that Frederic is attracted to a much younger girl, who treats her as "little less than an old woman" does "the horror" overcome her inhibition:

> The instant she had the first ideas of such an attachment, she flew to Frederic and in a manner truly heroick, spluttered out to him her intention of being married the next Day. . . . he not being the least terrified boldly replied,
>
> "Damme Elfrida—*you* may be married tomorrow but *I* won't."
>
> This answer distressed her too much for her delicate Constitution. She accordingly fainted and was in such a hurry to have a suc-

Miss Ann. Elliot.

16. Anon., *Miss Ann Elliot* (1811). From Jesse Foot, *The Life of Arthur Murphy, Esq.* Reproduced from the original held by the Department of Special Collections of the Hesburgh Libraries of the University of Notre Dame.

cession of fainting fits, that she had scarcely patience enough to recover from one before she fell into another.

 Tho', in any threatening Danger to his Life or Liberty, Frederic
was as bold as brass yet in other respects his heart was as soft as cotton and immediately on hearing of the dangerous way Elfrida was
in, he flew to her and finding her better than he had been taught to
expect, was united to her Forever—. (*Juvenilia*, 11–12)

This comical narrative forecasts the story of *Persuasion*—the story
of an engaged couple who cannot marry because of the lady's nice con-
siderations. Growing older, the woman has to see her beloved's sexual
attention turning to another younger object—until she intervenes and
changes the situation. The young Jane Austen who wrote "Frederic and
Elfrida" can have had little idea of the passion and grief within such a
situation. The author of *Persuasion* knows. *Persuasion's* story concerns a
woman who broke off an engagement not out of false delicacy but because she was persuaded the marriage was not for her lover's good. This
heroine never faints and cannot bluntly voice her feelings. Her inter-
vention is unintentional—Anne shows her worth at the time of Louisa's
accident. Slowly, Frederick Wentworth, knowing nothing of the ordeal
Anne has undergone, recognizes that he still desires her.

 The name "Frederick" has a special resonance. In Smith's *Emmeline*,
Delamere's handsome youth, his impetuosity, his ardor were qualities
the ironic contrarian reader Jane Austen insisted on seeing as superior
to the virtues of supposedly preferable Godolphin. The association of
this name with impetuous desire extends to the teenaged "Frederica" in
Lady Susan. Qualities young Jane liked in Delamere are given to the impetuous and courageous Frederick Wentworth. Between Elfrida's Frederic and the mature Captain Wentworth we find the privileged swagger-
ing Captain Frederick Tilney, heir apparent of Northanger Abbey. He is
certainly "bold as brass," if "soft as cotton" in the presence of his father.
In all instances of a "Frederick" Jane Austen seems to investigate what
masculinity might be and how women see it. Smith's Delamere was an
interesting avenue to the contemplation of erotic males. And in *Persuasion* the name is the best tribute to the author of *Emmeline*—herself an
apparition in the pages of the haunting story of death and resurrection.

Names in *Sanditon*

SURNAMES IN *SANDITON*

Heywoods and Parkers

Variously spelled "Haywood" or "Heywood," the heroine's locative surname comes from Old English *haeg* + *wudu:* "enclosed wood" or stand
of oak trees. Several small Midland towns are called "Haywood." The
name evokes simple "hay." Mr. Heywood, "Hale" and "Gentlemanlike,"
first seen "among his Haymakers" suggests the sturdiness of Old England and the English rural life (*Sanditon, Later Manuscripts,* ch. 1).
But that opening can also remind us of the comic opening of "Henry
and Eliza," where the parental landowners are first seen in the hay field:

> As Sir George and Lady Harcourt were superintending the Labours
> of their Haymakers, rewarding the industry of some by smiles of ap-
> probation, and punishing the idleness of others, by a cudgel." (*Vol-
> ume the First, Juvenilia,* 38)

It is as if young Austen parodied in advance that image of Farmer
George rewarding the hay maker. In this last novel, Mr. Heywood seems
deliberately overdone as an English rural type—John Bull making hay,
a parodic Farmer George. A prodigy of begetting, he fathered fourteen
children, vying with the Willmots of "Edgar and Emma." Deconstruc-
tion in "Henry and Eliza" of the benevolent landowner (with knowing
reference to the forced nature of rural labor) casts its playful shadow—
or streak of light—over the opening of *Sanditon.* We should not readily
determine that the "point" of the unfinished novel is simply to make us
appreciate traditional values and rural life, as against modern speculations by the barren seashore.

The most celebrated eighteenth-century "Haywood" or "Heywood"
is the novelist Eliza Haywood, author of *Love in Excess* (1719), *The History of Miss Betsy Thoughtless* (1751), and other works. Eliza Haywood
specialized in delineation of the passions, the power of Eros, and female
experience of constraint. A name so strongly associated with fiction
prompts us to look at *Sanditon* as a fiction about fiction. Fiction figures
within the story itself, not only in a beachside library and an evocation
of *Camilla* but also in Sir Edward Denham's ravings in favor of (male)
erotic passion in modern narrative (ch. 8). Haywoodian "love in excess"

is parodically represented. If *Persuasion* is a response to Scott's critique, *Sanditon* is a riposte.

Yet, rather than fixing its gaze upon poetry or prose, this novel focuses on the fictions of capitalism. Advertising is everywhere—of clothes, of houses, of seaside resorts. Rather than passion, people search for pleasure and money. After the generosity and courage of characters in *Persuasion,* who more than sufficiently counteract the mean, it is disconcerting to come into such self-centered postwar materialism. Advertising to do with health is commercially dominant. Mrs. Griffith, educator and guardian of a young heiress, competently fends off others' attempts to meddle with her charge's health. Just as we are thinking this admirable we find that Mrs. Griffith makes an exception "in favour of some Tonic Pills, which a Cousin of her own had a Property in" (ch. 11).

The Parkers' name suggests staid fixity in a bounded location, but the couple is moving when we first see them, just before their carriage overturns in the "rough Lane" outside the Haywoods' home. The name "Parker" originally indicated a man who enclosed land or "man in charge of a park." In Austen's time the most notable "Parker" was aristocratic John Parker of Saltram, created first Earl of Morley in September 1815.[79] Austen seems to have become acquainted with Frances, his second wife, Countess of Morley, through Henry, who may have visited Saltram in Jane's lifetime.[80] But the most interesting "Parker" with the Morley title is a man of the Tudor period.

Henry Parker, tenth Baron Morley (ca. 1480–1556), was educated in the house of Lady Margaret Beaufort. Like other powerful "Beauforts," Lady Margaret descended from one of the bastards of John of Gaunt born to Katherine Swynford. Margaret had married Edmund Tudor, and after his early death remained a Tudor supporter. Formidable and pious, she was praised by Henry Parker to the Catholic princess who became Queen Mary I. Baron Morley had much to endure under the rule of Henry VIII. A supporter of the old religion, he was required to furnish armed men to put down the Pilgrimage of Grace. Connected with the Boleyns, Henry Parker was driven, during the period of Anne Boleyn's trial in 1536, to convict his own son Lord Rochfort of misbehavior with the queen and hence of treason (ensuring Rochfort's beheading). The presence of the name "Parker" relating to "the Anne Boleyn complex" so important to Jane Austen is striking in combination with another name with similar associations in the case of Lady Denham (née Brereton) (see below).

We may surmise that *Sanditon*'s Mr. Parker, an antihero confident in his own well-meaning, will be careless of the welfare of others, even committing some act that looks like betrayal, as well as finding himself entrapped, betrayed, and ruined. A certain extravagance associated with the Parkers of Saltram suggests that Austen's Mr. Parker, if faithful as a husband (unlike famous contemporary Parkers), will come to financial grief. In Saltram a delightfully furnished Chinese bedroom had a (non-Chinese) marble fireplace, bearing images of bears robbing beehives and the motto "Take what you want says God. Take it and Pay for it."[81] This might be a motto for the Parkers of Saltram—and the Parkers of Sanditon.

Austen's Mr. Parker is the latest in her series of British land enclosers and land exploiters. Rather than privatizing agricultural land, Mr. Parker is treating sea and shore as a kind of "park"—his site for development and takeover. His admiring wife is incapable of argument, and the rest of his family (except his brother Sidney) does what they can to assist. This new form of "imparking" requires mobility and communication— the Parkers live in a flutter of newspapers, letters, advertisements, and searches, wheels a-rolling and post a-flying. (They seem to be waiting for the telegraph to arrive—as it soon will.) Their business and bustle may reflect Jane's observations of her brother Henry and his banking business. Its flurry of success quickly ran into failure before Waterloo year was out. Henry was a bankrupt in March 1816. Henry's crashed bank took a lot of other family money with it.[82] The Austen family's game of "Speculation" had led to defeat.

Hollies and Briars: Lady Denham's Prickliness

Mr. Parker's coadjutor in his busyness is a lady with a very Anglo-Saxon surname: "valley homestead or farm" (*denu* + *ham*). The surname was famous chiefly on account of John Denham the poet of "Cooper's Hill." Lady Denham possesses a real park, spoils of her second marriage to now deceased Sir Harry Denham of Denham Park: "For the Title, it was to be supposed that she had married" (ch. 3). Late in life she became a "Lady." Her maiden name was Brereton—surname of her young relative Clara. Anglo-Saxon "Brereton" (*brer* + *ton*) is a farm amid the briars. Lady Denham's family seems to have arisen from the briar patch. The only notable real-life ancestor would have been the William Brereton who was executed at the time of the execution of Francis Weston— and of Parker's son Rochfort—on trumped-up charges of adultery with

Anne Boleyn. William Brereton probably had no flirtatious link with the queen; his beheading seems to have been ensured by Thomas Cromwell as a payback. William Brereton had been deeply involved in taking over and pocketing the wealth of dissolved abbeys. Here again in Jane Austen's fiction, a character profits from ruthless ancestors who found their advantage in the Dissolution. Lady Denham, solid Saxon with an eye to the main chance, has something in common with General Tilney and his ancestors.

Lady Denham's first husband, Mr. Hollis, was "an elderly Man" when he married. The most interesting "Hollis" of Austen's time was Thomas Brand; of low birth, he accompanied Thomas Hollis on the Grand Tour and was left Hollis's property in 1774, taking his friend's surname. He spent money for support of groups promoting science, political reform, and Dissent, and bequeathed all his Hollis property to a friend in 1804 (*ODNB*). This example of homosexual emancipation exhibits property movement according to choice, without reference to bloodlines or marriage. Such transfer aside from bonds of blood or obligation connects with the position of childless Lady Denham, inheretrix of property that she can dispose of at whim. But her deceased husband in acquiring his wealth seems to reflect the Tudor Sir William Hollis (or Holles) who snapped up property by tricky business deals, making loans and then suddenly foreclosing. (He obtained lands from Sir William Fitzwilliam and Sir Thomas Elliot, among others.) Though anti-Protestant, Holles profited from the Dissolution. He "speculated in the lands of dissolved religious houses" (*ODNB*). Perhaps one of Lady Denhams's Hollis in-laws will be one too many for the Parkers.

On her first husband's death "Mrs. Hollis" acquired all his property, including "a large share of the Parish of Sanditon, with Manor &Mansion House" (ch. 3). When she marries Sir Harry Denham of Denham Park she is "too wary to put anything out of her own Power," and her second husband "cd. not succeed in the veiws [*sic*] of permanently enriching his family" (ch. 3, *Later Manuscripts*, 416). The Hollis property remains, still hers to bequeath as she wishes. No entail, will, or promise binds her. She is perfectly free to speculate with her property—even to waste it.

The final lines of the manuscript present images of the two dead husbands in Lady Denham's "sitting room." Dead Sir Harry is represented by a "whole-length Portrait of a stately [originally "portly"] Gentleman, which placed over the Mantelpiece caught the eye immediately,"

while dead Mr. Hollis is represented only in "one among many miniatures in another part of the room." In death they are divided. "Poor
Mr. Hollis!—It was impossible not to feel him hardly used; to be
obliged to stand back in his own House [originally "room"] & see the
best place by the fire constantly occupied by Sir H. D." (ch. 12). Lady
Denham values the dead men according to their status alone. It will
serve her right to lose Mr. Hollis's "own House."

"Hollis" is "Hollies," a descriptive locative, "dwelling by the holly
trees." A certain prickly quality may be expected of a Hollis—and a
doubly prickly quality in Lady Denham, formerly "Hollis" (née "Brereton"). She is scratchy as briars and prickly as hollies. In the manuscript
we can follow Austen's understanding of that point when she describes
the fencing of the grounds of Sanditon House with "rows of old Thorns
& Hollies." (Hollies, valued of old as winter cattle feed, might abound
in ancient hedges.) Austen thought better of that phrase, and drew
a line through "& Hollies" as overegging the pudding (ch. 12, *Later
Manuscripts,* 551).

Lady Denham is the oldest active person in Austen's oeuvre—
seventy years old at the time *Sanditon* opens. Physically lively and mentally commanding, she is Mr. Parker's partner and chief investor in
what we might call "Sanditon Limited." Concerned with making the
seaside resort a money-making operation, Lady Denham possesses inadequate economic insight. She desires numerous visitors to reward her
investment—but without any corresponding increase in local demand
for service and foodstuffs, which will raise wages and prices. Mr. Parker
endeavors in vain to explain to Lady Denham the harmony of market
forces. (Parker, probably like Jane Austen, seems to have read some
Adam Smith.)

> "My dear Madam, they can only raise the price of consumeable
> Articles, by such an extraordinary Demand for them & such a dif-
> fusion of Money among us, as must do us more Good than harm.—
> Our Butchers & Bakers & Traders in general cannot get rich with-
> out bringing Prosperity to *us.*—If *they* do not gain, our rents must be
> insecure—& in proportion to their profit must be ours eventually in
> the increased value of our Houses." (ch. 6)

Lady Denham obstinately clings to the values she knows: "But I should
not like to have Butcher's meat raised, though—& I shall keep it down

as long as I can." She resists bringing in a resident physician: "It wd. be only encouraging our Servants & the Poor to fancy themselves ill, if there was a Dr. at hand" (ch. 6). Enticing invalid visitors to Sanditon while banning medical attendants, she plans to fob invalids off with the use (for a fee) of her deceased husband's exercise machine (his "Chamber Horse") and the milk of her asses. Lady Denham, self-willed and prickly, comically combines grasping conservatism with an expansionist greedy capitalism. As Charlotte decides, Lady Denham is "Sordid" (ch. 7). Her boasts about her own perfect health may be hubristic. Lady Denham might suddenly depart this life, leaving the finances of Sanditon up in the air. The death of Mr. Parker's partner may have been planned as one of the complications plunging Sanditon into its inevitable crash. Yet Lady Denham is so lively and irritating that we cannot imagine her failing to survive.

Workers and Visitors

Many common persons with common surnames visit or work in Sanditon. The central penumbra of names is also the setting. We hear of a poor family named "Mullins," whom Mr. Parker wishes to assist, "as their distress is very great" (ch. 12). "Mullins," Norman but not all grand, is a form of *mulliner* ("mill worker"). Appropriately, William *Heeley* is a shoemaker and shoe seller. ("Heeley"/"Healey" is the name of a town in Yorkshire.) Mr. Parker rejoices at seeing in Mr. Heeley's window "Blue Shoes, & nankin Boots!" (the kind of boots that Emma Watson could not afford). These are to Mr. Parker "Civilization, Civilization indeed!" (ch. 4). As D. A. Miller notes, "Heeley" is another of the many names beginning with "H" in Sanditon, including Heywood, Hastings, Hailsham, and Hollis. Miller identifies this as "Anti-Style," a sign of incipient death in "the undoing of Style by wordplay."[83] But wordplay in Austen is creative life, not death. The repeated aspirate serves to highlight puns in, for example, "Hastings" and "Heeley." The Parkers' old house is temporarily occupied by one "Hillier" who thus dwells in the valley while the Parkers have moved to the top of the hill—so the Hilliers are really Valley-ers, and the Parkers are Hillier (ch. 4). The consistent aspirate is also hidden comic prophecy of what will blow the house down.

A "Jebb" (from short form of "Geoffrey") who owns a shop has a name appropriate to south Sussex, unlike "Whitby," owner of the shop tended by Mrs. Whitby. "Whitby's" is the circulating "library," bookstore, and trinket mart. Mr. Whitby's family originated in Yorkshire's Whitby—another seaside town. (Unlike brand-new Sanditon, Whitby is historically important for an abbey and famous abbess.) The Parkers are trying to encourage "old Stringer" as a grower and seller of vegetables, while they have their own gardener, old Andrew. "Stringer," ancient occupational term for one who makes bowstrings, is "a common Yorkshire name" (Reaney & Wilson). Low or working-class names suggesting northern origin keep cropping up in Sanditon, indicating postwar mobility. The English population is moving about, going to the south coast where new jobs are once the fear of invasion has gone.

"Mr. Woodcock," the hotel keeper, who assists the Parker sisters in getting out of the carriage, bears the name of an edible bird (Old English *wudocuce*). The name was probably at first a nickname, "later used to mean 'a fool, simpleton, and dupe'" (Reaney & Wilson). Polonius's phrase comes to mind: "Ay, springes to catch woodcocks" (*Hamlet,* act 1, sc. 6; *Shakespeare Plays,* 8:156). Mr. Woodcock has probably invested deeply in his new hotel; if so, this poor woodcock will be one of the earliest major victims of the crash, caught in the "springe" that Lady Denham and Mr. Parker have set to entrap others' money—and themselves.

In the sixth chapter of *Sanditon* Austen accesses a new means of producing a festival of low or absurd names. At the outset of *Persuasion* she gave us the arranged informational focus on one family's name in a list of short entries in the *Baronetage.* By contrast, in *Sanditon* we are shown a different (parodic) objective informational source, this time an informal list of "Subscribers" at the library. This random list of discrete unimportant persons disconnected from each other is the reverse of the organized account offered in Sir Walter Elliot's favorite volume. Mr. Parker eagerly peruses the list but is disappointed by names he understandably judges "without distinction." These are lower-class names—not a high-class Norman in sight. With one exception, the featured names have no direct relation to land or landscape. They tend to refer to towns, occupations, or parts of the body. "Mrs. Mathews" and her female offspring can shed no social grace upon the town. The Gospel of Matthew records Christ's warning us against building on sand. "Brown" (substituted for "Henderson" in the manuscript), referring originally to skin or hair color, is one of the commonest and dullest English surnames after "Smith," also represented in the Subscribers' book by "Lieutenant Smith."

"Mr. Richard Pratt" hints at the delightfully ridiculous. "Richard" is always wrong. "Pratt" is tricky name. Is this tricky Dick perchance Lucy's uncle? "Captain Little" is an oxymoron giving and then denying authority. "Captain Little" with touching social naïveté gives his home address as "Limehouse." If not quite the slum it became later, Limehouse in London's dockland was insalubrious and crowded. Site of lime kilns (*lym* + *oasts*) since the fourteenth century, Limehouse was always industrial, a place for shipbuilding and ropewalks. Charles Dickens's godfather owned a sail-making business here. Captain Little, retired on a small pension now the war is over, lives in a cheap and familiar place near shipping. "Limehouse" nicely cuts against the pseudo-gentility of "Sanditon."

The Rev. Mr. Hanking's surname is a diminutive derived from "hand." A "little hand" is not rendered any grander by belonging to a mere curate. Mr. Beard of Gray's Inn represents another part of the body. "Mrs. Jane Fisher," a widow, may have come to *fish* for a husband for herself or her daughter, Miss Fisher. They arrived with "Miss Scroggs," whose wonderfully ugly surname is unromantically Scottish. It means "someone who lives by the brushwood"; there were many Scroggses around Peebles. "Mrs. Davis," with a name associated with Wales and Saint David, appears to have traveled with "Miss Merryweather." This most attractive of these personal epithets caps the comical list. "Merryweather," description in the common riddle pattern (*myrige* + *weder*), is appropriate only to blithely cheerful persons. It may indicate that we will in the end come into merry weather.

True Norman names are represented elsewhere in the two Misses Beaufort (*beau* + *fort*, "beautifully strong" or "well fortified"). These two young ladies with "Miss Lambe" make up the entire "seminary" attributed to Mrs. Griffiths. Their surname is aristocratic—but the Beauforts (historically connected with Parkers) were descendants of bastards. Possessing "tolerable complexions, shewey figures, an upright decided carriage & an assured Look," these unconsciously vulgar visitors intend "to be the most stylish Girls in the Place." Showing off their harp, their sketching and themselves, the sisters attempt to attract male attention. Their object is "to captivate some Man of much better fortune than their own" (ch. 11). That description is so definitive that it is hard to imagine such characters unfolding any nuances of personality. But this pair is obviously intended to figure later in group or party scenes. The historical connection between "Parker" and "Beaufort" may even indicate that one or both will have a role in development of events, even in precipitating the crash. Their name hints that they are too well fortified to injure themselves seriously in any crash or conflict.

Miss Diana Parker dwells in a confusing and magnifying fog of friends and friends of friends. For six hours she massaged the ankle of a coachman, servant of her friend "Mrs. Sheldon," whose name chimes with the general themes of hypochondria and bizarre treatment of the body (ch. 5). John Sheldon (d. 1808), anatomist and surgeon, fell in love with a dying young lady and had her corpse embalmed and preserved, keeping this relic at home. Upon John's death Mrs. Sheldon gave the mummified beloved to the Royal College of Surgeons (*ODNB*). Diana habitually supplies a penumbra which (unlike that of Mrs. Elton, for instance) directly affects developments in the story. Diana trusts in communication with her particular friend Fanny Noyce. (This surname [*noyous*] indicates something annoying, as in *noisome* or *noisy*.) Through the annoying Fanny Noyce's particular friend Miss Capper ("maker of caps") Diana has made remote contact with a Mrs. Darling ("little dear") who was on good terms with a Mrs. Griffiths. The truly Celtic name "Griffiths" was Breton before coming to Wales. The Parkers' butler Morgan has a Welsh surname derived ultimately from Pictish. Three Welsh names (Davis, Morgan, and Griffiths) are encountered in a very short work. The novel integrates ethnic diversity—British ethnic diversity. Antique names not descended from Anglo-Saxon or Norman— "barbaric" names—turn up in unusual number in *Sanditon*. These "low" names, not ruling-class appellations, mark persons rising into respectability and visibility. They are indicators of a population becoming increasingly mixed and mobile.

Through Fanny Noyce, Diana assured herself of the advent of Mrs. Griffiths, supposed to be bringing West Indians to Sanditon. Through a quite different friend, Mrs. Charles Dupuis ("of the pit or well"), she had distant contact with a male resident of Clapham teaching at a seminary for young ladies in suburban Camberwell. Sanditon was thus recommended to that seminary. Two roundabout circuits collapse into one. The imagined two groups (one, a family of "West Indians"; the other, a girls' school in Camberwell) prove to be one and the same. Mrs. Griffiths brings three young ladies, one a West Indian, a Creole heiress of mixed blood.

This Miss Lambe, age seventeen, is black and wealthy, presumably the heiress of a plantation owner. Miss Lambe, "half mulatto, chilly

& tender" (ch. 11) seems a lamb ready to be thoroughly fleeced. The ugly but exact phrase "half mulatto" says that her mother was of mixed race, product of sexual encounter between a white man (likely a plantation owner or his relative) and a black woman (most likely a slave). Jane Austen takes us closer to the West Indies than she did in *Mansfield Park*. Austen may well have been influenced by a recent novel—the anonymous *The Woman of Colour,* published in 1808, hard on the heels of the Act ending the slave trade. Its heroine, Olivia Fairfield, "a mulatto West Indian" as she calls herself, is the illegitimate daughter of a planter by Marcia, an enslaved black woman. Olivia travels from Jamaica to England because her father's will left her a fortune which is to go to her cousin Augustus Merton if he is willing to marry Olivia and change his surname to "Fairfield." If Augustus is not willing to marry her, the money will go to Augustus' rude elder brother and even more disagreeable wife. Olivia and Augustus do marry, but a resurrection of Augustus' supposedly dead first wife renders that marriage invalid. At the end of the story Olivia returns to Jamaica to work on the education and welfare of black women and women of color.

Olivia Fairfield, central epistolary narrator of her novel, has more confidence and sense of humor than we may expect from Miss Lambe. Miss Lambe's venture into Sanditon society may, however, include some of the trials encountered by Olivia. Her future sister-in-law on first meeting will not touch Olivia's hand: "I held out my hand, and that lady was *very near* taking it in hers; but I fancy its *colour* disgusted her, for she recoiled."[84] One of Augustus's female friends says to him "upon my honour she is not near so dark as I expected to find her"–which Olivia overhears (*The Woman of Colour,* 117). Who can doubt that Miss Lambe is both toadied and snubbed by the strong conceited Beauforts?

The younger Miss Beaufort is "Letitia," from the Latin noun "*laetitia*" meaning "joy," "gladness" or "pleasure." (A certain slightly fake classical paganism colors *Sanditon.*) The best known "Letitia" was Anna Laetitia Barbauld, a well-known writer, critic, and editor.[85] The name refers us again to the study of fiction.[86] But there is an immediately relevant fictional predecessor. In *The Woman of Colour* the disagreeable blonde woman who will not touch Olivia's hand is "Letitia Merton." We may expect the social conjunctions of the Beaufort girls, their West Indian schoolmate, Lady Denham's relatives and other inhabitants of Sanditon to be fraught more or less hidden disagreeableness.

FIRST NAMES IN *SANDITON*

The first name of Sanditon's "heroine"—or central point-of-view personage—is "Charlotte." Austen employed this name throughout her career. In "Frederic and Elfrida" Charlotte Drummond, a rector's daughter too willing to oblige, accepts two proposals and then drowns herself (*Juvenilia,* 5–9). Most of Austen's "Charlottes" are good-natured but more calculating than Miss Drummond. Like Goethe's Lotte, they have a strong streak of practicality, avoiding imprudence and wastefulness. Charlotte Luttrell in "Lesley Castle" is more concerned with spoilage of the wedding feast than with the death of her sister's fiancé. Charlotte Lucas in *Pride and Prejudice* (another cook—she makes mince pies) does not let Mr. Collins go to waste. A Charlotte Davis, mentioned bitterly by Isabella, was allegedly dangled after by Frederick Tilney during his last two days in Bath—"I pitied his taste" (*NA,* II, ch. 12). But that offstage Charlotte apparently packed the captain off to his regiment without getting embroiled.

At age twenty-two, Charlotte Haywood is the oldest of Austen's heroines save Anne in *Persuasion*—and, unlike Anne, she has had no former experience of love. Neither is Charlotte Heywood an "imaginist" like Emma Woodhouse, although her imagination responds a little to the situation of the orphaned Clara. Charlotte seems the Austen heroine least likely to become entangled in emotional difficulties. She is neither vulnerable like Marianne, Fanny, and Anne, nor prone to enthusiastic mistakes like Catherine, Elinor, Elizabeth, or Emma. Charlotte's emotions are not to the fore. More surprisingly, we cannot feel they would be interesting—it is her dry inner remarks on others' foibles and her own that provide interest. *Sanditon* is not really a "love story." From the outset, we are effectually promised that the heroine's emotional development will *not* be at the center of concern. Charlotte surely will find a satisfactory young man without our worrying much about her. Yet—the double meaning hidden in reference to the "Heywood" who wrote *Love in Excess* might hint at possible passion or perplexity (though these may affect only Miss Lambe).

Sadly, we do not yet know Miss Lambe's first name (Viola would be a nice choice). Some of the first names in this unfinished work are common Austenian, while others are unusual. Mr. Parker is a Thomas ("Tom" to his relatives). With his impulsive desire to meet people whom he does not yet know, he seems a bit like Tom Bertram. His wife's name, "Mary," has been passed on to their little daughter. The narrator criticizes Mrs. Parker's passive complicity, providing no check on her husband's follies. She is not a whiner like Mary Musgrove, a tedious plodder like poor Mary Bennet, nor a charmer like Mary Crawford. But all four have in common a certain weakness, an unconscious self-indulgence.

"Susan" is "Susannah," heroine of the Apocryphal story of chastity falsely accused. Beauty, however, like display of chastity or cunning seductiveness (such as we see in *Lady Susan*), is comically absent from Susan Parker. Her body, however, is emphasized in a singular manner. Instead of adorning or cosseting her physical being, hypochondriac Susan Parker insults her body with somatic drama—as in having three teeth drawn on the spur of the moment. The only thing she has in common with the Apocryphal Susannah is that she may bathe (in the mode approved at Sanditon). She shares with Lady Susan Vernon and Susan Price (and probably with the ur-version of Catherine Morland) a concern with the physical and diurnal and an aversion to books, theory, rational consideration of the future, and abstract contemplation.

Diana Parker bears the name of the Roman goddess of the moon, hunting, and chastity. One of the pagan names of which Camden complained, "Diana" is unusual in Austen's time—though there was adulterous Lady Diana Beauclerk who married her lover (to Johnson's disapproval). Beauties like the Duchess of Devonshire were painted with the attributes of the moon goddess. Diana punished the hunter Actaeon who spied on her bathing by having him torn to pieces by his own hounds. The story of the beautiful woman spied on links the story of Diana and the Apocryphal Susannah; Renaissance artists deal with both scenes as opportunities for display of the female body, fantasies of voyeurism and punishment. Diana Parker, determined to bathe with the help of a bathing machine, comically lacks *any* pornographic promise as a bathing beauty. In Burney's *Camilla* (invoked in this narrative), there is a comic and distressing scene in Southampton: the heroine and vulgar Mrs. Mittin, though not bathing, are caught and trapped by jeering men in "one of the little rooms prepared for the accommodation of bathers."[87] Sir Philip *Sidney*—whose surname also appears among the Parkers—had written in his *Arcadia* quite a hot scene of a lover (disguised as a woman) looking at beautiful sisters naked in the water. We may well suspect that an important scene to come in *Sanditon* was going to involve a comic version of the Arcadian erotic, a scene of a bathing machine, women, the sea, and one or more gazers.

The chastity of Diana Parker is unquestionable. Both Parker sisters have turned against sexuality. Busily destroying themselves with violent medical treatments—and with chaste anorexia and herbal teas—the Parker spinsters need not worry about a love life. Diana is a busybody, a little like Mrs. Norris, proving her importance by rushing into projects, and repaying herself by insane binges of hypochondria, outdoing even the expert Mr. Woodhouse. Diana refers to the moon, and the moon can cause lunacy. Diana and Susannah work hard at turning their brother into an hypochondriac too. The terms "chilly" and "tender" and the theme of hypochondria appear in *The Woman of Colour;* Wealthy nabobs returned from exploiting India complain about the cold; Mrs. Ingot encourages her teenaged son to huddle in cashmere and lie on the sofa—"my tender sensitive sapling Frederic" (*The Woman of Colour,* 109).

Diana Parker is not the only character with a pagan first name. Clara Brereton's adjectival name is Latin for "clear," "bright," or "famous." Its relation to "Clarissa" is surely an influence on Sir Edward's decision to seduce her in the best Lovelacean tradition, but we are assured that "Clara saw through him, & had not the least intention of being seduced" (ch. 8). It is most likely that in the end he will marry her.

The niece of Lady Denham's deceased second husband, however, is named after Queen Esther, the heroine whose name entitles a book of the Hebrew Scriptures. Esther courageously spoke out even in face of the displeasure of the king, her husband, risking death in order to help her people. "Esther" (originally Persian, relating to the goddess Ishtar) has often been favored among English Christians but was not much in use in Austen's own time. Haughty and silent to supposed inferiors, Esther flatters Lady Denham. The perfect sycophant, she seems extremely unlikely to stand up against power—unlike her heroic Jewish namesake. But Esther Denham might surprise us.

Edward Denham has a Saxon and kingly first name. The first name of Austen's richest brother, it served the ambiguous Edward Ferrars. This Edward has the surname of a poet. But he talks arrant nonsense, consumed by a jargon of Romanticism. No "guardian of treasure," he imagines himself a seducer and destroyer, a Lovelace. He supposes Clara will fit in his scenario, but she is too well defended, too prickly—with that briar-patch surname. (But then, a Tudor ancestor with her surname met a sticky fate on a sexual charge.) This Edward seems oddly sterile. The fact that he is "running up a tasteful little Cottage Ornée, on a strip of waste Ground" epitomizes his folly (ch. 3). He is situated firmly in the marginal wasteland, even before we hear what hash he makes of literary terms, genres, and enthusiasms.

Tom Parker's youngest brother, Arthur Parker, at age twenty-one, has learned from his sisters the privileges of hypochondria. Deluding his enablers (happy to endow him with lumbago), he chooses no profession. Indolent cocoa-drinking Arthur totally contradicts the patriotic name of the heroic King Arthur who led the Knights of the Round Table—although he is drawn to the table. Sidney Parker, the middle brother, has another patriotic name, a surname made into a first name. This is only the second occasion (the first being Fitzwilliam Darcy) of Austen's use of that formula for the name of a prominent character. "Sidney" flies the Whig flag.

We meet Sidney Parker in the very last fragmentary chapter. Remarks quoted by his family indicate some wit and a sense of humor. Enriched by a personal inheritance, Sidney appears skeptical of the family projects of resort development and hypochondria. Austen's original title may have been *The Brothers,* putting the three Parker brothers at the center.[88] Different reactions to the creation and effects of the crash will be seen in Mr. Parker, Arthur, and Sidney—as doubtless the Austen brothers displayed themselves variously during Henry's bankruptcy.

Sidney Parker also seems the right age ("about 7 or 8 & 20") to offer a love interest to Charlotte. Yet all we are told about him on the first meeting is that he will stay at the hotel with friends, and not with his relations, and that he is "very good-looking, with a decided air of Ease & Fashion, and a lively countenance." This is altered from the more negative "very much the Man of fashion in his air" (ch. 12, *Later Manuscripts,* 550). Even the revised phrases are no endorsement. Austen's heroines do not marry for "Ease & Fashion." Sidney Parker seems like an upgrade of Tom Musgrave, similar—but inferior—to Frank Churchill. Entanglement with the Parkers seems hazardous to one's health and finances. That this young man has such a Whiggish name seems an indication that he is not to be an Austen heroine's final choice.

Sidney may be more impressive to the teenager, Miss Lambe. Some critics have overemphasized the fact that Miss Lambe does not speak, but she has only just arrived in Sanditon at the point where Austen stops writing.[89] *Mansfield Park* and *Emma* exhibit in Mary Crawford and Jane Fairfax Austen's disconcerting ability to create what I have called "a counterweight heroine." Arriving on our scene later than the settled heroine, the counter-heroine is talented and dark or dark–haired. (Elizabeth Bennet, though a true heroine, with her brown skin and quick wits—in marked contrast to the conventionally lovely Jane—partly originates this Austenian type.)

It is on the cards that Miss Lambe is designed as the important counterweight to Charlotte. Lonely and displaced, this alternative heroine of *Sanditon* is surrounded by developers who wish to exploit her fortune. She has no relations nearby; unlike placid Charlotte and tough Clara Miss Lambe will be emotionally vulnerable. "Chilly and tender" is a description emanating from exploiters, however, and may not be the whole truth about who she really is. Edward Denham, so openly crass, is unlikely to be Miss Lambe's heartbreaker—Sidney Parker is a more dangerous candidate. The "hero" who will marry Charlotte may not yet be visible. He might be one of the friends of Sidney Parker—and Sidney would function better as an "Anti-hero"—to use the term in "Plan of a Novel." Sidney, however, surely would not be the "totally unprincipled & heart-less young Man, desperately in love with the Heroine" ("Plan of a Novel," *Later Manuscripts,* 227). Perhaps we should attend to Sir Edward, comic opponent of *Sanditon*'s heroine. Sir Edward, muddled in poetry, fiction, Romanticism, and Lovelace, expresses in his comic disquisition on the Novel (ch. 8) a belief that hero and villain is the same thing nowadays. He may well be right. The real "hero" *and* "villain" of this financial adventure story is Mr. Parker, abetted by mean Lady Denham whose pride in her own perspicacity renders her certain to fall. Base fictions of health, wealth, and success constantly intrude on the sea and sunshine. The confused sterility of advertisement compasses most characters, and all language tends to become subsumed into advertisement. Mr. Parker even considers his handsome brother Sidney an attraction to lure women to Sanditon. Realities of body and mind are sucked into the fictions of the wasteland, the beach of salt sand.

PART III

Places

Chapter 8

Humans Making and Naming a Landscape

A place can be a small piece of earth's surface, a room, or a kitchen garden. In the eighteenth century, "place" often meant a mansion amid fine grounds. Henry Crawford encourages Edmund to make "improvements" to his parsonage, to "raise it into a *place*" (*MP*, II, ch. 7). But each of us lives in some place; some spot of earth—a "birthplace" has defining power. "Place" feels like something outside us, yet intimate. The body itself, however, might be considered the first place. Neither quite "self" nor not-self, it feels like the home of personality, site of emotion and decision. It deteriorates, very much like a property, if faster. This first of places is never stable, as it must move through space. Our inevitable experiments in space can be dangerous. Marianne runs, and falls. Louisa Musgrove jumps through space—and falls.

Many eighteenth-century poets gloried in graveyard settings, but eighteenth-century novelists (unlike their nineteenth-century successors) do not—partly because ladies did not attend funerals and graveyards chiefly served the poor.[1] Austen shows us only one funeral monument; respectable Mrs. Tilney's epitaph is placed on the church wall, as befits her rank. Buried under the church floor, not raw earth, Mrs. Tilney is abstracted into her plaque. Catherine is right—the monument cannot prove the corpse; it is but words, displaced from the body they purport to represent. Death hovers over Austen's fiction, though part of her excellence is being able to distract us from that shadow. The body is a place that won't last. But before we lose that place, we will have lost some others, changed and moved about, timidly or expansively, on our region of the globe.

The vulnerable body is always close to the center of Austen's vision. It is easy to understand why a Mr. Woodhouse chooses immobility. Immobility, seemingly safe, is rarely achievable. Austen's characters are often not fixed in place, but in the process of moving to new places. Homes (especially those of young women) are not permanent. Pleasure, health, marriage, war, or financial fluctuations bring on change of location. Change of place (even of a mere three miles) may be a stress or a tonic. A body in motion is a body displaced. One's place on the earth as well as in social station is treated as "nature." Place, however, is not "Nature," but a concept caught in the apparatus of history, law, and language. Beneath human "places," however, is the earth itself—claimed but not possessed.

Making a Place

England was once a true "wilderness"—imitated artificially on gentlemen's grounds, as at Sotherton. Before history, the "British Isles" were covered in deep forest. In the Iron Age human beings began hacking down the trees and making clearings. This process accelerated after the Saxon invasions. What happened in the colonies in North America from the seventeenth to the nineteenth century happened in England from the sixth century onward. The same program applies: clear a patch in the forest, create a crude dwelling, grow some food, take named possession. The Saxons made a determined push into the wilderness, just as their successors were to do in the New World. They chopped down trees, cleared fields, and built houses and settlements. Saxons acquired children, neighbors, houses, and barns. The population of England, like that of much of Europe, was on an upward curve. The Black Death terribly reduced that population. England had nearly six million people around 1350, but after the ravages of the great plagues only some three million. Succeeding eras looked very favorably on population increase. In the eighteenth century England reached its old medieval population level. Between 1700 and 1800 the population of England and Wales doubled in size—from about four million to about eight million. The eighteenth century is a young person's century.

There was scarcely time to rejoice. Before the century's end, after a sequence of bad harvests and wartime austerities, the Rev. Thomas Robert Malthus published his gloomy tract *An Essay on the Principle of Population* (1798), warning Britain of the danger of overpopulation. Population, Malthus warned, grows by geometrical progression; food production, by mere arithmetical progression. We cannot afford—at least the poor cannot afford—to go on begetting; the food supply would run out. Overpopulation is the central problem. (It didn't seem to occur to

Malthus—any more than to his modern successors—that the overconsumption of earthly resources by the rich might be curtailed.) The procreation of the poor was to be prevented. Partly from alarm at Malthusian prophecy and partly in order to determine wartime manpower and resources, the English government (following the Americans) decided on a ten-year census. The first census of 1801 gave England (for the first time since the Domesday Boke) some idea of who lived where and how many people there were, county by county. The results may be surprising to any reader of Malthus—the numbers inhabiting even the large prosperous southern counties seem small, scarcely enough to make good-sized modern town. Yet the total of well over eight million was more than expected. The first census is probably a serious undercounting, but the relative size of counties appears trustworthy. Most of England was still deeply rural, much of its populace living in small villages and hamlets, engaged in agricultural work and its support.[2]

The place names of any country or region seem a kind of "found poetry," a tribute to the relations of humans with a place within "Nature." In his invaluable work *The Making of the English Landscape* (1955) W. G. Hoskins points out that the majority of English village names, like the villages themselves, existed in the Middle Ages: "Nearly every village we know today had appeared on the scene by 1086."[3] Larger towns came into existence later, often founded as the result of deliberate planning by landowners, including bishops and religious foundations. "It is remarkable how many English towns have come into existence since the Norman Conquest, most of them as a result of 'the fever of borough creation' in the twelfth and thirteenth centuries." At Stratford-upon-Avon, for example, "The bishop of Worcester in 1196 . . . laid out, on the edge of the Saxon village . . . a piece of his demesne covering 109 acres. This was marked out in building-plots . . . and six streets were planned, three running parallel with the river and three at right angles to it." Shakespeare's Stratford was a planned town. The town (or cathedral "city") of Salisbury (or "New Sarum") was "the bishop of Salisbury's creation," its original gridiron plan laid out by Bishop Richard de le Poore in 1220–25. As well as straight streets the town plan included a market place and a guildhall.[4]

Names speak of the original creators of settlements. Sometimes the effect is macaronic, a mixture of tongues, as is the case with "Salisbury," based on a Celtic name *Serviodunum* (fort [*duno*] at Sorvio) with the Saxon suffix -*burh* attached. (The form "Sarum" arose in the fourteenth century from a misreading of old documents.) Roman terms could be layered upon earlier place names, as in "Towcester" in Hampshire, which combines an old Celtic name for a river (the Tove or "slow-moving") with the Roman *ceaster*. Place names in Cornwall, Wales, or Scotland are Celtic in origin; even in the center of England root words from the pre-Saxon inhabitants, the earlier Britons or Romano-Britons, survive. The majority of villages and small towns, however, sustain Anglo-Saxon names. Most English place names refer to an original settlement and may tell us what kind of settlement this was or what landmarks distinguished it. There are notably different names for groups of trees. The word "forest" (as in other parts of Europe) stands for the original wildwood, outside the world of settlement and civilization. A "coppice" is quite different, a managed stand of trees supplying perpetual growth and new shoots for cattle feed. A "shaw" is woodland set apart, or trees around a field. "Hay" is a hedge, or a field surrounded by a hedge.

The common suffix *-ham* indicates an enclosure, a land possessed— hence our word "home." The word *-ton* can indicate something larger, an enclosure with a set of buildings. This suffix is different from *don* (or *dun*) which means "hill." "Estate" is a misleading word apply to a *ton;* most *tons* were not what we would consider "towns" but farmsteads, each a messuage with main house, barns, a shelter for cattle (byre), and other outbuildings. The suffix *-thorp(e)* implies a secondary holding, a hamlet or a dairy farm at a distance from its parent farm. But many a "thorpe" becomes a self-standing entity. The prefix *carl* or *charl* indicates Old English "churl," commoner or serf, as in "Carleton" (*ceorl* + *ton,* a place for serfs' dwellings). "Hampden" means settled enclosure in a valley (*ham* + *dene* [valley]). The element *wick* carries the Roman *vicus;* a "wick" indicates a dwelling place on the basis of a similar Roman settlement. "Particularly in the West Country-wick and -wickham names are often close to Romano-British settlements."[5]

Place names in England are a surviving repository of Anglo-Saxon, the Old English which not even the Conquest was able to erase. There were many indicators of boundaries and division. *Stane* or *stone* may indicate a boundary stone. The prefix or suffix *bourn(e)* first means a stream; streams offered natural boundaries, so "bourne" came to indicate a boundary or border. Boundaries could also be marked by hedgerows or earthworks, in the Early English period and in later times. Crosses of stone served several important functions:

> Crosses were frequently erected to mark the boundaries of townships, monastic land-holdings, warrens, estates, sanctuary and other

territories. They were also placed in non-boundary locations to mark the venues of preaching or markets, while the erection of a cross could be a condition of the holding of land from the Knights Hospitallers [*sic*].[6]

Frequent documentary references to crosses and "cross" place names are evidence of their common use. Hence we have a believable name like "Uppercross" in *Persuasion,* indicating a stone boundary marker set in medieval times (which may still be there).

Hedges were an important feature of the English landscape from early settlements to the mid-twentieth century; they kept off marauding cattle and sheltered birds which fed on insects that threatened crops. Hedgerows in the fertile southern counties could be quite large and variegated installations. They often consisted of two lines of tall growth with a track between them. Hazel, walnut, and thorn trees, both blackthorn and whitethorn, contributed to hedgerows. Holly was valued not just as a prickly barrier, but on its own account, as a winter cattle feed. This old sustainable system of the hedgerow has been put under "assault of unprecedented severity."

> By using air photographs, it has been estimated that, of around 5000,000 miles of hedge existing in England and Wales in 1946–7, some 140,000 miles had been removed by 1974.[7]

Further miles of hedges have disappeared in the onslaught of mechanized farming and new motorways—a loss of habitat for birds and small animals. Hedges had provided man-made boundaries even in prehistoric Britain and emerge into history in legal documents. "References to hedgerows in Anglo-Saxon charters are abundant, with the hedges frequently being employed as boundary-markers."[8] In Austen's time the hedgerow was an important working part of the human landscape. Digging drainage ditches and planting hedges was among the hardest labor of the poorest paid rural laborers, "hedgers and ditchers." We must imagine Jane Austen's handmade landscape as worked by human beings creating and maintaining visible functional boundaries.

In his *Memoir of Jane Austen* the novelist's nephew J. E. Austen-Leigh describes hedgerows at Steventon:

> A hedgerow, in that country, does not mean a thin formal line of quickset, but an irregular border of copse-wood and timber, often

wide enough to contain within it a winding footpath, or a rough cart track. Under its shelter the earliest primroses, anemones and wild hyacinths were to be found. . . . Two such hedgerows radiated, as it were, from the parsonage. One . . . proceeded westward, forming the southern boundary of the home meadows. . . . the other . . . led to the parish church, as well as to a fine old manor house. (*Memoir,* 23–24)

These two hedgerows functioned as boundaries, marking off the meadows and the lands of the Steventon manor house, rented during Austen's early life by a family of gentlefolk with the bucolic name of Digweed, but later to come into the possession of Edward Austen Knight. W. G. Hoskins bears out Austen-Leigh's observation, noting a decline in quality of new enclosures of the eighteenth century: "The new fields were hedged around with quickset, whitethorn, or hawthorn, to give its alternative names, with a shallow ditch on one side."[9] New hedges offer thin if prickly obstacles to men and cattle, lacking fruit, flowers, or nuts. Richard Muir observes that "medieval and older hedges" tend to include a greater variety of species, including "crab apple, field maple, oak . . . hazel. . . . and various others that are lacking in younger hedges."[10]

The hedgerow at Steventon described by Austen-Leigh is a *medieval* style of hedgerow. The reference to "copse-wood" shows that it was used not only for shelter but also for cattle feed. "Coppicing," or cropping the tops of young trees, encouraged the sustainable repeated production of new green shoots that could be used to feed cattle. This type of old hedgerow is evoked to great effect in *Persuasion.* But there is a lighter glimpse of old hedgerow in *Emma.* The heroine, enjoying some cheering news (Frank Churchill is actually coming!) after a period of discomfort and frustration, looks out her carriage window. On this February day, Emma sees something to remind her of new life: "When she looked at the hedges, she thought the elder at least must soon be coming out" (*Emma,* II, ch. 5). The elder in the old hedges around Donwell Abbey lands will soon be springing—not yet into flower but into new green leaf.

The creation of man-made visible boundaries inevitably reminds us that the "Early Modern" period from Tudor times to the Victorian era saw an enormous land grab by the well-to-do. Common land was steadily seized, enclosed for the use of private owners. The single biggest grab had been King Henry's Dissolution of the Monasteries in the 1530s, removing valuable lands altogether from serving the public good and transforming them into private property. Powerful families were to follow suit in seizing land that was traditionally "common" to the people and eventually acquiring also an ideology explaining the beauty of the concept of private property. Throughout Austen's work we can find an implicit criticism of this privatization. She often differentiates between older practices and newer ones, especially when new ways of dealing with the land cause destruction for the sake of showing off. John and Fanny Dashwood at Norland destroy old walnut trees and what is evidently an old thorn hedge at the brow of a hill, a natural protection to insect-eating birds and a windbreak sheltering both humans and crops.

What Could Austen Know about Saxon Place Names?

We are entitled to ask if in Austen's time an ordinary reader could have known the implications of terms, the connections of traditional verbal labels with the land and its man-made settlements? Could Jane Austen have known what she was doing when she composed her place names?

Interest in English geography and the history of places and their names was not new. In the 1570s, during the reign of Queen Elizabeth, William Camden (1551–1623) began research for his important treatise *Britannia*. This topographical study of England, Scotland, and Ireland took him some thirty years; a version was published in 1586, and a larger edition in 1607, in the reign of James I. A serious production in Latin, intended primarily for European readers, *Britannia* was soon translated into English by Philémon Holland and went into many editions. Camden, deeply concerned with facts, also writes *con amore;* Edmund Gibson, his translator of 1695, says that allowance must be made "if in some places there appear more of the *Poetical* Style than is usual in Prose; which could not be avoided without deviating from the Original, because . . . Mr. *Camden*'s Style . . . leans much to the Poetical way."[11] Camden's work goes through Britain county by county, with details relating to landscape, buildings (extant and ruined), and historical connections. He searches out traces left by successive waves of different inhabitants.

Subsequent editors and translators shared Camden's interests, making corrections and adding new information. Handsome engraved maps and other visual images proliferated. Gibson's translation/edition of 1695 was republished and expanded. A second edition came out in 1722—in time to influence Daniel Defoe's *Tour thro' the Whole Island of Great Britain* (1724–26). A third edition of Gibson's version appeared in 1753. Gibson, Bishop of London, a serious scholar of Anglo-Saxon, speaks in his own "Preface" of the love of his country as his motive. In his *Britannia; or, A Chorographical Description of Great Britain and Ireland, together with the Adjacent Islands,* Gibson adds considerably to content and word count with "new discoveries," just as Camden himself had hoped. As Camden says in his own preface, "A new age, a new race of men, will daily produce new Discoveries. It is enough for me, that I have broken the Ice."[12] Information regarding the meanings of the names of persons and places was rendered readily available to the general reader—at least, to a reader with access to a good library. Camden's translators ensured vernacular access to clearly presented information about—among other things—root meanings of traditional names. Camden originally offers his reader explanations of many English names of noblemen or gentlemen, which Gibson retains, adding explanations of place names:

> Mr. CAMDEN had furnished his Reader with some General Rules for discovering the Original and Import of the ancient English Names of PERSONS; but it seemed to be a Defect in the Undertaking, that there was no Help of the like kind, to discover the Original and Import of the names of PLACES; especially in a Topographical Work. Which defect is now supplied.[13]

We can see the "General Rules to know the names of places" following upon "The Names of the English Saxons" in the front matter of Gibson's *Britannia* (fig. 17).

In Jane Austen's lifetime a new production of Camden's great work appeared. In 1789 Richard Gough published *Britannia; or, A Chorographicall Description of the Flourishing Kingdoms of England, Scotland, and Ireland, and the Islands Adjacent; From the Earliest Antiquity.* Gough says that this edition is "the result of twenty years journeying, and a longer term of reading and enquiry; the labour of seven years in translating and enlarging Mr. Camden's valuable work; and of nine more in attending this edition through the press."[14] Gough's heroic labor of love as translator and editor took—like the work of the original author—some thirty years. Gough modernizes spelling and organization and adds greatly to the contents. He gets rid of Gibson's antiquarian etymological rendition of county names such as "Suth-Sex" ("South Saxon," which is what "Sussex" means) or "Ham-Shire" for the now customary "Hampshire." Gough retains word lists of Anglo-Saxon names and components of personal names (1:cviii–cix), as well as adding "names of places . . . improved from Mr. *Lye's* dictionary." Gough

Rad. red. rod.   RAD. *red.* and *rod.* differing only in dialect, signify *counsel*; as *Conrad*, powerful or skilful in counsel: *Æthelred*, a noble counsellor: *Rodbert*, eminent for counsel. *Eubulus* and *Thrasybulus* have almost the same sense.

Ric.   RIC. denotes a *powerful, rich*, or *valiant man*; as Fortunatus has told us in those verses.

> *Hilperice potens, si interpres barbarus adsit*
> *Adiutor fortis hoc quoque nomen habet.*

Hilp'ric Barbarians a *stout helper* term.

So, *Alfric* is altogether strong: *Æthelric*, nobly strong, or powerful. To the same sense are *Polycrates, Crato, Plutarchus, Opimius.*

Sig.   SIG. was used by them for Victory; as *Sigebert*, famous for victory: *Sigward*, victorious preserver: *Sigard*, conquering temper. And almost in the same sense, are *Nicocles, Nicomachus, Nicander, Victor, Victorinus, Vincentius*, &c.

Stan.   STAN. amongst our forefathers was the ter-
† Vid. Sax. mination † of the superlative degree. So, *A-*
Gram. de *thelstan*, most noble: *Betstan*, the best: *Leof-*
Adjectivis. *stan*, the dearest: *Wistan*, the wisest: *Dunstan*, the highest.

Weard.   [WEARD. whether initial or final, signifies *watchfulness* or *Care*; from the Saxon peanban, to ward or keep.]

WI.   WI. holy. Thus *Wimund*, holy peace: *Wibert*, eminent for sanctity: *Alwi*, altogether holy. As, *Hierocles, Hieronymus, Hosius,* &c.

Wig.   [WIG. being a termination in the names of men, signifies *war*, or else a *Hero*, from pıʒa, a word of that signification.

Wiht.   WIHT. an initial in the names of men, signifies *strong, nimble, lusty*; which are implied in that word, being *purely Saxon*.]

Willi.   WILLI. and *Vill.* among the English Saxons (as *Billi* at this day among the Germans) signified *many*. So *Willielmus*, is the defender of many: *Wildred*, worthy of respect from many: *Wilfred*, peace to many. Which are answered, in sense and signification, by *Polymachus, Polycrates, Polyphilus*, &c.

Win.   [WIN. whether initial or final in the names of men, may either denote a masculine temper, from pın, which signifies in Saxon *war, strength*, &c. or else the general *love* and esteem he hath among the people; from the Saxon pıne, i. e. *dear, beloved*, &c.]

Wold.   WOLD. and *Wald.* with them, signified a *ruler* or *governour*. From whence *Bertwold*, is a famous governour: *Æthelwold*, a noble governour: *Herwald*, and by inversion *Waldher*, a General of an army.

But here let us stop; since others, as well as myself, will think I have said too much upon so trifling a subject.

The name   It may perhaps be more considerable if I tell
Britain re- posterity, supposing these papers to have the good
newed.   fortune to live, what I myself am † an eye-witness
† Circ. Ann. of; That as Egbert ordered this nearer part of
1607.   Britain, then his own dominion, to be called
England; so now, after about * 800 years,
* Now, about while I my revising this work, King † *James*
900.   being by the favour of heaven, and his own he-
† Jac. 1. reditary title, invested with the Monarchy of this Island, to the general satisfaction of all good men (that, as the island is but one, encompassed with one sea, under one person, and one crown, with the same language, religion, laws, and judicial process; so, to settle it in lasting happiness, and to remove all old quarrels, it might
* Jac. 1.   be called by one name:) King * *James*, I say, in the second year of his reign, did by Proclamation assume the stile and title of *King of Great Britain* in all cases whatsoever, except in the instruments of Law.

[*General Rules, whereby to know the* ORI-
GINAL *of the* NAMES *of* PLACES
in ENGLAND.

AB, in the beginning of names of Places, is oft-times a contraction of *Abbot*, and implies, either that a Monastry was there, or that the place *belonged* to some Monastry.

AC, AK, being Initials in the names of Places, signify an *Oak*, from the Saxon Ac, *an Oak.*

AL, ATTLE, ADLE, do all seem to be corruptions of the Saxon Æþel, *noble, famous*; as also ALLING and ADLING, are corruptions of Æþelınʒ, *noble, splendid, famous.*

AL, ALD, being initials, are derived from the Saxon €alꝺ, *ancient*; and so is oft-times the initial All, being melted by the Normans, from the Saxon ealꝺ.

AL, HAL, are derived from the Saxon Þealle, *i. e.* a *hall*, a *palace*: So, in Gothick, *alh* signifies a *temple*, or any other *famous* building.

ASK, ASH, AS, do all come from the Saxon æʃc, an *Ash-tree.*

BAM, BEAM, being initials in the name of any place, usually imply it to be, or at least to have been *woody*, from the Saxon beam, which we use in the same sense to this day.

BARROW, whether in the *beginning* or *end* of names of places, signifies a *Grove*; from beaꞃpe, which the Saxons used in the same sense.

BRAD, being an initial, signifies *bread, spacious*, from the Saxon bꞃaꝺ, and the Gothick *braid.*

BRIG (and possibly also BRIX) is derived from the Saxon bꞃıcʒ, a *bridge*; which to this day in the northern Counties is called a *brigge*, and not a *bridge.*

BRUN, BRAN, BROWN, BOURN, BURN, are all derived from the Saxon boꞃn, bouꞃn, bꞃunna, buꞃna; all signifying a *River.*

BUR, BOUR, BOR, come from the Saxon buꞃ, an *inner chamber*, or *place of shade and Retirement.*

BURROW, BURH, BURG, are derived from the Saxon buꞃʒ, byꞃıʒ, a *City, Town, Tower*, or *Castle.*

BYE, BEE, came immediately from the Saxon by, byꞃıʒ, *i. e.* a *dwelling.*

CAR, CHAR, in the names of places, seem to have relation to the British *Caer*, a City.

CASTOR, CHESTER, are derived from the Saxon ceaʃteꞃ, a *City, Town*, or *Castle*; and that, from the Latin *Castrum*; the Saxons chusing to fix in such places of strength and figure, as the Romans had before built or fortified.

CHIP, CHEAP, CHIPPING, in the names of places, imply a *market*; from the Saxon cyppan, ceapan, to *buy* or *traffick.*

COMB, in the end, and COMP in the beginning of names, seem to be derived from the British *kum*, which signifies a *low situation.*

COT, COTE, COAT, all from the Saxon coꞇ, a *Cottage.*

CRAG, is in British a *rough steep rock*, and is used in the same sense in the northern Counties at this day.

DEN, may signify either a *Valley*, or a *woody place*; for the Saxon ꝺen imports both.

DER, in the beginning of names of Places, is generally to be derived from ꝺeoꞃ, a *wild beast*: unless the place stand upon a river; for then it may rather be fetched from the British *dur*, i. e. *water.*

ER,

17. "General Rules to know the names of places" (1753). From Camden's *Britannia,* edited and translated by Edmund Gibson (London), clxxi–clxxii. Photograph: © The British Library Board.

largely retains though he does not enthusiastically pursue the botanical information about rare local plants in each county that Gibson had included (based on the work of "Mr. Ray"). Gough notes that Camden was not interested in listing manufactures or in cataloging plants. True, because William Camden did not have time, but he might well have approved of such additions.

This stupendous edition of 1789 consists of three (later four) handsome and thick folio volumes, illustrated with maps and other pictures in copper-plate engraving. *Britannia* becomes more and more detailed, in some regions showing every mile or half mile filled in. This work fulfills some of the objectives of the Ordnance Survey maps—but the Ordnance Survey is a military project. Begun chiefly as a response to the Scots invasion of 1746, it was made more urgent by the threats from France at the end of the century. The Ordnance Survey (the original GPS) is in a kind of competition with the peaceable Camden. Successive editions of *Britannia* added abundantly to the maps, fulfilling what was evidently Camden's own desire, if not within his capacity in 1607. Richard Gough in his own Preface (patriotically dated "*St. George's Day,* April 23, 1789") modestly states that he has not traveled as extensively through the kingdoms as the original author did, and he acknowledges informative material from other sources. (Gibson, however, is actually superior in supplying detailed bibliographies.) Gough also knows that he is writing for readers of an age accustomed to tourism—an activity aided for over a century by Camden's topographical guide:

> I warn the reader not to complain of a disappointment if he does not trace me in every part of the kingdom; and if I request him to content himself in many cases with the researches of others, though I will not offer such an insult to his discernment, as to intrude on him the rude observations of every rambler, now the rage of travelling about Britain is become so contagious, that every man who can write or read makes a Pocket Britannia for himself or others.[15]

Even before the age of cell-phone photos and blogging, Gough evidently feels too many people are now capable of writing their own travel books.

Gough compliments his immediate predecessor as translator and editor:

The republic of letters has great obligations to Bishop GIBSON. For if Camden first restored Antiquity to Britain, and Britain to Antiquity, his lordship restored Camden to himself, rescuing him from the confusion of that universal translator, *Philemon Holland,* and building on his latest and most improved edition a valuable superstructure.[16]

Camden intended his introductory essays to offer a history of England and the English people from the Britons through the Romans and the Anglo-Saxons, Danish incursions and the Norman invasion. The meanings of familiar place words are supplied. Camden enjoyed such etymological work, adding to it in the supplemental *Remains concerning Britain,* published modestly in 1605 as the "outcast rubbish of a greater and more serious work." In the *Remains,* Camden goes into the formation of surnames and the meanings of Saxon and other names, an encouragement to future editors to retain and even amplify linguistic material.

Few readers of *Britannia* will have gone from start to finish, but it is an excellent book for dipping into. The reader would be most likely to look up counties or towns of greatest personal interest. The narration is varied. Camden throws in stories told in quick but entertaining ways—such as, for example, the martyrdom of Saint Edmund.[17] The beautifully illustrated 1789 *Britannia* is the kind of book that a country gentleman would wish to purchase for his library. It is not unlikely that Jane Austen first came upon Gibson's *Britannia* in her childhood. (Although a decided Whig, nicknamed "Walpole's bishop," Edmund Gibson the scholar—author also of a famous tract on family prayers—might support Fanny Price's rhapsody upon the name "Edmund.") Later, Austen could have seen the new Gough *Britannia*, with its more modern spellings and usages.

Successive editors always tried to include more places and were evidently besieged by complaints of landowners whose estates did not yet figure. Camden warned that he didn't intend to publish information about every little castle and manor, but late eighteenth-century publishers knew their best customers. Greater efforts were made to include relatively small landowners and minor historical sites. The Knight family of Godmersham—the estate to be inherited by Jane Austen's brother Edward—were likely purchasers of the 1789 version. Godmersham would have been even more inclined to acquire the second edition in 1806, which, as well as the Brydgeses' Goodnestone, includes their estate:

> *Godmersham* . . . was another residence of the priors, much improved by priors Chillenden and Selling: the old hall remains, with the figure of the former carved over the porch. The estate belongs to Thomas Knight, Esq.:[18]

An unusual strength of William Camden's work (honored by his editorial successors) is his steady attention to the sites and histories of former religious foundations. The revised Gough edition sets Godmersham itself within that history; Godmersham is originally a *priory*—hence, perhaps, the amusement of Jane and Anna Austen at "Newton Priors." Recovering the memory of religious foundations is central to Camden's enterprise, desire for such recovery a major motive of this Elizabethan historian. Camden began his work when the Dissolution was only some forty years in the past—well within human memory. Recollections and ruins were still fresh. A great change had come over the spiritual and physical landscape of England in a very short time. Camden desired not only to record that alteration but to fix the memory of what had been. To preserve that memory he was willing to undertake a taxing and prolonged labor, arduous mentally and physically. In his own "Preface" William Camden takes note of this aspect of his book:

> There are some, I hear, who take it ill that I have mentioned Monasteries and their Founders. I am sorry to hear it; but (with their leave) they are possibly such who are angry, and would have it forgotten, that our Ancestors were, and we are, Christians; since there are not any more certain and glorious Monuments of their Christian piety and devotion: nor were there any other Seminaries for the propagation of Religion and Learning; however, in a corrupt Age, weeds might run up which were necessary to be rooted out.[19]

That Camden does not approve of what was done to the religious houses is made abundantly clear at the end of the section "Division of Britain":

> Till the reign of Henry VIII. there were, if I may be allowed to say so, monuments of the piety of our ancestors, erected to the honour of God, the propagation of Christianity and learning, and support

of the poor, religious houses, viz. monasteries or abbies, and priories, to the number of 645. ... About the 36th year of Henry VIII. a storm burst upon the English church like a flood breaking down its banks, which, to the astonishment of the world and grief of the nation, bore down the greatest part of the religious with their fairest buildings. For what the Pope permitted the Cardinal to do, the king with consent of parliament took the liberty of doing. In 1536 all the religious houses, with all their revenues ... were granted to the king. The next year, under the specious pretence of destroying the remains of superstition, the rest, with all colleges, chantries, and hospitals, were surrendered to the king. ... These were almost all shortly after destroyed, their revenues squandered away, and the wealth which the Christian piety of the English had from the first conversion of England dedicated to God, in a manner dispersed, and, if I may be allowed the expression, profaned.[20]

Gough introduces the "tempest" that arguably we encounter in Catherine Morland's first night at Northanger Abbey. Gibson is truer to Camden's original Latin in deploying the imagery of a torrent, a *flood* bearing things away with it. Sir John Denham's *Cooper's Hill* (1655; 1668) is an implicit meditation on Camden. This celebrated "topographical" poem (admired by Dryden and Pope) taught successors how to describe a view. The poet looks along Thames valley with a historical eye—seeing abbeys, their ruins, storm, and torrent:

> The adjoyning Abby fell: (may no such storm
> Fall on our times, where ruine must reform).

Denham follows the image of the river, whose smooth flowing his own writing would like to imitate "Strong without rage, without o'erflowing full." Denham ends with the river uncontrollable and destructive:

> No longer then within his banks he dwells,
> First to a Torrent, then a Deluge swells
> Stronger, and fiercer by restraint he roares,
> And knows no bound, but makes the bounds his shores.[21]

The tranquil stream becomes a raging tyrant, like Henry VIII— Camden's "torrent." The genius of the poem is its combination of past with present. Far from a tranquil observation of a pleasant view,

Denham's poem—directly inspired by Camden—is a contemplation of disaster. Observation of topography makes us witnesses to crime.

To contemplate a landscape truly is to know its history, which invites a sense of anxiety, even when mixed with overt complacency. Jane Austen's fictional landscapes are often suffused with an awareness—sometimes very uneasy awareness—of former things. The period in which Jane Austen lived saw increasing interest in the history of the places, peoples, and languages of the British Isles. In mid-century the poet Thomas Gray had experimented with verse forms and ideas derived from Welsh or Old Norse. In 1761 James Macpherson published "Fingal," the first of the poems allegedly by the Dark Ages bard "Ossian." Macpherson was embroiled in controversy well before his *Works of Ossian* were published in 1765. Dr. Johnson debunked the Ossian works as "forgery," while others, especially Scots like James Boswell and Hugh Blair, defended them as genuine heroic epics of Scottish (or Irish-Scottish) heroes of antiquity. Macpherson's poetry, a modern production tailored to mid-eighteenth-century tastes, was yet based on traditional lore and some orally transmitted lays. The concept of an oral tradition was unwelcome to critics (like Johnson) bred on manuscript and print transmissions. British Celts could have no claim to a "literature" if oral culture were to be excluded. The controversy turned fresh attention to the transmission of culture before the printing press. New prominence was given to oral works like ballads. Goethe, Napoleon, and Thomas Jefferson continued to admire Ossian.

The Ossian controversy stimulated interest in literature of the margins. In 1770 the Irish surgeon Sylvester O'Halloran published his *Introduction to the Study of the Antiquities of Ireland;* O'Halloran contributed to Charlotte Brooke's translations of Irish narrative poems and ballads, in her *Reliques of Irish Poetry* (1789). Brooke's title alludes to Thomas Percy's well-known *Reliques of British Poetry* (1765). Walter Scott's *Minstrelsy of the Scottish Border* (1802–3) represents a determined new endeavor to collect actual folk material and oral literature of Lowland Scotland. Austen would have known Scott's collection; she quotes Scott's poetry and is stylistically acute enough to be confident in identifying him as the author of the anonymous *Waverley* (28 September 1814; *Letters,* 277).

Thomas Moore's *A Collection of Irish Melodies* appeared in installments from 1808 to 1815. This important work infiltrated England through domestic musicians. Moore's *Irish Melodies* come to Jane Fairfax along with her mysterious pianoforte. (They will permit double-tongued Frank to keep up the private jest with Jane regarding Emma's mistaken suspicion of an Irish attachment on Jane's part.) The first song we hear Jane play, however, the Scots and Irish song "Robin Adair," is by Lady Caroline Keppel, although the air is the Irish melody "Eileen Aroon." In this popular song, the woman laments the loss of her beloved Robin, now cold to her. Indeed, obstacles impeded the course of the love of young Lady Keppel and the real Robert Adair, a military surgeon; after separation, the pair was united in marriage. The song is unusual in permitting a woman to express her own erotic feeling for a man. Jane's singing of it in Frank's presence is a code. A clever reader could divine right here that this couple are in some sense separated but will find union at last. The vogue for Irish melodies encouraged the Romantic interest in the harp. Mary Crawford (herself Celtic by descent) presumably is acquainted with works like Moore's, as well as "Scotch airs."

Austen's lifetime coincides not only with the French Revolution and the Napoleonic War, but also with a new era of English—or British—patriotism. Academic scholarship, primary research, tourism, popular culture, and inventive composition were combining both to stimulate and feed curiosity about the history and nature of Britain itself—its religions, its tribes, its languages, its multiplex history. Fanny Price is not the only person of her time who wishes to "warm her imagination with scenes of the past" (*MP*, I, ch. 9). The new taste for the British past was met by expensive productions in folio, fit for the libraries of great houses, reflecting an interest in archaeological remains of the Dark Ages as well as in medieval illustrations and manuscript records. Images of ancient things could now be scientifically reproduced in handsome engravings, presented along with diagrams and explanatory drawings. Joseph Strutt took a keen interest in representing English (Anglo-Saxon) people, language, and customs. In 1775 (the year of Austen's birth) Strutt published *Horda Angel-cynnan; or, A Compleat View of the Manners, Customs, Arms, Habits, &c. of the Inhabitants of England from the Arrival of the Saxons till the Reign of Henry the Eighth*. This large production was followed by *Glig Gamena Angel Ðeod; or, Sports and Pastimes of the People of England. Illustrated by Engravings selected from Ancient Paintings. In which are represented most of the POPULAR DIVERSIONS* (1801). Although "the Enlightenment" is often associated with casting off all that was medieval, the eighteenth century actually saw a strong interest in reviving knowledge both of the Middle Ages and of the medieval English. Camden trains his reader in linguistic history by offering early versions of the Lord's Prayer, working on up from "ancient Saxon" in 700 through 900 and circa 1200 to the late medieval period.[22] The taste for the "Gothic" in decor and fiction corresponds with a dominant interest in connections between past and present. Readers became engaged in cultural archaeology, including a wider interest including not only in structures like Stonehenge, but even the games of earlier centuries. In her taste for such "sports and pastimes" as cricket and baseball, Catherine Morland proves herself true Anglo-Saxon (fig. 18). *Britannia's* understanding of "Englishness" (or "Britishness") is in the background of eighteenth-century travel writers of all kinds, including the aesthetic William Gilpin in his many *Observations,* starting with *Observations on the River Wye and Several Parts of South Wales* (1782). The works of Gilpin are well known to Henry Tilney and Marianne Dashwood, as they were to the young Austen, although she makes fun of the new touristic interests.

"*Gilpin's* Tour to the Highlands" (*Observations . . . on the Highlands*) is alluded to in "Love and Freindship" where it inspires "a Tour to Scotland" (*Juvenilia,* 136). Laura in "Love and Freindship" dwells picturesquely on the Welsh fringe, in a cottage in the Vale of Usk. "A Tour through Wales—in a Letter from a young Lady" mocks the vogue for Welsh travel. The three women on their Gilpin-inspired "ramble" (a rather dangerously sexual term) counteract Gilpin by going much too fast to contemplate any scenery at all:

> My Mother rode upon our little poney and Fanny and I walked by her side or rather ran, for my Mother is so fond of riding fast that She galloped all the way. You may be sure that we were in a fine perspiration. . . . Fanny has taken a great Many Drawings of the Country, which are very beautiful, tho' perhaps not such exact resemblances as might be wished, from their being taken as she ran along. (*Juvenilia,* 224)

Gilpin offers us "Many Drawings" of structures and landscapes; the Johnson family, however, want to get Wales over with and allow no time for contemplative "Observations." The picturesque cannot exist in acceleration.

The well-informed William Gilpin can perform, often in Camden's manner, feats of instructing the touristic eye, celebrating—in determined Protestant vein—the beauties of Britannia. Some of Gilpin's effects depend on historical reconstruction, in making us feel the presence of real historical beings that lived or died here in the past. *Obser-*

18. Joseph Strutt, *Bat and Ball* (1801). Plate viii from *Glig Gamena Angel Ðeod; or, Sports and Pastimes of the People of England. Illustrated by Engravings selected from Ancient Paintings. In which are represented most of the POPULAR DIVERSIONS* (1801). Reproduced from the original held by the Department of Special Collections of the Hesburgh Libraries of the University of Notre Dame.

vations on the Western Parts of England is full of historical descriptions or references that modulate into imaginative sympathy, as in the story of King Alfred at Athelney, for instance, or the remarks on Monmouth's defeat at "Sedgmore" and the fate of his followers. (See below, chapter 11.) But Gilpin never views the monasteries and convents with any sympathy. To him the original abbeys are but a waste of resources. As we have seen, he rejoices (almost gleefully) at their overthrow, celebrating only their ruined survival as picturesque beauty spots. In justifying the ruination of the abbeys Gilpin is the anti-Camden. In making readers aware of layers of historical association and potential meaning, Gilpin is a child of Camden.

Camden and his subsequent editors all encourage awareness of Saxon influence upon the elements of place names. Gibson and Gough both not only retain but even expand the list of common components of place names. Gibson added a list of such elements in personal names, in very digestible form. As we have seen, a reader could easily find out that "BERT is the same with our *bright;* in the latin [*sic*] *illustris* and *clarus.*" "EAD . . . denotes *happiness,* or *blessedness.*" As well as "The Names of the English-Saxons" we are also given "General Rules, whereby to know the ORIGINAL of the NAMES of PLACES."[23]

We will learn in names of places to detect Saxon origin in the compound of Saxon elements:

> "BRUN, BRAN, BROWN, BOURN, BURN, are all derived from the Saxon born . . . burna; all signifying a *River.*" "THORP, THROP, THREP, TREP, TROP, are all from the Saxon, þorp, which signifies a *Village.*" "TON, TUN, are derived from the Saxon tun, *a hedge* or *wall;* and this seems to be from dun, *a hill;* the towns being anciently built on *hills,* for the sake of defence and protection, in times of war."

The reader is offered assistance in gaining some grasp of the Saxon linguistic elements within place names. At the front of the *Britannia* the reader of Gibson or Gough is offered an elementary key to the Saxon languages and the commonest components of place names such as the following: *-bury* (dative of *burh,* a fortified place, a term later applied to a manor house, then to village or town); *-by* (Scandinavian for farmstead or settlement); *-dun* for hill; *-ham* (Old English for homestead, manor, estate); *-hurst* (Old English, "wooded hill"); *-ley* (Anglo-Saxon, originally *leah,* a wooded area, then a man-made clearing in the wood, hence eventually open space, meadow); *-ton* from Old English *tun* (fortified private land, as in farm dwelling, manor house, or settlement).

The Norman Conquest of 1066 changed the language. Invading Normans as a superior aristocracy imposed their own language on England's inhabitants. Yet most place names remain true to the Anglo-Saxon. The typical Anglo-Saxon "English" place name is a compound of two syllables (more rarely three), each of which is a complete word. The expression thus breaks down readily into its component parts ("Wick-ham,"

"Ash-ford") in the manner most suited to a "charade" or "enigma" (e.g., "woe-man," "court-ship"). English place names are well suited to decoding and to wordplay. Austen enjoys them—and, even more perhaps, making up (or borrowing) names of places that sound historically convincing, realistically Saxon in their elements ("Mery" + *ton*; "High" + *bury*; "Woods" + *ton*). Austen takes great care to attach place names (real or made up) to persons who also have a convincing personal name of the right flavor. But place names above all others carry the poetry of England and the story of a relationship with the land—and the land is central to Austen and to her poetics of naming.

Chapter 9

Placing the Places

Regions and Locations

Place is central to Jane Austen's fiction. Many of her works open with a reference to a place—county or estate. To name the place is to set the tone of the novel. Description of place in a work of fiction strongly shapes or modifies a reader's vision of what we call a "character." The name of a real place evokes strong and complex elements of human history as well as of what we traditionally term "Nature"—rocks, soils, trees, waters. "Place" has a kind of sacredness. Whatever humans may do to the earth—including plastering a name upon some piece of it—is temporary. Austen is acutely aware of landscape and a great respecter of place. She will not invoke or invent a place name without meaning. As we will see, she weaves together the names of her characters with the names of places (real and imaginary) to create a complex web of significance.

Readers not living in the British Isles may not be aware of the implications of references to regions or features of landscape. Residents of the United Kingdom still know terms widely used in Austen's time, though this knowledge is eroding. In the eighteenth century most people would have known the difference between a forest, a coppice, a spinney, a shaw, or hay. The word "hangar" was neither archaic nor strictly regional for a "hanging wood," a wood on a steep slope. Every one of Austen's important settings has a realized landscape, although she usually sketches these firmly and quickly. (The long description of Pemberley in *Pride and Prejudice* and the walk to Winthrop in *Persuasion* are notable exceptions.) Jane Austen draws us into an unfolding history of human relations with an area of the earth.

Places are often mediated through descriptions and reactions offered by the characters. These may not be easy to interpret. In an important passage of *Sense and Sensibility* Marianne calls attention to the beauty

of Barton valley. Edward Ferrars quells her enthusiasm with prosaic remarks: "These bottoms must be dirty in winter . . . among the rest of
the objects before me, I see a very dirty lane" (*S&S,* I, ch. 16). (Note:
Edward is riding a horse while the young women are on foot. Who has
more right to complain of the dirt?) A short while later, Edward turns
against Marianne's enthusiasm for the picturesque, announcing an utilitarian credo. "I call it a very fine country . . . the woods seem full of fine
timber, and the valley looks comfortable and snug . . . it unites beauty
with utility" (I, ch. 18). We *think* we are supposed to take Edward's
"rational" side. But the context renders everyone's remarks suspect. Nobody here is objective. Marianne is trying to console herself for the loss
of Norland (which Edward has recently seen) by enacting delight in her
new area of Devonshire. Elinor, also unhappily reminded of Norland,
speaks repressively to her sister, mocking her memories of the past: "It
is not every one who has your passion for dead leaves" (I, ch. 16). Elinor
is harsh because she senses something different about this Edward who
has just come from "friends near Plymouth." Edward in his implicit
rebuke deliberately pushes against Marianne's sensibility in striking a
pose as a practical man, a man of sense who sees in nature only what is
fit to exploit.

We have no indication that Edward ever enjoyed prolonged experience of country life. He certainly possesses no estate—though he *might*
get one in Norfolk if he obeys his mother, Charles Musgrove pronounc-
ing on the potential productivity of a landscape would be worth hearing.
But Edward amid the hills of Devon is putting on an act, impersonating
a pragmatic male proprietor. In doing so he carelessly injures Marianne's
endeavor to make *herself* in exile appreciate her new environment. In
Marianne's own fashion, she is practicing patience. Impatience at his
own situation colors Edward's view and his conversation. Everything is
dirty, spoiled, demeaned. Nothing exalts the spirit. His mother and his
sister are partly speaking through him. But his bleak mood, in which
beauty is hardly to be found and materialism is all that counts, results
from too much contact with Lucy and pessimism about his own future.
No character present can give a just idea of the "objects before them."
The reader is pulled about from view to view, through various uneasy in-
terpretations, including memories—Marianne's, which are transparent
to us, and Edward's, which are opaque. The more the place is conjured
up for us, the less we know precisely how we are to react to it.

This sequence reminds us that we do not just "see"—we always interpret. We bring what we term "meaning" to our consciousness of

the world. Yet we do not make that world. Contours of land, water, vegetation—these things, deeply important to individual and communal survival, are outside of the individual's absolute will. Austen's novels at their core deal with the difficulty of survival. We are not able to be at one with the phenomena that constitute "place." Yet we are always making demands of a "place" which not only nourishes but identifies us.

English regions offer important information and identification. A most important geographical division is between North and South. The South has been the wealthiest region with the most arable land. During the Industrial Revolution (from the mid-eighteenth century) the North and the northern Midlands began to find a new prosperity. Some great aristocratic families had been headquartered in the northern region, but the chief settlements of the gentry and most prosperous traders were to be found in areas that in the twentieth century became called the "Home Counties." Near London and the south coast, these counties have continually been among the richest and most populous: Hertfordshire, Kent, Hampshire, and Surrey. Jane Austen herself was born in Hampshire and lived much of her life—especially of her creative life—in the same county, despite residence in Bath (Somersetshire) and visits to Kent, her father's county. Upon the death of Thomas Knight in 1794 the use of his house was left to his widow, but Mrs. Knight in 1798 decided to move to Canterbury and allow Edward Knight (né Austen) to take over Godmersham in Kent as sole proprietor as well as heir.[1] Henceforward, Jane and Cassandra made regular alternate visits to Godmersham. Edward had married Elizabeth, daughter of Sir Brook Bridges (or "Brydges") of Goodnestone Park in Kent (an estate that also found its way into *Britannia*). For the first years of their marriage Edward and Elizabeth lived on an estate called Rowling, near Goodnestone. Jane visited Rowling and Goodnestone in the 1790s; she visited Goodnestone again in 1805, also attending balls in Canterbury.

Austen's stories are often set—or *seem* to be set—in familiar southern counties at the center of England's prosperity. The normal move of the prosperous is from north to south and from west or east toward the center. Characteristic families of different eras (the Elliots, the Bingleys) move from north to south. It is customarily desirable to move from the periphery, from areas at or near the "Celtic fringe." The reverse move is seen as a socioeconomic fall. Austen can surprise us with changes in setting. The Dashwood women from Sussex must move to Devon—from the old center to a periphery. Fanny Price, born in a dynamic if rowdy economic center in Portsmouth on the south coast, is removed to Mansfield Park in Northamptonshire, in the north Midlands, of England, a long distance from Portsmouth and a considerable journey from London. The elder Ward sisters, however, moved from the east westward toward the central axis when Maria Ward married Sir Thomas Bertram.

Differences between east and west are important. Generally, the West County is rural and unprogressive, with fertile lands, decided hills, and green valleys, in counties such as Dorset, Somerset, and Devon. The two major western cities, Bristol and Bath, in the west—but not in the extreme west—are relatively easy of access from London. Bristol, a major seaport first chartered in 1155, was until the Industrial Revolution one of the top three cities in England for population and industry. Bristol's port gives access to the Severn estuary, where the longest English river meets the sea in the narrow and calm Bristol Channel. Bristol was famous—or notorious—as a center of the trade in sugar and slaves until the slave *trade* (not slavery itself) was stopped in 1807. Coastal development in the southern counties was held back in the medieval period by justified fear of French incursions, but from the sixteenth century southern coastal areas gained strength and activity through ports like Southampton. Southern coasts became again vulnerable to the threat of French invasion in Austen's time.

Eastern England was more flourishing in the Middle Ages than it became later. In the Civil War southeastern counties tended to be pro-Puritan. This area is the homeland of Oliver Cromwell (born in Huntingdonshire, MP for Cambridgeshire) and John Bunyan (Bedfordshire). The University of Cambridge became a powerhouse of Puritan theory. The flat eastern region, less beautiful than the West Country, is good for agriculture, cattle raising, and horse breeding. Charles II made Newmarket (near Cambridge) the center for horse racing, the kind of place that attracts the bachelor Tom Bertram. In the eighteenth century the eastern counties became a leading region for agricultural experiments and development, carried out by landowners like Thomas William Coke of Holkham Hall, Norfolk. Influenced by his neighbor "Turnip Townshend," Coke went in for crop rotation, importing and cultivating new grasses and breeds of sheep. In the Midlands and the North, new industries were beginning to emerge in Austen's time: pottery-making in the Midlands (in Staffordshire in particular, with Wedgwood in the lead) and cotton-spinning, especially in Lancashire. (Raw cotton from American colonies was made into fabric in the homeland.) Coal was mined ever more eagerly, though miners never benefited from the mine owners' riches.

During and right after the Napoleonic wars efforts were made to unite various regions of the country with better communications and routes for traffic and commerce.[2] Austen's contemporary Thomas Telford (1757–1834) in effect invented modern civil engineering, after starting as a stonemason and then working in the 1780s in Portsmouth dockyards. Nicknamed by Robert Southey "the Colossus of Roads," he was a brilliant innovator in roads, canals and bridges, creating the world's first suspension bridge. Telford answered England's felt need for connection. Tourists had sought carriage roads in order to enjoy Gilpin's style of aesthetic tourism, and scenic areas were opening to new industry; Arkwright put his early factory in Bakewell in Derbyshire.

Liverpool, northwestern port near the Lake District (but neither fashionable nor scenic), was central to the slave trade and to cotton import and export. Manchester was to be dominant by the mid-nineteenth century, but long-settled Birmingham ("home of the *ingas* of Beorma": Mills) was already associated with commerce, scientific development, and the new manufacturing classes—and was looked down upon on that account. "They came from Birmingham, which is not a place to promise much, you know. . . . One has not great hopes from Birmingham," says disdainful Mrs. Elton (herself the product of trade and commerce), looking down on the manufacturers, latest class to arrive (*Emma,* II, ch. 18). Mrs. Elton of the Bristol area is a trifle sensitive regarding slavery, asserting that her brother-in-law "was always rather a friend to the abolition" (II, ch. 17).

Counties

Jane Austen of Hampshire in her mature works tells us—with the one notable exception of Lady Susan—the native county of her heroes and heroines. She knows where they come from. Although English spatial divisions are small compared to those of North America, differences can run deep, even now. English counties are as meaningful to the English of Austen's time as the states of the United States are to contemporary Americans. Most of these counties were once separate kingdoms, with their own histories. They were on different sides during wars. Counties constituted the state's main political and administrative divisions (a fact changed only since the 1970s). Each county had its own particular county seat, or small capital. Census information was collected county by county. It makes sense to refer to the counties as the first of the place names that give meaning and color to Austen's fiction. We notice how

careful the author is to produce the information at or near the very outset of a novel.

House and Class

Houses give much away regarding a family's or an individual's history, pretensions, expectations. Like it or not, our dwellings locate us
in history, economics, and gradations of class. Since houses, furnishings, ornamental trees, and so on, can be bought with money, dwellings
represent "class" rather than pure "rank." For many centuries British
people have upgraded and improved their homes, intending to gain
not only in comfort but also in position. The big push in Austen's time
among the top classes was to remodel not just houses but grounds also
for ornament, pleasure, and display, a process delineated in Alistair
Duckworth's *The Improvement of the Estate* (1971). Strictly speaking,
an "estate" is a large landholding capable of supporting sustained farming. The true estate owner rents out his agricultural acreage to farmers
and lives on his rents. A dwelling with nicely landscaped grounds
around it (like Mr. Palmer's Cleveland) is not at all the same thing. The
claim to gentility as *power* is expressed through possession of an agricultural "estate," while "taste," reflected in decor and landscaping, becomes acutely important in establishment of nuanced social claims. Yet
in theory productions of "taste" exist only to serve the higher interest
of the estate itself, a durable sign of English culture as well as a means
of production.

That the ideology of the estate is not dead at the outset of the twenty-
first century can be seen in the success of the British TV series *Downton
Abbey* (first series 2010). The "abbey" on film is a nineteenth-century
architectural invention. (General Tilney might perhaps have liked it;
Gilpin would have hated it.)[3] *Who will inherit the estate?* This Trollo-
pean question, pertinent even now (judging by that TV series' success),
is at or near the heart of the plot of most English novels of Austen's
lifetime (sentimental, radical, or "Gothic"). The question is repeatedly
raised in her fiction as well as in her own relatives' lives. The fictional
estate to be inherited for good or ill is always to some extent a stand-in
for England itself.

Remodeling of grand—and less grand—houses reflects self-
announced identity and aspirations. Not everybody changed at once.
Many gentry families in the eighteenth and nineteenth centuries—and
even in the early twentieth century—lived in uncompromisingly un-

comfortable houses like Nancy Mitford's "Alconleigh," a fictional delib-
eratly unglamorous representation of her childhood home:

> Alconleigh was a large, ugly, northfacing, Georgian house, built with
> only one intention, that of sheltering, when the weather was too bad
> to be out of doors, a succession of bucolic squires, their wives, their
> enormous families, their dogs, their horses, their father's relict, and
> their unmarried sisters. There was no attempt at decoration . . . it
> was all as grim and as bare as a barracks, stuck up on the high hill-
> side. Within, the keynote, the theme, was death . . . the death of war-
> riors and of animals, stark, real. On the walls halberds and pikes and
> ancient muskets were arranged in crude patterns with the heads of
> beasts slaughtered in many lands.[4]

The gentry's ethos of possession, war and shooting was not necessarily
always remodeled into charm.

To render family dwellings a statement of culture was the objective
of many among the Georgian upper classes. But refashioning had its
dangers. Owners of new habitations give themselves away, even contradicting their fresh claim to established privileged status by overeager
stylishness. E. M. Forster in *Howards End* represented his horror at
"Suburbia" –a negative force menacing the real England. "Into which
country will it lead, England or Suburbia?"[5] In Austen's novels we can
feel the coming threat of "Suburbia." "Place" as authenticity is menaced
by a descent into trite reduplication allowing the "gentry" (old and new,
landed or pretending to be so) and the newly rich commercial classes
together to reinvent domestic style. Pretenders dwell amid pretentious
nominal signs evoking an older world that has just vanished and a relation to nature no longer extant. The American poet Billy Collins succinctly presents this irony:

> All I do these drawn-out days
> Is sit in my kitchen at Pheasant Ridge
> Where there are no pheasant to be seen
> And last time I looked, no ridge.
>
> . . . .
>
> I could drive over to Quail Falls
> And spend the day there playing bridge,
> But the lack of a falls and the absence of quail
> Would just remind me of Pheasant Ridge.[6]

Developers' names are inane phrases honoring contours of earth that have been flattened out and a life amid wild creatures (e.g., pheasants) suited to gentry pursuits, where neither the game nor the landmarks exist any longer (if they were ever there to begin with). The comical melancholy evoked by Collins is a reflection of the suppressed but efficient wish of modernity that natural landmarks and actual creatures would disappear. Consciousness of Suburbia, omnipresent in E. M. Forster's *Howards End* in 1910, is already present—if not treated with such fear and loathing—in Austen's novels a century earlier.

Chapter 10

Counties, Towns, Villages, Estates

REAL AND IMAGINARY PLACES IN THE "STEVENTON" NOVELS

Names and Places in *Northanger Abbey*: Wiltshire, Somerset (Bath), and Gloucestershire

REAL PLACES IN *NORTHANGER ABBEY*

In *Northanger Abbey* we feel Austen's new confidence in portraying places—as she had been learning to do since *Catharine*. For Catherine Morland, movement from place to place is, until near the end, a source of joy, whereas in *Lady Susan* and *The Watsons* change of place is difficult—even menacing. The Morlands and the Allens live in Wiltshire, in a fictional village called "Fullerton," which Mrs. Allen says is eight miles from Salisbury—though her husband says the distance is nine miles. (The lady wishes to make less of the distance that carriage horses have to travel for shopping.) Catherine accompanies the Allens to Bath in Somersetshire. In Bath she meets Mr. Tilney, "of a very respectable family in Gloucestershire," and subsequently travels eastward to Gloucestershire to visit the Tilneys in their impressive home, Northanger Abbey.

The early life of Catherine Morland is associated with outdoor living and physical activity. She is the most energetic and sportive of heroines of the period, "fond of all boys' plays"; Catherine "greatly preferred cricket, not merely to dolls but to the more heroic enjoyments of infancy, nursing a dormouse, feeding a canary-bird, or watering a rosebush" (I, ch. 1). This seems a dig at stories written for children, in particular Maria Edgeworth's tales featuring Rosamond, a little girl who constantly requires to be tamed into reasonable and productive behavior. "The Hyacinths" and "The Rabbit" show the child heroine's adventures in gardening, nurturing a damask rose, or learning, like Catherine under Elinor's tuition, "to love a hyacinth (II, ch. 7).[1] It is indeed not at all "wonderful" that Catherine the girl "should prefer cricket, base ball, riding on horse back, and running about the country" to ladylike (and husband-catching) accomplishments (I, ch. 1). Jane Austen is credited with being the first fiction writer to mention "base ball"—but her cousin Cassandra Cooke anticipates her in her historical novel *Battle-ridge* when the young man now under a Puritan regime complains of loss of sports: "'Ah!' says he, 'no more cricket, no more base-ball, they are sending me to Geneva.'"[2]

Catherine is a kind of New Woman of her era. Writers had become increasingly interested in the physical energies and activities of female characters. Even demure Fanny Warley of Susanna Minifie's *Barford Abbey* (1768)—the first "Abbey" novel!—learns (like Fanny Price) to ride: "Mr. Morgan has presented me a pretty little grey horse . . . and hopes, he says, to make me a good horsewoman."[3] Catherine Morland displays physical strength and adventurousness. In fiction of the 1790s this type is ably represented by the Welsh Ellen Meredith, Agnes Maria Bennett's heroine in *Ellen Countess of Castle Howel* (1794):

> The education of Ellen had indeed been extraordinary; she had learnt to read of the Rector . . . and to ride of the Bailiff: In this exercise she was so expert, that it was common for her maid Winifred and herself to catch a horse on the mountain, no matter whose, and gallop two or three miles without bridle or saddle; she was very famous for discovering birds nests, and minded not any height to get at them; ready to follow any body's hounds through thick and thin, and was even an excellent shot. With all these accomplishments she was now but in her fifteenth year.[4]

Ellen Meredith in her teenaged manifestation is both naive and strong. She is unfortunately tamed into ladylike behavior during schooling in Bath. Worn down by her family into accepting the hand of Lord Castle Howel, a family benefactor, she is injured by a bad marriage and the malice of town life. Ellen's story, influenced by Georgiana Cavendish's *The Sylph* (1779), seems also to be partly modeled on the life story of that novel's author. Cavendish and Bennet both lead the way in creating country-born female characters of great integrity and energy who are also innocent misreaders.

Catherine Morland, Austen's most naive heroine, comes from the West Country. Like Austen's Catharine Percival of Devonshire, she is an inhabitant of Wessex. (Thomas Hardy's "Wessex," based on the historical land of the West Saxons, comprises Devon, Wiltshire, Somersetshire, and the edges of bordering counties.) The West Country is traditionally perceived as healthy, if a little wild and backward—a good environment for a hardy and active childhood. The first third of *Tom Jones* is set in Somerset, the scene of Tom's—and of Henry Fielding's—birth and earliest youth. Squire *West*ern is an archetypal old-fashioned uneducated West Country rural squire. West Country people were often presented as yokels with thick accents. In the 1970s a British TV ad for apple cider ran, "Cotes comes up from Zummerzet where the zoider apples greow." From Shakespeare's time to the present, British actors could offer a sketchy stereotypical rendition of what by the twentieth century became termed "Mummerset." In *King Lear,* Edgar in disguise as a harmless—if mentally defective—beggar speaks in a mock West Country dialect, Shakespearean "Mummerset." The accent alone can get a laugh, from the understanding that these are backward if pleasant people. Wiltshire even today is decidedly rural, with a low density of population. In the first census in 1801 the county population was registered as 185,107.

Topographically, Wiltshire is largely a series of chalk and limestone ridges with deep clay valleys. Salisbury plain is a chalk plateau. Warm and rainy but not heavily forested, the region early attracted early human settlers. Flourishing in the Neolithic and Bronze ages, these settlers left some artworks, imitated in later centuries, like the white horse carved into a chalk hillside. Medieval Wiltshire prospered in sheep farming and became highly developed, with large Cistercian monasteries, organized agriculture, and wool exports. Its inhabitants were able to build and support considerable towns, including Salisbury, with its beautiful cathedral (built 1220–58). In 1320 the Salisbury Cathedral was completed with an ambitious spire (still the tallest church spire in the United Kingdom), reinforced by Christopher Wren at the end of the seventeenth century, and restored by James Wyatt in the eighteenth century. John Constable visited Salisbury on his honeymoon and was fascinated by views of the cathedral spire in the landscape. We get a glimpse of the famous cathedral in *Northanger Abbey.* Coming home in embarrassing circumstances, Catherine "rather dreaded than sought for the first view of that well-known spire" (*NA,* II, ch. 14).

Catherine Morland's imaginary village of Fullerton, nine miles from Salisbury, cannot be far from prehistoric and mysterious Stonehenge. Stonehenge attracted attention in the eighteenth century, starting with William Stukeley's landmark attempt at historical and scientific archaeology, *Stonehenge. A Temple Restor'd to the Ancient Druids* (1740) (fig. 19). Stukeley (1687–1765) was a friend of Isaac Newton (whose memoir he wrote) and of Edmund Halley, who assisted in him in calculat-

19. William Stukeley, *A direct view of the Remains of the Adytum of Stonehenge* (1740). From *Stonehenge* (table xviii). Photograph: © The British Library Board.

ing Stonehenge's alignment to magnetic north. Stukeley contends that the ring of giant stones is a temple of the Druids, "those famous philosopher priests," who "came hither as a *Phoenician* colony" bringing the purest Abrahamic religion. Their descendants and "the primitive Celts" built Stonehenge, "a true master piece." "Every thing proper, bold, astonishing," the author claims, beautifully adding "it pleases like a magical spell."[5] Stukeley's *Stonehenge* inspired subsequent theorists like John Smith who wrote *Choir Gaur. The Grand Orrery of the Ancient Druids* (1771), asserting mathematical and scientific knowledge and design in the ancient edifice. James Easton's *Salisbury Guide* (for tourists) promises not only an account of the antiquities of Old and New Sarum but also "An Accurate Description of Stonehenge" along with stately homes like Wilton.[6] Frances Burney incorporates elements of Stukeley's theory in writing the Stonehenge scene in *The Wanderer* (1814). Stukeley's argument served a new nationalism, favoring an England not only pre-Norman but even pre-Saxon—and defiantly non-Roman. According to this fresh nationalistic view, England had no need of European missionaries of *any* kind, for in England art, science, and religion had long been advanced. According to his narrative, a once despised people, thought ignorant and backward, are given new status, overturning con-

ventional history and adulation of Roman civilization and influence.
If we take Stukeley's thesis as a story in which supposed primitive simplicity trumps assumed sophistication—then that is the thematic story
of *Northanger Abbey* as well.

The Wiltshire of Catherine Morland's time was less progressive than it
had been in earlier eras, although it boasted—and boasts—some "stately
homes" in Stourhead and Longleat. At the turn of the century the Kennet and Avon Canal was cut through Wiltshire to facilitate Bristol-
London traffic. This canal connected two rivers with an immense system of over 100 locks, nearly 90 miles. Tunnels went through Sydney
Gardens, Bath, site of the company headquarters. Approved in 1794,
the project's last stretch was ready for traffic in 1810. Obviously this was
a time of energetic works and disruption, not to be equaled until the
coming of the Great Western Railway. In this novel Austen makes no
references to technological change in the rural hinterland. Wiltshire's
marketable products were modest; the region was known for cheese and
other dairy products. As well as "the Stilton cheese" (from Huntingdonshire), Mr. and Mrs. Cole served "the north Wiltshire" at the dinner
that Mr. Elton describes so minutely to Harriet (*Emma,* I, ch. 10). The
county was best known for wool and things made from wool. In 1741
the first loom at Wilton received a patent for carpet manufacture; production was highly successful, particularly during the French wars when
imports were limited. Other British carpet-making centers arose in the
West Country. The products pleased British consumers—though not
William Gilpin. He complains, "The British carpet . . . has *too much
meaning*. It often represents fruits, and flowers . . . and other things . . .
improperly placed under our feet."[7]
    Wiltshire in Austen's time was unspoiled, underdeveloped, and even
after the canal a little out of the way. To say one came from this county
was not to announce a claim to intellect. Not to put too fine a point on
it, Wiltshire people were thought to be a bit thick. They are deficient in
wit and imagination. Unsurprisingly then, we are told that Catherine
Morland's parents are "plain matter-of-fact people, who seldom aimed
at wit of any kind" (*NA,* I, ch. 9). Wiltshire folk were known as "Wiltshire moon-rakers." Francis Grose gives a brief explanation in his *Provincial Glossary:* "Some Wiltshire rusticks, as the story goes, seeing the
figure of the moon in a pond attempted to rake it out."[8] Wiltshire folk,
however, have their own version of this story, or joke against them. According to their own legend some men of Wiltshire, engaged in smug-

gling, went on a moonlit night to rake up a cask of brandy hidden in a pond. When questioned by authorities, they claimed they were trying to rake up the moon. In another version, the Wiltshire yokels sound even more like simpletons. They said, pointing to the moon's reflection, that they saw a large round cheese in the water and were trying to rake it out. Their ostensible simplicity deceived officials; Wiltshire folk know how to play upon their reputation for simplemindedness. Wiltshire folk still sometimes call themselves "moonrakers" in honor of their smuggling past—and even more in honor of their capacity to delude fancied superiors through creative exhibitions of stupidity. The recent appearance of a large number of "crop circles" in Wiltshire, may lead us to believe that Wiltshire "yokels" have yet again fooled their assumed "betters."[9]

Catherine Morland is a "moon-raker." She is not deceptive; she genuinely wants to catch the moon—to see her ideal realized, to grasp it in her own life. Yet she unwittingly deceives others who do not discern her true intelligence. Though Catherine has been called Jane Austen's stupidest heroine, she has insight and native wisdom, seeing through the deceptiveness of official historians and of many conventional notions.

Traveling to Bath, Catherine changes counties. Somerset, just east of Wiltshire, is also rural and ancient. In the far west is fabled Glastonbury, where the thorn tree is said to have blossomed from the staff of Joseph of Arimathea, disciple who supplied Christ's tomb and later (according to legend) became the first Christian missionary to Britain. Once the site of a great abbey, ancient Glastonbury (Celtic for "stronghold of the people living at woad place": Mills) is the alleged location of the tomb of King Arthur, "once and future King." Glastonbury registers *British* rather than Anglo-Saxon national pride. The name "Somerset" supposedly comes from *sumorseaete,* meaning "people dwelling at Somerton." It is pleasanter to think of Somerset itself as "summer's county." One area of this county is rich in caves and chasms, including the celebrated Cheddar Gorge, where cheese has been made since the twelfth century. Somerset's rushing streams were useful in the eighteenth century for powering mills for flour and paper. Yet Somerset as a whole remained underdeveloped. Conscious need for improvement is visible in the founding in 1777 of the Bath and West of England Society for the Encouragement of Agriculture, Arts, Manufacture and Commerce.

In coming to Bath, Catherine departs from rural simplicity to a town built for pleasure. First constructed when the invading Romans took over sacred hot springs and a shrine dedicated to the local goddess Sulis, the spa town fell into disrepair after the Romans left. The region was settled by Saxons and attacked by Danes. King Alfred fought a battle here and supposedly designed the new town; King Edgar was crowned in Bath Abbey in 973. Bath Abbey, rebuilt in 1500, was subject to the Dissolution in 1539, but in 1590 Queen Elizabeth gave a royal charter to the city, and the abbey church was restored as Bath's central church. Physicians prescribed Bath for their patients, who were to drink the mineral waters and to take the baths. Other spa towns in England were developed in different periods (Leamington, Cheltenham, Tunbridge Wells, and Harrogate), but none of these prospered like Bath from the late seventeenth century to the early nineteenth. Bath benefited from its ease of access. The growth of American colonies led to the expansion of the nearby port of Bristol. Bath shops could sell luxury goods, and hotels could offer costly comforts. Catherine Morland's Bath had become the major city of Somerset. In the census of 1801, Bath had a population of over forty thousand, making it one of the largest cities in Britain. A center not of productivity but of pleasure, a bit like Las Vegas, it relied on visitors to bring money, which went into more rental property for more visitors, in new well-designed squares and crescents. Henry Fielding's patron Ralph Allen, owner of stone quarries, had an architect-designed house at Prior Park built out of the local white and golden stone as a sort of advertisement. Bath is built on hills—making walking literally uphill work, odd in a center for invalids; there were sedan chairs for hire, and stout-legged porters (mostly Irish) to carry them. Bath's topography is hierarchical; the most desirable residences are in the higher regions, made magnificent by the Crescent. Visitors rented accommodations suited to their financial resources, thus admitting their status. The Thorpes in Edgar's Buildings, a developer's townhouses, are not in as glamorous a location as the Allens in Pultney Street (a broad modern street that won't ask too much of Mrs. Allen as a walker.) Milsom Street was the main shopping thoroughfare.

A sanctuary for the sick and disabled, Bath offered employment for those attending the invalids as well as to those who minded the shops. Bath produced the first purpose-made wheelchair, the "Bath chair," visible in Thomas Rowlandson's "The Pump Room." Given an excuse, visitors came for cures or pain relief, for dances and gambling, for entertainment and sociability. After London, Bath was the chief site of the marriage market, a place where one might go to search for a marriage partner—as do Isabella Thorpe, Augusta Hawkins, and Mr. Elton. Almost everyone of importance in the eighteenth century comes here at some point or other. Mrs. Piozzi (Hester Thrale) lived in Bath for a time, and so did Mary Wollstonecraft, as a rich woman's companion. Some stayed on—permanently—in the churchyard. Cassandra Leigh had recently buried her father in Walcot Churchyard when she married George Austen in Saint Swithin's Church, Bath, in 1764. Rev. George Austen died in Bath in 1805 and is buried in the crypt of Walcot Church. Frances Burney's husband General D'Arblay, who died in Bath, is buried in Walcot Churchyard; Frances decreed that when the time came she should be buried beside him. John Feltham in his *Guide to all the Watering and Sea-Bathing Places* worries that the many monuments to people who had come only to die could affect visitors "even in the enjoyment of the highest health" while "on invalids, it must have a very injurious effect."[10]

Bath in the late eighteenth century is a sort of island, a scene of hectic but attractive artificiality combined with a dark and gross reality. The excuse of drinking the waters brought sick and well to the Pump Room: "All persons who are decently dressed, without any regard to fashion, may freely perambulate the Pump-room," according to Feltham.[11] If you took the waters regularly, you were expected to pay "about a guinea a month." In *The Valetudinarian's Bath Guide,* Philip Thicknesse warns against excess, recalling the awful fate of his brother "who dropt down dead as he was playing on the fiddle . . . after drinking a large quantity of Bath Waters, and eating a hearty breakfast of spungy hot rolls, or *Sally Luns.*"[12] Dances were regularly held both in the Upper Assembly Rooms and the Lower Assembly Rooms (referred to collectively as "the Rooms"). In *The New Prose Bath Guide* Thicknesse comments, "we much doubt, whether it be true that the Upper Rooms shew Female Beauty so advantageously as the Lower. There is a certain Degree of Light to see Nature, as well as Art, to Advantage."[13] The Upper Rooms, he contends, are too brightly lit. Catherine Morland fails to attract attention in the crush of the Upper Rooms but succeeds better in the Lower Rooms, where she dances with Henry Tilney. The difference might be mortifyingly attributed to the searching glare of the over-illuminated Upper Rooms.

Bath offers music and dancing, pastry and bonnets with red ribbons—yet it has a strong flavor of mortality. *The New Prose Bath Guide* warns that Bath's most famous church has an infamous smell:

> It is very doubtful whether the *Abbey Church* is not . . . a very improper Place to attend Divine Service at, from the Number of Bodies

buried within the Church, and *near the Surface,* and the Frequency
of the Ground being opened, before the Effects of the Putrifaction
[*sic*] is over . . . for the Truth of this Observation we refer every Body
to the Evidence of their own Senses when they *first enter* that vener-
able Mausoleum.[14]

One can only hope that some remedy was found. Catherine and Isabella planned to attend "divine service" together in "the same chapel"
(probably Saint Margaret's Chapel); but an interesting association of
ideas is suggested when after the service they go first to the Pump Room
and then to the Crescent "to breathe the *fresh air* of better company"
(I, ch. 4, ch. 5, italics added). Bath's mixture of invalidism and pleasure
seeking, of fashionable bonnets and wheelchairs, of death and sex, must
have given it a considerable charge.

Jane Austen had visited Bath in the 1790s. After writing a first version of *Northanger Abbey,* the author on her father's retirement in 1801
was forced to live in this city she didn't care for. Later, expecting the
novel to emerge in print at last in 1816 or 1817, she prepared an "Advertisement by the Authoress." (Perhaps the title was now intended to be
Catherine; a letter now refers to "Miss Catherine" [13 March 1817; *Letters,* 333].) Austen's "Advertisement" says, "this little work was finished
in the year 1803 and intended for immediate publication." That novel,
rewritten during her Bath residence (with the title *Susan*) was sold
to Crosby & Company for ten pounds but never published. We have
the letter of 5 April 1809, in which the author tries to reclaim "a MS.
novel in 2 vol. entitled Susan," sent "in the Spring of the year 1803." She
writes as "Mrs. Ashton Dennis," giving her the excuse to sign with the
angry "MAD." Crosby in reply acknowledges that they have a manuscript novel "entitled *Susan*" but require to be repaid before they restore it to her; the firm also makes clear that she cannot, as she threatens, have it published elsewhere (5 April; 8 April 1809; *Letters,* 174–75).
Jane Austen could not afford the ten pounds and had to wait until she
had some money of her own. Her brother Henry then bought it back in
1816, letting Crosby know only after the transaction was completed that
the writer was the author of *Pride and Prejudice.*

Austen says in her letter to Crosby that she is "willing to supply You
with another Copy." She has not actually lost the *book,* just the publication. Possessing another complete manuscript, she might still have
gone ahead with rewriting the novel; possibly she already had made
important alterations *before* securing Crosby's copy and her legal right

to publish. Some old core original dating from the mid-1790s was extensively rewritten in Bath between 1801 and 1803, when the author of *Susan* could be at no loss for details of setting—and when she could have read *Belinda* (1801), referred to in *Northanger Abbey* (*NA*, I, ch. 5). After 1809, Austen, settled at Chawton, renewed her dedication to her career, and could undertake some defiant rewriting of the old story. A change in the heroine's name might have been one facet of a complex planned defense against Crosby. There are strong signs that Austen rewrote *Susan* during her mature phase, perhaps as early as 1809–11. Most striking is the introduction of *style indirect libre* in the second volume, about the point in the narrative where that device becomes strongly featured in *Sense and Sensibility* (also a reworked fiction). After a new start, Austen may have hesitated, realizing that the rewritten novel, if not identical to the story offered to Crosby, would still be recognizable, indissolubly tied to the parodic use of the "Gothic" fiction so popular in the 1790s. Preparing (she hoped) to publish in 1816 or 1817, the author designs a prefatory note asking the reader to bear in mind that "thirteen years have made comparatively obsolete" some parts of the book. She could not cut references to the "Gothic" novels—but as we have never let go of the "Gothic" mode, *Northanger Abbey* is always current.

If Jane Austen did not like Bath, it got her attention. It is the "real life" setting that she used at greatest length and most attentively. In both *Northanger Abbey* and *Persuasion,* the heroine is changing from one state of being to another, and from one role to another—or takes on a sequence of different roles. Bath is a place of transition and metamorphosis.

Isabella Thorpe comes to Bath literally from a different direction than Catherine. The home of the Thorpe family is Putney, some five miles southwest of Charing Cross. The Thorpes probably originated in some modest thorp. But, like Putney, they are becoming urban. Putney (Puttenhuthe, "landing place of the hawk": Mills), officially a separate village, was what we should call a suburb of London. Birthplace of Thomas Cromwell and Edward Gibbon, it is historically most famous for the "Putney Debates" of 1647 in which the victorious Oliver Cromwell put down the too-egalitarian Diggers and Levellers. Putney was valued for fresh air and recreation on its bowling green, although Putney Heath was a dangerous haunt of highwaymen. By the eighteenth century a few of the elite lived on Putney Hill. William Pitt the Prime Minister lived in the Bowling-Green House in Putney—and fought a duel with an MP on Putney Heath. Putney was—and is—a pleasant area by the Thames with riverside views (advantageous during the Oxford-Cambridge Boat Race). In Austen's time (and now) middle-class Putney differs greatly from the West End of the rich and fashionable and from more coveted riverside settlements. Isabella fantasizes about marrying someone who can keep her in one of the "charming little villas about Richmond"—a very different (and ultraexpensive) Thameside location (I, ch. 15).

The Thorpes keep trying to leave Putney behind. Isabella can compare the fashions of Bath with those of Tunbridge. Before investing in the Bath excursion Mrs. Thorpe evidently took her daughter to market in the smaller Kentish spa of Tunbridge Wells, setting of important scenes in *Camilla*. John Thorpe, a member of the same Oxford College as James, forsakes Putney to frequent the Bedford Coffee House in Covent Garden, where he runs into General Tilney; here Tom Musgrove of *The Watsons* also meets friends. (In Smith's *Emmeline* the Bedford figures gruesomely as the site of the candlelit duel between Delamere and Bellozane, in which the impetuous Frederic receives his death wound.) The Bedford had been the hunt of wits like Goldsmith and Garrick, but that greatness was in the past.

John Thorpe incessantly tries to prove himself a gentleman by making bets on his driving prowess and recounting implausible exploits in the hunting field. John boasts of bold riding—an attribute of country gentry. He even claims to hunt habitually in Leicestershire: "Fletcher and I mean to get a house in Leicestershire, against next season. It is so d— uncomfortable, living at an inn" (I, ch. 10). Leicestershire was celebrated for excellent foxhunting. To ride with the Quorn was the privilege of gentry and wealthy farmers.[15] It is highly doubtful if the son of a Putney lawyer could afford the expense of lodging, as well as the cost and upkeep of several "hunters"—costly horses able to leap fences and hedges. John, however, asserts that he owns three horses of high value: "I would not take eight hundred guineas for them." This sum would be a third or a half of his father's annual income, even if the deceased Thorpe senior was an extremely prosperous solicitor.

John Thorpe is drawing an extremely long bow. His rattle has an objective—to establish himself as a gentleman, instead of a suburbanite offspring of the midprofessional class. If John were *truly* indulging in such upper-class pastimes—expenses more suited to a Tom Bertram— he would gallop his parents swiftly into financial ruin. We may believe he is merely playing a role. John Thorpe is not unaware of the advisability of finding a rich wife in Bath, but his manners could captivate no lady. His outrageous boasts excite himself—he lives a rich fantasy life. Almost every character in this novel centering on fiction indulges in fiction of one sort or another.

Catherine Morland, the country girl who loved "riding on horseback, and running about the country" (I, ch. 1), is partly immobilized in Bath. She must walk in company and cannot go outside the city without being taken. She passes up an excursion to Clifton, a rival spa just outside Bristol (setting for most of the action in the last volume of *Evelina*). Catherine had wished to see "Blaize Castle," imagining it a genuine relic of antiquity, though it is but a folly, a sham castle built in 1766, on a hill with a picturesque view. The more substantial Blaise Manor House, created in 1796–98, boasted grounds designed by Repton. The Thorpe party bothers with neither castle nor manor house. They entertain themselves by taking the waters, eating a meal at the York Hotel, shopping and eating ice cream. Such conventional touristic activities do not interest Catherine, who can still fancy Blaize Castle a real relic of the Middle Ages—many things have a "blaze" of superficial glory about them, like Isabella Thorpe.

As Janine Barchas points out, had the Thorpe party gone the same distance from Bath in the opposite direction, they could have come upon a genuine castle at Farleigh Hungerford, site of a crime of the sort that Catherine imagines—a famous sixteenth-century case of wife imprisonment and attempted murder.[16] The husband allegedly made repeated attempts to poison a wife he had imprisoned in his tower; she could eat nothing offered by the household and was kept alive by the kindness of poor local women.

The Hungerfords' story is even more sensational than Barchas describes. Sir Edward Hungerford, father of the wife-imprisoning Sir Walter, was a courtier of Henry VIII. Sir Edward Hungerford's second wife, Agnes, had killed her first husband in order to marry him—perhaps with some collusion on Sir Edward's part. After his death, Agnes was tried and hanged for murder (1523). Sir Edward's son Walter (by a first marriage) entered the service of Thomas Cromwell in 1533. Walter's fortunes fell with Cromwell's; his mistreatment of his wife came out. Walter was accused of treason and witchcraft and also found "guilty of buggery" (*ODNB*). He was executed on the same day as Cromwell in 1540; his imprisoned wife was free and could marry again. This family history (in one of Austen's favorite periods) richly illustrates the miseries of marriage and its potential for complex violence.

In traveling to Northanger Abbey, Catherine changes counties again, moving eastward to a county that is partly in Wessex and partly in the Midlands. In earlier times, Gloucestershire thrived on agriculture and sheep. Water power supported flour mills. John Thorpe and James Morland stopped in the little town of Tetbury, Gloucestershire, on their way from Oxford. Named for Saint Tetta, the town flourished even before the Conquest, prospering in the wool trade; Tetbury is now a tourist's delight for the houses of medieval and Renaissance merchants. In this novel, we travel by old routes. Returning to London from Bath, John Thorpe is due to stop at Devizes (*castrum ad divisas*), "camp at three boundaries." This Wiltshire town had grown around the Castle built by the bishop of Salisbury in 1080 and was important in the Civil War, when Oliver Cromwell took its Castle. Devizes was a crossroads from early times; in Austen's era the construction of the Kennet and Avon Canal was linking Devizes with Bristol and London. Throughout this region, monastic foundations had played an important part in improving agriculture and providing centers of trade. Austen in this novel keeps her heroine clear of big modern towns, like London or Bristol. She—and we—travel on a partly medieval road, through places like Salisbury, Tetbury, Devizes. This scheme of reference quietly stresses the genuine ongoing medieval tradition of England, without the "Gothic" trappings supplied in Georgian fiction

Jane Austen's family connections with Gloucestershire were in the eastern side of the county, the Cotswold area around Saxon Adlestrop (once Tedestrop, "outlying farmstead . . . of a man called Taetel": Mills). Cassandra Leigh had been born in a rectory at Harpsden in Oxfordshire, but her aristocratic ancestors had Gloucestershire connections. In July 1806, Jane went with her mother and Cassandra to visit Mrs. Austen's cousin, Rev. Thomas Leigh, at Adlestrop Rectory. Here Repton had redesigned the grounds and "merged the grounds of the rectory with those of Mr. James Leigh at Adlestrop House."[17] That visit to Adlestrop was disturbed by the exciting news that death and a defective will had left uncertain the inheritance of a major Leigh property, Stoneleigh Abbey (in Warwickshire, just over the border). Thomas Leigh or—even better—Mrs. Austen's brother James Leigh-Perrot might claim the title. Mrs. Austen and the Rev. Thomas Leigh at once visited Stoneleigh, formerly a Cistercian abbey. Here a royalist ancestor had once sheltered Charles I. Mrs. Austen, Jane, and Cassandra could—like Catherine Morland—enjoy living "under . . . the roof of an abbey!" (*NA*, II, ch. 2). Mrs. Austen had feared "long Avenues, dark rookeries & dismal Yew Trees" but was happy to report "here are no such melancholy things." There was, however "the State Bed chamber with a high dark crimson Velvet Bed, an *alarming* apartment just fit for a Heroine"[18] Mrs. Austen may be affected by her cousin Cassandra Cooke's *Battleridge* where the heroine has cause for alarm:

> "I was carried up a winding staircase: a third door was opened, I saw by the dark lanthorn . . . nothing but armour. . . . A woman . . . entered . . . I followed her up into a dismal room. . . . Oh! What a dismaying chamber it was! An old uncurtained bed, made of black ebony, and carved with frightful faces!"[19]

Secret hopes for a share in Stoneleigh's fine establishment with its "26 Bed Chambers in the new part of the house" persisted for a while. Eventually the claim of Mrs. Austen's brother Mr. Leigh-Perrot was bought out with a sum of money.

Catherine remains in South Gloucestershire, at the opposite end from Adlestrop and its neighboring Stoneleigh Abbey. Northanger Abbey, we are told, is only thirty miles from Bath, to the north and east. On the journey "in two equal stages" General Tilney stops at Petty-France in South Gloucester "a two hours' bait" (II, ch. 5) in order to change horses and allow time for taking refreshment. Petty-France, then a mere coaching stop, is very near Great Badminton, seat of the Beaufort family. Deirdre LeFaye thinks the Tilneys' home "must be somewhere near Dursley in the Vale of Berkeley"[20] At Petty-France the party has fifteen miles to go. It may be simpler to imagine that their destination is just on the other side of the Beaufort estate.

IMAGINARY PLACES IN *NORTHANGER ABBEY*

Northanger Abbey, less rich in invented names than Austen's later works, displays more interest in place invention than do her earlier fictions. Catherine was born and lives in Fullerton, "a village in Wiltshire." Mr. Morland probably serves several adjoining parishes and churches with small congregations. He has a living he can spare to pass on to his son James—as George Austen was able to pass something on to *his* son James.[21] Austen knew that the engrossing of church livings was sometimes condemned as "pluralism" and that this was a current issue.

Catherine's clergyman father Richard Morland appears, however, un-
ambitious for himself; he does not seem to be trying to improve connections with Salisbury, the bishop's seat and abode of clerics. He can
afford to educate his sons; James goes to Oxford. Yet the family does
not live grandly, and Mrs. Morland, unlike Mrs. Bennet, is truly a slave
to her children's education. The name of the village—"Fullerton"—
sounds unromantic. There is a real Fullerton, a village in Hampshire,
not Somerset; Mills gives its origin as *Fugelerestune*—"village of the
bird-catchers." But the imaginary "Fullerton" could get its name from
Old French *fouleor* (anglicized as "fuller") + *tun/ton*.) A "fuller" cleans
cloth or raw wool, scouring and brightening raw wool or woven cloth
with substances such as "fuller's earth." As the wool and cloth trades had
long been important in this part of Wiltshire, the village's name seems
appropriate. The work of the fuller, the ancient dry cleaner is mentioned
in the New Testament: "And his raiment became shining, exceeding
white as snow; so as no fuller on earth can white them" (Mark 9:3). This
is a place that is clean—that is, innocent. "Fuller-ton" is a place where
one goes to be cleansed—as Henry Tilney is cleansed of some of the degrading avarice of Northanger when he comes to seek Catherine. Its inhabitants are "full"; that is, they are satisfied, they're not on the hunt for
anything more. That seems to be true not only of the Morlands but also
of the Allens. A yet-unstained innocence of ambition or greed underlies
the naive James's willingness to marry Isabella, a girl with no fortune.
Luckily for him, his modesty is not reciprocated.

The main issue of the novel is arguably *place*—in both topographical
and social senses. The best invention of a place name in this novel appears in its title. "Northanger" refers to a northern "hangar" or "hanging wood"—a wood on the slope of a steep hill. Presumably the direction is taken from the original abbey; that is, the hill slope and its woods
are to the north of the abbey, breaking the effects of wind and storm.
Catherine is assured

> of Northanger Abbey having been a richly-endowed convent at the
> time of the Reformation, of its having fallen into the hands of an an-
> cestor of the Tilneys on its dissolution, of a large portion of the an-
> cient building still making a part of the present dwelling although
> the rest was decayed. (II, ch. 2)

King Henry VIII notoriously rewarded supporters and hangers-on with
gifts from these confiscated lands. This abbey "fell" into greedy out-

stretched Tilney hands. General Tinley's ancestor put his thumb into Henry's great pie of prizes and pulled out a juicy one.

In employing an abbey as a setting Austen is stepping into Charlotte Smith territory. An important setting of Smith's *Ethelinde* (1789), a novel read by young Catharine Percival, is "Grasmere Abbey," formerly "dissolved by Henry the Eighth . . . given . . . to the family of Brandon" (I, ch. 1). When we encounter it, the abbey is owned by Sir Edward Newenden, a baronet. The heroine, Ethelinde Chesterville, is a relative of the baronet's newly rich wife. Lady Newenden's mother had "gone to the East Indies early in life" to capture a rich husband (as George Austen's sister Philadelphia and Catharine Percival's friend Miss Wynne had been compelled to do). Her catch, Mr. Maltravers ("bad crossing") is certainly rich, with a house in Hanover Square. The daughter of that union, Lady Newenden (née Maltravers), a spoiled creature accustomed to town luxuries, travels to Cumberland most unwillingly. Smith produces an extensive comic scene of an entry into an abbey at twilight. Sir Edward's wife, complaining of chilly discomfort, disparages the old edifice. Smith's design requires that Lady Newenden should be a silly and even bad wife, but the reader is likely to sympathize with her refusal to worship this antique sign of success and status. When her husband welcomes her at the door of the hall, she begs him not to keep her "in this great cold place; it strikes as damp as a family vault." A furnished room gives her little pleasure:

> A settee of rich cut velvet, with massy gilt feet, was in the room; which seemed to have in its time supported many of the venerable figures . . . represented in the great portraits that covered the wainscot. On this settee or sopha Lady Newenden sat down; and, wrapping her cloak round her, complained of the excessive coldness of the house. By this time an old housekeeper . . . appeared, and in the broad dialect of the northern country, enquired—"Wat my lady wad please to have aufter her journey?"
>
> "Have!" exclaimed her Ladyship, with evident marks of disgust; "why I would have a little warmth, good woman, if it is possible in these rooms."[22]

The housekeeper expostulates—her late lady never had a fire until the beginning of October. We may sympathize with the reluctant urban visitor, who rebukes her husband for bringing her "to this cold[,] damp, desolate place . . . fit only for the nuns and friars." Her sister-in-law protests against such disparagement of the aristocratic residence of her ancestors, "a family with which at least *mere modern opulence* may be proud to boast its alliance." Lady Newenden refuses to be impressed:

> "Not to-night, dear Ma'am—do not inform me to-night; for I am really fatigued to death, and cannot keep myself awake to hear any more about your ancestors. Doubtless they were all knights and esquires of high degree; only I wish their old-fashioned nunnery had fallen into the lake, before I had been dragged a thousand miles to catch my death in it."[23]

Catherine Moreland's entrance into Northanger Abbey seems contrived in deliberate contrast to the scene of arrival at an abbey in *Ethelinde*. Although the weather has turned dreary and rainy, Northanger Abbey is warm and dry, comfortable and fashionable:

> The furniture was in all the profusion and elegance of modern taste. The fire-place, where she had expected the ample width and ponderous carving of former times, was contracted to a Rumford, with ... ornaments over it of the prettiest English china. The windows, to which she looked with peculiar dependence, from having heard the General talk of his preserving them in their Gothic form with reverential care, were yet less what her fancy had portrayed. To be sure, the pointed arch was preserved—the form of them was Gothic ... but every pane was so large, so clear, and so light! (*NA*, II, ch. 5)

In Catherine's own room "the walls were papered, the floor was carpeted" (II, ch. 6). General Tilney has relentlessly modernized the place. His abbey, unlike "Grasmere Abbey," would meet the approval even of Lady Newenden. As a mischievous Austen well knows, Northanger would evoke the scorn of Gilpin, who laments over the modernized Ford (or Forde) Abbey in Dorset (now in South Somerset). Once the abbey was a picturesque ruin:

> Now, alas! It wears another face. It has been in the hands of improvement. Its simplicity is gone; and miserable ravage has been made through every part. The ruin is patched up into an awkward dwelling; old parts and new are blended together, to the mutual disgrace of both. The elegant cloister is still kept; but it is completely repaired, white-washed, and converted into a green-house. The hall

too is modernized, and every other part. Sash windows glare over pointed arches, and Gothic walls are adorned with Indian paper.

Gilpin expands upon the iniquity of such changes:

> When a man exercises his crude ideas in a few vulgar acres, it is of little consequence. . . . But when he lets loose his depraved taste, his absurd invention, and his graceless hands on such a subject as this, where art and nature cannot restore the havoc he makes, we consider such a deed under the same black character . . . as we do sacrilege and blasphemy in matters of religion.[24]

Oddly, Gilpin thinks people should refrain from domestic use of ruins once dedicated to sacred use—though he despises that use. He feels no anxiety about the "sacrilege and blasphemy" of seizing the religious foundations in the first place. God intended these places to be enjoyed *as ruins*. The improver of Forde Abbey has apparently blasphemed against the god of good taste—the deity whom General Tilney has also offended. By Gilpin's standards he is "depraved" and "graceless." And by Austen's own too—though for different reasons. Northanger Abbey is the opposite of Blaize Castle, a sham that Catherine imagined would be real. Northanger Abbey was once *real*—a real abbey—and is now a kind of sham. It is a fancy proposition projecting the self-image of greedy and self-satisfied General Tilney and his rapacious ancestors. Catherine may wish to live in a piece of the past, but the novel reminds the acute observer that the injuries of the past are still unrepaired. General Tilney has placed both his sons strategically in bulwarks of authority and mastery—Frederick in the Dragoons, Henry in the Church. Both sons in different ways are guards and defenders of the family's property.

The story of the big takeover of abbey lands is the truly "Gothic" story within this mock-Gothic tale. Like Isabella's infidelity, it is a banal instance of human heartlessness. An original "crime"—an outrage never to be mentioned but perpetually renewed, and committed with impunity—does not fear light of day. Catherine's first night within the walls of Northanger Abbey is fraught with a "Gothic" storm, recalling the image of Camden (and his translators) of the time when "a storm burst upon the English church."

The primal greed of the Tilneys is literally enacted by General Tilney. Austen ironically comments on the kitchens where "the General's improving hand" has been seriously at work: "His endowments of this spot alone might at any time have placed him high among the benefactors of the convent" (II, ch. 8) The irony here has nothing to do with Catherine's naïveté but reflects those who willfully "endow" their own appetites as "benefactors" only to themselves. Roger Moore's article "The Hidden History of *Northanger Abbey:* Jane Austen and the Dissolution of the Monasteries" delineates Austen's dark satire of a chaotic establishment that turns the land into property devoted to the feeding of one person. Moore suggests that Catherine's dissatisfied observations "introduce a note of social critique that is in the spirit of Cobbett."[25] The religious, human, and economic service of the old abbey, prayer and work marked by sacred hours—all that has been replaced by General Tilney's attention to his meal times.

Abbeys were customarily named after the nearest village or town, but "Northanger" refers to no community. Its original name is in disuse. The Tilneys' abbey is named after the wooded hill—an aesthetically pleasing view which also functions as a possession. The abbey church would once have had a saint's name, but that has disappeared. (If a Cistercian foundation, the abbey's church would have been dedicated to Saint Mary—another missing mother.) The capacity to erase places, to change geographies and rename them, is the true work and sign of power—as revolutionary movements know. Such erasure is radically destabilizing.

Henry Tilney, detecting Catherine's unspoken accusation of murder—a suspicion regarding his father that the son finds suspiciously easy to divine—defends his father from wife murder on the basis of cultural geography. He never says, "My father could never do such a thing! You don't understand him!" Instead, he asks Catherine to take her bearings from geography and history: "Remember that we are English, that we are Christians.... Does our education prepare us for such atrocities? Do our laws connive at them?" (II, ch. 9). Rhetorical questions are not convincing as answers. Camden reminds his readers that our ancestors were "Christians" and yet beloved Christian foundations were destroyed. Christians slaughtered other Christians in Tewkesbury Abbey—and in Drogheda under Cromwell. Sir Walter Hungerford had attempted murder of a spouse, and his stepmother had succeeded. Henry's Whiggish confidence reposes on the "neighbourhood of voluntary spies" (II, ch. 9). Rational paranoia, newspapers, and some cultural conditioning constitute the only credible restraints to inhibit a General Tilney.

Catherine, ashamed, hears Henry out—although at another level it is

Henry who should be ashamed of his brutal father and ancestral crime. In a comic mixture of innocence and insight Catherine insists on taking Henry extremely literally. She mentally acts as if what Henry is doing is setting out a *geographical* proposition. Ironically, she is quite right. Having seized the abbey and renamed it, the Tilneys—with Henry as their voice—are able to redefine it as a safe place incapable of sheltering "atrocities." Catherine takes what Henry says to be true of "the central part of England" though she would have "yielded the northern and western extremities" (i.e., the "Celtic fringe") (II, ch. 10). Yet in many eyes Catherine herself comes from the "western extremities." Her area of Wiltshire near Stonehenge might be read (through Stukeley and others) as a wild and mysterious part of England, associated with Druid rituals, and a Celtic—maybe even Phoenician—population. To rely on a delineated geography is unadvisedly to rely on a transitory political power enabled to draw lines. The powerful can only momentarily "define" regions perpetually subject to changes of name, definition, human belief, and human function.

Henry's assertive but circular argument arises from a shallow Whig progressivism, unconsciously self-interested. His statements *prove* nothing. Had Catherine been a sharper Tory antagonist, she might have retorted with reference to Hungerford Castle. More telling still, she might have referred to recent British history and Hanoverian treatment of a royal wife. In 1714 the Whigs brought in George Ludwig, Elector of Hanover, as King of England. George had married Sophia Dorothea of Celle (1666–1726) in order to unite two Germanic territories, even though Sophia Dorothea was legitimated by her parents' marriage only after her birth. Having had two children by this spouse, George fell in love with his mistress Melusina and effectually abandoned his wife. Mistakenly thinking sauce for the gander might be sauce for the goose, Sophia Dorothea entered into an affair with the Swedish Count von Königsmarck.

Retaliation was swift. Königsmarck was murdered in 1694; Sophia Dorothea was imprisoned for the rest of her natural life. The erring wife was kept a strict prisoner in the Castle of Ahlden for thirty years (*ODNB*). Matters were a trifle awkward when George I succeeded to the British crown and questions were asked as to the whereabouts of a queen who might be expected to figure in a coronation. English historians rarely dilate upon this episode. Oliver Goldsmith splendidly fudges the matter: "Pursuant to the Act of Succession, George the First, son of Ernest Augustus, and his princess Sophia, grand-daughter to James the first, ascended the British throne."[26] What a thumping lie! Sophia Dorothea never set foot in Britain and was not allowed to "ascend" anything. George II hated his father for what he done to his mother and never forgave him. King George I had committed murder (through agents) and kept his wife locked up—and yet he took the Coronation Oath.

Henry Tilney declares that his immediate territory is safely under control. Yet Henry—a mere second son—is not really in charge of the abbey, any more than Edmund Bertram will be in charge of Mansfield Park. In any case, who controls the controllers? Henry's "objective" criteria could always be challenged by facts. Henry projects everything he does not want to think about upon the "Gothic" fiction, whereas through her reading Catherine has come to suspect—rightly—that bad things are real. She has learned about good and evil. Henry remaps the geography of central England as "safe," but we see only a vista of spies and hear a shaky assurance that civilization precludes nasty deeds— even by those who have committed a gigantic theft and are living off the proceeds.

Henry Tilney holds—but does not of course possess—a parsonage at Woodston, with some glebe lands. Here he is making modest improvements. Nothing will belong to him, however; everything belongs to the Church of England, although the living is in the gift of its local patron (General Tilney). Catherine Morland does not acquire any *more land* by this marriage. The imagined village has a modest name— "Woodston" (*wudu* + *ton*), "settlement in the woods." This little Saxon settlement almost certainly predated the great (imaginary) abbey— probably once called "Woodston Abbey." Woodston has not progressed much since it was a clearing in the woods, about 800 AD. In 1800 it is probably losing population. Woodston, however, with its fields, and the puppies Catherine plays with, is a pleasanter place than the aggressive abbey. Mrs. Henry Tilney will spend most of her time here. She is never going to be mistress of Northanger but will have to defer to Frederick's wife, whoever that may be. Henry and Catherine are always going to be under the control of Northanger Abbey and its owner. After their wedding they will not escape the supervision of the commanding General Tilney. A few more dogs and some children in Woodston parsonage may, however, render the aging general less eager to inflict a ceremonial visitation on Henry Tilney and his wife.

The abbey itself in this novel is the central force from which anachronism spins. The Gothic novel in creative conscious anachronisms contributes to Catherine's, and our, recognition that we are living in a world of history—and that this is seriously shocking. Catherine of Wiltshire, the moonraker, is willing to seem stupid in order to pursue a reality that she suspects is not truthfully accounted for, not seriously told. History's aggression and confusions render our apprehensions chaotic and worrying. Henry tries to combat anachronism, the colliding multiple layers of living, by asserting a tidy clean space of modernity, an unmoving centrality unrelated to violence, passion, and confusion. This is as dishonest in its way as John Thorpe's flamboyant carelessness about time and distance. "Real solemn history" provides an inefficient anodyne to the pain of living *in* history. Relief from the pressures of living within multiple temporal charges is perhaps best provided by are things that are born, grow, and die, like puppies and the hyacinth, not concerned with fashion and never out of time.

Names and Places in *Sense and Sensibility*: Sussex, Devonshire, London (Town) — and a Touch of Dorset

REAL PLACES IN *SENSE AND SENSIBILITY*

Sense and Sensibility almost aggressively declares that it is sticking close to England. Colonel Brandon has been abroad to the East Indies (i.e., India) fighting the wars for colonies against the French. Elinor says he talks well about his experiences, but the reader hears nothing of such travel tales, only the substitutes provided by the mockery of Willoughby and Marianne:

> "That is to say," cried Marianne contemptuously, "he has told you that in the East Indies the climate is hot, and the mosquitoes are troublesome." . . .
> "Perhaps," said Willoughby, "his observations may have extended to the existence of nabobs, gold mohrs, and palanquins." (*S&S*, I, ch. 10)

The laughing pair discount anything that Brandon might have to tell, limiting him by caricature. This is a way of erasing the significance not only of what the wounded empire builder has done, but of the British Empire itself. Brandons roam. Colonel Brandon's sister (whom we never meet) is abroad, in Avignon, once a resort of Jacobites.[27] The woman who will be Marianne's sister-in-law has gone abroad only for health; Brandon seems to be surrounded by sickly women. Aside from such slight references to a world outside, the persistent focus in this novel is on England. Willoughby and Marianne want to stay safely in England. Unlike Catherine Morland, who liked to be "reminded" of the south of France (known to her only through Emily's travels in *Udolpho*), Marianne is not transported by her reading to Mediterranean shores. Her reading lies entirely in contemporary English poets like Cowper, who write about England.

Sense and Sensibility opens with the memorable and ironic sentence "The family of Dashwood had long been settled in Sussex" (I, ch. 1). Sussex itself is a long-settled county, inhabited since prehistoric times, as witnessed by Chanctonbury Ring, an Iron Age hill fort. Camden describes this county of Suth-Sex:

> The sea coast of this County . . . has very high green hills, call'd the *Downs,* which, consisting of a fat chalky soil, are very fruitful. The middle-part, chequer'd with meadows, pastures, corn fields, and groves, makes a very fine show. The hithermost and north side, is shaded pleasantly with woods, as anciently the whole Country was, which made it impassable.

Antiquaries say that the forest, the "Weald" (wildwood, like German *Wald*) was originally "a desert and vast wilderness; neither planted with towns, nor peopled with men, but stuff'd with herds of deer, and droves of hogs only."[28] In the earliest inhabited periods it was known for "Iron-mines all over," with furnaces and forges; in later ages the region went in for "casting of Cannons" and also gunpowder: "Near *Hastings* also are two powder-mills, where is made very good Gun-powder."[29] Sussex had a technological and industrial turn from the Stone Age onward, early undertaking metalworking. The Weald became smaller and more built upon. In the late eighteenth century the destruction of timber, loss of a formerly abundant fuel, starved some once-thriving industries (such as glassmaking). The serious problem of finding available wood in Sussex highlights the carelessness of John Dashwood in cutting down trees.

This land of the South Saxons was a kingdom in the Dark Ages. The Sussex coast was attacked successfully by the Normans. Intending to keep his new possessions, William (and his successors) strengthened the ports and built or refortified numerous castles along the south coast, putting the most trusted confederates in charge. A close associate of William the Conqueror, Hubert de Burg (or De Burgh), was made constable of Dover Castle. (We may imagine this invader was a direct ancestor of Lady Catherine's husband.) The Normans moved Sussex's bishopric to the city of Chichester where the cathedral was dedicated in 1108. Flourishing under Saxon kings, Sussex continued to thrive under the Normans and subsequently under Plantagenets and Tudors.

Sussex, with its own culture and industries, was never far from centers of power. Under William III and his eighteenth-century successors great efforts were made to improve roads, resulting in a system of turnpike roads and enhanced communication. Coastal towns played an important part in the defenses of England during the Napoleonic War. Brighton on the coast of Sussex was not only the Prince Regent's leisure center but also a fortified place preparing to repel invaders. In *Lady Susan,* Sussex is the abode of the aristocratically named Charles Vernon and his wife, a Norman-descended De Courcy of Kent. His banking makes Charles Vernon seem a bit Whiggish; Lady Susan remarks, "Charles is very rich I am sure; when a Man has once got his name in a Banking House he rolls in money" (Letter 5, *Later Manuscripts,* 10). This seems a fling at Henry Austen, who had "set himself up as an army agent and banker" about the time of his father's retirement.[30] The Vernons' life in Sussex strikes Lady Susan as surpassingly dull, and we may find it so too. Norland in Sussex does nothing to dismiss that impression. We shall return to Sussex in *Sanditon,* but to a different part of the county, the coast and not the fat hinterland inhabited by "the family of Dashwood." Norland, the Dashwoods' long settlement, is obviously in the county's tranquil middle with its "meadows, pastures and corn [i.e., wheat] fields." Yet Sussex at the beginning of the nineteenth century was suffering from agricultural depression and popular resentment at low wages (conditions that John and Fanny Dashwood will certainly do nothing to ameliorate).

"The family of Dashwood had been long settled in Sussex"— delightful ironic sentence. We rapidly learn that the term "family" does not include women, but refers to males with the correct surname. The Dashwood women to whom we become attached are not be "settled in Sussex" at all. They are explicitly excluded by Fanny Dashwood, who argues that her husband's half sisters "were related to him only by half blood, which she considered as no relationship at all" (*S&S,* I, ch. 2). Primogeniture, the right of the eldest male to take all, is generally believed to have come in with the Normans. In pre-Conquest Kent and parts of Sussex, land tenure had became independent of service to the lord. "*Socage*" permitted paying rent in money alone; land values measured in money meant land could become "partible." Anglo-Saxon *Gavelkind* (an Anglo-Saxon term of puzzling etymology essentially connecting with rent of land) seems an evolution of *socage;* it allowed property to be divided by will. In accord with Gavelkind a property owner could dispose leave separate parts of his wealth to his wife and kin. As Edward Hasted explains, in *The History and Topographical Survey of the County of Kent,*

> Lands in *gavelkind* descend to all the sons alike in equal portions, and if there are no sons, then equally among the daughters; and as to the chattels, it was formerly part of the custom of this country to divide them into three parts.[31]

Imagine Mrs. John Dashwood's horror if all the nice things in Norland had to be divided into three parts ! Male children were entitled to an equal share of the father's property, the widow had a share and even the female children (though these had to be legally represented). Jane Austen, whose richest relatives lived in Kent, probably knew that Kent and parts of Sussex had maintained the more equitable Saxon inheritance system.

> The Custom of Gavelkind is in many Towns in *Sussex;* but that scarce any two Places agree in any other of the *Kentish* Customs, but that of the Descent. The Lands lying within the Port of *Rye* in *Sussex* are partible among Males, and the Wife is endowed of a Moiety, as in Gavelkind.[32]

Gavelkind arguably has "a more noble Original" than primogeniture, "being descended from the Universal Law of the whole World" whereby children of the same parents, "entitled to the same Affection and support . . . partook alike of the Possessions," until some found it necessary "to raise Distinctions where Nature made none."[33] This is the view of Mrs. Bennet whose silly notion is backed also by Adam Smith and William Blackstone.

Gavelkind can benefit the women (at the very least, the widow) without reliance on fragile promises made by a son to a father on his deathbed. Lady Catherine in Kentish Rosings can proclaim that entail "was not thought necessary in Sir Lewis de Bourgh's family" (*P&P,* II, ch. 6). Jane Austen goes to some trouble to show the reader that Norland is tied to male heirs by the will—or whim—of a particular man who chooses unnecessarily to respect primogeniture and is also charmed by a male infant. No ineluctable entail impends, rendering inheritance by the male heir legally inevitable, as in the case of the Bennets. The will of the man referred to as the "Old Gentleman" (common synonym for the Devil) sends the Dashwood females into exile. In *Sense and Sensibility* it is Edward Ferrars's mother who has oddly benefited from absence of primogeniture—though not because of her county. Mr. Ferrars's property is not tied up for the eldest son; Mrs. Ferrars possesses not only the property with its income, but also the disposal of it. Neither the Old Gentleman nor Mrs. Ferrars enters into the spirit and principles of Gavelkind.

How did Mrs. Ferrars gain such control? This widow's entire control over property signals that this family, though exceedingly wealthy, is not highborn. Their wealth has little to do with ownership of land. Does the unpleasant Mrs. Ferrars benefit from the mere accident of a husband's sufficiently low birth—not quite gentry? Mrs. Ferrars herself does not seem of gentle birth. We cannot "place" Mrs. Ferrars—we don't know who her family was or where she was born. We don't even *know* where Edward and Robert were born, but probably in London, where the family lives on the proceeds of—what? There is no home estate. There is an estate in Norfolk that Mrs. Ferrars *might* give to Edward if he should marry to her liking; this, however, is not a family home but something more like an incidental investment, an acquisition rather than an inheritance. The Ferrars money must have derived originally from trade and commerce, and then from shrewd investments. Fanny Ferrars in marrying the heir of an estate is marrying up—no matter how substantial her dowry.

In *Sense and Sensibility* Austen makes the kind of move she intended to perform in *The Watsons,* snatching her orphaned girls away from their original setting. Readers too are abruptly snatched away from Sussex, sent a considerable distance into rural Devon with its lovely but steep hills and muddy lanes. Sir John Middleton's estate with its cottage is some four miles from the small but thriving cathedral "city" and market town of Exeter. A Roman foundation on the river called by the Celts "Exe" (meaning "water"), "Exe-*ceaster*" was once a Roman camp. This town flourished in the Middle Ages and the Tudor era because of the wool trade. Exeter, 171 miles from London, prospered again in the eighteenth century; central market town of the western region, it was the sixth largest city in England. Yet Exeter's population in the first census of 1801 is given as only twenty thousand persons.

The expensive New London Inn, which could handle three hundred

horses a day opened in Exeter in 1794. This seems just the place to attract Robert and Lucy, who stop there on a wedding journey from London. The time taken to travel by stagecoach from London to Exeter was
just under thirty-three hours; a private carriage might go more rapidly.
Austen is exactly right regarding the length of Mrs. Jennings's journey to
London with Elinor and Marianne: "They were three days on their journey" (*S&S*, II, ch. 4). Exeter, endeavoring to catch up with the modern
world of speedy coach travel, was not too out of the way for traffic to
Bath and Bristol, although Bath is seventy miles away and Bristol sixty-
six. Devonshire, to which the Dashwood women must go, has both
agricultural hinterland and extensive seacoast. The Dashwoods do not
go to the seacoast—although Ang Lee's film (1995) wished otherwise.
Their story stays inland. It is Lucy Steele who is strongly associated with
the coast; she comes from Dawlish, and her uncle lives further west,
near Plymouth.

Plymouth, not a direct setting for the novel's action, is important
as Edward's shadow world. Bounded by two rivers, the Plym, and the
Tamar (marking the boundary with Celtic Cornwall), Plymouth was
the home port of Sir Francis Drake. According to legend Drake paused
to finish his game of bowls in Plymouth Hoe before going on to defeat
the Armada. In 1620 the Pilgrim Fathers set sail in the *Mayflower* from
Plymouth. More disturbingly, after the 1780s gangs of convicts were
shipped off to Australia from this port. A new mile-long breakwater,
long in the planning stages, was begun in the year after *Sense and Sensibility* was published. Plymouth, former "principal naval base in the
war against Spain," declined sharply from the mid-seventeenth century.
Communications were poor, and it ceded importance to the new port
at "Dock" (later "Devonport"). Frequent references to "Plymouth" in
Persuasion correctly reflect the importance of "Dock"(or Plymouth
Dock), a great naval installation; "by 1801 Dock was the largest town
in Devon."[34] Mrs. Ferrars, however, sends her elder son to the suburbs
of old Plymouth—a most unlikely far-western spot, near an antiquated
port devoted to the duller forms of sea traffic—to be privately educated
by Mr. Pratt. Such lonely schooling in a remote unfashionable place
seems extremely odd for someone of the standing to which the Ferrars
family pretends. After Edward's distressing revelation, Robert claims
that he expostulated with his mother:

> "Why would you be persuaded by my uncle, Sir Robert, against your
> own judgment, to place Edward under private tuition . . . ? If you had

only sent him to Westminster as well as myself, instead of sending him to Mr. Pratt's, all this would have been prevented." (II, ch. 14)

Robert has been given the benefit of one of the best schools in England, the only one of the great "public schools" located in London itself. Westminster produced some famous sons, including Dryden, and can hardly be blamed for the folly of Robert.[35] Jane's brothers had been privately taught by George Austen before going to Oxford. But Edward Austen Knight of Godmersham sent his sons away to school; perhaps he regarded home schooling as a compromise with poverty. Edward Ferrars is certainly no advertisement for private schooling. Although Robert may be an indifferent advertisement for a "public" school, Westminster would certainly pay off in social advancement. Uncle Robert always favored the boy named after him.

Why was Edward sent to Mr. Pratt in Plymouth? Robert's impression is that his mother "was persuaded . . . against her own judgment." Did the persuasive uncle raise the point of Edward's distressing shyness? Physical awkwardness, extreme bashfulness, or some juvenile disability might well have prompted the uncle to suggest stashing the boy away (a little like Austen's mysteriously defective brother George). Did he develop a stammer like "little Lord Lymington" whose mother "grew alarmed at the hesitation in his speech" and after a month took him away from George Austen's care? (But that mama took the stammering child to a speech specialist in London.)[36] Little Lord Lymington did not get better; he became obsessed with funerals ("Black Jobs"). As Earl of Portsmouth he developed vampiric tendencies—which one hopes is not Edward's case.[37] In Austen's own mother's family, Edward Leigh the heir, after a brilliant start, deteriorated mentally; placed in a private asylum, he was treated by doctors Monro and Willis (later to treat "mad" George III). In 1774 Edward Leigh was declared officially "Lunatic" and was kept hidden away in Stoneleigh Abbey, a "Gothic" fate.[38] His will caused the confusion about inheritance that raised Austen hopes of Stoneleigh after "mad" Edward's sister died in 1806. Mrs. Austen expressed pleased surprise that there were no Gothic horrors at Stoneleigh, but she may have known of one—her lunatic relative hidden away for years.

Were Mrs. Ferrars and her brother concerned that Edward might be mentally defective—or at least backward? The adult Edward is shy and awkward; he might indeed not have stood up well to the rough and tumble of Westminster. But why is he sent to Plymouth—so very distant? Perhaps the Ferrars had business interests there, trade with American colonies and former colonies. Who was "Mr. Pratt"? He is never referred to as a clergyman, though the Steeles would surely voice any such claim to gentility. He successfully prepared Edward for Oxford, so Pratt must have had sufficient Latin and Greek. Given the strong associations of his name with the legal profession through the brilliant Pratt who became Lord Chancellor, this Pratt may be a lawyer with time on his hands. Putting Edward to school with a Pratt might strengthen family hopes that the youth will choose the right profession. And with young Edward hidden in a small domestic establishment in Plymouth, where a Pratt's home is his castle, nobody from the fashionable world would be likely to catch sight of this hobbledehoy. He won't disgrace the family. But they should beware: "Pratt" is a name dangerous to "Ferrars."

The coastal town of Dawlish attracts Robert Ferrars, who has his fingers on the pulse of fashion. Dawlish ("dark stream," a Celtic river-name) was a fishing village making a determined bid to become a seaside resort in the new style. John Feltham in his *Guide to all the Watering and Sea-Bathing Places* says that Dawlish "has, within a few years, risen into a state of comparative elegance" (like Lucy Steele herself). "There are now building five large houses upon the cliffs, commanding a picturesque view of Torbay . . . and, as the Princess of Wales has lately honored this place with her residence, there is no doubt but Dawlish will rapidly rise into consequence."[39] The presence of Caroline of Brunswick (who visited in April 1806) might be a mixed blessing.

Jane Austen had visited Dawlish; during Mr. Austen's retirement, the Austens went on summer holidays to seaside resorts, one year to Sidmouth, the next (1802) to Dawlish and Teignemouth. In August 1814 Jane remembers the library at Dawlish as "particularly pitiful & wretched 12 years ago" (10 August–18 August 1814; *Letters*, 267–69). Holidays in Devonshire at the turn of the century gave Austen background for the setting of *Sense and Sensibility*. It may have been during the time at Dawlish that she encountered the good young clergyman, a suitor to whom Jane was reputedly attracted, but who died untimely, according to confused family recollections.[40] The possibility that her last incomplete romance took place in Dawlish makes it the more piquant that Austen should choose Dawlish as the birthplace of Elinor's vulgar rival and a honeymoon resort for the fop Robert and his vixen Lucy.

Devonshire was making a conscious effort to modernize and to attract tourists. Yet Devonshire was still considered the abode of yokels. It appealed to poets and novelists. In Charlotte Smith's *Celestina,* the hero's paternal estate, Alvestone, is "between Sidmouth and Exeter." The heroine exiles herself from London, where she fears the marriage of the man she loves will soon take place, betaking herself to a cheap lodging in "a small new built brick house" on the edge of a dreary heath: "Winter had alike divested the common of its furze and heath blossoms, and the few elms on its borders, of their foliage."[41] In the winter of her discontent, Celestina can, however, almost see Alvestone, home of her beloved George Willoughby:

> By the help of a telescope lent her by her landlord, Celestina had discovered a clump of firs in Alvestone Park; and though they were near ten miles distance, and without a glass appeared only a dark spot above the rest of the landscape, she found a melancholy pleasure in distinguishing them, and would frequently . . . in their pensive rambles, fix her eyes on that distant object.[42]

Marianne Dashwood at Cleveland seeks out an eminence from which "her eye, wandering over a wide tract of country . . . could fondly rest on the farthest ridge of hills in the horizon, and fancy that from their summits Combe Magna might be seen" (*S&S,* III, ch. 6). "Combe Magna" is the name of Willoughby's estate in Somersetshire—still in the West Country. The name in its mixture of Old English noun (*cwm, cumbe* = *valley*) and Latin adjective (*magna* = big) indicates antiquity. Combe Magna may be attractively located, but it apparently brings Willoughby only about six to seven hundred pounds a year. We never see it directly.

At least, Marianne Dashwood does not avail herself of a telescope to try to see Combe Magna. Celestina, however, has some excuse, as she was brought up at Alvestone. When Willoughby comes back to rural Devon unmarried, he invites Celestina back home:

> The snow, which had covered every object with cold uniformity, had now given place to the bright verdure of infant spring; the earliest trees and those in the most sheltered situations had put forth their tender buds; the copses were strewn with primroses and March violets, and the garden glowing with the first flowers of the year.[43]

Austen does not engage openly with such tropes of Devonshire beauty; she gives us an impression of the great hills, the muddy valleys, fresh air, and space. Yet the movement from autumn through winter to spring is important to Jane Austen in *Sense and Sensibility* (as it is also in

Pride and Prejudice and *Emma*). Marianne's recovery takes place in the Devonshire countryside in spring.

The London section of the novel contrasts markedly with the scenes in the country. The right time to visit London is during "the London season" from January to June. The "Season" started soon after the New Year, grew more dashing after Easter, and came to a grand finale at the King's official birthday, on the fourth of June. During this period new plays, concerts, and operas were produced; rich visitors vied with each other and with the permanent residents to give elegant parties. The Dashwood girls go to London only for the first half of the Season, and their entertainments are neither expensive nor very exclusive—for example, they do not spend an evening at Almack's, where one of the titled patronesses had to vouch for a girl before she could enter. Elinor and Marianne are not debutantes. Their brother and his wife should have entertained them, brought them into London society, and made sure the girls met some eligible young men. Of course they do nothing. Elinor is nervous of their visiting Mrs. Jennings, fearing that she and Marianne will be introduced to an inferior set of City people, thus barring themselves out of the world of the gentry. Elinor's fear seems to us embarrassingly snobbish but is realistic.

"London" was notoriously divided between "City" and "Town." The City of London is the original area, based on the old fortified square mile. Long self-governing, it elected its own mayor and aldermen and held out for a considerable degree of independence. Proud of being citizens of their own city, commercial denizens of London were ridiculed for centuries as vulgarians and money-grubbers. After the Restoration the slang term was "Cits," represented in Restoration comedies as joyless Puritans or greedy vulgarians, worthy only of being cuckolded by Cavaliers. The City was then—and now—the center of British commerce and finance; it is close to the port and to "low" waterside regions like Wapping. "Town," well to the west, is traditionally centered upon the royal court at Saint James and is the region of palaces, Parliament, and parks. Theaters and elegant shops engage the gentry. "Going to London" can mean two entirely different things.

The inhabitants of these different worlds rarely met socially. City identity precluded gentility. Mrs. Jennings, who formerly lived in the City but now lives in Town, is one of the few *characters* who actually dwell in London. Most characters—the Dashwoods, the Middletons, the Steeles, Willoughby, Colonel Brandon—are renting or visiting. Mrs. Ferrars, another permanent resident in London (as Robert must be also), has a grand address in Park Street. That street was the address of the wealthy widow Maria Fitzherbert, when she and the Prince of Wales first began their relationship in her bijou town house, where the couple went through a ceremony of marriage. An ultraexpensive Park Street residence seems both too grand and too louche for Mrs. Ferrars—but we never see her at home. She does not entertain her own relatives; Fanny and John must invite her to dine in the house they rent. It is hard "to place" Mrs. Ferrars. Radically unsociable, Mrs. Ferrars exhibits many of the marks of the person who has come up in the world through wealth alone. She could certainly *afford* a better tutor for her son, but, beyond a point, the "breeding" or lack of it of a Mr. Pratt would not worry her.

Mrs. Ferrars's social isolation stimulates doubt of her pretensions. Was Lord Morton's daughter ever *truly* a genuine marriage prospect for either of her sons? We may speculate that Mrs. Ferrars has achieved secretly—starting out on slightly higher ground—what Mrs. Jennings has obtained openly, with little pretense: a rise into a rank and class above that of her birth or background. Lucy, with more capacity for social observation than either Mrs. Ferrars or Mrs. Jennings, wishes to do as these women did. Mrs. Ferrars, cunning and enclosed, resembles Lucy, save in total ignorance of the arts of compliment.

Fortunately for Elinor, Mrs. Jennings lives in an acceptably fashionable area, in "Berkeley-street" near Portman Square. This is not far from the imaginary lodging of Lady Susan in Upper Seymour Street, near Portman Square, where she entertains her illicit lover Manwaring and writes Reginald a dismissive letter. In 1801–2 Henry Austen and his second wife, the dashing Eliza de Feuillide (née Hancock), were living "quite in style in Upper Berkeley Street, Portman Square," according to Philadelphia Walter.[44] Portman Square, frequently mentioned in fiction of this period, was first developed in the Restoration. More valuable as Town moved westward, by the 1770s this square had some claim to fashion. In Frances Burney's *Cecilia* the newly rich and disastrously extravagant Harrels dwell in Portman Square, in a town house fated to be overrun by bailiffs and creditors. At that time, Portman Square was just opposite the Tyburn gallows. Since 1855 Marble Arch has stood near the lethal spot, a shiny white distraction from somber history. Perhaps executions ceased to be produced at Tyburn because *Cecilia*'s critique in 1782 of the traditional procession from Newgate along Oxford Street, formerly "Tyburn Road," brought to developers' attention a certain negative effect on their rising residential properties. The procession to Tyburn was abolished in 1783. If not the very *best* address, Portman Square is acceptable, if a mere extension of the old or true West End.

The Middletons rent a house in "Conduit-street," in the center of what came to be known as "Mayfair," after the "May Fair" held in Shepherd's Market. Now running between New Bond Street and our Regent Street (the latter designed in the 1820s and unknown to Austen), Conduit Street in the eighteenth century, near Burlington House and highly expensive shops, was utterly fashionable. Nowadays Conduit Street is home to Tiffany and a host of international designers' shops; the jewelers' windows can damage your eyes with the glare of diamonds. The Steele sisters, when ejected from this earthly paradise, have to take refuge again with their relatives in Bartlett's Buildings, a purpose-built tenement in Holborn (the same social no-man's-land as Burney's Evelina finds herself in when she stays with her vulgar grandmother). Strangely, the Middletons are staying in a more glamorous address than John and Fanny Dashwood, who have rented lodgings, "a very good house for three months," in "Harley-street"" (II, ch. 12). Harley Street—not yet associated with medical offices—is just west of the perfect West End squares; it is presentable, if less glamorous than the Mayfair address. The Dashwoods in this instance are not extravagant; visiting only for the early part of the Season, they do not intend to take on the higher rents charged for the post-Easter period. They do commonplace touristic things, like taking their little boy "to see the wild beasts at Exeter Exchange" (II, ch. 11). Named after Sir Thomas Cecil, Earl of Exeter, the house on the Strand was a remodeled Elizabethan mansion turned into a sort of zoo.

Single men can find good lodgings cheaply, and are not expected to hold fashionable dinner parties. John Willoughby lodges in "Bond-street," center of the area devoted to the most expensive shops, close to the parks and to club land. George Willoughby in *Celestina* likewise lodges in Bond Street when in town. Colonel Brandon "lodges in St. James's-street," an excellent address, if temporary; presumably his bachelor's lodgings are a couple of rooms. After the repudiation by faithless Willoughby and Marianne's heartbreak, the Dashwood girls' London season of enforced gaiety is a Lenten affair indeed. They depart before Easter.

There follows a brief disastrous visit in Somersetshire, haunted by illness and danger. Return to Devonshire spells health. The West Country cures the ills of London. At the end of the story four major characters are all living in Dorsetshire, native county of Colonel Brandon. Dorset's county town, Dorchester (*Dornwaraceaster*), was once a Roman en-campment based on a Celtic settlement. Dorset is just west of Hampshire, with Somerset to the northwest and Wiltshire to the northeast. Remains of prehistoric settlements show that it has long been friendly to human habitation; its climate is relatively warm; it has rich arable land and pastures. In the Victorian era it was to supply London with butter. On the Channel coast, Dorset in Austen's time is beginning to develop bathing resorts, Weymouth being the most famous. Frank Churchill and Jane Fairfax will meet in Weymouth. The sharp rise in this resort's fortunes came when George III, recovering from his first attack of what has been later diagnosed as porphyria (manifested at its worst in symptoms of insanity), went on holiday to Weymouth in 1789.

Despite the loyalty aroused by George III's curative visits, Dorset has a history as a standing ground of rebels. Much of this county was staunchly pro-Parliament in the Civil War; many of its inhabitants supported Monmouth when he landed at Lyme Regis in 1685. The Bloody Assizes were held in Dorchester and Taunton. After Jane Austen's time (but in the lifetime of her siblings) Tolpuddle in Dorset was known for the "Tolpuddle Martyrs," pioneers in union rights. In 1832, six agricultural workers banded together as a Friendly Society to demand better wages and working conditions. These men were found guilty on the technical charge of taking an oath and transported to Australia. The outcry was so great that the government was eventually forced to let the "Tolpuddle Martyrs" return. Agricultural problems and labor unrest were brewing in Austen's lifetime.

Although it participated in stirring historical events, Dorset was—and is now—a deeply rural place. In the census of 1801 the population of the entire county was under 102,000. As Dorset was known for dairy products, it is appropriate that married Edward and Elinor want "rather better pasturage for their cows" (III, ch. 14). They are settling into the bucolic style of the region.

IMAGINARY PLACES IN *SENSE AND SENSIBILITY*

In *Sense and Sensibility* Austen goes further than she has done before in inventing a number of imaginary estates. (*Lady Susan* has two, and *Northanger Abbey* but one.) In the background of the entire story is the "family" property of Norland Park—a punning name. "Norland," which sounds like a contraction of "North-land," reminds us that the heroines have neither house *nor* land. Before inheriting Norland, Mr. Dashwood and his family have been residing at a more modest place called "Stanhill" ("stone-hill"). Mr. Dashwood dies not long after he inherits, leaving a widow and three daughters. The three sisters' half brother John Dashwood, the heir, takes the entire property, abetted by his wife, who is determined that her husband should give his sisters and stepmother nothing. Breaking with tradition (of which she may be ignorant) she refuses to acknowledge any claim of theirs to residence in the patriarchal home. The home of Mitford's "bucolic squires" was expected to house "father's relict" and the squire's "unmarried sisters," but that is not how town-bred Fanny sees an estate. On meeting Elinor in London, John Dashwood tells her he has made a purchase of "East Kingham Farm," which he has bought from "old Gibson." "Kingham" indicates a "settlement lived in (or owned by) the King"; John Dashwood even seizes formerly royal land in his land hunger. He complains to Elinor of the "inclosure" of Norland Common as "a most serious drain" on his financial resources—though it represents an expansion of his acreage and increase of potential wealth (*S&S*, II, ch. 11). A "Common" was common land, on which the poor villagers could raise a few cows, sheep, and geese, and so on. John Dashwood's enclosure will put more stress upon the lower orders in their struggle to survive. Privatizing of common land went on for generations from the sixteenth through the eighteenth century, supported by the new theory giving all power to *contract* and none to customary rights. Ownership as absolute possession displaced stewardship and continuity. Whig political philosophy allowed no claim to use of land unless an absolute right of possession were conferred in a clear written contract. (The English deployed these theories equally smartly in the New World, taking land from the indigenous people because they did not have the proper papers.)

Sense and Sensibility plays throughout upon the loss of custom to contract. Mrs. Ferrars and her children Fanny and Robert, Whiggish to the bone, have no regard for obligation not battened down by *contract*. Fanny seizes on the fact that John promised his dying father no *specific* donation to the widow and children. There was no contract on that deathbed. Annuities specifically left in a will subjected Mrs. Ferrars to unpleasant obligations to old servants, obligations she would have avoided if she could. Much of the novel circles around the difference between obligation and contract—Willoughby proves capable of relying on the absence of contract in the cases of both Eliza and Marianne. Marianne does not understand that love—unlike an engagement— is not a *contract*. John and Fanny understand very well that they are bound by no contract to care for the Dashwood women; John does not even buy his sisters a pair of inexpensive earrings in the jewelers' shop. Sir John Middleton and Colonel Brandon may have an older view of charity or hospitality. The commercially minded find no challenge posed by charity. They substitute gimcracks—like the "huswifes" Fanny Dashwood buys, giving the Steele sister each "a needle book, made by some emigrant," shorting both needy maker and recipient (II, ch. 14). We watch John Dashwood in the process of cutting the last ties to custom under the urging of his wife who genuinely sees no obligation in words said to a dying parent as long as they are not specific. Only with the binding of contract can obligation be reluctantly admitted. Lucy Steele goes a bit further in the general trend when she suits herself by denying both custom *and* contract.

John's land hunger is matched by his wastefulness of land once he has it. One sign of his defectiveness is that he cuts down trees, partly in order to make a space for "Fanny's greenhouse . . . upon the knoll behind the house":

> "The old walnut trees are all come down to make room for it. It will be a very fine object from many parts of the park, and the flower-garden will slope down just before it, and be exceedingly pretty. We have cleared away all the old thorns that grew in patches over the brow." (II, ch. 11)

Walnut trees would make a much better sight than the glassy artifice of a greenhouse. In order to erect this expensive structure (which will eat up fuel) John rashly cuts down the protective thorn trees—which have their own beauty:

> White hawthorn . . . is the oldest of the hedgerow trees . . . used in Saxon times to make impenetrable fences. . . . In the Midlands it is the tree one sees most often: and for a brief spell in early summer it is the most beautiful . . . with its continuous miles of white may-blossom glimmering as far as the eye can see. . . . From the hedgerow trees near and far come the calls of countless cuckoos, and the lesser sound of an infinite number of small birds.[45]

Thorns not only mark a boundary but also provide shelter from the wind on the brow of the hill. Once Norland's thorn trees are gone, the knoll will be subject to the fierceness of sun and wind; flowers may wither, and it is quite on the cards that the greenhouse may eventually blow down.

John and Fanny are not trying to make the land bear better; they are going in for decoration, replacing the wilds with something "exceedingly pretty." We note this word's use in description of the nicely furnished reception room at Northanger Abbey—"the prettiest English china" (*NA,* II, ch. 5). Johnson's first two definitions for the adjective "pretty" are "Neat; elegant, pleasing without surprise or elevation" and "Beautiful without grandeur or dignity." He also remarks that it is used "in a kind of diminutive contempt" (Johnson, *Dictionary,* vol. 2). "Pretty" in Austen's writing always seems more negative than positive. Lady Catherine indulges her own "diminutive contempt" in referring to the Bennet's shrubbery as "a prettyish kind of a little wilderness" (*P&P,* III, ch. 14). John and Fanny Dashwood's displacement of John's sisters and stepmother is of a piece with their view of property as something to play with. They have no idea of public good—not even the good of their extended family. And they cannot see the land in terms of its good. They caricature the actions of pioneer ancestors who cut down the wildwood.

The little family of women goes to Devonshire because Sir John Middleton of Barton Park offers them a cottage on his property at a minimum rent. "Barton" is a fairly common place name (*bar + tun,* or "barley-farm"): "outlying grange where barley is stored" (Mills). As Anne-Marie Edwards points out, "Barton is so common among Devon place names that it is not surprising Jane should choose it for the name of the valley, the large house and cottage and nearby village in her novel." Edwards believes that Austen saw something of the Exe valley during the family holidays in Devon in 1801 and 1802. She espouses the view that Barton Park with its village is modeled on Upton Pynes. "Pynes," great house of the Northcote family, served as the model for Sir John Middleton's house, while the location of Barton cottage is drawn from the farm at Woodrow Barton, "about a quarter of a mile from Pynes."[46] Such a search for exact parallels can be misleading, but Jane Austen knew the area that she describes.

Like Sir John himself, Barton Park seems unpretending, somewhat old-fashioned. Once a homely farmstead subordinate to a manor—or a priory—this Barton has become an enclosed (parked) estate with manorial rights to hunting and shooting. Sir John likes men who hunt and shoot, like himself, but is less desirous of male guests who will go after his game. Yet Sir John is not merely a sportsman. He undertakes some active land management: he has new "plantations" at "Barton Cross"— unlike that other John, he plants trees rather than cutting them down.

Barton Cottage is not the lowly kind of cottage used by laborers, but the former home of an agent or steward. The Dashwood women's house mirrors the home of the author by the time the novel was published in 1811. In 1809 Mrs. Austen, Jane, and Cassandra were offered Chawton Cottage as a place of residence by Edward, who himself had inherited not only Godmersham but also Chawton Great House and estate in Hampshire. The Great House property included the more lowly Chawton Cottage. At least Barton Cottage does not possess the disreputable history of Chawton Cottage, at one time a low-class inn or pub with a couple of killings to its credit.[47]

Elinor Dashwood, willing—like West's virtuous Louisa Dudley—to resign herself to life in an inferior habitation, is unaware that her new county harbors an antagonist to her happiness in the person of Lucy Steele, hovering at a distance on the coast. Lucy's uncle Mr. Pratt lives in a town or hamlet near Plymouth called "Longstaple"—a combination of elements from "long" (as in Longleat, Wiltshire) and "staple" (from Barnstaple, Devon). The latter name means "post or pillar of the battle axe" (Mills), but Austen is probably thinking of the word "staple" as applying to wool—although a battle-ax would suit Lucy also.

Near Barton Park is the estate at Allenham, in the hands of the redoubtable if invisible Mrs. Smith. As in *Northanger Abbey*, the introduction of the name "Allan/Allen" seems to evoke barbarians. "Allen"+ *ham* would be "the home settlement of Aluns," parallel to the "Huns" in Mr. Collins's "Hunsford" in *Pride and Prejudice*. About twelve miles from Barton Park, there is an estate called "Whitwell," belonging to Colonel Brandon's brother-in-law. That Brandon has relatives in the vicinity serves to explain how he has fallen into the company of Sir John and Lady Middleton and of Lady Middleton's mother Mrs. Jennings. The owner of Whitwell, husband of Brandon's unnamed sister, is not present, but under the auspices of Colonel Brandon a party plans to enjoy the pleasures of the grounds, including a sheet of water on which boats can be sailed. "Whitwell" or "white well" would seem to refer to a priory well, belonging to the White Friars (Carmelites). Marianne later hopes to visit the ruins of an old priory on or near Sir John's estate. This area of Devonshire near Exeter was formerly rich in religious foundations, including some established by Saxon kings. Sir John's lands include "the Abbeyland," the remains of an abbey and its surroundings—within walking distance for Marianne. Sir John's "Barton" would have been an outlying grange or farm of that dissolved ecclesiastical establishment. Nobody in this novel reads "Gothic" fiction, but we find here some of the concerns of *Northanger Abbey:* the Dissolution, use of church lands, remnants of the past. The anachronistic pressure and presence of the historical past is introduced gradually and piecemeal. Yet it presses on us in a novel in which the past threatens to overcome the present: the seduction and mistreatment of Eliza and her daughter, Edward's rash engagement. Dead leaves swirl around us; happy are those who can learn to love them.

A different estate is encountered in Somersetshire when Elinor and Marianne visit Cleveland, home of Mrs. Jennings's daughter Charlotte Palmer and her husband:

> Cleveland was a spacious, modern-built house, situated on a sloping lawn. It had no park, but the pleasure-grounds were tolerably extensive; and like every other place of the same degree of importance, it had its open shrubbery . . . a road of smooth gravel winding round a plantation . . . the house itself was under the guardianship of the fir, the mountain-ash, and the acacia. (*S&S,* III, ch. 6)

This is not a great holding, not even, apparently, a true agricultural estate. It is a charming house in the country. House and grounds have been recently done up, with landscaping in the modern style. The lawn is "dotted over with timber," but the dots are calculated effects; oaks and elms are ornaments like the "Grecian temple" that graces one eminence. (It is hard to imagine sulky Mr. Palmer, or Charlotte of the terrible laugh, suitably inhabiting a Grecian temple.) Acacia and Lombardy poplar are recent arrivals, newly fashionable trees. Lombardy poplars—or rather "a plantation of Lombardy poplars"—appeared in "Evelyn" (1792), a mockery of perfection, in which an excess of fashionable vegetation and a rage for symmetry are combined (*Volume the Third, Juvenilia,* 231). Mr. Palmer is almost as fashion conscious as Robert Ferrars.

"Cleveland" is one of the best historical jokes hidden in Austen's novels. Barbara Villiers, only child of Viscount Grandison who died in the Civil War, was one of Charles II's most beautiful and flamboyant mistresses—and the most highborn. As we have seen, this young female royalist married *Roger* Palmer, made first Earl of Castlemaine as a reward for cooperative cuckoldry. Barbara and Roger quietly separated in 1662. Barbara Villiers (also known as Barbara Grandison, Barbara Palmer, and Lady Castlemaine) bore King Charles II five children. Charles in requital made her "Duchess of Cleveland" in her own right, with special permission to allow the dukedom to descend to her eldest son (by the king), Charles Fitzroy. "Fitz-roy" is Norman, meaning *fils,* "acknowledged illegitimate son of" a king (*roi*). (This indicative surname was used by Austen in "Frederic and Elfrida" for Rebecca and Jezalinda Fitzroy.) "Cleveland" seems a very appropriate name for the cloven sex; we may suspect some pun-ful ingenuity on King Charles II's part.

The novel's Mr. *Palmer,* then, his name so closely if oddly associated with *Cleveland,* probably ought to be considered to be a result of this illicit heritage (along with the real-life Anthony Eden and Princess Diana). Perhaps his ancestor was even a hidden "Fitzroy," passed off as a "Palmer." Presumably one of his progenitors named the estate in honor of the title of the adventurous female founder of their fortunes. The wealth and importance of the aspiring MP Mr. Palmer are based on the illicit sexual success of a high-born and beautiful ancestress. Not all "fallen" women end up like Brandon's disaster-ridden first or second Eliza. City people who marry up will soon be tangling with Norman bastards, or perhaps with blue-blooded cuckolds.

"Delaford" ("of the ford") is Colonel Brandon's estate in Dorset, inherited unexpectedly. His elder brother—the one who stole Brandon's girl (the orphaned heiress), married her, and then cast her off—predeceased him. The estate's name mingles French and English elements; it is the ancient site of a water crossing, a splashy ford. Places where men, animals, and wheeled traffic might cross watercourses without a bridge were important to rural economy; see the ford in John Constable's "The Hay-Wain." Delaford estate brings in some two thousand pounds a year, but it is not a showplace. Despite Henry Tilney's strictures on the use of the adjective, Mrs. Jennings rightly insists that Delaford is "a nice place."

> Delaford is a nice place, I can tell you; exactly what I call a nice old fashioned place . . . quite shut in with great garden walls that are covered with the best fruit-trees in the country; and such a mulberry tree in one corner! Lord! how Charlotte and I did stuff the only time we were there! Then there is a dove-cote, some delightful

stewponds, and a very pretty canal . . . and, moreover, it is close to
the church, and only a quarter of a mile from the turnpike-road, so
'tis never dull." (*S&S*, II, ch. 8)

Delaford, humbly named after its useful site, is "old fashioned." Whatever the sins of the previous proprietors, Brandon's father and brother
did not try to "improve" it. Delaford's various attributes—espaliered
fruit trees on a southern wall, dovecot, canal, stew ponds (where fish are
kept for the table)—suggest a place where time has stood still. Like the
Leighs' Adlestrop manor (purchased by Thomas Leigh in 1553), Brandon's house was probably built in the mid-sixteenth century, house and
grounds being revised at the turn into the seventeenth century. The like-
lihood of some connection between our Colonel Brandon and Charles
Brandon, Duke of Suffolk, increases when we consider that Thomas
Leigh's father-in-law originally purchased Stoneleigh Abbey from
Charles Brandon and that the abbey went to Thomas Leigh's second
son, while his eldest son got Adlestrop manor.[48] Austen's models for
Northanger Abbey and a model for Delaford Park are connected. The
traditional old elements of Adlestrop manor were done away with in
Austen's lifetime by Repton and the ambitious cleric. The only other
Austen imaginary estate with fish ponds, "the old Abbey fish-ponds,"
is Donwell Abbey (*Emma,* III, ch. 6). The reference to Delaford's mulberry tree suggests Shakespeare; the felling of the old mulberry tree
in Shakespeare's garden in 1756 had excited historians and souvenir
hunters. Brandon's country manor house seems a Tudor holding; it
has not set itself apart from road or church or community. Repton has
come nowhere near. Even the ornamental portions of the estate produce food: fish, peaches and apples from the fruit trees, mulberries on
which one can "stuff." Yet no scenes of the main novel are set here, and
we never see it directly.

Dorset's Delaford seems haunted by passions of the past. The heroines transplanted from Sussex remain true to Wessex. Yet the hope
that here we may find what we seek seems slightly misguided. There
is a troubling lack of energy about virtuous Colonel Brandon's peaceful Delaford—which we know only through the jocular greed of
Mrs. Jennings. It is a little off-putting that it is "quite shut in"—so much
a refuge as to be imprisoning. Brandon wants to live in the past on his
emotional estate as on his father's lands. Dorset seems more confining
than the Devonshire to which the Dashwood sisters first come. Delaford is not only small but exclusionary, a defensive burrow. Important

people left out include Eliza Williams and her child by Willoughby. Where are they? How is Brandon caring for them? Neither Elinor nor Marianne expresses any interest in seeing the "the little love-child"—in marked contrast to Richardson's Pamela who takes in Mr. B.'s illegitimate child and brings her up with her own children. There is no overflow of powerful affection.

Because we have not accompanied the central characters to their final dwelling place, the novel seems to fade off, to leave us in a muted world. The story has been full of predators, reflected in the names of criminals and sinners. The story of Laurence Shirley, Earl Ferrars, was commonly told to illustrate British justice. But we look in vain for much justice at the end of the story. Green Devon hills might offer beauty, possibilities of growth. But this narrative is shadowed by negatives—autumn, crime, sin, dead leaves, showers of rain, pain, illness, regret. Hope seems to turn back on itself, finding uneasy refuge in ironic resignation. The sense of adventure diminishes in favor of making the best of things, seeking a sanctuary wherein the less aggressive emotions of the past can simply repeat themselves. Elinor will continue to delude herself about Edward, even as she has found him a job, a house, and wife; she will write the sermons and get him to the church on time. Marianne is loved for her resemblance to somebody else who lived in the past and makes do with the aging husband she didn't really desire, but to whom she is compelled to be grateful. There is no sharp pain and no sharp pleasure. Spiritual search, like erotic search, seems to be over. We don't actually seek for the remnants of the spiritual past, the ruins of the White Friars' abbey—though Marianne thinks of doing so. Nobody seems to go to church—an odd omission in story that will demand "ordination" for one of its characters. One supposes Elinor attends church punctiliously once she has married a clergyman; Edward must attend since services are his business. But in London the party takes advantage of "so beautiful a Sunday" to go to Kensington Gardens (*S&S*, III, ch. 2). The peace of Delaford feels analgesic, not creative. Yet Dorset's history of restlessness and rebellion may make us wonder whether the old fish ponds and mulberry trees can satisfy forever—or whether esteem and a flannel waistcoat really make up for loss of erotic love.

Names and Places in *Pride and Prejudice*: Hertfordshire, London (City), Kent, and Derbyshire

REAL PLACES IN *PRIDE AND PREJUDICE*

Sense and Sensibility ends on muted notes. The heroines retreat and make do. In *Pride and Prejudice* almost everyone's favorite Austen heroine refuses to give in and make do. Elizabeth dares fate and sallies forth with an almost impudent confidence that matters will turn out well. Yet this heroine, sometimes as naive as Catherine Morland if wittier, has almost as much against her as Elinor and Marianne. Primogeniture is an idol honored in the law of entail. That ruthless law is starkly clear (to all save the protesting Mrs. Bennet). Girl children get nothing. Gavelkind does not apply. The heroine was born and lives on—but cannot remain on—an estate called "Longbourn" in Hertfordshire, a small but prosperous county in southern England just northeast of Greater London. Flat and accessible, this county was well populated even in the Neolithic era. The Romans took it over without much struggle; the region capitulated equally easily to the Saxon invaders and then the Normans. In 1800 the area offered country living in close proximity to London. That county now borders on the region served by the London Underground; even in the Victorian period Potter's Bar in Hertfordshire marked the beginning of London. In *Howard's End* E. M. Forster located his titular house in Hertfordshire, precisely because his imaginary ancient manor Howards End is meant to be on the border between the truly rural and the new urban. It marks a resistance to "Suburbia." A century earlier, the same forces were in play. Hertfordshire is very different from the West Country, the counties of Wiltshire, Somerset, Devonshire, and Dorset so important in *Catharine, Northanger Abbey,* and *Sense and Sensibility.* Hertfordshire is on a crossroads, close to the urban center.

Another center of modernity has an important role, even though the main story does not go there. Lydia falls for—and to—Wickham in Brighton, at once a defended port, military camp, and highly fashionable resort. Brighton in Sussex, settled from early Saxon times, was originally "Brighthelmstone," *tun* of a man called *Beorhthelm* ("bright helm"). Brighthelmstone was a quiet seaside settlement until the late eighteenth century, when the Prince Regent bought an old farmhouse and got Henry Holland to remodel it. This new Royal Pavilion was an ongoing production from 1787 onward. The prince lived there for a while with his mistress—or wife—Maria Fitzherbert. This most glamorous of seaside resorts (owing to the prince and his pavilion) inevitably became associated with entertainments and illicit sex. Two seaside resorts figure in the offstage action of *Pride and Prejudice*. Ramsgate is another seaside resort. In *Mansfield Park* Tom Bertram in Ramsgate encountered the Sneyds, a middle-class family perhaps trawling for husbands for their girls. Roger Sales points out that the realistic reference to "Albion Place," abode of the Sneyds in Ramsgate, quietly raises the question of what the young of "Albion" (i.e., England) should be or do.[49] A small fishing port grown rich, according to Feltham, on Russian trade, Ramsgate, by now competing for the lucrative seaside pleasure market, rates a pullout picture in Feltham's *Guide*. The name offers rich resources in sexual puns.[50] In Ramsgate, Georgiana and her dowry nearly tumbled into Wickham's power. In Brighton, Lydia falls, evidenced in her letter's allusion to "a great slit" in her gown—an obscene reference that tells us her "great slit" has been opened (and won't be mended) (*P&P*, III, ch. 5). Both resorts encouraged dangerous mingling—and both required defending against invasion. In July 1803 Jane's brother Francis William Austen was put in command of the North Foreland unit of the "Sea Fencibles" to defend the coast and countryside in the event of a French landing. He was headquartered at Ramsgate, where he met the girl he married. Jane Austen visited Frank in Ramsgate.[51] Austen's novels are very conscious of places where the enemy might make a breach in defenses, might invade and take over. The military war underlies the erotic war, the stories of sexual attack and yielding.

Pride and Prejudice starts off in the agricultural countryside. Some dangerous action takes place on the coastal edge of England, but the plot makes London central, serving as the hinge or crossroads of the story. Every important character (save Mrs. Bennet) lives in or visits London. Via London, Elizabeth gets from Longbourn to Kent—and ultimately to the estate of Pemberley. Caroline Bingley and her sister drag Bingley away from his new rented estate in Hertfordshire to London—to Town—in November, shortly after the Netherfield ball; Darcy goes shortly after to his own town house in London (we never find out where it is). Bingley soon resides with Darcy while Caroline Bingley stays with her sister at Mr. Hurst's house (presumably rented) in Grosvenor Street, in the fashionable area of the West End. That street was the address of Harriet Byron's cousins the Reeves, whom she visits on her first sojourn in London. (Later, Harriet's friend Charlotte [née Grandison] and her husband Lord G. reside, more grandly, in Grosvenor Square itself.)

Wickham seduces Lydia in Brighton but takes her to London—
not to Gretna Green. Mrs. Younge, Georgiana Darcy's ex-governess,
rents (presumably) a house in the West End, in Edward Street (later
destroyed to make Langham Place). Lady Susan's immoral friend Alice
Johnson lived in Edward Street, so it appears twice as an address for an
Austen character up to no good. Mrs. Younge keeps a lodging house;
one would not put it past her to be engaging—if ultragenteelly—in
other activities requiring multiple rooms. Unable to supply lodgings
to the wandering couple, she directs them to an address in or near the
Strand (on the borderland between Town and City), where they are discovered by Darcy. Their wedding is at last solemnized in the church of
Saint Clement Dane in the Strand, because Wickham was living with
Lydia in that parish.

Jane Bennet also goes to London—to the City, not the fashionable
Town. Elizabeth visits Jane and the Gardiners in Gracechurch Street in
the City of London, the Gardiners' home. Gracechurch Street is near
Threadneedle Street (site of the Bank of England) and Lombard Street,
which derives its name from pawnbroking and money exchange carried
on by the original medieval bankers from Lombardy. Gracechurch
Street in Austen's day was at the heart of commerce.[52] The family dwelling is within sight of Mr. Gardiner's warehouse, though we don't know
exactly what he deals in.

As we have seen, landed gentry mocked and even shunned such
"Cits" as low and materialistic, at best uneducated, greedy, ignoble,
and lacking in culture. They are probably Puritanical, hypocritical like
Pope's Sir Balaam in the *Epistle to Bathurst*. The Gardiners are neither
vulgarly materialistic nor Puritanical. Their marriage is strongly based
and affectionate. The name "Gracechurch" originally referred not to
theological "grace" but to "grass"—this was in olden days the site of
"the church in the grass-market." Yet in this novel some elements of an
allegorical divine "grace" seem to cling about the characters who dwell
in Gracechurch Street.

Small towns surrounding London are mentioned in relation to the
probable route taken by Wickham and Lydia *if* they were endeavoring to
elope to Scotland. Wickham took Lydia from the gay and well-manned
Brighton to Epsom in Surrey, known for horse racing and bourgeois
dissipation. (See discussion of Box Hill in *Emma*, chapter 11.) Wickham
hired a post chaise and fast horses, at sufficient expense to make credible an elopement to marry. But the trail petered out; there was no evidence of Wickham and Lydia going north through Barnet or Hatfield

as they should have done after Clapham had they been heading for the Scottish border. Clapham, an Anglo-Saxon town with a name meaning "homestead on a hill," was a center for changing directions and vehicles long before the railway attached "Clapham" to "Junction." That Wickham hires a common hackney coach indicates that he intends to go into London, not away from it. Predecessors of later taxis, hackney carriages were individually numbered, and thus a vehicle might be traced. There is a touch of the Sherlock Holmes pursuit in the efforts to trace Wickham, but Colonel Forster, Mr. Gardiner, and Mr. Bennet have insufficient clues. Jane writes to Elizabeth,

> After making every possible enquiry on that side London, Colonel F. came on into Hertfordshire, anxiously renewing them at all the turnpikes, and at the inns in Barnet and Hatfield, but without any success, no such people had been seen to pass through. (*P&P*, III, ch. 4)

The pursuers' efforts resemble the attempt by Frederic Delamere's father Lord Montreville and his agent in Smith's *Emmeline* to trace Emmeline Mowbray and Frederic, believed to be eloping:

> By this delay, and the blunders of the affrighted servants . . . it was near nine o'clock before his Lordship and Sir Richard left London. At Barnet, they heard of the fugitives, and easily traced them from thence to Hatfield; after which believing all farther enquiries useless, they passed through Stevenage . . . without asking any questions which might have led them to discover that Delamere and Emmeline had gone from thence towards Hertford only an hour and an half before their arrival.[53]

Frederic's outraged father finds clues that he does *not* want to see indicating that his son has gone northward to Gretna Green. Lydia's friends, on the contrary, are saddened to deduce that she is *not* traveling to Gretna Green. Wickham and Lydia have *not* passed through Barnet or Hatfield, north of London, to change horses or take a new equipage for the road to the North. Neither Smith's nor Austen's couple is actually heading toward a Scottish wedding, though for different reasons.

Wickham is at last trapped or bribed into marriage. He will indeed go to the North—but not by choice. Having joined—or been joined to—the regular army, he is to be sent to Newcastle-upon-Tyne. This grimy city (named after its "new castle" after the Norman invasion) shipped coal from the mines of county Durham in the northwest of England, supplying the Industrial Revolution with fuel. Fear of working-class unrest is the likely reason for keeping troops there. Distance does not staunch Mr. and Mrs. Wickham's appeals for money nor curb their aptitude for parking themselves on the Bingleys when they can.

Characters in *Pride and Prejudice* are largely on the move—they move outward from the first supposed center in Longbourn and Meryton where we start. These young people are particularly restless. They go off in various directions—to London, to Brighton, to Kent, to Derbyshire, to Newcastle. Important characters spend a large amount of time in places not their native home—as Darcy and Bingley both do in their sojourn in Hertfordshire in the first part of the novel. Netherfield is only rented; Charles Bingley moves away from it twice, the last time after his marriage when he does not want to be too near his in-laws. The Bennet parents are the only people of importance who stick close to their original center. The Bennets' home is "only twenty-four miles" from London. By setting out early in the morning, travelers can arrive at the Gardiners' house in the City by noon (II, ch. 4).[54] Mr. Bennet, however, is averse to moving through space. It is his vegetable ambition never to stir; he cannot even bring himself to attend an assembly at Meryton for an evening. Too indolent to take advantage of proximity to London, in his courtship days he settled for the prettiest of the Meryton girls. Until the Lydia affair, when he goes on his ineffectual journey to London, Mr. Bennet has apparently never bothered to travel. He remains a fixture in his own estate in his own county of Hertfordshire. The name of the county, however, is based on movement; it derives from its chief town, Hertford, which means "the place of the deer crossing" ("hart" + "ford"). The correct pronunciation ("H*a*rtfordshire") lends itself easily to wordplay, as "the place where hearts cross—and meet."

Elizabeth travels to Kent, a very different county from Hertfordshire—larger, more historically important, much wealthier and more populous. Hertfordshire's population in the census of 1801 was 97,577; in 1811 it had gone up to 111,654. Kent's population was three times the size: in the census of 1801 it was 307,624; in 1811 it had grown to 373,095—perhaps partly because of the wartime defensive activity since 1803. One of the warmer counties of England, Kent—whatever Mrs. Elton may say—is traditionally known as "The Garden of England." Camden comments that the inland or uppermost parts are "most healthy and rich."

"As for good meadows, pastures, and corn-fields, it has these in most places, and abounds with apples beyond measure; as also with *cherries.*"[55] The county's name (Julius Caesar's *Cantium*) refers to its geographic position, from Briton *Cantus* ("rim" or "edge"). Kent is cornered by the Thames and the sea. Major towns include Maidstone, the county town; Chatham, site of naval dockyards along the river Medway; Tunbridge Wells, the inland spa resort; and Canterbury, the cathedral city. The famous white cliffs of Dover are part of Kent's extensive seacoast. The ports of Rochester on the east coast, and Dover and Deal on the south facilitated trade but made the region vulnerable to attack.

This is Jane Austen's ancestral county. Her important great-uncle Francis lived in Sevenoaks, in West Kent. A lawyer and land agent, Francis Austen became wealthy and influential; he seems to have maneuvered Edward's adoption by the Knights. Kent is the county of the manor of Godmersham Park of which Jane's brother Edward became the adoptive heir. He married a daughter of the family of Bridges (or Brydges) in Goodnestone, Kent. Jane's father was born in this county, in Tonbridge, where he was brought up by his aunt Hooper after his mother's death. Jane's father's family can be traced back with certainty to "John Austen ... of Horsmonden in Kent, who was born around 1560 and died in March, 1620."[56] Jane Austen's close associations with Kent include her surname, which comes ultimately from Saint Augustine, who brought Christianity to England.

Kent is important in the history of the Church of England, so comically represented in this novel by Mr. Collins. In 557 Pope Gregory I appointed Augustine the first Archbishop of Canterbury. Camden comments that Canterbury belonged to the king "till King Ethelbert gave it with the royalty to Austin upon his being consecrated archbishop of the English nation." The cathedral was famous: "Christ church in the very heart of the city rises with so much magnificence to the clouds, as to inspire even distant beholders with religious awe." There was another church of Saint Austin "for the burying place both of the kings of Kent and of the archbishops."[57] Canterbury acquired its own local saint because of a famous murder. On 20 December 1170 knights of King Henry II murdered the Archbishop of Canterbury in his own cathedral Canonized in 1173, Thomas à Becket became a popular English saint. King Henry II had to do penance.[58]

One curiosity of Kentish history is its numerous rebellions. Leaving aside the murder of Thomas à Becket—a violent act not to be blamed on the Kentish populace—Kent seems curiously bloodthirsty. Camden praises the Kentish for their courage, noting that this county's men were always put in the front of an English army, but some attach that war-spirit primarily to the eastern Jute-descended "Men of Kent." Kent would not readily submit to other rulers. According to Kent's own story, "Men of Kent" from east of the Medway (fierce descendants of "Jutes," i.e., Goths)and western "Kentishmen" sent a surprise delegation to William. Carrying boughs—like Birnham Wood marching to Dunsinane—they took the Conqueror by surprise. This delegation made it clear that if not allowed to retain their customary laws, such as Gavelkind, Kent would fight on. William gave in; henceforward Kent termed itself "*Invicta*"—"Unconquered." The Elizabethan poet Michael Drayton in *PolyOlbion* praises noble Kent for throwing off "the servile yoke" of primogeniture, "Not suffering foreign laws should thy free customs bind."[59] Mrs. Bennet would prefer to shake off "the servile yoke." In the eleventh century Earl Godwin, ordered by the king to punish the people of Kent, turned against his nominal lord, King Edward the Confessor, and undertook a military attack. The Bridges' Goodnestone Park (*Godwines + tun*) may have belonged to that Godwin. Even the Normans ran into some trouble here and conceded to Kent a qualified independence as a County Palatine, allowing the people to keep some of their own old laws and customs. Other Kentish conflicts follow: Wat Tyler's Peasants' Revolt, 1381; Jack Cade's rebellion, 1450; Wyatt's rebellion against Queen Mary I, 1554. Kent was not easy to govern.

During the Napoleonic Wars, naval and mercantile sea traffic was swinging westward, to Brighton and Portsmouth. Yet Kent was presumed to be a central object—perhaps *the* central object—of French plans of invasion. Fortifications dotted the Kentish coast. Possibility of attack became most acute in 1805. During part of that year Jane Austen was a visitor at Goodnestone Farm, very close to the coast. She repeats what seem to be family or local jokes about the "evil intentions of the Guards" in mockery of male landowners' fears that the Guards might disturb the game birds or even engage in poaching (30 August 1805; *Letters,* 112 and note 384). The Guards had been sent to defend the Kentish coast; the danger had lifted only a few days before Jane wrote that joking remark.

In using Kent—her ancestral county—as a setting for an important sequence of her second novel to be published, Austen places the imaginary "Rosings" inland, west of the county center and away from the coast. Mr. Collins tells us exactly where Rosings is when he uses a real place name, dating his letter from "Hunsford, near Westerham, Kent." The real Westerham ("dwelling or settlement in the west") is less than ten miles west of Sevenoaks (of which it is now a parish). Westerham is nearly ten miles from Saxon Bromley (*Brom-ley,* "clearing where the broom grows"). Now a borough of Greater London, rural Bromley in Austen's day usefully offered an inn stop for refreshments and fresh horses on the road from Hastings to London. Lady Catherine unnecessarily recommends using her name to get attention at the (real) Royal Bell Inn.

Did Mr. Collins date his letter from "Westerham" as it was the local postal town—or because he wished to sound as if he lived at a more important place than Hunsford?[60] Westerham was a manor belonging to Godwin, Earl of Kent, and then to his son Harold, ill-fated king of England. It is mentioned in the Domesday Book. Pitt the Younger took country breaks in Westerham. More stirringly, General Wolfe (1727–59), who took Canada from French control and died in a famous battle, was born in Westerham vicarage. One doubts if any hero will emerge from Mr. Collins's vicarage in Hunsford.

Kent was well known to Austen as the source of blood and name. Why, then, does Kent emerge as a comical place of jangle in *Pride and Prejudice*? We can see in the *Letters,* and in the comments of certain descendants, some signs that Jane Austen was treated with condescension or coldness by these grander and richer connections, the Bridges of Goodnestone and the Austen-Knights. The recollections of her niece Anna Lefroy (née Austen) bear this out:

> I have intimated that of the two Sisters Aunt Jane was generally the favorite with children, but with the young people of Godmersham it was not so. They liked her indeed as a playfellow, & as a teller of stories, but they were not really fond of her. I believe that their Mother was not; at least that she very much preferred the elder Sister. A little talent went a long way with the Goodneston Bridgeses of that period; & *much* must have gone a long way too far. (Anna Lefroy, "Recollections," *Memoir,* 158)

Here we may have a key to the riddle. *Pride and Prejudice* overtly resists domination, condescension, and conventional judgments. A certain bloody-mindedness and recalcitrance are evident in the scenes that take place in Kent—but Elizabeth, not the locals, takes on the role of Kentish rebel. Elizabeth balks at the position in which she is placed,

talks back at those who express disapproval, and mocks assumptions of
superior importance.

In Darcy's explanatory letter we find out about the negative role of
Ramsgate—another fallen site in Kent. Nowhere in the narrative is
Kent permitted to be good. We may recollect that in *Lady Susan* "Park-
lands" in Kent is the abode of the aristocratic but fretful De Courcys,
nursing pride, Norman blood, and infirmity within their enclosure.
Kent is a fallen kingdom. In *Pride and Prejudice,* Kentish stubbornness,
vainglory, and sense of entitlement are expressed in Mr. Collins and
Lady Catherine and reflected in Darcy. Elizabeth sets herself against
the Kingdom of Kent's claims. In the drawing room at Rosings, she sees
Darcy as implicated in these claims:

> "You mean to frighten me, Mr. Darcy, by coming in all this state to
> hear me? But I will not be alarmed.... There is a stubbornness about
> me that never can bear to be frightened at the will of others. My
> courage always rises with every attempt to intimidate me." (II, ch. 8)

But Darcy is not trying to intimidate her with Kentish authority—he
is drawn to her. Earlier he said "I have been used to consider poetry as
the *food* of love" (*P&P*, I, ch. 9), quoting and refashioning the famous
opening speech of Shakespeare's Orsino (a bearish name):

> If musick be the food of love, play on;
> Give me excess of it;
> (*Twelfth Night,* act 1 sc 1; *Shakespeare Plays,* 2:353)

Elizabeth rejects the notion that poetry can be the food of any but a
stout full-grown love, and the couple never discuss poetry further. But
at Rosings Elizabeth does supply the music, and draws her Orsino's attention; he moves "towards the pianoforte" and "stationed himself so as
to command a full view of the fair performer's countenance" (II, ch. 8).
Her music is a food of his love. The novel touches upon the realm of
romance and pastoral comedy; as Easter approaches the spring waxing
in rural Kent gives promise of violets and recognition. This is only one
of the many touches of pastoral comic joy that touch the novel and play
against its satire, doubt and rebellion. False claims to authority (civil
and religious) abound. The county excites no warm admiration in either
the heroine or the hero (who both come from elsewhere), as we see in
their cool exchange on the subject:

"Are you pleased with Kent?"

A short dialogue on the subject of the country ensued, on either side calm and concise. (*P&P*, II, ch. 9)

"Garden of England" though Kent may be, offering the setting for the spring movement of the novel as its trees regain their greenness, Elizabeth (like her author) refuses to rhapsodize—particularly when indoors.

IMAGINARY PLACES IN *PRIDE AND PREJUDICE*

The Bennet's estate is "Longbourn"—that is "long stream" or "long boundary" (long + *bourn*[e]). The name apparently applies to a settlement around the Bennets' home and to the family's estate. The estate presumably was once bounded by a stream. Shakespeare's Hamlet employs the word in his famous soliloquy: "The undiscover'd country, from whose bourne / No traveller returns" (*Hamlet*, act 1, sc. 2; *Shakespeare Plays*, 8:209). Hamlet's use partially remakes the word, implying that *bourn(e)* is not just the border or frontier but the undiscovered country itself, a territory contained within borders. The Bennet females, though living within a homeland, bounded territory, cannot rely on that border to protect them. Mr. Collins will inherit Longbourn and move in as soon as Mr. Bennet dies. The women will have to step over that border and never return. There is no long home for any of the girls in Longbourn. But one's "long home" can mean the grave, so in getting away from Longbourn the women are getting away from death—or at least from Mr. Bennet's kind of stagnation.

Mr. Bingley takes an estate called "Netherfield"—an unpretentious locative, meaning the "lower field," presumably in former times attached to the Longbourn estate. The "nether" suits Charles Bingley's slightly inferior status. He only *rents* Netherfield. It is a "park," but the term is seldom used in connection with the name of this unpretentious manor. We hear of other small estates nearby in Mrs. Bennet's unrealistic rhapsody over potential homes for Lydia and Wickham. As well as "the great house at Stoke" with its too small drawing room, there is "Haye-Park" ("hedge" + "park") and distant "Ashworth" ("enclosure with ash-trees"). There is also "Purvis Lodge" with its "dreadful" attics (III, ch. 8). Nothing will purvey a neighborhood home for the Wickhams, though "Ashworth" suggests their need for repentance.

The village nearest Longbourn is "Meryton." The name is close to a real name, "Merton" ("farmstead by a pool," *mer* + *ton*), but Austen's country town is a pun ("merry" + *tun/ton*). As Fay Weldon pointed out, this is a merry town, offering sex and shopping, bonnets and dancing. It also supplies gossip, choric disapproval, and opportunities for people to spy on each other. There must be sufficient work for Uncle Philips, who succeeded Mrs. Bennet's father as the local attorney, Mr. Gardiner's son having gone off to business in London. The Bennet girls frequently walk to Meryton. Similarly, Jane and Cassandra used to walk several times a week to the little town of Dean near Steventon. Anna Lefroy says she remembers her two aunts "& how they walked in wintry weather through the sloppy lane between Steventon & Dean in pattens. . . . I thought it so very odd, to hear Grandpapa speak of them as 'the Girls.' 'Where are the Girls?' 'Are the Girls gone out?'" (*Memoir,* 157).

The Bennet girls live a slightly vulgar rural life, finding amusement in the entertainments of Meryton, the parties given by their cheerfully vulgar aunt and her husband, "broad-faced stuffy uncle Philips," who (on his one appearance) smells of port wine (I, ch. 16). There is the occasional modest assembly. The Bennets are on a boundary or borderland—a *bourn*—between country and London, between gentry and bourgeoisie, between Pastoral and "Suburbia." Longbourn is the girls' (temporary) home but not their center. The novel explores what it means to live in a borderland, as most of the characters are doing. Mr. Collins and Charlotte live in a borderland between village and estate, but they are also in a temporal borderland between past and future—when they will inherit Longbourn. Hunsford indicates a place where barbarians ("Huns") cross the stream. Perhaps Austen was thinking of the fierce Jutes, whose name means "Goths," barbarian ancestors of the "Men of Kent." No character could be less like a warrior Goth than Mr. Collins—although in manners, morals and intellect he is unwittingly barbarous. Hunsford, site of Mr. Collins's parsonage, is a very small village on the estate of Rosings Park. Rosings is to be inherited by Lady Catherine's daughter Anne. As Lady Catherine explains to the less fortunate Elizabeth, "I see no occasion for entailing estates from the female line.—It was not thought necessary in Sir Lewis de Bourgh's family" (II, ch. 6). The ancient force of Gavelkind in Kent does its work. But Lady Catherine's attempts to govern are not happy.

Rosings, as Lady Catherine sees it, encompasses all human magnificence; Mr. Collins fortunately reflects her views. Rosings, however, is not central to the narrative, but comically subordinated to places in Hertfordshire and Derbyshire. Our "first impression" will associate the name "Rosings" with the scented colorful flowers that do indeed grow well in Kent. There is a light pattern of reference to the Wars of the Roses: Bingleys come from Yorkshire, while Darcy has Lancashire connections. The name "Rosings" may seem pretty—but it means something like "settlement of followers of a man named Ross" or "of a *rus* (red-haired) man"; the common suffix *-ing* or *-ingas* means "people related to, belonging to or following" some particular leader. Rosings, then, was once a Saxon settlement, probably first cleared by a redheaded man. The family has lived and flourished here since Norman times. The term "Park" spreads during a long period of enclosures and was unlikely to have been attached to Rosings earlier than the seventeenth century. Despite claims to antiquity registered in its awkward Saxon name, Rosings Park has modernized itself. The grandiose house was recently built by Sir Lewis De Bourgh, "a handsome modern building" (II, ch. 5). This new house is situated "on rising ground," bearing out the observations of Mr. Parker in *Sanditon* that moderns build on hills whereas in the old days people built in valleys: "Our Ancestors, you know, always built in a hole" (*Sanditon,* ch. 4).

The house of Rosings is on rising ground, yet the metaphorical "house," the family, is quietly sliding downhill. Rosings' battery of boastful windows exhibits the sin of pride, showing off the ability to afford not only glazing but the window tax. The many apartments, the "fine proportion and finished ornaments" of rooms pointed out by Mr. Collins—all these indicate to skeptical Elizabeth "mere stateliness of money and rank" (II, ch. 6). A character such as Lady Susan or Mary Crawford might be called an "exciting freelance," a female interloper and social heretic who irrupts into a domestic scene and is felt to pose an aggressive threat. Elizabeth Bennet seems to the Bingley sisters an irritating freelance, attracting hostility and faultfinding similar to that accorded Lady Susan or Miss Crawford. Here Elizabeth bursts aggressively into Lady Catherine's scene, an exciting free spirit fighting her own battles. To Lady Catherine De Bourgh, she is an inferior and an interloper. To an ordered world that should have been settled once for all by the Conquest Elizabeth is indeed a threat.

The comic Kent of *Pride and Prejudice* is proud and prejudiced, keeping its hereditary traits of independence, pride of rank, and rose-bush prickliness while its real importance is dwindling. Profusion and ostentation serve to conceal decline. The De Bourgh family is winding down; its sickly heiress is neither marriageable nor likely to survive (one of the darker truths behind the ostensibly light narrative). Rosings's projected inheritors will desert it—Darcy will live in Derbyshire, Anne De Bourgh will die. Will Rosings come to Colonel Fitzwilliam in the end? Even that trustworthy sycophant Mr. Collins and his Charlotte will move away to take over Longbourn. The wealth of Rosings, ascended from Saxon settlement to Norman landholding to Georgian great house, is now dwindling into consumerist riches, with no one to love this land or ensure the estate's integration into a modern economy.

Rosings is imaginary, but it is given a site on a real map, and Austen expects us to know without authorial travelogue what places of importance are near any region she emphasizes. We are, I believe, meant to know about Stonehenge near Salisbury in Catherine Morland's Wiltshire. Imaginary Rosings is very near real Westerham, and Westerham is less than nine miles from the nearest major "stately home," Penshurst Place. Penshurst was the home of Sir Philip Sidney, Elizabethan poet, novelist, statesman, and soldier. His *Arcadia* (written 1580, published 1590), often considered the first English novel, is certainly England's first long prose fiction centering on a love story (or stories). *Arcadia* was a favorite work of one of Austen's heroes, King Charles I.[61] Samuel Richardson, who took the name "Pamela" from Sidney's fiction, also reprinted *Arcadia*. That the novel was known in Austen's time is indicated by such casual reference as we find in, for example, Susannah Gunning's *Anecdotes of the Delborough Family* where the heroine's grandmother claims "though I live here secluded from the world . . . I am nevertheless as romantic as any nymph of Sydney's Arcadia, and would go as far, if I was able, after an adventure, as Don Quixote."[62]

The house at Penshurst, a beautiful medieval and Elizabethan dwelling, is everything that Rosings—that pompous Georgian structure—is not. But the green landscape connects Penshurst with the areas of Rosings Park in which Elizabeth likes to wander. In his pastoral novel Philip Sidney composed one of the most memorable of imaginary places—*Arcadia*. Here he paints a beautiful springtime world:

> Which by and by . . . welcomed *Musidorus*'s eyes . . . with delightful prospects. There were . . . humble vallies, whose base estate seemed comforted with the refreshing of silver rivers: meadows, enamelled with all sorts of eye-pleasing flowers; thickets which being lined with most pleasant shade were witnessed so too, by the cheerful disposition of many well-tuned birds . . . here a shepherd's boy piping, as though he should never be old.[63]

The intensification of nature was informed or inspired not only by reading Greek pastorals but also by Sidney's youthful experience of the lanes, fields, and groves of Kent's Penshurst—not far at all from the pleasant paths favored by that determined walker Elizabeth Bennet. In such a pastoral green space on the very edge of spring Darcy emerges from "within the sort of grove which edged the park" (II, ch. 12) to hand Elizabeth his important letter. *Pride and Prejudice* is realistic, questioning, sometimes flippant, even cynical—but Arcadia is always just about to happen. Some very tough truths are told in this novel in which everyone goes wrong, but our hearts are light as we read because we are never far from the land of green promise.

The most memorable and most fully described of imaginary places in *Pride and Prejudice* is Pemberley—long unseen target of our expectations. Far from home, as a tourist in the north country, Elizabeth (unencumbered by parents and sisters) can meet and converse with Darcy once again, when spring has turned into high summer. Mr. Darcy's estate is in Derbyshire, a rugged county in the north Midlands, bordering on Staffordshire and Yorkshire. Darcy's county is ornamented with several "stately homes," the most gigantically impressive of which is the Duke of Devonshire's Chatsworth. Despite arguments in favor of Chatsworth as the model, laid out by Donald Greene in his essay "The Original of Pemberley" (1968), the house at Pemberley is definitely, even defiantly, *not* Chatsworth.[64] It is not grand, not baroque in wings and portico. Chatsworth had come to seem passé and meretricious. In his descriptions of the Lake District and Derbyshire, William Gilpin disparages Chatsworth:

> Chatsworth was the glory of the last age, when trim parterres, and formal water-works were in fashion. . . . . The house itself would have been no way striking; except in the wilds of Derbyshire. . . . There are few pictures in the house.

Gilpin saves his praise for the beauties of Matlock Vale:

> A romantic, and most delightful scene. . . . The river Derwent, which winds under this semi-circular screen, is a broken rapid stream. In some places, it is visible, in others, delving among rocks and woody projections, it is an object only to the ear.
>
> It is impossible to view such scenes as these, without feeling the imagination take fire. . . . Every object here, is sublime, and wonder-

ful. Not only the eye is pleased; but the imagination is filled. We are carried at once into the fields of fiction and romance.[65]

Austen has turned the tables by taking over descriptions of Matlock Vale and adapting them to her house of "fiction and romance."

The house at Pemberley has the advantage of being imaginary. We are left, like Mr. Gardiner, "conjecturing as to the date of the building" (III, ch. 1). Subtle signs indicate it should be Elizabethan—appropriate to the heroine's first name. It is "a large, handsome, stone building." We may imagine it as a Tudor edifice, with medieval foundations and some improvements made during the building boom of the early seventeenth century. This house was not torn down and rebuilt in the eighteenth century for modern display (like Rosings) or remodeled for inane show (like Sotherton). Austen's contemporary traveler Viscount Torrington (in a diary Austen could not have known) comments caustically on the "the foolish glare, uncomfortable rooms, and frippery French furniture" of Chatsworth: "The Dutchess has made a fine display of French tables, gilt chairs, uneasy sofas, and all what is call'd charming furniture."[66] Not everyone was charmed by Chatsworth. Mrs. Gardiner says she does not care for such repetitive displays: "If it were merely a fine house richly furnished . . . I should not care about it myself; but the grounds are delightful. They have some of the finest woods in the country" (II, ch. 19). Pemberley does not make an artifice out of Nature. The house is furnished for use, not show: "It was neither gaudy nor uselessly fine" (III, ch. 1). Chatsworth *is* "gaudy and uselessly fine." Pemberley is *not* an elaborate Chatsworth but an anti-Chatsworth.

Where exactly are we? Elizabeth at the inn at Bakewell asks if the family are at home; relieved to find Darcy absent, she consents to go on the expedition to Pemberley, near the imaginary village of "Lambton." "Lambton" seems innocuously pastoral, but a real Lambton, much farther north in county Durham on the river Wear, was the site of a manor house that once belonged to a northern branch of D'Arcy's and came into possession of the earls of Durham.[67] Our Darcy's Lambton is within five miles of Darcy's house and within an easy morning's drive from Bakewell. Darcy's (imaginary) estate thus is locatable as ten miles or less from (real) Bakewell in Derbyshire, some thirty miles southeast of Lancashire's Manchester. Bakewell, a bustling market town of Anglo-Saxon foundation (*Badecanwelle*), was not yet known for "Bakewell Pudding" and "Bakewell Tart." As Gilpin says, Bakewell on the Wye is pleasantly situated:

> Here [at Ashford] we fall into a beautiful vale fringed with wood, and watered by a brilliant stream. . . . The vale of Ashford continues with little interruption to Bakewell, where it enters another sweet vale—the vale of Haddon; so called from Haddon-hall, a magnificent old mansion, which stands in the middle of it, on a rocky knoll, incompassed with wood. This princely structure, scarce yet in a state of ruin, is able, it is said, to trace it's [*sic*] origin into times before the conquest.[68]

Although Donald Greene insists that Pemberley's stream is the Derwent, we are equally entitled to guess that Mr. Darcy's stream might be the river Wye, which also runs by beautiful Haddon Hall with its historic picture gallery and plentiful windows. Pemberley is a compound of suggestions supplied by several old Derbyshire mansions, including Hardwick Hall, built in the sixteenth century by that formidable Elizabeth, Bess of Hardwick, and designed with more glass windows than customary in Elizabethan domestic dwellings. Hardwick Hall was famous for its Long Gallery, hung with pictures illuminated with natural light from the generous windows. Elizabeth Bennet at Pemberley rejoices in windows that offer both light and prospects and in pictures that present persons whom she knows. "The picture-gallery" exhibits among family portraits "a striking resemblance of Mr. Darcy," preparing her for his imminent epiphany, his manifestation in the flesh (III, ch. 1).

Austen has partly reinvented lost Haddon Hall to suit herself, drawing on and reshaping the ruined edifice presented by Gilpin in creating her own livable mansion, a rebuke and contrast to the pretentious gilt and mahogany of Chatsworth. First built in the eleventh century, Haddon Hall's major reconstruction took place in the Tudor period. The beautiful grounds harmonize with parts of the description of Pemberley. Haddon Hall is connected to a love story of a lady named Vernon—a name Austen had already used. Dorothy Vernon eloped with the second son of the Earl of Rutland of the Manners family—a young man of whom her father disapproved. But the lady owned the great and beautiful estate, and the Manners family held on to it. Family emblems appeared in the topiary and elsewhere; a boar's head (emblem of the Vernons) and a peacock (emblem of the Manners family). These could stand for Prejudice (or at least stubbornness) and Pride.

"Pemberley" is an Anglo-Saxon locational description, "place on the barley field near a hill." "Pember" would originally have referred to a man owning a barley field or fields. "Pember," a surname, was a not uncommon element in cognate place names/surnames, like "Pember-ton."[69] Such names are first associated with Lancashire. Derbyshire was once under the rule of the duchy of Lancaster; the original founder of the manor of Pemberley presumably had Lancashire connections. The *ley* is pure Anglo-Saxon. "Pemberley" means "Pember's clearing"—"clearing of a man who grows barley." Darcy's estate, named at its heart after basic *ber*—barley—returns us to simplicity, to the primal work of loving Nature and raising food in it.

Lady Catherine in memorable horror inquires of heaven "Are the shades of Pemberley to be thus polluted?" (III, ch. 14). Is she referring to Pemberley's shady woods—or to the spectral presences of noble an-cestors? The riddle is answered apparently in the ending when Lady Catherine "condescended to wait on them at Pemberley, in spite of that pollution which its *woods* had received" (III, ch. 19; italics added). Now Lady Catherine is climbing down. Surely she originally referred to the spirits of great ancestors tainted by ignoble marriage. But Pemberley's name is not grandiosely noble or romantic.

The practical old name indicates a genuine antiquity traceable to an original Saxon farm holding. Mr. Darcy, probably still a man who grows barley, is a conservator of the land. Darcy sustains the woodlands and appreciates the woods that delight Mrs. Gardiner—in contrast to such foolish inheritors as John Dashwood. One of the pleasant images of the novel, even experienced through Elizabeth's agitated embarrassment at her encounter with Darcy, is the walk through Pemberley's grounds by the river. A descriptive reference that may completely elude the modern reader comes in the description of the walk back down "to the edge of the water":

> It was a spot less adorned than any they had yet visited; and the val-ley, here contracted into a glen, allowed room only for the stream, and a narrow walk amidst the rough coppice-wood which bordered it. (III, ch. 1)

Austen picks up the Scottish word "glen" to describe the narrow valley but uses an old and very English term, "coppice," for the vegetation on this narrow border. A "coppice" might well date from early medieval times. "The two essential forms of woodland management were wood-pasture, recorded in Domesday as *silva pastilis,* and coppiced woodland, known as *silva minuta.*"[70] "Wood-pasture" entailed pollarding the trees, cutting them at the top to keep livestock from browsing at will. Coppiced trees were cut close to ground level; coppiced trees are still alive and grow slender shoots, "crops of leafy fodder and poles."

> When managed as a coppiced crop that is felled every few years, the trees are regularly reinvigorated and will live virtually indefinitely: coppiced beeches in southern England could be a thousand years old. Coppice woodland was cut on rotations which varied according to the nature of the fodder, fuel or timber required.[71]

Cattle were not allowed to browse among the coppices, but the new shoots, product of the cut stumps, were used as cattle fodder. (The practice seems largely to have died out in the late Victorian period.) An eighteenth-century "coppice wood" is practical and durable, a traditional example of sustainability. A "coppice" is a recyclable resource, providing implements as well as food for cattle. Pemberley's grounds are in total contrast to modern landscape design, seen, for example, in Cleveland's fashionable ornamental trees. Pemberley does not just display the natural, it is working with Nature, using the products of the land in a sustainable way in a true conservatism. Austen consistently endorses the use of land for sustainable cycles of production, primarily of food. Pemberley, no mere exhibition of groupings of trees and shrubbery, has nothing of Suburbia about it. It is a place based on food production and sustainable growth.

The quiet rhythms of the description, its leisurely details, blend in with the *largo* pace of the Gardiners' pleasure: "Mr. Gardiner . . . was very fond of fishing, and was so much engaged in watching the occasional appearance of some trout in the water . . . that he advanced but little." The gentle ease is comically varied by Elizabeth's agitation and embarrassment, *allegro andante,* especially when Mr. Darcy approaches. To Elizabeth's surprise Darcy soon invites Mr. Gardiner "to fish there as often as he chose, while he continued in the neighbourhood" (III, ch. 1). Derbyshire's excellent fishing was famous, not least because of references in one of the most popular travel books ever written, Izaak Walton's *The Compleat Angler; or, The Contemplative Man's Recreation. Being a Discourse of Rivers, Ponds, Fish and Fishing not unworthy the Perusal of most Anglers.* Part 1 was published in 1653; part 2, by the poet Charles Cotton, was added in 1676. This attractive work, perfect for country house libraries and often printed in the eighteenth century, is a great outdoor how-to-do-it book. Walton, friend of Donne and admirer of Herbert,

writes a quietly poetic treatise, combining travel description with curious lore, natural history, verse, and anecdote. A pastoral rich in honey-
suckle, pubs, recipes, lyric quotes, and advice on tying artificial flies, *The
Compleat Angler* on first appearance must have seemed a perfect antidote to the Civil War and Cromwellian rule. Both Walton and Cotton
are fond of the border area joining Walton's native Staffordshire to the
wilder Derbyshire. The second chapter of Cotton's continuation offers
a joyous description of Derbyshire fishing, with accounts of the various
rivers. The characters are "Piscator Jr." (Fisherman the Younger) and his
new acquaintance "Viator" (Traveler), once "Venator" (Hunter), now
converted into a fisherman. The pair cross a stone bridge over the little
river Henmore going into the town of Ashbourn—still named "Viator's
Bridge" in honor of the *Angler*'s character. The traveler may find the
Derbyshire peaks, as Piscator Jr. admits, "a little terrible to a Stranger,"
but he persuades this traveler that the country is admirable, and that
Derbyshire rivers are the best for fishing, starting with the river Dove:

> And this River, from its Head, for a Mile or two, is a black Water (as
> all the rest of the *Derbyshire* Rivers of note originally are; for they all
> spring from the Mosses) but is in a few Miles travel, so clarified, by
> the Addition of several clear and very great Springs . . . which gush
> out of the Lime-stone Rocks, that before it comes to my House . . .
> you will find it one of the purest chrystalline Streams you have seen.

After describing the Trent, "not only one of our *Derbyshire* rivers, but
the chief of them," Piscator turns to the Wye:

> The River *Wye* . . . has its source near unto *Buxton,* a town about ten
> Miles from hence . . . a black Water too at the Fountain, but by the
> same Reason with *Dove,* becomes very soon a most delicate clear
> River, and breeds admirable *Trout* and *Grayling,* reputed by those
> (who, by living upon its Banks, are partial to it) the *best of any;* and
> this running down by *Ashford, Bakewell,* and *Haddon* . . . falls into
> *Derwent,* and there loses its Name.[72]

Cotton's description covers the area Elizabeth visits. Before meeting Darcy she has seen some of the wonders of the Peak District. "Matlock and Dove Dale" she later discusses with Darcy in their flustered
effort to keep conversation going. Ancient Matlock (*Matlac,* "the meet-

ing oak") was by Austen's day a little spa town. Dove Dale, the valley of the river Dove, was a celebrated beauty spot. The stream that runs through Pemberley may arise from one of those mossy streams, dark at first, "black Water," running through woodland, cleared by the addition of waters from the clear limestone rills. The *Compleat Angler*'s imagery plays on the contrast between the challenge of the unknown and rugged "ill Landscape" and the gentle and varied beauty and fecundity of the Derbyshire rivers. An entity which may seem black and formidable at first can become "one of the purest chrystalline Streams you have seen."

This minidrama of *The Compleat Angler* parallels the psychodrama of *Pride and Prejudice.* Derbyshire is the right location for Mr. Darcy's birth and home. He doesn't play well to strangers; to the stranger he can seem "a little terrible." The Derbyshire gentleman's personality is rugged, and sometimes dark, his motives cloudy—like "black Water." Yet he is benevolent, his motives and feelings will clear, and his spirit can eventually manifest itself as "purest chrystalline."

That Darcy is a fisher is a great point in his favor. Hunting, Walton indicates, is the province of princes and nobles, bossy men who love to rule. The "plot" of Walton's Part 1 of *The Compleat Angler* is the conversion of Venator from hunter to fisherman. Fishing is fit for those who want to learn contemplation; "the very sitting by the River Side, is not only the quietest, fittest Place for Contemplation, but will invite an *Angler* to it."[73] Thus the narrator sees beautiful sights that "fully possessed my Soul with Content."[74] Fishing is conducive to appreciation of God's world. Quietness of soul, a disposition to be pleased, are qualities achieved by a fisherman. Good men enjoy fishing, Walton insists— and so they do; this novel's two best men, Mr. Gardiner and Darcy, are fishermen. Mr. Bingley and Mr. Bennet are shooters—as admittedly is Darcy—but we don't hear of their fishing.

When Elizabeth comes to Pemberley she has been touring the Peak District, escaping somewhat suburbanized Hertfordshire. She has gained an education in the beautiful and sublime. She is becoming Northern. Mr. Darcy is a man of the North, and so is Bingley. Each can, as it were, "pass" as a gentleman of the English South, but their hearts are not in it. Bingley finally purchases his estate, not in the south near London as his sisters wish—not even next door to Darcy—but "in a neighbouring county to Derbyshire" (III, ch. 19). The biggest and most obvious county bordering Derbyshire is Yorkshire (fig. 20). Despite Bingley's sisters' preferences, his swerve to the south was not per-

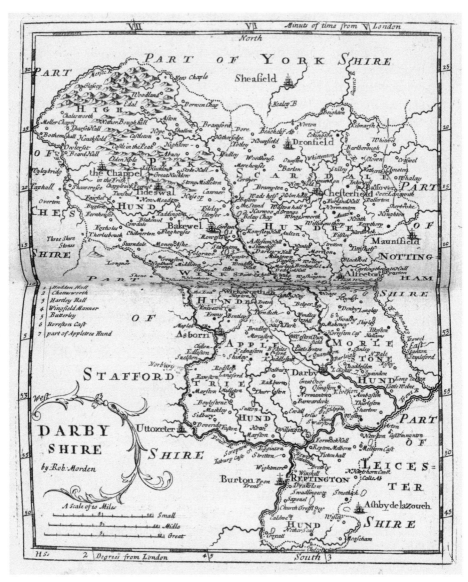

20. Robert Morton, *Darbyshire* (1704). From *The New Description and State of England, containing Maps of the Counties of England and Wales*. Photograph: © The British Library Board.

manent. He returns home—to Yorkshire. That will be Jane's home too. If he settles somewhere not far from Sheffield, Bingley will be within traveling distance of the Bakewell area, as the map shows.

Derbyshire is already at the center of the new manufacturing industry. In 1777 Richard Arkwright had built Lumford Mill at Bakewell, and, at nearby Wirksworth in the Peak, the first cotton mill with a steam engine. By the time of Elizabeth Bennet's tour, parts of Bakewell were being rebuilt to accommodate modern industry. Derbyshire was becoming steadily industrialized. Austen picks up the name "Lambton," associated with both D'Arcys and coal mining.[75] One edge of Derbyshire borders on Manchester, which had begun to vie with active Birmingham to the south as a manufacturing and commercial center. Derbyshire's industries at the turn into the nineteenth century were largely new and modern. In making Derbyshire her permanent home, Elizabeth Bennet is uniting herself not only with the traditions of agricultural and rural Pemberley, but also with the nineteenth century's future.

Chapter 11

Real and Imaginary Places in the "Chawton" Novels

Names and Places in *Mansfield Park:* Huntingdonshire, Hampshire (Portsmouth), and Northamptonshire

REAL PLACES IN *MANSFIELD PARK*

In *Pride and Prejudice* we see a heroine from a small agricultural southern county unite her life with that of a superior gentleman from a more impressive county where he has a large estate. This scenario—a gentleman from a large flourishing county somewhat remote from London takes in marriage a woman from a small agricultural county—is played out like a variation on a theme at the very beginning of the next novel, *Mansfield Park*. This novel exhibits a more complex use of place than Austen's previous works. Although the novel is named for one massively immoveable center, place references are wide ranging. The wars in the Mediterranean in which William Price is engaged bring in Gibraltar, Malta, and Sicily. William buys the amber cross in Sicily, although the amber is in origin a Baltic product. Fanny in her reading of Lord Macartney and his (failed) embassy can travel in imagination outside of the modern West by going to China. The desire to reach through space is felt in this novel, curiously intertwined with a counteractive desire to stay put or to fence others in. The story combines the maximum of movement with the maximum of restriction.

Reaching through Spaces: Vessels, Geography, Stars

The names of the naval vessels scattered through the narrative are both imaginary and "real." Ship names display the glorious arbitrariness of all naming, offering a wild poetry scrambling geography and mythology. William's first ship was the "H.M.S. Antwerp," sketched by young William and labeled "in letters as tall as the main-mast" (I, ch. 16). The ship named after a Flemish town is a place within a place, attached to the wall in Fanny's room. Ships' names are not representations of towns or anything else, but transmutations of ideas projected upon movable places. Austen borrowed the names of vessels associated with her sailor brothers. Frank Austen was captain of the HMS *Elephant,* and had served on the *Canopus* in 1805–6, in the Battle of Saint Domingo. The *Thrush* may lie at Spithead "Near the Canopus." The *Canopus* is named after an Egyptian town, an ancient port on the Nile Delta. Reference to the *Canopus* and the *Cleopatra* would remind Austen's first readers of the battle for Egypt—the Battle of the Nile, or Battle of Aboukir, fought 1–3 August 1798. General Napoleon Bonaparte intended to take over Egypt and the eastern regions of the Mediterranean, designing to cut Britain off from India. In the Battle of the Pyramids (21 July), Bonaparte had defeated the Egyptian Mamluk forces in a land battle. Nelson and his fleet sped down to grapple with the French fleet by the Delta. The Battle of the Nile was a decisive naval victory for Nelson; almost all of the French fleet's seventeen ships were captured or destroyed. "Canopus" may be the original name of the French ship or a refitted capture renamed. The ship's name commemorates an ancient town and a potential new territory in Egypt. Unlike a topographical spot on land, this *Canopus* is a highly mobile "place."

The *Thrush,* humbly named after a common English bird, gains new associations. Mr. Price tells William of his ship: "She lays just astern of the Endymion with the Cleopatra to larboard." The name of the famed Egyptian queen is abruptly connected with the Greek hero who fell in love with the Moon (and was to supply John Keats with the title of an early poem). Austen's brother Charles served on the *Endymion* as midshipman and then on the *Cleopatra,* taking command in 1810. How could Austen resist the fantastical and poetic resonance of such names! Genders are interestingly mixed. A ship is a "she" though her crew are all males. To lie between Cleopatra and Endymion is to share male and female passion—and beauty. You cannot put the map of the world together, for the world is in an energetic kind of chaos. Metamorphosis is everywhere.

In Fanny's cold East room at Mansfield, the *Antwerp* appears as William drew it, disproportionate, reduced to two dimensions. Dislocated visual allusions to places appear in the "transparencies" "where Tintern Abbey held its station between a cave in Italy, and a moonlight lake in Cumberland" (I, ch. 16). The images on Fanny's walls are all failures, stressing hunger for representation and its impossibility. In Fanny's East room, her almost-private space, we find images of the mind longing for change of place, playing upon transparent or imperfect images of elsewhere. There are other "places" too, beyond the terrestrial globe.

Edmund refers to Arcturus; Fanny adds "I wish I could see Cassiopeia" (I, ch. 11). Arcturus and Cassiopeia are among the lofty names
that humans in a particular culture have given to configurations of
stars. Cassiopeia, arrogant queen of Ethiopia, boasted that she and her
daughter Andromeda were more beautiful than the Nereids, daughters
of Ocean. The queen was punished by Poseidon, who placed her in her
chair in the sky. This star myth might be a comic reflection upon Lady
Bertram and her most beautiful daughter Maria—certainly all that
Lady Bertram does is *sit*. The myths entertain us, but the names we give
to stars and our fantasies of what we see in constellations offer consum-
mate examples of arrogant naming. Austen in 1799 jokes, "I have nothing to do, but to invent a few hard names for the Stars" (9 January 1799;
Letters, 34). In naming stars (whether as mythographers or astrono-
mers) we cannot even pretend to consult the natives. Planets, stars, and
constellations are not (in 1800) objectives for tourism or active coloni-
zation, but playthings of mental geography—a game honoring colonialism by expanding it, claiming metaphysical power over distant reality.
Naming stars fosters a sense of "being in place" in the universe as well as
in the world. Those who most enjoy escaping to these grand imaginary
entities may be the very persons who have least power over their own
lives—like Fanny, who cannot even be permitted to go out on the lawn
by herself for stargazing.

Counties and Colonies

In *Mansfield Park*, Austen also deals most emphatically with the differences between English places. The obvious contrast is between Portsmouth on the coast of Hampshire, England's busiest naval port—full of
males and masculine endeavor, a bit brutal, quite dirty, and boisterous—
and Mansfield Park itself, inland, peaceful, enclosed within Northamptonshire, an epitome of determined and calm gentility. Both places
provide major settings for the novel's action. There are, however, two
invisible centers of production: the first delivering persons, and the second wealth—and both anxiety. These are Huntingdonshire and Antigua. The distant Caribbean island is the source of much of Sir Thomas's
wealth and importance, while from little Huntingdon come the three
Ward sisters. From the matrix of generative Huntingdon most of the
characters spring—not only Lady Bertram, Mrs. Norris, and Frances
Price, but also Tom, Maria, Edmund and Julia Bertram, as well as Fanny
and William Price and all their siblings.

The Invisible Influence of Huntingdonshire

The novel begins with a contrast between Huntingdonshire and Northamptonshire.

> About thirty years ago, Miss Maria Ward of Huntingdon, with only seven thousand pounds, had the good luck to captivate Sir Thomas Bertram, of Mansfield Park, in the county of Northampton, and to be thereby raised to the rank of a baronet's lady, with all the comforts and consequences of an handsome house and large income. All Huntingdon exclaimed at the greatness of the match. (I, ch. 1)

Huntingdon, meaning "hunter on a hill," is the county town of the shire named after it. Huntingdonshire is—or was—a very small county just west of Cambridgeshire, in the flat eastern area of England. The name suggests "hunting," a subtheme of the novel. In some versions of the story of Robin Hood, the celebrated outlaw who robbed from the rich and gave to the poor was Robin, Earl of Huntingdon. Mythical Robin is customarily a man of the North. Yet the issue of the redistribution of wealth hangs over Austen's story. Huntingdonshire was always small—Camden calls it "This little Shire."[1] The population in the 1821 census was 48,771. Quiet and unprepossessing, this county is now extinct, having been swallowed up in the late twentieth century by Cambridgeshire, of which it has become a mere district. Even in an earlier era, it shared administration with Cambridgeshire, the two having one High Sheriff.

Huntingdon the town, some sixty miles from London, was a small market town on the River Great Ouse. It was once given by King Stephen to King David of Scotland, but Henry II rescinded the donation and perhaps David didn't miss it. Huntingdon received its original charter from King John, traditional archenemy of Robin Hood. Before the Black Death, the region was well populated, with enough engineering skill to build a famous bridge across the Ouse. There was some valuable timber on well-forested hills. Camden says, "It is a very good Corn Country."[2] (The word "corn" in British English always means wheat or barley—until the late twentieth century the term never refers to maize.) Huntingdonshire, flat and well watered, suited grass and cattle raising, though water meadows could turn into marsh. The Abbey of Ramsey stood "where the rivers stagnate in a spungy kind of ground."[3] The settlement of Elton, or "eel-town," was nearby; spongy land and river provided a nourishing environment for eels. Muddier lands unsuited to wheat or sheep were good for vegetables.

As for famous inhabitants, Huntingdon's one claim to greatness is that it is the birthplace of Oliver Cromwell, who was born there in 1599—as Jane Austen knew; her marginal comment on Goldsmith's page declares that Oliver's father's patrimony was more than he deserved. Cromwell was actually born in the village of Hinchingbrooke, one-half mile from Huntingdon. Dryden mocks a "dire Usurper": "his birth, perhaps, some petty Village hides."[4] In 1628 Cromwell represented Huntingdon as MP. Cromwell, however, was to part with his Huntingdon land; his later life was more closely associated with property inherited from his mother in Ely. His religious conversion seems to have postdated his departure from Huntingdon. He was later elected as MP for Cambridge, intellectual powerhouse of seventeenth-century Puritanism.

Travelers to little Huntingdon in the eighteenth century speak of it as a place whose day, if it had one, is past. "This Town has nothing remarkable in it," declares the author of *A Pocket Companion of Roads of the South Part of Great Britain* (1724). He adds, "'tis a long continued Street, pretty well built, has three Parish churches, and a pretty good Market-Place."[5] Camden seems to have been struck by the robustness of its working people: "Nor is there a Town in the Kingdom that has a greater number of lusty stout Husbandmen."[6] This sounds like a rural population in an overgrown village. Defoe dwells on the terrifying pleasures of local Stilton cheese, which "is brought to Table with the Mites, or Maggots round it, so thick, that they bring a Spoon with them for you to eat the Mites with, as you do the Cheese." Defoe compliments Huntington's "beautiful Meadows," but, save for the old bridge, finds little otherwise of interest: "This Town has nothing remarkable in it; 'tis a long continued Street, pretty well built."[7] After Defoe's death, Samuel Richardson revised and expanded his *Tour*. Richardson dramatically caps the account of Huntingdon with a gruesome local story that has "made so much Noise." A family in nearby Warboys (or Warbois) was executed for practicing witchcraft to the injury of a rich family's child: "And thus three unhappy Persons were sacrificed to Ignorance and Superstition."[8] One of the accusers was Lady Cromwell, grandmother of Oliver Cromwell.

The Witches of Warboys had become legendary; there is an illustration in Richard Boulton's *A Compleat History of Magick*, 1715 (fig. 21). The village of Warboys, extant on the lands of Ramsey Abbey since before the Domesday Book, was only seven miles from Huntingdon.

21. Richard Boulton, *The Witches of Warboyse* (1715). From *A Complete History of Magick, Sorcery, and Witchcraft*. Photograph: © The British Library Board.

After the execution in 1593, the Throckmorton family, not content with hanging poor aged Alice Samuels as well as her unlucky husband and daughter, asserted its role as righteous victim in perpetuity. The wealthy Throckmortons endowed a memorial: a fellow of Queen's College, Oxford, was to preach a sermon against "Witchcraft" annually on the celebration of the Annunciation (Lady Day, 25 March) at the church in Huntingdon. This practice continued until 1812. Well before that date, Queen's College speakers had deliberately lost the plot. Contradicting a Throckmorton descendant, Martin Joseph Naylor of Queens insists that "the Society of Queen's were not such slaves of odious superstition as he ungenerously imagines. The sin of witchcraft has long since ceased to be the theme of their annual discourses, nor has the subject ever been mentioned, except to explode, and deprecate the lamentable effects of, such miserable delusions."[9] Naylor, who published the four endowed sermons he preached from 1792 to 1795 against "vulgar superstitions," holds up the executed Samuels family as a painful example of "the odious and mischievous powers of bigotry and ignorance."[10] Austen's Oxford-educated brothers presumably knew about this by now rather embarrassing endowed sermon on the Witches of Warboys. Warboys occasionally surfaced in the news in relation to draining fenland for agricultural use.

Huntingdon comes off in all accounts as a backwater, a small market town, essentially a town of one street, with a population (on market days) of stout farmers and laborers. The portion of population with any claim to any degree of gentility must be small indeed. On the occasion of Sir Thomas's proposal for the hand of Maria Ward, if "all Huntingdon exclaimed at the greatness of the match" multitudes were not involved (*MP*, I, ch. 1). In a one-horse—or one-street—town a few people were surprised. The Wards' money would have been made in cattle or agriculture, but they are wealthy only in relation to other denizens of their area. Maria's dowry (seven thousand pounds) is not commensurate with what a Northamptonshire estate owner like Sir Thomas Bertram might command on the marriage market. But the girl is healthy and handsome—and, moreover, unlikely to feel entitled to criticize or disobey.

The Wards lived in no great style. Maria's uncle is a mere "lawyer," that is an attorney (like Mr. Philips in *Pride and Prejudice*). None of the three Ward sisters (the novel's older generation of females) is at all well educated. The three girls are credible descendants of the "lusty Husbandmen" of this muddy region. Their rise in class is not something well understood or managed by them. It seems, however, that on her rise Maria and her elder sister Elizabeth prudently threw off ties with Huntingdon: the only relationship they sustain (if intermittently) is with sister Frances. Nobody in the story ever refers to any relation or friend in Huntingdonshire or makes any move to visit this ancestral home.

Northamptonshire, just west of humble Huntingdonshire, is a contrast in size, importance, and wealth. Its population in the 1801 census is given as 131,757; by 1821 it had risen to 141,353. In literature, Northamptonshire is the abode of Harriet Byron, the English heroine of *Sir Charles Grandison*. Two manor houses in Northamptonshire provide settings for important scenes of that novel, especially in the "cedar parlor," the paneled room with its wide window seats. Austen-Leigh tells us, "Every circumstance narrated in Sir Charles Grandison, all that was ever said or done in the cedar parlour, was familiar to her [Jane Austen]" (*Memoir*, ch. 5, 71). On her marriage, Harriet moves south from Northamptonshire, away from the provinces toward the center, uniting with Grandison who owns a large estate in the South and has London connections.

Northamptonshire, still highly rural, was on the north-south axis. New efforts were under way to create a much better communications network. "Stoke," market town nearest to Mansfield, is Stoke Bruerne, a village gaining importance with the advance of the Grand Union Canal. This project, for which Parliament voted funding in 1793, linked waterways (natural and man-made) in the South and the Midlands, making for speedier transportation. The canal was declared completed and the last tunnel opened by Telford in a ceremony at Stoke on March 25, 1805, attended by five thousand spectators.[11] So Mary Crawford's harp could come from London by water transport—not possible a few years before.

Prosperity long marked Northamptonshire. The wealthy had gone in vigorously for enclosures; the region distinguished itself in the creation of parks. The English "park" is a proclamation of rights over land. Land so "enclosed," taken over and set off with a formal boundary, is required to offer nothing to anyone but the owner (and immediate dependents). The common people bitterly resented enclosure, which took common land away from the poor and gave it to a wealthy private family. The prized right to hunt or shoot on a manor belonged to the landowner. The poor were punished if they attempted to hunt, fish, or shoot. Austen is highly alert to manorial rights to game—those remnants of Norman forest law. Mr. Bingley in leasing Netherfield gains the right to shoot there. Sir Walter Elliot grudges giving Admiral Croft such rights at Kellynch, but Mr. Shepherd knows that this must be included in the rental agreement. Mrs. Bennet offers Mr. Bennet's grounds at Longbourn for the young men to shoot over, and Mr. Darcy offers Mr. Gardiner the right to fish in his stream. Almost the only energetic attribute of Mr. Rushworth is his zeal in pursuing poachers. Tom and Edmund Bertram are both shooters of birds on Mansfield grounds.

Great "parks," true stately homes with extensive lands, result from a series of expansions. "Apthorpe Park in Northamptonshire was enlarged in the time of James I after the king had been a guest there." Finding the deer park "neither large enough nor sufficiently stored with covert," King James directed the earl of Westmoreland "to take in and impale another 314 acres." "At Althorp and Deene, in the same county, the Spencers and Brudenells were constantly adding to their deer parks by purchases and exchanges of land in the late sixteenth and early seventeenth centuries. Many expanding parks began swallowing up good cornland in this period there are frequent complaints about this development."[12] "Good cornland" of course means land capable of bearing abundant wheat and barley. Great landowners might demote farming to enhance the Norman and ruling-class pleasures of the chase.

Mansfield Park is a later version of the homes of Norman hunt lovers. It is what Bernard Shaw called "Horseback Hall." The Bertram girls ride well, and Mary is taught to ride by Edmund, who keeps horses suited to hunting; Edmund and Tom are both foxhunters. Henry Crawford and Edmund have been enjoying a fox chase when Henry's horse loses a shoe, forcing Henry to walk the horse quietly back. He thus accidentally explores Thornton Lacey.

Northamptonshire in the central southern Midlands is a very good locale for a novelist looking for a wealthy region somewhat remote from London, hospitable to great houses and the privileges of "parks." The county was famous for "stately homes," like the estate of the Spencers at Althorp, where Princess Diana (née Spencer), was buried in 1997. The county was also a setting for conflict. Divided between Royalists and Puritans, it has major Civil War associations. Important battles were fought in Northamptonshire—above all the fatal Naseby in June 1645, when the defeat of the Royalist forces spelled doom for King Charles.

The imaginary estates Mansfield Park and Sotherton in Northamptonshire are prosperous—and yet a little out of the mainstream. Sir Thomas Bertram, we are told, has been an MP representing his region; we are not told of his affiliation to any party, but he seems much less Tory than Whig. Desire for protection of his colonial plantations would incline him in the Whig direction; Tories traditionally objected to yielding taxes to pay for naval dominance and colonial wars. Sir Thomas's position as an MP has entailed prolonged absences in London, which Lady Bertram—surprisingly—prefers not to visit. In plays and novels from the Restoration through the Regency, a visit to London is notoriously the desideratum of country ladies with any claims to wealth, position, or fashion. Members of the Bertram family are encouraged to remain on the estate. Agriculture still provides income. Hay making, and consequent shortage of carts, is referred to. But, at the Mansfield we know, much of the land appears given to pleasure— the rural pleasures of gentlemen and ladies. Lady Bertram has her rose garden. The Norrises plant an apricot tree, and Mrs. Grant a shrubbery. Mrs. Grant's new shrubbery—unlike an old hedgerow—performs no agricultural functions. In a famous instance of search for exact detail, Jane Austen wished to know "whether Northamptonshire is a Country of Hedgerows" (29 January 1813; *Letters,* 202) Evidently she rightly decided it was not. Hoskins remarks on "this comparative scarcity of trees in the East Midland hedgerows—in Northamptonshire and Leicestershire especially," attributing this absence to foxhunting.[13] There is a casual reference to a man "mending a hedge" in Henry's description of Thornton Lacey (*MP,* II, ch. 7), but this was likely one of the coarser single-line hedges of the eighteenth century. Austen saves up the proper hedgerow, the medieval hedgerow, for a great scene in *Persuasion.* In *Mansfield Park* we get no beautiful landmarks or signs of the beneficial human labor working with nature. Sport is found within the landscape—by killing something. Bertram males both hunt and shoot. Tom Bertram knows that he can deflect his father's scolding by turning the conversation to the pleasures of shooting:

> "I have hardly taken out a gun since the 3d. Tolerable sport the first three days. . . . The first day I went over Mansfield Wood, and Edmund took the copses beyond Easton, and we brought home six brace between us, and might each have killed six times as many." (*MP,* II, ch. 1)

Mansfield insists on the pleasures of shooting, not only in blood sports but also the erotic war—Henry Crawford desires to make a small hole in Fanny's heart. Moral actions and thoughts are colored by shooting and being shot at. Edmund's position (reflecting his namesake King Edmund) as the man who gets shot at suits the park with its perpetually lethal amusements. William Price also gets shot at—very literally—in warfare defending the outwardly placid England of Mansfield Park.

The sources of Sir Thomas Bertram's income pose something of a puzzle. Mansfield has gently morphed into a kind of stagnant ornament and recreational space. Unlike Pemberley, it isn't open to visitors—it is not grand enough to be a literal showplace. It benefits nobody outside its own denizens. There is no lively village or little town like Meryton, no reference to connection or community—work with a school, for example, as in *Emma.* The ladies (or at last Fanny) do sewing for the poor, though we don't see these "poor"; rough calico lies ready at hand in the "poor-basket" (I, ch. 7). (Ladies' labor at these rough garments takes work away from poor women and is of much less value than a cash donation.)

Activity at Mansfield is in uncertain relationship to the business activities in the Caribbean. Much of the wealth of the Bertrams for many years has evidently flowed in from plantations in Antigua. That distant center of productivity is becoming problematic at the time of the novel's main action. The characters' "wealth" depends on sea journeys. Sea battles protect the trade routes to the Caribbean and the colonies themselves. There is thus a real economic relation between the seafaring William Price (and his father, the former Marine) and the aloof and spiritually landlocked Sir Thomas with his landlocked immediate family.

Fanny Price, born at the outer edge of Hampshire, is the one Austen heroine who is her author's compatriot. Fanny, however, comes from the lively coast, not the inland peace of a Steventon. Camden describes "Hantshire" (or "Hamshire") as "a small county, abounding with corn, pleasantly interspersed with thick woods and rich pastures, and happy in its communication with the sea by its many creeks and harbours convenient for trade."[14] Portsmouth, flourishing trading port in the Middle Ages, was in 1194 turned by Richard Coeur de Lion into a military and naval center. It was frequently sacked by the French, taken four times between 1338 and 1380. Henry V seriously fortified it, and Henry VIII made it the heart of the Royal Navy. In Portsmouth the King Henry and his courtiers watched the launching of his great battleship *Mary Rose* and looked on with horror as it sank. Camden admired the Portsmouth of Elizabeth: "Queen Elizabeth at great expense fortified it so strongly with new works that nothing is wanting to make a place of the greatest strength."[15]

Portsmouth was worth fortifying; it offered protection to Southampton, a port at the end of a protecting channel well suited to mercantile traffic. Portsmouth made a perfect dry dock and was suited to large naval operations. Many ships at once could be berthed there: "The safe and spacious road of *Spithead* between Hampshire and the Isle of Wight is 20 miles long and in some places three broad."[16] From Portsmouth Nelson set out in the *Victory* to fight and die in the Battle of Trafalgar in October 1805. Portsmouth was the headquarters of the small fleet that after 1808 was to police the coast of Africa, pursuing slave ships in support of the new ban on the slave trade—an activity in which Francis Austen was an active participant. From 1807 to 1809 Jane Austen had lived with her sailor brother Francis and his family in Southampton. Thus she had come to know the region much better than she could have known it in 1783 when the ill-fated relocation of Mrs. Cawley's "school" to Southampton led to serious illness. "Beware of the stinking fish of Southampton," warns Isabel in "Love and Freindship" (*Juvenilia,* 105); young Jane may have been told that Southampton's malodorous air caused her terrifying fever. Typhus, however, results from infection by a louse; Ann Cawley took the children into unclean quarters, in a town inundated with returning servicemen who had been living in unhygienic close quarters. Typhus killed Jane Cooper's mother and nearly killed young Jane Austen. Indirectly, these females are victims of war.

Portsmouth in Fanny Price's era (and even ours) is an interesting island fort, with a varied accumulation of defenses and impressive buildings. "God's House" or "Domus Dei" was a name for the Hospital of Saint Nicholas established in 1212. It was the scene of a scandalous murder in 1450 when a group of sailors killed an unpopular bishop. The town was put under excommunication. In expiation, a chapel was built. Taken over by Henry VIII in 1540, the former religious foundation hospital became an armory, then a governor's house. The chapel remained in constant use; in 1662 it was the site of the wedding of King Charles II and Catherine of Braganza. That chapel, restored in 1767, became known as the "Garrison Church." Here, perhaps more for patriotism than for piety, the Price family goes every week—and here Henry Crawford joins them one bright spring Sunday. (This chapel is still visible, though in a new state of ruin, as it was bombed in January 1941.) Unlike her author, Fanny is connected with the sea. Fanny is also urban in her birth, in that respect resembling the London-bred Crawfords rather than the rural Bertrams. Urban characters in novels tend to have a large acquaintance. Though we don't think of Fanny as urban, she actually has the largest circle of acquaintance of any central character in *Mansfield Park,* with the exception of (secondary) Tom, whose references to numerous friends exhibit his restless desire to escape from enclosure and social limitation.

Fanny, the city child, threatens to bring the vulgar taint of town air, of streets and crowding, to Mansfield Park. Sir Thomas warns of signs of class inferiority in the child they are about to take in: "We . . . must prepare ourselves for gross ignorance, some meanness of opinions, and very distressing vulgarity of manner" (*MP,* I, ch. 1). Mansfield Park is in the most literal sense *exclusive*—guarding its doors, it keeps others out. Unlike Bennets, Woodhouses, Musgroves, or even Elliots, the Bertrams do not refer to friends and acquaintances and dining out. (They seem to dine only with their own dependent and protégé, the parish clergyman.) How surprising we find it that the Bertrams know a sufficient number of people to give a ball—and that somebody would come! Although Sir Thomas Bertram travels, he never mentions any other men as associates in politics or plantations or in clubs. Superlatively "unclubbable," this unsociable patriarch is more self-enclosed and narcissistic than General Tilney or Sir Walter Elliot. Fanny threatens the taint not only of plebeian streets, but of other people.

The woman hiding behind the title "Lady Bertram" was once Maria Ward. Maria Ward's marriage forced the passive girl to enter a world to which she is not at all accustomed. Maria Ward is capable of bearing healthy, good-looking children—probably a prime motive for Sir Thomas's choice in marriage. Once she has given him the four children she has no further use or any heavy duties. Sir Thomas does not demand intelligence, so she is all right there. Her "upward mobility" has really meant "upward stasis." Lady Bertram has been training herself for years to desire nothing from the outer world—certainly not the company of persons of her husband's social level. She keeps trying to "pass," coping with her new class by taking Sir Thomas's "advice." Her efforts are largely successful, though a little of the old background seeps out, as in her repeated "I will tell you what, Fanny" (III, ch. 2). Waiting to be told what to do, Lady Bertram is fixed, splendidly sedentary, not daring any spontaneity that might give herself away. Frightened of putting a foot wrong, Maria the First, thus reshaped, sits eternally upon the sofa. Lady Bertram cannot possibly educate her children, as she is totally ignorant. Unacquainted with books or society, and unequipped with either the etiquette or principles suited to her station, she learns by mimicry, when necessary.

Lady Bertram's behavior is more comprehensible—and her character more sympathetic—if we consider that this first young Maria was acutely aware of insufficiencies in her own background and felt compelled to conceal her "low" self. Her first weeks at Mansfield at age eighteen were probably uncomfortably similar to Fanny's experience at age ten. Inertia is less a temperamental defect than a strategy. She needed to conceal from Sir Thomas any "gross ignorance" or "distressing vulgarity of manner." Maria the First follows a policy of watchful waiting, of sitting tight. Panic and anxiety may have provoked her brain to seize up, so that even games of cards are beyond her—but she may not always have been so stupid.

In her act as "Lady Bertram" Maria can just about manage be taken for an incorrigibly indolent fine lady. Hence her extraordinary reluctance to go to London. Social ordeals demanding complex behavior—meeting the wives of other MPs, attending parties in the Season—threaten her imitation of breeding. Mrs. Norris is less exact in masquerading as a clergyman's wife, and her veneer of breeding often slips. Like practically every inhabitant of Mansfield Park, Maria Ward as Lady Bertram has been *acting*—acting so successfully that the restraint became second nature. In fact, Mansfield Park seems so full of daily acting that it really *cannot* take any more theater. The advent of actual theatricals tips the balance over into emotional reality. The passions claim their rights. Maria Ward's experience long before we know her—smothered, even drugged, though she may appear by prosperity and worldly success— prefigures Fanny's in important respects. Both are transplants who must try to act in accordance with new proprieties. Fanny is also caught up in the cruel domestic theater, forced perpetually to enact gratitude and suppress any sense of grievance—or of self. Her statement "I cannot act" is necessarily false. She is *always* trying to act as the superlatively grateful child the family would have her be—masking self-pity, resentment, and her feelings toward Edmund. As she grows older it is harder to dissemble her love for Edmund—a guilty horrifying incestuous love that she covers, acting sufficiently effectively to deceive Sir Thomas when he asks if she rejects Henry Crawford because there is somebody else.[17]

What we begin to see—once we focus on the fact of little Huntingdonshire and its cultural deprivation—is the absence of mental forces beyond the peasant level in all three of the Ward sisters. If they dwell in a town—the tiny town of Huntingdon—when Sir Thomas first encounters them, not many generations back their family must have been purely of the shire, offspring of the "stout Husbandmen." Mrs. Norris consistently gives the game away. Boosted—and constrained—by her sister Maria's rise, Elizabeth Ward, the eldest sister, was "obliged" to be content with the clergyman to whom her patron Sir Thomas could give a living. But Mrs. Norris is not fit to be the wife of a clergyman of the Church of England. At Sotherton, in a moment of tell-tale revelation, we hear her peasant voice and outlook as she offers the gardener a mode of treatment for his grandchild: "She had set him right as to his grandson's illness, convinced him it was an ague, and promised him a charm for it" (*MP*, I, ch. 10).

Offering charms for sickness belongs to a country world already archaic. Elizabeth Norris's diagnosis could even be harmful. She is getting dangerously close to a Witch of Warboys. (The Ward sisters might even have come from Warboys, that little village near Huntingdon.) Mrs. Norris displays the "Ignorance and Superstition" associated with

Huntingdon. Mrs. Norris's clerical husband, who would have taken a BA degree at Oxford or Cambridge to qualify for ordination, was to some minimal extent a man of letters. Mr. Norris certainly ought to have educated his wife out of such superstitious notions—but apparently didn't bother. Probably he paid as little attention as he could to this lowborn spouse (illiterate, bad-tempered but well connected), refraining from conflict to avoid complaints to his patron.

Mrs. Norris has been left to go her own way. She has not truly been successful in learning to join the class—or, rather, the *rank*—to which she has become artificially attached through her sister's marriage. That renders all the more amusing her assumed superiority when she puts on an act by asserting the sacredness of the hierarchy: "People are never respected when they step out of their proper sphere. Remember *that*, Fanny. . . . The nonsense and folly of people's stepping out of their rank and trying to appear above themselves, makes me think it right to give *you* a hint, Fanny" (*MP*, II, ch. 5). Mrs. Norris, having stepped out of her rank, is with indifferent success trying to "appear above herself." Like her predecessor Cromwell, she is a "Usurper" from Huntingdon, or from a nearby "petty Village." Mrs. Norris is not unique in adopting a false self. In this novel almost every character—including Fanny—is in moral or social masquerade and can be placed under the label of Parasite, Pretender, or Usurper.

Of all Jane Austen's characters, Mrs. Norris is most in the manner of Balzac, who deals with the dangers posed by "*Les parents pauvres,*" poor relations. True, unlike *la cousine Bette,* Elizabeth Norris is not likely to foster a handsome young Polish sculptor or spend years in devious revenge. But the peasant's hidden suspicions and sense of resentment—these are present. Aunt Norris also bears some resemblance to George Eliot's Aunt Glegg in *The Mill on the Floss.* All three novelists are dealing with characters who have to adjust from an old way of life to another. Change distorts them, evoking deep defensiveness. Mrs. Glegg, out of date in an expanding industrialized town, supports herself on an ideological inheritance of Puritanism, signaled in passive-aggressive reading of Baxter's *Saints' Everlasting Rest.*

Mrs. Norris has no ideology that could be accounted for by—or related to—books of any sort. The *logos* is as nothing in her sight. Elizabeth Norris is not interested in religion, not even formally. She has two copies of the Book of Common Prayer in her house but never looked into them—until she decides to not to send either to her goddaughter. She hypocritically sounds a slightly religious note while trying to impress Sir Thomas in the first conversation, but this style is not congenial to her and we never hear her repeat it. (Was this a slightly false start by Austen?) Mrs. Norris's archaic "charm" against ague represents the genuine unreconstructed peasant woman. She shrewdly keeps away from any tasks requiring reading or knowledge. She may abet her nieces' ridicule of Fanny's incapacity—but prudently does so only in general terms. Like Fanny, Mrs. Norris could not "put the map of Europe together." (At a higher range of jest, this difficult task is what the deputies of the Allies are endeavoring to do—with great difficulty—in 1814.)

Mrs. Norris's real religion is luck. "Fortune" and "luck" run though the novel from the first paragraph. That the proposal from Sir Thomas is a stroke of "good luck" for Maria Ward is an idea that affects all her family (I, ch. 1). Mrs. Norris is deeply aware that luck can run out, so she safeguards herself by hoarding, saving money, and patching things together. Outsiders are to be regarded with suspicion, potential rivals for a slim maintenance. The harder we look at Mrs. Norris the more clearly she proclaims her true background. Her proposed arrangements for bringing Fanny from Portsmouth entail putting her own servant "Nanny" up at the London dwelling of Nanny's cousin the saddler and having the child Fanny come by herself all the way from Portsmouth, to meet Nanny at the saddler's and get a bed there. Certainly, this is not the plan Sir Thomas would adopt. But such arrangements would have been the way in which former Wards made journeys; it hasn't been long since they were putting up at the homes of relatives who were saddlers or something similar. Such arrangements not only answer the demand for frugality, but also keep the traveler safely within familiar relationships of reciprocal obligation and control. Dealing with strangers should be avoided. That is an axiom. Another axiom is that one must seize any small good that is going. Mrs. Norris is genuinely proud of her ability to seize small chances of good fortune—to take her meals at the Great House, to get a free baize curtain. Aware at some level of her resemblance to Fanny (both hangers-on of the Bertrams, and competitors for their bounty), she needs to keep Fanny down.

Mrs. Norris's life is based on an intuition that survival is a competition. With superiors she guards herself by rapid talk and flattery. While she has a kind of intimacy with her own servant, she is unused to formal service and is uneasy at "the passing of the servants behind her chair" (II, ch. 7). Perhaps she suspects that servants at Mansfield or Mansfield Parsonage make fun of her or at least (rightly) identify her as close to themselves in original station. Yet, when talking to Mrs. Whitaker, the housekeeper at Sotherton, Mrs. Norris treats her as an equal. When she is "spunging" (as her niece Maria says) cream cheese, heath, and pheasants' eggs, she is functioning at her own true level. Spunging Mrs. Norris has come from her spongy ground to take what she can. At Sotherton she is about as relaxed and happy as she ever gets. Her little riff of pleasure at the idea of nurturing the pheasants is not entire affectation:

> I shall get the dairy maid to set them under the first spare hen, and if they come to good I can have them moved to my own house and borrow a coop; and it will be a great delight to me in my lonely hours to attend to them." (I, ch. 10)

She rejoices at returning to the familiar poultry yard.

Mrs. Norris's sense that life is a zero-sum game is unnervingly justified by the end of the novel. The losses of the Bertrams are the gain of the Price family. The loss experienced by both Mary Crawford and Edmund Bertram is a gain to Fanny Price. Sir Thomas is certainly obtuse—his obtuseness enhanced by the Puritan legalism in his makeup. He never spotted the prosperous peasant in his wife's elder sister and for years foolishly trusted Mrs. Norris, his flatterer, as coadjutor. Nothing in her peasant mentality guides her regarding proprieties or moral scruples— she is not at all accustomed to thinking about moral matters. She is strict in the sense of putting down people who seem to challenge her worth, but she has no "moral sense" of the kind that either a philosopher or a curate could recognize.

Mrs. Norris belongs to a class that does not think abstractly about morality at all. This fact—or this absence—makes her appear more liberal, more "modern" on sexual matters. Historians tell us that among English peasantry heterosexual couples' coming together before marriage and a certain level of sexual experiment were tolerated—sometimes even encouraged. Certain forms of misbehavior might be seen as topics for rude jokes rather than for exclusion on moral-religious grounds. (What was not readily countenanced was leaving a brat for the parish to support, but Maria Rushworth [née Bertram] will make no demand on taxpayers.) Puritanism modified these attitudes to a considerable extent, but Puritanism did not "take" with the Ward family. Mrs. Norris airily advises Edmund regarding the play, "If there is anything a little too warm (and it is so with most of them) it can be easily left out," and she adds, "We must not be over precise, Edmund." She uses the old negative word for Puritanical morality. No "precisian," she disclaims all Puritanism. Mrs. Norris is most willing to stick to the adulterous Maria.

Sir Thomas, in contrast, may well have some genuine Puritan ancestry. Despite the use he makes of the conveniences of the Church of England, he seems a true and natural Roundhead, if secularized. He forbids and censors. On his return to Mansfield he tears down the young peoples' theater and destroys the playbooks—repeating notorious acts of the 1640s. He will not explain, argue, or even converse about the issue. Sir Thomas Bertram's destructive censorship should suffice to set everyone right. His house bears the name of Luther's birthplace, but his attitudes smack more of Calvinism. Lutheran "Justification by (unearned) Grace" is never available in his house. As a dictator he has a true Cromwellian flavor. Unfortunately for him, his two sons in their very different ways seem natural Cavaliers, while his wife and her sister are unaffected by religion or philosophy—or indeed by any coherent morality or ideology. Mrs. Norris is tolerant where we would expect intolerance, for we—like Sir Thomas—have read her incorrectly. She chooses to live with the adulterous and fallen niece. The vision of their tormenting one another is one of the few false notes that enter into the ending. Jane Austen sins against her own lights in making Lady Bertram comprehend the terrific wrong of which her adulterous daughter has been guilty. Lady Bertram has never exhibited understanding of any principles behind the strange rules to which she must adhere in her new place. The *concept* of "principle" is not available to her. Maria the First has performed obedience with the best mimicry she can supply. Lady Bertram never refers to religion, and she presumably shares the beliefs—or, rather, lack of them—shown more clearly if accidentally in Mrs. Norris. Lady Bertram will, perforce, acquiesce in Sir Thomas's dictates and assent to his strictures, shedding occasional puzzled tears on her own,. wondering why she can never see her elder daughter.

Sexuality doesn't particularly interest Mrs. Norris. She is a pre-Puritan, no "precisian." Sir Thomas satisfies his Puritan conscience by getting rid of contamination, shaking Maria off. He will send her money at a distance but refuse to see her or take her back into his home: "He would not by a vain attempt to restore what never could be restored, be affording his sanction to vice" (III, ch. 17). Denied reunion with her family, the fallen Maria, young and healthy, will undoubtedly be found by some future suitor attracted by her charms. In "Lesley Castle" Austen had adumbrated a twenty-first-century kind of resolution to marital bust-up. In *Mansfield Park* Austen feels constrained to say that Maria must withdraw "to a retirement and reproach, which could allow no second spring of hope or character" (III, ch. 17). But second springs *do* come—something Austen explores in her last completed novel.

Putting Maria into perpetual wardship is faintly ridiculous—she will cross that ha-ha, she will get through the gate. The possibility of marriage to Henry is denied, but the possibility of marriage to someone is *not* closed to a divorcée. Austen was an acquaintance of Elizabeth, Countess of Craven, later the merry Margravaine of Anspach. Comebacks, pleasures, and second springs are available. If a second spring in Anne Elliot's style is not possible, a recrudescence like that of Mrs. Clay is quite achievable. Maria's life is not over—we collude with Sir Thomas in supposing it must be. If Maria takes up with a man able to soothe her financially, Mrs. Norris as the girl's companion will quietly go along with the arrangement, even at the risk of alienating further an already estranged Sir Thomas, whom Elizabeth Norris does not understand and has never cared for. He has been a source of goods, not a revered moral authority. He thought she bought his notions, but she never did. Elizabeth, eldest and least flexible of the Ward sisters, might have been much happier if she had never left Huntingdon.

Frances, the youngest Ward sister, will have none of the Bertram way of life and chooses a man whose sexuality and energy are what she wants. Of the three sisters she is the most true to her own feelings and inheritance. At the outset we see her marriage from the Bertram point of view: Frances "married . . . to disoblige her family, and by fixing on a Lieutenant of Marines, without education, fortune, or connections, did it very thoroughly" (I, ch. 1). But these deficiencies are natural to the Wards. Frances Ward has baulked at taking advantage of her sister's rise to rise in rank. Sir Thomas rebukes Fanny for throwing away a chance closely similar to what he offered Maria Ward:

> You think only of yourself. . . . And are, in a wild fit of folly, throwing away from you such an opportunity of being settled in life, eligibly, honourably, nobly settled, as will, probably, never occur to you again. (III, ch. 1)

Fanny Price's rebellion against such pressure and such standards of value is, in its way, heroic. It will not occur to her—and probably not to the reader—that her rebellion is a repetition of Frances Ward's rebellion, a generation ago, against the Bertrams and their way of life. The older

Frances, rejecting the opportunity to be sublimed into an imitation Bertram, had also not repressed "every tendency to that independence of spirit" which Sir Thomas finds "prevails so much in modern days . . . and which in young women is offensive and disgusting" (III, ch. 1).

Fanny Price in adulthood learns to look down upon her mother and has always disliked her father, so she cannot comprehend the good side of their lives. Yet in many important respects Frances Ward experiences the most productive outcome of the three Ward sisters. Fanny judges her mother (who has borne ten or more children) harshly as "a dawdle, a slattern" (III, ch. 8)—though she has never thought to judge her aunt Bertram as a lazy imbecile. Fanny, taking mental revenge for love denied, has no inducement to enter into the hardships of her mother's life. On an income of about four hundred pounds a year the Prices are clinging precariously to the middle class. Unsentimental Frances Price has survived giving birth to and rearing so many children in fairly good shape. Although her husband's disability and drunkenness have posed unexpected setbacks, Frances's life is probably not very different from the life she envisioned. Unlike the denizens of Mansfield Park, Mrs. Price does not have to expend time and psychic energies in acting or adjusting her Huntingdonshire habits to the burdens of that "handsome house and large income." The terror behind the glazing of Maria Ward (remolded into Lady Bertram), the tension and disjunctions in her angry sister Elizabeth, may evoke sympathy for both these warped characters—even the Mrs. Norris whom we all love to hate.

Beyond little Huntingdon with its poverty of knowledge and judgment, beyond even the enclosed, stagnant, and repetitive Mansfield, there is a much wider world. No other novel among Austen's works so abounds in references to places on the geopolitical globe. Allusions to various places in England include Midland towns like Huntingdon, Northampton, and Peterborough but also new emphasis on ports such as Brighton, Deal, and Liverpool. The Crawfords, as often noted, introduce the urban world of money and sophistication, with a thorough comprehension of London's social geography. Mary thinks Fanny and Henry should get married in Saint George's Hanover Square—a most fashionable church. A friend lived in "one of the best houses in Wimpole Street," which Mary approves as a residence for the newly married Rushworths in their foray into the Season. Maria will have "got her pennyworth for her penny. Henry could not have afforded her such a house" (III, ch. 9). Yet Wimpole Street, not quite Mayfair, is mere Marylebone.

Admiral Crawford must be more than merely well-to-do; his London home is in Hill Street in Mayfair (between Shepherd's Market and Berkeley Square). He is able to procure "a cottage at Twickenham for us all to spend our summers in"; it was "excessively pretty," but he disrupts it by improvements (I, ch. 6). Twickenham, a riverside suburb, former site of Pope's home and grotto and then of Walpole's Strawberry Hill, was only a little less fashionable than ultraexpensive Richmond, whither in Smith's *Emmeline* Lady Frances Crofts repaired to engage in adultery. Henry goes to Richmond to pursue his brief affair with Maria, visiting in nearby Twickenham (*MP*, III, ch. 14). One of the subthemes of *Mansfield Park* is Admiral Crawford's unkindness and unfaithfulness to his wife, evoking Mary's resentment and suspicion of marriage, not allayed by a close view of the Grants' domestic life. Admiral Crawford presumably had private reasons for finding a "cottage" in this riverside environment; we have deduced that he was assisted by his useful aides the Aylmers, who also assist the illicit conjunction of Maria Rushworth and Henry Crawford. Admiral Crawford in Twickenham diverted his females' attention unpleasantly by inflicting the mess of improvements, "all dirt and confusion" (I, ch. 6)—the only injury that Mary can openly mention. For this mild criticism she is censured by Edmund and Fanny, nervous of any assault upon the patriarch. But Mary is complaining (if in code) of female oppression, silent hiding and enduring sexual dirt, and resultant emotional confusion.

Mary Crawford is not simply a Londoner nor (despite generations of critics) does she represent only or even primarily modern London town life. As we have seen, Mary, her sister and her brother-in-law Mr. Grant, her brother Henry and her uncle Admiral Crawford are all of Scottish extraction, an identity registered in their names and the names of Mary's chosen friends. Both Henry and Mary have lost an original region or nation. They are *in the process* of becoming English, rather as the Ward sisters (and their children) are *in the process* of becoming Northamptonshire gentry. Most of the major characters—with Fanny at the center—are in a state of flux and immigration.

Antigua: The Invisible Source

Sir Thomas carries about with him invisibly the West Indies of his wealth. His journey to the actual place divides the novel. Maaja Stewart points out that Elizabeth Inchbald's *A Simple Story* (1791) also is bisected by the journey of stern Lord Elmwood, ex-priest, to the West

Indies: "The patriarch's authority is weakened by his absence," and sexual transgression and rebellion ensue.[18] Sir Thomas is always an absentee from one of his estates, even though he stresses that his son should live in his parish.[19]

Antigua is not contiguous with Mansfield, but is yet an invisible center, as well as a distant place on the globe. Jane Austen could have known something of the West Indies. The sons of George Austen's half-brother William had settled in Jamaica. Tom Fowle, Cassandra's fiancé, went with Lord Craven on the West Indies campaign as chaplain and died of yellow fever in San Domingo in 1797. The Willoughby family figured prominently in Antigua history. George Austen at Oxford had tutored James Nibbs, whose family owned sugar plantations in Antigua. George Austen later asked this wealthy young man to be godfather to his son. Rich James Nibbs sent his own son to Mr. Austen to educate and named George Austen potential trustee for his Antigua estate.[20] If Nibbs had died when his heir was a minor, Jane's father would have had the charge of several plantations in Antigua—which might well have stimulated research into the island on the part of Austens. Nibbs later "took his spendthrift son on a voyage to Antigua" and eventually disinherited him.[21]

The name "Antigua" or "Ancient" derives from the antique image of the Virgin Mary and the Christ Child in Seville Cathedral; on his second voyage Christopher Columbus named the island "Santa Maria de la Antigua." In 1632 English settlers from Saint Kitts (Saint Christopher) on moving in used the short name "Antigua." In 1683 Christopher Codrington, a brutally efficient entrepreneur, introduced plantation-style sugar cultivation, beginning the importation of large numbers of slaves. "Plantation" is to us inevitably fraught with evil memory. The term has—or had—an innocent primary meaning, referring to any extended area of new plantings of trees, bushes or large vegetation, like Sir John Middleton's new "plantations" at Barton Cross. That familiar and even virtuous word at first supplied a kind of green-world cover for an evil system. The term, however, had a long association with the "planting" of colonies. Slavery supported the development of capitalism in England and North America. An impression of the backbreaking work on the plantations can be found in William Clark's 1823 depiction of cane cutting in Antigua (fig. 22).[22] The modern visitor to the island is struck by the energy and early technology insanely dedicated to torturing fellow beings in quest of sweet stuff.

Antigua was a turbulent source of riches. Rebellion was feared, and

22. William Clark, *The Cutting of the Cane* (1823). From *Ten Views in the Island of Antigua*. Photograph: © The British Library Board.

not all governors were able. While Austen was designing the novel, the governor was the failed diplomat Hugh Elliot, made Governor of the Leeward Islands from 1809 to 1813 thanks to the operation of his brother Gilbert Elliot, Baron Minto (see above, chapter 7). In 1710 Governor Daniel Parke had been murdered—dismembered in the streets of St John's—by a riotous mob of whites (chiefly Assemblymen). In 1701 slaves rebelled when the plantation owner refused to give them Christmas Day off. They cut off his head and soused it with rum.[23] (Presumably, they were turning him into a Christmas pudding.) In 1736 a great ball was planned for 11 October, in belated celebration of the coronation of George II. The slaves were prepared with different tasks and signals. "Tomboy" the carpenter was to build the platform and seats, affording opportunity for strategic placement of gunpowder. In Mansfield Park, too, theatrical carpentering threatens proper order. Unfortunately for Antiguan freedom fighters, the ball was postponed to 30 October; in the interval, the plot leaked out. Panicked hearings were followed by draconian punishments, included breaking five men on the wheel and burning over seventy at the stake.[24] In this display of "civilization" the whites could triumph but were forced toward the recognition (if partially suppressed) that the workers necessary for the gain for which they came were permanently desirous of their overthrow and death. The ball that did not take place in October 1736 is the most famous of the "balls of Antigua."

Sir Ralph Payne, Governor of the Leeward Islands from 1771 to 1775, kept the peace and was highly popular with sugar planters; Sir Thomas Bertram can be imagined as having known Payne when both were MPs. Payne, now an Irish baron, Lord Lavington, made a comeback as governor in 1799. Lavington died in 1807, an event that probably stimulated Sir Thomas's decision to look after his own interests now that the planters' friend was gone.

Antigua (only 108 square miles) is an important Atlantic gateway to the Caribbean. From its highest point "French" islands like Guadeloupe and Montserrat are visible.[25] Saint John, the central port, was the administrative capital of the Leeward Islands. A number of free persons of color worked in the towns, especially Saint John (they were forbidden to own land). Their semi-independent presence might have disconcerted a newly arrived plantation owner.[26] The official enquiry into the alleged great conspiracy of 1736 argued that inequality of numbers of white and black inhabitants was a menace. Planters should reside on their estates. Other recommendations were that slaves should not become craftsmen or tradesmen and that more servants should be white. Such advice proved too difficult to follow, but the sight of a free black craftsman might cause twinges of unease in a proprietor. Such an aficionado of nice gradations of inequality as Sir Thomas would have found this mix offensive and confusing. Even the unfree engaged publicly in some trade. Janet Schaw remarks on their sale of produce: "The Negroes are the only market people. No body else dreams of selling provisions. Sunday . . . they are all at liberty to work for themselves."[27] Black enslaved persons thronged the markets of Saint John, along with free blacks and "mulattoes" and white men at a loose end. Bustle, trade, drinking, and sexual activity must have increased upon the burgeoning of English Harbour and the addition to the island population of multitudes of sailors in rich variety, from Britain, the Americas, and the Indian subcontinent.

In 1784, Horatio Nelson (not yet a national hero), heading the Squadron of the Leeward Islands, was sent to develop a naval dockyard. The Duke of Clarence (later King William IV) served under Nelson as captain of the *Pegasus;* Clarence House, Antigua, was built as his residence. It still exists, as does the naval yard now called "Nelson's Dock-yard," restored as a touristic site and museum. This well-planned dock-yard, which made English Harbour a center of industry, permitted ships to have their hulls scraped and repaired and to be refitted with masts. Dockyard workers included not only sailors but multiple skilled workers such as carpenters, many of these free black laborers. Austen would have known, if only from Southey's *Life,* about Nelson's use of dancing and theatricals to keep his men's spirits up in Antigua:

> When the hurricane months confined him to English Harbour, he encouraged all kinds of useful amusements—music, dancing, and cudgelling among the men; theatricals among the officers; anything which could employ their attention, and keep their spirits cheerful.[28]

Nelson's theatricals must have entailed multiple gender impersonations and a certain racial and class mingling. Did they continue—and disgust Sir Thomas? Sir Thomas did take note of "the balls of Antigua," describing them to the Grants' dinner party and listening to William Price on "the different modes of dancing" in foreign places (*MP,* II, ch. 7). Did Sir Thomas refer to the hospitality of Lord Lavington? The departed governor was famous for dance parties, if a trifle eccentric on some points:

> His lordship . . . was a very hospitable man . . . his Christmas balls and routs were upon the highest scale of magnificence; but he was a great stickler for etiquette and a firm upholder of differences of rank and *colour.* It is asserted, he would not . . . receive a letter or parcel from the fingers of a black or coloured man, and in order to guard against such horrible defilement, he had a golden instrument wrought something like a pair of sugar tongs.[29]

In his Parsonage chat or travelogue Sir Thomas would have described with amusement and some contempt the dances of the mixed social levels of whites. Did he stress the low Scots shop boys and former servant girls, along with the "Houris" with "dark brilliant eyes"?[30] He might discourse on the enthusiasm of the "negroes" at their own dance parties, dancing country dances, or choosing "native dance, and their music of the *Bangoe* and *Tum-tum,*" in a "ball-room . . . decorated with branches of the cocoa-nut . . . while boughs of the Pimento . . . and the orange tree . . . impart a pleasing fragrance."[31] The "favourite colours" of "the fair sex" are "pink, blue, and bright yellow . . . but the manner in which these several shades are arranged defies all description."[32] Holding a proper English ball at Mansfield, with properly dressed modest young white ladies (in white), would reassert true English properties, counteracting grotesque foreign recollections.

Englishmen traveling on ship to or from the island could expect French assaults—although Lady Bertram does not worry about this possibility. In danger of imminent attack by "a French privateer," Sir Thomas on his way home *almost* gets shot at (II, ch. 1). William Price in his naval service goes to the West Indies and may well find himself in Nelson's Dockyard. Antigua links Nelson with a William Price, hard-worked midshipman (later lieutenant), and also with the English baronet holding onto his sugar plantations.

R. W. Chapman's argument that *Mansfield Park* follows the calendar of 1808–9, with Fanny's ball taking place on Thursday, 22 December, seems sound.[33] That is, the novel is set in the fraught period after the Act against the Slave Trade, passed in 1807, had begun to be enforced in 1808. The Allies' blockade of European coasts added to the difficulties of selling sugar, while the ending of the slave trade—though not yet of slavery itself—posed labor problems. Current financial uncertainties suggest good reasons why Sir Thomas feels he must visit Antigua at this particular juncture, although he always exaggerates his own efficacy. An ongoing problem was the rapacity of middlemen, estate managers, and agents. John Luffman, in *A Brief Account of the Island of Antigua* (1789), describes the freedom with which the managers for absentees used their employers' income and the slave labor for their own purposes:

> To be the manager of an estate of an absentee, in this isle, I am well satisfied is one of the best situations in it, altho' their stipends amount to no more than from eighty to one hundred pounds sterling, per ann. . . . This discription [*sic*] of men sport several dishes at their tables, drink claret, keep mulatto mistresses. . . . These people, Sir, raise on the grounds of their employers, stock of every kind . . . which they feed principally with the grain, &c. belonging to the estate on which they live. . . . There are of these men, or at least their wives who occupy the time of from twelve to twenty negroes daily on this business to the manifest injury of their masters.[34]

An estate's "Attorney" would receive "from half a guinea, to a guinea, for every hogshead of Sugar he ships." No doubt Sir Thomas found the first thing he had to do was to fire his manager. But getting an efficient and honest replacement would be no easy matter. Luffman describes a more peaceable time in the 1780s, whereas by the time of Sir Thomas's voyage the war was raging through the Caribbean. War entailed a varied influx of newcomers and transients, while the old settled plantations looked less secure of profit. As well as new problems in securing labor, there was a steep decline in sugar's profitability. Britain's own blockade of the Continent separated consumers from product. Napoleon, cut off from French islands in the Caribbean by the British blockade, in 1813 banned the import of cane sugar altogether in the lands he controlled. European production of sugar from beets was amplified and improved. A glut of cane sugar caused prices to drop—and they were to drop again after Waterloo.[35]

In the eighteenth century, demand for sugar had risen enormously. The availability and relative cheapness of sugar in the early nineteenth century stimulated interest in what we call "candy" and more cakes. In Austen's novels the youngest generation manifests a keen desire for sugar. Spoiled little Annamaria Middleton is pacified with "sugar plums" and "apricot marmalade" (S&S, I, ch. 21). Mary Musgrove's boys require to be pacified by their grandmother with "trash and sweet things" (Persuasion, I, ch. 6). Sugar consumption had rendered the sugar boycott, an antislavery protest first mounted in 1791, of some effect. Consumers, in the first use of a new democratic political instrument, refused to use products of the sugarcane—sugar and also molasses and rum. (Mr. Price, we note, perseveringly drinks rum.) In this political action, women played an important part. King George III and Queen Charlotte joined in the boycott—inviting ridicule of the "Anti-Saccharrites" by plantation owners' supporters (fig. 23). Austen's favorite poet William Cowper was an important propagandist for the abolition of slavery. In Cowper's satiric poem "Pity for Poor Africans" (1788), the worldly speaker politely laments slavery but argues that it is unrealistic and peculiar not to trade in or use sugar.

The adjective "sweet" is noticeably used negatively or very skeptically by Austen throughout her works.[36] The desire for female "sweetness" expressed in Mansfield Park seems ironically appropriate to an establishment basing its wealth on the cruel production and commercial sale of sugar. The first edible mentioned here is the sour-sweet "gooseberry tart" which fails to comfort the homesick little girl on her first arrival at Mansfield (I, ch. 2). The strongest contemporary example of sweet-sour in literature is William Cowper's abolitionist poem "Sweet Meat

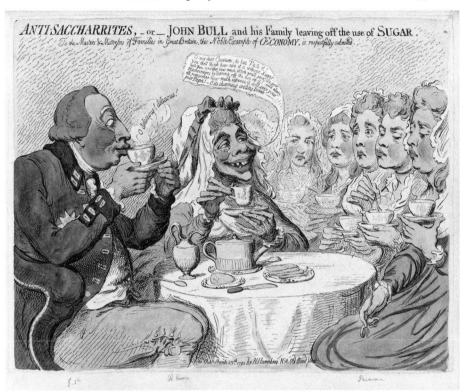

23. James Gillray, *The Anti-Saccharrites; or, John Bull and his family leaving off the use of sugar* (1792). Photograph: © National Portrait Gallery, London.

Has Sour Sauce" (1788).[37] Abolitionist writings tend to try to turn the reader off sweetness with unpleasant associations; in *Mansfield Park* Austen appears to follow (with some subtlety) the abolitionist lead. Throughout the novel we have dashes of great sourness along with too much bland sweetness—found even in the "biscuits and buns" that Fanny sends for when unable to bear the family meals at Portsmouth. (III, ch. 11). Antigua remains a sour sweet spot in the invisible center of *Mansfield Park,* a location of slavery, anxiety, and sugar. It is paralleled in the main narrative by the flower garden where Fanny endures a parodic slavery in the heat gathering summer roses for potpourri (a source of "sweet" domestic fragrance composed of dead things) (I, ch. 7). Antigua's name means "old," "ancient"—and much that is unwholesomely "old" peers out at us in *Mansfield Park.* Sotherton, peasant values (like those of Mrs. Norris), potpourri, and slavery are all *old.*

IMAGINARY PLACES IN *MANSFIELD PARK*

Stones and Ravens—and Rushes

Some lesser imaginary places add to the poetic effect. Stanwix Lodge is the name of a place near Mansfield Park that Henry Crawford thinks of renting. The name is from Saxon *stan-wic,* that is, "stone place." (There is a real Stanwick near Northampton.) "Everingham" is the name of Henry Crawford's estate in Norfolk, where (according to himself) he made great aesthetic improvements in his first youth. We don't know how this young man with the Scottish name came to inherit a Norfolk estate with a Saxon name, presumably from *ebur* or *efer* (a boar) + *ing(as)* + *ham.* The name would then mean "the settlement of the followers of the man with the boar's head helm," or "of the man as strong as a boar" (as in "Ever-hard" or "Everard"). The "boar's head helm" would match with the "bright helm" of the Bertrams; it reflects on a man who is stubborn and greedy. The open irony in this case comes from the dominant first syllable "ever" in the supposed home of a man who cannot be faithful or keep at anything consistently.

Rushworth mentions his friend Smith's Compton, a small estate improved by Repton. "Compton" suggests computation, though it means "farmstead or village in a valley" (Mills). "Ecclesford" in Cornwall is the home of Lord Ravenshaw, where young Mr. Yates was going to perform *Lover's Vows.* "Eccles" (from "Ekklesia" meaning "church") might mean a ford or water crossing by a church—or away from the church. Alternatively, the root might be *aigles,* "eagles" (as in Eccles in Kent)—a place where eagles cross. The more striking locative is undoubtedly in Lord Ravenshaw's name, "the stand of trees full of ravens."

Sotherton—so ripe for "improvement"—has a rather dull name for a great estate with an Elizabethan house. The merely locative term means merely "south-place," "south settlement." Once it was south of something more important—perhaps a priory? Maria's remarks as she approaches Sotherton are quite in keeping with landscape designer Humphry Repton's disdainful views of any rural community: "Those cottages are really a disgrace. I am glad the church is not so close to the Great House as often happens in old places. The annoyance of the bells must be terrible" (I, ch. 8). Alistair Duckworth in *The Improvement of the Estate* points out that Maria's tastes and Rushworth's vague plans exhibit an owner aestheticizing his duties out of existence. Silly Mr. Rushworth and Maria are alike devoid of any religious senses of stewardship:

"The displacement of their concern from the function to the appearance of Sotherton will neglect the traditional emphasis on 'use' as the basis of landed existence."[38]

The hot day of wandering about the grounds and coming upon yet more boundaries and pales is frustrating. Sotherton feels like an extension of Mansfield Park. Yet Sotherton has some things Mansfield does not. Its owners in the distant past had the privilege of holding their own courts. And Sotherton has its own chapel—"fitted up as you see it, in James the Second's time" (I, ch. 9). This interesting tidbit dropped by the incurious Mrs. Rushworth raises the possibility that the Rushworth family were at one time secret Catholics, emboldened by accession of the Catholic King James II to create their own place of worship in their home (not the parish church). In the same period the first Duke of Devonshire built Chatsworth and created a very fancy baroque chapel in the European Catholic style. The Sotherton chapel as we see it is very plain, denuded of the romance that Fanny hopes for. It is certainly nothing like Scott's Melrose Abbey in *The Lay of the Last Minstrel* (1805) to which Fanny alludes, not altogether inappropriately, as Scott's poem deals obliquely with the transition from Catholicism and feudalism.[39] Sotherton's chapel is one of the riddles or paradoxes secreted in this novel. History produces strong Puritan Rushworths and some Catholic Rushworths. One possible historical backstory to this imaginary Sotherton is that at the Restoration the estate passed from a Puritan family to a Catholic branch. But the *Rush*worths are wavering reeds shaken in every wind. This is the only occasion on which this narrative enters a church, and this scene deepens an impression that religion has been abandoned. The chapel is an empty space. Sotherton, the emptiness at the heart of the novel, signals a world of the absence of God and grace. All the references to piety and morality in all that follows—including ordination—can simply reinforce the view of social order dominant, spiritual reality abandoned. Patriarchal power and lectures of morality do not replace religion. In fact, they degrade it beyond recognition.

The Weight of "Mansfield"

"Mansfield" is a complex, rich, and resonant name. The name (originally Germanic) matches well with the *beorht helm* of the Germanic "Bertram." Mansfield is the German town where Luther was born—suiting the most Protestant of Austen's novels. Mansfield is the real name of a small town in Nottinghamshire: "A market town of good resort, whose name some bring in to confirm the claim of the German family, Mansfield, to antiquity. . . . Kings used to repair hither for the pleasures of the chace."[40] *Britannia* comments that this town is on the edge of Sherwood Forest, with a remnant population of deer; so Mansfield—like Huntingdon—carries associations with Robin Hood, as well as with deer hunting. In *Sir Charles Grandison,* Miss Mansfield, an old maid in her thirties, is persuaded to benefit her slumping gentry family by marrying the wealthy and cantankerous Lord W. Like "Hartfield" and other names in Austen, the word can be read as a kind of riddle depending on a pun—or puns. It's a "Manse-field," place of a mansion, or a parsonage—and this estate has both. Read as "Man's Field," it is the field of this world in which we are all placed, a field full of folk. But it is "*Man's* field," a male preserve with very masculine controls.

The most important English historical association with "Mansfield" is its connection with William Murray (a Scot), who became Lord Chief Justice in 1756, when he was created Baron Mansfield (later first Earl of Mansfield). The most famous decision of this Lord Chief Justice, highest appeals judge, concerns the Somersett case. James Somersett, a slave in Boston, escaped when his American master brought him to England. The master claimed him back as property. When the case was heard in 1772, Lord Mansfield in his judgment said, "The state of slavery . . . is so odious, that nothing can be suffered to support it but positive law" (*ODNB*). Once Mansfield determined that the law of England did not support slavery, his decision implied that all slaves within England and Wales (although *not* in the British Empire at large) were free. This led to the freedom of some fourteen or fifteen thousand persons and to the saying that any man or woman who set foot on English soil is a free person.

The irony of the name of "Mansfield" being attached to a place whose owner is connected with slavery appears too pointed to be accidental. This connection, emphasized by Margaret Kirkham in 1983, is denied by John Wiltshire, in favor of connotations of "general Englishness."[41] Having caught the significance of "Pratt" in *Sense and Sensibility,* I am even more inclined than before to think the reference to Lord Mansfield is intended. The connection of the title of *Mansfield Park* with Lord Mansfield's decision is strongly supported by Paula Byrne, among others.[42]

Byrne points out that Mansfield was known to support black equality in more than legal judgments; he effectually adopted his nephew's illegitimate daughter by a black enslaved person named Maria Belle. The child, Dido Belle (ca. 1761–1804), was brought up by Lord Mansfield (her great-uncle) as a companion to Lady Elizabeth, his niece and heir, whom Austen met in 1805 but thought had "astonishingly little to say for herself" (24 August 1805; *Letters,* 107). Belle served her great-uncle as a secretary; it is a question whether her presence in his life influenced Mansfield's most famous decision. Left a small legacy, Belle married an Englishman, John Davinier, in Saint George's Hanover Square; they had three sons.[43] Her story is the basis of the British film *Belle* (2013), directed by Amma Asante. Austen will move closer to such a young woman in *Sanditon.*

That Jane Austen thought about slavery we cannot deny. Austen proclaimed herself "in love with" the writing of Thomas Clarkson, the leading historical and moral exponent of abolition (24 January 1813; *Letters,* 198). Cowper, Austen's favorite poet, was a strong voice for the abolitionist cause. There is ample evidence that Jane's siblings supported the abolition of slavery, from an early article by James in *The Loiterer* to the more active expression of her brother Frank, whose naval duties entailed chasing slave traders. Frank said that England, "jealous . . . of her own liberty[,] . . . should pay equal attention to the inalienable rights of all the nations, of what colour so ever they may be."[44]

Mansfield Park focuses upon unease regarding the conduct and self-excuse of the ruling and wealthy classes. Austen's doubts about her own gentry class and the assumptions of her culture go very deep—she is always looking into whatever original rapacity created the comfortable cushion of wealth that lends itself so nicely to respectability and secret oppression. Oppression and acquiescence are central to the action of *Mansfield Park,* most troubling of her novels. In this version of "Cinderella" there is no perfectly happy ending. A twisted economy has its way with the characters. "I wish he [William Price] may go to the East Indies, that I may have my shawl. I think I will have two shawls, Fanny," says Lady Bertram, dreaming of cashmere, careless of East Indies or West (II, ch. 13). Her nephew should risk his life on a long and dangerous voyage to get her a shawl. This is one of the most stupidly cruel and exploitative statements in the novel—a work in which such statements abound.

There is a second element in the estate's name: it is "Mansfield *Park.*" The term "park" denotes a large enclosure in which game could be held for private hunting. Samuel Johnson gives the word extensive treatment in his *Dictionary:*

A place of ground inclosed and stored with wild beasts of chace, which a man may have by prescription or the king's grant. Manwood, in his forest-law, defines it thus: a park is a place for privilege for wild beasts of venery, and also for other wild beasts that are beasts of the forest and of the chace: and those wild beasts are to have a firm peace and protection there, so that no man may hurt or chase them within the park, without license of the owner: a park is of another nature, than either a chase or a warren; for a park must be inclosed, and may not lie open; if it does, it is good cause of seizure into the king's hands: and the owner cannot have an action against such a hunt in his park, if it lie open.

The next quotation Johnson offers is from Bacon:

We have parks and inclosures of all sorts of beasts and birds, which we use not only for view or rareness, but likewise for dissections and trials.

For the verb "to park"—which does not bear our modern sense—Johnson gives the definition "to inclose as in a park" and offers the quotation from Shakespeare:

How are we park'd, and bounded in a pale?
A little herd of England's tim'rous deer,
Maz'd with a yelping kennel of French curs.

Johnson's definition repeatedly emphasizes the enclosure of animals behind a fence (or "pale") for the purpose of human (male) pleasure. The Bacon quotation oddly modernizes the idea to include a place of experimentation on animals. In a bounded *park* the animals are the property of the owner. Only those given permission can hunt or chase them—or conduct experiments upon them. We have noted the novel's constant allusions to hunting and shooting. Sir Thomas, owner of this park, can offer Henry Crawford the metaphorical license to "hurt or chase" his Fanny. Subsequently, in a Baconian manner he commits a little experiment upon Fanny, "a medicinal project upon his niece's understanding, which he must consider as at present diseased" (III, ch. 6). Sir Thomas is not aware that Tom, his Regent, has earlier given Henry implicit license in Sir Thomas's absence to play at hunting Maria and Julia. All three of these women suffer from enclosure, limitation, and inspection. No wonder Maria is revolted by the iron gate and the boundaries confronting her on the grounds of Sotherton. Her allusion to Sterne's starling who cannot get out applies not only to Sotherton but to the enclosed world of the home in which she, like Fanny and Julia, is "park'd and bounded in a pale."

Falling among Thorns: Thornton Lacey

Thornton Lacey is the site of Edmund's future parsonage. "Thornton" is Old English ("thorn" + *tun*), an enclosed settlement with thorn trees marking its boundaries. Again we find boundaries, enclosure. "Lacey" indicates that this settlement was once part of the properties of the De Lacy family, like Kingston Lacy in Dorset. Thornton Lacey, an Anglo-Saxon homestead taken over by Normans, may well be superior in age to Mansfield Park.

Henry Crawford, who comes centuries too late actually to dissolve English religious houses, makes no open ideological claim in his enthusiastic plans to revise the parsonage. It has, he pleads, "so much the air of a gentleman's residence, so much the look of a something above a mere Parsonage House. . . . You may raise it into a *place*" (II, ch. 7). A *place* evidently offers a higher way of being, transcending low matter such as the farmyard, the blacksmith's shop—and religious services. Henry may unconsciously be affected by Sotherton and its cold inane chapel. Making Thornton Lacey parsonage into a gentleman's residence would be a kind of parallel cover-up, tactfully privatizing, secularizing while upgrading. It is another form of Dissolution.

What Henry Crawford only *proposes* doing to Edmund's future parsonage uncomfortably resembles what Jane Austen's mother's cousin, the clergyman Thomas Leigh, had *actually* done in 1799 to his rectory in Adlestrop. He called in the landscaper Humphry Repton (admired by Rushworth and Mrs. Norris for his costly consultancy) to combine the rectory grounds with the estate. The new design meant that the village green was planted over, the village cottages having been removed. Repton's secularizing "improvements" could be seen by Cassandra Austen and her daughters when they visited in 1806. As Duckworth says of Henry Crawford, such "plans to 'clear away,' 'plant up,' and 'shut out' features of the landscape are to be read as a rejection of the traditional shape of reality."[45] There is no stronger example of Austen criticizing her own family as rulers than Henry's proposed revision of Thornton Lacey in exactly the manner of Thomas Leigh.

When he is to be ordained, Edmund leaves Mansfield to stay with a friend of his own age surnamed Owen. (The family includes young ladies, which makes Mary Crawford uneasy.) The Owens reside in a village or estate called "Lessingby." The name seems largely inspired by Lessingham in Norfolk, a Saxon "settlement of the *ingas* of Leofisige" (Mills). But the suffix -*by* indicates an area formerly settled by Danes. The strange name was perhaps partly suggested by Leasowes, the poet Shenstone's little estate near the town of Hales*owen* in Shropshire.[46] Edmund is ordained in Peterborough, now under the dominion of Cambridgeshire, a settlement in the fen country from Roman times. This "burgh of St. Peter," a reference to its former abbey of Saint Peter, enjoyed considerable independence, and a famous cathedral. It seems odd to us that nobody in Edmund's family suggests seeing him ordained; evidently, unlike Anglican practice in the twentieth or twenty-first century, this ceremony was not considered a sight for families. A sense of estrangement accompanies the ordination. Something peculiar has happened to Edmund in a place far away—rather like Tom's fall. The name "Lessingby," a comical invented word, sticks close to this off-stage event. "Lessingby" sounds like a place where one becomes *lesser*—odd in a story that is *officially* on the side of ordination. At the end of the story Edmund, defeated in love, wears out his attachment to Mary and is content to settle for Fanny, pushed by others and soothed by Fanny's care. Fanny's unyielding devotion is instinctive and ruthless, like Helena's in *All's Well*—the young man stands little chance. Edmund has "lessened." He never developed spiritual strength. His ordination is in complacent obedience to a very worldly father. And we may uncomfortably suspect (as Maaja Stewart suggests) that, despite Sir Thomas's strictures against absentee clergy, Edmund will not yield Thornton Lacey upon moving into Mansfield parsonage and the Mansfield living.

Jane Austen's clergymen are unsatisfactory—obedient to rich fathers like Henry Tilney and Edmund Bertram, or limply lacking any vocation like Edward Ferrars, whom Elinor pushes into a home and an income and a job. Edmund will go dutifully through the services; his sermons will be no duller than the next man's (if not as good as Blair's, as Mary suggests). But spiritual calling and energy of soul are lacking. A man conditioned by terror of being shot down has limitations. Edmund's letters and conversations reveal him as self-centered, anxious, and indecisive. There is no sign that he has ever associated with or cared for the poor. He is willing to let London go to the dogs. He is caught among the thorns of his destined settlement. (Did his *Thornton* influence Brontë's

Thornfield Hall?) "Thorns" evoke uncomfortable recollections of Christ's "Parable of the Sower," in which the seeds (of spiritual truth) variously are eaten by fowls or fall "upon stony places." (Stones and fowls appeared already: "Stanwix," the stones of Sotherton, and ravens and crows.) "And some fell among thorns; and the thorns sprung up, and choked them" (Matthew 13:4–7). Readers are all alert to Henry's flaw in redesigning the parsonage but deaf to what has already gone wrong, the ignoring of spiritual life; the Word gets choked by other concerns. Without assistance from Crawfords, deep within the moral narrative, the parsonage and church at Thornton Lacey are choked by thorns.

Edmund's description of his rural presence as a clergyman omits both sacramental and pastoral functions. Edmund will operate chiefly, if not quite as a constable of manners in his father's fashion, as a kind of self-identified model. Parishioners will have the benefit of "observing his general conduct." This comic and painful "line" sounds as if it comes straight from Sir Thomas (I, ch. 9). Edmund's advice will be feeble and self-conscious. I would pay money to keep him away from my deathbed.

Why Edmund is as he is we understand through our knowledge of the warped environment of Mansfield Park. Save for the Portsmouth episodes and the excursion to desiccated Sotherton, the central action takes place within Mansfield's strict bounds. It ceases to imprison only to eject. The Woman taken in Adultery (see John 8:3–11) turns into a hopeless castaway, all grace forbidden her. This is morality of a sort—but has little to do with Christianity. The religion that Edmund has been truly ordained into is the religion of Mansfield Park—ultimately the emptiness of Sotherton's chapel.

Mansfield Park is far from a happy story. The ending has many ironic touches, even if we detect some desperate efforts on the author's part to turn back from what she knows. We can make it happy if we must. Edmund will have to take on the job of permanent acting. As Claudia Johnson points out, Edmund has never shown any sexual interest in Fanny.[47] Under benevolent paternal pressure, Edmund—who never comes first with his father in any matter—must pretend to be sufficiently in love with Fanny, even though he has said farewell to Eros. The characters' acting entangles them. Products of history and perverse training, they cannot tell the true from the false. Efforts to reach beyond the pale, to touch the genuine, are felt as threats; all acceptable persons must stay within the park. This is a wonderfully effective, ironic, and deeply compassionate story about damaged people.

Names and Places in *Emma*:
The Royal County of Surrey

REAL PLACES IN *EMMA*

Emma is set in only one location and never leaves its own county. True, Highbury is only sixteen miles from London. Tara Ghoshal Wallace rightly calls London "a constant stage-sharing presence" in *Emma*. Goods can be easily obtained and moved; Wallace points out the difference from rural Northamptonshire where transporting Mary's harp would interfere with hay making.[48] Frank Churchill goes to London to get his hair cut (really to order a piano from Broadwood). Mr. Elton carries Emma's portrait of Harriet to be framed in Bond Street. John and Isabella Knightley and their children live in Brunswick Square, in the region of London we now call "Bloomsbury." Brunswick Square, developed in the latter eighteenth century, was named in honor of Caroline of Brunswick, the unfortunate woman whom the Prince Regent was forced to marry; it was the site of England's first orphan asylum.[49] Indirect embedded references to the queen, Caroline of Brunswick, and to the Royal House of Brunswick-Lüneberg perpetuate the theme of kingship and the game of claimants so comically conducted throughout *Emma*.

Brunswick Square takes up part of the grounds of the Foundling Hospital. Established by Captain Coram, the Hospital admitted the first infants in 1741; the orphanage building was finally constructed on part of the Earl of Salisbury's estate, in Bloomsbury Fields.[50] In the eighteenth century the Brunswick Square area, neither too populous nor industrial, was known for green fields and clean air, explaining Isabella's boast. She probably has never bothered to tell her father about the neighboring Foundling Hospital, and as he never goes to London (and apparently doesn't read) he cannot be alarmed. Isabella's square offered a large garden for residents in its center. The John Knightleys have a very good address but not a great one—well suited to the rising barrister. Harriet (illegitimate quasi-orphan) visits the Knightleys of Brunswick Square and accompanies the family, including their children, to Astley's Circus. There she falls in again with Robert Martin and completes her own circuit in the comical Circus of Love. Despite these London touches, no direct dramatic scene really takes place in Town. We remain fixed with Emma in Highbury, in Surrey.

A quiet theme regarding the care of the poor circles in the background of Austen's fourth published novel. The condition of the poor in the rural areas and provincial towns was a concern of the times. Frederick Morton Eden in 1797 notices the poor men's Friendly Societies and the management of poorhouses and workhouses in different parts of the country, including detailed descriptions of the typical diets—in which gruel figures prominently. During the Napoleonic Wars, hardship was greater than in 1797; matters worsened after Waterloo, under pressure of food scarcity, with too few jobs for returning veterans. In *Emma* Mr. Woodhouse (with a little help from Isabella) consumes gruel, treating himself like a charity. Paradoxically, his anorexia entails consuming food meant for the poor. There was fear of unrest even in Austen's Hampshire.

Unlike Gilpin, Eden regrets the loss of the medieval institutions:

> Grateful as I am for the blessings of the Reformation, the transfer of tithes from the clergy to lay-contractors is not that part of it which I contemplate with the most satisfaction.[51]

Highbury's post-Reformation church and abbey must keep up to the mark and fulfill their original functions. The rulers of Highbury must look outside themselves.

"Surrey" (from *south-rie* or "south of the river") is a fertile region, sheltered but central, with good river communications. The county's history from Saxon times is studded by coronations and the claims of kings. Camden gives the tribal name as "Regni" indicating different rulers of various tribes. There was some dispute about the term, but John Aubrey in *The Natural History and Antiquities of Surrey* is clear. "It [Surrey] was under the *Romans,* with *Sussex,* stiled REGNI, as some say, because their generous Conquerors granted them their former Priviledge [*sic*] of living under a *Regal* or *Kingly* Government."[52] Surrey kept its own kings.

This past, if partly imaginary, is perfectly suited to the world of *Emma.* Highbury, both commonplace and magnificent, is a center of pretensions and clashing royalties. Everyone who comes to Highbury either sets out to be a king/queen or has the privilege of living under "a *Regal* or *Kingly* Government." (This makes it all the more comical that when completing *Emma* Austen really did run into the "*Kingly* Government" of the Prince Regent.) Rival queens include Queen Emma

Woodhouse, Queen Jane Fairfax, and would-be Empress Augusta Elton. The invisible but powerful Mrs. Churchill, named after a woman
who claimed equality with Queen Anne, also sets herself up as a ruler.
King George (Knightley) rules the largest piece of land, while old King
Cole, who looked harmless before, is rising into power. A new and "aimable" Prince Francis may bring in a French element. Historical allusions
in *Emma* tend to be royalist. As we have seen, however, "Weston" is
a perfect—and perfectly dangerous—courtier's name, introducing the
sexual intrigue and cruelty of the hazardous court of Henry VIII.

Emma offers multiple place names suggesting both pre-Conquest
Saxon history and Norman rule, a subtle web of references to royalty
of various eras. Many of the places mentioned have an honorably old
history. Cobham, a market town twenty-one miles southwest of central
London, is not exactly royal, but it is proud and ancient. Settled in the
Iron Age, Cobham ("Cobb's" or "Cofa's" *ham*) prospered in the Saxon
period; it was held by Chertsey Abbey at the time of the Conquest.
"Cobham gives both name and title to its barons," including Alexander Pope's friend Richard Granville Temple, Baron Cobham.[53] Pope's
Epistle to Cobham deals with the variability and unaccountability of the
human mind and character—a theme most appropriate to *Emma*.

Mr. Knightley rides to Kingston (King's-*tun*/*ton*), and others have
business dealings there. Kingston-upon-Thames (as it is now called) is a
market town near Cobham, ten miles southwest of London. Prosperous
in Saxon times, the town bore this name before the Conquest. Kingston
was the site of coronations of early monarchs and also of their funerals;
seven Saxon kings are buried there. Camden discusses the buried Saxon
kings; Gough adds that their portraits used to be shown in Saint Mary's
chapel until taken down in 1730 and notes that urns and old coins have
often been found in Kingston.[54]

"Guilford" or "gold-ford" (*gylde* + ford; nowadays "Guildford"),
mentioned in that other Surrey novel *The Watsons*, also has strong royal
associations. The golden name fits in well with its former existence as
the site of the Anglo-Saxon Royal Mint, center of the treasury in the late
tenth century. William the Conqueror took it over and built a defensive
castle, which later became a hunting lodge. "I think most highly of the
situation of Guildford" Jane wrote to Cassandra in May 1813, having admired its views en route to London. (20 May 1813; *Letters,* 209).

Cobham, Kingston, Guildford—old Saxon towns, associated with
Mr. Knightley. Highbury seems ringed about and guarded by enduring Saxon settlements. "Richmond" we associate with Frank. It is on

the Richmond Road out of Highbury that Harriet encounters the gyp-sies. Modern Richmond is expensive; idiotic Isabella Thorpe imagined living with James in a "charming little villa" in Richmond (*NA*, I, ch. 15). Unlike "Cobham" or "Kingston" its name is Norman French, meaning "rich" or "strong" hill (*riche* + *mont*). This name was bestowed by the victorious Henry VII, winner of the Wars of the Roses and founder of the Tudor dynasty, when he took over this pleasant place on the Thames, renaming it "from the county from where he took the title of earl be-fore his accession to the crown"[55] The tide comes up the Thames as far as Richmond, making it useful to medieval (and later) shipping. Its earlier medieval name was Shene—or "Sheen"—on account of its shin-ing beauty. In this town Queen Elizabeth died. Here too passes away the (presumably) disagreeable Mrs. Churchill, imperious ruler of her own family and of Frank's fortune. Perhaps Mrs. Churchill ought to be buried at Kingston, with other English monarchs, as she has been such a strong queen—at least in the eyes of her husband and adopted son.

Windsor, not strictly in Surrey but not far from Highbury, is also associated with Frank. In Austen's time, as now, the Royal Borough of Windsor could supply luxurious accommodations and good shops. Mr. Churchill and Frank betake themselves here to wear out the first shock of Mrs. Churchill's death. Escaping from the Surrey rulers, Frank becomes king of himself in this royal demesne. Camden notes that its old name is "*Windleshora*," "perhaps from the windings of the bank."[56] Eton School is just across the river from Windsor.

Monastic property at the time of the conquest, Windsor was taken over personally by the Norman king, appearing "proper and conve-nient for a royal retirement on account of the river and its nearness to the forest for hunting," according to the charter.[57] The right to hunt in Windsor was through many centuries reserved to blue bloods. Site of Windsor Castle and Saint George's Chapel, Windsor is associated with chivalry and the founding of the Order of the Garter, with its sexy back-story and motto *honi soit qui mal y pense* (evil be to him who thinks evil of this). Once upon a time Windsor was the abode of Charles II's mis-tress Nell Gwynn. Shakespeare's *The Merry Wives of Windsor* seems to have stimulated Austen's imagination in creating *Emma*. False match-making, disguise, riddles, pretensions, and food all figure in Shake-speare's play, as well as a character named "Frank Ford." (See discussion above, chapter 7). Isabella Knightley, Anne Weston, Emma Knightley, Harriet Martin, and even perhaps Augusta Elton either are—or will be—more or less "merry wives."

Looking down from Box Hill on the Surrey landscape spread below them, Frank Churchill says, "Let my accents swell to Mickleham on one side, and Dorking on the other" (III, ch. 7). Dorking introduces the comic motif of poultry; readers might imagine the sound of cackling of "some milk-white Hens of Dorking" at the mere mention of the name.[58] In *The Watsons*, set in and near Dorking, the family was most appropriately served "a Turkey" for dinner. Turkeys figure too in Highbury; Mrs. Weston has a poultry house and is robbed of "all of her turkies" (III, ch. 19). Other poultry houses are robbed too, so frightening Mr. Woodhouse that (desiring a male protector in his house) he is willing to consent to his daughter's marriage.

Mickleham, "large settlement" (Old English *micel* [great] + *ham*) near the old Roman road, is mentioned in the Domesday Book. Mickleham's recent associations, however, were with the French Revolution; in 1792–93 Juniper Hall was leased to a group of distinguished émigrés including Mme de Staël and General Alexandre D'Arblay. Austen must have known that Frances Burney the novelist and her future husband D'Arblay met there; Mickleham was the scene of their courtship. The D'Arblays married in the local church and knew Jane's godfather, rector of Great Bookham. Jane herself would have had opportunities for sightseeing in Surrey when visiting Samuel and Cassandra Cooke only four miles from Box Hill.

The important scene on Box Hill in *Emma* represents an unusual use by Austen of a real and specific outdoor site. In a most interesting departure the action moves away from the settlements (Saxon and Norman) so strongly insisted on elsewhere in the novel. We enter a kind of no-man's-land, not quite civilization. The expedition transports everyone to a pocket of time as well as an alternative space. Donwell Abbey's strawberry party took place on Midsummer Eve, 23 June (also Harriet's birthday; her power waxes). The Box Hill fiasco takes place on Midsummer Day; this festival of emotions is a daytime evocation of *A Midsummer Night's Dream*. In a wild and unpossessed territory, Midsummer madness reigns. The wooded hill on the North Downs of Surrey is named after the wild box trees growing there. The hill affords a beautiful view or "prospect." William Gilpin spends some pages in admiring description of Box Hill:

That boast of Surrey, the celebrated Box-Hill, so called from the profusion of box which flourishes spontaneously upon it. This hill, from its downy back and precipitous sides, exhibits great variety of pleasing views into the lower parts of Surrey; and the higher parts of neighbouring counties. But we have here only to do with it, as itself an object in a retiring scene; in which it fills its station with great beauty; discovering its shivering precipices and downy hillocks.[59]

Gilpin, though noting that cultivation has removed much of the indigenous box, comments on the happy view "towards Box-hill; which presents its flanks in these partial views, with a very mountain-like appearance. The whole scene makes a good Alpine picture."[60] It thus resembles the newly fashionable tourist objective "Swisserland" that Frank Churchill—and perhaps Austen's brother—yearned for (*Emma*, III, ch. 6).[61]

There is more to be said of Box Hill—a curiously indecent history, elided by Gilpin. Douglas Murray was the first to open the Pandora's Box of Box Hill's interestingly disreputable history.[62] John Aubrey discusses it briefly in the fourth volume of his *Natural History and Antiquities of Surrey:*

> The great Quantity and Thickness of the *Box* Wood yielded a convenient Privacy for Lovers, who frequently meet there, so that it is an *English Daphne.* The Gentry often resorted hither from *Ebbisham* [Epsom] but the Wood is much decayed now.[63]

The reference to "Daphne" is an elegant periphrasis; as Douglas Murray explains, "Daphne" refers to an erotic site outside ancient Antioch. Box Hill was closely associated with the pleasures of nearby Epsom, famous for horse racing and a resort useful to what we call "weekends" for middle-class businessmen from London and environs. (It was only an hour's journey from Croydon.) John Macky in *A Journey through England* (1714) speaks of Epsom as "the Place in the world the freest from Censure and Observation; for Mankind seems to be here *Incognito* all the Week."[64] (Wickham, characteristically, is familiar with Epsom.) The pleasures on offer are various, including racing, dancing, card playing and raffling: "From this Account, it is plain we are not quite in Heaven here, though we may justly be said to be in Paradise."[65] Box Hill is a central topos of this earthly "Paradise":

> On *Sundays* in the Afternoon, the Company generally go to a Charming place called *Box-hill,* about Six Miles off . . . and it's very

easy for Gentlemen and Ladies insensibly to lose their Company in these pretty Labyrinths of *Box-Wood,* and divert themselves unperceived. From hence one hath a most delicious commanding Prospect of a fine Country, and it may be justly called the Palace of VENUS.[66]

Defoe's *Tour* offers a detailed account of Box Hill, a place of opportunity for "abundance of Gentlemen and Ladies from *Epsome,* to take the Air, and walk in the Box-Woods; and, in a word, Divert, or Debauch, or perhaps both, as they thought fit." A vintner of Dorking, "taking notice of the constant and unusual flux of Company thither," established a little pub on the hill, but this got a bad reputation as a sort of brothel.[67] That era is remembered in Edward Beavan's awkward "Box Hill. A Descriptive Poem" (1777): "There late arose so gay, / A crowded pile,* incontinence's delight; / That Virtue, lovely maid, at length suppresst"[68] (8). The asterisk points to a footnote: "A house of ill fame, now abolished." Not "Virtue" but some young men of Dorking blew the pub or "Vault" up with gunpowder one Saturday night. Various writers allude to the open—or almost open—sexual congress associated with this site. Yet, after a censorious account, Defoe immediately refers favorably to the vale below Box Hill as a center of strawberry cultivation, "the Country People gathering such great quantities of *Strawberries,* as they carry them to Market by *Horse-Loads.*"[69] We find in Defoe the association of strawberries and Box Hill that we find in *Emma:* a scene of near fulfillment and frustration among the red berries brings on the storm of sexual frustration and anger on Box Hill.

Strawberries are traditionally the fruit of Venus. Mrs. Elton's desire for a strawberry party intimates sexual desire. But it is Mr. Knightley who says suggestively, "Come, and eat my strawberries. They are ripening fast" (III, ch. 6). *He* is ripening fast and needs to make more haste in the service of Venus—though it is not with Mrs. Elton that he wishes to enjoy strawberries. (Mrs. Elton's lack of staying power in berry gathering perhaps points to a deficiency in sexual stamina.) Mrs. Elton commands the excursion to Box Hill, although Emma had tried to make Mr. Weston conduct a more elegant party to the scene. In the novel's opening we are tightly supported and girdled by royal towns—and so again near the end with references to Richmond and Windsor. The series of royal centers offers a sense of security and rules—a sense mocked by the feelings coming unglued in the combination of the strawberry party and the Box Hill scene. Command and control, "Government," give way to unsatisfied sexuality and feelings that won't be ignored.

If the newly married Mrs. Elton wishes to "explore" Box Hill, she may be unconsciously wishing to explore further sexuality or to induce her husband to do so. The very name of the place is mildly obscene. ("Box" and "Hill" are slang names for sexual parts of the female body.) The party brings its own refreshments, presumably the "pigeon-pies and cold-lamb" envisaged by Mrs. Elton—refections that comically suggest victims and dupes, lambs and pigeons (III, ch. 6). There is one sole reference to the presence of another party of "explorers," a group in an Irish jaunting car. On a fine summer day numerous parties would most probably have shown up—some in definite search of decidedly intimate rendezvous in the green world. Austen's Box Hill is homely and yet seems distant and wild, a theater for libidinous passions barely kept in check. This day—or two days—of midsummer madness can teach Emma that after all the course of true love *never* did run smooth. The thick, resistant dry box groves are a contrast to the warm, juicy strawberries of the day before. There are various flickering feelings. Mr. Elton is not yet quite "over" Emma, which pushes him to be more disagreeable than necessary to her and to the despised Harriet. Mrs. Elton's jealousy at hearing Mr. Weston's and Frank's adulation of Emma is ungracious, but not causeless. Augusta Elton tries to take charge of Jane, who, sidelined, is constrained to conduct in code a breaking of her engagement. Frank, secretly hurt, is sulkily angry and wants reassurance of his manhood. Emma, unconsciously aware that Frank means nothing and is not really talking to her, savages the old maid whom she fears she may yet resemble, guardian of Emma's unacknowledged rival. Even Mr. Knightley is jealous, misreading the scene as Frank's success with Emma. Erotic desires are aroused and rebuffed. Hurt feelings and anger—not sexual delight—result. Moral rule gets pushed aside, and the endurance and kingly rule of the old Saxon towns is far below this brief height of uncanny exaltation.

Flirtation, insult, rejection, and momentary heartbreak are offered in this Temple of Venus. Like Puck, Venus has set the characters by the ears when they stray into her woods. The ambiguities of this Mount of Venus are felt throughout, if no direct allusion is made to its impolite and decidedly impure history. Even in Gilpin's genteel aesthetic description, the language seems sensuously tactile and curiously sexual with its "shivering precipices" and "downy hillocks."

As Frank and Jane Fairfax conduct their coded breakup on the summit of Box Hill, Frank remarks—overtly in reference to the Eltons who met at Bath—that it is ridiculous to marry "upon an acquaintance formed only in a public place!" (III, ch. 7). As Frank is well aware, he and Jane became engaged after a brief acquaintance at the seaside resort of Weymouth in Dorset at the mouth of the River Wey. (There is a delicate hint in *Sense and Sensibility* that Charlotte Palmer caught her husband when Mrs. Jennings took her to Weymouth, perhaps in the same journey that took the mother-daughter pair on their one visit to Brandon's Dorsetshire estate, where they tacitly decided they might do better.) Weymouth in *Emma* is an invisible center of offstage action in the immediate past. It too has royal associations. In 1789 King George III came to Weymouth (where the duke of Gloucester had built a lodge) to celebrate and further his recovery from his illness—his first serious bout with the menacing porphyria. George III visited fourteen times between 1789 and 1805, greatly enhancing Weymouth's reputation. Feltham calls it "the most fashionable of all the sea-bathing places," reverently remarking: "The sea here is remarkably tranquil.... at all times of day, immersion in the briny flood is safe and delightful. The sands are as smooth as carpet."[70] In 1804, when Cassandra was at Weymouth, Jane joked about her sister's impressions of the place:

> Your account of Weymouth contains nothing which strikes me so forcibly as there being no Ice in the Town . . . Weymouth is altogether a shocking place I perceive, without recommendation of any kind, & worthy only of being frequented by the inhabitants of Gloucester. (14 September 1804; *Letters,* 92)[71]

In *Emma,* Mrs. Elton objects to the "shocking" lack of ice: "She was a little shocked . . . at the poor attempt at rout-cakes, and there being no ice in the Highbury card parties" (II, ch. 16). Mrs. Elton misses ice cream. The only reference to use of ice in the 1791 edition of Hannah Glasse's popular *The Art of Cookery* is in the recipe "To make ice cream."[72] Ice cream is on Jane Austen's mind as she looks forward to a dinner party: "I shall eat Ice & drink French wine" (30 June–1 July 1808; *Letters,* 139).

Frank Churchill was able to visit Weymouth where he met and courted Jane because his invalid aunt, the imperious Mrs. Churchill, fancied the resort would do her good. Mr. Dixon on a Weymouth sailing party saved Jane from unwanted "immersion in the briny flood," stimulating Emma to imagine a love between these two. A girl's falling in love with a man who saves her from the water in a sailing accident recalls Sheridan's Julia Melville whom Faulkland rescued; the romance of the situation is counteracted by Lydia's sensible comment when Julia remarks on the "obligation": "Obligation!—Why a water-spaniel would have done as much! Well, I should never think of giving my heart to a man because he could swim!" (*The Rivals,* act 1, sc. 2).[73] The light—but consistent—motif of "madness" in *Emma* is not lessened by the allusions to Weymouth, the very name of which carries a delicate reminiscent allusion to the madness of a king. That illness, no longer able to be hidden, brought on the Regency in 1811. All the contending monarchs in *Emma* are a little mad.

There are no waves or cooling waters anywhere in the Box Hill scene; all is desiccated. By contrast, the novel constantly refers to the sea. John Knightley took his family to "Southend on Sea," a modest seaside resort, thriving on proximity to London. (Jane Austen's brother Charles had taken his family there for a holiday.) Cromer ("lake of crows"), unreasonably recommended by Mr. Woodhouse, is a resort far to the east on the chilly eastern coast of Norfolk. We may feel required to look down on this new rage for visiting the seaside—and yet we share the longing. Emma says "I must beg you not to talk of the sea. It makes me envious and miserable;—I who have never seen it!" (I, ch. 12). Emma is tactfully trying to close down the dispute about resorts and make peace by mock enactment of frustration—but her art conceals some real wistfulness. Emma lives on a very short tether. For all her energy, she is allowed very little movement in space.

There is something sad about Emma's never having seen the sea. We think better of Mr. Knightley as erotic partner rather than as mere mentor because on their honeymoon he gives Emma "a fortnight's absence" from Hartfield, "in a tour to the sea-side" (III, ch. 19). Nobody else has offered her relief from looking after her father (except perhaps Mr. Perry), but Mr. Knightley appears to have noticed at last that she needs a respite. The imminent prospect of being himself shut in with Mr. Woodhouse has sharpened his perception, perhaps. It is hard on Mr. Knightley to leave Donwell; his going on honeymoon is a gift to Emma of himself. And both will benefit from the sea.

In these later Austen novels, the human relation to the ocean is treated in many complex ways—including its uses in trade and war. In personal encounters the sea offers a source of renewed energy. The walk of Henry and Fanny on the Portsmouth ramparts on a March day with the view of the ocean is salutary and beautiful: "The ever-varying hues of the sea now at high water, dancing in its glee and dashing against the ramparts with so fine a sound" (*MP,* III, ch. 11). The reader catches the erotic energy and momentarily begins to pull for Henry as the better partner for Fanny. But Fanny soon becomes tired—too readily tired for her age. In *Persuasion* and *Sanditon* major scenes take place by the sea. In *Emma* it becomes a separate place, not mere individual resorts but an *idea*—"the sea." Something that must be experienced rather than discussed, "the sea" is an earthly "place" not exactly locatable. It is a place that becomes both energy and a feeling.

IMAGINARY PLACES IN *EMMA*

There is a real Highbury, beyond Islington, long swallowed up by Greater London. The geographical information given about Emma's Highbury, "the large and populous village almost amounting to a town," does not fit that real Highbury—or any other place. We are told it is sixteen miles from Brunswick Square in London, and near Cobham, Kingston, and Windsor. The suffix "bury" (like *-burg*) meaning a fortified place is common Saxon for a settlement. Like so many terms in *Emma* dividing easily into syllables—including, as Mr. Weston illustrates, the heroine's first name—"High" + "bury" lends itself to wordplay, to "charade." It is "high" in its pretensions, but also a place where one can feel *buried*. It might have been suggested by the childhood home of Burney's *Evelina*; "Berry Hill" is also a place where the heroine is buried, unseen or stifled. In *A Gossip's Story* Jane West anticipates Gaskell's *Cranford* in the invention of her old-maid narrator "Prudentia Homespun" and the gossipy small town of Danbury. Her Danbury, where single women play important roles, seems an influence upon Highbury.

Highbury is the essence of the small town; "high" can be used both as "elevated" and "main" ("High Street" is England's "Main Street"). Large enough to support a prosperous apothecary and lawyer, the settlement grows around Donwell Abbey as it has done from the Middle Ages. Highbury in Emma's time is in danger of becoming almost a dormitory town. It isn't quite rural and if it does not—to some extent—become "Suburbia," it would remain dull and third rate. Standing outside Ford's shop Emma can look at what activity the place affords:

> Much could not be hoped from the traffic of even the busiest part of Highbury;—Mr. Perry walking hastily by, Mr. William Cox letting himself in at the office door, Mr. Cole's carriage horses returning from exercise, or a stray letter-boy on an obstinate mule, were the liveliest objects she could presume to expect; and when her eyes fell only on the butcher with his tray, a tidy old woman travelling home-

wards from shop with her full basket, two curs quarrelling over a dirty bone, and a string of dawdling children round the baker's little bow-window eyeing the gingerbread, she knew she had no reason to complain. (II, ch. 9)

The view here gives Emma at least some glimpse of those so far below her on the social scale that she does not know their names but has to recognize their activities, just as they can see her dawdling outside Ford's awaiting Harriet. The "high" in Highbury jokes with the propensity of some of its inhabitants to look vertically, not horizontally. Looking down on others provides a comic motif of *Emma*. That Box Hill offers a view from a height (fairly rare in pre-airplane days) connects the expedition with the theme of looking down; the experience makes some giddy and reckless.

In *Juvenile Indiscretions* (1786) Agnes Maria Bennett sets the action in East Sheen and Esher, presented as middle-class to lower-middle-class Surrey localities. Initial attention is largely focused on the practices and defects of boarding schools for both boys and girls. Dickens must surely have read this novel before writing *Nicholas Nickleby*.[74] We first see the heroine, Clara Elton, at age fourteen residing at Mrs. Napper's school (pretentious and poorly run). Clara is the soon-to-be-orphaned daughter of the reserved Mr. Elton, a merchant whose dealings with America have led to bankruptcy after the American Revolution. Clara Elton resembles both Harriet Smith (resident at a school) and Jane Fairfax (orphan facing destitution)—but in *Emma* the name "Elton" is used for a character the reverse of heroic. Fictional associations with Surrey, combined with Austen' own brief experience of the Abbey School in Reading, may have prompted the centrality of Mrs. Goddard's school—a contrast to Mrs. Napper's school in being unpretentious, financially sound, and comfortable, if almost equally unglamorous.

We hear about a couple of estates that are not in or near Highbury—not in Surrey at all. "Balycraig," family seat of Mr. Dixon in Ireland, is the new home of the former Miss Campbell. Miss Campbell's Scottish identity might have made attaching to an English landed proprietor seem too difficult, although she had a dowry of twelve thousand pounds. "Baly"—more customarily nowadays "bally"—is a version of *baille,* a common English component of place names, meaning "homestead." But in Ireland "bally" is more likely to be anglicized Irish, from *bealach,* a pass or passage, here combined with "craig" meaning "crag" or "rocky outcrop." "Balycraig" would indicate a pass through the rocky rise or even a homestead on the rocks. In neither case does the name promise rich arable land. Mr. Dixon, we are told, is "rich and agreeable" if "certainly plain" in appearance (II, ch. 2, ch. 3). Who is the guarantor of his riches? The estate's name does not promise wealth—though craggy Balycraig may indeed be picturesque. (Mr. Dixon has made attractive drawings of it, perhaps to advertise himself.) If Mr. Dixon were not rich—or not as rich as painted—then Miss Campbell's twelve thousand pound dowry would indeed be welcome. (Compare Edgeworth's *Castle Rackrent*.) Irish bachelors—see O'Brien in *The Watsons*—have a reputation as fortune hunters.

The Churchills' Enscombe is far off in Yorkshire. *Combe* is Old English, ultimately Celtic, a valley between hills running from the sea. "Enscombe" presumably means a place in such a valley. Either Austen nodded when she put such a place name in Yorkshire—for *combe* is rather a West Country term—or she indicates that the original owners of this estate (where Frank's mother was born) had lived elsewhere and gave their northern home a reminiscent name. Frank's fearsome aunt, Mrs. Churchill, is married to Frank's uncle, "of a great Yorkshire family" (I, ch. 2), but that does not mean *she* was born or bred in the northern region. "She has taken it into her head that Enscombe is too cold for her," Mr. Weston says contemptuously (II, ch. 18). Some people named "Braithwaite" (a Yorkshire name) are expected to visit Enscombe, but Mrs. Churchill doesn't like them. She may never have liked Yorkshire or its people. Perhaps Mrs. Churchill married the wrong man and lived in the wrong place, with Frank the one bright spot in her life. Quite likely she did not realize that Frank saw her as a domineering and disagreeable, a tyrant like another "Mrs. Churchill," Sarah Churchill, Duchess of Marlborough. She thought he adored her as a mother. Mrs. Churchill escapes, coming south to die. A backstory that we will never hear: the mistaken marriage of Mrs. Churchill. Mr. Weston enjoys abusing Mrs. Churchill; Frank tries to defend her a little but won't openly contradict his father. (Blaming situations on Mrs. Churchill is useful to both.) In *Emma*, Austen consistently makes us question assumptions and perspectives. Possibly Mrs. Churchill's story may be read altogether differently—we have been charmed into accepting Mr. Weston's interpretation. In a novel that plays so intelligently with perceptions, illusions, and *blunders* we cannot achieve absolute certainty.

Within Highbury, we know of "Randalls," purchased by Mr. Weston; an old farm once belonging to a man named Randall, it may well be older than Hartfield. Its unpretentious name is realistic.[75] Mr. Weston has enough money not only to purchase but to renovate the farmhouse. "Randalls" is now a consumer's, not a producer's, establishment—no longer a source of income, not a farm nor properly an "estate" at all, but a place where Mr. Francis Weston and his wife can live on the income he has gained through trade. Mr. Weston, working in a business in London and residing in Highbury, has lived the life of a modern suburban commuter.

"Hartfield," home of Emma and Mr. Woodhouse, is a "charade" in Harriet Smith's sense. The word divides easily into "hart" (stag) + "field," an open space where deer are found. The name also puns on the other "heart"—"hearts" can play in this "field." The White Hart, traditional emblem of Richard II, is a sign of innocence, peace, and purity; in Arthurian legends it symbolizes the start of quest. Jane Austen would have known the famous old White Hart pub on the main road outside Sevenoaks, Kent. In *The Watsons,* the White Hart inn is the scene of the ball. The legend of the White Hart is also intermixed with the story of Herne the Hunter, used in Shakespeare's *The Merry Wives of Windsor.* "Hartfield" has a made-up sound. Austen is recycling a fictional name. In Charlotte Smith's *Desmond* (1792), "Hartfield" is the name of Desmond's guardian's small country estate; Mr. Bethel goes there to withdraw from a world that has been too much for him. Mr. Woodhouse's Hartfield is a place of cozy retirement, but it is not rural. There are no fields, no deer. It is like a *memory* of the country. Not a traditional estate like Longbourn or Mansfield Park, Hartfield is a modern residence with some grounds, part of the almost-town: "Highbury . . . to which Hartfield, in spite of its separate lawn and shrubbery and name, really did belong" (I, ch. 1).

How can this be said to differ from the abode of Mr. Tomlinson "the Banker" in *The Watsons,* with his "newly erected House at the end of the Town with a Shrubbery & sweep" (*The Watsons, Later Manuscripts,* 276)? Mr. Tomlinson wants to consider his house "in the Country," while Emma has to admit that hers is really in the village. We are told through Emma's defensive inner process that Mr. Elton *should* have realized "that the Woodhouses had been settled for several generations at Hartfield, the younger branch of a very ancient family." Yet even Emma has to admit that their lands are nothing much: "The landed property of Hartfield certainly was inconsiderable, being but a sort of notch in the Donwell Abbey estate, to which all the rest of Highbury belonged; but their fortune, from other sources, was such as to make them scarcely secondary to Donwell Abbey itself" (I, ch. 16). Hartfield allows Mr. Woodhouse sufficient space in which to take his daily walk outdoors for a quarter of an hour, but the grounds do not supply enough space for young and energetic Emma. There is a reference to Hartfield pork. Most people, not just the poor, seem to have been accustomed to raising pigs in a pen on their premises and did not mind the smell. (We remember Charles's pigsty in "Jack and Alice"; Mr. and Mrs. Collins keep pigs, as did the Austens.) There is no other reference to produce from the land. The Woodhouse money is in stocks ("other sources"), the proceeds of trade. The Woodhouses are new capitalists, not antique gentry.

Mrs. Elton, once arrived in Highbury, boasts incessantly of her brother-in-law's establishment, "Maple Grove" near Bristol. We never see Maple Grove, but we hear Mrs. Elton's tireless references as she endeavors to advance her own status. Maple Grove is very modern. The house, freshly built with its grounds laid out with the modern desirable "shrubbery" and other ornaments, would hardly constitute an "estate" in the older acceptation of the word. But Mrs. Elton cannot be entirely wrong when she irritatingly and insistently compares Maple Grove to Hartfield. (Even Austen's fools and knaves always speak some sense.) And the narrator seems in this instance to support Augusta Elton:

> The very first subject after being seated was Maple Grove . . .—a comparison of Hartfield to Maple Grove. The grounds of Hartfield were small, but neat and pretty; and the house was modern and well-built. Mrs. Elton seemed most favourably impressed by the size of the room, the entrance . . . "Very like Maple Grove indeed! . . . . And it is not merely the house—the grounds, I assure you, as far as I could observe, are strikingly like. The laurels at Maple Grove are in the same profusion as here . . . just across the lawn; and I had a glimpse of a fine large tree, with a bench around it, which put me so exactly in mind!" (II, ch. 14)

This is almost Proustian in the way it captures a certain high bourgeois style and mode, as Marcel does in describing Elstir's seaside villa.[76] Mrs. Elton, trying to aggrandize her own position, does not see how greatly she irritates Emma. Emma Woodhouse harbors unconscious pretensions about her family and her home—including her grounds. (Hartsfield's are only "neat and pretty"—how damning!) Augusta Elton challenges Emma's pretensions, although all that Mrs. Elton is doing is to try to establish her own credentials. But Mrs. Elton is correct. Hartfield *is* like Maple Grove. Both are the establishments of members of the bourgeoisie who can afford them. Each offers a modern convenient house and pleasant, nonproductive ornamental grounds. Suburbia is arriving. There is some similarity even in the names "Hartfield" and "Maple Grove"—so like the inventions of developers and realtors."Hartfield" begins to sound like the kind of name given by to houses with grounds when the wild creatures have long gone from the area. (Compare Billy Collins's "Pheasant Ridge").

This tame place belongs to Mr. Woodhouse. But there is the wilder "Hartfield," in which an Emma, the picture of health like Emma Hart (Lady Hamilton) holds all the wildness of her beauty and energy and where she postures in her attitudes. This "hart-field" is more at home with Herne the Hunter; it is a place where the wild things are.

Donwell Abbey, like Northanger Abbey, is an (imagined) religious foundation taken over by Henry VIII during the Dissolution and given to private owners. This abbey had a large demesne, including many arable acres, a mill, and fish ponds. Members of the strawberry-gathering party after luncheon go to look at "the old Abbey fish-ponds" (III, ch. 6). The most famous abbey in Surrey was Chertsey Abbey, a Cistercian abbey whose church was also the burial place of kings—more kings! Donwell seems to be partly based on Chertsey. One of the remarkable things about Chertsey was that it had an engineered river, its course designed during the Middle Ages to power the water mill. In Austen's novel, Abbey-Mill Farm is named after the abbey's water mill, a strong medieval survivor, still working. The "river making a close and handsome curve around it" could have been designed in medieval times for that purpose (III, ch. 6). Emma in a little rhapsody of patriotism (which we should partly discount) rejoices in language borrowed partly from Gilpin: "It was a sweet view—sweet to the eye and the mind. English verdure, English culture, English comfort, seen under a sun bright, without being oppressive" (III, ch. 6). The repetition of "sweet" is one element making the rhapsody suspect. Emma has seen nothing but England, and but little of that.

One notable element of the green English scene that Gilpin highly prizes is *not* to be found here—a *ruined* abbey. Donwell Abbey and its mill are still functional. They do not adorn the landscape with picturesque broken stones. The disapproval of the whole project of transforming a monastery into a self-serving showcase of comfort and display—disapproval so notable in *Northanger Abbey*—is absent in the presentation of Donwell Abbey. The name seems almost as overtly allegorical as names in *Piers Plowman*. Mr. Knightley has "done well" not only in a material but also in a moral sense. Langham, "long settlement"—"long home" is a hamlet near Donwell, evidently within the Abbey lands. Mr. Knightley speaks of "moving the path to Langham, of turning it more to the right that it may not cut through the home meadows" (I, ch. 12). He would have the power to change the paths of the laborers who live in this Saxon named settlement (which probably predates the abbey itself), but he would not break ancient rights of passage and has no will to cause "inconvenience to the Highbury people." Donwell, a product of the dispossession, exists in a continuum with the past.

This most important estate in the area, source of jobs and crops, Donwell Abbey is, strictly speaking, not in Highbury (we are told), but in the adjoining parish. The two parishes must be amalgamated, however, for Mr. Knightley has a great deal to do in parish meetings—he appears to be a warden—and Mrs. Elton boasts of her husband's working with him, though she says this is "the most troublesome parish that ever was," adding, "We never heard of such things at Maple Grove."

> "Your parish there was small," said Jane.
> "Upon my word, my dear, I do not know, for I never heard the subject talked of."
> "But it is proved by the smallness of the school, which I have heard you speak of, as under the patronage of your sister and Mrs. Bragge; the only school, and not more than five-and-twenty children." (III, ch. 16)

This exchange demonstrates that Jane Fairfax no longer feels obliged to be perfectly meek to Mrs. Elton. Her display of logic amazes that lady: "What a thinking brain you have!" Pursuing Jane's capacity for deduction, we recognize that Highbury has a number of children and that the population and the church congregation show no signs of dwindling—a fact that would be pleasing to Miss Bates but not to the Rev. Thomas Robert Malthus. Highbury, in defiance of Malthusianism, is truly a "large and *populous* village" (I, ch. 1, italics added). This prosperous area will produce more laborers, and more poor people, and there will be real work for any clergyman worth his salt.

Even if it still represents the takeover, Donwell Abbey has not wholly yielded to privatization. There is a sense of community obligation. Food production is immensely important. Indeed, from one angle *Emma* can be seen as a sustained riposte to Malthus, who had so alarmed Britain and the world with his gloomy predictions in his *Essay concerning Population*. Thomas Malthus was born in Surrey in 1766 and later served as a curate near Albury—which might have affected Austen's "Highbury." Malthus was still in the news, revising his influential *Essay* and publishing pamphlets such as *The Present High Price of Provisions* (1800). His most recent pamphlets (1814; 1815) defended the "Corn Laws" banning importation of grain into England. Ostensibly Christian, Malthus advocated the sad necessity of denying food to the poor. Charity extended to keep people from dying constituted a danger to the economy. Malthusian ideas stimulated Darwin to think of natural selection, supported Herbert Spencer's speculations on the survival of the fittest, and drove Engels and Karl Marx to antagonistic analytical response.

Austen engages in no overt philosophical commentary or argument as to whether it is right or inevitable to let the poor starve and die. But her Surrey novel is a quiet sustained retort to the Surrey theorist. A child is conceived and born during the course of the narrative—sex and procreation. Food abounds in this novel—pork, boiled eggs, Stilton and Wiltshire cheese, baked apples, sweetbreads and asparagus, apple tart, arrowroot, cake, wine. In Highbury people are constantly engaged in feeding each other. Not only do Highbury people give dinner parties, but they also feed those who are below them in status or income. Even Emma's slightly ridiculous act as Lady Bountiful visiting a poor family and ordering soup for them has its good side. The poor get food and are taught to read in the church school. If people don't get food, they will steal it—as somebody steals Mrs. Weston's "turkies." "Other poultry-yards in the neighbourhood also suffered.—Pilfering was *housebreaking* to Mr. Woodhouse's fears" (*Emma*, III, ch. 19). The narrative ridicules Mr. Woodhouse's definition, even though the thieves indeed broke into an enclosure. Austen here indirectly casts ridicule on the "Alton Association," wealthy landowners offering a reward of two guineas for information regarding stealing of poultry from enclosed ground—precisely what has occurred in the "poultry-yards" of Highbury. The Association zealously seeks to punish hungry persons who take turnips from the fields. Early in *Persuasion* we meet a similar implicit critique of the principles of the Alton Association. Mr. Shepherd recalls Wentworth's brother, the curate, as settling amicably, without legal remedy or reprisal for the offense, a theft of apples from his walled orchard. "Very odd indeed!" (*Persuasion*, I, ch. 3).

Food in *Emma* moves down the social scale—the Perry children get Mrs. Weston's wedding cake, Mr. Knightley's apples feed the Bates family. But people "lower" on the scale can also be charitable to those technically "above" them, as the wife of the baker kindly attends to the needs of the Bates family. The conversation between Miss Bates and Mr. Elton regarding the former clerk who now needs parish care is not at all faultfinding or tax defensive regarding either the old man requiring parish relief or his son, hostler at the inn. The sympathetic tone emanates from Miss Bates: "Poor old man, he is bed-ridden, and very poorly with the rheumatic gout in his joints—I must go and see him to-day" (*Emma*, III, ch. 8). Mr. Elton has been good to the family of his predecessor, allowing deaf old Mrs. Bates and her daughter to occupy the Vicarage pew. He is rewarded in acquiring Miss Bates as a sort of unpaid curate. She knows all about what goes on in the parish. We are accustomed to despising or ridiculing Mr. Elton, because he is conceited and made a great blunder. But as a working vicar Elton is the best of Austen's clergyman—and he has not been shooed into position by his kinship to the landowner.[77]

The best response to the problem proposed by Malthus is to raise food for England. This solution is quietly endorsed throughout the novel. Donwell is a working estate, with an unknown number of farmer tenants. Robert Martin is one of these tenants, and the flourishing condition of Abbey-Mill Farm speaks well for Mr. Martin's work and for Donwell Abbey's general health and productivity. Robert Martin is the other knight and noble soul upholding Highbury in balance with George Knightley. Mr. Knightley, unlike John Dashwood and Mr. Rushworth (or Mr. Bennet), is fully engaged in food production. No gentleman of leisure, not given to the sports of chasing or killing things, he is deeply concerned in "the plan of a drain, the change of a fence, the felling of a tree, and the destination of every acre for wheat, turnips, or spring corn" (I, ch. 12). George Knightley is a farmer and dresses like one, walking in "thick leather gaiters" (II, ch. 15). Generous to those around him, giving his last apples to the Bateses, this "Farmer George" spends little on himself. He turns his profits largely back into the land and into new, improved farming methods. Emma teases him about his interest in "shows of cattle, or new drills" or "the dimensions of some famous ox" (III, ch. 18). Emma's money, both dowry and inheritance—almost entirely liquid capital—is going to be plowed back into the Donwell Abbey estate.

The work on the land is the battle of life against death. And death is always waiting. Death plays a greater role in Austen's novels than we are commonly aware of. Emma's mother has died; Frank's mother died. Both of Jane Fairfax's parents died—one from warfare, the other from what is obviously tuberculosis. Jane has inherited the consumptive disease her closest relatives fear, hence the fuss (ridiculous to readers since antibiotics arrived) over Jane's colds or wet feet. Mr. Woodhouse is slowly dying. Emma has suppressed her fears of the future and allows herself to face the prospect fully only after Mr. Knightley has proposed: "Such a partner in all those duties and cares to which time must be giving an increase of melancholy!" (III, ch. 15). Austen told some of her relatives that Mr. Woodhouse died two years after Emma's marriage and that Jane Fairfax "survived her elevation only nine or ten years." The Austen-Leighs add, "Whether the John Knightleys afterwards settled at Hartfield, and whether Frank Churchill married again, may be legitimate subjects of speculation."[78] It is hard to believe that having spent all those years and much energy on a career as a barrister, John would care to be mewed up in Hartfield. As for Frank—who cares? The striking thing is that Jane Fairfax, like Mr. Woodhouse, is slowly dying, all the time, though we don't know it. We *refuse* to know it—like Frank, who sees in his beloved's pallor only the refinement of a beautiful and valuable object. But there is much to be done before we die. Everybody is a bit mad and yet quite sane. Against the shadow of death we fight back with communal feeling. There are supplies of food and care—against the Malthusian grain (or Malthusian meanness with grain). Emma herself joins—as it were—the Malthus party only once: her vicious attack upon Miss Bates tacitly proclaiming that the rich and powerful need not support the poor and powerless and that some people should not exist. But that is only for a moment. At the end the game of thrones turns at least partly into a generous exchange. Eros is not frustrated. Queen Emma rules—if not as she had thought. The old Saxon wars and Tudor dangers are comically thwarted. We can hope. Everyone is saved, England is saved, and Malthus is wrong.

Names and Places in *Persuasion*: Somerset, Dorset, and the Rebellious Trail of the West Country

REAL PLACES IN *PERSUASION*

Persuasion, like *Emma,* uses one main county—Somersetshire—as its central location. Anne Elliot is another West Country heroine, native, like Catharine Percival and Catherine Morland. Unlike Emma, this heroine constantly moves about. Yet, in going from her father's Kellynch Hall to her sister's home at Uppercross (three miles away) and then to Bath, she remains in her native county. The visit to Lyme takes her into Dorset—somewhere new, excitingly close to the sea.

Taunton ("settlement on the River Tone"), Somerset's county seat, is the most important town near Kellynch and Uppercross. Since the fourteenth century, law courts met in county seats to choose administrative committees and to conduct trials. Capital cases were saved for the Assizes or periodic "sittings" of visiting judges. Against this background of law, Kellynch is let. Mr. Shepherd, Sir Walter's lawyer and agent, is "attending the quarter session at Taunton" when he meets with Admiral Croft to negotiate the rental of Kellynch (I, ch. 3). This must be the Midsummer session, as the Crofts take possession at Michaelmas. Croft says, "I thought we should come to a deal my dear, in spite of what they told us at Taunton"; opinions of Sir Walter have reached that far.

Prosperous Taunton, a center of the wool trade, had a turbulent history. Site of important battles in the Wars of the Roses, it also participated in the "Cornish uprising" of 1497, supporting the claim of Perkin Warbeck. During the Civil War, Taunton was a Parliament stronghold, successful against fierce Royalist attack owing to the leadership of the Puritan defender Robert Blake, who later became chief admiral and reorganized the navy. Admiral Blake (whose surname is given to the amiable ten-year-old Charles Blake encountered at the ball in *The Watsons*) is a model of organization and courage. Nelson said he didn't reckon himself the equal of Blake. Taunton supported Monmouth, illegitimate son of Charles II who tried to take the throne from James II. For its "treason" Taunton was the scene of some of the worst retributive sentences against the common people during the Bloody Assizes. Judge Jeffreys's mockery of those he sentenced adds a dark pun to the "taunt" in Taunton.

Taunton had ugly associations for Austens and Leighs. Jane's aunt, Mrs. James Leigh-Perrot, had been tried at the Assizes in March 1800 for felony. Her alleged crime: theft of valuable lace from a Bath shop. Had Jane Leigh-Perrot been convicted of this capital charge, she would have been transported to Australia. Her long imprisonment awaiting trial meant months of anxiety, and the trial itself surely left scarring memories. That trial attracted some two thousand spectators; "the fashionable *Lady's Magazine* had a reporter and an artist on hand."[79] Jane Leigh-Perrot's very public ordeal ended in deliverance, and so ultimately does the ordeal of Austen's inwardly stressed heroine.

In contrast to the royalist references in *Emma,* which evoke grandeur and rightful rule, geographical and historical references in *Persuasion* are reminders of insurgency and upheaval. Rebellion runs under this text. Settings recall protest and fighting, war and execution. As noted earlier, Monmouth's mistress, Henrietta Wentworth, is recalled within Austen's text in the presence of a "Henrietta" and a Wentworth. Henrietta Wentworth (1660–86), daughter of the fifth Baron Wentworth, in her teens became mistress of the young James Scott, Duke of Monmouth, despite her family's efforts to separate them. Monmouth, who had been forcibly married off at age fourteen, protested he had no real marriage; he and Henrietta thought of themselves as husband and wife. Henrietta followed him into exile in Holland and was instrumental in raising money for his invasion through sale of her jewels and the credit for personal wealth. Matters went very badly; the duke was defeated, swiftly tried, and beheaded in 1685. "On the scaffold after the rebellion's defeat Monmouth renewed his pledges of devotion to Henrietta" (*ODNB*). She did not long survive him, dying the following year. The ill-fated young duke, whose program promised freedom of religion to Catholics and Protestants, is the Stuart claimant whom the young Jane Austen in her annotation of Goldsmith's *History* called "Sweet Man!"

The novel's surrounding atmosphere, a sort of spiritual setting, is war—as Mary Favret pointed out. Naval warfare is the center of Austen's war. Names of ports abound; in Plymouth, Wentworth found timely refuge for the battered *Asp* and his prize, and from Plymouth in a later year he sped to Portsmouth to break the news of Fanny Harville's death to Benwick "and never left the poor fellow for a week" (*Persuasion,* ch. 8, ch. 12). Recent times brought on death, battles, and the chance of Captain Wentworth going to the bottom without Anne's even knowing of it. The opportunity of peacetime (which may threaten wartime's social bonds) is tinged with anxiety. Unprecedented physical injury enters Austen's narrative. What now? Change is certain—but what sort of change? Letting Kellynch (a break with the past) is possible because of the new treacherous peace of 1814.

Many characters still live mentally in the war, insensibly separated from nonparticipants like the Elliot males who (unlike Musgroves) are untouched by danger or loss. But the naval officers are bound by positive emotional bonds. In this novel Austen deals most fully with love—not just erotic love, but a variety of loves. Among these, men's love for men rates very high. Counteracting war's destruction, the men inhabit an invisible moving tent of affections. They move rapidly toward each other, reaching through space in comfort and support. The entire novel endorses the male capacity to love, underwriting Harville's memorable claims in the important dialogue with Anne at the White Hart and supporting our idea of Wentworth's capacity to love Anne Elliot, since he loves Benwick and Harville with such practical and unwavering loyalty. In *Mansfield Park* Fanny loathed the poverty of the house at Portsmouth. Here the Harville's poor little rented house with its battered furniture is seen longingly by Anne as a haven of the affections, an enviable capital of the good community. "'These would have been all my friends,' was her thought; and she had to struggle against a great tendency to lowness" (*Persuasion*, I, ch. 11).

Names of ships no longer have the dreamy poetry of ship names in *Mansfield Park*, suited to Fanny's dreams and William's hopes. The names of vessels in *Persuasion* are hard and dangerous: *Asp, Grappler, Laconia* (I, ch. 8; ch. 12). That Wentworth captained the *Laconia* (true Greek name for "Sparta") indicates the Spartan hardiness beneath his geniality. As well as love, there is in this novel an undercurrent of rage on many sides—in Anne and Wentworth not least. Each resents the others' stance. Land workers are still remembered in this story, but concern for them is subordinated to—or merged with—awareness of the Government's callousness toward its fighting men. Wentworth in a brief satiric outburst articulates his resentment:

> "The admiralty . . . entertain themselves now and then, with sending a few hundred men to sea, in a ship not fit to be employed. But . . . among the thousand that may just as well go to the bottom as not, it is impossible for them to distinguish the very set who may be least missed." (ch. 8)

In the eyes of the Admiralty, sailors (including those of Wentworth's socioeconomic class) are but poor working men, interchangeable, even disposable. A serene ruling-class callousness regarding "the thousand that may just as well go to the bottom as not" becomes familiar to us in the pronouncements of sedentary Sir Walter Elliot, so unlike Sir Walter Raleigh. Anne is sharing that callousness in her view of Dick Musgrove. Elliotishness infects the nation.

Bath, a peacetime center, is the novel's setting through the second volume. Anne never liked this city, associating it with her mother's death, school, and the loss of Wentworth. It rains in Catherine Morland's Bath—but soon clears up. The rain falls more steadily on Anne Elliot's Bath. When the sun shines, the buildings of white stone hurt the eyes—"the white glare of Bath." Jocelyn Harris has described in detail the Bath of Anne's time—and the time of Austen's residency in the first years of the new century.[80] The town was increasingly smoggy and crowded, its population swollen (so we feel in the novel) by the advent of pensioned veterans and the war wounded. Previous overbuilding combined with depression and wartime uncertainty meant empty buildings, or low-rent housing often jerry-built, suggesting recollections of infectious fevers. The democratic projects that had looked so promising in the earlier period had been largely forgotten or overturned by the fashionable, who now set their own rules and did not attend mixed assemblies, of the kind so useful to Catherine Morland. Anne resents the stupidity of private parties to which she is confined.

Austen lets us know in exactly what part of the city everyone—or nearly everyone—has lodgings. As Harris emphasizes, the city is hierarchical. The best people live at the top of the hills, and the poorer sort down in the flat, near the inns and the stables. Unlike Catherine Morland, who has no contact with anyone in ill health (Mr. Allen's ailment being but a happy excuse), Anne has to visit an old friend who is poor and crippled, temporarily bedridden. Mrs. Smith has lodgings in Westgate Buildings, in the bottom of the town, noisy from the traffic of the Old Bridge. This lodging was suggested to the Austens: "Miss Lyford . . . gave my mother such an account of the houses in Westgate Buildings, where Mrs. Lyford lodged four years ago, as made her think of a situation there with great pleasure." Jane knows that Cassandra would oppose this idea, but happily their father "has now ceased to think of it entirely" (14–16 January 1801; *Letters*, 73). Lady Dalrymple and Miss Carteret take a house in Laura Place, on the other side of the Avon, away from the worst nuisances of horses, manure, garbage, barges, prostitutes, and street sellers—a total contrast to Mrs. Smith's humble pair of rooms. Laura Place, named after Sir William Pultney's daughter, was a high-class development of the 1790s. Mr. Austen (a little unrealistically) wished to live there: "At present the Environs of Laura-place seem to be his choice . . . he grows quite ambitious" (14–16 January 1801; *Letters,* 73). On first arrival the Austen family stayed with Aunt and Uncle Perrot in Paragon Buildings, which looked up toward Camden Place.

Bath has its own Bond Street, where Sir Walter "counted eighty-seven women go by . . . without there being a tolerable face among them." He does not spare his own sex: "As for the men! they were infinitely worse. Such scarecrows as the streets were full of!" (*Persuasion,* II, ch. 3). Feltham finds the sight of sick people as troubling as the tombs: "Amidst all the gaiety of Bath," he is distressed by "the sight of so many miserable victims of disease as here present themselves."[81] Sir Walter doesn't admit—or care—whether people he sees are pitiably sick or wounded; they are just inferior. He does not care if they avoid death as long as *he* does. Sir Walter can look down on them—literally, for he lives in Camden Place, on Beacon Hill, at or near the very top of Bath. Philip Thicknesse (obsessed with "Putrefaction") recommends the heights of Bath: "It is said . . . that old Age itself is nothing more than a tendency to Putrefaction; if this be true, Men in Years should prefer a high situation for their Dwelling."[82] Sir Walter's "lofty, dignified situation, such as becomes a man of consequence" would suit not only the baronet's inordinate sense of superiority but also his lust for self-preservation—his immortality project (II, ch. 3). Lady Russell resides only somewhat below him, on Rivers Street, and the Crofts are further down, at a respectable address in Gay Street. Mr. Elliot's Bath address remains curiously unascertained. (Was he lodging with a mistress?)

As Jocelyn Harris points out, Camden Place, purpose-built terrace overlooking the Avon, could not be completed owing to landslips. Sir Walter's haughty new home on unstable ground suits him "as an isolated and crumbling relic of the aristocracy."[83] It is, however, a good address. Ironically, it reiterates the name of the author of *Britannia* whose patriotism opposes Sir Walter's attitudes in every respect. The connection is not accidental. Camden Place, Bath, is named after the estate of the first Earl Camden, Lord Chancellor, whose "Camden Place" in Kent near Bromley occupied land formerly owned by the Elizabethan historian. Here we connect with someone encountered before. Charles Pratt—successful prosecutor of Earl Ferrers, the jurist who turned every Englishman's home into his castle—became Lord Chancellor and the first Earl Camden. Charles Pratt as Baron Camden and then Earl Camden remained a staunch supporter of liberty, equality, and rights; he argued against imprisoning Wilkes and spoke favorably of Americans in their argument against the Crown (*ODNB*). London's Camden Town, of which he was one of the developers, is named after him. For different reasons every town called "Camden" in North America is named for Pratt's sake, ultimately in acknowledgment of his principles. A grandiose project at the top of Bath celebrates a champion of the underdog; a lurking Pratt challenges the upper reaches of snobbish Bath. Patriotism and liberty strain against Elliot snobberies. Modest rebellion or independence slides in even under the posh address of the stagnant father. The name of the first Camden, defender of the vanished monasteries, the name borrowed by the defender of liberty, presides over Bath from a height.

This novel presents an unusually effective setting antipathetic to the heroine; the heroine becomes happier in a place with which she is not at all in harmony. There are no green, growing things around; everything is man-made. Vegetation returns only when Wentworth and Anne have been reunited; they exchange confidences at Elizabeth's party while pretending to admire "a fine display of green-house plants" forced and partly artificial (II, ch. 11). Whatever its shortcomings of deception, dirt, and artificiality—and its barely concealed intimacy with death and physical disaster—Bath allows meeting and crossing of paths, reunions and unions.

Aside from dislikable Bath, *Persuasion*'s most important scenes in a real setting take place in Lyme Regis, Dorset. Originally named after the river Lim (a Celtic word for stream), Lyme, a port long before the Normans arrived, was transformed into "Lyme Regis" ("of the King") when given a charter by King Edward I in 1284. The often restored "Cobb," the long breakwater, predates the fourteenth century.[84] It provides an attractive, even somewhat romantic, vista (fig. 24). Here in this little bay on 11 June 1685 the Duke of Monmouth arrived with a small number of ships for his ill-fated attempt on the crown. He received strong support in the immediate area during his brief disastrous bid for power. Lyme Regis, watery site of the failed invasion, remains an attractive—and small—seaside town. One can still see the landscape and buildings that Austen describes. Every visitor walks on the Cobb. The coasts and cliffs and rock falls that Anne Elliot and her author enjoy are still present, but science has transformed our vision of the coast, now known as "the Jurassic Coast." In Austen's own day, a girl named Mary Anning (1799–1847) was working with her brother finding fossils to sell to tourists. Mary's father the cabinetmaker is mentioned by Jane

24. Copplestone Warre Bampfylde, *The Harbor and the Cobb, Lyme Regis, Dorset, by Moonlight* (before 1791). Photograph: Bridgeman Art Library.

Austen, who did not agree with his estimate for replacement of a lid (14 September 1804; *Letters,* 94). Austen would have seen the fossils that Richard Anning exhibited outside his premises. Mary Anning, who has steadily gained respect as a scientific predecessor of Darwin, is credited with finding the first *Ichthyosaurus* (which got its name in 1817).[85] The museum at Lyme Regis is currently divided between two women: Jane Austen and Mary Anning (fig. 25).

Geological observation enters Austen's descriptions of Lyme: "Pinny, with its green chasms between romantic rocks . . . many a generation must have passed away since the first partial falling of the cliff prepared the ground for such a state." (I, ch. 11). Part of the attraction of that coast is its changeability, a creative instability beyond the rhythmic temporal passing of crops and seasons. Austen in *Persuasion* begins to exhibit a surprising sense of geological time, characteristic of Victorian poets and novelists in the future. In *Persuasion* Austen offers different processes happening at different rates at the same time: the tempo of reverie and human memory, the human memory that includes history over several hundred years, the personal memory of eight years ago, the

25. B. J. Donne, *Painting of Mary Anning made after her death at the Geological Society* (1847). Photograph: © Natural History Museum, London.

ineluctable aging, the pain or inspiration of the hour, the shock of a minute, the slow rhythms of the earth and those who work the land, the cycles and cataclysms of the earth apart from man's designs. . . . Here indeed is innovation. This represents a fresh departure in Austen's lively cultivation of anachronism, whereby one "time" overlaps, shuffles into, or bleeds through others.

Louisa Musgrove's fall happens in an instant on one particular bright morning. Monmouth set foot on this shore on one particular day, and his armies marched along the Cobb. Monmouth's fall was rapid and distressing. Allusions to Taunton and Crewkerne as well as the announced distance (seventeen miles) from Uppercross to Lyme suffice to let us see that the armies of Monmouth and King James II must have moved near or even across the lands of Kellynch and Uppercross in 1685. This novel's imaginary estates and settlements can scarcely be any great distance from the historical battlefield site of Sedgemoor. Gilpin's description of the area connects fields and hedgerows with the site of Monmouth's battle:

> The whole country, I believe, is a scene of cultivation, and the woods little more, in fact, than hedge-rows. But one row succeeding another . . . the whole appears, in the distance, as one vast bed of foliage.
>
> On the left we had the same kind of country. . . . Among the savannahs on this side, shoot the extensive plains of Sedgmore [*sic*], which stretch far and wide before the eye. Here the unfortunate Monmouth tried his cause with his uncle James; and all the country was afterwards the scene of those acts of brutality, which Kirk and Jefferies committed, and which are still remembered with horror and detestation.[86]

If we look at the map of the movements of Monmouth we can see that Anne's routes follow his fairly closely—although she does not begin at Lyme. The novel itself seems to be about rebellion, about questioning hierarchy and finding a new way out, a new way to live. Its historical geography—marked by pain and failure—consistently supports this daunting endeavor.

IMAGINARY PLACES IN *PERSUASION*

Kellynch Hall, which plays a paradoxically important part in the story *because* it is abandoned, is obviously a grand estate. The name is not Norman and at first glance does not seem Saxon. Janine Barchas plausibly suggests that it was named with the real estate of "Redlynch" in mind. Redlynch in Somerset, three miles from the village of Charlton-*Musgrove* was the site of a grandiose property belonging to the great Whig family of Fox. This gigantic showplace was first put up for auction in 1797, and its household items were auctioned in 1801.[87] "Redlynch" was once *Redlisc* (*hreod* [reed] + *lisc*), "reedy marsh." Austen substitutes the harsh and unfamiliar first syllable "kell." In Irish names, *Kill* or sometimes *kell* means "church" or "churches." But Old English or Norman *Kell* comes from *kelda,* Old Norse for "spring," found in many Irish and some English place names (e.g., Kellet, Lancashire). Camden explained these linguistic elements.[88] "Kellynch" would be a marshy place with a spring or springs. (The word might add an extra pun to finding "a second spring"). The Old Norse element estranges the name; it sounds like "kill"—killing by inches. The name might have been brought here by a family originating further north than Cheshire, where the Elliots' official story begins according to Sir Walter's "favourite volume," the *Baronetage* (I, ch. 1). The Elliot estate has been modernized, with the usual shrubbery and flower gardens; it has space for game birds and shooting. We know there are fields and pastures, as the Crofts later admire them, but the estate seems to be regarded by its owner as an ornamental and comfortable set of social signals, not as a center of production.

"Monkford" is apparently the name of the village where the clergyman or curate of Kellynch's parish resided; Frederick Wentworth's older brother Edward was curate of "Monkford" when Frederick visited him in 1806. The name tells us that there was once a monastery or abbey near Kellynch; the monks were presumably the original cultivators of the land. This imaginary name is modeled on real ones such as "Monkleigh" (Devon) and "Monksilver" (Somerset). At "Monk-ford" the monks (and other travelers) crossed a stream. Nobody mentions the ruins of an abbey, but there must have been one—yet another ghostly abbey, just the faintest whisper of ruins somewhere, perhaps lying under the heavy body of Kellynch.

Kellynch Lodge is the rented home of Lady Russell, the tenant of Sir Walter, her "attentive landlord." A "lodge" is the home of a gatekeeper of a great house or manor, placed at the entrance. A lodge keeper is supposed to keep watch over comings and goings. Sir Walter has already been driven to economize on a lodge keeper. Lady Russell tries to make a good substitute, but she cannot supervise his affairs.

Uppercross realistically refers to a crossroads, and a boundary marker, a stone cross, or stone with a cross marked on it, dating to the Middle Ages. It is here that Anne begins her superior ordeal ("upper" + "cross")—meaningful affliction that will lead to a happy issue. "Uppercross" seems a normal local term. That there is no separate grand name for the manor house is, paradoxically, a mark of its genuine antiquity. Uppercross village until recently was "completely in the old English style," the only two gentry houses "the mansion of the 'squire . . . substantial and unmodernized" and the parsonage "with a vine and a pear-tree trained round its casements." Charles upon his marriage has embarked on the improvement of a farmhouse elevated into a "cottage." Fashion impacts Uppercross Cottage with "its viranda [*sic*], French windows and other prettinesses" (I, ch. 5). The term "prettinesses" combines amusement with mild disparagement. Such adornments cannot compete in attractiveness with the twining vine and pear tree just mentioned. But allowance is made for change as well as continuity, even while we note the unpretentious original nature of the Great House. The old must be admitted into a novel that ultimately desires change in a changing world.

One of the outstanding natural descriptions in Austen's work occurs in *Persuasion,* in the sequence of the November walk. The walk from Uppercross to Winthrop is undertaken for practical reasons; Louisa Musgrove designs it, determined that Henrietta shall make up with Charles Hayter of Winthrop and thus leave Captain Wentworth for Louisa herself—if she can get him. A pleasant pastime is actually a calculated move. The Nature we are in is not wild but deeply inhabited, signaling layers of human use. On their way back from Winthrop, the party walk up a long strip of meadowland—the shape of a medieval field. Charles Musgrove whacks with his stick at nettles—another symptom of long human occupation. On the walk, Charles chases a weasel (*mustela*), an enemy to mice, but itself traditionally fought as a threat to grain.

Mary Musgrove (née Elliot) with customary Elliot haughtiness looks down upon her husband's family, disdaining their poorer and more rustic cousins. She wishes neither sister-in-law to connect her further to this inferior family, although Charles Musgrove sensibly argues for the value of cousin Charles Hayter:

> "Please to remember, that he is the eldest son; whenever my uncle dies, he steps into a very pretty property. The estate at Winthrop is not less than two hundred and fifty acres, besides the farm near Taunton, which is some of the best land in the country . . . whenever Winthrop comes into his hands, he will make a different sort of place of it . . . and with that property, he will never be a contemptible man. Good, freehold property." (I, ch. 9)

The path to Winthrop goes across the fields; the party seem to be walking on Musgrove lands and then on Winthrop property. Anne is walking not through "freehold property" but through a poetic landscape. She tries to escape into her own mind. The exchanges between Louisa and Wentworth pierce through and displace the "sweet scenes of autumn . . . unless some tender sonnet, fraught with the apt analogy of the declining year, with . . . the images of youth and hope, and spring, all gone together, blessed her memory" (I, ch. 10). Charlotte Smith's "tender sonnets" indeed describe youth, hope, love, and spring—all gone:

> Another May new buds and flowers shall bring.
> Ah! Why has happiness no second spring?[89]

Austen picks up Smith's phrase. Not many weeks later Anne will begin to feel tugs of hope "that she was to be blessed with a second spring of youth and beauty" (II, ch. 2)

Yet the landscape through which the party walk to Winthrop, no blank but scene of hopeful work, counteracts "poetical despondence":

> After another half mile of gradual ascent through large enclosures, where the ploughs at work, and the fresh-made path spoke the farmer, counteracting the sweets of poetical despondence, and meaning to have spring again, they gained the summit of the most considerable hill, which parted Uppercross and Winthrop, and soon commanded a full view of the latter. . . . Winthrop, without beauty and without dignity, was stretched before them; an indifferent house, standing low, and hemmed in by the barns and buildings of a farm-yard. (*Persuasion,* I, ch. 10)

The food-bearing earth and the uncompromising *thisness* of the farm are reassuring, gifts of highest value. Both Anne and her sister are deflected from this truth, Anne by sorrow and Mary by pride. Mary haughtily refuses to enter the Hayters' low dwelling; Anne finds her a seat "on a dry sunny bank, under the hedge-row." Anne soon hears "Captain Wentworth and Louisa in the hedge-row, behind her, as if making their way back, along the rough, wild sort of channel, down the centre" (I, ch. 10).

The messages that we are getting from Jane Austen's landscape are contradictions of Mary's standards. What we are looking at—looking *down* on—is a very old settlement. Winthrop bears out what is said con-

temptuously in *Sanditon* by the modernizing Mr. Parker: "Our Ancestors, you know, always built in a hole" (ch. 4, *Later Manuscripts,* 427).
In dignity of age, Winthrop can vie with any estate in Austen's oeuvre.
A humble messuage, it has been here since early Saxon times—possibly
long before. The name is Anglo-Saxon, from Old English "Win-thorpe,"
meaning "outlying farmstead of a man named *Win*" or *Wina* (Victory).
"Winthrop" convincingly indicates a settlement and farm predating
the Conquest; a series of houses and outbuildings will have occupied
this space. This Anglo-Saxon farm has no trace of a chase or park devoted to killing game; all is planting and husbandry. The farmyard, the
current assemblage of "barns and buildings," low roofed and modest—
contemptible in Mary Musgrove's eyes—looks like a seventeenth-
century farmstead on a medieval basis. The hedgerow marking a boundary is also old—very old. It is the thick medieval hedgerow with the
path down the center, like the hedgerows near Steventon parsonage.
Winthrop's great hedgerow contains a variety of vegetation, including
hazel trees, an excuse for Louisa to draw Captain Wentworth away "to
try for a gleaning of nuts in an adjoining hedge-row." The hazel trees
are the material source of Wentworth's parable of the nut. Anne is protected by "a bush of low rambling holly"—a plant encouraged as winter
feed for cattle by farmers and husbandmen since medieval times.

The old boundary-marking stone that gives Uppercross its name
likely arrived some centuries after the foundation of Winthrop. Unpretending Winthrop is no mere antique curio, or memorial, or poetic
theme—and never a showplace. It has been "good freehold property"
for a long while. Charles Musgrove is justifiably annoyed at his wife's
devaluing it—but what better could be expected from one reared in
ostentatious Kellynch? The Hayter family of Winthrop is probably
much older than the migrating Elliots, who are really Scots removed
by some generations from their geographic origin. The name "Hayter"
("dweller by a hedge") turns up in England from the thirteenth century
onward. It is a most suitable name for the family connected with the
novel's important hedgerow, itself an installation of centuries' endurance. Place becomes Time. Winthrop tells us that England has endured
and will endure, will be victorious. If we look into Austen's novels for
a place that is the *opposite* of Winthrop, we have two choices, I think—
Maple Grove (with no roots) and Mansfield Park (all "dignity," caught
in Norman dominance and ruthless imparking).

Place names real and imaginary in *Persuasion* combine to remind us
of stress and conflict—even bloodshed—combined with hope for re-

newal through perseverance and the operation of natural forces. But despite reverence for deeply settled Winthrop, the ending frees Anne from settled establishment or stasis. Frederick's new "fortune," some twenty-five thousand pounds, is less than many dowries—only half of what Miss Grey brings Willoughby. With less than two thousand pounds a year, this couple may not purchase a house.[90] Anne in the end has no home—but she has a carriage, the landaulet.[91] Mobility and freedom are the prizes. Anne in finding her freedom traces paths taken before by people rising up in rebellion. She moves across spaces marked by others' bloodshed and despair, even as she moves through time marked by her own quiet despair and loss. She turns toward the real and reunites with a man who has done real things. Mr. Knightley and Captain Wentworth differ from all the other "heroes" of Austen's fiction as they effect changes in the world.

The tribute to the visual arts paid in the novel's hidden joke of the reference to "Charles Hayter" is paralleled by the hidden tribute to the poetic and novelistic art in the novel's use of "Mrs. Smith." The poor friend, sick and enclosed and in some pain, is related by the magic craft of the artist—herself an artificer, a "smith"—to the author of the sonnets that consoled Anne and of the fiction that delighted and instructed the young Jane Austen. Here is a brilliant use of anachronism in a form of doubling. The heroine's crippled friend connects with the dying writer—now dead, but as a novelist and poet still living beyond death, one whom Austen honors. The interval within Mrs. Smith's confining sickroom and the moment of sadness, fresh air and poetic recollection in the fields near Winthrop become one time, one place.

In *Persuasion,* Time and Place are uniquely and strangely united. Place becomes Time, and Time becomes a Place of its own. In extrovert *Emma,* Time is marked by social time, religious festivals and celebrated seasons. In *Persuasion,* Time is multiple, currents flowing at different speeds and rhythms, interbraiding but never lost in total unity. Time is both interior and exterior, running through body, emotions, land, manmade entities and cliffs. Time moves the rocks on which everything appears to stand. Place is where Time crystallizes and becomes visible, seen (briefly) through the transparent plane of individual reality, language, and imagining.

Names and Places in *Sanditon*:
Sussex — Inland and Coast

REAL PLACES IN *SANDITON*

This is the third novel in which Austen uses Sussex for a setting. In *Lady Susan,* the family of Charles Vernon lives in Sussex; in *Sense and Sensibility,* Elinor, Marianne, and Margaret Dashwood, born in Sussex, must move to Devonshire. In both works, Sussex is presented as peaceful, prosperous, and inert. In *Sanditon,* on the contrary, the seacoast of Sussex is jittery, on the make, inflamed by building, advertising, and development fever. Further inland, the Heywood home seems inert, virtuously unalterable to a parodic degree. In the story, people come to Sanditon from as far away as the West Indies, while the Parker sisters scatter their whimsical charity far and wide, to Worcestershire or Burton-on-Trent in Staffordshire. But Sussex remains central, if curiously unsatisfactory. The right man—if and when he appears—may take Charlotte away not only from hectic, unstable Sanditon but also from the stolid, unsociable rural Sussex in which she has been fixed for her first twenty-two years.

Charlotte visits Sanditon to enjoy herself and "with excellent health, to bathe & be better if she could" (ch. 2, *Later Manuscripts*). Sanditon is a mixed destination, like Bath sought by the restless, the sick, and the hypochondriac. Jane Austen herself had become a seeker after health; a sharp attack of an unidentified illness seems to have occurred in 1816, just as she was finishing *Persuasion.* This was probably the beginning of whatever killed her. It may not have been the beginning but a continuation, a dire sequel to an earlier story. The forced move to Southampton at age seven caused Austen's worst juvenile illness. It also probably sowed the seeds of her early death. Linda Robertson Walker has pointed out that typhus can recur and proposes that Austen's last illness was "recrudescent typhus," demonstrating that Jane's symptoms fit the profile.[92] The childhood encounter with a louse in poor lodgings at a seaside town left the seeds of a lurking destruction beneath all the health and dances and long outdoor walks of Austen's prime. It seems ironically fitting that in her last work she should inspect the seaside resort and the reckless, overoptimistic, or fanciful pursuit of perfect wellness. Jane Austen was in a mood to understand the enchantment of a universal panacea:

The Sea Air & Sea Bathing together were . . . a match for every Dis-
order, of the Stomach, the Lungs, or the Blood; They were anti-
spasmodic, anti-pulmonary, anti-sceptic [*sic*] anti-bilious & anti-
rheumatic. Nobody could catch cold by the Sea, Nobody wanted
appetite by the Sea. (*Sanditon,* ch. 2)

Sussex, land of the south Saxons, settled long before the Saxons got
there, boasted commercial ports before Roman times. Its seacoast
was important to its economy. Recently prepared for defense against
a French invasion under Napoleon, that coast was dotted with lookout
points (Martello towers); soldiers had been dispatched to defend ports
and strongholds. Many places mentioned in this unfinished novel are
associated with recent anxieties about invasion. After 1815, government
defense funds dried up; ports and settlements along this seacoast were
turning to what we call the "tourist industry." In references within *Sanditon* to real towns and villages, Austen in effect offers us two categories
(sometimes overlapping): first, a list of places connected with the Norman invasion and recent invasion threats; second, a subtle list of towns
and villages undergoing fresh development as seaside pleasure places.

Mr. Parker insists that Sanditon is different, that it is comparable to
"East Bourne" and one full mile closer to London. Eastbourne, abode of
the comical "Mr. Gell" who married "Miss Gill," was a port, its name indicating "bounded on the east by the stream." Eastbourne would thrive
as a resort in the Victorian era and well into the twentieth century—
despite its pebbly beach. Brighton was Sussex's pleasure resort par excellence. An old coastal settlement in West Sussex is also mentioned,
Worthing (*Weorth* + *ingas,* "family or followers of a man called *Weorth*
or "valiant"). Little Worthing pushed its way steadily into the top list,
assisted by a visit from Princess Amelia in 1798. (The building of Worthing's Park Crescent postdates Austen but is very much in the spirit of
the developments in Sanditon.)[93] Such newly fashionable resorts with
abundant lady visitors might encourage Sir Edward Denham in his
postwar plans for seduction.

The coast of Sussex is known for its historic vulnerability to invasion.
According to the Parkers, "Two hours take us home, from Hailsham"
(ch. 1). The village of Hailsham in East Sussex, an Anglo-Saxon settlement ("Haegel's *ham*") by now site of a livestock market, had recently
been heavily defended against Napoleon. Hailsham Barracks was built
to house soldiers who were to defend coastal fortifications, especially

Pevensey Castle (some six miles from Hailsham and three from East-bourne). Once the invasion threat had gone, Hailsham Barracks were closed, and Hailsham sank back into village life.

The second place name mentioned in *Sanditon* is "Hastings." The Parkers are coming from Tunbridge, the inland spa town in Kent, by now a fading old-fashioned resort. They are traveling "towards that part of the Sussex Coast which lies between Hastings and E. Bourne" (ch. 1). Hastings, prosperous before Roman times, was of old known for iron mines. The Saxon name is *Haestingas,* "Haesta's folk" (*-ingas*). Power-ful Hastings remained a kingdom separate from that of the South Sax-ons, nominally at least, until the eleventh century. The fateful Battle of Hastings took place on 14 October 1066, when the English force encountered the invading Normans. William of Normandy and his men were victorious, killing Harold Godwinson, King of England, and began their rapid takeover of the whole country. As we have seen, Hast-ings was vividly remembered in Jane Austen's time, a memory height-ened by de Loutherbourg's picture. The actual battle took place a few miles north of the little port, at a hill later called "Senlac Hill" (*sangue-lac,* "from the blood there shed"). The monument to victory followed shortly thereafter.

> The Normans, exalted with this victory, erected an Abbey in mem-ory of the Battle, and dedicated it to St. *Martin* (which he [William] call'd *Battle-Abbey,*) in that very place where Harold, after many wounds, died in the midst of his enemies; that it might be an eter-nal monument of the Norman victory.[94]

Battle Abbey—oddly dedicated to peaceable Saint Martin—was to suffer under the Dissolution, and its privilege of sanctuary was eradi-cated "by authority of Parliament." After William's victory, Hastings was fortified with a large Norman castle; amalgamated with Pevensey it become one of the Cinque Ports, the five ports most important to the first Norman kings. Later it underwent eclipse, battered by waves and tides and French incursions. Fishing and smuggling were Hastings's chief industries until its refashioning as a seaside resort once the dan-ger of Napoleonic invasion vanished. Hastings had a population a little over three thousand at the turn of the nineteenth century; the town built new crescents and squares and advertised itself with some success.

Charlotte Heywood lives in an imaginary Willingden, Sussex, near the real Willingden ((also referred to). Feltham calls Willingden "a very pleasant village, about two miles from East Bourne."[95] In *Sanditon*, Mr. Heywood tells the erring Parkers that the Willingden they seek, "Great Willingden, or Willingden Abbots," is seven miles away, "on the other side of Battel." This Willingden bears the term "Abbots" because it once belonged to Battle Abbey. "Battel" (Old French *bataille*) is the site of the now disused Battle Abbey, at or near the battlefield itself. The novel very decidedly reminds us of the Battle of Hastings throughout the first chapter; repeated references introduce us to conflict, danger, and defeat. *Sanditon,* the unfinished novel, refers us to the Norman invasion in ironic counterpoint to its story of the coming of a new age of commercial development—and exciting new possibilities of overthrow.

Camden rejects a popular etymology for the name "Hastings": "Some there are who ridiculously derive it from *Haste,* in our tongue."[96] Austen uses the pun: "Hastings" does suggest "haste"—a leading characteristic of members of the Parker family and a quality of the modern world. The comedy of this meaning does not overrule a floating melancholy. Hastings bears the unhappy reminiscence of defeat. It is a negative interface where the English have to admit the foreign. Not accidentally did Agatha Christie name the original English sidekick for Belgian and French-speaking Hercule Poirot "Hastings," as the site at which the powers of the foreigner make their way into English society. At Hastings for the first and only time the English were truly vanquished. They lost—seriously lost—to an invader. The fact that in the opening scene Mr. and Mrs. Thomas Parker are moving toward Hastings is one of the numerous indications of their future overthrow, which is also immediately enacted through the overturning of their carriage.

IMAGINARY PLACES IN *SANDITON*

Willingden, home of the Heywoods, indicates Anglo-Saxon origin. Possible it merely signifies "well in a valley" (*welle* + *dun*), or "Willowvale,"—or perhaps just "area of the *ingas* of a man called 'Willa.'" Charlotte's native village is one of two "Willingdens." In following up the newspaper advertisement, Mr. Parker should have gone to the other one, the *real* Willingden by Battle Abbey, but Austen creates a double, the false Willingden, abode of the Heywoods. This saucy liberty comments on this novel's willful reflection of reality in a kind of doubling. Everybody here is *will*ful—including the stubbornly realistic but perhaps shortsighted Heywoods. The Heywoods's private "Willingden" is insistently rural—literally pastoral, for Mr. Heywood has a shepherd.

This self-willed lair of pastoralism and hay making seems to question the stable values of the Hayters and Winthrop introduced in the preceding novel. The punning name, "valley of willing," points up a passive-resistant will embodied in the fifty-seven-year-old Mr. Heywood. Mr. Parker exhibits the urgency of a loose but active will believing in its easy power to transform.

The most important and ingenious invented name is "Sanditon" ("sandy" + *tun/ton*), a *tun* built on or by the sand. A sandy beach to boast of had recently become important. Sanditon is a new development, an artificial town whose prosperity is literally to be built on sand. It is an ominous name, if one recollects Christ's parable:

> Therefore whosesoever heareth these sayings of mine, and doeth
>   them, I will liken him
> unto a wise man, which built his house upon a rock.
> And the rain descended, and the floods came, and the winds blew,
>   and beat upon that
> house; and it fell not for it was founded upon a rock.
> And every one that heareth these sayings of mine, and doeth them
>   not, shall be likened
> unto a foolish man, which built his house upon the sand:
> And the rain descended, and the floods came, and the winds blew,
>   and beat upon that
> house: and it fell: and great was the fall of it.
> (King James Version, Matthew 7:24–27)

Sandy foundations can be swept away in a moment. Radical instability and ephemeral life are heralded in this name, as they are in Richardson's "Sandoun" (or sand-dune), estate of Robert Lovelace (invoked in *Sanditon* as a model by Sir Edward). In *Sanditon,* the sand is literal. We may hope, however, for some partial escape from the crash predicted in the first few sentences of the work. The Parkers, "being induced by Business to quit the high road, & attempt a very rough Lane, were overturned in toiling up its long ascent half rock, half sand" (ch. 1). If *half* is rock, then half may endure.

Mr. Parker rushes into advertising language: "Excellent Bathing—fine hard Sand . . . no Mud—no Weeds—no slimey rocks—" (ch. 1). He is trying to counter the bad repute of the Sussex coast, long-standing since Camden in *Britannia* gave a decidedly negative picture of it. (Camden uses the word *atrox*—atrocious.) It lacks good ports and is bad for shipping: "The sea being very dangerous by reason of Shelves and Sands, which make it rough: and the shore also is full of Rocks."[97] Philémon Holland translated and elaborated: "It hath few harbours, by reason that the sea is dangerous for shelves, and therefore rough, and troublous, the shore also it selfe full of rocks, and the South-west wind doth tyrannize thereon, casting up beach infinitely."[98] Mr. Parker, like a good advertiser, counteracts negative propositions before they can be asserted. We are no longer to be concerned with shipping or fishing but with beach culture. In a magical reversal, shelving sands, dangerous to shipping, are now *good*. He emphatically contrasts the good "Sanditon" with the evil "Brinshore," lying "between a stagnant marsh, a bleak Moor & the constant effluvia of a ridge of putrifying Sea weed" (ch. 1). "Brinshore" is a made-up locative, clearly intended to mean "briny-shore," or "saltwater shore."[99] Clearly, Brinshore is to be repudiated, and Sanditon to be embraced. The rocks of the Sussex coast that Camden and his successors observe are a danger to shipping, but Sanditon as pleasure place must rise and fall on sand.

Arriving in Sanditon we find there are several parts to it. The Parkers' own old homestead lies in a valley. "The Church & real village of ["original" crossed out] Sanditon" are at the foot of a hill (*Later Manuscripts,* ch. 4). New Sanditon is on the brow of the hill and the cliff, overlooking the sea. Below this new cliff-top development, on the seashore, there is the sandy bathing place with bathing machines. There is also a small fishing settlement, probably pre-Roman. The description of Sanditon is very close to Feltham's account of Dawlish, which also combines objective description with boosterish delight. Austen seems to have composed her Sanditon not only from her own experience of seaside resorts, especially Dawlish, but also from the style of description in Feltham's admiring *Guide*.

Lady Denham's Sanditon House, inherited from the deceased Mr. Hollis, is halfway up the hill. We enter Lady Denham's property in the last chapter, noting its misty enclosure and the paling's intermittent elms and thorn trees, indicating a park of considerable age. Sir Edward and Clara are overseen in converse, although "Privacy was certainly their object" (ch. 12). Charlotte, an involuntary spy, thinks that as "secret Lovers" they are ill-used. The thick air and the thorns make the place the reverse of attractive as an erotic *pleasaunce*. The house itself, "large & handsome" with old and well-kept furniture, contrasts with the flimsiness of Mr. Parker's abode but feels moribund, harboring images of dead husbands. Edward Denham is "running up a taste-

ful little Cottage Ornèe [*sic*], on a strip of waste Ground lady D[en-
ham] has granted him" (ch. 3). That augments his silliness, but Lady
Denham's domain as a whole seems a kind of "waste Ground." It would
be fun if by some twist of plot the upshot of the financial story made
Miss Lambe the beneficiary of Lady Denham's callously acquired inane
riches. Perhaps the girl does not need to marry—nor unromantic Charlotte either; a commentator at the end of *The Woman of Colour* remarks
to the author "you have not rewarded Olivia even with the usual meed
of virtue—*a husband!*" (*The Woman of Colour,* 189).

Sanditon's new developments are budding into the bourgeois names
fashionable among architects and urban developers. Charlotte sees "a
Prospect House, a Bellevue Cottage, & a Denham Place" (ch. 4). A
"view" or "prospect" has become a kind of property to be marketed.
Lady Denham, however, insists on imposing her own name. Above all,
there is Mr. Parker's pride, the new "short row of smart-looking Houses,
called the Terrace, with a broad walk in front, aspiring to be the Mall
of the Place. In this row were the best Milliner's shop & the Library....
the Hotel & Billiard room" (ch. 4). The Terrace serves as a social and
entertainment center.

Mr. Parker's new residence, we know before meeting it, is windy: he
absurdly boasts, "the Wind meeting with nothing to oppose or con-
fine it around our House, simply rages & passes on" (ch. 4). "Trafalgar House" is "a light elegant Building," its trees too new for shade. It
perches on the highest point, for its sea view, "not an hundred yards
from the brow of the Cliff"—so Austen first wrote, then cut the "not"
and substituted "about" (ch. 4, *Later Manuscripts,* 439). Did the "not,"
foretelling danger, give too much away? This building so light and in-
substantial, like Chaucer's House of Rumour (in Pope's version) is "Per-
vious to Winds, and opens ev'ry way."[100] This vain House of Rumour
may blow down. Or the sandy cliff may crumble, following the landslip
examples of Lyme. There is a strange revising reassurance that the cliff
is "steep, but not very lofty," a fact of importance if the house fell to the
beach. The crash to come may be literal ruination. The view from the
Venetian window enjoyed by Charlotte begins with "the miscellaneous
foreground of unfinished Buildings." Nothing is yet completed.

Mr. Parker comments on the name of his cliff mansion: "which by
the bye, I almost wish I had not named Trafalgar—for Waterloo is more
the thing now. However, Waterloo is in reserve—& if we have encouragement enough this year for a little Crescent to be ventured on . . .
then, we shall be able to call it Waterloo Crescent" (ch. 4). In drawing

the enthusiastic Mr. Parker, Austen picks up what we would term a *virtual* quality to his hobby, speculation and play. In some ways Mr. Parker is like a novelist himself. He lives in fantasy—love in excess. In *Sanditon,* fantasy plays in and through geographical "place" and through the body, itself becoming a fictionalized site. Health and sickness are objects of mental play, folding with uncanny ease into rumor, advertising, and romantic appetite for the immoderate, even to immolation. "Waterloo is in reserve"—yes, indeed. Mr. Parker will undoubtedly meet his Waterloo. England defeated the French in 1815, but the English are going to defeat themselves in an era of bubbles and speculations. The novel is waiting to spin about giddily. It builds up in the reader an appetite for the inevitable crash.

Conclusion

What kind of novelist is Jane Austen? Sir Walter Scott, in his comprehensive review, finds in Austen the virtues and defects of a devout realist. "Instead of the splendid scenes of an imaginary world," Austen offers "a correct and striking representation" of the world as it is, treating "such common occurrences as may have fallen under the observation of most folks." He compares her work to that of the Flemish school of painters—not a very high ranking, as Austen would have known from Reynolds's *Discourses*. Jane Austen, in Scott's view, omits love and romance in favor of calculation, determined to "couple Cupid . . . with calculating prudence," displacing romantic love by "more sordid and more selfish motives."[1] The word "sordid"—important to Frederick Morton Eden—seems to have stuck with Austen after Scott's review. In *Sanditon*, Charlotte is shocked at Lady Denham's meanness and annoyed with herself for politely not disputing the righteousness of the lady's misshapen principles:

> And I am Mean too, in giving her my attention, with the appearance of coinciding with her.—Thus it is, when Rich People are Sordid. (*Sanditon*, ch. 7, *Later Manuscripts*, 486)

Scott had not comprehended—or refused to admit—that this is a "sordid" world. We are all—even young lovers—affected by our own struggle for survival and by our world's assumptions regarding what is correct and successful. Not one of us, not even a heroine, escapes the taint. In various ways we are *persuaded* to conform—as is shown, perhaps in a kind of answer to Scott, in *Persuasion*.

A decade later, Scott saw more in Austen. Rereading *Pride and Prejudice* in 1826, he praises her manner and style:

The Big Bow-wow strain I can do myself like any now going; but the exquisite touch, which renders ordinary commonplace things and characters interesting . . . is denied to me.[2]

His comment fits with Austen's own well-known ironic self-praise, suggesting that *Pride and Prejudice* is "rather too light & bright & sparkling," wanting some intermittent and irrelevant introduction of the "Big Bow-wow strain," masculine stuff such as "a critique on Walter Scott, or the history of Buonaparté" (4 February, 1813; *Letters,* 203). The "exquisite touch" makes Austen a type of Pope's spider: "The Spider's touch, how exquisitely fine, / Feels at each thread, and lives along the line."[3] For Swift, the spider disgustingly epitomizes the modern, spinning "original" material out of her own entrails.[4] Austen, however, certainly turns to the outer world, to which she does not merely submit (as Scott implicitly complains). In acknowledging the external she lets us see more of it (past passions, old causes) than mere staid realism thinks desirable. True, Austen is never content with inner life alone—certainly not with her own inner life. But the sensitivity that links her to each thread of her narrative, and to her own poetics, raises the danger that she will be trapped by others, an exhibit in a glass-walled terrarium of style.

Indeed Austen has at times been caught—trapped and exhibited—as the perfect stylist. D. A. Miller lays out that view:

> Here was a truly out-of-body voice, so stirringly free of what it abhorred as "particularity" or "singularity" that it seemed to come from no enunciator at all. . . .
>
> And in the other constituents of person—not just body, but psyche, history, social position—the voice was also deficient, so much so that its overall impersonality determined a narrative authority and a beauty of expression both without equal. The former, bare of personal specifications that might situate and hence subvert it, rose to absoluteness, while the latter, likewise emptied of self, achieved classic self-containment. No extraneous static encumbered the dictation . . . such thrillingly inhuman utterance was not stylish; it was Style itself.[5]

For Miller, Austen's style is a triumph of absences—and absence of person and specifics. She has whittled herself down to nothing, to "Style itself." A dried husk with but a voice left, she pathetically resembles

Ovid's Echo. Thin and elegant, her work denies the earth and all substance. No wonder she was incapable of "the Big Bow-wow style"! I agree with Claudia Johnson in her repudiation of Miller's characterization of the author as "anorectic."[6]

My own examination of her novels through the names of places and persons has revealed to me a Jane Austen very different from Miller's. She is not general but particular, not abstemious but replete. Rather than austere, she goes perilously close to over the top, muddling deliberately the combinations of elements of her startling particularities. The world may not be quite ready for her surreal and unholy mixtures. The world was not quite ready in 1816 to read *Emma*. Maria Edgeworth, taking her cue from the anorectic Mr. Woodhouse, could see nothing more than chitchat about gruel and couldn't finish her complimentary copy. Assumptions about realism have often got in readers' way, occluding Austen's treatment of angles of vision and the role of assumptions and biases and habits in creating what passes for "reality." Many readers still blame Austen for *Emma*'s notions transmitted through *style indirect libre*. Craving the authoritative narrator, we think we are walking on a solid surface, but we tread unsteadily on crumbling shale or sliding cliff, as in the disconcerting geology of *Persuasion*. Austen reassures us at one level, for she is attentive to the world outside the self. Yet she profoundly questions the procedures and habits by which characters and readers compose individual and social reality. Her attentiveness and questioning are combined, not separable.

In 1993, in the introduction to *Catharine and Other Writings*, I said that Austen in her early works had struck out a new and powerful line of nonrealistic comedy. The contents of the young Austen's three notebooks or "Volumes" had been conventionally looked at, when examined at all, as mere juvenile rehearsals for the recognized six published novels. I felt—and feel—that is the wrong way to read them. I had only G. K. Chesterton to back me up. Introducing *Volume the Second* in 1922 he had praised this freshly discovered Austen as a comic artist in the line of Rabelais and Dickens.[7] I lamented the necessity that had forced the exuberant and tough author to suppress original dynamic talents and produce more soothing and regular courtship novels: "she had to pretend that the world was better and its general fictions more reliable than she knew them to be."[8] Jane Austen's earliest known works defy realism. They deploy the rhetoric and tropes of conventional fiction in order to set narrative on its ear. These early fictions are brilliantly discordant and nonrealistic, sometimes merely parodic but more often pushing through the parodic into the fantastic and splendid. Jane is a mistress of the surreal. Austen, so it seemed to me, had sacrificed a great deal not only of her original humor and wit but of her vision of the world, in order to please the circulating libraries and get published at last.

I have now ceased my lamentations. At that point I had not realized the full magnificence of Austen's achievement. She had not let go of the surreal and fantastic and edgy elements so wonderfully present in the first works. Instead, she combined these elements with the decorum and concerns of the courtship novel. Her daring pretence to be *only* realistic is as good as a masquerade. But Austen used the popular motif of masquerade only once in "Jack and Alice," where the real masquerade is in language. Austen's full style creates a kind of masquerade in which the historical continuities of a pageant are broken up in kaleidoscopic fury. Think of putting an Elizabethan Dudley and Virgilian Camilla together or smashing together such warring atoms as the Whig billionaire Fitzwilliam and the Tory martyr Darcy! How can a murderous Ferrars court a blasphemous and luxurious Dashwood? What Russell could tolerate a Wentworth? And what is Marianne—a nation in need of cure—doing in sprinting down that Devon hill? There is a religious meaning to much of Austen's work, though one hesitates to say this, for that leads to the danger of merely allegorizing Austen. Assertive linear allegory she dislikes and defies. Still, how does a Darcy make his way at last to Gracechurch Street or a pupil of Lady Russell accept the divinity of uncertainty? Does Marianne ever make it to the holy "White well" or the "Abbey land"? Gilpin's multiple *Observations* tell us how to get along without charity by enjoying little thrills of aesthetic enchantment. Austen's narrative won't allow that kind of rapture (so seductive to the young Tilneys). For Austen, history is painful, rather than merely enchanting. Painfully exciting, it is not moribund. It is a continuous present. Austen makes sure that some stones remain for us to trip over. Yet her characters like Elizabeth and Wentworth rush through spaces for affection's deep sake, leaving radiant traces in the air.

Austen's variably textured and multilayered fiction could come into being partly because of the pioneer work of other fiction writers. The women writers of the 1790s, novelists who created historically based imaginary locations, like Bennett's Castel Coed or Smith's Grasmere Abbey, offered complex images of an iridescent historical reality, visible and invisible at once. Jane Austen was thus enabled to cover the ground more rapidly and allusively than her predecessors. Historical allusions

abound in her fiction—they are part of the consciousness of each novel
in itself. Combinations of place names and personal names point both
back and forward. Or rather, references and images are more than just
allusions; we find we are within history all the time. The writing is dense
with allusion, thick with multiple sensations and meanings.

Austen's sense of British history is closely linked to geographical
consciousness. Imaginary but accurate maps form the background of
each novel. The heroine's natal county functions as a distinctive *patria*.
"Places" apparently cannot contain these characters; they are on the
move. Yet in each case the central characters are visibly the products
of their place, as Catherine Morland is recognizably a product of Wiltshire. Austen seems particularly fond of the West Country. Catharine
Percival lives in Devonshire. Catherine Morland is born in Wiltshire,
and Anne Elliot in Somerset. They are natives of Wessex. (Until Hardy
no novelist had done more for Wessex than Austen.) These rural counties are out of the fashion (save for the cultural island of Bath on an edge
of Somerset). The younger, more naive, heroines from Wessex have time
in which to adjust their ideas. Even in Anne Elliot there are touches
of naïveté. South-central England faces outward from the old culturally powerful and historically dominant regions of Kent and Sussex.
Arrogant Kent is represented by Lady Catherine De Bourgh (with her
marital Norman surname of invader and controller), and the confident
South Saxons by the grasping Dashwoods. Elinor and Marianne, however, adopt Devonshire and then Dorsetshire, contradicting the more
conventional move made by Lucy Steele as she moves from coastal
periphery (Dawlish and Plymouth) to the center—to the West End of
wealthy London upon her marriage to Robert Ferrars. The successful
move is traditionally from coast to center, and (even more important)
from north to south—the track of the Elliots all the way from Scotland.
But Darcy returns to the north, and Bingley after a southward swerve
remains true to Yorkshire.

Through the language of names and the language of place, Austen
shows how each person is already shaped by the culture and history of
the birthplace. The English language speaks through us, but it is many
languages, and in one speech different eras drop out of our mouths. English persons contain Celtic, Danish, Saxon, and Norman possibilities
simultaneously. Places also speak, telling of former inhabitants; they are
multiple, made of shifting layers. With one strong exception in Emma
Woodhouse, Austen heroines must change places and are thus engaged
in running up against cultural differences. Counties are like magnets;

they pull—or require—new qualities from you when you get there. These qualities may be good, or they may be unwholesome, even malignant, as in the case of Lady Bertram (née Maria Ward) affected by her dire enclosure within a small area of Northamptonshire.

Anne Elliot recognizes the cultural difference between Kellynch and Uppercross, only three miles away. Elizabeth Bennet runs into cultural difference in her visit to Kent and enforced acquaintance with Rosings. But Darcy also changes places in visiting Netherfield; after his Hertfordshire experience he sees Rosings differently. Frank Churchill believes—or affects to believe—that cultural adjustment means no more than buying gloves at Ford's, which will make him "a true citizen of Highbury" (*Emma,* II, ch. 6). Few characters pretend to adapt so readily. Not only the heroines but other central characters are immigrants or nomads. This is true of Lady Bertram (and thus also of her children), and of Mrs. Norris, Fanny Price, and seafaring William—but also of the Crawfords, Scottish incomers to southern England. Maria and Elizabeth Ward both had great difficulties and are not at ease with a new and different local environment. The Huntingdon peasant lurks within them, haunting the family—a problem Fanny cannot recognize (though she inherits it).

The child Fanny, moved without volition from Portsmouth to Northamptonshire, really has two places to be not at home in. After revisiting (at the will of her uncle) her natal town of Portsmouth, Fanny returns to Northamptonshire; she will remain immobilized within the Mansfield enclosure. Isabella Woodhouse seized her chance to evade Suburbia. She can settle in London, saving herself from being buried in High-*bury,* in a life at home as the caretaker daughter—a mantle that seems to settle over Emma like an invisible cobweb. Elizabeth Bennet is born in cozy southern Hertfordshire, close to London, and threatened as Suburbia; on her marriage she moves north, moving away from and toward modernity in coming to Derbyshire, site of new industrial developments. Darcy belongs to Derbyshire; he seems like a southern gentleman when we first meet him but we are wrong—despite his Kentish ancestral ties. He returns to Derbyshire where Elizabeth must make a new place for herself. Her children will be northern, not southern—as will Jane's Yorkshire-born children by Bingley. The girls' old haunts in Hertfordshire will be largely forgotten.

It is necessary to have a place in which to be—the sensation of "being in place." Austen has memorable description of imaginary spots of earth where that sensation is especially satisfying: Pemberley, Winthrop.

Yet no sooner is one "in place" than "place" changes. Movement happens; other places run toward us. Everything slips, moves, falls through time—has been falling through time: "many a generation must have passed away since the first partial falling off the cliff prepared the ground" (*Persuasion,* I, ch. 11). The transitory makes life fascinating and dangerous. Everyone desires to have meaning in the world, some slender importance, though it may come to nothing more than a plaque on the church wall or a page in the *Baronetage* that will be soon rewritten. Sir Walter's fascination with his meager personal entry in the big book is contemptible but not without pathos. We all yearn to be registered in the Book of Life. Frederick gives voice to this desire when he recalls a near thing:

> "Four-and-twenty hours later, and I should only have been a gallant Captain Wentworth, in a small paragraph at one corner of the newspapers; and being lost in only a sloop, nobody would have thought about me." (*Persuasion,* I, ch. 8)

"Lost in only a sloop"—not where one would be caught dead in, not being in place. Born into a manufactured identity as we all are, Sir Walter knew Kellynch as his place—but forsakes it. He probably will not die there; he will depart this life in lodgings in Bath, like any Mrs. Smith.

We are all haunted without knowing it, but the "ghosts" are a reality within and without. Hartfield is haunted by the memory of an abbey, by recollections of farms—and by Maple Grove, specter of the future. References to actual historic sites and personages in Austen are neither realistic decor nor simple allegories. They pop up suddenly and inexorably, cheekily inviting and not caring about our approval or disapproval— Queen Elizabeth, Barbara Palmer (Duchess of Cleveland), Sarah Churchill, Battle Abbey. As soon as we become conscious of the impish presence of history we become uneasily aware that we are not merely surrounded by but plunged *within* it—within all these tensions and opposing stresses. In a brilliant move of estrangement, William Camden with his categorization by tribes and tribal regions of Britannia had begun to alienate English readers from accustomed acceptance of our place in the world as inevitable and continuous. "Here" is not consoling sameness. What have our tribes been up to? Place has a geographical or "chorographical" plotting of certainty—and a political and social and industrial and even geological uncertainty. So much is man-made, and both Nature and the human-made repeatedly change.

The movements of Austen's characters are credible, and the counties acutely chosen and observed. But while Austen magnificently deploys realism, reinventing it with uncanny scrupulousness in her novels (deceiving even Walter Scott), she is simultaneously setting up allusions and stirring them together to create an underlying surrealism that is all her own. Here victims of Tudor beheadings may play with Civil War victors; Saxon kings and modern courtesans wander through the new shrubbery. Everything shows how (as has been famously said) the past is neither dead nor even past. To be a person is to be caught not in a static ordered station but amid conflicting streams or dancing particles of history and human thought that cannot be still.

Consider the extraordinary world inside the poetic names and images in *Mansfield Park*. Everywhere Austen is a poet, without telling us so. We find a number of dead things: dried rose leaves, amber. A dying king shot with arrows twirls from a branch while the cannon of Napoleonic warships fight in the Mediterranean. Endymion and Cleopatra lie down together. Sugar lurks far beyond the sea, while a ha-ha laughs at an expanse of waste. Tintern Abbey holds its station between a cave in Italy and a moonlight lake in Cumberland. A ball is ordered, and a slave owner cuts his throat in a drawing room. The stars shine still, while Scottish intruders threaten and are threatened. Ravens and crows fly about, as in a "Ravens' shaw," and young men are adorned with dead birds. There are iron gates, golden chains, and a silver knife of discord. Three Ward sisters, three weird sisters, begin a story, the eldest engaging in witchcraft. Lovers' vows are false or stifled. Love is scarce. Outcasts are indeed cast out. A palace of dread must deny the existence of the dreadful—a worse experience than the "Gothic" acknowledgement.

Every novelist enters into competition with history, running—as Samuel Johnson noted of time—against an adversary not subject to casualty. History is a perfect Proteus, shape changing, artful, never quite defeated nor knowable. Austen's invocation of historical realities is her mode of the fantastic. Yet her representation also doubles back on itself to show us that little is actually "fantastic." Life *is* violent and absurd. Silly Catherine Morland believed a general might lock his wife away—but a King of England locks his wife away. An old crime of theft of Church lands for private enjoyment remains unspoken and unrepented. An earl shoots a servant to keep the secret of his abuse of his imprisoned wife—and is hanged for murder. Various particularities roost upon each other. Behind hot roses are carrion birds and witches. The horrible crime committed in a hot climate, the crime of slavery, is unspeakable and yet overt. Within the stones of a dignified Derbyshire mansion there lurks an old memory of a bloodstained scaffold at Tower Hill. We think we can keep the main story—the proper account—cleanly separate from mere *allusion.* But the embodiment of names keeps showing that these are not separate levels, but elements that collapse into one another or are fusing. Each of us living humans is likewise dwelling in a shifting set of allusions to something else.

One of Austen's greatest techniques proves to have nothing to do with interiority, or ease of style—nor even with rational knowledge, or psychological skill. Before they have thought and agency, all characters emerge from Britannia's whirling and colliding histories. They perk into being among and because of phenomena for which they are not individually responsible at all—any more than they are responsible for the English language in which they express their thoughts even to themselves. *Style indirect libre* is not exactly "free." A brilliant device with which to express complex limitation, it lets us in on the limitations of freedom, the comic inadequacy of consciousness trying to make terms with the rest of everything that is.

Where all is moving metaphor, then all is reality. But Austen forbids us to cry "Metaphor!"—For people do not live and die metaphorically. The Bloody Assizes in Taunton are not metaphorical. The most "fantastic" source is the reality we cannot quite take in, that which goes beyond the grasp—or wishes—of written history or of consciousness. Personages in the stories live within intense history. Frederick Wentworth fights Bonaparte's navy—with the memory of Nelson, the fallen hero, to keep him company. And beside and beyond the once unfallen Admiral there is a lovely woman dancing her attitudes in volcanic Napoli, the picture of health. And behind Wentworth—as behind Darcy—are the scaffold and the ax. A queen picks her way across hot plowshares. Suffering is always possible, but suffering itself requires images and memories—and energy. Joy is always possible, but it cannot be separated from facts as hard as the stones beneath the Cobb upon which Louisa fell.

Austen no longer needs the trappings of the "Gothic," for she has made the Gothic her own. She exhibits this in *Northanger Abbey* where she discards the capsule the Gothic first came in. But Austen (who never left off reading "Gothic" fiction) is grateful to the Gothic novelists— as Catherine Morland should be grateful—for teaching what a horror history is and how hard it is to come individually to any decent terms with social life. Austen notices things going wrong. Her favorite Shakespearean character seems in the end to be Cardinal Wolsey, for whom everything went wrong. Where'er we walk she lets us know there are stones, the ruined abbeys poking above the earth. Or there are bones beneath our country lanes and hedgerows, the men who died at Sedgemoor and elsewhere. The earth itself cannot afford to care, any more than it must care that you or I or Jane Fairfax or Anne Elliot—or Jane Austen—may think the last spring has come and gone.

Austen's works are decidedly earthy. She constantly brings us into contact with the earth that sustains us—and into which we shall disappear. Emma Watson and her sister Elizabeth splash along a muddy lane. The damp valleys of the lovely Devonshire hills create muddy roads displeasing to Edward Ferrars. Elizabeth with mud on her petticoats hops over the fields. The earth is always doing something, saying something, offering or removing something. Human beings are forever acting within and on it. In each novel, in different ways, Austen brings us back to our reactions to the earth. She insists on the particularity of each patch, each particular *place*. She senses the underlying "thisness," the "hereness" of land, its generosity and withholding, in the slightest hint of elder buds in February. The need for cultivation of the land, human work with plow or coppicing, with sheep or a few more cows—all this is noted, as is the desecration of sacrificing earth's s human use for the sake of inanely boastful decoration. The insistent presence of the land—this is a deep base melody to her song. Only in her later novels does she acknowledge the tremendous and powerful and bright presence of the sea, but she never loses touch with the land and its hold upon us. This land goes all the way down in the depth of her work, to the bedrock that we come upon at last, rockfalls at Lyme and the sliding sand of Sanditon.

We inherit the earth and the sins of the ancestors—like the Dissolution of the Abbeys. All human arrangements are incomplete and changeful. Our energies seek their "resources" in a more dangerous manner than Mrs. Elton. The energies of our predecessors and contemporaries may leave us in a fine pickle of mayhem. Gross and horrible things manifest themselves repeatedly, and we smooth them over in the history books, as we do the Dissolution or King George I's wife. On the whole Austen is not afraid of the mayhem but castigates the cover-up. At the same time, she doesn't make a Gothic fuss as if we could rid ourselves of human turbulence. That is the foundational error of Sir Thomas Bertram, whose stop-short efforts at repentance do not let him see the sin deep within himself that he cannot banish from Mansfield.

Nobody is separate from the sinners. Emma Woodhouse, "the picture of grown-up health," shares that status with the other Emma, the lowborn and beautiful Emma Lyon, later Hart, later Hamilton, who worked for James Graham's Temple of Health.

Austen's novels do not communicate a sense of people living in a truly settled world—despite our self-assurances that she is gratifying our desire for the peaceful, calm world of a mannerly past. As Mary Favret emphasizes, Austen is living in and describing a world at war. Not only so, the old wars are also still present—the Conquest, the Civil War. Places are products of somebody's gain, and somebody's loss. (Donwell Abbey is the result of a ruthless takeover; Mansfield Park battens on the proceeds of plantations worked by slaves.) Critical readers blithely assume that *The Romance of the Forest* and *The Children of the Abbey* (stories of abuse and displacement) are inferior books because Harriet Smith likes them. A strange reading of Austen's dodgy novel, which centers on the fallibility of assumptions! References to other works of literature, like historical allusions, punning and playful, get into our eyes like grit in the air and disturb our vision. We are partial, prejudiced, and ignorant. The energies of world and thought play through us just the same, while the earth hums and stirs beneath our feet, meaning to have spring again—and meaning to have winter.

Austen has many satiric excellences, but she is not in the *last* analysis a satirist. She does not want to lump up human dreadfulness in a safe container quarantined from love, affection, duty. Happiness and mourning appear together. Names create a poetic fabric of connections and relationships, parallels, parodies and memories. The Dashwood and Ferrars families bear the names of spectacular sinners; they and the Middletons walk over holy ruins. In the names of persons and places (real and imaginary) the author refers us to the work of different generations and tribes who have created names and human "places" in layers of coral-like accretions, leaving lively traces—including traces of distress and violence. Miss Bates wishes to think "good people" always get together (*Emma,* II, ch. 3), but the "good people" may sometimes be malicious, careless, or sordid.

Austen's characters live in time, inscribed by the past and proceeding toward the future. The last two novels (*Persuasion* and *Sanditon*) deal overtly with living in history in the process of formation. The land itself seems to be in formation, with its rock slips, uncannily reflecting or presaging the oncoming interest in fossils and geology associated with

Lyme and nearby regions. Earth is destabilized; everything may fall or tip over or be overset—a young lady jumping off a wall, a gentleman's carriage on a cart track. Certainty is unobtainable. Anne and Frederick at the end of *Persuasion* cannot *know* what will happen to Napoleon, the navy, or themselves. The author knows what happened to Napoleon at Waterloo but knows no more than her heroine what will follow. *Sanditon* (ironically not completed) stretches the exuberance of modern delight in the future. The Parkers are truly modern, in that they live for and in "the future"—but forget that the future is under no contract to be kind to them. The war is over, but wars are still with us. Conquest looms over this narrative.

Sanditon gives us new scenery—rocks, seaweed, shore. Oceans rise in Austen's late works; even Emma gets to the sea at last. The sea itself becomes unignorable in *Mansfield Park, Persuasion,* and *Sanditon.* In *Sanditon* we see something ludicrous in the desire to tame the sea, to subject it to the commands of advertising and the marketplace. How can we ever put a park pale around it? This commercial endeavor somewhat resembles taking over the abbeys, a private appropriation of something immense and complex, God-given and not meant for the presumption of human ownership.

Austen's view of "love" is compassionate and Christian. Love—erotic love—is too near the essence of the human to be idealized or rendered pretty. Put two sinners together—and watch out! A mortal reader put together with a character may go astray. We may, for instance, give way to the normal corruption of our own hearts under the inexpert guidance offered by the prejudiced consciousness of an Emma. Here are topics too big for satire alone, unless it is mere misanthropy. Presumption, "terrible blunders," and misreading are normal. The narrative device known as *style indirect libre,* or "free indirect style"—which Austen developed to such an extent that it dominates English fiction for over two hundred years—is perfect for conveying folly sympathetically. It works partly by making readers themselves fall into folly or wrong belief. The joke may be on us. Observing with the arrogated superiority of Emma or Mr. Knightley, we engage to ourselves (like Mrs. Elton) the right to look down on Harriet Smith. But every "Smith" in Austen is a maker, beating upon the anvil a new possibility. (Willoughby's relative in *Sense and Sensibility* and the crippled former schoolmate in *Persuasion* are salient cases.) Reading *Emma,* we fancy that judgment is the objective, and that we are on the right way to it. But beneath the comedies of "poor little Miss Smith" and her inadequacy—and the uses made of her by Emma and the narrator—there is more, and more gracious, irony still. Emma blunders around in her understanding of love in relation to others and herself. Under her guidance, Harriet blunders too. But Harriet has already encountered Eros and knows true love.

> He had gone three miles round one day, in order to bring her some walnuts, because she had said how fond she was of them—and in every thing else he was so very obliging! He had his shepherd's son into the parlour one night on purpose to sing to her. (*Emma,* I, ch. 4)

We can recognize this—or we can if we are readers like Austen: "here a shepherd's boy piping, as though he should never be old." Behold!— perfect pastoral, the thing itself! These images have been present in literature since the ancient Greeks. Rendered elegantly if apparently artlessly, the ideal is incarnate in Harriet's experience. While Emma and others must struggle and bargain for some love, to Harriet—the character we enjoy looking down on—is given the erotic ideal. Her namesake Harriet Byron, heroine of *Sir Charles Grandison,* went to a masquerade in the "dress of an Arcadian princess."[9] Harriet Smith does not have to dress up for her role. The last shall be first and the first last. Although her status is low in the worldly game of thrones played out in Highbury, in the competition of Eros Harriet has already won. Love, the great prize, is hers, and she is the princess of Arcadia.

NOTES

Chapter One

1. Jo Modert, "Chronology within the Novels," in *The Jane Austen Companion,* ed. J. David Grey, A. Walton Litz, and Brian Southam (New York: Macmillan Publishing Company, 1986), 53–59.

2. Francis Grose, *A Classical Dictionary of the Vulgar Tongue,* 3rd ed. (London: Hooper & Co., 1796), n.p.

3. [Francis Grose], *Lexicon Balatronicum. A Dictionary of Buckish Slang, University Wit, and Pick Pocket Eloquence* (London: C. Chappell, 1811).

4. George Holbert Tucker, *A Goodly Heritage: A History of Jane Austen's Family* (Manchester: Carcanet New Press, 1983), 82.

5. Chesterfield, *Letters Written by the late Right Honourable Philip Dormer Stanhope, Earl of Chesterfield, to his Son.* Published by Mrs. Eugenia Stanhope. 4th ed., 2 vols. (London, J. Dodsley, 1774), 1:559.

6. Alexander Pope, *The Rape of the Lock,* ed. Geoffrey Tillotson, Twickenham ed. (London: Methuen, 1962), Canto iii, line 110, 176.

7. At the end of the century we have *Hooper's New Puzzle Cap: containing a Collection of Riddles, Enigmas, Charades Rebusses . . . Conundrums &c. for the Diversion of Young Ladies and Gentlemen,* and the four-volume *The Masquerade: A Collection of new Enigmas, Logogriphs, Charades, Rebuses, Queries and Transpositions* (Southampton and London, 1797).

8. *Charades &c. Written a Hundred years Ago by Jane Austen and Her Family* (London: Spottiswoode & Co., 1895). In *The Watsons* Jane Watson, rebuking her husband, cites the sartorial example set by "Mr. Marshall and Mr. Hemmings" (*Later Manuscripts,* 124). "Marshall and Hemmings"—a constabulary pair, enforcers of uniformity and restriction. Perhaps Jane Austen did hate hemming.

9. Fielding, *An Apology for the Life of Mrs. Shamela Andrews,* in *Joseph Andrews and Shamela,* ed. Douglas Brooks-Davies, rev. Tom Keymer (Oxford: Oxford World's Classics, 1999), letter 1, 314.

10. Caractacus's speech, if not his own, was an "invention" not of a British but a Roman historian; Tacitus presents it as a model of courage and uncorrupted honor.

11. D. W. Harding, "Character and Caricature in Jane Austen," in *Critical Essays on Jane Austen,* ed. B. C. Southam (London: Routledge & Kegan Paul, 1968), 83–105.

12. John Mullan, *What Matters in Jane Austen? Twenty Crucial Puzzles Solved* (London: Bloomsbury Press, 2012), 3.

13. Ibid., 132–46.

Chapter Two

1. Ann Radcliffe, *A Journey made in the Summer of 1794, through Holland and the Western Frontier of Germany, with a Return down the Rhine, to which are added Observations during a Tour to the Lakes . . .*, 2nd ed., 2 vols. (London: G. G. and J. Robinson, 1795), 2:36–37.

2. "The Names of the English Saxons," in Camden-Gibson *Britannia* (1753), clxix–clxx.

3. Linda Colley, *Britons: Forging the Nation, 1707–1837,* rev. ed. (New Haven CT: Yale University Press, 2009), 14.

4. Recently banned, foxhunting remained a sign of status. It was always expensive, requiring highbred horses capable of jumps. The high social place given to deer hunting in Scotland through the twentieth century is registered in the film *The Queen,* and series 3 of *Downton Abbey.*

5. See E. P. Thompson, *Whigs and Hunters: The Origin of the Black Act* (London: Allen Lane, 1975). The severe laws against poaching in an Act of Parliament known as the "Black Act" were "occasioned directly by an episode of bloodshed in Windsor Forest on 9 April 1723" (69). Four men were executed for murder. Authorities had hoped to turn the trial of poachers into a trial for sedition but had to fall back on "the old sin of deer stealing" for which six men were transported. The "Black Act" (passed before the trial) made deer stealing a capital offense and turned many offenses into major felonies, including maiming cattle and cutting trees. The "Black Act" renewed objections to the "Norman yoke."

6. David Hume, *The History of England from the Invasion of Julius Caesar to The Revolution in 1688,* 8 vols. (London: A. Millar and T. Cadell, 1767), 1:247.

7. Philippe Jacques de Loutherbourg (1740–1812), scene painter and innovator of lighting effects at Drury Lane Theatre, was one of the artists commissioned by Robert Bowyer to paint a series of pictures for a special edition of Hume's *History.* Artworks were displayed in Bowyer's "Historic Gallery" at 82 Pall Mall. *The Battle of Hastings,* exhibited in 1804, appeared as engraved illustration to the first volume of Hume's *History.* Copies of engravings could be purchased separately.

8. Footmen are a remnant of an older power structure. The strength of a feudal lord was measured in the retinue of young males whom he could command (originally for service as a private army).

9. Devoney Looser, *British Women Writers and the Writing of History, 1670–1820* (Baltimore, MD: Johns Hopkins University Press, 2005), 190.

10. Charlotte Smith, *Desmond,* ed. Antje Blank and Janet Todd (Peterborough, ON: Broadview Press, 2001), 90–99.

11. William Gilpin, *Observations Relative Chiefly to Picturesque Beauty, made in the Year 1773, On several Parts of ENGLAND; Particularly the Mountains and Lakes of Cumberland and Westmoreland,* 2 vols. (London: R. Blamire, 1786), 1:12.

12. Gilpin, *Observations on the River Wye, and Several Parts of South Wales &c. Relative chiefly to Picturesque Beauty made in the Summer of the Year 1770* (London: R. Blamire, 1782), 35.

13. Gilpin, *Observations on the Western Parts of England, Relative chiefly to Picturesque Beauty.* (London: T. Cadell and W. Davies, 1798), 138–39.

Chapter Three

1. Tucker, *Goodly Heritage,* 56.

2. Colonel Pride and his troopers stood at the door of Parliament, admitting no MP who had not indicated that he would vote for the death of the king. "Pride's Purge" supports the royalist claim that the "trial" was totally illegal.

3. Information is offered in Alton's church, where the bronze memorial to Colonel Boles with commemorative verse is visible. Written histories rely largely on William Curtis's *History of Alton* (1896).

4. Monmouth's first attempt is the subject of John Dryden's *Absalom and Achitophel.* This poem failed in its primary objective, which was to have Shaftesbury executed for treason.

5. Samuel Johnson, *A Journey to the Western Islands of Scotland* (London: J. Pope, 1775), 104.

6. Claudia L. Johnson, *Women, Politics and the Novel* (Chicago: University of Chicago Press, 1988); see especially ch. 1, "The Novel of Crisis."

7. Hester Lynch Piozzi, *Anecdotes of the late Samuel Johnson, LL.D. During the last Twenty Years of His Life,* 2nd ed. (London: T. Cadell, 1786), 84.

8. Frederick Morton Eden, *The State of the Poor; or, The History of the Labouring Classes in England,* 3 vols. (London: J. Davis, 1797), 1:451.

9. "Alton Association" large handbill or poster, 1809 ("Pinnock, Printer, Alton"); copy supplied by Jane Hurst of Curtis Museum, Alton, Hants.

Chapter Four

1. Lawrence Sterne, *The Life and Opinions of Tristram Shandy, Gentleman,* ed. Melvyn and Joan New (London: Penguin Books, 2003), vol. 1, ch. 19, 47.

2. Alastair Fowler, *Literary Names: Personal Names in English Literature* (Oxford: Oxford University Press, 2012), 2.

3. Only recently under the pressure of immigration did France drop its list of acceptable first names.

4. According to William Camden; see *Remains concerning Britain,* ed. Leslie Dunking (Wakefield, Yorkshire: EP Publishing Ltd., 1974), 105.

5. Ibid., 58; cited also in Fowler, *Literary Names.*

6. Victoria Huxley, *Jane Austen and Adlestrop: Her Other Family* (Adlestrop, Gloucestershire: Windrush Publishing, 2013), 34–35.

7. In fiction the name is appropriate to low, conniving characters, like Fielding's "Peter Pounce."

8. Cassandra Cooke (unusually) deals with King Kenneth of Scotland in *Battle-*

ridge, perhaps an indication that the author had Scots ancestors. See *Battleridge: An Historical Tale, Founded on Facts.* By a Lady of Quality. 2 vols. (London: G. Cawthorn et al., 1799).

9. "Taffy," a derisive nickname for a Welsh person, derives from the Welsh pronunciation of "David"—as in the abusive rhyme beginning "Taffy was a Welshman, Taffy was a thief."

10. Park Honan argues that Mary is partly inspired by Gray's poem "A Long Story." The poet is summoned to the ancient great house for a trial attended by "ghostly prudes" astonished by the modern Viscountess's kindness to the poet. One exclaims, "Madam Bridget, / Why, what can the Viscountess mean?" and notes "the times are alter'd quite." (Park Honan, *Jane Austen: Her Life* [New York, NY: St. Martin's Press, 1987], 340.) That the apparitions "in peaked hoods and mantles tarnish'd," once "garnish'd / The drawing room of fierce Queen Mary!" makes clear the Catholicism of the ghosts.

11. Camden equates the name "with Agricola"; *Remains,* 80.

12. Ibid., 107.

13. Napoleon Bonaparte, a fan of Ossian, asked by his former fiancée Désirée in 1799 to name her baby, named the infant Count Bernadotte, "Oscar." That baby became King Oscar I of Sweden. All modern Oscars come from the tradition of Ossian, including Oscar Wilde—and Hollywood's film prize.

14. Ibid., 109, 56.

15. Maggie Lane, *Jane Austen and Names* (Bristol: Blaise Books, 2002), 23.

16. Camden, *Remains,* 101.

17. Ibid., 57.

18. George Austen, letter of 17 December 1775, *Family Record,* 30; Nokes, *Life,* 51.

19. Maggie Lane is not quite right in indicating that Emma never uses the respect form regarding Harriet, but absolutely right in noting that in private conversations Emma speaks to "Harriet" while Harriet uses the respectful form "of someone addressing a superior." See Lane, *Names,* 35.

20. Ibid., 33.

21. See note by Claudia L. Johnson and Susan J. Wolfson to Longman edition of *Pride and Prejudice* (I, ch. 8) (New York: Pearson Education Inc., 2003), 42.

Chapter Five

1. Tom Keymer, "Rank," in *Jane Austen in Context,* ed. Janet Todd (Cambridge: Cambridge University Press, 2007), 387–96; 387.

2. Samuel Richardson, *Pamela; or, Virtue Rewarded. In a Series of Familiar Letters to her Parents: And afterwards, In her Exalted Condition,* 3rd ed., 4 vols. (London: Printed for S. Richardson, 1742), 3:207.

3. Keymer, "Rank," 391.

4. Ibid.

5. Austen does not use "Dame" in her adult fiction, perhaps considering it too old-fashioned, even demeaning. In the twentieth century the British government chose "Dame" as the suitable title of honor for a woman.

6. Taken from Nicholas Harris Nicolas, *The Dispatches and Letters of Lord Admiral Nelson* (1846), as cited in Roger Knight, *The Pursuit of Victory: The Life and Achievement of Horatio Nelson* (New York: Basic Books, 2005), 518.

7. Tobias Smollett treats the story of the "Annesley Claimant" at length in *The Adventures of Peregrine Pickle,* 4 vols. (London; Printed for the Author, sold by D. Wilson, 1751). Smollett warmly espouses the case of the Claimant: "The hapless youth had not any relative alive . . . whose interest it was not to connive at his destruction" (4:213).

8. Francis Grose, *Dictionary of the Vulgar Tongue,* 3rd edition (London: Hooper & Co., 1796); see under "NOK" (n.p.).

9. See my *A Natural Passion: A Study of the Novels of Samuel Richardson* (Oxford: Clarendon Press, 1974), 249–51.

10. Donald J. Greene, "Jane Austen and the Peerage," originally in *PMLA* 68, no. 5 (1953): 1017–31, as reprinted in *Jane Austen: A Collection of Critical Essays,* ed. Ian Watt (Englewood Cliffs, NJ: Prentice-Hall, 1963), 155.

11. Donald Greene, "The Original of Pemberley," first published in the first issue of *Eighteenth-Century Fiction* (1968): 1–23, as reprinted in *The Selected Essays of Donald Greene,* ed. Lawrence Abbott (Lewisburg, PA: Bucknell University Press, 2004), 322.

12. Elizabeth Jenkins, "The Marriage Registers at Steventon," *Collected Reports of the Jane Austen Society* (1965): 294–95.

13. Claire Tomalin remarks on Jane's imagining a "Jack Smith" as bridegroom "one would like to know more about that particular dream." *Jane Austen: A Life* (New York, NY: Vintage Books, 1999), 77.

14. The surname turns up in contemporary fiction. Agnes Maria Bennet's "Percival Evelyn" is the rather shy beloved of the heroine of *Ellen of Castle Howel* (1794).

15. James Boswell, *Life of Johnson,* ed. R. W. Chapman and J. D. Fleeman with an introduction by Pat Rogers, World's Classics (Oxford and New York: Oxford University Press, 2008), 188.

16. Janine Barchas, *Matters of Fact in Jane Austen* (Baltimore, MD: Johns Hopkins University Press, 2012), 44–49; I also benefited from Professor Barchas's illustrated talk at the ASECS annual meeting in Vancouver, March 2011.

17. Barchas, *Matters of Fact,* 256–57.

18. *Further Memories of the Whig Party 1807–1821. With some Miscellaneous Reminiscences by Henry Richard Vassall, Third Lord Holland,* ed. Lord Stavordale (London: John Murray, 1905), 256.

Chapter Six

1. Barchas, "Artistic Names in Austen's Fiction: Cameo Appearances by Prominent Painters," *Persuasions* 31 (2009): 145–62.

2. Barchas, *Matters of Fact,* 57–68.

3. Camden, *Remains,* 67.

4. Alexander Pope, *Dunciad* (1744), Twickenham ed., Book IV, line 90, 755.

5. Barchas, *Matters of Fact,* 116–17.

6. Ibid., 103–4.

7. Mary Robinson, *Angelina*, 3 vols. (London: Hookham and Carpenter, 1796), 1:147.

8. Camden, *Remains*, 79.

9. Barchas, *Matters of Fact*, 170.

10. Delarivier Manley lived with Barbara Villiers after leaving her own husband but was expelled from the household for flirting with the duchess's son.

11. Tucker, *Goodly Heritage*, 60; Barchas, *Matters of Fact*, 163.

12. The scene in the third volume of *Celestina* is the reverse of the situation in *S&S;* Willoughby, weakened by illness, is shocked to see at a party the woman he loves with another man. "Mortified tenderness" afflicts him at the moment when Celestina catches sight of him: "the well known figure, the well known face of Willoughby, emaciated and pale as they were, instantly struck her." (*Celestina*, ed. Lorraine Fletcher [Peterborough, ON: Broadview Books, 2004], 374–75.) Lorraine Fletcher comments on the relation of the two novels in a section of her "Introduction," 38–42.

13. Barchas, *Matters of Fact*, 202–4.

14. Peter Sabor in annotating *Pamela* said that Mr. B. is "Mr. Brandon" if his house is "Brandon Hall"; Jocelyn Harris suggests Austen "may have commandeered Mr. B's new name for Colonel Brandon." *Jane Austen's Art of Memory* (Cambridge: Cambridge University Press, 1989), 37.

15. Patrick Parrinder, *Nation and Novel: The English Novel from Its Origins to the Present Day* (Oxford: Oxford University Press, 2006), 91.

16. Barchas suggests a link with the Duke of Suffolk in *Matters of Fact*, 164–65.

17. Hume, *History*, 1767 ed., vol. 4, ch. 33 (under "1546"), 276.

18. Austen Papers, cited by Tucker, *Goodly Heritage*, 66.

19. Harris, *Art of Memory*, 48.

20. Pope, *The Rape of the Lock*, Twickenham ed., Canto iii, lines 177–78, 232. Critics have observed a play upon *The Rape of the Lock* in *S&S*. See Jocelyn Harris, *Art of Memory*, 63. Edward Copeland notes "the rich erotic subtexts" of Pope's poem in the scene where Willoughby cuts Marianne's lock, commenting that Belinda's "screams of horror" are "heard only later" from Marianne (Cambridge ed., 454).

21. E. E. Duncan-Jones, *The Times Literary Supplement*, 10 September 1964, and elaborated on by Harris in *Art of Memory*, 54.

22. Jane West, *A Gossip's Story*, 2nd ed., 2 vols. (London: T. N. Longman, 1797), vol. 1, ch. 14, 185. Critics like A. Walton Litz have recognized this parallel in West but treat West dismissively. The description of the dull house and run-down district to which the elder sister and her father move is a triumph of socioeconomic observation.

23. West, *Gossip's Story*, vol. 1, ch. 15, 190.

24. Each of these novelists sees the positive side of her Marianne's aspirations and outlook; the antiquated snobbery of Marianne Dudley's mother-in-law Lady Clermont is neither the girl's fault nor that of the French Revolution. West offers more complexity and liveliness than she is usually given credit for. A perennial problem within Austen criticism is the desire to look down on all female writers of the period who are not Austen.

25. See Maurice Agulhon, *Marianne au combat: L'imagerie et la symbolique républicaines de 1789 à 1880* (Paris: Flammarion, 1979); also as *Marianne into Battle: Republican Imagery and symbolism in France, 1789–1880*, trans. Janet Lloyd (Cambridge: Cambridge University Press, 1981). Website (*Site Officiel*) of Puy Laurens gives the Occitan text with translation into modern French.

26. Camden-Gough, *Britannia*, 1:223.

27. "Great store of plate, both gold and silver, much money, and many jewels of great value, were found deposited by Hubert in the Temple." Edward Hasted, *The History and Topographical Survey of the County of Kent. Containing the Antient and Present State of it*, 2nd ed., 12 vols. (Canterbury: W. Bristow, 1797), 1:140.

28. Camden-Gough, 3:44.

29. Regina Maria Roche, *Children of the Abbey*, 4 vols. (London: William Lane for Minerva Press, 1796), 2:27–29.

30. Katherine Philips's husband, however, was a leading Puritan republican, a "regicide" who voted for the execution of Charles I.

31. Mary Robinson, *The Natural Daughter*, in *A Letter to the Women of England and the Natural Daughter*, ed. Sharon M. Setzer (Peterborough, ON: Broadview Press, 2003), ch. 14, 133–34.

32. [Susannah Minifie Gunning], *Barford Abbey*, 2 vols. (London: T. Cadell, 1768), 1.21–22.

33. Amanda Foreman's biography of Georgiana Spencer, Duchess of Devonshire, was the basis of the film *The Duchess* (2008).

34. The dismal prognosis for Anne De Bourgh has largely escaped comment. In P. D. James's sequel, *Death Comes to Pemberley* (2011), Anne is already dead.

35. John Dryden, *Alexander's Feast; or, The Power of Musique* (1697), lines. 96–97, in *Poems and Fables*, ed. James Kinsley (Oxford: Oxford University Press, 1962), 507. The poem remained popular as song in its setting by Handel.

36. Mary Waldron, *Jane Austen and the Fiction of Her Time* (Cambridge: Cambridge University Press, 1999), 52.

Chapter Seven

1. Tobias Smollett, *The Expedition of Humphry Clinker*, 2nd ed., 3 vols. (London: W. Johnston, 1772), 3:105. See Tara Ghoshal Wallace, *Imperial Characters: Home and Periphery in Eighteenth-Century Literature* (Lewisburg, PA: Bucknell University Press, 2010).

2. Adam Nicolson, "Dominance: The Lascelles," in *The Gentry: Stories of the English* (London: Harper Press, 2011), 211–41.

3. Ibid., 240.

4. Camden-Gibson, *Britannia*, 2:443.

5. Peter Knox-Shaw, *Jane Austen and the Enlightenment* (Cambridge: Cambridge University Press, 2004), 180. Frank Gibbon first made the link in his important article "The Antiguan Connection: Some New Light on *Mansfield Park*," *Cambridge Quarterly* 12 (1982): 298–305.

6. Moira Ferguson, "*Mansfield Park*: Slavery, Colonialism and Gender," *Oxford Literary Review* 13 (July 1991): 118–39.

7. John Norris is read by Clarissa Harlowe and Anna Howe in Richardson's *Clarissa.*

8. Camden-Gough, *Britannia.*

9. Not all connotations are unfavorable. A virtuous young naval officer named "Lieutenant Stornaway" in *Emmeline* cares for a sick wife; stranded in France he is rescued by helpful Godolphin.

10. Hence the Cam was called "Granta" (the name "Grantabrigga" mutated into "Cambridge").

11. Barbara K. Seeber uses this and other references to illustrate Austen's critique of field sports, connecting killing of birds and animals with masculine mastery of women, lands, plantations, and slaves. *Jane Austen and Animals* (Farnham, Surrey: Ashgate Publishing Co., 2013).

12. *Delphine* regrets the betrayal of the Revolution and looks for the renewal of ideals. The character Sophie de Vernon subtly illustrates the evils of the ancien régime. *Delphine* achieved instant fame when an infuriated Napoleon immediately exiled Mme de Staël. If Austen's novella is (as I firmly believe) an experiment inspired by *Delphine,* that makes the date of composition consonant with the watermarked paper dated 1805 found in the fair copy.

13. Henry Austen (by now in his clergyman phase) tells us that Jane Austen once turned down a London dinner invitation on hearing that Mme de Staël was to be present (Henry Austen, "Memoir of Miss Austen," *Memoir,* 149–50). The refusal might have resulted less from Austen's own wish than from the kind of pressure earlier put upon Frances Burney to put an end to association with the immoral Mme de Staël. See Doody, *Frances Burney: The Life in the Works,* (New Brunswick, NJ: Rutgers University Press, 1988), 199–200. Burney complied but grumbled "I wish the World would take more care of itself and less of its neighbors."

14. Germaine de Staël, *Delphine,* trans. Avriel H. Goldberger (De Kalb, IL: Northern Illinois University Press, 1995), letter 6, 18.

15. Ibid., letter 41, 171.

16. Ibid., letter 43, 187.

17. In *Jane Eyre,* Rochester occasionally uses "Janet" affectionately for "Jane." But "Janet" would not be an acceptable name for a truly English lady.

18. Sales, *Jane Austen and Representations of Regency England* (London: Routledge, 1996); see especially ch. 4, *"Mansfield Park:* The Regency Crisis and the Theatre," 87–131.

19. Victoria Huxley, *Jane Austen and Adlestrop,* 46–50; *Letters,* letter of 12–13 May 1801, 85.

20. See Lane, *Names,* 16.

21. St. Edmund Hall, Oxford ("Teddy Hall") is named for a different and lesser English saint, an Oxford-educated Edmund who became archbishop of Canterbury. The big "Saint Edmund" is the martyred king.

22. Camden-Gibson, 1:450.

23. Edmund Gibson, *Family-Devotion; or, An Exhortation to Morning and Evening Prayer in Families,* 18th ed. (London: E. Owen and W. Johnson, 1750), 14.

24. Margaret Kirkham notes the following surnames in *Emma* found in the

social columns of the *Bath Journal,* 1801–2, when Austen was in Bath: "Knight-ley," "Cole," "Campbell," "Perry." See Kirkham, *Jane Austen: Feminism and Fiction* (Brighton: Harvester Press, Ltd.; Totowa, NJ: Barnes and Noble Books, 1983), 139–40.

25. Laurie Kaplan refers to Colleen A. Sheehan's suggestion that "two of the teachers at Mrs. Goddard's school—'Miss Nash' and 'Miss Prince'—refer to two of the Prince's paramours, by whom he may have had illegitimate offspring" (Kaplan, "*Emma* and 'the Children in Brunswick Square,'" *Persuasions* 31 [2009]: 238).

26. The song "The Campbells Are Coming" was composed in 1715 for an occa-sion when the Campbells under the Earl of Mar were fighting the English.

27. Samuel Richardson, *Pamela; or, Virtue Rewarded. In a Series of Familiar Letters to her Parents: And afterwards, In her Exalted Condition,* 4 vols. (London: Printed for S. Richardson, 1742), 4:341.

28. Charlotte Brontë may have responded more favorably to Austen than she lets on in her indignant letter to G. H. Lewes. Jane Fairfax's predicament under Mrs. Elton's pressure to take a job may be recollected when Mr. Rochester assures Jane Eyre that he has found a good position for her as a governess undertaking "the education of the five daughters of Mrs. Dionysius O'Gall of Bitternutt Lodge, Con-naught, Ireland." He adds, "You'll like Ireland, I think: they're such warm-hearted people there, they say." *Jane Eyre,* ed. Margaret Smith (Oxford: World's Classics, 2000), vol. 2, ch. 8, 251.

29. Barchas, *Matters of Fact,* 3–4.

30. Catherine Bailey has traced the ugly story of coal mining and the Wood-houses in the nineteenth and twentieth century in *Black Diamonds: The Rise and Fall of an English Dynasty* (London: Viking Penguin, 2007). In 1842 Commissioners reported on abuse of children and women in their mines throughout Yorkshire.

31. Grant Holly, "*Emma*grammatology," *Studies in Eighteenth-Century Culture* 19 (Lansing, MI: Colleagues Press Inc., 1989): 39–51.

32. Samuel Richardson, *Clarissa,* 3rd ed., AMS rpt., 7 vols. (New York: AMS Press, 1990), vol. 1, letter 36, 238.

33. Jocelyn Harris, *Art of Memory,* 169–87.

34. Janine Barchas observes this also; see *Matters of Fact,* 53.

35. Roche, *Children of the Abbey,* vol. 2, ch. 24, 117.

36. Ibid., 121–22.

37. In the twentieth and twenty-first centuries St. Martin-in-the-Fields, con-scious of its patron saint and its mission to the poor, has been a center for the Lon-don homeless.

38. Alban Butler, *The Lives of the Fathers, Martyrs, and Other Principal Saints: Compiled from Original Monuments, and other Authentick Records,* 4 vols. (London: no printer, 1756), 1:616. The "Life of St Martin" is based on the traditional account by Sulpicius Severus.

39. Butler, *Lives,* 4:630.

40. Stafford, "Introduction," in *Emma* (London: Penguin Books, 2008), xiii.

41. Cavendish's *Life of Wolsey* and the Wyatt poem are both quoted in the Weston *ODNB* entry.

42. Francis Weston appears as a character in Hillary Mantel's *Bring Up the Bodies* (2012).

43. Cassandra Cooke, *Battleridge,* vol. 1, ch. 6, 89.

44. Lane, *Names,* 13.

45. Camden notes that she was also called by the Saxon name Elgiva ("help-giver"); *Remains,* 102.

46. Smollett, *A Complete History of England,* 4 vols. (London: Rivington and Fletcher, 1757–58), vol. 1, book 1, 191–92.

47. Hume, *History of England,* 1:173.

48. David V. Erdman, *Blake; Prophet against Empire,* 3rd ed. (Mineola, NY: Dover Publications, 2010), 46–47. Blake painted a historical series indicting the tyranny of Earl Goodwin and King Edward.

49. Cornelia Knight, *Autobiography* (first published 1861), quoted in Roger Knight's *The Pursuit of Victory: The Life and Achievement of Horatio Nelson* (New York: Basic Books, 2005), 310.

50. Scott's review article (*Quarterly Review* 14 [October 1815]) is not only a re-view of *Emma* but of Austen's work to date, with the singular omission of *Mansfield Park.*

51. Tucker, *A Goodly Heritage,* 53.

52. *Life and Letters of Sir Gilbert Elliot,* letter of November 1792; 2:73.

53. Jocelyn Harris, *A Revolution Almost beyond Expression* (Newark: University of Delaware Press, 2007), 224n88.

54. Barchas, *Matters of Fact,* 252–53.

55. Noted also by Jocelyn Harris, *Revolution,* 224.

56. Richardson, *Clarissa,* 3rd ed. rpt., 7 vols., 7:305–6.

57. Barchas, *Matters of Fact,* 242.

58. Smith, *Emmeline,* ed. Lorraine Fletcher, vol. 1, ch. 13, 116–17.

59. This north Midlands name also provides the title of John Parker, new Earl of Morley.

60. Mary Wollstonecraft, *A Vindication of the Rights of Woman* (1792), ch. 4, ed. Miriam Brody (London: Penguin Classics, 1992), 150.

61. Was Arthur Conan Doyle affected by *Persuasion* when in 1893 he named his thickheaded family of loyalists in "The Adventure of the Musgrave Ritual"?

62. Mary Favret, *War at a Distance: Romanticism and the Making of Modern Wartime* (Princeton, NJ: Princeton University Press, 2010), 169.

63. Originally painted for Benwick's former love, Benwick's miniature is to be "properly set" for his new fiancée, Louisa. Barchas suggests "the need for a new setting hints at a possible inscription or enclosure meant for Fanny"; perhaps "a similar portrait of Fanny Harville . . . survives still among the captain's things." Janine Barchas, "Artistic Names," *Persuasions* 31 (2009): 157–58.

64. Charles Hayter, *An Introduction to Perspective, Adapted to the Capacities of Youth, In a Series of Pleasing and Familiar Dialogues between the Author's Children. By Mr. Hayter, Portrait Painter* (London: Printed for the Author, and sold by Black, Perry & Co. et al., 1813), 152.

65. Ibid., 157.

66. Ibid., 11.

67. Ibid., 3.

68. See Douglas Murray on *looking* in Austen's fiction, "Gazing and Avoiding the Gaze," in *Jane Austen's Business,* ed. Juliet McMaster and Bruce Stovel (New York: St. Martin's Press, 1996), 42–53.

69. Prints of Raphael's much-admired Hampton Court Cartoons were widely available. Mark Twain in *A Connecticut Yankee in King Arthur's Court* makes fun of the fishing disciples' picture on grounds similar to those of Croft's critique of the print he is looking at—absence of realism and lack of perspective.

70. Joshua Reynolds, *The Works of Sir Joshua Reynolds, Knight; Late President of the Royal Academy*, 2nd ed., 3 vols. (London: T. Cadell Jun. and W. Davies, 1798), "Discourse I," 1:85. Reynolds gave an annual "Discourse" to students and colleagues of the Royal Academy.

71. Favret, *War at a Distance*, 162.

72. Smith, *Elegiac Sonnets,* 7th ed. (London: A. Strahan for T. Cadell, 1795).

73. "He has his Winter too of pale misfeature, / Or else he would forego his mortal nature"; "The Human Seasons," lines 13–14, *John Keats: The Complete Poems*, ed. John Barnard (London: Penguin Books, 1988), 232.

74. Charlotte Smith, "Preface," in *Marchmont,* 4 vols. (London: Sampson Low, 1796) 1:xi, viii.

75. Harris, *A Revolution*, 77.

76. The repetition was too much for the 1995 BBC film dramatization. Hayter's name was changed to "Henry"—also awkward, as "Henrietta" is its feminine form.

77. Harris, *Revolution*, 146.

78. Jesse Foot, *The Life of Arthur Murphy* (London: J. Faulder for John Nichols & Son, 1811), 188. Foot, a surgeon, wrote works in support of plantation owners; his works were likely to be found in great houses.

79. Happily freed of his first wife by divorce in 1809, John Parker married the beautiful Frances Talbot. Upon her husband's elevation, Frances Parker of Saltram became a countess—the same Countess of Morley (her title still fresh) who wrote a charming response to her complimentary copy of *Emma.* Austen was not to know that the countess thought this novel inferior to its predecessors, as she told her sister-in-law (Nokes, *Life,* 479).

80. See note to "Morley" by Deirdre LeFaye, *Letters,* 557. By 1820 Rev. Henry Austen was domestic chaplain to the Earl of Morley (Tucker, *Goodly Heritage*, 147).

81. See Ronald Fletcher, *The Parkers at Saltram, 1769–89: Everyday Life in an Eighteenth-Century House* (London: BBC Books, 1970); this book accompanies a documentary.

82. Uncle Leigh-Perrot had to pay ten thousand pounds and Edward Knight twenty thousand pounds toward a suretyship; the other brothers had to pay some hundreds. Jane Austen herself lost just under twenty-six pounds kept in the Austen bank—recent proceeds from the novels (Deirdre LeFaye, *JAAFR*, 234). The family insisted that no breach was made by this debacle, but it is impossible to believe that there was no resentment or stress. Jane Austen's sudden loss of health has been related to the shock of this failure. Henry was officially declared bankrupt on 23 March 1816.

83. D. A. Miller, *Jane Austen; or, The Secret of Style* (Princeton, NJ: Princeton University Press, 2003), 89–90.

84. Anonymous, *The Woman of Colour* (1808), ed. Lyndon J. Dominique (Peterborough, ON: Broadview Press, 2008), 71.

85. Anna Laetitia Barbauld produced in 1804 an edition of Samuel Richardson's correspondence with a prefatory essay. In 1810 her great collection of *British Novelists* included an important prefatory essay "On the Origin and Progress of Novel-Writing."

86. Austen probably noticed Barbauld's contention in "On the Origin and Progress of Novel-Writing" that by the late eighteenth century the power of novel writing had passed to women writers.

87. Burney, *Camilla; or, A Picture of Youth*, ed. Edward A. Bloom and Lillian D. Bloom (Oxford: Oxford University Press, 1972), book 8, ch. 1, 609.

88. Information from a granddaughter of Jane's brother Francis in a letter to R. W. Chapman, 1925. See introduction to *Literary Manuscripts*, lxxx.

89. See Sarah Silah, "The Silence of Miss Lambe; *Sanditon* and Contextual Fiction of 'Race' in the Abolition era," *ECF* 18, no. 3(2006): 329–54.

Chapter Eight

1. "Graveyard Poets" include Edward Young of *Night Thoughts* and Blair of "The Grave." In *Tom Jones* the churchyard is treated as a comic site for a peasant "battle," as only poor villagers are buried in the earth around the church.

2. See Kathrin Levitan, *A Cultural History of the British Census: Envisioning the Multitude in the Nineteenth Century* (New York: Palgrave Macmillan, 2011).

3. W. G. Hoskins, *The Making of the English Landscape,* rpt. with introduction by Keith Thomas (London: Hodder & Stoughton, 2005), 59.

4. Ibid., 84–85.

5. Richard Muir, *The New Reading the Landscape: Fieldwork in Landscape History* (Exeter: University of Exeter Press, 2000), 182.

6. Ibid., 81.

7. Ibid., 89. Muir is quoting a report of the Nature Conservancy Council of 1984.

8. Ibid., 84.

9. Hoskins, *Landscape,* 158.

10. Muir, *New Reading,* 89.

11. Edmund Gibson, "Preface," to Gibson's edition of William Camden's *Britannia,* 3rd ed. (1753), vol. 1, sec. 1.

12. "Mr. Camden's Preface," trans. Edmund Gibson, in Camden-Gibson *Britannia,* vol. 1, K2V.

13. Camden-Gibson, *Britannia,* vol. 1, D1R.

14. Richard Gough, "Preface," in Camden-Gough, *Britannia* (1789), 1:viii.

15. Ibid., 1:vi.

16. Ibid. 1:vii.

17. Camden-Gibson, *Britannia,* 1:450.

18. Camden-Gough, *Britannia,* 2nd ed. (London: printed for John Stockdale by

J. Nichols and Son, 1806), 1:354 (under "Kent"). Entry is outdated by 1806; Thomas Knight died in 1794.

19. "Mr. Camden's Preface," trans. Edmund Gibson, in Camden-Gibson, *Britannia,* vol. 1, K2V.

20. Camden, "Division of Britain" (last paragraph), trans. Gough, in Camden-Gough, *Britannia,* 1:cxxxiv; compare Gibson's version in Camden-Gibson, 1:ccxxxi.

21. John Denham, *Cooper's Hill* (1668 version), ed. Jack Lynch, lines 115–116, 355–358. http://andromeda.rutgers.ed,/~jlynch/Texts/cooper.html.

22. William Camden, "Languages," in *Remains,* 22–29.

23. "The Names of the English Saxons and General Rules to know the ORIGINAL of the NAMES of PLACES in ENGLAND," in Camden-Gibson, *Britannia* 1:clxx-clxxiv. See figure 17.

Chapter Nine

1. LeFaye, *JAAFR,* 87, 108–9.

2. During the post-Waterloo depression the government instituted a budget for public works, for which Telford served as advisor (Roland Paxton, "Telford," *ODNB*).

3. The edifice appearing in the ITV series as "Downton Abbey," supposedly located in Yorkshire, is "Highclere," a nineteenth-century fantasy built upon the palace of the bishop of Winchester in Hampshire.

4. Nancy Mitford, *The Pursuit of Love* (1945), rpt. (New York: Vintage Books, 2010), 43.

5. Forster, *Howards End* (1910), rpt. (New York: Barnes & Noble Classics, 2003), ch. 3, 15.

6. Billy Collins, "The Golden Years" (2006), rpt. in *Aimless Love* (New York: Random House, 2013), 104.

Chapter Ten

1. Maria Edgeworth began writing children's stories in *The Parent's Assistant* (1796) and continued in *Early Lessons* (1801), with stories featuring Rosamond.

2. Cassandra Cooke, *Battleridge,* 1:2. Claire Tomalin points out a reference to "Base-Ball" in *Little Pretty Pocket Book* of 1744 (*A Life,* 297–98).

3. [Susanna Minifie], *Barford Abbey,* 1:212.

4. Agnes Maria Bennet, *Ellen Countess of Castle Howell,* 4 vols. (London: William Lane at the Minerva Press, 1794), 1:52.

5. William Stukeley, *Stonehenge. A Temple Restor'd to the British Druids* (London: W. Innys and R. Munby, 1740), 2–5.

6. James Easton, *Guide to Salisbury,* 6th ed. (Salisbury, 1780).

7. William Gilpin, *Observations on the Western Parts of England,* 275.

8. Francis Grose, *A Provincial Glossary with a Collection of Local Proverbs and Popular Superstitions* (London, 1787), n.p.

9. The Wiltshire Crop Circle Information and Co-ordination Centre is located near Devizes. The beautiful circles boost tourism.

10. John Feltham, *A Guide to all the Watering and Sea-Bathing Places . . . new and improved*. Illustrated with Maps and Views (London: Richard Phillips, 1810), 53. This work, originally published in 1806, expands in reprintings.

11. Ibid., 45.

12. Philip Thicknesse, *The Valetudinarian's Bath Guide; or, The Means of Obtaining Long Life and Health* (London: Dodsley, 1780), 12.

13. Philip Thicknesse, *The New Prose Bath Guide for the Year 1778*, 2nd ed. (London: Printed for the Author, 1780), 37.

14. Ibid., 30.

15. In 1750 Hugo Meynell established a pack of hounds at his home near Quorn in Leicestershire. The hunt, known as "the Quorn," became the most prestigious of all hunts.

16. Janine Barchas, *Matters of Fact*, ch. 3, 93–112. See also her "The Real Bluebeard of Bath: A Historical Model for Northanger Abbey," *Persuasions* 32 (2010): 115–34.

17. Nokes, *Life*, 303. Tucker postulates "that the idea of employing Repton at Sotherton . . . originated in Jane Austen's indignation over similar 'improvements' to William Leigh's pleasant, old-fashioned garden at Adlestrop." William Leigh (1604–90) had created seventeenth-century ornamental gardens "with a canal, fountain, and several alcoves, and expensive shewy summer houses" (Tucker, *Goodly Heritage*, 57–58).

18. Cassandra Austen, letter of 13 August 1806 to her daughter-in-law Mary Austen, in Le Faye, *JAAFR*, 156–57. See *A Family Record*, 177–79. See also Nokes, *Life*, 306; Tomalin, *Jane Austen: A Life*, 199–200.

19. Cooke, *Battleridge*, vol. 1, ch. 9, 203–5. A pioneer in historical novel and detective story, Cassandra Cooke precedes both Jane West and Walter Scott in producing a historical personage (Oliver Cromwell) as a character.

20. Deirdre LeFaye, *Jane Austen: The World of Her Novels* (London: Frances Lincoln Ltd., 2003), 214.

21. James's first curacy was at Stoke Charity near Steventon, and he soon added the curacy of nearby Overton. The influence of his mother's relations enabled him to add "the parishes of Cubbingon and Hunningham in Warwickshire to his haul of ecclesiastical livings" (Nokes, *Life*, 107.) James Austen apparently never visited these Warwickshire parishes.

22. Charlotte Smith, *Ethelinde; or, The Recluse of the Lake*, 5 vols. (London: T. Cadell, 1789), 1:35–37.

23. Ibid., 40–43.

24. William Gilpin, *Observations on the Western Parts of England*, 277–78.

25. Roger Moore, "The Hidden History of *Northanger Abbey*," *Religion and Literature* (Spring 2011): 55–80, 68.

26. Goldsmith, *History*, 4:194.

27. The Old Pretender had lived in Avignon and so, briefly, had Bonnie Prince Charlie. Avignon, taken from the Papal states by revolutionary France in 1791, was made part of the department of Vaucluse in 1793. Austen represents it as still visitable. Brandon's sister might have gone over during the brief Peace of Amiens in 1802.

28. Camden-Gibson, *Britannia,* 1:195.

29. Ibid., 1:196.

30. LeFaye, *JAAFR,* 130–31. This internal joke adds support to a date of writing in the early years of the new century. Henry had a partner, another officer named Henry Maunde; in 1807 they joined with James Tilson, forming a new firm, "Austen, Maunde and Tilson with offices at 10 Henrietta Street, Covent Garden" (Tucker, *Goodly Heritage,* 140).

31. Hasted, *The History and Topographical Survey of the County of Kent,* I; 315.

32. Thomas Robinson, *The Common Law of Kent; or, The Customs of Gavelkind,* 2nd ed. (London: his Majesty's Law Printers for P. Uriel, 1788), 35.

33. Ibid., 9.

34. W. G. Hoskins, *Devon,* first published 1954, rpt. (Andover, Hampshire: Phillimore & Co. Ltd., 2011), 453–56, 210. Plymouth delayed obtaining passable roads even to Dock. Turnpike trusts made roads better at go-ahead places like Exeter and Honiton, but the journey from Exeter to Plymouth and back must have been slow (ibid., 150–53).

35. Ed Copeland cites Cowper's strictures on public schools in "Tirocinium; or, A Review of Schools" (1784), a poem quoted in *Mansfield Park,* to support belief that Austen also repudiates public schools—the more as her father was a private tutor. See Copeland, ed., Cambridge *S&S,* 485.

36. See *A Family Record,* 29.

37. See Paula Byrne, *The Real Jane Austen,* 20–21. Search "John Charles Wallop, 3rd Earl of Portsmouth 1767–1853" in Wikipedia and elsewhere (no entry in *ODNB*). See "The Strange Case of the Vampyre Lord of Hurstbourne Priors," http://timedetectives.wordpress.com. Some of our information comes from Byron, whose solicitor compelled the earl to marry his daughter, apparently employing the threat of being locked up for lunacy.

38. Victoria Huxley, *Jane Austen and Adlestrop,* 22–26. Edward fifth Lord Leigh was a close relative; the expectations of James Leigh-Perrot and Cassandra Austen were stimulated upon his sister Mary's death in 1806.

39. John Feltham, *Guide* (1810), 219–21.

40. The strongest support of this vague story is that it emanated from Cassandra, who apparently confided something of it long after Jane's death. See Austen-Leigh, *Memoir,* 29. James Edward does not recollect the place; his sister Caroline says it was "in Devonshire" (Appendix, *Memoir,* 188). Familial recollections are collected and evaluated by George Holbert Tucker in *Jane Austen the Woman: Some Biographical Insights* (London; Robert Hale, 1994), 60–64.

41. Smith, *Celestina,* 1:58, 122.

42. Ibid., vol. 1, ch. 12, 135.

43. Ibid., 143.

44. Tucker, *Goodly Heritage,* 140; quoted from *Austen Papers, 1704–1856,* ed. R. A. Austen-Leigh (private printing; Spottiswoode: Ballantyne & Co. Ltd., 1942), 133.

45. Hoskins, *Landscape,* 161–62.

46. Anne-Marie Edwards, *In the Steps of Jane Austen,* 3rd ed. (Newbury, Berkshire: Countryside Books, 1991), 102–6.

47. Fifteen years before the Austen women moved in, Chawton Cottage had served as a low pub, the "New Inn," and earlier "Petty Johns." It was the scene of a murder or manslaughter in 1775. In 1790 a worse killing took place there. Only after these darks doings did the bailiff come to purify "Chawton cottage" with respectability. Despite Henry Tilney, murders do occur in England. See Nokes, *Life,* 357-59.

48. Huxley, *Jane Austen and Adlestrop,* 7-8.

49. Roger Sales, *Jane Austen and Representations of Regency England,* 95.

50. Although the original name of Ramsgate (Middle English *Remmesgate*) meant "a gap in the cliffs where wild garlic grows," the name taken simply as "the gate—or entryway—of a ram" certainly offers sexual connotations.

51. Jane Austen visited her brother Francis (Frank) in Ramsgate in 1803, but fell into no danger. Sir Egerton Brydges saw her there and could recollect only "Cheeks a little too full." See Nokes, *Life,* 262; Tucker, *Jane Austen the Woman,* 76.

52. At the end of the eighteenth century Gracechurch Street was the location of the main office of Packwood, maker of razor strops, who initiated the most ambitious advertising campaign seen hitherto, a media campaign alluded to in Maria Edgeworth's *Belinda* (1801).

53. Smith, *Emmeline, The Orphan of the Castle,* ed. Lorraine Fletcher (Toronto: Broadview, 2003), vol. 2, ch. 6, 180.

54. On the basis of such information, one critic has worked out that Meryton should be Harpenden, in Hertfordshire: Kenneth Smith, "The Probable Location of 'Longbourn' in Jane Austen's *Pride and Prejudice," Persuasions* 27 (2005). A village called "Redbourn," Smith believes, inspired the name "Longbourn." To reason thus is to imagine too exactly.

55. Camden-Gibson, *Britannia,* 1:215.

56. Austen origin in Kent: see Tucker, *Goodly Heritage,* 16; LeFaye, *JAAFR,* 1-4.

57. Camden-Gough 1:216.

58. Resenting the humiliation of a monarch, Henry VIII not only had Becket's shrine demolished during the Dissolution in 1538, but ordered that his bones be scattered.

59. Quoted by Hasted, *The History and Topographical Survey of the County of Kent,* I; 318.

60. There were fine houses in the Westerham vicinity, including Squerryes Court, used for some Hartfield scenes in the 2009 BBC TV version of *Emma.* Churchill chose Chertwell near Westerham as his country residence. During World War II the danger was so great that the Churchills could not use it until the war was over. Similar dangers menaced Kent in the Napoleonic period.

61. Charles was mocked by republicans for quoting the prayer of the princess Pamela, Sidney's heroine, in *Eikon Basilike,* the king's book of self-defense.

62. Gunning, *Anecdotes of the Delborough Family,* 5 vols. (London: William Lane for Minerva Press, 1792), 5:98.

63. Sidney, *Arcadia,* in The *Works of the Honourable Sir Philip Sidney, Kt. in Prose and Verse,* 14th ed., 3 vols. (London: E. Taylor et al., 1725), 1:10-11.

64. Greene's "The Original of Pemberley," rpt. in *Essays,* 321-23.

65. Gilpin, *Observations, Relative Chiefly to Picturesque Beauty,* 2:220-23.

66. John Byng, *Torrington Diaries,* 4 vols. (London, 1934), vol. 2, cited by Claudia L. Johnson and Susan J. Wolfson, appendix to Longman edition of *P&P,* 419.

67. Lambton Castle was built in the nineteenth century on the ruins of Harraton Hall, a seventeenth-century mansion belonging to the D'Arcys.

68. Gilpin, *Observations, Relative Chiefly to Picturesque Beauty,* 2:219.

69. "Pemberton" is used by Frances Burney in *Cecilia* for the heroine's teasing friend, the young aristocrat Lady Honoria Pemberton; her name might have influenced Austen's invention of "Pemberley."

70. Richard Muir, *New Reading,* 5.

71. Ibid., 8–9.

72. Izaak Walton and Charles Cotton, *The Compleat Angler; or, Contemplative Man's Recreation.* In Two Parts with Notes by Moses Browne. 7th ed. (London: Henry Kent, 1759), Part II, ch. 2, 229–32.

73. Ibid., Part I, ch. 1, 19.

74. Ibid., Part I, ch. 4, 57.

75. Lambton in Durham became known for somewhat ruthless coal mining that affected "Lambton Castle," built there in the nineteenth century.

Chapter Eleven

1. Camden-Gibson, *Britannia,* 1:510.

2. Ibid., 1:501–2.

3. Ibid., 1:504.

4. John Dryden, *Annus Mirabilis,* line 851.

5. Herman Moll, *A Pocket Companion of Roads of the South Part of Great Britain,* 2 vols. (London, 1717) 2:167. The BL copy belonged to George III and was donated by George IV.

6. Camden-Gibson, *Britannia,* 1:501.

7. Daniel Defoe, A *Tour thro' the Whole Island of Great Britain.* Divided into Circuits or Journies. 3 vols. (London: G. Strahan, W. Mears et al., 1724) 2:166–67.

8. Defoe [and Richardson], *A Tour thro' the Whole Island of Great Britain.* Divided into Circuits or Journeys. 4th ed. 4 vols. (London: S. Birt, T. Osborne et al., 1748), 3:45.

9. Martin Joseph Naylor, "Preface," in *The Inantity* [*sic*] *and Mischief of Vulgar Superstitions* (Cambridge: Printed by B. Flower for J. Deighton and W. H. Lunn, Sold in London by Rivington et al., 1795), ix.

10. Ibid., ii.

11. "Stoke Bruerne Canal Village," http://www.stokebruerne.org.uk.

12. Hoskins, *Landscape,* 136.

13. Ibid., 159.

14. Camden-Gough, *Britannia,* 1:115.

15. Ibid., 1:120.

16. Ibid., 1:139.

17. John Wiltshire analyzes the degree of acting on Fanny's part in ch. 2 of *Jane Austen and the Body* (Cambridge: Cambridge University Press, 1992), 62–109.

18. Maaja Stewart, *Domestic Realities and Imperial Fictions: Jane Austen's Novels in Eighteenth-Century Contexts* (Atlanta: University of Georgia Press, 1993), 110.

19. Ibid., 115–16.

20. The Austen family's association with Antigua was clarified by Frank Gibbon's article "The Antiguan Connection," *Cambridge Quarterly* 11, no. 2 (1982). See Ruth Perry, "Austen and Empire: A Thinking Woman's Guide to British Imperialism," *Persuasions* 16 (December 1994): 95–106.

21. Park Honan, *Life,* 341. Honan compares Nibbs's design to detach his son from undesirable acquaintance by a voyage to the West Indies with Sir Thomas Bertram's treatment of Tom. We might note that the "medicinal project" upon Fanny follows a failed medicinal project upon Tom, entailing similar dislocation.

22. *Ten views in the Island of Antigua. In which are represented the Process of Sugar Making, and the Employment of the Negroes in the Field, Boiling-House, and Distillery.* From drawings made by William Clark During a Residence of three Years in the West Indies, upon the Estate of Admiral Tollemache (London: Thomas Clay, 1823). Practically nothing is known of Clark. Vice-Admiral John Richard Delap Tollemache (born "Halliday"), whose death is recorded in the 1837 *Gentleman's Magazine,* owned or had part in at least six lucrative Antigua estates. In 1839 his executor successfully fought off in his name a claim on Delap's estate, of which Tollemache was declared owner, including 268 enslaved persons. See the UCL online database "Legacy of British Slave-Ownership."

23. See the blogs "Past Imperfect" and "Antigua's Disputed Slave Conspiracy of 1736" (2 January 2013).

24. See David Barry Gaspar, *Bondmen and Rebels: A Study of Master-Slave Relations in Antigua* (Durham NC: Duke University Press, 1993), ch. 1.

25. Britain took Guadeloupe briefly in 1759, restoring it in 1763, recapturing and losing it again in 1794.

26. By 1805 there were 1,300 "free coloured" persons in Antigua according to John Davy in *The West Indies before and Since Slave Emancipation* (1854); his statistics are quoted by Susan Lowes in "'They Couldn't Mash Ants': The Decline of White and Non-White Elites in Antigua, 1834–1900," in *Small Islands, Large Questions,* ed. Karen Fog Olwig (London: Cass, 1995), 5–6. "Mrs. Lanaghan" describes this "higher class of coloured persons." Surprisingly, she acclaims them as "the possessors of warm and generous thoughts—the doers of high and noble actions" (*Antigua and the Antiguan: A Full Account of the Colony and its Inhabitants . . . Interspersed with Anecdotes and Legends,* 2 vols. [London: Saunders and Otley, 1844], 2:170).

27. Janet Schaw, *The Journal of a Lady of Quality; Being the Narrative of a Journey from Scotland to the West Indies, North Carolina and Portugal in the Years 1774 to 1778,* ed. Evangeline Walker (first published by Yale University Press, 1921), rpt. with an introduction by Stephen Carl Arch (Lincoln: University of Nebraska Press, 2005), ch. 2, 88.

28. Robert Southey, *Life of Nelson* (London: John Murray, 1813), ch. 2; rpt. (Amazon digital Services, Kindle), 40–41.

29. "Mrs. Flannigan," in *Antigua and the Antiguan,* vol. 1, ch. 12, 136. Mrs. Flannigan, an Irish visitor pre- and post-Emancipation, married an islander and stayed in Antigua, where she is best known as Mrs. Lanaghan.

30. "Mrs. Flannigan," in *Antigua and the Antiguans,* 1:199. The author here describes a ball at St. Kitts interrupted by an earthquake in 1833.

31. "Mrs. Flannigan," in *Antigua and the Antiguans,* vol. 2, ch. 38, 107–8. This author, publishing well after slavery is abolished, is officially in favor of abolition. The unsurprising condescension grates, but the detail is valuable. Antiguan "Christmas balls" became famous in the nineteenth century.

32. Ibid., 109.

33. John Wiltshire in his introduction to the Cambridge edition comes down on the side of the 1808–9 dating ("Introduction," in *Mansfield Park,* xliii–xlv). The only real contradiction is the reference to Crabbe's *Tales*—if his *Tales in Verse* (1812) is intended. On the other hand, other small touches—including Mary's reference to Lady Lascelles—support the 1808–9 time scheme.

34. John Luffman, *A Brief account of the Island of Antigua, together with the Customs and Manners of Its Inhabitants, as well White as Black.* (London: T. Cadell, 1789), letter 11, 43–45.

35. See Peter Macinnis, *Bittersweet: The Story of Sugar* (Crow's Nest, NSW: Allen & Unwin, 2002), 135.

36. Isabella Thorpe's "sweetest girl in the world" is an adolescent cliché. On Fanny's first entry "her voice was sweet," winning favor (I, ch. 2). Yet "sweet"—a word that recurs in *Mansfield Park*—is often clichéd or ironic. Fanny Price's reference to "this sweet wood" at Sotherton is both (*MP,* I, ch. 9). Mary says that in Fanny Henry will have "a sweet little wife" (II, ch. 12). Edmund refers to Mary's "sweet peculiarity of manner" (III, ch. 4). Henry says that Fanny has given her name "such reality of sweetness," (III, ch. 3) Earlier he expatiated on her "modesty and sweetness," the narrative voice amplifying: "that sweetness which makes so essential a part of every woman's worth in the judgment of man that though he sometimes loves where it is not, he can never believe it absent" (II, ch. 12). Craving for sweetness may mislead.

37. Cowper's "Sweet Meat Has Sour Sauce; Or, The Slave Trader in the Dumps" was not accepted as an official abolitionist poem, because of its gruesomely cheerful list of torture implements and the unrepentant tone of the slave trader. See Suvir Kaul, *Poems of Nation, and Anthems of Empire* (Charlottesville: University of Virginia Press, 2000).

38. Alistair M. Duckworth, *The Improvement of the Estate: A Study of Jane Austen's Novels* (Baltimore, MD: Johns Hopkins University Press, 1994) (rpt. of 1971), 49–50.

39. John Wiltshire objects that Austen errs, as a "profusion of mahogany" is not in the style of the 1680s (note to *Mansfield Park,* 664). There could have been an updating under the Hanoverians, but mahogany was in use by the late seventeenth century. The chapel as originally designed in the 1680s might have been different, with more Catholic emblems. Stoneleigh Abbey had its own chapel so the Leigh family did not have to pray for the usurping monarch as they would in the parish church. Presumably the same motive was behind Sotherton's chapel, but Mrs. Rushworth would not wish to bring up something so unpleasantly discordant.

40. Camden-Gough, *Britannia,* 2:396–97.

41. See Kirkham, *Jane Austen, Feminism and Fiction,* and John Wiltshire, "Intro-

duction," in *Mansfield Park* (Cambridge, 2005), xlv–xlvi. The connection of Austen and slavery was raised by Edward Said in a famous essay of 1989, "Jane Austen and Empire" (reprinted in his *Culture and Imperialism*); he argues that Jane Austen entirely acquiesced in slavery and took for granted its benefits to her class.

42. Byrne, *The Real Jane Austen*, 213–23.

43. Jane Austen met Elizabeth Murray (now Mrs. Finch-Hatton) in 1805 and may have been acquainted with Dido Belle.

44. James in *The Loiterer* supported the Abolition Bill debated in 1789. Francis Austen said that even putting legal restraints on slaveholders was not enough: "Slavery . . . modified is still Slavery." Frank's remarks appear in a document "Remarks on the Island of St. Helena" written in April 1808, quoted in Knox-Shaw, *Jane Austen and the Enlightenment*, 164. In his reference to "inalienable rights" Frank seems to have picked up some of the language of the American Revolution. That sentence was omitted by the Hubbacks who quoted part of the document in *Jane Austen's Sailor Brothers* (1906).

45. Duckworth, *Improvement of the Estate*, 52.

46. Halesowen ("Owen's Hollow") was given by King Henry II to the Welsh Prince Owen.

47. Johnson, *Women, Politics and the Novel*, 117.

48. Tara Ghoshal Wallace, "'It Must Be Done in London': The Suburbanization of Highbury," *Persuasions* 29 (2007): 67–78.

49. Laurie Kaplan suggests that one reason Austen hesitated to dedicate *Emma* to the prince was its reference to his hated wife and its side glance at the Foundling Hospital: Kaplan, "*Emma* and 'the children in Brunswick Square,'" *Persuasions* 31 (2009): 236–47.

50. The Foundling Hospital was removed in the twentieth century, permitting the development of a park of seven acres in Coram's Fields.

51. Frederick Morton Eden, "Preface," in *State of the Poor*, 1:xi.

52. John Aubrey, "Introduction," to *The Natural History and Antiquities of the County of Surrey*. Begun in the Year 1672. 5 vols. (London: E. Curll, 1719), 1:xxiii.

53. Camden-Gough, *Britannia*, 1:228.

54. Ibid., 1:176.

55. Ibid., 1:169.

56. Camden-Gough, *Britannia*, 1:151. Windsor inspires Camden's Latin poem "The Marriage of the Thames and Isis," a possible influence on Gray's "Eton Ode."

57. Camden-Gough, *Britannia*, 1:151. Camden quotes the charter whereby William the Conqueror obtained Windsor from the abbot of Westminster.

58. See Edward Lear, "The Courtship of the Yonghy-Bonghy Bò," verse 2.

59. William Gilpin, *Observations on the Western Parts of England*, 1:11. F. W. Bradbrook noted Gilpin's description and its possible influence upon *Emma* in *Jane Austen and Her Predecessors* (Cambridge: Cambridge University Press, 1966).

60. Gilpin, *Observations on the Western Parts of England*, 1:27.

61. In July 1816, wealthy young William Cotton traveled with James Austen and two of Austen's "agreeable nephews" from Paris to the vale of Chamounix; see Gerald Hamilton-Edwards, *The Leisured Connoisseur* (Plymouth, Devonshire: private printing, 1954), 107–13. Jane may have known the year before of James's desire

to get to Switzerland, even a plan to escort Edward's sons. In a late letter Austen comments on Miss Bigg "being frisked off, like half England, into Switzerland" (22 May 1817: *Letters*, 341).

62. I am grateful to Douglas Murray for sharing with me his unpublished article on Box Hill.

63. John Aubrey, *Natural History and Antiquities of Surrey*, 4:174.

64. John Macky, *A Journey through England, In Familiar Letters from a Gentleman here, to his Friend Abroad* (London: J. Roberts for T. Caldecott, 1714), 71.

65. Ibid., 1:80.

66. Ibid. 1:72.

67. Defoe, *Tour*, 1:101–102.

68. Edward Beavan, *Box-Hill, A Descriptive Poem* (London: J. Wilkie, 1777), 8.

69. Defoe, *Tour*, 1:103.

70. Feltham, *Guide to all the Watering and Sea-Bathing Places*, 429–30. Like other visitors, the king went into the sea in a bathing machine, of the sort we hear of in *Sanditon*. According to Feltham, Weymouth was recommended by "the celebrated Ralph Allen," and here "the first bathing machine seen on the beach was constructed for his use." Weymouth offered diversions—"the best comedians [actors] from the London and Bath theatres frequently exhibit their talents here"—which Frank would appreciate (*Guide*, 430–31).

71. By "Gloucester" Austen seems to mean the inhabitants of Gloucester Lodge, i.e., the royals.

72. Hannah Glasse, *The Art of Cookery made Plain and Easy. To which are Added One hundred and Fifty New Receipts, a copious Index, and a Modern Bill of Fare*, 20th ed. (Edinburgh, 1791). There are multiple references to dishes and cookery in *Emma*. Mr. Woodhouse, ironically, seems to be trying to keep to pauper's fare in order to preserve life. Frederick Morton Eden includes diets offered by poorhouses in the 1790s in *The State of the Poor*. Gruel—or worse, "water gruel"—often figures in these stern menus.

73. Sheridan, *The Rivals*, 3rd ed. (London: J. Wilkie, 1776), 11.

74. The "tall, thin, overgrown lad" found at Puffardos's seminary, ill dressed in tattered garments, anticipates Smike.

75. R. W. Chapman noted in his edition of *Emma* that a house near Leatherhead bore the name Randalls.

76. Marcel Proust, *A l'ombre des jeunes filles en fleurs* (1919), vol. 2 of *A la recherche du temps perdu*. See translation by C. K. Scott Moncrieff and Terence Kilmartin, "Within a Budding Grove," vol. 2 of *Remembrance of Things Past* (New York: Vintage Books, 1982), 892–93.

77. Irene Collins came to much the same conclusion, although disliking Mr. Elton more than I do; see *Jane Austen and the Clergy* (London: Hambledon and London, 1994), 100.

78. *A Family Record*, 281.

79. Tucker, *Goodly Heritage*, 82–91.

80. Harris, "The White Glare of Bath," in *Revolution*, ch. 9, 160–87.

81. Feltham, *Guide to All the Watering Places* (1810), 53.

82. Thicknesse, *New Prose Bath Guide*, 79.

83. Harris, *Revolution*, 164.

84. Camden defines "Cob" as "a forced harbour for Ships, as the cob of Linne in Dorsetshire." (*Remains*, 122).

85. Mary Anning's presence in Lyme as a contemporary of Jane Austen is noted by Peter W. Graham, "Why Lyme Regis?," *Persuasions* 26 (2004).

86. William Gilpin, *Observations on the Western Parts of England,* 149.

87. Barchas, *Matters of Fact*, 235–38.

88. Camden gives "Schell" and "Skell" as elements in surnames indicating spring or well; *Remains*, 123, 124.

89. Charlotte Smith, "Sonnet II," in *Elegiac Sonnets,* 5th edition (1789), 2. See "Names in *Persuasion*," above.

90. Janet Todd estimates Frederick's annual income at £1,250. If Sir Walter eventually does fork over Anne's dowry, that would be another five hundred pounds—but still less than Mr. Bennet's or Colonel Brandon's income. Todd, note to *Persuasion, 359.*

91. Sandy Lerner argued in a talk at JASNA meeting 2013 that Frederick's income could not realistically have risen to the upkeep of a landaulet.

92. Linda Robertson Walker, "Jane Austen's Death: The Long Reach of Typhus," *Persuasions On-Line*, 31 (Winter 2010). Many explanations have been postulated for Austen's final illness: Addison's disease, tuberculosis, inadvertent arsenic poisoning, cancer. Walker's convincing suggestion explains why Jane might die early while her siblings did not.

93. This minor resort is comically celebrated in Oscar Wilde's *The Importance of Being Ernest* as the source of Jack Worthing's name: as a baby he was found in a handbag in a train "on the Brighton line."

94. Camden-Gibson, 1:209.

95. Feltham, *Guide* (1810), 234.

96. Camden-Gibson 1:210.

97. "Suth-Sex," in Camden-Gibson, 1:195.

98. Camden, *Britannia*, trans. Philémon Holland, as *Britain; or, A chorographical Description of the Most Flourishing Kingdomes, ENGLAND, SCOTLAND, and IRELAND, and the Islands adjoyning.* Beautified with Mappes. (London: Printed by F.K. R.Y. and I.L. For Andrew Hur, 1637), 360.

99. Actual place names beginning with "Brin-" refer to the property of a man called *Bryni*, or to burning; in Welsh *bryn* means hill.

100. Pope, "Temple of Fame," line 427, *Poems of Alexander Pope*, 185. Pope's poem of 1715, a version of Chaucer's *House of Fame,* exhibits the temple of true fame in contrast to the whirling house of rumor and lies: "a Structure fair, / Its Site uncertain, if in Earth or Air; / With rapid Motion turned the Mansion round" (lines 420–422, 185). This home of gossip and advertising comports with Austen's "rototory [*sic*] motion," fashionable and giddy-making moving in "circles" (*Sanditon,* ch. 11).

Conclusion

1. Scott's review of *Emma* and the earlier published novels (except *Mansfield Park*) was published in the *Quarterly Review* 14 (March 1816): 188–201. It is reprinted in *Jane Austen: The Critical Heritage,* ed. B. C. Southam, 2 vols. (London: Routledge Kegan & Paul, 1968), 1:58–69.

2. Scott, journal of 14 March 1826, as quoted by Lockhart.

3. Pope, *Essay on Man,* I, line 217.

4. Swift's contrast between the spider and the bee is found in *The Battle of the Books* (1704).

5. Miller, *Secret of Style,* 1–2.

6. Claudia Johnson, *Jane Austen's Cults and Cultures* (Chicago: University of Chicago Press, 2012), 29.

7. G. K. Chesterton, "Preface," to *Love and Freindship and Other Early Works by Jane Austen* (New York: Frederick A Stokes Co., 1922), xiii–xv.

8. "Introduction," to *"Catharine" and Other Writings* (Oxford: World's Classics, Oxford University Press, 1993), xxxviii.

9. Richardson, *Sir Charles Grandison,* ed. Jocelyn Harris, 3 vols. (Oxford: Oxford University Press, 1972), vol. 1, letter 22, 115. Richardson implicitly criticizes the fashionable falsehood of the costume that obscures the true Arcadian nature of Harriet Byron, but the episode looks back to Sidney's *Arcadia.*

INDEX